THE PORTUGUESE, INDIAN OCEAN AND EUROPEAN BRIDGEHEADS 1500-1800

PROF. DR. K.S. MATHEW

THE PORTUGUESE, INDIAN OCEAN AND EUROPEAN BRIDGEHEADS 1500-1800

Festschrift in Honour of Prof. K.S. Mathew

Edited by
PIUS MALEKANDATHIL
T. JAMAL MOHAMMED

MANOHAR
2023

First published 2001
Second edition 2023

© Editors 2001, 2023

All rights reserved. No part of this publication may be reproduced or transmitted, in any form or by any means, without prior permission of the editors and the publisher

ISBN 978-93-90729-60-9

Published by
Ajay Kumar Jain *for*
Manohar Publishers & Distributors
4753/23 Ansari Road, Daryaganj
New Delhi 110 002

Printed at
Replika Press Pvt. Ltd.

CONTENTS

Introduction to Second Edition   6
1. Introduction   9
2. A Joy for Ever **A.R. Kulkarni**   23

I. PERSPECTIVES ON INDO-PORTUGUESE HISTORY

3. Globalisation of the Earth? Reflections on the European Expansion and its consequences **Eberhard Schmitt.**   32

4. The Portuguese in India and the Indian Ocean: An Overview of the Sixteenth Century **M.N. Pearson**   49

5. Precedents and Parallels of the Portuguese Cartaz System **Luis Filipe F.R. Thomaz**   67

6. German Participation in the India Fleet of 1505/06 **Stephan B.G.C. Michaelsen**   86

7. Outgoing Carreira Ships in the Indian Ocean (1550-1575) **Joseph Velinkar**   99

8. Contribution of Malabar Rulers in Delaying Dominance by Foreign Powers in Malabar Region **K.K.N. Kurup**   111

9. Cristãos e Especiaria: The Portuguese Impact on the Malabar Christian Community **Jan Kieniewicz**   119

10. Paravas and Portuguese. A Study of Portuguese Strategy and its Impact on an Indian Ocean Seafaring Community **Kenneth McPherson**   133

11. Non-Portuguese Westerners Trialed by the Goa Inquisition (1563-1623) **John G. Everaert**   149

12. The Convent of Saint Monica and its Inhabitants in the early Decades of the Seventeenth Century **Carlos Alonso Vañes**   163

13. India or Brazil? Priority for Imperial Survival in the
    Wars of the Restauração **George D. Winius** 181

14. A Brazilian Commercial Presence beyond the
    Cape of Good Hope, 16th-19th Centuries
    A.J.R. Russell -Wood 191

15. The Nayaks of Tamil Country and Portuguese
    Trade in War-Animals **S. Jeyaseela Stephen** 212

16. The Salsette Campaign of 1658 - 1659: Issues of
    War and Peace in Bijapuri - Portuguese Relations
    during the Mid-17th Century **Glenn J. Ames** 223

17. Merchants, Markets and Commodities: Some Aspects
    of Portuguese Commerce with Malabar
    Pius Malekandathil 241

18. Hunting Riches: Goa's Gem Trade in the Early
    Modern Age **João Teles e Cunha** 269

19. The Portuguese and Aspects of Trade in Ports of
    South Kanara **Nagendra Rao** 305

20. Decline of the Portuguese Naval Power: A Study
    Based on Portuguese Documents **K.M. Mathew** 324

21. José Custodio de Faria in the History of the
    World of Psychology: A Dialogue Between Indian and
    European Psychologies **Hannes Stubbe** 337

22. Hinduism in the Quotidian of the Christians of Goa
    in the 18th Century
    Maria de Jesus dos Martires Lopes 354

23. Goan Women in other Lands
    Fatima da Silva Gracias 364

II. INDIAN OCEAN AND MARITIME ACTIVITIES

24. Indian Traditions of Boat-building **B. Arunachalam** 376

25. Historical Contacts Between Quilon
    and China **Haraprasad Ray** 387

26. Maritime Trade and Cultural Interactions in the
    Indian Ocean (1500-1800) **T. Jamal Mohammed** 403

27. Sanskrit in Magindanaon: Implications on Pre-Islamic Trade and Traffic **Juan R. Francisco**   412

28. India and Greece : A Cultural, Historical and Linguistic Symphony **Francis Arakal**   440

III. INDIA AND ASPECTS OF EUROPEAN EXPANSION

29. Orientalism, Occidentosis and other Viral Strains: Historical Objectivity and Social Responsibilities. **Teotonio R. de Souza**   452

30. A Critical Evaluation of the Political and Administrative Policies of the Dutch East India Company in Kerala **M.O. Koshy**   480

31. The Trade in Indian Textiles and the Industrial Revolution in England **Dietmar Rothermund**   495

32. Anglo-Carnatic Relations of the Eighteenth Century **B. Sobhanan**   507

33. Asian States and Mercantilism in the Indian Ocean Economy: Bengal Nizamat and the English Company in 18th Century **Ujjayan Bhattacharya**   523

34. Milestones of the Mughal Period in the Haidarabad Region (Andhra Pradesh) **Jean Deloche**   549

35. West European and Mughal Interaction during the Reign of Aurangzeb **J.B.P More**   558

36. The French at Surat, 1693-1701 **Aniruddha Ray**   587

37. French Notices on the Drugs and Medical Practices of Medieval India **P. Hymavathi**   616

38. Colbertism and the French East India Company's Trade with India during the Seventeenth and Eighteenth Centuries. **B. Krishnamurthy**   635

39. French Connections with Mahe in the Eighteenth Century **Joy Varkey**   652

40. Appendix : K.S. Mathew - A Bibliography   663

41. Names and Addresses of the Contributors   669

INTRODUCTION TO SECOND EDITION

The waters of the Indian Ocean served not as a barrier, but as a bridge to get connected with a wide variety of human enclaves located on its rim, but mutually dependent on one another. The cycles of monsoon winds—with which the waters Indian Ocean used to get activated, with which the nature of commodity-flow and wealth flow through it used to take different directions, with which the pattern of agrarian and craft production used to undergo different rhythms of progression, with which cycles of work, leisure, cultural performances and entertainment were organized at different time junctures—used to bring commonality and unity of immense nature among the settlers on the rim of Indian Ocean. The Monsoon factor used to determine the time of agricultural processes, the time for market operations, the time of navigation, the time for war and peace, the time for religious festivities, and the time for academic activities. Among the societies bordering the Indian Ocean one can find a great amount of cohesion and cogence, particularly unity of immense nature. Interconnectedness among them is followed by commonality in food culture, dress culture and language culture. However, the people under the spell of Southwest Monsoon exhibit certain unique features and traits, which are different from the ones seen among the people under the spell of Northeast Monsoon, which suggests the evolution of region-specific commonality in this water space over years.

The meanings of European expansion into the Indian Ocean have become an important area of historical study in the recent past. The frequent commercial voyages between Portugal and India and the concomitant colonial projects that the Portuguese formulated for India were intrinsically intertwined and the unravelling of their logic highlights the nuances of the early phase of European expansion and the plurality of ways how the natives responded to it. Interestingly the Indian Ocean served as a bridge for the European powers to interact with Indian society and for the integration of its multiple regional economies with the evolving Atlantic-centric World system, even before their amalgamation within the national frame. An analysis of the process shows that one geography after another was slowly integrated with this system on the basis of their resourcefulness and ability to supply commodities and products that were in high demand in Europe. The diverse politico-commercial policies of the Portuguese, the Dutch, the French and the English at different time points facilitated the different parts of India to get glued to the Atlantic-centered World System, often at the deprivation of freedom of local people to produce goods of their choice, the denial of the locals of the right to trade with merchants of their preference and the increasing reduction of the chances for surplus to remain in their hands.

The sixteenth century was relatively a long span of time for the Portuguese to conduct a variety of experiments on the ways how to conduct trade in the non-European world without disturbing their balance in wealth reserve, on the modality of power forms to be deployed for controlling rulers, merchants and commodity traffic, on the type of cultural mechanisms that should be resorted to for penetrating into areas, where weapons of war happened to be weak and futile. The economic, social, political and cultural dimensions of the interactions that the Europeans starting from the Portuguese till the English got engaged in in the Indian Ocean form the core part of this volume. The work sheds light also on the meanings of European expansion, the nuances of local resistance to it, the multiple layers of trade and their significance, the operational part of mercantilism and Colbertism in India, and also the adaptability of different languages to accommodate, absorb and assimilate the new concepts and new idea-denoting vocabularies brought through these processes of interactions.

"The Portuguese", "the Indian Ocean" and "European Expansion" form the three major thematic areas on which Prof. K.S. Mathew concentrated his academic research for more than three decades and hence the Felicitation volume, originally prepared in 2001 to pay tribute to him on his sixty-second birthday, has taken this wider thematic frame. Prof. Mathew entered the field of historical research at a time when the historiographical approaches to these themes were radically changing especially by mid-1970s against the backdrop of changing perceptions of international geopolitics with colonial moorings still in the air and the Indian Ocean emerging as a zone of great importance and serious concern for the Indians.

Prof. Mathew was a leading stalwart among the new trendsetters in the historiography on Portuguese India, which took a decisive turn

Introduction to Second Edition

with the entry of a new generation of historians, like C.R. Boxer, Vitorino Magalhães Godinho, Luis Filipe F.R. Thomaz, M.N. Pearson, George Winius, Anthony Disney and Teotonio R de Souza. The new historiographical school exploded the various myths regarding Portuguese expansion in the East that were spread with political motives during the time of Salazar's regime. It was concomitantly followed by attempts to study the meanings of Portuguese activities in India from an Indo-centric perspective. Prof. Mathew played a decisive role in institutionalizing this new trend in Indo-Portuguese historiography along with John Correia-Afonso, Teotonio R. de Souza, Luis Filipe F.R. Thomaz and Teodoro de Matos by launching a series of International seminars on Indo-Portuguese History (ISIPH), which are organized alternatively in India, Portugal and occasionally in Brazil every three years.

In our efforts to felicitate Prof. Mathew by putting up a volume on areas, which were central to his academic concerns we got immense help, support and scholarly papers from a large body of academicians from across the world, to whom we are deeply indebted. We sincerely thank all the renowned scholars who contributed these highly well-researched articles almost 22 years back, when it was first published. With the passage of time, its copies were soon sold out and during my last 15 years of teaching at Jawaharlal Nehru University, New Delhi as a Professor in History, my students and many researchers brought to my notice about the difficulty in accessing this book for their research pursuits. At this juncture Manohar Publishers came forward to re-publish this work and make it available to the large academic community. We express our deep gratitude to Mr. Ramesh Jain and Ananya Jain of Manohar Publishers for having taken up this publication project and brought out this work so excellently on par with its academic content.

17 May 2023   PIUS MALEKANDATHIL
                                                        (Former Professor of History, JNU)

                                                         T. JAMAL MOHAMMED
                                                              (Trivandrum)

1

INTRODUCTION

"The Portuguese", "the Indian Ocean" and "European Expansion" form the three major thematic areas on which Prof. K. S. Mathew concentrated his academic researches for more than three decades and hence the Felicitation volume, prepared to pay tribute to him on his sixty-second birthday, has taken this wider thematic frame. Prof. Mathew entered the field of history at a time when the historiographical approaches to these themes were radically changing especially by the middle of 1970s against the backdrop of international political developments, and when colonial moorings were still in the air and the maritime space of Indian Ocean was increasingly becoming a matter of great importance and serious concern for the Indians. He was a leading stalwart among the new trend-setters in the historiography on Portuguese India, which took a decisive turn with the entry of a new generation of historians, like C.R.Boxer, Vitorino Magalhães Godinho, Luis Filipe F.R. Thomaz, M.N.Pearson, George Winius, Anthony Disney and Teotonio R. de Souza. The new historiographical school exploded the various myths regarding the Portuguese expansion in the East spread by Salazzar's regime and tried to reconstruct the Portuguese activities in India in an objective and scientific way, where Indo-centric dimensions were given the focus. He played crucial role in institutionalizing this new trend in the Indo-Portuguese historiography along with John Correia - Afonso, Teotonio R. de Souza, Luis Filipe F.R. Thomaz and Teodoro de Matos by starting International Seminars on Indo-Portuguese History, which are organized alternatively in India and Portugal every three years.

I

The scholars of this movement ushered in different trends of historical writing: Vitorino Magalhães Godinho resorted to the analytical style of Annales school in *Os Descobrimentos e a Economia Mundial* (4 vols.,Lisboa, 1981-4), where as Luis Filipe Thomaz with his command of several non-Portuguese languages and mastery of Portuguese sources has given a new understanding to the Portuguese expansion in *De Ceuta a Timor* (Lisboa, 1994). He evolved the concept of the Portuguese "network" and not an "empire" to describe the *Estado da India* and thus he tries to purge the pejorative connotations attached to it. In the Anglo-Saxon world, the new Indo-Portuguese historiographical tradition was heralded by M.N.Pearson in his work *Merchants and Rulers in Gujarat:The Response to the Portuguese in the Sixteenth Century* (New Delhi, 1976). The commercial aspects of the Luso-Indian relations are highlighted in K.S.Mathew's *Portuguese Trade with India in the Sixteenth Century* (New Delhi, 1982).His works *Portuguese and the Sultanate of Gujarat (1500-1573)* and *Emergence of Cochin in the Pre-Industrial Era: A Study of Portuguese Cochin (Pondicherry, 1990)* belong to this tradition. Recently the Indo-Portuguese history is made quite familiar to the English-speaking people through the works of Sanjay Subrahmanyam, who epitomizes this new trend in his work *The Portuguese Empire in Asia 1500-1700: A Political and Economic History* (London, 1993). The first twenty-two essays, dealing with Indo-Portuguese themes, and included in the first part of this volume, are either representatives of this tradition or are indicative of the newly emerging historiographical trends in different parts of the world.

A.R.Kulkarni, who was the former chairman of ICHR and former Vice Chancellor of Tilak Vidya Pith, Pune, was also the teacher of K.S. Mathew. He introduces the person of Mathew and his academic evolution for the Felicitation volume. He muses on the pleasure of being a guru by looking into stages through which the student-Mathew got transformed into Historian-Mathew. The academic part of the Festschrift starts with the article of Eberhard Schmitt of Bamberg University, Germany, who looks at the globalization phenomena ushered in with the geographical discoveries as well as European expansion and argues that this development was followed by an imperceptible formation of a world wide traffic network and a gradual linking up of the world through commerce, trade and European culture. According to him the discovery of eastern sea-route to Asia along with the western one, besides the discovery of America led to the high-level interaction on a global basis, which accelerated the process of European expansion, carried out with adaptations to the local practices of trade. M.N.Pearson of the University of New South Wales, Australia gives a broad overview of the Portuguese and their activities by locating them in the context of Indian Ocean in the 16th century. He examines the various politico-commercial strategies and machineries of the Portuguese, which were devised to realize their fundamental aim: "to buy spices cheap and to sell them dear in Europe, thus undercutting the traditional Mediterranean route." Luis Filipe F.R. Thomaz of the Universidade Nova de Lisboa, Portugal brings out the precedents and parallels of the Portuguese *cartaz* system and refutes the traditional view that it was a Lusitanian innovation and challenges the argument that before the Portuguese expansion the Indian Ocean was a free zone, where everybody could navigate. He argues that the basic intention of the various systems of control was to encourage the trade of certain goods if conducted by friends and to forbid the traffic of others and in general the commerce of foes, even though these control systems had different focuses.

Stephan B.G.C.Michaelsen from Dortmund, Germany discusses in detail the German participation in the India fleet of 1505/06 and sketches the movement of German traders to the sources of supply of high-value oriental goods. He also tries to see its impact on the spice market in Lisbon and also analyses the reasons for the Germans for not being able to conduct contract-trade with Portuguese India for the next seventy years. Joseph Velinkar of St.Xavier's College, Bombay, India outlines how the *carreira* ships were organized into a system of convoys, routes and relief stations in order to reach the Indian subcontinent safely and to take back precious wares to Portugal in the third quarter of the sixteenth century. He says that the trans-oceanic movement of the *carreira* ships, with men and provisions for the feeding of the establishments of Portuguese India, depended on many factors like the weather, stock of provisions, date of rounding the Cape, health of the passengers, sea-worthiness of the ship and the opinion of the mariners. K.K.N.Kurup, Vice-Chancellor of Calicut University, Kerala, India traces the contribution of Malabar rulers including the Zamorin and his Muslim allies in delaying dominance by foreign powers in Malabar region. He argues that India's national interests are tied up with its sea waters and says that the native strategy to expel the Europeans from the waters of Arabian sea gradually helped to evolve a conceptualization of maritime India.

Jan Kieniewicz of Warsaw University, Poland tries to see whether the Portuguese succeeded in exerting impacts on the native Christians of Malabar and to see whether they evolved as reaction to assorted stimuli. According to him what actually took place was an encounter in the form of relations between two cultures, two social systems, in which mutual impacts were counterbalanced and which generated a *sui generis* joint space deprived of all symptoms of domination and subjugation. Kenneth McPherson of Indian Ocean Centre, Curtin University of Technology, Australia studies the impact of the Portuguese on the indigenous sea-faring community of the Paravas, who were living outside the central points of the *Estado da India*. He argues that the Portuguese intervention not only saved some sections of the Parava community from economic decline, but created a new caste with its own internal economic and social dynamics moulded by the economic forces unleashed by the process of intervention. John G.Everaert of Ghent University, Belgium deals with the non-Portuguese West Europeans put on trial by the Goa Inquisition during the period from 1563 to 1623. He shows how the Goa Inquisition chased the heretic westerners principally the protestants, Muslim renegades as well as sodomites and he argues that the Inquisition activities against

Introduction

them in the seventeenth century were motivated more by political hostility against the Dutch and the English than out of religious necessity. Carlos Alonso Vañes of Estudio Teologico Agustiniano, Valladolid, Spain speaks of the history of the convent of Saint Monica, the first Nunnery in Portuguese India, and gives detailed account of its early inhabitants. He also depicts how this convent turned out to be the leading monastic center for the women all over Asia till its suppression in 1834, where the ladies of the noble and aristocratic descent including the daughter of the king of Jaffnapattanam entered in order to carve out spiritual identity for their womanhood.

George D.Winius, who has recently shifted his academic activities from USA to Portugal, attempts to show that when the Portuguese immediately after the restoration (1640) had to fight three simultaneous wars, one on its border with Spain, another in Brazil and the third in Indian Ocean(the latter two against the Dutch) and when Lisbon administration could not stretch its limited resources to directions more than two, the Portuguese were compelled to opt for either Brazil or India, an option that had to be taken at the cost of the other. He points out how the decision of the king and his councillors to send men and supplies to Brazil and not to India played vital role in shaping the subsequent history of Asia and America. A.J.R.Russell-Wood of The Johns Hopkins University, Baltimore, USA, traces the historical developments by which the Brazilian ports became more prominent way stations for vessels outward-bound from Portugal providing opportunities for Brazilian goods to enter Asian markets and also shows how Brazil replaced Portugal as the final destination for the vessels from India. He highlights the emergence of inter-colonial trade, by a powerful merchant community with great political clout, linking the ports of Brazil with Africa and India, which operated without dependence on metropolitan capital or on Portuguese vessels.

S.Jeyaseela Stephen of Viswa Bharati University, Calcutta, India, deals with the Portuguese trade with the Nayaks of Tamil country in war animals, which enabled the Lusitanians to gain control over the ports of the Nayaks and to exercise influence at the royal courts in the hinterland. He also points out how the commercial activities of the Portuguese were linked to the military objectives of the Nayaks, whose demand for horses eventually gave way to the demand for elephants after the battle of Talikotta in 1565. Glenn J.Ames of the University of Toledo, USA examines how the strained relationship between Ali Adil Shah of Bijapur and the Portuguese culminated in the Bijapuri invasion of Salsette in 1658-1659. He argues that the defeat of Ali Adil Shah in 1659, enabled the Portuguese to re-establish effective rule in Goa and undertake reforms while Bijapur, whose weakness was evidently exposed in the war, was heading towards its own doom, which culminated in its annexation by the Mughals in 1686.

Pius Malekandathil of Goa University, India looks into the impact of Portuguese commerce on the various mercantile groups and on the market structure of Malabar. He argues that the challenges raised by the entry of the Portuguese in the markets of Malabar were eventually responded by maintaining parallel streams of commerce, in which one stream operated in Cochin-Goa-Lisbon commercial axis, while the other, operating outside Portuguese control systems, fed the traditional caravan route that terminated in the ports of Mediterranean. João Teles e Cunha of the Centro de Estudos Damião de Gois, Lisboa, Portugal says that the gem-trade in India carried out by the Portuguese, a traffic in which Goa played no less significant position, subsisted because it was all done through private merchants and their networks survived especially in centres far away from the official presence. He also points out that though trade in gem was free in the sixteenth century, it was highly regulated in the beginning of the seventeenth century, as a result of which precious stones were increasingly smuggled out to Europe either through the Cape-route or the Levant. Nagendra Rao of Goa University, India examines how the arrival of the Portuguese accelerated the volume of trade transactions in the ports of South Kanara. According to him the external demand from the Portuguese accelerated the agrarian production in the hinterland and general economic activities in the region under study, as a result of which symptoms of capital accumulation began to appear in South Kanara.

K.M. Mathew, former Dean of Social Sciences, Goa University, India analyses the reasons for the decline of the Portuguese naval power in the Indian Ocean region. He views that it was chiefly the decadence in the art of shipbuilding and navigation that ushered in Portuguese decline in the East. Hannes Stubbe of the University of Cologne, Germany looks into the role of the Goan personality José Custodio de Faria, who developed the theory of suggestion or the psychological theory of hypnosis for the first time, in the history of world of psychology. He shows how Abbé Faria, a complete outsider in the movement of European hypnotism of that time, was able to formulate the theory of *"sommeil lucide"* thanks to his acquaintance with the therapeutic techniques and religious-ethnopsychological practices of India and how it developed as a result of the dialogue between the Indian and the European psychologies.

Maria de Jesus dos Martires Lopes of Lisboa looks into the various Hindu religious practices and cultural traditions that penetrated into every day life of the Goan Christians of the 18th century. She argues that on the one hand the interpenetration of religious elements in both Christianity and Hinduism created harmonious synthesis, while on the other hand the increasing access of the natives to priesthood favoured this interpenetration to the extent of indianizing the religious ways. Fatima da Silva Gracias from Goa, India analyses the phenomenon of migration of the Goan women to different parts of the world, an activity that started during the Portuguese period but gathered momentum in the post-liberation days, and discusses the various socio-economic and religious conditions that favoured female-emigration. She argues that though the woman-migrants turned out to be active ambassadors of Goan culture as well as traditions and helped to improve the economic conditions and level of standard of living in Goa, the absence of mother from home has created many problems in the family, where at times it led to the breaking up of the family.

II

Prof. K.S. Mathew is also one of the pioneers in the field of Indian Ocean Studies and Maritime History, which are already being developed as disciplines of historical study with the efforts and cooperation of Satish Chandra, Ashin Das Gupta, M.N.Pearson, Sinnappah Arasaratnam, Kenneth McPherson, B.Arunachalam and Lotika Varadarajan. The more purposeful academic attempts to study the Indian Ocean came from Satish Chandra, who set the stage ready for the new branch of study by publishing the book *The Indian Ocean Explorations in History, Commerce and Politics* (New Delhi, 1987). A significant contribution in the field of Indian Ocean-oriented study was made by K.S.Mathew, especially in his edited work *Studies in Maritime History* (Pondicherry, 1990). His works *Mariners, Merchants and Oceans* (Delhi, 1995), *Indian Ocean and Cultural Interaction A.D. 1400-1800* (Pondicherry, 1996), *Ship-building and Navigation in the Indian Ocean Region A.D.1400-1800* (Delhi, 1997) also represent this historiographical tradition. Kenneth McPherson's work *The Indian Ocean: A History of People and the Sea* (Delhi, 1993) analyzes the different cohesive factors that worked in the maritime space of Indian Ocean for bringing in an organic unity. The diverse maritime traditions of the sea-faring people of India were brought to lime light by the various articles of B.Arunachalam, the former Professor of Geography, Bombay University, India. In this volume he discusses the Indian sea craft building during the sixteenth and the seventeenth centuries and brings to limelight the traditions of boat-building preserved by the sea-farers in the form of ship/ boat songs, ballads and astrological verses. He says that proximity to the timber-yielding forests in nearby accessible areas influence the location of boat-yards and that timber with high density and compressibility, with capacity to withstand saline water and the wood-borers were preferred for boat-building.

Introduction

Haraprasad Ray of the Asiatic Society, Calcutta, India locates Quilon in the historical context of Indian Ocean and traces the emergence and development of this port as a result of its contact with China and West Asian world. He maintains that the dwindling phase in Quilon's trade history started with the measures taken by the Chinese government to stop the drainage of China's metallic currency to Malabar, which restricted gold, silver and copper from flowing out of China. T.Jamal Mohammed examines the aspects of maritime trade and cultural interactions in the Indian Ocean during the period from 1500 to 1800 and points out that the colonial expansion in India went side by side with the cultural interactions between the colonial power and the colonized. According to him the general trend of the Portuguese in their interaction with the local society during this period was characterized by the attempts to do away with the existing social customs and manners for the sake of replacing them with those of the Europeans especially of Portugal.

Juan R.Francisco, former Professor of Indology, University of the Philippines, Philippines looks into the process through which Sanskrit and Indian cultural elements entered in coastal Magindanaon, which was at the farthest end of the maritime trade and traffic routes in the South East Asian region. He says that one of the important intellectual goods adopted by Magindanaon region in the process of trade and traffic was the language of Sanskrit. Francis Arakal of Sree Sankaracharya University of Sanskrit, Kalady, India, looks at the mutual contacts and interactions between India and Greece and tries to show that the cultures, civilisations and philosophies of India and Greece are not as independent of each other as are being thought of. Linguistic analysis shows areas of affinity in culture and highlights the various dimensions of historical contacts between the two.

III

The different aspects of European Expansion are themes of perennial discussion for scholars and Prof.Mathew's interest in themes of European Expansion gets diversified with his teaching-cum- research guiding activity, defined by the post of Professor in History at the University of Pondicherry, which was the former base of French possessions in India. There began a new trend in the historiography on European expansion with the works of M.E.P.Meilink-Roelofsz, Niel Steensgaard and Om Prakash, who looked at the developments in Asia and at its trading activities against the background of European expansion. K.S. Mathew looks into the various aspects of German collaboration in Indo-Portuguese trade and European expansion in his work *Indo-Portuguese Trade and the Fuggers of Germany* (Delhi,1997). What happened in Asia and India in an age of mercantilism and capital formation in Europe was a matter of utmost interest for most of these scholars. The various aspects of mercantilism and Indian trade are discussed in detail by Dietmar Rothermund in his work *Asian Trade and European Expansion in the Age of Mercantilism* (Delhi, 1981). On the other hand K.N.Chaudhuri in his work *The Trading World of Asia and the English East India Company, 1660-1760* (London,1978) has focused attention on the trends and patterns of Indian trade against the backdrop of English expansion in India. K.S.Mathew's books *French in India and Indian Nationalism, 1700- 1963 A.D.* (2vols.New Delhi, 1999), and *Indo-French Relations* (New Delhi, 1999) which are chronologically of later period, follow the same tradition in analyzing the problems of European expansion.

Teotonio R. de Souza of the Universidade Lusofona, Portugal draws attention to multicultural diasynchrony of the human mind with reference to the challenges posed by Eastern cultures. To him contemporary thought is essentially diasynchronic, which is a complex philosophical heritage, a co-existence of various philosophies of various times and cultures. He argues that Western pluralism falls short of multiculturalism, while the East, which has always lived multiculturalism with a manifest reciprocity, throws much light in this direction. M.O.Koshy, Pro-Vice-Chancellor of Kannur University, India evaluates the political and administrative policies of the Dutch East India Company in Kerala to see how the Dutch penetrated

Introduction

into Kerala's markets and maintained hold over its economy. He opines that these policies were dictated by the objectives of maximizing profits from the Eastern trade, for which a variety of machineries and devices were deployed.

Dietmar Rothermund of South Asian Institute of Heidelberg University, Germany dwells on the trade in Indian textiles and the Industrial Revolution and points out how the import of white cotton cloth mainly from Bengal as intermediate product to London for the endeavours of the cotton printers declined steadily after 1750s because of import substitution, i.e., spinning of cotton and weaving of cotton cloth in England. He argues that trade in Indian textiles, which had created an enormous demand and generated a great deal of income for the merchants participating in it, was the pre-condition for the development in British cotton industry, with which began the industrial revolution. He also calls for the revision of theories dealing with India, particularly the capitalist world system and the industrial revolution as well as the theory propounded by the British Marxist writers that the plunder of Bengal financed the British Industrial revolution.

B.Sobhanan of the Kerala University, India analyzes the Anglo-Carnatic relations in the eighteenth century and shows how the one-time independent Carnatic rulers were made dependent on the English through their carefully chalked out strategies. He argues that the English converted the kingdom of Carnatic as the most suitable base to commence their imperial designs in the south, which entered a decisive phase with the establishment of British paramountcy there through the subsidiary treaty. Ujjayan Bhattacharya of Goa University, India attempts to show how far the activities of the English East India Company in Bengal were guided by the mercantilist policies chalked out in the mother country and he analyzes the reaction and behaviour of the Asian states to the mercantilist policies of the Europeans by studying the Bengal of the eighteenth century. He says that the growth of the practice of revenue farming and the evolution of the commercial strategies, that varied from the procurement of investments through *dadni* or contract system to a more direct method of procurement through *gomastas*, were in fact the East India Company's responses to the changing economic and political compulsions of the 18th century Bengal.

Jean Deloche of the Ecole Française Pondicherry, India examines the stone pillars and turrets, which were erected in the vicinity of Haidarabad and Machilipattanam as route-indicators during the Mughal period. He points out that these stone pillars which were cut from the rocks and were bulb-shaped at the top, were arranged by pairs and are suggestive of a different system for demarcating roadway in the south of the peninsula. J.B.P.More from Paris, traces the interaction between the Mughal empire under Aurangzeb and the West European traders including the Portuguese, the Dutch, the English, the French and the Danes, who had established themselves at various nodal centres of exchange. He says that the Mughals allowed the West Europeans to establish settlements at Surat and Bengal to gain various types of customs duties from trade and thus increase their budgetary resources, besides ensuring supply of precious metals and other goods necessary for the empire, and highlights the fact that the Indian merchants had taken full advantage of the presence of the Europeans to increase their participation in maritime trade.

Aniruddha Ray of the Calcutta University, India looks at the functioning of the French factory at Surat from 1693 till 1701against the competitive commercial background created by the other European trading companies and the pressure brought on them by the Mughal authorities. He argues that the changes of the fortunes of the French at Surat were linked mainly with the politics in Europe, wider problems of piracy, the response of the population towards the Europeans, the restrictions imposed by the Mughal governor and the responses of the native merchants, who played very decisive role in the trade of Surat. P. Hymavathi of the Kakatiya University, India traces the art of healthy living and healing techniques practiced by the Indians of the later medieval period from the accounts of the French travellers and physicians. According to the author, though these accounts failed to bring out the deep-rooted underlying aim of traditional practices, French travelogues form an important part in the heuristics of Indian medical history.

B.Krishnamurthy of Pondicherry Central University, India tries to analyze the main features of Colbertism that evolved as a French version of mercantilism and to see how far this policy influenced the activities of the French East India Company in France and in India. He is of the opinion that under Colbertism the French company evolved into an organization that was more royal than mercantile in its approach and attitude towards the Indian trade and India and views that it had earned for the French more enemies than friends among the natives as well as Europeans. Joy Varkey of N.A.M. College, Kallikkandy, Kannur, India traces the history of French connections with Mahe in the eighteeth century and highlights Mahe's position in the French empire as a seaboard emporium of pepper trade, as a source of sepoys to the French military, as a motor of diplomatic interaction with local rulers and as an intermediary point in the exchange of communication. According to him the geographical location of Mahe, the resources of the hinterland and local political factors together with France's financial constraints played vital role in the French commercial operations carried out from here.

In our efforts to felicitate Prof.Mathew by putting up a volume on areas, which are central to his concerns we got immense help and collaboration from the academic world, to which we are deeply indebted. Our special thanks are due to Fundção Oriente, Lisbon for coming forward to take up the publication of this volume by granting us financial support. Right from the beginning Exmo.Sr.Dr.João de Deus Ramos, the Administrator of Fundção Oriente- Lisbon, Dr.Adelino Rodrigues da Costa, the former Delegate as well as Dr.Sergio Mascarenhas de Almeida, the present Delegate of Fundção Oriente Indian Delegation,Goa showed keen interest in seeing this volume through, for which we are extremely happy and grateful. We place on record our indebtedness to the Chairman

21

of the Malabar Educational Society for Human Resource Development and Research (MESHAR), Mahe for having taken up the initiative to get this work published under the series of the Institute for Research in Social Sciences and Humanities of the MESHAR.

We are also thankful to Fr.Jose Pulloppillil, Nirmala Computer Academy, Muvattupuzha for according us facilities for bringing the present work to fruition. Our indebtedness is also due to Sr.Jesina CMC for taking care of the language correction, to Mar Mathews Press, Muvattupuzha for having done an excellent printing job.

June, 2001   **PIUS MALEKANDATHIL**
                              Goa University

                              T. JAMAL MOHAMMED
                              Trivandrum

2

A JOY FOR EVER

A.R. Kulkarni

If somebody asks me, which is the happiest moment in your life, as a teacher, I would say unhesitatingly-when I hear or see that my students have gone ahead of me. The achievement of your student, is a joy for ever, - really a 'thing of beauty'. I am one of those fortunate teachers who can claim that at least a few of my students have not only attained a place of honour for themselves, but also have carried my name along with them to distant places. Professor K.S. Mathew, the founder of History Department of the Pondicherry Central University is one of such rare species.

I distinctly remember those good old days, when I first met this young, lean and of medium height 'Father' coming from Kerala to Pune in 1971 for post-graduate studies in the Department of History of the University of Pune. The historic city of Pune, which has produced many eminent historians, and had established a separate University in 1949, to promote history and culture of the region, had no department of history till 1969. A few senior teachers from the constituent colleges were invited to conduct the post-graduate programme of the University. They used to meet once in a week in a small classroom which could accomodate hardly a dozen students.

When I took over the charge of the Department in 1969, as its founder Professor, I was keenly interested in strengthening the Department both quantitatively and qualitatively. I was particularly in search of good students who could, in the long run, put the Department on the academic map of India. I persuaded the University authorities to liberalize the rules of admissions and permit students of some autonomous institutions like De Nobili, Spicer colleges and similar institutions after thoroughly scrutinizing their under-graduate courses. I could recommend Mathew's application on the basis of his graduation from the Lateran University, Rome with distinction(1966) without hesitation and thus Mathew joined the Department and successfully completed his course in History in 1973 with first class, a rare grade in those days.

I liked mixing with the students to understand their problems and observe their aptitudes. It also helped to create cordial atmosphere in the Department. Dr. Mathew once invited me for lunch in his residence of the St.Ignatius Parish at Khadki, a suburb of Pune, where I had a free talk with him about his future plans. Hailing from Kerala, where the Portuguese descended first on this sub-continent, I thought while enjoying the simple lunch, that Mathew would be the best person to be groomed for Portuguese studies, for which I had a great fascination. I always felt that the history of West-coast and Konkan, would be incomplete without a proper exploration of the Portuguese and the Dutch sources particularly of medieval times. Earlier I had persuaded a Jesuit Provincial of Pune to grant permission to my another student, Dr. Teotonio R. de Souza of Goa, to pursue doctoral thesis, which was not a common practice among the Jesuit Priests in those days. Mathew, being trained for priesthood was also facing a similar difficulty. I requested Mar Sebastian Valloppilly, the Bishop of Tellicherry (Kerala), to allow him to do research, and I was happy to know that the head of the diocese respected my letter.

Dr.Teotonio R. de Souza did his Ph.D. under my supervision, but I had a different plan for Mathew in my mind. I recommended his application to the Centre for Historical Studies of the Jawaharlal Nehru University, Delhi for admission to the M.Phil. and Ph.D. degrees as a test case, and I was quite happy that eminent historians like Professors S.Gopal and Romila Thapar gave him a green signal. Earlier, I had also recommended

A Joy for Ever

one of my students Dr. Lalima Varma, to the School of International Studies of the J.N.U. and she was not accepted for M.Phil. and Ph.D. courses, but was later on absorbed into the staff of the Department. When students are acceptable to well-known academic centres, naturally one would feel quite contented.

Dr. Mathew, thus got an opportunity to study at JNU in 1973 where he completed his M.Phil. in History, obtained a Diploma in Portuguese Language and secured the most coveted degree- Ph.D. in History in 1978. He had the benefit of working under the supervision of Dr. K.N. Panikkar, Dr. R. Champakalakshmi and Professor S.Bhattacharya, the well-known scholars in the field of History.

I did not know much of the family background of Dr. Mathew till I visited a couple of years back his ancestoral house at Kurumalloor, in the Kottayam district of Kerala. I was at Palai(Kerala) for a seminar, and Dr. Mathew who was its co-ordinator was very keen on taking me to his village and introducing me to his elder brothers and other relatives who were pursuing their family calling-agriculture. I received a very warm welcome from his family members. Mathew was born as the seventh and last child of his parents Mr. and Mrs. Skaria Kuzhippallil in a Syrian Catholic family on 2nd June, 1939. After completing his early formal education, he underwent rigorous training for seven years in Philosophy, Sociology, Latin, Syriac, Theology and Bible in the St.Joseph's college Alwaye, Kerala. He then obtained a Bachelor's degree in Humanities from the Lateran University, Rome in 1966. Between 1966 and 1971 he worked in collaboration with the National Extension Block, Calicut and diocese of Tellicherry for developmental activities for the newly migrated people in the northern part of Kerala, the Malabar region.

However, this did not satisfy Dr. Mathew's urge for higher studies, for which he came to Pune and from there shifted to Delhi, and successfully completed all his academic pursuits.

Dr. Mathew's stay at the JNU, was quite rewarding. He came into contact with many Indian and foreign scholars visiting the University. He got the ICHR fellowship for visiting European archives for data collection for his research project. He also secured the prestigious Gulbenkian Foundation(Lisbon) fellowship for two years to work in various archives and Libraries in Lisbon and other archival centres in Europe. As a consequence of these two fellowships he could acquaint himself with many other archives in Spain, Paris, Rome, Venice, Florence, London, and so on. He came into contact with senior scholars like Professor Magalhães Godinho of Lisbon, Professors C.R.Boxer, J.B.Harrison and Kenneth Ballhatchet of London. His doctoral thesis *'Portuguese Trade on the Malabar Coast 1500-1530'* based mostly on the hitherto unexplored fresh Portuguese materials was highly appreciated by scholars, and it also gave him boost to do further research in the field of his choice.

He entered into the teaching profession at M.S.University of Baroda(1979), and later on shifted to Central University of Hyderabad, A.P. as Professor(1985) and worked as Head of the Department of History till December 1987. He finally settled down as Founder Professor and Head of the Department of History, Pondicherry University, another Central University since 1987. His main thrust areas of research are socio-economic history of Malabar and Maritime History of India, and he devoted most of his time for developing them individually and through his pupils. He encouraged many sholars from Baroda, Hyderabad and Pondicherry to study the Portuguese, the French and the Dutch records and even obtained for them fellowships from the Gulbenkian Foundation for data collection from the foreign archives. A cursory glance at the list of successful Ph.D. dissertation completed by his students under his supervision and the various research projects finalized by him personally, bear an eloquent testimony to his achievement in the field of historical research.

One of the major pre-requisites for a researcher in History, particularly medieval history, is a good linguistic equipment. This enabled him to go to the originals directly, instead of depending on their translations made by some one else. Dr. Mathew is one of the very few Indian historians, knowing many Indian and foreign languages and becoming most trustworthy and successful researchers of medieval India. Besides Malayalam, his own mother tongue, Dr. Mathew knows, Hindi, Sanskrit, and many foreign languages like Latin, Portuguese, German, Spanish, French, Syriac and Greek, a rare combination indeed.

Dr. Mathew, it appears from his successful career, was born for history. The rigorous training and discipline which he acquired while preparing himself for priesthood, has been skillfully utilized by him for developing his personality as a teacher and a disciplined research scholar. For a long time, I had cherished the desire of developing Portuguese and Dutch studies in the Department of Pune University. I often felt that the study of Maratha country-particularly of its economy and society would remain incomplete without consulting the Portuguese and Dutch records besides the English along with the indigenous sources. But I did not know any of these foreign languages except English. I just thought what I could not do, my students should do it. Historical research, I believe is a team work, and for an indepth study of a region or a period, a net-work of scholars interested in various aspects of history alone could help to reconstruct its history. I tried to get either Dr.Teotonio R. de Souza or Dr. K.S. Mathew as my colleagues in the Department to give shape to my ideas. But that was not to be.

Dr.Mathew did not miss a single opportunity to declare me publicly as his 'guru'. In fact, while I was in Lisbon, he acted as my friend philosopher and guide and brought to my notice the relevance of Portuguese records for better understanding of Maratha history in certain aspects. He would sit by my side, and read for me some selected documents and summarize them in English. We used to spend the whole day either in Torre do Tombo, or Bibliotheca Nacional, and return to the Seminario dos Olivais, Lisboa in the evening, a residence which he had secured for me. I could hardly forget the services rendered by him during my stay in Lisbon.

Dr. Mathew always looked after his students not only as a teacher, but as a person. His students always found themselves quite comfortable with him and admired him wholeheartedly. I have met most of them, and know that they consider it as an honour to serve him. Knowing that Dr. Mathew was my student for sometime, they treat me also as their 'guru's' guru. A tradition is thus unwittingly set up.

Dr. Mathew's achievements in the field of historical research are highly commendable. He has more than 16 books and a number of research articles reaching a century to his credit. They not only speak for his industry and urge for research, but also indicate the steady progress that he has attained in producing qualitative research pieces.

As founder Professor of the Department of History of the Pondicherry University, he made it internationally known within a short period. I had the privilege of inaugurating the Department, and I have watched its development under the stewardship of Dr.Mathew, all these years. He is a good organizer of academic activities like seminars or symposia at the national or international levels. The seminars/symposia he conducted on Indo-Portuguese studies, Indo-French Relations, Maritime History of India, Ship-building and Navigation and so on, attended by many eminent Indian European and Asian scholars, speak not only for his efficient organization, but also for his varied interests in historical research. Generally, the papers presented and discussed in such academic bodies are forgotten. But one of the special features of these academic programmes of Mathew is that he worked hard and got the proceedings published as fast as he could. This method of working, perhaps, induced the scholars to respond to his invitation, as they were sure that their efforts would not be wasted, and they would be printed at the earliest.

Professor Mathew, thus could carve out a niche for himself in this vast world of scholars, because of his hard work, earnestness, and relentless pursuit of his plan of research, in his chosen field mainly the socio-economic history of Malabar region and the Maritime History of India. Dr.Blanco, the Administrator of the International Service of the Gulbenkian Foundation, Lisbon encouraged him by financial support for his research, whenever he needed it, as he was convinced of the potentialities of Dr.Mathew. The very fact that he was invited as Visiting Fellow at Wisconsin University, Madison, U.S.A., Ottawa University, Canada, the Institut d'Histoire Universite, Michel de Montaingne - Bordeaux III, France, Maison de Sciences de l'Homme, Paris, proves how he was acceptable to the international advanced centres of Research. In view of his academic contribution U.G.C. awarded the prestigious national fellowship of two years (1993-1995) meant for eminent professors.

Professor Mathew is a widely travelled person. He visited Australia, Portugal, Spain, France, Germany, Austria, the Netherlands, Belgium, England, Italy, Norway, United States, Canada, Hungary and Macao. There is a Marathi proverb which says that the great advantage of travel *(deshatan)* is the friendship with the learned people *(pandit maitri)* and entrance into their assemblies *(Sabhet Sanchar)*. By his sojourns in various parts of the world, Dr. Mathew has achieved both - friendship of scholars, and association with international intellectual bodies.

As a man, Mathew always respects the elders; he is generous in his help to the needy students, without reservations, adjusts with his academic rivals, by his mild temperament and sobre character; he is a good judge of men and above all mindful of his responsibilities towards his family. I have often seen in his house, nephews and nieces staying with him for their higher education. He thus indirectly indicated his indebtedness to his family.

Dr. Mathew is a great lover of books, and has collected old and new books from various parts of the world. His large collection is open to his students and other scholars without any restrictions. In fact he has designed his house in Pondicherry in such a way that the Library room could be detached from the main apartment with a separate entrance from outside, so that the students can use the Library without disturbing the residential part.

Dr. Mathew has a long career ahead. I can speak from my experience that a retired person is more busy than one who is in service. I am sure that there are still more academic honours,- national and international- waiting for him. I only wish him good health and long life so that he could implement all that he had planned for his retirement.

While taking a resume of Professor Mathew's achievements, I could not avoid the temptation of making a self-assessment, and I must confess that he has gone far ahead of me, which makes me proud of him. This is in fact a victory for the 'guru', because, as the great poet Keats puts it, it is 'a thing of beauty-a joy for ever'.

I
PERSPECTIVES ON INDO-PORTUGUESE HISTORY

3

GLOBALISATION OF THE EARTH?

Reflections on the European Expansion and its Consequences.

Eberhard Schmitt

"The greatest event since the creation of the world, apart from the incarnation and death of Him who had created it, has been the discovery of the Indies [i.e. America]."[1] Whoever, in 1992, tried to grasp the consequences of the European expansion was in danger of succumbing to the concentrated power of this sentence. It originates in the year 1552, coined by the chronicler Francisco López de Gómara, secretary to Hernán Cortés, as an attempt to convince the emperor Charles V of the importance of the New World's evangelisation. But it could have originated in our times almost as plausibly, being uniquely modern in its propensity to unduly intermingle entirely different things and perceive them as aspects of one coherent, teleological chain of events.

To avoid an oversimplifying interpretation of the elapsed demi-millenium, and not to repeat Gómara's error, we will therefore have to recall the fact that the process of European expansion commenced, not with the discovery of America in 1492, but as early as the end of the 13th century. Neither was it set off by transposing the medieval efforts of christianisation into the far West, beyond the Pillars of Hercules, nor by a genuinely European urge, inspired by a lust for adventure and thirst for knowledge associated with renaissance Europe, of unveiling, as it were, the world beyond the horizon.

The European expansion was not a development that grew from - so to speak - „internal causes". Quite to the contrary, it was the reaction to a mighty challenge which, at that time, had already been tempting the Occident for no less than two thousand years, tantalisingly rousing a certain predatory mentality especially among the Europeans of the Mediterranean.

This challenge was the Orient, then seeming opulent and miraculous, with its precious commodities and phantasy-rousing mirabilia, having forcefully refreshed its position in European consciousness only recently through manifold contacts during the era of the crusader states and the *Pax Mongolica*.

For the historian, several distinct threads of continuity spanning the range between the phase of late-medieval European-Oriental encounters and the beginning of early modern expansion can be discerned. Three prominent ones shall be mentioned here to clarify the temporal and spatial scope of these early connections.

There was, as a first factor, the role of the Italian maritime republics that had contributed to the spread of news but also to the knowledge and esteem of eastern luxury goods like silk, sugar, pepper, ginger, nutmeg, cloves and cinnamon in Europe. On these they had prospered, maritime cities like Venice and Genoa, through them they had risen in political power and wealth they were straining to keep after the fall of the crusader states. For the Genoa of 1291, the year in which the last stronghold of the crusaders, Akkon, fell, the sources witness that members of the merchant patriciate set off on two galleys to sail through the Strait of Gibraltar and then along the African coast „unto the shores of India, whence to fetch commodities which promised good profits"[2], so the chronicler Jacopo Doria informs us. The idea not to somehow try to pry open the islamic bolt that had kept the gateway to the Orient shut since the end of the crusader states, but rather to circumnavigate that bolt, door and the roads lying behind it on a new route altogether, had ever since been kept alive, especially among the burgeoning colonies of Genovese citizens in Lisbon and Sevilla. It became one of the decisive motors of the beginning of Portuguese expansion along the

African coast and was still ruling principle for the voyage of Columbus in 1492.

As a second thread of continuity we may well see the role of the Papal Curia as the confluence of the most important factual knowledge about the Orient and Africa in the late Middle Ages. From there intensive encouragement issued for Portugal to seek the mentioned sea-route arose until the end of the 15th century. Since 1143, the times of the early campaigns against the Moors, still conducted in the region of the Tejo estuary, Portugal had been under the immediate suzerainty of the Popes, and in 1456 the curia issued to Portugal and the Portuguese Order of Christ the monopoly for taking possession of new countries and islands on a route along the coast of Africa „usque ad Indos"[3], as far as where the Indians live. On the Portugese model of early encounters with non-christians in black Africa the curia was to shape it`s missionary concept which differed from the rigorous policy of annihilation that had been the customary mode of contact with the muslim archenemy. A new concept that later contributed to the Indio-protection-policy for the achievement of which the catholic orders (i.e. mainly the Franciscans), among others, fought in America.

A third thread of continuity is discernible in the origins and composition of European leadership élites from the period of the crusades down to the so-called „Great Discoveries" and the *conquista* of the New World: those who left the borders of Europe were mainly later-born sons of the lower nobility, usually professional soldiers, accompanied by troops of hired mercenaries, who intended to obtain the resources for a living as befitted their social position, to maintain that position, or to enhance it.

This observation applies to both early Portuguese expansion and Castilian-Spanish expansion alike. Almost always everything was at stake then, it meant „make or break": Returning from a spoils-expedition at sea with empty hands or from a *conquista* without treasures of gold and silver would have meant hopelessness in aspiring social consolidation, and therefore in the last consequence also the loss of honour to every single of these noble leaders. Philipp von Hutten, knight and *conquista-entrepreneur* for the Augsburghian Welser-company, who was searching for *El Dorado* in Venezuela around 1530-46, strikingly reduced this circumstance to a trivial slogan: „Be it God's will, the land or my body must pay for it."[4]

These, among others which are less apparent, are the three principal strands of continuity in which Columbus's voyage of 1492 was embedded. In its own time it was not a singular, outstanding event. In 1493 his voyage was acknowledged in Spain, but it was hardly realised in the rest of Europe, especially since no one learned where exactly Columbus had been to. As long as the Catholic Kings believed Asia to now be accessible on a western route, and therefore „*las especierías*", the spice emporia of the Orient, opened to them, they were in consent with Columbus if only concerning the estimation of his achievement as a discoverer. However, this harmony faded when contemporaries like Vespucci realised in 1502 that the world discovered by Columbus was a continent hitherto unknown, a *mundus novus*. From then on, this „New World" was essentially regarded as a mere obstacle on the way to Asia. More than one expedition was sent out o find a passage through the „annoying barrier" that was America.

What really caused a sensation in these years, and leads our considerations directly to modern times, was the opening of the eastern sea-route to India by Vasco da Gama in 1498 and the ensuing establishment of a wide-meshed Portuguese maritime ascendancy covering the Indian Ocean as far as the *Insulinde* with its spice markets. The wealth and marvels of the Orient now appeared to lay open before the Occident, just like it had been hoped for in Southern Europe since the era of the crusaders.

This splendid success of opening up an eastern trade route to India consequently, and completely, eclipsed the discovery of the „New World" in the European consciousness. Or, as Fernand Braudel once put it, „America was not everything"[5]. And it might have stayed that way, America might have remained a Sleeping Beauty serenely removed from the course of history; a state which, if not perpetual, might at least not have changed for a long time to come, comparable to the status Australia seems to maintain to this day.

Things inadvertently changed, however, in 1522. In that year, the handful of survivors from the great Magalhães-expedition of 1519 returned, having, in defiance of their orders, circumnavigated the globe on the return voyage from the Moluccas, their destination, instead of returning via the Pacific. This voyage proved that the westward route to Asia was substantially longer than Columbus and the Catholic Kings had anticipated, an insight which led to the conclusion that the westward voyage to Asia would not be worth while as regarded spice trade. In this light, Columbus's great conception had finally met with failure 30 years after the discovery of America.

And yet, the result of Columbus's first voyage acquired significance within that same period of time, and almost overnight America commenced to be intrinsically valuable in European eyes. The reason for this was Hérnan Cortés's completing the conquest of the Aztec Empire, that silver-brimming Mexican kingdom that caused a sensation in the Old World in 1521. Now the New World was recognised as home to advanced civilisations rich in precious metals. A vast inrush of people set in, and in 1526 emperor Charles V extended the permission to emigrate to his non-Spanish subjects.

America quickly became the epitome of possibilities of unexpected gain and rise, the new land of wonders and wealth, the land in which a position in life could be achieved by one's own capability, the land of - we are tempted to say - „unrestrained possibilities", though the expression did not yet exist then.

Ultimately, then, neither the exploration of the eastern sea-route to Asia had in itself a lasting impact on history, nor that of the western one, nor that fortuitous result of Columbus' expedition, the discovery of America, but the interaction of the three. They resulted in an acceleration of the European expansion and, especially in the western direction across the Atlantic, an intensification thereof, which would not have occurred as it did, had Columbus actually made landfall in east Asia in 1492. Was it then that the globalisation of the Earth began?

The following history is indeed the history of the almost imperceptible formation of a world-wide traffic network and a gradual linking up of the world through commerce and trade, and, not least, elements of European culture: their fleets enabled the Portuguese and Spanish, and from the turn of the 17th century onward the Dutch and the English, to reach virtually every point on the map that had any significance with regard to economic exchange; soon firmly-established shipping lanes criss-crossed the seas, the South Atlantic, the Indian Ocean, and, after the Urdaneta expedition in 1565, the Pacific Ocean as well, which was traversed by the route of the Manila Galleon.[6]

As this world wide traffic system evolved, however, a fundamental structural difference developed, which distinguished the maritime traffic between America and Europe from that to Asia: the Atlantic route soon surpassed the traffic to Asia in terms of goods carried and passengers conveyed by the manifold. People from Europe settled permanently in the New World, maintaining relations of all kind with the Old World, buying and selling everyday necessities and thus creating the need for comprehensive interaction, which in effect enclosed the Atlantic within a few decades as an Iberian - after 1600 - a Western European inland sea.

The Atlantic was to remain such a ‚European inland sea' for quite a while. Spaniards and Portuguese settled and colonised the western hemisphere along the Atlantic coast from Patagonia to Florida, around the Carribean Sea and the Gulf of Mexico. Englishmen, Swedes, Dutch and Frenchmen took root from the Gulf of Mexico up to the region of the St. Lawrence River. Western European bridgeheads on the far side of the North Atlantic evolved into gateways for land-hungry settlers, gradually driving the native population into the *hinterland* on the entire continent.

In contrast, in Middle and South America, the Iberian powers tried to mould the natives into subjects of their crowns: a policy of integration, co-ordinated with christianisation under the auspices of the state's religious patronate, forced upon the Indios the adoption of European language, European practices of agriculture and crafts, European-shaped settlements, European life-style and European civilisation, as far as possible. But the Indios remained second-class citizens at best, and could not normally hope to exceed the position of indentured semi-free labourers, with a few exceptions in Mexico and Peru. In this light it is probably less decisive, whether they were materially better or worse off in the old indigenous cultures, as being maintained by a recent line of research[7], but the point rather is that they entirely or to a large extent lost their cultural identity. Much was taken away by the Iberian powers, however, some they did give in return.

In North America, the Europeans destroyed the indigenous ethnic groups and cultures to a far greater extent, though they themselves prospered a lot more in the process than they would have in the Old World or in Middle and South America: when later the thirteen North American colonies were to revolt against England they understood themselves as the „better Europe", acting according to civil theological principles, which adopted the best of European political theory, philosophy and ethics of the enlightenment - all that which, in their opinion, might well have been deliberated in degenerated Ancient Europe, but could not be put into political practice there. Never was America to be more European than during the phase of North American independence beginning in 1774

Remarkably, European settlement outside of the Americas, in Africa, Asia and Oceania, was reluctant and numerically insignificant. Around 1800 there were only four permanent European settlements housing more than two thousand residents of European descend in the entire eastern hemisphere: Portuguese Goa, Spanish Manila, Dutch Batavia (now Jakarta), and Capetown, Dutch as well, the latter two only since the 17th century.

This minor European presence mirrored the actual position of Europeans in the eastern hemisphere: the superior technology and armament of their ships enabled them to swiftly establish naval supremacy wherever they chose, and elicit profits out of piracy or forcible barter, but the point was never far when they had to revert from confrontation to co-operation with the locals in order to establish real commercial relations which guaranteed sustained revenues and profits through regular trade relations. Corresponding to this state of affairs, European presence in Asia - limited to the coast in most cases - was predominantly borne by exquisitely balanced agreements between Europeans and local princes, increasing or decreasing with the emergence of new factors, and quite frequently remaining extremely precarious until the late 18th century.

Furthermore, the Europeans in the Orient busied themselves only to a lesser extent with the trade between Asia and Europe. As Vitorino Magalhães-Godinho has proven, the most important commodities of European-Asiatic long-distance trade (pepper, ginger, cinnamon, mace, nutmeg, and cloves) represented only about 14% of the overall 16th century inner-Asiatic maritime trade, half of which reached Europe via the Cape route, the other half via the Levant. The remainder of the production, about 86%, was traded and consumed within Asia itself: and it was this inner-Asiatic trade that the Europeans gradually entered, because it was more lucrative than long-distance trade with Europe.[8]

The not too surprising result was a far-reaching European adaptation to the practices of the trade, which had developed over the course of centuries. In other words: it was the Europeans who submitted, ultimately, to local and regional circumstances, and not the markets that submitted to the Europeans. Thus out of a factor of ephemeral disruption of the maritime trade system in the East, the Portuguese in the course of the 16th century developed into well-adjusted Asiatic trade- and tribute-lords. With the Dutch and the English it was basically the same until well into the second half of the 18th century. Only then did the realities begin to shift, as the two powers' East-India-Companies were persuaded by their military to occupy extensive territories, in which they anticipated tendencies of the imperialism that was to develop later - including all its consequences.

If we compare at this point western versus eastern hemisphere European expansion, one thing becomes obvious: in America, Europe had firmly established itself, in a rejuvenated and, consequently, rather ruthless fashion, as it were. Simultaneously, there it had the opportunity to shirk a tendency of comprehensive social disciplining which had begun to gain ground in the societies of European absolutism. Into Africa, Asia and Oceania, on the other hand, Europe had only set foot in acquiring a host of bases; there might have been between five and six hundred around 1800 - if we include all the meanwhile abandoned ones into the count. Moreover, in many of these bases European presence was tolerated rather than maintained on its own power. Nowhere had the eastern hemisphere been branded with its mark, as one might be led to believe when browsing through a school atlas depicting large parts of it as European colonies. Nothing could be further from the truth: the spreading out of the Europeans across the globe did not yet have any direct consequences on the Orient.

The mightier were those it had on America, where a rapid deterioration of the native population's conditions and an equally rapid expansion of the whites' ascendancy were concomitant to the coming into power of the white, yet already genuinely American independence movements of the late 18th and early 19th centuries. For even if in Europe the urge to spread out over the entire globe had substantially abated, temporarily, after the American Europeans' secession from their European motherlands, in America itself, and especially in the newly formed United States it had only become the more pronounced. A veritable sub-colonialism was emerging.

This, too, is where we find the origins of the concept of America's inexorable and providential rise, serving progress' purpose. Hegel, conservative ideologist of European ethnocentrism, had had the idea of introducing the concept of a *Weltgeist* into the philosophy of history, which was constructed from the outset with the inherent propensity to transmigrate from protestant-progressionist Prussia to the United States of America, where - in the populist Hegelian view - it has been settling ever since the year 1917 at the latest, when the United States took the stage of world history.[9]

And it has only been since the middle of the 19th century that the history of the USA is connected to that of Columbus. Since then, a myth has been forged which made Columbus a figure of light, bearer of a torch the sheen of which has become brighter throughout human history: he was now looked upon as initiator, as founder of a global, irreversible process which had led to an incessant improvement of human civilisation. His deed, the myth maintains, had begotten, as an inevitable next step, the formation of the United States, building a new and better civilisation and having risen, barely two hundred years after its coming into existence, to be the most powerful nation in the world, and, moreover, the spearhead of the morally superior, of the completion of creation itself. In actual fact, though, Columbus and the emergence and subsequent history of the United States, remarkable as it may indisputably be, have but little to do with each other. Columbus's feat was not the cause of the development North America underwent in the 19th and 20th centuries, it was a condition opening the possibility.

Prerequisite to all further efforts of Europeanising the world - whether they now originate in Europe or North America - was beyond doubt the intellectual and simultaneous technological development of the 19th century in particular. Owing their technological superiority (the use of steam power having triggered a stimulation of industrialisation which in turn made possible fast cargo and passenger transportation over long distances), Europe and North America managed to bring a large part of the world under their control during the age of imperialism. A certain messianic turn of mind, which dated back to the times of early christianisation and of the Enlightenment, having undergone a process of gradual secularisation, was instrumental in enabling them to endow themselves with several fundamental legitimising principles, most prominent among which was the notion of a European international law, to justify their actions.

One contemporary of this inclination to bring the world the salvation of Europe was the German propagandist of colonialism, Carl Hager. In 1886, he formulated what could be read ten thousandfold in similar testimonies from these decades: „It is the ancient and glorious privilege and obligation of Europe to enlighten the other parts of the world with the achievements of its civilisation, its moral and political convictions, its technology and science, to civilise the other countries. The notion of the solidarity of humankind, the ideal of civilising the entire globe has, in the course of time, in the wake of geographic discoveries gained ground and vigour, until it has, in our times, embellished with economic aspirations, become an unchallenged claim towards European humanity."[10] Thus, was Europeanisation a necessary precondition for all further development of civilisation on earth?

In the struggle for Europeanisation in the era of imperialism the actual military occupation of territories overseas by European or US forces probably was not even the decisive factor. Anyway, it scarcely lasted longer than a century. What the determined Europeanism of the 19th and 20th century did bring about, independent of the gain of formal territorial acquisition, was a certain convergence of major parts of the world in terms of a technical minimum standard concerning the infrastructure, as it existed in Europe and North America and which went beyond the established network of trade-routes and shipping lanes. This was achieved through the construction of roads and railroads, the introduction of a modern communications-system, and also the partial assumption of European organisation concerning police forces, mail, school- and health-system, but also by an imitation of European work ethics and the like.

Of far greater significance than the forcible appropriation of overseas territories during the age of imperialism, carried out in accordance with European international law, was the fact that Europe succeeded in arousing and sustaining, an interest in its material and intellectual culture among the native élites. Evidently this culture even today provides a power reservoir an orientation towards Europe can selectively draw upon, even in such cases where basic behavioural patterns are anti-European.

Rather conspicuous was the fact that the Europeans and their „sub-colonial cultural relatives" of the 16th to the 20th centuries, i.e. the emerging white civilisations of Ibero-America, North America, Sibiria, South Africa, Australia and New Zealand and, ultimately, Israel (what today we are customarily calling the „West") advanced, from the outset, not only into the inhabited, but also into the uninhabited and even the uninhabitable corners of the earth, searching for unexploited deposits of natural resources. Rare woods, precious metals, medicinal herbs, narcotics and spices, pearls, gems, furs, fish and train oil, salt, tar, guano, coal, ores, minerals, mineral oil, and mineral gas: these and similar raw materials and products were the objectives of the acquisitive European grasp no less than human civilisations, tribes, states, and markets or overseas soil and sea as such. Practically all non-western states of the world have adopted this predatory turn of mind from the Ancient West; yet protagonists of a counter-movement are not to be found in the „third world", but come from the West itself, massively and not without impact.

Has the world beyond the western-dominated regions become more European since then, or more American (which in this case means the same)? Has, since then, owing to four hundred years of European expansion, owing to an almost complete Europeanisation at least in terms of science and technology, come about something like a globalisation of the world along European lines?

In my view, the answer has to be a two-fold one, stemming from the ambivalent nature of what we call „the West".

One answer is: one manifestation, the West, incarnated as a number of multinational business corporations, indeed does control a large portion of the world, notwithstanding legal and political decolonisation, by means of a global network into which it continually feeds new technologies.

The other manifestation of the West, in contrast, and that is the second answer, represented by the governments of the major industrial states, draws little direct benefit from the non-western world. Quite on the contrary, it supports it, e.g. by diverse (albeit not always entirely altruistic) development aid projects and by debt relief programmes of extensive scope.

Nonetheless, the question remains unanswered of whether European, or rather, western, initiatives have effected a process of global standardisation, or how justified the postulation of such a process is for the future. As Huntington has recently pointed out in his best-selling (and frequently rather oversimplifying) „Clash of Cultures", the adoption of western technologies, certain trends in fashion, even isolated patterns of behaviour, for centuries outside an extant European network of global commerce, production, and communication, has contributed very little towards a Europeanisation of the world, just as the use of Japanese cars and cameras has hardly resulted in the Japanisation of America or Europe.[11]

Does technical and technological globalisation incur a standardisation of the world or not? Well: the standardisation we observe in global cultures is merely superficial. The effects it produces, i.e. the reactions it incurs in the depths of individual cultures, are rather to the contrary, namely conscious regionalism, conscious clinging to cultural individuality, revitalisation of domestic cultural values. „Globalisation", therefore, seems to me to be a rather deceptive term, a phenomenon which does not substantially touch upon the peculiarities of individual cultures and their historical development. The emphasis put on globalisation these days may bring something into the focus of attention which might not actually be of vital importance for the life and coexistence of the world's civilisations. This is because human beings and the communities they live in will continue to explore not only the points they have in common, but more than ever their peculiarities by a faculty of comparison which is strongly encouraged by globalisation. In the worst conceivable case, the consequence of getting to know each other more intimately is for cultures to do the exact opposite of converging.

As Marília dos Santos Lopes has recently observed for the early modern Europeans' familiarisation with Africa, the more intimate the Europeans' perception of the Africans became, they grew not more acquainted to them, but rather more estranged, the Africans were increasingly labelled „savages" and progressively lost their individuality.[12]

One is forced to add, in this context, that racist, religious, cultural, ideological and other concepts of separation and segregation are always apt to interfere with a standardisation of the world, and are frequently called back to memory and reinforced.[13] One example is that, with a tendency towards differentiation among virtually all larger societies of the world, an inflation of newly-formed written languages has occurred, which, having evolved from everyday language or dialect, are now claiming equality with older, firmly established official languages. It may well be that in another half century there may exist twice as many languages with formally stylised grammar as today. This phenomenon can hardly be attributed to a tendency of global standardisation, although it benefits from modern communication technologies, from a globalisation which provides it with impromptu contributors and sympathisers all over the world.

Therefore: is there going to be a globalisation in the sense of an in-depth standardisation penetrating even the innermost core of human existence? Or will globalisation, rejected as a threat to cultural identity, set off a diametrically opposite process, engendering further cultural self-awareness and diversification? The following interpretation seems possible: The existence of western techniques and technologies may not mean nothing at all - but it does not appear to mean very much. Let the possibility of exchanging information from anywhere around the globe within a fraction of a second be called globalisation, of obtaining and comparing data on virtually every subject within minutes. Defying widespread euphoria: the sheer mass of said data, it would appear, has the effect of invalidating it, and the more there is, the smaller the chance of their being processed into genuinely new information, providing us with an opportunity to extend our outlook on everyday life or life in general, that they might bring about a uniformed culture more stringent, globally, than we have today. One is involuntarily reminded of the files compiled by the former GDR's *Staatssicherheit* (i. e. secret service - department of the interior in this context): atomistic information, in quantities that thwarted every effort of ever systemising, let alone make use of it, obscured the view towards the essential, „un-focused" the gaze, as it were, by no means engendered creativity and consequently failed in that task of „moulding together" the society the said *Staatssicherheit* had been created for.

One has to see clearly that globalisation by way of giving access to communications-systems and data does not mean westernisation. The great cultures of the earth are to a high degree immune to influences that recommend themselves only by their technology and ways of transmission.

There are other phenomena, though, which might have a certain, albeit minimal chance of becoming big sellers for the West to export to the rest of the world: western humanities and social sciences for example, which have, through their remarkable, highly developed differentiation, succeeded, not only in making the functional principles of Europeanism itself an object of scholarly research, but the intellectual and religious foundations of other cultures of the world as well - a scientific approach hitherto without parallel in any other cultural system (which might serve to show that Europe was, in the course of expansion, influenced by the outside world to a far greater extent than vice versa). Secondly, a system of values which comprises the acquirement of tolerance, embracing equally non-Europeans in terms of race, religion, and ethic, and which has found its expression in the UNO-charter (not unchallenged, naturally: many states are clamouring about „human rights imperialism"). Thirdly, the working out of procedures, especially in Latin America, of stemming the inbred overseas Europeanism by means of invigorating the surviving native traditions with the help of the Europeans (though the success is subject to discussion,) -

indigenism at the cost of the Europeans, as it were, but developed with their direct or indirect intellectual help.

So it may seem that an advancing westernisation of the world is not due to the extant, western-controlled trade and communications network, but that it might be, to a certain degree, be brought about by the attractiveness and magnetism of a western community of values. But at the same time the West might be putting a stop to that: namely by having these tendencies subverted - as has been the case in every saeculum of European expansion to this date - by exploitation techniques applied in part openly, in part clandestinely, by certain western groups and interests protected by theorems of superiority, which have almost always and everywhere accompanied the West, like „unequal brothers", again and again enabling non-Europeans to appreciate European culture as well as, at the same time, denouncing it for being two-faced. The West is ambivalent: possibly Europe will continue with its propensity to bungle with one hand what it built with the other, or clandestinely take back what it has benevolently given.

Translation: *Christian Rödel* assisted by *Rosa Karl*.

References:

1. Span. orig. cit.: „La mayor cosa después de la creación del mundo, sacando la encarnación y muerte del que lo crió, es el descubrimiento de las Indias", in Francisco López de Gómara, *Historia General de las Indias y Vida de Hernán Cortés*, 1st ed. Zaragoza 1552. Here cit. according to the ed. of Jorge Gurria Lacroix. Caracas 1979, p. 7.

2. Latin orig. cit.: „... ut per mare occeanum irent ad partes Indie mercimonia utilia inde deferentes", in Jacobi Aurie [Jacopo Doriae] Annales ad annum 1291, in *Annali Genovesi di Caffaro e de' suoi continuatori dal MCCLXXX al MCCLXXXIII*. Vol. V, Nuova edizione a cura di Cesare Imperiale di Sant' Angelo. Roma 1929, p. 124.

3. Cf. the Bull „inter cetera" of Pope Calixtus III (13th March 1456), in *Monumenta Henricina*, Vol. XII (1454-1456), Coimbra 1971, pp. 286-288.

4. German orig. cit.: „Aber ob Got wil, das Land oder mein Leib muß es bezalen ...". in Eberhard Schmitt/Friedrich Karl von Hutten (eds.), *Das Gold der Neuen Welt*.

Eberhard Schmitt

Die Papiere des Welser-Konquistadors und Generalkapitäns von Venezuela Philipp von Hutten 1534-1541, 2nd ed., Berlin Verlag Arno Spitz, Berlin, 1999, p. 104.

5   German orig. cit.: „Amerika war nicht alles". in Fernand Braudel (ed.), *Europa: Bausteine seiner Geschichte*, Frankfurt am Main, 1989, p. 10.

6   Cf. Eberhard Schmitt (ed.), *Wirtschaft und Handel der Kolonialreiche (= Dokumente zur Geschichte der europäischen Expansion. Vol. 4)*, München, 1988.

7   For exemple among others Horst Pietschmann, *Die Eroberung des Aztekenreiches durch Hernán Cortés oder besiegte Sieger und siegreiche Besiegte*, Münster, 1998.

8   Vitorino Magalhães Godinho, *L'économie de l'empire portugais aux XVe et XVIe siècles*, Paris 1969, pp. 577-596.

9   Unsurpassed the analysis of Ernst Fraenkel, *USA - Weltmacht wider Willen*,Berlin 1957.

10 Carl Hager, Deutschlands Berufs in Ostafrika [german origin. cit.: „Ein altes herrliches Vorrecht und der Beruf Europas ist es, den übrigen Erdteilen die Errungenschaften seiner Kultur, seiner sittlichen und politischen Anschauungen, seiner Technik und Wissenschaft mitzuteilen, die anderen Länder zu zivilisieren. Der Gedanke von der Solidarität des Menschengeschlechts, das Ideal der allgemeinen Zivilisierung des Erdballs hat im Laufe der Zeiten im Gefolge der geographischen Entdeckungen an Boden und Kraft gewonnen, bis er in unserer Zeit, vermischt mit materiell-wirtschaftlichen Bestrebungen zu einer unbestrittenen Forderung für die europäische Menschheit geworden ist"], in Jutta Bückendorf, "Schwarz-weiß-rot über Ostafrika!", *Deutsche Kolonialpläne und afrikanische Realität*, Münster 1997, p. 262.

11 Samuel P. Huntington, *The Clash of Civilizations and the Remaking of World Order*, New York 1996 [several reprints].

12 Marília dos Santos Lopes, " Wie die Wilden immer wilder wurden. Afrika als neue Welt", in *Jahrbuch für Europäische Überseegeschichte* 1 (2001), pp. 45-57.

13 Cf. Thomas Beck:, *Globalität und Ethnogenese* (habilitation thesis Univ. of Bamberg, before issue).

4

THE PORTUGUESE IN INDIA AND THE INDIAN OCEAN: AN OVERVIEW OF THE SIXTEENTH CENTURY

M.N. Pearson

Just over 500 years ago Vasco da Gama opened up the sea route between India and Europe. Many people have said that this was a very important event in the history of the world. Indeed, the famous Indian author and diplomat K.M. Panikkar said that there was a "Vasco da Gama era" of Asian history, which started in 1498 and ended when the European powers gave up their colonies. What I aim to do in this short essay is to provide a rounded view of the Portuguese and their efforts in the sixteenth century. This is not done to denigrate their achievements, nor to praise them; rather I want to try and sketch how they were located in the context of the Indian Ocean in the sixteenth century. I hope that this very broad overview will provide a background for the more detailed studies which will follow it in this volume very fittingly dedicated to the achievements of Professor K.S. Mathew.

Let me first attempt a very general statement to locate the Portuguese in the Indian Ocean world. The Portuguese identified quite quickly the main choke points and strategic places around the Indian Ocean littoral. Indeed, the early correspondence and histories and other accounts devote much effort to this sort of identification of where was vital to control.

Goa, Colombo, Melaka, Hurmuz, Diu and Aden were seen as most strategically located to serve Portuguese ends, and all except the last were taken. These port cities were all flourishing before the Portuguese conquest, and all had strategic implications. Goa was centrally located to control the Arabian Sea. Colombo also was well located, and also provided access to cinnamon. Melaka and Hurmuz were located to control choke points, and both were also major emporia. Possession of Diu provided control over the entrance to the Gulf of Cambay, and access to the rich production areas around the eastern shore of the Gulf. In the case of east Africa, Mozambique in the south had several advantages. It was conveniently located to control trade on the southern coast, and to block trade from the hostile Muslim world down to the gold available in Sofala. Also, and here Mozambique was unusual as compared with the other ports which they conquered, it was to be the vital way station for the *carreira* from the colonial capital of Goa to the metropolitan capital of Lisbon, thus fulfilling the same function that the Cape of Good Hope later provided for the Dutch. In theory this voyage was to be done in one passage, but in practice the great ships often needed to call in on the African coast to heal their sick, to get supplies, on the outward voyage to collect cargo for India, or to await the next monsoon. Mozambique then became the vital link in the chain between Goa and Lisbon.

These strategic sites were acquired with several ends in view. Their conquest helped the Portuguese to undermine the Muslims who had previously dominated Indian Ocean trade, and especially that in spices. They functioned as nodes in the vast seaborne network of the Portuguese maritime empire. They provided facilities for the vital armadas, and the *carreira* to Portugal. They were beach-heads from which conversion drives were launched. They provided places where the Portuguese elite could give themselves fancy titles and indulge in an anachronistically feudal life-style, and from which they made vast private profits during their terms of office. In a more general sense the Portuguese were trying to create or impose a hierarchy *de novo* in the Indian Ocean. From a situation of autonomous port cities and free trade in which competition was economic but not military, they now wanted to establish an articulated structure where Lisbon controlled Goa, and Goa controlled all the conquered port cities. The nature of the political aspiration, and also its extent, have to be seen as quite revolutionary.

There was an underlying and little-discussed coherent economic imperative also. At least in material terms, the Portuguese were in Asia to buy spices cheap and sell them dear in Europe, thus undercutting the traditional Mediterranean route. To forbid this trade to all others was one thing, and in any case this effort met with little success, as we will see. But the Portuguese still had to be able to buy the spices themselves, for they monopolised, partially, sea trade only, and not land trade let alone production. Nor did they have the domestic resources to be able to send large amounts of money out from Portugal. This requirement, to find money to pay for the spices, meant that the Portuguese were soon intricately linked into the country trade of Asia, a matter which has been much discussed in the case of the English and Dutch, rather less so for the Portuguese.

East Africa provides an excellent case study of this matter. The Portuguese quickly found out that a commodity which could be used to pay for the spices was available in east Africa, namely gold from the Zimbabwe plateau. If they could secure supplies of this, or better still a monopoly, then payment for spices would be no problem. But it soon also became apparent that gold had to be paid for too. It could be acquired only in exchange for goods, and not Portuguese goods either..

Similarly with east Africa's other priced export, ivory. Here the Portuguese had no hope of controlling supply, for elephants were hunted in very far flung areas. However, perhaps they could block its export. Again, however, they still had to be able to pay for it. The only items in demand on the plateau and elsewhere were beads and cloths from Gujarat; these were the traditional trade items which the producers of gold and ivory wanted, and here, as in so many other areas, the Portuguese then had to fit in to existing patterns. A continuing supply of

Gujarati cloths to east Africa was essential in their wider designs. Thus were the Portuguese immersed in an intricate web of country trade in the Arabian Sea, in this case cloths from Gujarat to exchange for gold and ivory which then could pay for spices which then could be extracted from the Indian Ocean network and sent outside it to European markets.

With this very broad background, we can turn to the vexed question of the importance of the arrival of the Portuguese in the Indian Ocean. I will look at several themes, but very briefly. Some have suggested that this linked, for the first time, Asia and Europe. But this is hardly a tenable claim, for these two continents had been linked for centuries via the Red Sea and Persian/Arabian Gulf. Rome had an extensive trade with India 2000 years ago. Later, Asian products continued to get to the Mediterranean and European markets. Spices were in great demand here. Europeans needed them to preserve meat, and to flavour it. This was certainly an important trade for the European consumers, and for the Asian producers and traders. It was also important for the Mamluk rulers of Egypt, for a significant amount of their revenue came from taxing this trade.

Historians consider this trade, and then sometimes claim that while certainly there had been some contact before 1498, commercial connections between Europe and Asia were greatly strengthened because the Portuguese had discovered a new, faster and more efficient route to join the two, that is the route around the Cape of Good Hope. It is true that the Cape route was, at least in theory, faster than the more difficult route from the spice production areas in the Malukus, across the Indian Ocean, up the Red Sea, and then overland to Alexandria. The Cape route also was cheaper, because taxes did not have to be paid to land controllers en route, especially the Mamluks. Furthermore, at this time sea transport was substantially more cost-effective than was transport over land.

In practice it turned out that the Cape route was not really so much better. It was, after all, a long and arduous sea voyage which took many months. Quite often Portuguese ships were lost on the way, or had very long passages. Mortality was very high, so that often ships from Portugal had to stop over in Mozambique to cure their sick before they set off again for India. Often the ships were overloaded, and the cargoes poorly stowed, so that the spices and other cargo reached Lisbon in very bad condition. Over the whole sixteenth century about 10% of those on board died, and just under 10% of the ships were lost, mostly due to shipwreck.

But much of the blame for the failure of the Cape route to outdo the Red Sea was a result of the policies of the Portuguese themselves. It is significant that the Dutch, and even the English, did much better sailing around the Cape in the seventeenth and eighteenth centuries than did the Portuguese in the sixteenth. The central Portuguese aim was to monopolise the transportation of spices from Asia to Europe. They tried to prevent anyone else from trading in these products. For a time, may be forty years from about 1500, they were quite successful. Most Asian spices did get to Europe in Portuguese ships via the Cape of Good Hope, and the Portuguese made large profits. However, the existing trading networks in the Indian Ocean, most of them Muslim, soon recovered and were able to find ways to get around the Portuguese trade control system. A lot of spices went overland via the Gulf. The Portuguese never controlled the entrance to the Red Sea, so that Asian merchants could easily avoid Portuguese fleets trying to block the entrance, and so proceed to the head of the Red Sea. The Portuguese attempted monopoly was also very expensive to enforce: they spent vast sums on fleets and forts.

The Portuguese were strong at sea, but not on land. This meant that they had to have good relations with the land powers which surrounded their ports and forts, and to achieve this they often let these Indian rulers send off spices to the Gulf and the Red Sea. It was also very difficult to control all the areas where spices were produced. The fine spices - mace, nutmeg, cloves, and cinnamon - came from quite restricted areas; the first three from the Maluku islands, and cinnamon only from Sri Lanka. However the Malukus were right on the edge of the area where

53

the Portuguese operated, and they seldom were able to control trade in these spices very tightly. The only bulk spice was pepper, and this was even harder to monopolise, for it was grown in several areas: Malabar, Malaya, and several areas of Indonesia. The Portuguese simply lacked the military and naval capacity to be able to patrol all these areas and block trade in spices. For all these reasons the monopoly soon collapsed, and at least by 1550 as many spices were getting to the Mediterranean via the Gulf and the Red Sea as got there in Portuguese ships via the Cape.

However, it was not just spices that were traded between Asia and Europe in the sixteenth century. Another very important product was bullion. The Spanish in the Americas exported large amounts of gold across the Atlantic to Iberia from early in this century, and from mid century even vaster amounts of silver, especially from the incredibly rich mine at Potos' in Peru. Much of this bullion flowed through Europe and so on to the Indian Ocean and Asia. However, again the Portuguese and the Cape route were far from being dominant in this trade. It is clear that much more bullion came into the Indian Ocean area via the Red Sea than came around the Cape of Good Hope. Thus there certainly was a vast drain of bullion from the Mediterranean to the Indian Ocean, but most of this was not handled by the Portuguese.

There are two other matters that we need to consider in this context. First, European historians have written extensively about changes in the spice trade to Europe. What we can say here is that this trade was no doubt important for Europe, but not nearly so much for Asia. Only about one-tenth of Asia's total production of spices went to Europe. Most of them were consumed within Asia. China, for example, was a huge customer for ginger and pepper, as was the Mughal empire. Thus to focus only on the spice trade to Europe is to ignore the bulk of this trade, which was never destined to go anywhere near the Mediterranean. The Portuguese had very little control of this intra-Asian trade.

It could be that we are using the wrong geographical categories here. I have been writing of "Asia" and "Europe," but may be this familiar terminology disguises more than it elucidates. When we write about this early modern period there is often an undertone of a successful dynamic Europe as compared with a static, even backward, Asia. We might do better to think of an area called Eurasia. This would include the eastern Mediterranean, and thus would take in part of the Ottoman Empire. The area then extends down through Egypt to the Red Sea, and so into the Arabian Sea. These areas have all been intricately linked for centuries, even millenia, by trade and the movement of people. If we take this perspective then we could say that the Cape route opened up an alternative to trade within Eurasia, but that this route did not take over from the more traditional ones for some time yet.

If then the opening of the Cape route had a rather minor significance in terms of trade between the Indian Ocean area and Europe, what can we say about the effects of the arrival of these first Europeans on the major states of the Indian Ocean area at the time? I will sketch five areas of contact. In East Africa south of the Sahara the only major state was the Mutapa state or Monomotapa, located in the area which is now Zimbabwe. This state had no sea access, though it produced large amounts of gold and ivory which were taken down to the coast, to Sofala or Kilwa, and then exported. The Portuguese had very little effect on this trade. They tried to monopolise it, but achieved very little. Gold exports had been in decline before they arrived, and this decline continued in the sixteenth century. Ivory was an important export for the Portuguese, but this product was also traded by various Muslim groups. In any case, the basis of the power of the Mutapa rulers was in land and cattle, not in the export trade to the coast. Later in the sixteenth century the Portuguese penetrated far inland up the Zambezi valley. One of the first was the intrepid Jesuit Fr. Gonçalo de Silveira, who was killed at the Mutapa court in 1561. Later other Portuguese established estates, or *prazos*. Sometimes these recognised the authority of the Mutapa ruler, sometimes they did not. The Mutapa state declined in the seventeenth century, and Portuguese activities may have contributed a little to this.

Moving on north, the Portuguese had various diplomatic and military dealings with the Ottoman Turks. This strong and expansionist Islamic state was a source of great concern for the Portuguese authorities. In the first half of the sixteenth century it took over Egypt, and the Red Sea area, including the Islamic Holy Places. It also established itself in Iraq, in the area around Basra and Baghdad. Turkish fleets raided the east African coast in the 1580s, and caused the Portuguese much concern: they responded by building the huge Fort Jesus in Mombasa. Much more famous was the expedition to Diu in 1538, where a strong Ottoman fleet acting in conjunction with Gujarati forces besieged the Portuguese fort, and were defeated only with very great difficulty. The Ottomans remained a feared adversary for the rest of the century. However, this land oriented power was much more focused on the Mediterranean and the Middle East, especially Iran, than on the Indian Ocean, and Portuguese fears were largely unnecessary.

The next major state with which the Portuguese had contact was Safavid Iran. This state was founded in 1500, just as the Portuguese were establishing themselves in the Indian Ocean. It fought a series of wars with the Ottomans in the sixteenth century, and for this reason the Portuguese tried to have good relations with the Safavids, and encouraged them to confront the Ottomans. Pepper was allowed to pass through the Straits of Hurmuz to Iranian ports, and silk was provided by the Persians in return. Yet this tacit alliance was built on sand, for in 1622 the Safavids and the English combined to take over Hurmuz from the Portuguese.

The *Estado da India*'s main interlocutors were two important Indian Muslim states, Bijapur and the Mughal empire. Bijapur was of course contiguous to the Portuguese capital of Goa; indeed Goa had been conquered from them in 1510. Relations were tense throughout the century. The local controllers of Ponda, right next to Portuguese territory, were often a worry, while in 1570 Bijapur joined in a major attack on Portuguese areas. It may have been because of these tense relations that Goa did not trade very much with Bijapur. One major trade item, cotton cloths, were obtained from Gujarat in preference to Bijapur, and Goa's food came mostly from the Kanara area further south. Certainly Portuguese activities had very little influence on the progress of Bijapur. The area was conquered by the Mughals in the 1680s, but the Portuguese played no role in this.

The *Estado*'s relations with the Mughal empire are rather more complex. The great emperor Akbar conquered Gujarat in 1572, thus bringing his empire into direct contact with the Portuguese. Like the other great Islamic territorial states, the Mughals concentrated on the land rather than the sea. This meant that most of the time Portuguese maritime activities did not bother the Mughals. On occasion the Portuguese would attack or capture a ship belonging to the Mughal elite, and then the Mughal state would respond. However, the main area where the Mughals were concerned was the pilgrimage to Mecca. The port of Surat, in the seventeenth century one of the most important ports in the world, was the main exit point for Indian Muslims going on hajj, and the Mughals were concerned that this passage not be blocked. On the other hand, the Portuguese knew that their forts in Gujarat, in Diu, Daman and Bassein, were vulnerable to attack from the land. Equally important, Goa relied on Gujarat for the bulk of its export products, and especially cotton cloths. Thus they could not afford a long war with Gujarat, and nor could they allow any blockade to go on too long, for this would mean that Portuguese trade all over the Indian Ocean and to Europe was denied goods to trade. It was thus in effect a stand-off, with both sides prepared to be conciliatory most of the time. The Portuguese tacitly allowed the hajj passage to continue, and gave the Mughals "free" passes for some of their ships. Portugal's other contact with the Mughals had to do with their well-known attempts to convert the emperors. The Jesuit missions to the court failed, of course, to achieve this, but their activities have provided us with some fascinating accounts of life at the Mughal court.

In southeast Asia the Portuguese were not faced with any major maritime or territorial power, but this was not the case in China. The Ming dynasty there was powerful in the sixteenth century, and extremely ethnocentric. Foreigners had to behave with due subservience to Chinese officials, and the Ming accounts present the Portuguese as cannibals or malicious goblins. The Portuguese were very much in an inferior position. In the early 1520s a Portuguese fleet was heavily defeated by a Chinese coast guard fleet. Later, in the mid 1550s, they were allowed to establish themselves in Macau, but always on terms of strict subordination to Ming officials. From late in the century, however, the Portuguese were able to fill a gap and profit from a very lucrative trade which linked Macau and Japan. The conclusion has to be that Portugal's relations with major states around the Indian Ocean in the sixteenth century were mostly civil enough, in part because the maritime interests of the Portuguese seldom conflicted with the major interests and activities of these land-oriented states. Certainly it is impossible to see the arrival of the Portuguese as affecting the progress or decline of these states in any significant way.

Another area where we are told that the opening of the Cape route made a huge difference, ushered in a momentous change, is in the area of religion. The Portuguese, of course, had both economic, political, and religious aims. One thing Vasco da Gama was looking for was the mythical Christian potentate Prester John. At first they thought that the inhabitants of Malabar, except of course the Muslims, were some sort of schismatic Christians. During the sixteenth century the Portuguese secular authorities spent much time and effort facilitating conversions. The main drive was led by the new and enthusiastic Society of Jesus, led by St. Francis Xavier. This effort did have some success. It has been estimated that by the end of the century there may have been 175,000 Christian converts in all of India, most of them poor fisher folk. Descendants of these converts are to be found all over India, and Asia, today. No doubt this is a substantial achievement, yet there are some hesitations to be expressed also. First, India had a population in this century of about 140 million, so from this perspective the missionary success was rather limited. The greatest success was of course in the city of Goa itself, where at this time about two-thirds of the population were Christian. However, in the whole territory of Goa, the Old Conquests, Christians at most made up one-quarter of the total.

The Portuguese and others found it hard to convert people who already, at least to an extent, belonged to one of the major world religions, namely Hinduism. It was much easier when one was working amongst people who had more rudimentary religious beliefs, such as the situation the Spanish found in the Philippines. Here they had great success, converting virtually everyone in the area they controlled, the whole of the northern Philippines, in a matter of a few decades.

A second point is that of course the Portuguese did not bring Christianity to India. A strongly supported legend claims that the apostle St. Thomas proselytised, and died, in India. His tomb can be seen in a southern suburb of Madras to this day. The Portuguese found several Christian communities when they arrived: Nestorians, "St. Thomas" Christians, and various others. Late in the sixteenth century the Portuguese church, influenced by the militant notions of the Counter Reformation, began to bear down hard on these indigenous Christians, for it was considered that they were deviant, even heretical.

A final observation is in order. Despite the intolerance of the Counter Reformation, and many of the Jesuits, it was not simply a matter of a "European" religion being transmitted to India. Rather it was a two way process, as indeed is always the case when people convert to a new religion. In many social areas Hindus who had converted to Christianity retained their old customs. Various food prohibitions and notions of pollution continued to be influential. Sometimes Indian Christians seem to almost merge in with Hindus, in an eminently tolerant way. Thus the feast day of St. Francis Xavier in Old Goa is celebrated by all the inhabitants, whether Hindu, Christian or neither. But the best example, and the most studied, is the continuance of caste notions in families who have been Christian for centuries. Christianity in India then owed as much to its local environment as it did to the norms of Rome.

But surely the Portuguese, being Europeans, stood out in Asia? Surely many of their feats, and many of the things they introduced, could not be emulated by Asians? Well, not really. One of the few areas where the Portuguese were unusual was in their naval prowess, for they had mastered the art of mounting cannon on board ships. This ability enabled them to achieve considerable maritime success all over the Indian Ocean, though they certainly never came near to controlling the seas and all ships on them. In any case, one could argue that the Portuguese timed their arrival in the Indian Ocean area very well. A century earlier the great Chinese expeditions under Zheng He (Cheng Ho) had ranged far and wide over the whole ocean, as far as the Red Sea and the east African coast. These were massive expeditions in very large and powerful war junks. The first one in 1405 included 62 large ships, some of them over 100 metres long. There were about 28,000 men in this expedition. By comparison, the total crew on Vasco da Gama's four small ships in 1498 numbered 170 at most.

There is no doubt that no Portuguese fleet would have been a match for these Chinese ones. Indeed, many famous historians have speculated that Zheng He could have sailed around the Cape of Good Hope, up the West African coast, and colonised Europe. But instead his political masters back in China terminated these expeditions. And on this matter we need also to remember that the Ottoman Turks, at least, had very powerful navies, as seen in Diu in 1538, and later off the East African coast, and of course in the Mediterranean. But luckily the Ottomans never concentrated all their forces, or even any significant part of them, in the Indian Ocean area.

We can say then that the Portuguese to a limited extent stood out for naval expertise. In what other areas did they differ from the Indian people they interacted with? In a material sense, we know that the Portuguese introduced from America many crops which today are thoroughly acculturated in India. The list includes chilli peppers, pineapples, maize, cassava, cashew trees, cucumbers, avocados, guava, and tobacco. But again we must be careful not to exaggerate the Portuguese achievement. These crops came from the Americas, and so would have been transmitted on from Europe to the Indian Ocean via the land routes in any case.

In a more cultural area, it is sometimes claimed that the Portuguese brought the fruits of Renaissance Europe to India. This is a problematic claim. First, Portugal in fact did not share fully in the series of developments collected together as the Renaissance, especially as the Church, and the Counter Reformation, were too influential. The persecution of Portugal's important Jewish population, which persisted after they had either converted or been expelled, also had long term effects on Portugal's intellectual life. As a specific example, what of the printing press, often considered to be a great symbol of the whole loosening up of the dissemination of knowledge which is characteristic of the Renaissance? A printing press arrived in Goa in 1556, thanks to the Jesuits. By 1679 it had published 40 books, but only three of these were on secular subjects. The most famous of these is of course the work by Goa's great savant, Garcia d'Orta, *Colloquios dos simples e drogas*. The other 37 were all on religious subjects, and some of them were mere anti-Jewish or anti-Hindu propaganda. And it is symptomatic that d'Orta's work had much more impact on the rest of Europe than it had in Portugal.

More generally, it is clear that many Portuguese in India acculturated and fitted in to the Indian environment. Portuguese doctors, including even Garcia d'Orta, recognised that often Indian remedies were better than European ones. Some aspects of pollution were picked up from Hindu practice. There was copious sexual interaction, and hence reproduction, between Portuguese men and Asian and African women. The result was the creation of a very large *mestiço* population. Even in their capital city of Goa the Portuguese were far outnumbered by Indians: the total population in 1600 was about 75,000, of whom 1500 were Portuguese or mestiços, 20,000 Hindus and the rest local Christians. Most significant of all is the way so many Portuguese chose to live outside of the small coastal areas controlled by the state. Rather they lived all around the littoral of the ocean, on the northern Swahili coast, on the Coromandel coast, and in insular southeast Asia. These men married local women, seldom had the chance to take the sacraments, and generally fitted in to the very rich, complex and cosmopolitan trading world of Asia in the sixteenth century.

If we take a very long term view, can we say that the Portuguese opened the door for other Europeans to come in and change Asia profoundly? Were they harbingers of a future when most areas in Asia were colonised by Europeans powers, with very dramatic and deleterious consequences? Again this claim is difficult to sustain. As we have been pointing out, in many areas the Portuguese had no particular advantage over the Asian states and peoples with whom they had dealings. They were, if you like, as premodern or early modern as anyone else. Generally speaking westerners had no superiority in any area at this time. This was obviously the case in terms of culture, society or religion, and it would be racist to say otherwise. However this also applies in material matters, such as the production of goods, trade practices, technology, etc. Inequality appeared only when western Europe industrialised, and for the first time we have a rich world and a poor world. This happened only from late in the eighteenth century. One consequence of industrialisation in the west was that they now had the technological capacity to take over large areas of Asia, and this is what happened. However, my argument is that the increasing economic and military power of the west led inevitably to their colonising Asia; this would have happened even if the Portuguese had not rounded the Cape in 1498. The Portuguese effort then must be seen as a tour de force, that is a prodigious effort which however had no flow on and no consequences, in short a one-off achievement.

Finally let us look at trade control, for it is often claimed that the Portuguese were able to control the trade of the Indian

Ocean in the sixteenth century. When the Portuguese sailed around the Cape and up the East African coast in 1498 they entered a sea which was almost completely *mare incognita* to them. True, they had some information from Venetians and others who had traded in the area for many years. In Mozambique Gama was met by a native of Fez, in Morocco, and in Calicut by two Muslims from Tunis who spoke Genoese and Castilian. Further, Gama had been told to try and reach Calicut, whose reputation as a trade emporium was well known in the Mediterranean. Nevertheless, the Portuguese had a lot to learn. But one thing they were clear on, that this was an expanse of water over which no one previously had claimed title. Thus, they proclaimed, they had a right to impose for the first time a system of trade monopoly and trade control, for there was no preceding title which they had to take account of.

What was the situation in the Indian Ocean in 1498? There certainly had been violence at sea before the Portuguese arrived. Piracy was very widespread indeed, something which took a heavy toll on merchant shipping. There even are a few instances of Asian states at this time or in the past using sea power, such as Gujarat, Srivijaya, and the Chola state. However, it does not seem that any of these powers had very effective navies. We should see their maritime efforts as being completely adjunct to their land ones: their navies were only auxiliaries to their armies. Similarly, the controllers of the various port cities, such as Calicut, Melaka, Cambay, Hurmuz, made no attempt to force ships to call to trade. The bait with which they attracted merchants was that they provided low taxes and security. This is a complete contrast with the Portuguese, who established an essentially maritime empire. Sometimes this empire is called a network, by which sea routes linked up a series of port cities all around the Indian Ocean. In short, it is not too much of an exaggeration to say that the Portuguese introduced politics into the Indian Ocean.

This then provided the quasi-legal underpinning for the Portuguese system of trade control. This has been much studied, notably by Professor Mathew, and I will only touch on a few salient points here. Right from the start the Portuguese claimed the right to direct trade, and to say what goods could be traded. All ships trading in the Indian Ocean were meant to take a pass or *cartaz* which laid down where the ship was sailing to, and specified what people, armaments, and goods were not to be carried. Trade with the Red Sea, considered to be a hostile Muslim area, was discouraged or stopped. Turks were not allowed to trade in the Indian Ocean. More important, spices were declared to be a Portuguese monopoly, and anyone trading in them was liable to have his ship captured, or even sunk and the crew killed. Later in the century another element appeared, a rather more peaceful one. The *cartaz* had always required that Asian trading ships call in at Portuguese ports to trade. This became very much an imposition once the Portuguese established customs houses at their ports, for now these ships had to call, and also had to pay customs duties. These were established quite early in Cochin and Goa, later in Diu, and much later again in Daman and Chaul. Revenues from this made up the vast bulk of the *Estado*'s total revenue late in the sixteenth century. One thing to note here is that this shows that Portuguese policy throughout the sixteenth century did change; this is only one example of the way their presence and policies in the Indian Ocean in this century were by no means monolithic or static.

Many historians have also tried to estimate the success of the Portuguese in this effort to control, and later to tax, Asian trade. As we noted above, their main aim, which was to monopolise the spice trade, was not achieved. Even before the middle of the century more spices were getting to Europe via the Red Sea or the Gulf, and then the Mediterranean, than were taken in Portuguese ships around the Cape of Good Hope. As to the *cartaz* system, it worked in certain restricted areas, usually those close to a Portuguese fort. Thus it had some success around Mombasa, and on the other side of the ocean Melaka. The Bay of Bengal was hardly affected at all, but the west coast of India was heavily patrolled, and it was difficult to Indian traders to avoid the Portuguese fleets. They were most successful of all around the Gulf of Cambay and the Persian/Arabian Gulf, for their forts at Diu and Hurmuz enabled them to inspect most ships. Hence the massive customs revenues from these two places.

Obviously then the trade control system was only partially successful. There were various problems with it. One was the failure to take the port of Aden, which would have let them control the entrance to the Red Sea. Another was what we would today call corruption, where Portuguese officials were bribed to allow "illegal" trade - indeed some officials themselves engaged in this. The Portuguese also were at times constrained by political realities, especially their need to conciliate their landed neighbours. Several rulers on the west coast of India were kept on side by being allowed to trade in spices, or trade to the Red Sea, despite this being outside the normal practice allowed by the Portuguese. More generally, the Portuguese were trying to control a vast maritime space, as any glance at a map will make clear. A small distant country of less than 2,000,000 people could not hope to police such vast ocean wastes.

More generally still, we need to look at fundamental Portuguese aims. At least in material terms, the Portuguese were in Asia to buy spices cheap and sell them dear in Europe, thus undercutting the traditional Mediterranean route. To forbid this trade to all others was one thing, and in any case this effort met with little success. But the Portuguese still had to be able to buy the spices themselves, for they monopolised, partially, sea trade only, and not land trade let alone production. Nor did they have the domestic resources to be able to send large amounts of money out from Portugal. This requirement, to find money to pay for the spices, meant that the Portuguese were soon intricately linked into the country trade of Asia, as we noted at the beginning of this essay. This in turn meant that increasingly over the century the Portuguese were more concerned that trade continue and expand, rather than their being so strict in attempting to enforce their system that trade suffered and evasion increased. We can put forward two conclusions about trade control: first, the Portuguese aims changed considerably during the course of the century, and second that they never got very close to achieving the sort of control they had hoped for.

All this may seem very negative and belittling of the Portuguese. This is not my intention at all. What I have tried to do is present a modulated overview of their activities, one which locates them in the context of the Indian Ocean in the sixteenth century. There is no need to denigrate their achievements, which were many; indeed I have sketched some of them in this article. Their nautical prowess was exemplary, their courage and daring admirable. But we do not need to accept the grandiose claims of some historians which see them as bringing civilisation to Asia, or as achieving mastery over the ocean. Nor do we need to accept the hostile interpretations of some Indian nationalist or chauvinist writers, who claim that they were a completely negative presence which opened the door for Asia to be colonised by Europe. If we situate them in the historical milieu in which they operated we will get a less heroic, and less destructive, result, but one which I hope reflects better their real significance.

Further Reading

This sketch is based on my own research, and that of others. Three useful surveys are:

C.R. Boxer, *The Portuguese Seaborne Empire, 1415-1825*, London, 1969;

M.N. Pearson, *The Portuguese in India*, Cambridge, 1987;

Sanjay Subrahmanyam, *The Portuguese Empire in Asia, 1500-1700*, London, 1993.

5

PRECEDENTS AND PARALLELS OF THE PORTUGUESE *CARTAZ* SYSTEM

Luís Filipe F. R. Thomaz

In a previous article we have already tried to react against some old ideas about the Portuguese *cartaz* system that still prevail [1]. The traditional view is that, whereas before the Portuguese expansion the Indian Ocean was a free one, where everybody could navigate, from the beginning of the sixteenth century onwards, it fell under the control of the Portuguese, who claimed a right of sovereignty on it and restricted the right of sailing therein to purchasers of the *cartazes* delivered by their authorities. We tried to show that, although containing a certain element of truth, such a simplistic view of things needed some qualification.

The aim of the system was, in fact, manyfold: though originally conceived to assure the blockade of the Red Sea, it was along the times used for a variety of purposes. It is possible to distinguish three or four kinds of control: a strategic control, aiming at the embargo of spice trade through the Red Sea route; a political control, aiming at harming the enemies of the *Estado da Índia;* and a fiscal one, aiming at protecting the Crown monopolies and implementing the forcible taxation imposed by the Portuguese on some lines of commerce. Roughly during the first two thirds of the sixteenth century there was also a certain social purpose, aimed at restraining the activities of Portuguese private merchants and preventing soldiers from becoming traders.

The safe-conducts, which were issued for a small fee, seemingly paid to the clerk who drew them up, were not a direct source of income to the State; but they contributed to its revenue in two different ways, that of the booty the system occasioned and that of forcible taxation it assured. The former was given up by the Crown in 1570, but the latter continued in force or even developed in the subsequent period. It was applied to the traffic through the Gulf of Cambay which was taxable in Diu; to the traffic between most of the western coast of India and the Red Sea, which was taxable in Diu or in Goa, according to the provenance of the vessel; and to the traffic between Ceylon, Orissa, Bengal, Southeast Asia or the Far East and the Arabian Sea, which was taxable in Goa. In later days forcible taxation was also applied to the traffic through the straits of Malacca.

The effectiveness of the control changed, more or less with the intensive presence of Portuguese vessels. The contrast ought to have been sharp between the Arabian Sea, where the Portuguese operated a series of *armadas* to enforce their control, and the Bay of Bengal, where after 1530 virtually no Portuguese fleet operated. This space of freedom was, nevertheless, often used by Portuguese mutineers and pirates, who, in so far as they could, imposed their own law. So, if the Arabian Sea was the normal theatre of Portuguese privateering, the Bay of Bengal often became a theatre of Portuguese piracy. None the less, though their effects were in practice the same, privateering, which was a regular and legal procedure, at least from the Portuguese point of view, cannot be equated to piracy, which was a marginal and illegal activity at the eyes of everybody.

In the present paper we only intend to deal with the juridical side of the problem, leaving aside its social and economic aspects. Our purpose is barely to add some precisions and to confirm some impressions we have expressed in the preceding article, on the basis of further documents we have meanwhile come across. These show that, as we had advanced, the system implemented by the Portuguese is not so original as it appeared to XIX century scholars, but, on the contrary, has several parallels and precedents, in the Atlantic and the Mediterranean as well as in the Indian Ocean.

The Earliest Extant Cartaz

To analyse the exact nature of the control claimed by the Portuguese it seems opportune to quote in full the purport of a *cartaz*.

Although the system had worked from 1502 onwards, in so far as we know, no XVI century *cartaz* is preserved. The reason seems to be that the original was delivered to the crew of the vessel concerned, and the register of the safe-conducts issued in each place was kept by the local factors, whose records have not reached us. So, quite curiously, the earliest extant *cartaz* is, to our knowledge, the English translation of that found in 1612 aboard a *Terrada* which was seized by the British captain Christopher Newport in the Persian Gulf. The seizure and the purport of the document is recorded by Purchas [2]:

> (...) This Terrada was about the burden of fifteene tunnes, her lading, for the most part, was victuals of those parts; as Rice, Dates and Wheat and such like. They had a Portugall passe, wich they shewed us, thinking at the first we had been Portugals. The Original whereof I translated out of the Portuguise language, because it might be knowne in what subjection the Portugals doe keepe all these Countrey people: without which Passe, they are not suffered to saile to nor fro, upon paine both of losse of life, ship and goods: the Copie whereof followeth, viz:
>
> *Antonio Pereira de Laserda, Captaine of the Castle of Mascat, and the Jurisdiction of the same, for his Majestie, & c.*
>
> *All those, to whome these Presents shall be shewed: know that I have thought good, to give secure licence unto this Terrada, of the burden of fiftie Candies, the Master whereof is Norradim a Moore, and Baluche, and a dweller in Guader, of the age of fiftie yeeres, and carrieth for his defence four Swordes, three Bucklers, five Bowes with their Arrows, three Calivers, two Launces and twelve Oares: that in this manner following declared she may passe and sayle from this said Fort, to Soar, Dobar, Mustmacoraon, Sinde, Cache, Naguna, Diu, Chaul and Cor. In going she carrieth goods for Conga,*

as Raisons, Dates and such like: but not without dispatch first out of the Custome house of this said Fort, which shall appeare by a Certificate, written on the Backside hereof. And to performe well the said Voyage, she shall neither carry nor bring any prohibited goods, viz., Steele, Iron, Lead, Tobacco, Ginger, Cinamon of Seilon and all other things whatsoever prohibited, and not tollerated by the Regiment of his Majestie. And in this manner shall the said Terrada make her Voyage, without let or hinderance of any Generalls, Captaines, or other of the said Signories Fleet, or ship whatsoever, which she shall happen to meet withall. And this shall be of force and sufficiency for one whole yeere, in going and comming. If it be expired, then to serve other so long time, as the making hereof.

Given from the said Castle of Mascat, this sixteenth of November, Ann. Dom. 1611.

I, Anthonio de Peitas, Notarie of this said Factorie have written this, & c.

Sealed and Signed

Anthonio Pereira

The Certificate written on the backe side hereof is this: viz. Registered in the Booke of Certificates, in Folio xxxij and so forwards.

Signed, Anth. Peitas

The terms used in Dutch *pascedullen* of the XVII century are roughly identical, since their control system was entirely moulded upon that of the Portuguese; the first known example is a sea-pass issued at Malacca three weeks after the Dutch conquest of the city from the Portuguese. Notwithstanding the Dutch pleadings for the freedom of the open seas, the *Heren XVII* or "Gentlemen Seventeen" who ruled the VOC considered that by the conquest of Malacca the Company had inherited all the rights and privileges claimed by the Portuguese, including the exigence of safe-conducts from all vessels crossing the straits and forcible taxation on them [3]. For our purpose, however, the Dutch system is less interesting, for it represents an aftermath rather than a precednt or a parallel of the Portuguese one.

The Medieval Safe-Conducts

The Portuguese arrived in the East with the burden of the medieval tradition of piracy, privateering and maritime war in the Mediterranean and adjacent waters.

During the Antiquity, as the Mediterranean was a kind of Roman lake, maritime law did not develop as a chapter of the *jus gentium* or international law, but rather as a part of the internal ordainments of the Empire. The situation dramatically changed with the split of the Roman Empire into two halves, Eastern and Western, with the coming on the stage of the Barbarians and, chiefly, with that of the Muslims. Such states were often fighting each other, on the water as well as overland, and so the need of a certain control over the seas arose.

By the end of the VI century, the Eastern Roman Empire began to issue *licentias navigandi*, "licences of navigation", which attested the nationality of the vessel, enrolled its crew and legalized its activities. This implies the existence of certain means of control, and at least a latent concept of sovereignty on the sea.

The concept of territorial waters developed in the West from the IX century onwards. Insofar as we know, the earliest extant document where it appears clearly expressed is the so-called *pactio Sicardi*, a five years truce between Sicardo, Lombard prince of Benevento, and the city of Naples, still formally Byzantine, signed in 836; both parties repeatedly engage to keep peace in "every castle or place of its dominion", *terra marique*, "ashore and on the water".

Nevertheless the limits of such *aquae nostrae*, "our waters", were not clearly defined; so, each state extended its control as far as it could. As could be expected, maritime powers and merchant republics went farther than landbound states: Venice claimed the exclusive right of navigation and control on the Adriatic Sea, and Genoa on the Ligurian Sea. Beyond the *aquae nostrae* lay the *pelagus* or open sea, where any violence could take place. The idea of freedom of the open sea, where no state could interfere with its peaceful utilization by another power, only developed in the XVII century, under the influence of the Dutch jurists, chiefly of Huigh de Groote, alias Hugus Grotius, coming to be generally acknowledged in the following century [4].

It is important to note that during the Middle Ages the boundaries between piracy and privateering were not clear in Europe. Plunderage was considered legal when there was war between two states; but merchants who had been illegally plundered or barely unpaid, and could not obtain indemnity were allowed to compensate themselves by seizing vessels or goods belonging to the other party, provided that they had obtained from their sovereign a *letter of marque*. This right to reprisal [5] engendered a kind of vicious circle of vendetta, which tended to perpetuate privateering as an endemic activity.

It is also important to note that the statute of neutral party was rather unclear. Neutral vessels were frequently plundered, in order to dissuade their overlord to support the other party, or to persuade him to honour a blockade. Hence the need of sea-passes or safe-conducts, which were the main European predecessors of the Portuguese *cartazes* used in the Indian Ocean. Several examples of such documents, issued by the Portuguese authorities to foreign merchants and vice-versa, dating from the twelfth century onwards, are preserved in the archives [6]. Some of them are granted to individual merchants, normally during a period of some months to a few years. None the less, others are collective, such as those bestowed in 1444 by the Regent Dom Pedro upon all the Breton merchants who intended to trade in Portugal, guaranteeing them safety of persons and goods for one year, from 1st January 1445 onwards [7]. It includes the condition that forbidden goods, which are not specified, should not be traded, and that duties should be paid on all the other items. Its validity was limited to the Portuguese coast between Viana (nowadays Viana do Castelo) and Cape St. Vincent. Other safe-conducts [8] were only valid north of Cape Espichel, near Setúbal, but the reasons for such a limitation are not specified and remain unclear.

As a sample, let us translate the safe-conduct granted in 1438 by the Regency to merchants from the Duchy of Brittany, bringing victuals and other goods, at request of the Municipality of Lisbon:

> Dom Afonso, by the grace of God King of Portugal and Algarve and Lord of Ceuta, to whomsoever this letter be shown: We make known that the council and the burghers of our very loyal city of Lisbon sent to warn us that, by God's will, this year hath been very scarce of bread and every other foodstuff; and that they, thinking of our service and general profit, agreed that every carrack or ship from the Duchy of Brittany could come merchantly to the aforesaid city of Lisbon, henceforwards for one year, notwithstanding any carracks, ships or merchandise of our realm they may have seized hitherto. And they besought as a grace that We give them our assurance thereto. And We, having seen what they besought, once examined by the Queen our mother, tutor and curator, and by our counsel the liberties and privileges that hereabout were granted by the most virtuous and victorious King Dom João, of good memory, our grandfather, and confirmed by the most excellent and mighty King Dom Eduarte, our lord and father, whose souls God may have, wishing to follow those lordships, from whose generation and right We come, with all the good-will and wishes We have to cherish above all the said city, as that which hath been and is always loyal to our very kingdoms. We take for good and hereby We ensure any carracks, ships, merchants and merchandises of the aforesaid Duchy of Brittany that may come merchantly to the aforesaid city of Lisbon with bread (i. e., wheat) and any merchandise or goods of their own, from the making of this letter onwards for one whole year, albeit there be war between them and us, lest they be caught or spoiled or arrested from the entrance of our haven, off Cascaes, and inside the aforesaid city; nor shall there be done to them any evil or harm inside our said haven of the said city of Lisbon. Rather We want and shall be pleased that they be there all the time welcome and well received, and may sell their merchandises at the said city and buy others from our realms, whichsoever they prefer, paying us our customary duties; and that they may lade those goods which they will, buy and depart whenever they want, paying us our duties.

And by this letter We exempt them from all the tithes on bread and vegetables they may bring into the aforesaid city during the aforesaid year. And beyond this, if any carracks or ships come and bring bread or vegetables into the aforesaid city, We hereby ensure them against all our nationals and subjects, from the mouth of Viana up to the inside of the havens of the aforesaid city of Lisbon, provided that the aforesaid carracks come laden with bread and vegetables, or at least bear one half of the load; and likewise We grant them that, after they come inside the said harbours, they be free to sell the said bread and vegetables at ease, and be acquitted of the said tithes, as hath been said; and they will pay the other duties in accordance with the customs of our realms. And if any of the aforesaid carracks that come into the aforesaid haven of Lisbon giveth bail for not harming or damaging the carracks of our realms, nor our nationals, until they return to Brittany, bearing certificate that they produced the said bail, We order our nationals to let them go securely to Brittany with their carracks. And if any of them be caught and show the certificate of the bail they gave at the aforesaid city, We are pleased that they be immediately disengaged. And therefore We order our admiral and captain-major of our fleet, and our skippers and privateers, and people of our realms, and any other officers, to keep and follow this assurance, and to have it kept and followed without any impediment; in testimony whereof We grant them this. Given at Thomar, the 23d september. So ordered the King, in accordance with the Queen his mother, as his tutor and curator. Martim Gil drew it up, in the year 1438 of the Birth of Christ.

The text appears particularly akin to the *cartazes* granted during the XVI century to ships from the ports of Canara coast, on condition that they brought foodstuffs to Goa. The exemption of duties is identical in both cases.

As the safe-conduct is generic and collective, the identification of the ship is absent, and this is the main difference between it and most of the *cartazes* that reached us. Collective *cartazes* are seldom found in the East. After the conquest of Malacca, Afonso de Albuquerque sent messengers offering *seguros* (assurances) to neighbouring countries, especially to non-Muslim ones, such as Siam [9]; these assurances appear to have been collective guaranties, as we often find in Europe during the Middle Ages, rather than individual sea-passes. In early times we also find many cases of delivery of a Portuguese flag instead of safe-conduct [10]; apparently it had a more symbolic role, since it signified the acceptance of Portuguese overlordship. These practices, however, disappeared quite soon — the last examples we know of date from about 1512 [11] — probably because they did not permit a clear identification of the vessel.

However, the intention is the same: to avoid spoliation of vessels deemed friendly and even useful to the State, and to bestow protection on them. Also the need of passes was the same in the Atlantic as in the Indian Ocean, for any vessel found without them was in both oceans susceptible of seizure.

The Mamluk Sea-passes and the probable Origin of the use of the Arabic Loan-word Cartaz in the Indian Ocean.

There are, also, some signs that safe-conducts were already used in the Indian Ocean before the Portuguese century. In Portuguese the word *cartaz* is a loan-word (from Arabic *qirṭâs*, "paper, document"), and a neologism, introduced into Indo-Portuguese in the first quarter of the sixteenth century. Unlike most of the Arabic loan-words in Portuguese, it does not exist in other Iberian tongues, such as Castilian and Catalan, which can be a sign that it was not borrowed from Arabic during the Muslim occupation of the Peninsula; it is nowadays quite current in Portuguese in the sense of "bill, poster, placard" but, as far as we know, this sense is not attested before the first quarter of the seventeenth century.

In the technical sense of safe-conduct it appears from 1518 onwards, significantly in documents written in the East[12]. Some texts which explain its sense suggest that the word was used amongst the Muslims of Kerala. For instance, João de Barros states: "...and he presented the assurance he brought to the captain [of Cannanore] Lourenço de Brito, which assurance is commonly called *cartaz* amongst the Moors, and at present amongst the ours..." [13]. This perfectly agrees with the expression of Gaspar Correia: "...those from Ceylon should send to Cochin, to take the certificate, which they call *cartaz*..." [14]

Already in 1505 we find references to ships sailing with *cartazes* issued by the Zamorin of Calicut [15]. Moreover, we know that in the sixteenth century the kings of Eli (Cannanore), Calicut and Cochin, issued *cartazes*, which were duly acknowledged by the Portuguese. Nevertheless, the fact that the name is an Arabic loan-word suggests a Near-Eastern origin rather than an Indian one. We think, therefore, that the word *qirtâs* was primarily used in Kerala for the sea-passes issued by the Mamluk Sultanate of Egypt for ships sailing to India, a practice that, seemingly, was at a further stage imitated by local rulers. In Arabic, their official name was indeed *amân*, "safety, assurance", whose equivalent in Portuguese is *seguro*, quite often also used to mean "safe-conduct", especially in former times; but it is very likely that familiarly people have called it *qirtâs*, "paper", and thus this latter name was perpetuated in Portuguese.

The Mohammedan *amân* continues the pre-islamic institution of *jiwâr*, whereby a foreigner received the protection of a member of another tribe for himself and his property. Mohammed gave it a religious meaning, replacing the tribal solidarity by a confessional one; in the Koran [16] he laid down: "if a heathen entreateth thee to give him thy *jiwâr*, bestow it upon him, so that he may listen to the words of Allah; and then let him go whithersoever he may enjoy security (*amân*)".

Any Muslim freeman was entitled to grant safe-conducts to individuals; but only the *imâm* could grant them to indeterminate groups or collective corporations, such as the citizens of a town or the members of a guild of merchants. The earliest collective *amâns*, granted for commercial purposes, we know of are inserted in treaties between the Muslim administrators of Egypt and Nubian chiefs, dating from 651-652 A. D. From the XII century onwards many safe-conducts of the same kind were given to Christian European merchants or pilgrims [17].

The *amân* was not always easy to get, in particular for voyages into the Red Sea, where since the first crusades all infidels were banned, by fear of any contact between the Christians of Europe and those of Ethiopia, which might bring about an anti-islamic alliance that would encircle Egypt. Pedro Tafur reports that Nicolo de' Conti, whom he met in 1436 in Sinai, had to wait for two years to get a pass enabling him to sail to the Indies.

As the Mamluk state increased its control on the circulation of persons and goods, individuals, even Moslems, needed a pass to go through the customs and check-points at the gates of towns. In 1325 or 1326 Ibn Battuta noted that in Damietta "no one who enters the city may afterwards leave it except by the governor's seal; persons of repute have a seal stamped on a piece of paper, which they show to the gatekeepers; other persons have the seal stamped on their forearms and must show that" [18]. People travelling overland towards Syria were controled at Qutya, the eastern entrance of Egypt, where they had to show their passes.

As merchants from the Indian Ocean were often maltreated and spoiled at Aden, the King of Ceylon sent in 1283 A. D. an embassy to Egypt, with proposals of direct commerce between both countries. Thereupon Sultan Qalâwûn decided to enhance such a trade, and in 1288 ordered the Mamluk Chancery to issue sea-passes to Hindus, Chinese and Yemenites that intended to visit Egypt for trading purposes [19].

Subhi Labib stresses the importance of this passport system created by the Mamluk Sultans of Egypt in the late Middle Ages, which is a noteworthy precedent of that put in practice by the Portuguese in the XVI century [20]:

> The way in which Egypt affirmed her sovereignty over the Red Sea and her interests in the Indian Ocean was not the construction of a fleet for state commerce, but the creation of a passport system. Every merchant who had a pass was under the immediate protection of the Egyptian Sultan, and was guaranteed safe passage through the Red Sea, without danger to life or property. (...) This pass system remained in use up to the end of medieval times.

The creation of this system is reported by several chroniclers; some of them, such as Ibn al-Furât and al-Qalqashandî [21], give the passport text in full. It begins with a praise to God, who created such a state of things that the justice of the sovereign bestows safety upon his subjects. His protection shelters traders departing from Egypt as well as those coming from Iraq, Persia, Byzantium, Yemen, India and China, whose lives and goods are put under Egypt's responsibility. Likewise, their trading stations ashore would be under the islamic protection. The document mentions the main kinds of goods that would be welcome in Egypt, above all mamluks, *i. e.*, slaves to be used as soldiers, whose importance was crucial to Islam. Traders bringing slaves would therefore be granted fiscal exemptions [22].

The main difference between these documents and the Portugueses *cartazes* is that the former lay stress on the articles of trade which are welcome, whereas the latter rather emphasize the prohibited items. However, the intention is roughly the same: to encourage the trade of certain goods, if conducted by friends, and to forbid the traffic of others, and, in general, the commerce of foes. No wonder that the importation of slaves into the Muslim domains is in one case stimulated and in the other forbidden.

Under the Mamluk dynasty, Egypt substantially strengthened her influence in the Red Sea and on the Hijaz coast, despite of the atempts of Yemen to bring them into her sphere of suzerainty. Thus, Egyptian sea-passes represented an effective protection, and became a real need to any vessel venturing to sail thither.

The Chinese Licences for Sea going Ships

In China, at least under the Ming (1367-1644) and Ch'ing (1644-1911) dynasties, as well as in Japan, merchant ships sailing to foreign countries had to carry imperial licences or passports. Like the Byzantine *licentia navigandi* and the Portuguese *cartaz* used in the Indian Ocean, such licences were individual, and contained the indentification of the vessel and of its owner, and the list of the armament it carried. The rule also applied to ships

Precedents and Parallels of the Portuguese Cartaz System

sailing from Macao, wherefore several of such licences are kept in Portuguese archives. Here is the purport of one of them, dated from 1759[23]:

> "By Imperial mandate, Commander Li ... (?), who is assigned to the Imperial Household Department and is in charge of the Kwangtung custom-house decrees this:
>
> *Upon presentation of memorials to the Emperor, Imperial instructions were given to the effect that, if Western ships from which customs have already been collected, are driven to other provinces by unfavourable winds and currents without intending to trade there, then, upon verification of the receipt and seal that testify to their customs payments, they shall be allowed to pass on and should not be double-taxed, as had originally been agreed upon, decided and laid down in the documents.*
>
> *Now, as the merchant Lei-Szu-Shan-Chi [= Luís dos Santos Resende (?)] , commamder of a foreign vessel, carries goods to Lu-Sung [= Luzon] for trade, and all duties have already been paid in accordance with the regulations, this licence is given to him; it is [hereby] handed out to this same merchant of the said ship and he should keep it. Guard houses and control posts, upon examination of this document, must let him pass and are not allowed to charge double taxes or to impede his way. The cannon and arms carried by the ship for its defense are also registered in this document, according to the old laws. The ship is not permitted to carry additional armaments or prohibited goods. To avoid the incovenience of confiscating [things] , the foregoing [instructions] must be observed.*
>
> *Happy journey!*
> *Twenty-eight foreign seamen.*
> *Ten shotguns.*
> *Six artillery pieces,*
> *Twelve piculs and six pecks of rice.*
> *Shipper's name: Mu-La-Tuo.*
>
> *This licence is entrusted to the foreign merchant Lei-Szu-Shan-Chi. [Issued] on the tenth day of the third lunar month, in the twenty-fourth year in Ch'ian-Lung's reign (1759). The Canton Custom House.*
> *May this respectfully be followed.*

79

The main scope of this system is, as in the preceding cases, to assure a certain control of private merchant navigation; the most noteworthy difference is that in China control was chiefly exerted inside the harbours and in shore, rather than in the opens seas, which were feebly patrolled by the imperial fleets. Therefore, rather than from the risk of seizure on sea, the passport protected the bearer from that of double taxation, chiefly in case of call at a port different from the intended destination; in such case it also prevented the payment of the official measurement fees owed by each vessel at its first voyage, which were reduced to one third at subsequent voyages. Moreover, in case of shipwreck on the Chinese coasts, the passaport also entitled the castaways to be repatriated at the expenses of the imperial exchequer.

Exactly as the Portuguese some times did with their *cartazes* in the second half of the XVI century, the Chinese system of licences was also used for a protectionist purpose: to limit the number of ships sailing from each port. In 1726 the maximum number of sea-going ships allowed in Macao was limited to twenty-five. In that year,

> the local [Chinese] official [who was in charge of Macao's port] was instructed to number all the ships, to brand the [respective] numbers [on them], and to issue a document to each vessel, with the names of the owner, the skipper, the sailors, the foreign merchants, and the commander in charge, all of which had to be filled in on [this document], so that [the data] could be verified, registered and sent to the Governor-general by the coastal control posts whenever a ship was about to leave a port [24].

In the course of time, some of the purposes of the system fell into oblivion, and thus only the limitation of the number of sea-going vessels fitted up in Macau was actually controlled. The routine brought about a paradox, which was described by the *ouvidor* (judge) Arriaga, in 1810, in the following terms [25]:

> As to the number of artillery pieces, the pilot's name, the crew number and other things listed in the licences — they do not correspond

to the facts in the least, because the Chinese deal with those matters in the most unintelligible and improbable way that one can conceive of. The Chinese emperors, since times immemorial, allowed the Portuguese citizens of Macao to employ, for their commercial advantage, twenty-five sail in all, wishing that in case of all these vessels, from the first to the last, there always be listed the same pilot's name, the same quantity of artillery and staff, etc — just as in the very first instance. This is done in such a way that, when a ship is sold, lost or taken out of service for reasons of age, the [new] vessel filling its position must use the same pilot's name and register the same number of guns and crew, even if it is only a brigg and not a large *nau*, as in previous times. Taking this in its own light, the owners and pilots are immortal beings and the crew is unchangeable, because it is now more than two hundred and eighty years that Macao became a colony of His Majesty and the individuals referred to are always the same in the minds of the Chinese.

In Japan a similar system of control appeared in the last decade of the XVI century. Japan was the extreme nook of the Old World and had been for centuries a very isolated country. External commerce was feeble and kept many archaic features; it took quite often the shape of an administered trade, directly conducted by the State or by corporations such as the Buddhist monasteries, rather than by private marchants. During the first centuries of her history and again under the Chinese dynasty Ming, Japan formally accepted to present it as an official tribute to China, even sacrificing her national pride to the wish of securing the importation of exotic products and manufactured goods from abroad [26].

During the Ashikaga period (1338-1573), the monopoly of the external commerce virtually fell into the hands of the abbot of Tenryuji or Heavenly Dragon Temple, a Zen monastery at Saga village, west of Kyoto. Therefore, ships conveying goods from or to China were known as *Tenryujibune*.

After the arrival of the Portuguese Japan had a period of political and economical opening, followed, as is well known, by a long era of seclusion, which lasted until the mid-XIX century. It was during this period of opening that a sytem of trade licences, called *shuinjo*, "red-seal passports", was adopted by the *Taiko* Hideyoshi; ships bearing them were known as *Go-shuin-sen* or "August red-seal ships". The first recorded issue of *shuinjo* for overseas navigation was made in 1592; the system lasted for more than forty years, up to the definitive seclusion of Japan, under the Tokugawa dictatorship. It is difficult to discern whether it was moulded upon that of Chinese licences for sea going vessels or upon that of Portuguese *cartazes*.

Anyhow, some differences are conspicuous. Out of eighty-two passports recorded during the Keicho period (1596-1614), 8 were granted to *daimyos*, 4 to *bakufu* (headquarters) officials, 14 to Europeans, 6 to domiciled Chinese and 50 to national merchants [27]. From these figures it becomes evident that the aim of the system was to control the exit of nationals as well as the entrance of foreigners, as it was also the case in China. As in China, too, the control was carried out in shore rather than on the high seas, where the *bakufu* had no means of intervention.

Whatever its origins may have been, the Japanese system appears thus especially akin to the Chinese system of bureaucratic control, rather than to the Western systems of strategic control we have analysed above.

Conclusion

By and large, these documents confirm that, as we had pointed out in our previous article, the Portuguese sea-passes or *cartazes* used in the Indian Ocean, far from being an innovation brought in by the Portuguese, or a peculiarity of their system of maritime control, have several precedents and parallels in different periods, contexts and parts of the world. Indeed, there are slight differences between the various systems, stress being laid some times on the conveyance of forbidden goods, sometimes on the payment of more or less forcible taxes, and so forth; but in every case the passport represents an assurance against the risks of spoliation and seizure on the sea, especially as a reprisal in the context of an open or latent conflict.

The main difference between the control exerted by the Portuguese, in the heyday of their hegemony in the Indian Ocean, and that exerted by other powers is its extent rather than its nature. It is, indeed, the spread of their presence throughout the Eastern Seas that appears as unprecedented; it enabled them *inter alia* to claim a right of control on the high seas and to enforce taxation on certain long-distance trade routes, not necessarily touching their domains.

Theoretically the extent of their control —which continued to be also exerted on the Atlantic, as in the Middle Ages — was almost world-wide. In the practice, nevertheless, it was limited to the oceanic areas their fleets could effectively patrol — exactly as the control carried out by other powers.

References:

1 Luis Filipe F. R. Thomaz, "Portuguese Control over the Arabian Sea and the Bay of Bengal: A Comparative Study", in *Commerce and Culture in the Bay of Bengal, 1500-1800*, ed. por Om Prakash & Denys Lombard, Manohar / Indian Council of Historical Research, New Delhi, 1999, pp. 115-162.

2 *Hakluytus Posthumus or Purchas His Pilgrimes, containing a History of the World in Sea Voyages and Lande Travells by Englishmen and others*, by Samuel Purchas, B. D., vol. IV, Glasgow, James Mac Lehore and Sons Publishers to the University, 1905. Chap. X: A Journall of all principal matters passed in the twelfth Voyage to the East Indies, observed by me, Walter Payton, in the good Ship the Expedition: the Captaine whereof was M. Christopher Newport, being set out, Anno 1612. Written by Walter Payton. § II: Their comming to the Persian Coast: the treacherie of the Baluches.

3 Marcus Vink, "Passes and Protection Rights - The Dutch East India Company as a Redistributive Enterprise in Malacca, 1641-1662" in *Moyen Orient & Océan Indien / Middle East & Indian Ocean, XVIe - XIXe s.*, 7 (1990), pp. 73-101.

4 Giulio Vismara, "Il diritto del mare", in *Scritti di Storia Giuridica*, vol. 7: Comunità e Diritto Internazionale, Dott. A. Giuffrè Ed., Milan, 1989, pp. 440 & sqq.

5 Ruy de Albuquerque, *As Represálias — Estudo de História do Direito Português (século XV e XVI)*, 2 vol., Lisbon, 1972.

6 Several examples in João Martins da Silva Marques, *Os Descobrimentos Portugueses — Documentos para a sua História*, vol. I, Lisbon, 1944 (repr., Instituto Nacional de Investigação Científica, Lisbon, 1988), doc. 329, p. 415 (granted to the Genoese merchant, settled in Lisbon, Francesco Usodimare for three years from 17.V.1442 onwards); supplement to vol. I, doc. 16, p. 26 (granted in 1308 by Edward III of England to Portuguese merchants); doc. 100, p. 128 (granted in 1438 by Phillip, Duke of Burgundy, to Portuguese merchants); doc. 309, p. 384 (granted in 1297 by Edward I of England to Portuguese merchants for 8 months, on condition of reciprocity); etc.

7 Issued at, Lisbon, 1.I.1444, ANTT, *Chancelaria de D. Afonso V*, livº 25, fl. 4; published in *Monumenta Henricina*, vol. VIII, Coimbra, 1967, doc. 147, pp. 233-234.

8 For example ANTT, *Chancelaria de D. Afonso V*, livº 24, fl. 15 v.

9 João de Barros, *Ásia de..., dos feitos que os portugueses fizeram no descobrimento e conquista dos mares e terras do Oriente*, Década II, Lisbon, 1553 (new ed. by Hernâni Cidade & Manuel Múrias, 4 vol., Agência Geral das Colónias, Lisbon, 1945-48), II, vi, 7; Gaspar Correia, *Lendas da Índia* por..., [written before1563], published (...) sob a direcção de Rodrigo José de Lima Felner, 4 tomes in 8 parts, Academia Real das Sciencias, Lisbon,1858-66, II, pp. 243, 263-265 & 381; F. Lopes de Castanheda, *História...*, III, lxxii-lxxiii; Afonso [Brás] de Albuquerque, *Comentários de Afonso de Albuquerque*, 5ª edição conforme a 2ª, de 1576, 2 vol., Imprensa Nacional — Casa da Moeda, Lisbon, 1973, III, xxv, xxxvi, xxxvii & IV, xx.

10 Barros, *Ásia*, Decade I, book vi, ch. 4; I, vi, 7; II, iv, 3, etc.

11 Afonso [Brás] de Albuquerque, *Comentários,* part IV, ch. xxxvii.

12 see Sebastião Rodolfo Dalgado, *Glossário Luso-Asiático,* 2 vol., Coimbra, 1919-21, reprinted Asian Educational Services, New Delhi & Madras, 1988, s.v.

13 João de Barros, *Ásia,* ii, 4;

14 Gaspar Correia, *Lendas da Índia,* I, p. 298.

15 Gaspar Correia, I, p. 523.

16 IX, 6; cf also XVI, 112.

17 cf J. Schacht, art. "Amân" in *Encyclopédie de l'Islam,* vol. I, Leyde & Paris, 1960, s.v.

18 H. A. R. Gibb, *The Travels of Ibn Baṭṭûṭa, A. D. 1325-1354,* translated with revisions and notes from the Arabic text edited by C. Defrémery and B. R. Sanguinetti, by..., Vol. I, Hakluyt Society, London, 1958, p. 36.

19 Aḥmad Darrag, *L'Égypte sous le règne de Barsbay, 825-841 / 1422-1438,* Damascus, 1961, pp. 198-199; Robert Irwin, *The Middle East in the Middle Ages - The Early Mamluk Sultanate, 1250-1382,* Southern Illinois University Press, Carbondale and Edwardsville, 1986, p. 74.

20 Subhi Labib, "Egyptian Commercial Policy in the Middle Ages", in *Studies in the Economic History of the Middle East, from the rise of Islam to the present day,*

edited by M. A. Cook, Oxford University Press, 1978, pp. 63-77.

21 Abû'l-Abbâs Aḥmad bin Alî al-Qalqashandî, *Subh al-casâ fî çinâcat al-inshâ*, 14 vol. Cairo, 1910-1920, vol. XIII, pp. 340-341.

22 Subhi Labib, *Handelgechiche Aegyptens im Spaetmittealte, 1171-1517*, F. Steiner, 1965, pp. 84-86, 160-161 & 394-397.

23 Arquivo Histórico Ultramarino (Lisbon), *Macau, caixa* 30, doc. 47; pub. in *Sinica Lusitana - Fontes Chinesas em Bibliotecas e Arquivos Portugueses - Chinese Sources in Portuguese Libraries and Archives*, vol. 1 [1668-1871], Fundação Oriente, Lisbon [2000], pp. 77 & sqq.

24 [Yin Kuang Jen & Chang Ju Lin] *Ou Mun Kei Leok* [Monography of Macau, 1st ed., 1751], translated by Luís Gonzaga Gomes, Ed. Quinzena de Macao, Macao, 1979, p. 112.

25 Note appended to the document transcribed above, and published therewith.

26 For further details *vide* Charlotte von Verschuer, *Le Commerce Extérieur du Japon - Des origines au XVIe siècle*, Maisonneuve & Larose, Paris, 1988.

27 C. R. Boxer, *The Christian Century in Japan, 1549-1650*, 2d ed., Carcanet Press, Manchester, 1993, pp. 249-250 & 261-267.

6

GERMAN PARTICIPATION IN THE INDIA FLEET OF 1505/06

Stephan B.G.C. Michaelsen

Why were Germans involved in the Portuguese-India trade? To answer that question, it might be useful to sketch briefly the German foreign trade in the relevant period.

Starting with the Northerns part of Germany, there was the association of "trading " towns called "Hanse", prominent members being Luebeck, Danzig, Rostock, Hamburg, Bremen and Cologne. The basic rationale was to monopolize trade in the hands of its citizens. Major commodities included grains, dried fish, cloths and furus. Major offices were located at Brugge, London, Bergen, Visby, Riga and Nowgorod in Western Russia, this indicating a preponderance of Baltic sea trade. Trade was also done to the Iberian peninsula, mainly in shipbuilding mateirals. The Hanse maintained its own army and fleet, mirroring the virtual absence of central power in Germany. The international power of the Hanse culminated in the 14th century when the peace accord of Stralsund 1370 confirmed domination of the Baltic sea. - By the beginning of the 16th century internal dissent and changes in the environment led to a deterioration of the association; Brugge lost to Antwerp, the London Stalhof closed by the 1560 s. The impact of the Discoveries took a little time to be understood in many Hanse towns, Hamburg being the first to allow full residency to foreigners, English "adventurers" and the emigrants from Portugal from around

1580, thus contravening the Hanse principle to reserve trade to its own citizens[1].

Traders in Southern Germany, mainly in Augsburg and Nuernberg, had traditionally close contacts with the "World Trade" centers in the Mediterranean region. With the help of offices in Venice, Genoa, Florence and Rome the South German companies were participating, not as importers but rather in a secondary trade position, in the marketing of high-value goods from the East. They attempted to obtain a stronger import position by forming a pepper-import cartel (from Genoa), but this idea was shelved when information of the Discoveries and notably news on the threat to the traditional supply routes through the Middle East became known in Venice and Genoa. The factors of the German companies reported on the perceived consequences on the importance and the eroding exclusivity of the Mediterranean area for the Orient trade.

Trade to Western Europe from Southern Germany had attendance at trade fairs at Lyon as a stepping stone. From there visits overland to Saragossa and Valencia were undertaken, and in December 1502 Simon Seitz, an employee of the Welser company at Augsburg, started his journey accompanied by Lucas Rem, through France and Spain to Lisbon to intensify trade there.

As an aside: Apart from trade, the South German companies, Fuggers and others, were coerced to loan large amounts of ready cash to Maximilian and later Charles V for their election expenses as kings and emperors. This financing eventually contributed to the downfall of the companies, since repayment of loans was at best erratic.

As shown above, the interest of the German traders was to get near the source of supply of high-value Oriental goods. The centre of their supply had shifted to Portugal and thus the German interest in Lisbon. From the side of Portugal there was a necessity to attract co-financiers for the development of the India trade, since with its limited resources in manpower and finance the effort was not sustainable.alone. Another important factor was Portugal's dependence on supply of materials for

87

shipbuilding and ordnance, like timber, pitch and tar, ropes and copper. Another peculiarity of the India trade had surfaced: demand for third and one half of the purchase price of pepper could be paid for in goods, the rest in metals, mainly silver and copper[2]. Now the copper mining and trade were almost a monopoly of the South German companies and they also enjoyed a strong position in silver. (Many mining concessions were obtained as collateral for loans to the Habsburg emperors).

When Simon Seitz arrived at Lisbon in January 1503, a contract for trade privileges was already prepared, with active mediation by Valentin Fernandez from Maehren, a long-time resident, translator and printer at Lisbon. On February 13, king Manuel ratified the *Privilegia*[3], which confirmed and substantially enlarged older agreements. It provided a basis for the Welser and also for other German companies to trade on par with Portuguese nationals, as long as a minimum of 10,000 ducats were invested. For future arrivals of goods from India the Germans were to get preferential customs treatment, though this was rather offset later by frequent changes in the pepper import policy. An attempt to participate financially to the extent of 20,000 ducats in the fleet to sail in 1504 failed, the king rather reserving the trade for the crown, and for Italian merchants, who had participated in practically all India fleets since 1500.

The agreement of February 1503 covered nominally all German companies, though it was obtained by and for the Welser. Other German companies, Fugger, Imhoff, Hirschvogel, Höchstetter obtained similar privilege-letters in 1503/04, and we find them all as partners in the 1505 venture.

After their non-acceptance for the 1504 fleet the Welser did not give up. Also the position of king Manuel changed; the crown realized its financial limitations. So Lucas Rem could conclude in August 1504 a contract with king Manuel, which allowed the Welser to send three ships with next year's fleet to India and buy their own account through their own agents. This sounded quite liberal, but the details showed the restrictions: The ships, under Portuguese captains and with Portuguese crew, had to be provided for a period of 18 months with all cost for charter, equipment and provisions borne by the Welser. Supreme command rested with the admiral of the fleet. In India, the royal factors were to determine prices, at which imported goods were to be sold, as well as the prices for spices etc., to be bought. The agents of the German/Italian companies were at liberty to sell and buy, under the above restrictions, as much as fund's availability and shipping space allowed. But their movements on Indian soil were severely curtailed[4].

On arrival in Lisbon, all spices were to be brought to the India House, where the goods were to be appraised and duties calculated. The crown was to get 1/4 plus 1/20, i.e., 30 per cent, and after this having been settled, the goods were contractually free to be sold or shipped out of Portugal without any further hindrance or charges. So much the contract; now we will see, what actually happened.

Lucas Rem was quite proud to have achieved direct access to the riches of India. The profit potential was very attractive: pepper at 3 *cruzados* per quintal at Cochin, landed cost in Lisbon around 8 cr, ruling price 40 to 20 cr. Of course there was also substantial risks in the long sea voyages given the shipbuilding and navigational expertise at the time and in the transport from Lisbon by sea and by land to the consuming markets.

Subsequent to the conclusion of the August 1504 contract the Welser formed as consortium of German and Italian companies to spread expenses and risks. Marchioni and other merchants of Florence and Genoa invested 29400 *cruzados/* ducats, Welswer had the biggest individual share with 20,000, Fugger and Höchstetter contributed 4000 each, Imhoff and Gossenbrott 3000 each and Hirschvogel 2000. The total investment was thus 65,400 *cruzados*[5]. The consortium chartered the three ships *San Jeronimo, San Rafael* and *San Leonardo*[6]. According to Venetian trade intelligence the *Rafael* loaded some 200 tons of copper, 10 tons of lead, 3 tons of vermillion, 2 tons of mercury, corals and some other unspecified goods. Furthermore, the ship was said to carry 80000 *cruzados* in cash[7].

The fleet of 1505 is unique in leaving to us two reports of Germans on board. One was Balthasar Sprenger, quite certainly an employee of the Welser house, He boarded the *Leonardo* at Antwerp and wrote a "travel report"of which some four similar versions are extant. The report, published in 1509, gives a detailed description of the voyage, without however touching the main objective of the venture, the commercial matters. Presumably those were reported separately to his principals. His report, *"die merfart....."* is the first printed German report on travel in Africa and India. Another German is Hans Mayr, employed by the crown as scribe/clerk, sailing on the *Rafael*. The report ascribed to him, originally in Portuguese, again is an interesting travel report without touching commercial matters[8]. - Ulrich Imhoff sailed, as a German agent, on the *Jeronimo*[9], but he died soon after his return to Lisbon and left nothing in writing.

We have explained the motivations and objectives of Germans getting involved in Luso-Indian trade. Now we will cover the voyage proper in a short manner and then get to the result of the venture.

The large 1505 fleet of 14 or 15 *naos* and 6 caravels assembled in Lisbon, loaded stores, men, goods and 3 dismantled brigantines plus 2 knocked down galleys for coastal duty in Africa and India. Finally the fleet under Francisco d'Almeida sailed out of the Tejo on March 25, 1505; in the confusion the *Leonardo* suffered slight collision damage and sailed a day later. - The passage around Africa was relatively smooth (Cape Verde April 7, blown down to appr. 40 (?) degrees S, Quiloa July 22, Mombasa August 8, from North of Melinde August 27 to Karwar/Anjediva September 12-15). We bypass the extensive ethnological contents of both Sprengers and Mayrs reports. In line with the kings instructions: assure supremacy on the East African coast, fortify Cochin or Cannanore, send the "trading" part of the fleet back in time - there were negotiations, war and plunder at Quiloa and Mombasa. The crews of the "German" ships were asked to fight along, but were cut off when distributing the considerable loot.

After getting the fort on Anjediva constructed to a defensible stage, the fleet proceeded down the coast; in Onor/ Honavar Portuguese authority was enforced, in friendly Cannanore a fortification was started, Calicut was bypassed. Cochin was reached by end of October 1505, just over seven months after departure from Lisbon.

Here Francisco d'Almeida assumed his position as viceroy and crowned the new Raja of Cochin with proper pomp and protocol. That being achieved and construction of a strong fort having progressed, spice loading could and did start. Some pepper had been ordered by the preceding fleet, and inspite of irritations like a punitive expedition to Quilon, a Calicut-inspired rebellion and efforts of Arab and other competing traders to boycott the Portuguese, loading proceeded quite smoothly. Anyhow, time was extremely short: wind condtions on the route to the Cape demanded departure from the Malabar coast by early January. So only two months were available, within which all the logistics from dealer to plantation and from dealer to warehouse - lighter - ship in different loading ports had to be price for the spices, and to "friction losses" between the Portuguese officials and the German and Italian merchants, whose limitations on authority and movement ashore we mentioned earlier.

Inspite of obstacles and time squeeze, Sprenger found time to report on the Indian social system, though superficially, and his *"merfart"* included the famous woodcuts on the Raja of Cochin.

The first group of ships comprising the *Rafael* with Fernao Suarez as admiral, *Jeronimo, Judia, Botafogo* and *Conceicao* sailed (on time) by January 2, 1506 after completing loading in just two months. The group had a smooth passage, though the *Conceicao* started leaking and had to repair at Mozambique. The four ships doubled Cape of Good Hope on March 8, two months after leaving India. So the total voyage time was just 14 months. - The *Conceicao* arrived about three weeks later. Goods could not be discharged for some time, since Lisbon was ravaged by a plague epidemy [10].

On January 21, 1506 the ships *Leonardo, Gabriel* and *Magdalena* sailed from Cannanore. Late as they were, they had a long, tedious passage. After repairs in Mozambique *Leonardo* rounded the Cape only by July 7, 5 ½ months after leaving India, arrival at Lisbon on November 15, i.e., 10 months since Cannanore and 20 months for the total voyage. *Gabriel* and *Magdalena* came in even later, early 1507.

The *Flor de la Mar* sailed still later from India, on February 2. She had to stay in East Africa due to "missing the season", transshipped cargo which arrived at Lisbon in 1507; the ship returned to India. So including *Flor*'s, cargoes of nine ships came to Lisbon. It was unique, that practically all the goods purchased in India did arrive in Europe, no cargo was lost and the investors were quite happy.

Now, what did the fleet bring back from India? A letter from Lisbon[11] mentions altogether 35600 *"zentner"* (appr. 1800 tons) of spices as expected arrivals. This is difficult to correlate with other, lower figures[12]. Haebler[13] figured out for the German/Italian group a pepper quantity of 120000 quintal of which thirty precent was to go to the crown (see above), leaving 8400 quintal to the group. Divided pro rata investment, Welsers part was 2600 quintal, Fugger and Höchstetter 500 quintal each, Imhoff and Gossenbrott 380 quintal each and Hirschvogel 240 quintal. Haebler mentioned just 2200 quintal of pepper for Welser[14]. Is this possibly calculated from the first two ships only? - Here we disregard other spices like ginger and cloves and other materials brought by the fleet and the "German" ships[15].

It will be recalled that the original contract with the Portuguese crown allowed the investors free access to their goods after payment of the 30 percent cess. In the meantime, arrivals of unexpected large quantities of pepper, mainly by the fourth fleet of Vasco da Gama, had led to a price collapse, from 40 to 20 ducats per quintal, and a minimum price of 20 was decreed[16].

New regulations from January 1505, that means even before the 1505 fleet sailed, cancelled the free access to the products. In 1506, the India House held considerable stocks of unsold pepper. So the newly arrived pepper was blocked in the warehouse, and the pepper belonging to the crown was to be sold before the investors could get hold of their pepper kept in the India House[17]. The private companies refused an offer by the crown to purchase their pepper, they feared not being paid properly and timely[18]. Messy and long court cases for breach of contract were the result; the accounts were still not settled by 1509 [19]. The Fuggers had in 1512 still claims on pepper stored in the India House[20.] The Welser came to a profitable cross-trade, where they contracted with the crown to buy fixed quantities of sugar from Madeira. When the crown could not supply, Welser could get hold of some of their pepper as compensation[21].

Inspite of all the hassle at the end of an otherwise fortunate venture, the German companies had a good return on their investments, even considering the long time it took to realize profits. As mentioned earlier, the landed price of pepper in Lisbon was around 8 cr/quintal. At 20 cr/ql the gross yield for the group could have been around 168000 cr., with an investment of 65400 cr. Of course, this is an approximation on the outcome. Haebler mentioned a margin of as much as 150 per cent.

One can well speculate, why a similar investment was not undertaken in the following years. Reasons were possibly the uncertainty in the final outcome of the 1505/06 venture, the insistence to buy from the Portuguese office at Antwerp, where traders could take delivery with reduced risk on transport and price development [22].

Decades later a contract system emerged, where the crown sold through one appointed party at prescribed minimum prices. Here the Welser and particularly the Fuggers became active again. Still, the 1505/06 venture with the substantial risk capital input was not repeated.

References:

1. Hermann Kellenbenz,*Unternehmerkraefte im Hamburger Portugal-und Spanienhandel 1590-1625,* Hamburg, 1954.
2. Franz Huemmerich, *Die erste deutsche Handelsfahrt nach Indien 1505/06,* Muenchen/Berlin,1922, p.85
3. Johann Philipp Cassel, *Privilegia und Handlungsfreiheiten, welche die Koenige von Portugal ehedem den deutschen Kaufleuten zu Lissabon ertheilt haben,* Bremen, 1771
4. Franz Huemmerich, *Die erste deutsche Handelsfahrt*,p.100
5. Konrad Haebler, *Die ueberseeischen Unternehmungen der Welser und ihrer Gesellschafter*, Leipzig, 1903, p.19 et al
6. Ibid .,p.18
7. Franz Huemmerich, *Die erste deutsche Handelsfahrt*,p.24
8. Translation in Franz Huemmerich, "Quellen und Untersuchungen zur Fahrt der ersten Deutschen nach dem portugiesischen Indien 1505/06", in *Abhandlungen der Koeniglich –Bayerischen Akademie der Wissenchaften, philosophisch-Philologische und historische Klasse*, XXX.Band, 3, Abhandlung, Muenchen , 1918,pp.134-149
9. Wolfgang Knabe,*Auf den Spuren der ersten deutschen Kaufleute in Indien,* Anhausen, 1993,p.86
10. Franz Huemmerich, *Die erste deutsche Handelsfahrt,* p.105
11. Franz Huemmerich, "Quellen und Untersuchungen zur Fahrt", pp.149-150
12. K.S.Mathew and Afzal Ahmad (ed.),*Emergence of Cochin in the pre-Industrial Era*, Pondicherry, 1990, p.133
13. Konrad Haebler, op.cit.,pp.22-29
14. Ibid.
15. Ibid.
16. Ibid.
17. Franz Huemmerich, *Die erste deutsche Handelsfahrt*,pp.139-143
18. Ibid
19. Ibid
20. Ibid
21. Ibid.
22. Ibid.

Bibliography

1. Braudel, Fernand, *Civilisation and capitalism, 15th-18th century, vol. II: The Wheels of Commerce; vol. III: The Perspective of the World*; tranlated by Sian Reynolds, London, 1983, 1984
2. Cassel, Johann Philipp, *Privilegia und Handlungsfreiheiten, welche die Koenige von Portugal ehedem den deutschen Kaufleuten zu Lissabon ertheilt haben,* Bremen, 1771

3   Cipolla, Carlo M. (ed), *Europaeische Wirtschaftsgeschichte*, Band 2: *Sechzehntes und siebzehntes Jahrhundert;* here: Kristof Glamann, "Der europaeische Handel 1500-1750, Pfefferhandel", Stuttgart, 1979.

4   Dharampal - Frick, Gita, *Indien im Spiegel deutscher Quellen der Fruehen Neuzeit (1500-1750)*, Tuebingen, 1994.

5   Ehrenberg, Richard, *Capital and Finance in the age of the Renaissance, A Study of the Fuggers...*, translated by H.M. Lucas, London, 1928.

6   Fitzler, Hedwig M.A., "Portugiesische Handelsgesellschaften des 15. und beginnenden 16. Jahrhunderts", in *Viertel Jahresschrift fuer Sozial - und Wirtschaftsgeschichte (VSWG)*, XXIV Stuttgart, 1932

7   Haebler, Konrad, *Die ueberseeischen Unternehmungen der Welser und ihrer Gesellschafter*, Leipzig, 1903.

8   Hinsch, J.D., "Die Bartholomaeus-Bruederschaft der Deutschen in Lissabon", in *Hansische Geschichtsblaetter*, XVII, Leipzig, 1890.

9   Huemmerich, Franz, *Quellen und Untersuchungen zur Fahrt der ersten Deutschen nach dem portugiesischen Indien 1505/06*, in Abhandlungen der Koeniglich-Bayerischen Akademie der Wissenschaften, philosphisch - philologische und historische Klasse, XXX. Band, 3. Abhandlung, Muenchen, 1918.

10. Huemmerich, Franz, *Die erste deutsche Handelsfahrt nach Indien 1505/06*, Muenchen/Berlin, 1922

11 Kellenbenz, Hermann, *Unternehmerkraefte in Hamburger Portugal - und Spanienhandel 1590 - 1625*, Hamburg, 1954

12. Kellenbenz, Hermann, *Die Fugger in Spanien und Portugal bis 1560*, Teil 1, Muenchen, 1990.

13 Knabe, Wolfgang, *Auf den Spuren der ersten deutschen Kaufleute in Indien*, Anhausen, 1993.

14 Lane, Frederic C., "Tonnages, Medieval and Modern", in *Economic History Review* XVII, no. 2, Utrecht, 1964/65

15 Mathew, K.S., "Cochin and Maritime Trade of India during 16th century", in *Journal of the Directorate of Archives*, Vol. VI, no.2, Goa, 1988

16. Mathew, K.S. and Ahmad Afzal (ed), *Emergence of Cochin in the Pre-Industrial Era*, Pondicherry, 1990

17. Mathew, K.S., *Indo-Portuguese trade and the Fuggers of Germany*, New Delhi, 1997

18 Nusser, Horst G.W., *Fruehe deutsche Entdecker: Asien in Berichten unbekannter deutscher Augenzeugen 1502-06*, Muenchen, 1990.

19 Rem, Lucas, *Das Tagebuch des Lucas Rem aus den Jahren 1494 - 1541, Ein Beitrag zur Handelsgeschichte der Stadt Augsburg*, mitgeteilt....von B. Greiff, Augsburg, 1861.

20 Poelnitz, Goetz Freiherr von, *Die Fugger*, Frankfurt, o.J.

21 Schaefer, Dietrich, "Das Zeitalter der Entdeckungen und die Hanse", in *Hansische Geschichtsblaetter* XXV, Leipzig, 1898

22 Schulze, Franz, *Balthasar Springers Indienfahrt, 1505/06*, Strassburg, 1902

23 Stier, H.G.C. (ed.trl.), *Vlaemischer Bericht ueber Vasco da Gama's zweite Reise 1502/03*, Braunschweig, 1887

Stephan B.G.C. Michaelsen

Some Data on Portuguese Fleets to East India from 1497 to 1506

a) First fleet, Vasco da Gama, 3 ships plus supply ship, departs 7/1497, Calicut 1/98, return to Lisbon 7/99 to 11/99.[1]

b) Second fleet, Pedro Alvarez Cabral, differing numbers: 10 or 12 or 13 ships depart March 1500, 8 or 6 or 5; return June 1501; Italian participation [2]. Bombardment of Calicut, relations with Cochin. Great loss in manpower and capital, rather small amount of spices arrives at Lisbon.

c) Third fleet, Joao de Nova, 4 ships (2 royal, 2 private) sail March 1501, Cochin end 1501, small purchase on local credit [3], return 1502.

d) Fourth fleet, Vasco da Gama, 24 (!) ships depart Febr/April 1502 of which 11 royal and 13 private [4], includes squadron under Vincente Sodre to blockade the Red Sea route [5], return Sept-Nov 1503 with 34000 quintal of pepper [6]. German gems dealer Joerg Herwart in Cochin, February 1503 [7].

e) Fifth fleet, Afonso de Albuquerque, 3 or 4 ships, from Lisbon 4/1503, on board trader Peter Holzschuher from Nuernberg, three ships of the previous year meet in the Indian ocean; via Gulf of Aden and Cambay to Cochin, from there 1/1504, Lisbon, 1504 [8].

Francisco de Albuquerque, from Lisbon 4/1503 to Cochin 9/1503, fortification at Cochin, 2 ships sail for Europe 2/1504, lost at sea [9]

Antonio de Saldanha, 3 ships sail middle April 1503 [10]

f) Sixth fleet, Lopo Soares de Albergia, 13 (or 11 to 14) ships, depart spring 1504, 11 ships return autumn 1505.

g) Seventh fleet, (viceroy) Francisco de Almeida, 14 or 15 ships[11] and 6 caravels sail 3/1505, some ships remain out East, trading ships back in Lisbon between 5/1506 and early 1507. See also data on ships in the fleet of 1505/06 given separately.

Fleet of Pero d'anhaya, 6 ships, from Lisbon 5/1505 [12], to build fort at Sofala

h) Eighth fleet, Tristao da Cunha and Afonso de Albuquerque, 10 (or 17) ships sail 8/1506, 4 ships return autumn 1507 [13]

Notes:

1. Generally based on Franz Huemmerich, *Die erste deutsche Handelsfahrt*, and on Horst G.W. Nusser, *Fruehe deutsche Entdecker*, pp. 78 - 101
2. Konrad Haebler, op. cit., p. 15
3. K.S. Mathew, *Emergence of Cochin*, p. VI.
4. Konrad Haebler, op. cit., p.24
5. Ibid., p.8
6. Ibid., p.25
7. Wolfgang Knabe, op. cit.
8. Konrad Haebler, op. cit., p.13; Wolfgang Knabe, op. cit., p. 84
9. Wolfgang Knabe, op. cit., pp. 85, 86, 383, 415
10. Franz Huemmerich, *Quellen und Untersuchungen*, p. 94
11. Konrad Haebler, op. cit., p. 15
12. Franz Huemmerich, *Quellen und Untersuchungen*, p. 40
13. Konrad Haebler, op. cit., p. 31

German Participation in the India Fleet of 1505/06

Distances on the West coast of India, in nautical miles (from Admiralty Chart 708)

Bombay to Goa	220
to Anjedive islands	45
to Honavar	37
to cape at Mt. Dili	145
to Cannanore	15
to Calicut	45
to Cochin	80
to Quilon	70
to Cape Cormorin	80

Some Data on Ships of the East India Fleet of 1505/06

1) JERONIMO, rather large ship, (viceroy) Almeida on board eastbound, captain Fernao d'Eca dies 8/1505 in Mombasa; German and Italian interest, on board Pero Fernandes Tinoco and Ulrich Imhoff; sails from India 2/1/1506, Lisbon 5/1506. Possibly already in fourth fleet[1]

2) SAN RAFAEL, somewhat smaller; captain Fernao Soarez, home port Porto; German and Italian interest, on board Hans Mayr; returns with *Jeronimo*. Possibly already in fourth fleet.

3) LEONARDO, captain Diogo Correa; German (and Italian?) interest, on board Balthasar Sprenger; sails 15/1/1505 from Antwerp to Lisbon, damage at Lisbon-Crossarm and Mombasa-rudder; sails from Cannanore 21/1/1506, Lisbon 11/1506. Possibly already in fourth and again in 1508 fleets.

4) JUDIA, captain Antao Goncalves, owner Fernando de Noronha; private; returns with *Jeronimo*. Possibly again in fleet 1508.

5) BOTOFAGO, captain Joao Serrao hurt in Mombasa [2], captain westbound Ruy Frere? [3] ; royal; returns with *Jeronimo*. Possibly again in fleet 1508.

6) CONCEICAO, captain Sebastiao de Souza; royal; eastbound part of the "slow" convoy, sails from India with *Jeronimo*, leaking near Cape of Good Hope, back to Mozambique, arriving Lisbon alone 6/1506.

7) GABRIEL, eastbound captain Vasco Gomes d'Abreu who becomes admiral westbound, captain westbound Diogo Fernandez; royal; "slow" convoy but joins with fleet at Mombasa 20/8/1505, returns with *Leonardo* and *Magdalena*. Possibly again in fourth fleet.

8) MAGDALENA, captain Diogo Fernando Correa; royal; "slow" convoy, returns with *Leonardo* and *Gabriel*. Possibly again in fleet 1508.

9) FLOR DE LA MAR, captain Joao da Nova who led third fleet and was in Quiloa and Cochin 1501; royal; sails late 2/2/1506, misses season, to Zansibar?, ship leaking, cargo transferred and arrives Lisbon 7/1507. Possibly already in fourth fleet.

10) BELLA, captain Pero Ferreira Fogaca; royal; old ship, eastbound disintegrates and sinks in the South Atlantic 28/1505.

97

11) ?, Captain Lucas Fonseca, return delayed, stays at Mozambique [4].
12) ?, Captain Lopo Sanchez, eastbound beached near Capo de Corrientes, all lost. Had one of the dismanted brigantines on board.
13) ?, Captain Fernao Bermudes; makes brief stop at Mozambique eastbound 7/1505, captain raises flag in Mombasa together with Ruy Frere [5].
14) ?, Captain Felepe Rodriguez
15) ???

Caravels:

C 1) SAN JORGE, captain Joao Homen; had trouble in Quilon 11/1505.
C 2) SANTA CATARINA, captain Goncalo de Paiva; with the "fast" convoy.
C 3) ?, Captain Lopo Chanoca; participates in suppression of rebellion at Cochin.
C 4) ?, Captain Antao Vaz; arrives Anjediva 24/9/1505.
C 5) ?, Captain Goncalo Vaz de Goes, stationed at Quiloa with one of the brigantines.
C 6) ?, Captain Nuno Vaz Pereira; brings pepper from Cochin to Cannanore 1/1505 [6].

Notes:

1. Wolfgang Knabe, op.cit., p. 62 et al
2. Franz Huemmerich, *Die erste deutsche Handelsfahrt*, p. 58
3. Ibid., p. 121
4. Ibid., p. 68
5. Ibid., p. 59
6. Ibid., p. 106

7

OUTGOING CARREIRA SHIPS IN THE INDIAN OCEAN (1550-1575)

Joseph Velinkar

Not long after the discovery of the sea-route to India, Portugal established the *Casa da India* in 1503 in order to regulate its spice trade (under royal monopoly) with India. The Carreira ships were slowly organized into a system of convoys, routes and relief-stations in order to reach the Indian subcontinent safely and bring back their precious goods.

The cargo of a 500-800-ton *nau* (heavy transport ship) consisted of the equipage of a running ship of the period: anchors, mast, sails, pumps, cordage, cannons, cannon balls, sloops, boats, etc.; the ship's provisions, chiefly many barrels of drinking water, wine and oil for the 6-month voyage, and last, the personal provisions – sometimes even live hens, pigs, sheep and cows – and luggage of each traveller. The freight, consisting chiefly of bales, barrels and boxes stacked high up on the upper deck, was later moved to the lower decks and hold as the ship sailed into the high sea.[1] The largest-capacity *nau* of the 1550's was the 1000-ton *'Graça'*.[2]

The crew of an Indiaman numbered about 112, about 50 of whom were sailors and an approximately equal number boatmen (*grumetes*).[3] The captain and higher officers, with the 11 artillerymen and their constables completed the crew. The passengers were mostly soldiers and a few merchants, clerics and travellers who sought to earn a living or make a fortune in the East. The 1558-flotilla consisting of four ships carried 2000 men.[4] In 1562 six ships with 3000 troops arrived in India.[5] In 1571 seven ships sailed out with a total of 4000 men,[6] the number on each being 500-600. But sometimes a ship carried even 800 persons on the last stage of the voyage (Mozambique-Goa).[7] And in 1568 the 'Chagas' left Lisbon with 830 persons on board.[8]

Passengers formed a motley group. A large number of soldiers recruited in Portugal during those years were sent to the East. A six-ship flotilla sailed with 3000 soldiers for India, though one ship 'São Paulo' was carried to Brazil by the equatorial tides and winds and returned to Portugal not long afterwards.[9] Orphan boys and a few merchants wishing to try their luck in the East got aboard too.[10] Women were not to be left behind. Already in 1524 Vasco da Gama had forbidden women to sail to the East under penalty of flogging, because of the hardships of the voyage. No man was permitted to take along even his wife or female slaves.[11] But as the years passed and circumstances changed, the annual route became better known and less risky. By 1562 a ship with individual cabins for about 30 women was constructed.[12] The same year three women reportedly sailed to India on the 'São Vicente'.[13] In 1565, 10-11 women travelled aboard a Carreira ship.[14] Some women stowaways hid in the irregularly stacked mass of cargo till the *nau* had passed Madeira and the supply caravel turned back. One woman moved about on deck, disguised as a man.[15] Occasionally public women connived with the crew to be stowed away.[16] At Mozambique many female slaves were purchased and brought aboard.

In 1549 Jorge de Cabral, first Governor to live with his wife in India, desired to spend the rest of his life with her in the Orient.[17] In 1558 Capt. Payo de Noronha took his wife Joanna Fajorada and daughter along to India on the 'Graça'.[18] In 1560 *fidalgo* D. Diogo Pereira de Vasconcellos took his wife Dona Francisca Sardinha and daughter Dona Constança on the 'São Paulo'.[19] Later several married men (*casados*) took their wives to India.[20] Finally, as mentioned in various accounts, there were some women on nearly every Indiaman. These had to suffer severe hardships, specially during shipwrecks.[21]

Being quite aware of the vulnerability of married and unmarried men, who were away from their families for a long time, Vicar General Miguel Vaz had suggested to King João III way back in 1534 that married men should be allowed to take their wives along with them to the East.[22] First Archbishop of Goa D. Gaspar too had requested Regent Queen D. Catarina in 1561 to arrange for the marriage of many parentless young women whom the court had sent to India.[23]

Other kinds of travellers too were found on these ships: an Indian who helped set up India's first printing press in 1556 was returning from Portugal, another who assisted in the kitchen on board,[24] and two other Keralites of the military caste (Nairs) in 1563.[25] On the 1568 voyage Viceroy D. Luis de Athaide had his select choir and musical band sailing with him.[26] At the morning dry Mass and in the evenings the musicians played their flutes, bagpipes and other instruments, while the choristers sang to entertain the voyagers. Among the important passengers over the years were Viceroys, Archbishops, Patriarchs, bishops, Provincials and Captains.

During this period, an average of five ships used to sail from Belem in Lisbon on the annual *Carreira*. They followed the fixed sea-lane, riding at anchor at Madeira, passing the Canary and Cape Verde Islands and the Gulf of Guinea. Before reaching the steamy, becalming doldrums, the escort caravel surrendered its sweet-water cargo and turned back home. If the Atlantic currents did not carry them off Brazil-wards, the flotilla proceeded to round the Cape of Good Hope. Only after doubling the Cape – which they frequently did not see –, did the captain have to decide whether he should navigate up to Mozambique or take the 'outer' route and cross the Ocean to Cochin.

Sailing straight across the Indian Ocean required making a decision, which depended on many factors: the weather, stock of provisions, date of rounding the Cape, health of the passengers, sea-worthiness of the ship and opinion of the mariners. According to a royal regiment already in force in 1567, any Portuguese ship crossing the Cape up to 8 July had to follow the less dangerous Mozambique Channel route, after that date it had to take the outer route.[27] And by another royal order, the captain had to sit in consultation with his officers before taking the decision.[28]

On the inner route after passing the Cape, the ships sailed north to leeward, skirting the south-east African coast. But the galleon 'São João' was wrecked off this coast in 1552, while passing Natal. The survivors were later transported to Mozambique. In 1554 the 'São Bento' sank off this coast too, but the passengers were saved.[29] The shoals of São Rumao and others of the Mozambique Channel were danger zones,[30] round which the pilot had to manoeuvre in order to reach port safely. In 1548 the 'São Pedro' found itself resting on a reef - which had wrecked a ship before, - but managed to float away.[31]

Mozambique, the last and obligatory port of call at the end of this run, had a dangerous bar. In 1548, a ship approaching it with a fair wind behind her struck a shoal several times till its rudder came apart. In 1561 a ship ran into a sandbank, but was refloated by a morning wind.[32] During the two years 1565 and 1566, two ships 'Flor de la Mar' and 'Tigre' were lost here.[33]

The ships usually crossed the bar at the beginning of July and anchored for nearly a month in the port. Late arrivals had to shorten their stopover, e.g. in 1562 the 'São Vicente' cut short its stay to only five or six days[34] to catch the tail-end of the monsoon, which would take it to Goa in September. Once the winds turned west, the ships had to stay in port till the onset of the next monsoon, as the 'Conceição' did in 1559.[35]

Mozambique, a narrow strip of land with a perimeter of barely three miles and a "stone's throw" broad, was a sandy island of palm trees and few freshwater wells. The land itself was considered 'unhealthy' and 'pestilential'.[36] Even the town and houses gave off a foul odour.[37] After 1569, a new fortress at the port, the church of Our Lady of the Bastion dominating the landscape and a hospital for sick voyagers – and still later churches of the Holy Spirit, St. Anthony, St Gabriel and the Misericordia - were its prominent features.[38] The population of the island consisted of a mere 100 Portuguese and about 200 Negroes and Indians. These had planted the few fruit trees on the island. The roosters made good and the pigs better food, but the hens from the mainland were rather small, their flesh not very palatable, and the fish very unwholesome.[39]

While the ship lay anchored, the sick were carried ashore and attended to. The hospital in Mozambique was too small to accommodate the large number of ill often brought from the Carreira ships. In 1556, over 100 from four ships [40] and in 1562, 400 from two ships[41] arrived ill. Each patient was placed on a bed. But when they were too many, some were laid out on beddings on the floor, and sometimes even two on a bed..[42]

The crew and passengers disembarked for purchases. Many slaves of both sexes, different origins and sizes were bought for re-sale elsewhere. The *'Chagas'* carried nearly 200 slaves to India in 1567.[43] In 1564 a ship with 250 slaves was so crowded that passengers "could not stretch out their legs".[44] And some slaves were so famished that they died two or three days after leaving port.[45] The typical articles available were ivory, ebony and gold. On the mainland, herds of wild elephants roamed the forests where local Negroes easily got their long tusks and meat, which was eaten dry and uncooked. Ebony of the finest Oriental variety was available in large quantities in the forest. And finally gold (dust or grain) was brought by the inhabitants and bartered for trinkets, knick-knacks and gimcracks because they lacked a suitable medium of exchange. But the exclusive right of dealing in these was the fort captain's, who could easily amass a fortune in a very short time.[46]

Life on board, described by several authors, had several interesting features. When two ships sailed side by side, passengers on one shouted across to those of the other.[47] When life was boring and the wind dropped, many brought out their fishing-rods and angled in the ocean.[48] Childbirth was a rare occurrence. Two births aboard the 'Graça in 1561,[49] a third of a baby girl[50] and a fourth of a still-born child in 1565[51] are mentioned.

Love and matchmaking were only to be expected on a long voyage. Once a woman fled from her lawful husband into the arms of her lover on board.[52] Marriages too were celebrated, one secretly, another publicly.[53]

Illness was rife, absence of it rare, the main reasons on the last leg of the voyage being: weakness resulting from the long voyage to Mozambique, polluted water drunk at the port when the casks ran dry, the "humid, feverish air" of the same port,[54] bad weather and finally serious illnesses contracted before leaving the port.[55] Common ailments were "fever", beriberi and scurvy.[56] Deaths were accidental, (falling off a running ship) or due to illness.[57] On the *Esperança* alone in 1565, over 130 persons died during the voyage.[58] The deceased were covered, given a ceremonial funeral and cast into the sea.

The last leg of the voyage (c. 900 leagues) lasted about a month. The ships tried to catch the strongest part of the monsoon (*monçao grande*) in August.[59] A 50-league-a-day speed was considered good for a *nau*, but the average was 30.[60] On reaching Goa, the captains were advised not to cross the bar before 3 September.[61]

Earlier (in 1548) a pilot, who had never steered a ship to India, strayed far off course.[62] But over the years, prominent sea-marks made the acquainted route less dangerous. Two days after sailing north-east, the ship passed Comoro archipelago, the main island being 15 leagues long and 7½ leagues broad. Mt. Kartala, 2500 m. high on the principal island, stood as the first land-mark for passing ships. But Carreira ships did not halt there for provisions, as the islanders were unfriendly to the Portuguese.[63]

On this stretch, there were few shipwrecks. A disaster struck the *São Filipe*, as it approached Goa in 1563. It had to withstand the worst storm known to have hit the west coast of India, lasting four to five days. While waiting for the rest of the flotilla on the high seas in order to reach the coast together, it sank losing all its merchandise and many lives.[64] Reaching the Goa bar straight had been a problem for many a pilot, the ship sometimes reaching a spot a few miles off Goa[65] at the Vengurla Rocks (*Ilheos Queimados*),[66] or at Kharepatan, or at Anjediva. After their arrival at Goa, the whole city turned out to welcome the ships. The flagship (on which the Viceroy travelled) led the procession of vessels into Old Goa port. In 1554 D. Pedro Mascarenhas, in 1558 D. Constantino de Bragança, in 1568 D. Luis de Ataíde and in 1571 D. Antonio de Noronha travelled on the Carreira ships and were received at the pier with much pomp and solemnity. D. Constantino, spent a day waiting at Panjim before proceeding to the city. The new incumbent first presented his patent of Appointment and Provision, signed the Terms and Autos, took charge of the *Estado da India* and only then entered the capital, proceeding to the Cathedral and Viceregal palace.[67]

The city had been preparing already 8 – 10 days before the advent of the ships. Beds, stretchers and other medical furniture were made available to the hospital.[68] On arrival, the seriously ill were quickly transferred to the Royal Hospital and the sick attended to. At Cochin the small, inadequate hospital was hard put to it for room. When four ships, with 400 patients, arrived together in 1568, some were accommodated in the hospital, and the rest in the Dominican and Franciscan friaries and honourable noblemen's houses.[69]

On the 1570 voyage, of the 4000 persons on board nearly 2000 kept good health. Those who died *en route* had been afflicted by some strange illness marked by some "very troublesome" fever and swollen legs. They had contracted a contagious disease the previous year in Portugal! On the '*Chagas*' alone, over 450 of the 900 persons died during the voyage, over 300 died on the '*Belem*' and similarly large numbers on the other ships of the Armada.[70]

At the beginning of 1571 during the Adil Shahi siege, the entire population of Goa suffered from a very serious fever.

The body was racked with pain, and the hands and feet were very limp. But the illness was not fatal. Hardly had the city recovered from this malady, when another more serious and dangerous epidemic spread in the city. The patient's temperature rose or his body turned cold with a new species of fever which, like a pestilence, ended his life in a short time.[71] Archbishop George Themudo too was not spared from this trial and breathed his last in St.Paul's College.[72]

The ships of that year (1571) too brought over 600 sick to Goa. These convalesced in the Royal Hospital for nearly two months. Before long, the epidemic had spread to Cochin and nearly everyone there was laid down, but only a few died.[73]

After the arrival of the ships, disembarkation of passengers and unloading of cargo, the ships were washed and readied for the onward voyage to Cochin, where the spices were usually loaded, and the return journey to Europe.

But the Indiamen that rounded the Cape of Good Hope late and sailed by the outer route had a worse tale to tell.. They had to face a hard and stormy voyage because of the fickle southwest monsoon-end winds, inexperienced pilots, imperfect charts and insufficient stock of victuals. Along this route the ships were battered by monsoon winds and their life-span considerably curtailed, gales forcing them off their destination or wrecking them in mid Ocean.

In 1556 the *Conceição* (Algaravia Nova) wrecked off the Peros Banhos , a rocky atoll of the Chagos archipelago (250 miles south of the Maldives), 500 leagues off the west coast of India. The captain, pilot and about 28 survivors set off in a little boat *(batel)* to seek for help. Another raft *(jangada)*, constructed from the remains of the wreckage, set off with another group, twelve of whom reached the Indian coast alive to tell the story! The remaining 160 stranded persons moved from atoll to atoll till they all perished of illness and hunger.[74]

The long voyage of the *'São Paulo'* to India is another sad but telling example of Carreira ship hazards. After a long wait off the coast of Guinea and being unable to cross the

Equator, many fell sick and some died. The captain decided to head for Brazil in order to replenish the dwindling stock of provisions and seek help for the many patients. He anchored at Bahia on 17 August. After resting the sick for 47 days, he weighed anchor on 2 October 1560 and sailed before the wind. Quickly crossing the Atlantic and passing between Ascension and Trinidad islands he reached the Cape on 15 November, too late to take the inner route! So he decided to cross the Indian Ocean.

A northerly wind carried them east-south-east and soon they were near the 38th parallel passing an island (Amsterdam or St. Paul?) at a distance of three to four leagues. Then they passed several (unidentified!) islands: Ilha dos Romeiros (Island of Pilgrims?), Islands of Seven Sisters (Seychelles?) and Island of Gold (Chryse Cherson on the Malay peninsula?) on the Equator, 30 leagues off Sumatra.

On 20 January the ship ran into a tempest. Sailing to windward in the face of a gale, the foresail of the prow snapped. The next morning (21 January) they landed on an islet off the coast of Sumatra. The ship was stuck in slime. There were many women and children on the vessel. After an arduous struggle with nature, with the help of natives and leaders of the region on land and with other sailing vessels at sea, they reached Sunda bay on 29 April. They reached Malacca only two months later and were received by Captain João de Mendonça. Later they were put aboard a ship and taken to Cochin in September, when the "small monsoon" winds began to blow.[75]

Several other shipwrecks occurred in the Indian Ocean. One occured on a Lakshadvipa island in 1555.[76] Of two other ships going towards Sri Lanka in 1560, one got stuck in the shoals near Jaffnapattanam, but was rescued by the Viceroy, who happened to be nearby in the region, negotiating with a king,[77] the other strayed into the islands of Diego Rodrigues of the Maldive Islands. Several other ships were wrecked and their masts and equipment were washed ashore on islands of the inner route.[78]

Of nearly every flotilla some ship or other had the misfortune of being delayed or obliged to sail directly to Cochin from the Cape. Some missed their destination and reached some other shore. Some were battered and many passengers fell ill and died. From Cochin they sailed up to Goa for unloading, repairs and refurbishing, before being reloaded for the return journey.

From all this we see that Portuguese soldiers and workers and African slaves were a Carreira cargo of persons, though with some Portuguese provisions and African products, all facing the outward voyage perils during the third quarter of the sixteenth century.

To this end, commercial and friendly political bonds were forged with other kings, the threat coming only from the Dutch and later from the English.

References:

1. J. Wicki ed., *Documenta Indica (DI)*, Rome 1948-84, V, 527; VI, 292; G. Schurhammer, *Francis Xavier: His Life, His Times (=FX)*, tr. J. Costelloe S.J., Rome, 1977, II, 6.
2. Diogo do Couto, *Décadas da Ásia (=DdA)*, Lisboa, 1973, VII (2), 17; *DI* III, 518.
3. *FX* II, 5-8.
4. F. C. Danvers, *The Portuguese in India (=Tpil)*, London, 1894, I, 511.
5. *Tpil* I, 524.
6. *Tpil* II, 2.
7. *DI* V, 545; VI, 308.
8. *DI* VII, 507.
9. *DdA* VII (2), 17.
10. *DI* II, 222, VI, 466.
11. Gaspar Correa, *Lendas da India (=LI)* Lisboa, 1860, II, 819-21.
12. *DI* V, 453.
13. *Ibid.* 530.
14. *DI* VI, 457.
15. *DI* V, 544.
16. *DI* V, 530.
17. *LI* IV, 680.
18. *Ibid.* 681.
19. *DdA* VII (2), 424-25; *DI* V, 443.

20 *LI* IV, 266.
21 *DI* I, 384; V, 441,489, 544.
22 *FX* II, 159.
23 *DI* V, 230.
24 *DI* V, 540; VI, 39.
25 *DI* VI, 385.
26 *DI* VII, 508.
27 *Ibid.,* 287.
28 *DI* VI, 535.
29 *DI* III, 442.
30 *Ibid.* 395-96.
31 *DI* I, 389.
32 *DI* V, 218.
33 *DI* VII, 286.
34 *DI* V, 528.
35 *DdA* VII (2), 185.
36 *DI* V, 499; VI, 456.
37 *DI* VIII, 436.
38 *DI* V, 276; VIII, 699.
39 *DI* VI, 536; VIII, 690-91.
40 *DI* IV, 119.
41 *DI* VI, 384.
42 *DI* VII, 288.
43 *DI* VII, 370.
44 *Ibid.* 249, 276.
45 *DI* V, 500.
46 *DI* VI, 536.
47 *DI* II, 199.
48 *DI* VII, 469.
49 *DI* V, 500.
50 *DI* VI, 455.
51 *DI* III, 457.
52 *DI* VI, 537.
53 *DI* V, 531.
54 *Ibid.*; *DI* VII, 292.
55 *DI* I, 392, 447.
56 *DI* II, 224; III, 112; V, 374, 532.
57 *DI* VI, 41.
58 *Ibid.* 468.
59 *DdA* VI (2), 282.

60 DI VI, 34, 384; VII, 293.
61 DI V, 529.
62 DI I, 428.
63 DI VI, 42, 277, 301.
64 DdA VII (2), 561; DI VI, 61.
65 DI III, 508.
66 DI V, 225.
67 DdA VIII, 3-4.
68 DI VII, 384.
69 DI VII, 693.
70 DdA IX, 50-51; DI VIII, 436-37.
71 DI VIII, 439-40.
72 DI VIII, 443.
73 DI VIII, 486.
74 DI III, 294, 356, 602-05; Alfonso Paes, *Relação da nao Conceição* II, 7, 15; B. Gomes de Brito, *História trágico-marítima*, Lisboa 1904, II, 5, 46.
75 DI V, 436-77.
76 DI III, 430.
77 DI IV, 834.
78 DI III, 443.

8

CONTRIBUTION OF MALABAR RULERS IN DELAYING DOMINANCE BY FOREIGN POWERS IN MALABAR REGION

K.K.N. Kurup

The arrival of the Portuguese in the medieval city of Calicut in 1498, in an organised effort for trade and commerce, political expansion and religious solidarity with the Christianity in the East Indies, was an epoch making event not only in the Asiatic history but also that of Europe. It was the inauguration of new historical forces which in the long run had far fetching impact on nations and nationalities under the process of formation. The regions like Malabar with their traditional kingdoms were exposed to the European expansion and colonial aspirations in this context.

A tiny state of Western Europe, namely Portugal, emerged as an important sea faring nation at the end of 15th century. Its inventions particularly related to trans-oceanic navigation, in matters like heavy tonnage of the vessel, mariners' compass, cartography of world and oceans made her to achieve the credit for discovering new sea routes. Although the achievements of Vasco da Gama were given laudable appraisals in all European text books related to colonial expansion, his role was not so significant one as perceived in such text books. The voyage upto Cape of Good Hope, the southern point of Africa, was effected earlier by Diaz and his companions. The Eastern coast of Africa had already established trade links with Western Coast of India even earlier as 12th century. Therefore the advent of the Portuguese on Malabar Coast was not a significant event as seen in the colonial text books. But this advent by the Portuguese became significant due to the development of historical forces which had taken place following that event. Malabar was the major territorial region which had witnessed such historical developments.

The four major kingdoms which had existed in Kerala during this period were Kolathunad, the Kingdom of Zamorin, Cochin and Venad. Each Kingdom had its own feudatories and subordinate principalities. Many of them were fighting each other for resource control and territorial expansion. The four Kingdoms which had enjoyed a predominant place and political power over all other smaller principalities were also in a struggle for power. In fact vassalage and political fragmentation had been the order of the day. There was no powerful state formation on account of the internal struggle, institution of caste hierarchy and meager state resources. Therefore the Kerala situation was quite permissive of any foreign intervention in its political and economic affairs.

Although a large number of political fragments or native kingdoms existed in Malabar during the sixteenth century, the Calicut Kingdom of the Zamorin was famous as an entrepôt on the western coast of India. The Malabar spices, particularly pepper and cardamom were highly demanded in the international markets of Aden and Ormuz. The trade links with these centres established by the Arabs made Calicut an international city where traders of different nations found their immense fortune.

The prosperity of Calicut among all the four Kingdoms had been mainly due to its maritime trade and commerce with the Arabs and the Egyptians. These nationalities had much contributed to the growth of Calicut as a medieval town on the Western Coast of India. Abdur Razzak, the Persian ambassador who visited Calicut in 1442 testified the prominence of Malabar trade with the Arab countries. He wrote:

"........the most wealthy merchants bring thither from maritime countries considerable cargoes which they unload and unhesitatingly send into the markets and bazaars without thinking in the meantime of any necessity of checking the account or of keeping watch over the goods......"

These commercial activities even turned to the establishment of Arab settlement in the town.

The advent of the Portuguese in the city of Calicut made them accessible to the gateway of Asia. The Portuguese rivalry in commerce as well as religion against the Moors or Muslims compelled the Zamorin to interfere in the dealings and maintain the law of his country and safeguard the interests of his subjects. Such confrontations against the Portuguese continued over a century, finally resulting in the total disintegration of the Zamorin's Kingdom.

The peaceful political climate of Calicut was much disturbed by the advent of the Portuguese. They cherished the ideas like the monopoly of trade and maritime enterprise in the Eastern waters originating from the Papal Bull to their nation. In fact such a claim by the Portuguese compelled them to project superiority over all other nationalities. This was an open declaration of enmity against the Zamorin and the allies, the Muslims.

During the hundred years of resistance against the Portuguese, the native kingdom of Zamorin, spent its money, men and resources and gradually upheld a new concept of maritime India. It was this resistance against the *conquistadors* that had made the Western Cost of Malabar a free zone although the fortified centres of the foreigners existed beyond the territorial limits of Zamorin.

The Portuguese could establish their settlements at Cochin and Cannanore, the Southern and Northern frontiers of Calicut Kingdom, respectively. The Rajas of Cochin and Kolathunad always tried to extend their states and power in confrontation with the authority of Zamorin. However their expansion was restricted by the Zamorin.

The Zamorin was courteous to extend hospitality to the Portuguese also as he had done to others. But the Calicut market dominated by the Arabs refused to deal with the new comers. When they were asked to pay the usual customs levy, an act of barbarism was shown against the soldiers of the ruler.

The northern ruler, the Kolathunad and the southern ruler of Cochin, extended welcome to the Portuguese to their markets, on account of commercial and political rivalry with the Zamorin. In the chequered history of the Kingdom of Calicut there had been compromises and confrontations by the ruling class. However, there had been one constant element that the Muslims or the Arabs with their native descendants known as the Mappilas hoisted the banner of revolt against the intruders.

The conflicts and stubborn resistance of Malabar had been responsible to compel Albuquerque to look for a comfortable place, other than Cochin on the Western Coast at Goa to establish a centre for Portuguese expeditions in Asia. For him it was possible to annex that territory from the vassals of Vijayanagar and establish some considerable territorial possession in Asia as a colonial experiment till 1961. However such an experiment was impossible in Malabar on account of the spirit of freedom shown by the Zamorin and the Mappila sailors. The Malabar sailors, who were more trained for a peaceful maritime trade which was either coastal or long distance one, were immediately converted into combatant mariners. They had to counteract the Portuguese piracy and also resist the order of the day that might was right.

Meanwhile Mohammed Kunjali Marakkar from Cochin, migrated to Ponnani and later to Calicut when it was not possible for a free enterprise at Cochin due to the intervention of the Portuguese. His search for a free commercial zone and political support against the Portuguese made him an ally of the Zamorin. The trading house of Kunjali was able to capitalise the Muslim loyalty of the coast and the Calicut town and organise a maritime force to cope with any emergency. The Marakkar was destined to be the first hereditary admiral of the Zamorin. The frequent confrontations in the sea made him an innovator of considerable reforms in the marine force. Smaller crafts called *'Pades'* were built for fast voyages. They could be rowed through narrow waterways and rivulets and lagoons. They were positioned at various strategic ports for giving warning as in the modern radar system. They were further manoeuverable to set fire to the Portuguese vessels. New strategies like 'hit and run', attack on the enemies from flanks in separate groups, or sector attack, the policy of forward from the sea, convoying of cargo ships being escorted by fighting vessels, sea control in the areas of interest, the policy of naval blockade, concentration of force as in a naval base and the offensive action were introduced by the Calicut mariners and their commandants. Such modern strategies and the introduction of modern brass guns and ammunition had effected drastic changes in the organisation of a navy, which had even conceived a maritime India, instead of the localisation of Malabar. This navy even escorted cargo vessels to Gujarat, participated in naval encounters at Rameshwaram; and Puttalam in Ceylon.

The Zamorin's fleet were very particular to intercept the Portuguese communications between Goa and the Malabar Coast. In such efforts all commandants of Calicut had given effective leadership. As early as 1530 Alfonso Mexio complained to the King of Portugal, that Indian seamen had complete control over the maritime trade that pepper was always taken to Mecca, Diu and elsewhere. For controlling the trade and traffic, the Portuguese introduced a system of *cartaz* or Pass system, but it gradually disappeared due to piracy and capture of native vessels. During the middle of the 16th century, the Portuguese domination of the sea began to decline. Admiral Pattu Marakkar or Kunjali III extended this activities to the Konkan Coast. Virtually it had cut off the Portuguese communications with the Malabar Coast. However the animosity continued, and Portuguese tried to establish friendly relationship with the Zamorin. But a constant policy of friendship was not possible as the Marakkar and the Muslims were not favourable for any compromise with the enemies. Fresh hostilities were begun and the Portuguese fortress at Chaliyam was besieged by the forces of the Zamorin.

The Zamorin even tried for an alliance with Turkish rulers, the Sultans of Bijapur and Ahmadnagar. However such alliances were not fruitful, and he was destined to continue his saga alone in the Calicut Kingdom. The Portuguese fortress at Chaliyam, on the southern bank of Beypur, was forced to surrender to the Zamorin's fleet in 1571. This was a heroic achievement of a joint action by the army and the navy. It was a turning point in the Portuguese activities in Calicut. They negotiated now for the possession of a point at Ponnani, and that was permitted by the successor of the Kingdom. Kunjali Marakkar III, who was in command of the fleet of Zamorin questioned the wisdom of this political development in the Calicut Court. Now the commandant consolidated his naval power in the northern point of the Kingdom at the mouth of Puduppattanam river, at Kottakkal. After the death of Kunjali Marakkar III in 1593, his nephew Mohammed Kunjali Marakkar continued his encounters against the Portuguese. Gradually a rupture had developed between the ruler and the vassal and the rupture was readily exploited by the Portuguese. In a joint campaign against the Kunjali Marakkar IV at Kottakkal in 1600, the native soldiers of the Zamorin and the Portuguese defeated the forces of Marakkar. He was captured and finally executed in Goa. It was the end of a heroic chapter of resistance of Malabar against the Portuguese expansion and the colonial policy of fortification and armed trade.

It was an irony of history, that the Zamorin who had been the Kingpin of resistance against the Portuguese, became an ally of the foreigners and turned against his own vassal Kunjali Marakkar IV. Furtado, the Portuguese Commandant was fortunate to capture the veteran commandant of Malabar alive and transport him to Goa for execution. Thus came the end of a chapter of heroic resistance of Malabar against the first adventurers. After the Portuguese the Dutch and the English came to the Malabar Coast. All of them had followed the same policy of trade and commerce and political ambition on the Malabar Coast. The Kingdom of Zamorin had almost deteriorated in its political stature and control. The northern part of the Kingdom became independent and fell under the control of Kolathunad. The southern frontiers were also encroached upon by independent chieftains like the Raja of Palakkad. In 1793, the Bombay presidency of the English East India Company annexed the entire region of Malabar with their political authority after the Treaty of Seringapatanam.

Within this brief framework of historical development, the 16th century was a crucial and determining period in the history of India. Although the powerful Mughals and the Vijayanagara rulers consolidated their political power, the coastal kingdoms and regions like Malabar were exposed to foreign conquests. Malabar had initiated its heroic resistance against the first wave of foreigners. With all ups and downs in the fortune of a small kingdom it had done wonders in defeating a colonial power. Nowhere in South East Asia or Latin America such a resistance for a century had taken place. But Kunjali Marakkars and the Zamorins created a chapter in the history of India.

A student of maritime history will appreciate that these encounters against the Portuguese particularly from the Calicut rulers or the Zamorins were responsible to maintain the freedom of sea and the land for a century in a coastal region i.e., Malabar. Although there had been efficient expeditions by the Portuguese to Malabar, they could not enforce a trade monopoly or control of the sea or territorial gains as in Goa. Even the peace negotiations and the settlements had no continuity for longer period in Malabar, as they had always jeopardised the native interests and freedom of trade and navigation. Therefore compromises were often violated and hostilities were restored. In fact it was a policy of prolonged confrontation against the foreign power not only for the freedom of trade and commerce but also for safeguarding the freedom of land and the sea. The native strategy to expel the enemy from the Arabian waters gradually evolved into a conceptualisation of maritime India. These encounters made Malabar a free territory till the end of the 18th century, promoting indigenous culture, language and literature. Even in a colonial situation its subnationalism was not defeated, as it had achieved considerable growth.

The origin of Indian navy is attributed to 1613, when the Indian Marine was commissioned by the British Agent at Surat who acquired a small number of *grabs* and *gallivants* for its formation. Subsequently it was shifted to Bombay in 1686 and known as Bombay Marine. When a reassessment of the historical situation is made, it can be very well evaluated that the Zamorin's navy and its mariners under the command of Kunjali Marakkars were the pioneers of Indian Navy with modern strategy and a practical approach to a maritime India. Even the convoy system of cargo vessels supported by armed sailors and marine force were introduced by a local ruler, much in advance of his time. Even the grand Mughals could not achieve such exploratory measures in the Arabian waters. There should be an organised effort on the part of the Indian navy and the Universities to reassess our maritime history. It is further recollected that this year brings home the heroic memories of 400th year of the martyrdom of Mohamed Kunjali Marakkar, who sacrified his life and fortunes for the freedom of land and the sea, not only of Malabar but also in a wider context.

History has taught us the valuable lesson that our national interests are tied up with waters. The words of Alfred T. Mohan have to be quoted: "whoever controls the Indian Ocean controls Asia. This Ocean is the key to the seven seas". The destiny of the world as well as our nation's history will be decided on its waters. The political and commercial history of Malabar and the role of its rulers mainly of the Zamorin and their Commandants highlight how they had delayed the exploitation of our resources by a foreign power for a period over a century. It is an era of achievements and limitations, success and failure.

Select Bibliography:

1. K.V. Krishna Iyer, *The Zamorins of Calicut* (Calicut University, 1999 edn.).
2. K.K.N. Kurup (ed.), *India's Naval Traditions* (New Delhi, 1997)
3. K.K.N. Kurup & K.M. Mathew, *Native Resistance against the Portuguese & The Saga of Kunjali Marakkars* (forthcoming)
4. William Logan, *Malabar*, Vol. I, (Madras, 1951 edn)
5. M.N. Pearson, *The New Cambridge History of India: The Portuguese India* (Delhi, 1990)

9

CRISTÃOS E ESPECIARIA :
THE PORTUGUESE IMPACT ON THE MALABAR CHRISTIAN COMMUNITY

Jan Kieniewicz

The Christians whom the Portuguese sought so persistently had been living in Kerala for more than a thousand years. Regardless of our estimates of sources concerning the beginnings of the Syro-Malabar Christian community we may assume that it dated back to the time when the caste system in Kerala had not yet assumed form.[1] Hence the Christians, together with other groups, developed as part of the local caste society.[2] It is noteworthy that the status held by the Christians differed markedly from the one of the Jews and Muslims living along the Malabar littoral. The Jewish communities were even older, but retained their distinctness despite the equally obvious acceptance of Judaism by the inhabitants of Kerala. The *Mapilla* - Muslims who had settled along the Malabar coast, were not exclusively the successors of migrants, and retained bonds with Arab settlers who entered Kerala from the period prior to Mohammed. The situation of the Christians, however, remained exceptional.

By resorting to European accounts we envisage the St. Thomas Christians as a separate community, similar to the Jews and Muslims. Meanwhile, social divisions in Kerala did not coincide with the professed religion. It is worth noting that the Christians upheld contacts with the Universal Church but did not model themselves on it. The sometimes lengthy severance of those contacts was a painful process, although apparently the native Christians did not consider themselves abandoned. Christian consciousness became a component of their identity, expressed in forms suitable for a caste society.[3]

I regard the economic, social and professional differentiation of the native Christians as a directive confirming their similarity to the *Nayars*.[4] The Christians seemed to have formed a caste cluster, with strong inner differentiation and hierarchic order.[5] Nonetheless, the latter did not possess a caste character owing to the absence of spatial separation. Furthermore, in relations with the outside world the Christians acted as an entity and not *via* inner divisions. Their prominent representatives were owners of gardens and organisers of pepper supplies, in other words, men who controlled the whole of the pepper trade in Malabar.[6] At the same time, the rather poor Christians who played host to the missionaries, with whom they shared "their scant property"[7], included the teachers of martial arts and probably the less prosperous, who formed suicide groups.

From the vantage point of the incomers the situation appeared to be obvious. Arabs, Persians, and traders from different parts of India had been arriving in Malabar ports from time immemorial. Jews from the entire Diaspora also maintained contacts with Malabar on a much smaller but equally effective scale. The incomers conducted their affairs and frequently settled down, finding in the Jewish and Muslim communities both support and cooperation. Seeking the Christians, the Portuguese hoped for analogous benefits, but reality proved to be entirely different.

This difference is frequently ascribed to the behaviour of the Portuguese and the specific properties of European civilisation. Today, we are aware of the fact that the employment of force in relations with Malabar was caused primarily by the circumstances of Portuguese involvement in the spice trade. As Christians and Europeans the Portuguese were not more inclined towards violence than other people engaged in exchange along the coast. From the very outset, they proved to be incapable of accepting the existing conditions for conducting business ventures. Violence supplemented their ever modest capital.[8] The practice of resorting to violence while struggling against competitors was not a European invention. Was the disillusionment which the native Christians caused the Portuguese the reason for the exceptional exploitation of force for the purpose of obtaining spices?

The Portuguese impact upon the Christian community of Malabar should be, therefore, interpreted as a reaction to assorted stimuli. The latter were composed of Portuguese undertakings, while the reaction can be discerned in those forms of Christian culture which permitted the Christians to live for centuries in a symbiosis with a Hindu surrounding. The accepted thesis claiming that Portuguese influence was slight and did not encompass the whole community calls for further verification.[9]

Indubitably, direct relations with Portuguese endeavours could have been maintained by Christians residing in the direct vicinity of Cochin, Quilon (Kollam) and Cranganore (Kodungallur). The Christian population scattered at the foot of the mountains was deprived of links of this sort. On the other hand, Portuguese impact stemmed the least from such associations. The Christians did not oppose the Portuguese, and by participating in commercial contacts with them they assumed stands known from relations along the coast. The Portuguese took a long time to learn Malayalam.[10] The native Christians began speaking Portuguese earlier, but for all practical purposes it would be difficult to assess the consequences of those individual cases.

It is possible to distinguish four groups of stimuli which had an opportunity to affect the Christian community.

1. Pressure exerted upon spice traders to sell their commodities only or primarily *via* Portuguese factories.

2. The establishment of military-political control wielded by the Portuguese in certain ports along the Malabar littoral.

3. The creation in Kerala of a local Latin Christian community.
4. Changes in liturgy and the recognition by the Malabar Church of the direct superiority of Rome.

What were the consequences of those undertakings? Before I try to answer this question it is necessary to define more closely the nature of the above listed stimuli, which, after all, in the course of the sixteenth century succumbed to changes also as a result of mutual impact.

I

The Portuguese created an offer of purchases which can be defined in monetary terms only approximately, due to the well-known fact that the factories in Malabar had at their disposal cash and goods which first had to be sold.[11] In addition, there existed an expanding "sector" of purchases made by the Portuguese on their own. From the beginning, however, the resources proved insufficient for meeting the needs. Already in the past I tried to demonstrate that the growth rate of the spice "production" could not equal the suddenly increased demand.[12] As a consequence, the requirements of the factories had to become competitive for the heretofore established buyers. Furthermore, purchases made by the factories were intended for the European market, up to then served by suppliers through Red Sea and Persian Gulf routes. Portuguese intervention disturbed Levantine trade systems albeit did not result in their breakdown. Presumably, during the sixteenth century European consumption could have risen owing to a growing buying power but not as a consequence of falling prices.[13] At any rate, the emergence of Portuguese factories revealed itself, above all, in the battle waged against competition involving suppliers and not in a price rise. Apparently, those events did not exert a direct impact upon the activity of the producers.

The configuration of relations within the spice trade was, in my opinion, characteristic for the segment structure of society and closely connected with the spatial conditions of the Malabar coast.[14] I do not know of any source basis for presuming that native Christians were relegated from the ports by the increasingly important Muslim agents. In the first place, we have testimonies of offers made and contracts signed with Christian suppliers in a given factory or port.[15] In the second place, I believe that the Christians basically did not deal with trade in the "export" sphere, but played an extremely important although not exclusive role in "the concentration of supplies", and thus in the direct hinterland of the ports.[16]

We know that for the Portuguese the basic but by no means the sole obstacle was created by trading conditions, including the inability to obtain high quality commodities.[17] I recognised that this fact was associated with the incapability of the factories to mobilise funds at the time when it was possible to purchase prime pepper. It also seems unquestionable that equal difficulties were encountered while organising capital intended for advance payments for the producers.[18] The inferior quality of the goods was also connected with other factors, including the malversations committed by Portuguese officials. Those circumstances, however, rather confirm the thesis about the absence of the direct impact of Portuguese demand upon the supply provided by the gardens of Malabar.[19]

In conclusion, we may say that in the course of centuries the Portuguese influenced a certain increase in demand for spices, albeit this was a process drawn out in time. In effect, I have the impression that growing export followed a production rise, and not *vice versa*.

II

The force applied by the Portuguese was, to a certain extent, meant to replace the lack of sufficient capital. Even if they did envisage the possibility of dominating all the ports, in practice this feat proved unattainable. The problem consisted of the fact whether the Portuguese joined the competition for hegemony or whether their activity rather provoked the intensification of tension between rulers. At any rate, sustaining the resistance of Cochin against the claims made by the *Zamorin* of Calicut denoted a stabilisation of relations along the coast.

Anticipations concerning military or political cooperation with native Christians were founded on a misunderstanding. Not only did the Christians never constitute a separate power, but as a community they were incapable of transgressing the accepted principles of conduct. From time to time they formed *ad hoc* armed groups for the purposes of defending concrete interests or persons.[20] We know of statements indicating that they had at their disposal armed forces, but I am unfamiliar with any evidence about the creation of permanent forces serving rulers - after all, there simply were no Christian rulers. True, the rajah of Udayamperur was known as the king of Christians, but according to the same principle as the rajah of Vadakkumkur bore the title of *rey da pimienta* . The reason was simply the presence of numerous Christians in his territory. In the second half of the sixteenth century, the title of protector was granted to the rajah of Cochin.[21]

The use of force was limited by existing possibilities and the necessity of arriving at an agreement about pepper, which all parties regarded as of utmost importance. The Portuguese were unable to subjugate the *Zamorin*, to deal with the activity of the Kunjalis and to guide uncontrolled export. They defended the position held by the rajah of Cochin although it is not totally clear whether his standing was truly threatened. Moreover, they provided subsidies to those rajahs who could influence pepper supplies from the mountainous regions, but were incapable of halting land export. In relation to the rajah of Cochin they could not execute their demands that he changed his approach towards converts to Christianity.

The armed activity of the Portuguese assisted their trade and permitted the existence of the factories. In addition, it guaranteed protection for undertakings in other domains, such as missions, but did not alter the pattern of forces. The introduction of the Portuguese into the political system along the Malabar coast did not change the position held by the Christian community.

III

Contrary to appearances, the most permanent impact was the one exerted by missionary undertakings - a truly Portuguese accomplishment due to *padroado real* and the ethnic composition of the majority of the clergy active in the sixteenth century. This particular issue, is, however, of a secondary nature.

Two phenomena appear to be essential. The Portuguese were incapable of convincing the Malabar Christians to reject relations with Chaldean bishops and to accept the superiority of the representatives of Rome. On the other hand, their activity led to the emergence of a Christian community among the converted Malayalis.

From the very outset it was probably conceived that a religious community would yield economic and political cooperation. In both aspects the Portuguese became disillusioned. True, the Christians were willing to recognise the Portuguese as an authority, but under the condition that they would fulfill the function of rulers *vis a vis* the social system.[22] There were no opportune chances for this to happen. The Portuguese imagined that winning supremacy would create opportunities for reaping economic benefits. This too did not take place despite the proximity of both Churches as regards doctrine, and marginal divergences concerning the forms of performing liturgy. A discussion about eventual "heresy" is totally futile and could help, at best, in understanding European attitudes towards the phenomenon in question.[23] The Portuguese conducted a policy of seeking a rapprochement, and were capable of convincing the Christians to accept certain reforms of the cult. However, they were unable to influence the conduct of the local community. In my opinion, the reason lay in the role played within it by the clergy and churches. In this domain too the Portuguese found it difficult to discover a common language.

After several decades of Portuguese presence and a number of spectacular missionary successes there emerged a new community. Conversion to Christianity signified expulsion from Malayali society without opening a path leading to the Portuguese community. For St. Thomas Christians the converted also turned into an outcast group. Good relations with the Portuguese could favour the maintenance of their high status, but all contacts with the converts were tantamount to a threat of losing one's position.

IV

The greatest puzzle, in my opinion, was the acceptance of Roman supremacy at a synod held in Udayamperur in 1599. I do not intend to delve deeper into the efforts undertaken in the first half of the century. The conclusion drawn from those experiences was unambiguous: spiritual impact on the Malabar Christians could be accomplished only by endorsing their culture. This is the reason why the work conducted by the Jesuit missions followed the course of accommodation, and started with learning the Malayalam and Chaldean languages. Attempts to purge the liturgy appeared to be quite easy, and much satisfaction was derived from the progress made in this field. The basic problem consisted of a striving towards the organisational subjugation of the clergy. Apart from other tasks bishops of the Malabar Church were entrusted with the role of liaisons with the Eastern Patriarchate and hence with Rome. This particular bond remained unquestioned. For centuries, attempts had been made to convince the bishops to accept not only Latinising reforms but also to recognise the direct superiority of the Catholic hierarchy.[24] Those endeavours, however, did not produce the expected outcome. Hence, I believe, the end of the sixteenth century witnessed attempts to realise a *sui generis* Church union, expressed in the synod articles and the appointment of F. Roz as the bishop of Angamali. Notwithstanding the efforts made by F. Roz and his acknowledgement of local customs, the decisions made in 1599 had to bring about an intervention in the functioning of the community. Undertakings aiming at a transformation of the *kathanars* into priests led to an attempted change of social relations. The ensuing response was a conflict, which in 1653 resulted in a severance of ties.[25]

Cristãos e Especiaria

So much for the stimuli. Characteristically, it is more difficult to formulate an opinion about the reactions. I am convinced that traces of Portuguese activity should be sought much later. There is, for all practical purposes, no sixteenth-century information produced by the community under examination, and the European descriptions are extremely one-sided. We are compelled to conclude about eventual direct consequences upon the basis of much later material. Let us start with the reactions.

1. I believe that the economic situation in distant markets and the activity pursued by buyers along the coast did not influence relations in the spice growing regions. Here, it is purposeless and outright impossible to distinguish the Christians. From a very remote perspective one may propose a hypothesis about connections between the economic demand for spices and ownership transformations, a process suggested by British reports from the beginning of the nineteenth century. If relations between the *kanamkarans* and the *janmakarans* really did take place, then they were not the effect of Portuguese ventures. On the other hand, we may say that the economic position of the Christians as producers, traders and financiers deteriorated between the sixteenth and the nineteenth century, a change, however, linked rather with non-economic factors.

2. Assorted types of military activity affected the Christian community to a minimal extent. In Kerala, the Portuguese did not become a power equal to the local rulers and thus could not occupy the position of protectors. Their financial support for the Christian community was not permanent, and frequently never even reached it. Christian settlements remained scattered and subjugated to rulers not always favourably inclined towards the Portuguese. The latter were incapable of executing rights which granted the new converts a status on par with that of the old Christians. This held true particularly for the principle of confiscating the property of persons accepting Christianity; naturally, it did not pertain to the *nazrani* . It remains an open question, however, whether outside observers could not have

identified baptism performed by the missionaries as conversion to the religion of the newcomers?

3. On the other hand, the development of Indian Christianity - the effect of conversion - did exert a distinct impact on the situation of the Malabar Christians. As a rule, the converts were members of lower castes or remained outside the caste system; with the possible exception of fishermen or pearl divers in the south, they regarded the *nazrani*, their high status and life-style as a model to emulate.[26] Meanwhile, it was precisely this feat which proved to be unattainable. The St. Thomas Christians did not accept the new converts, and decidedly opposed their presence in their churches.[27] In a longer-range perspective, the development of Latin Christianity along the coast diminished the prestige of the up to then privileged Christians.

The Malabar Christians did not disturb the existing order, and enjoyed both their rank and long-established relations. From the vantage point of the closely affiliated *Nayars* the professed religion remained insignificant. Meanwhile, the new Christians regarded their access as a manner of promotion, demonstrated, i.a. in transgressing bans concerning spatial segmentation - the use of roads and presence near the places of residence of the higher castes. Efforts to change attire brought about an analogous disturbance. Those ambitions, supported by the Europeans, undermined the position of the *nazrani*.

The fate of the initiative of a bilateral adaptation, made by the Franciscans and then the Jesuits, remains extremely characteristic. Regardless whether it assumed the guise of Latinisation or accommodation, the ultimate intention proved to be an attempt to alter forms of life. The *nazrani* resisted such an encroachment, ineffective due to the fact that it was addressed to the bishops and the *kathanars*, totally deprived of an opportunity to pass it further on. The absence of a Church organisation and vertical hierarchy excluded the perspective of overcoming resistance against issues which the Malabar Christians did not regard as religious.

4. The acceptance of a union and the introduction of subjection to European Church structures, denoted a transition to an attempt at regulating Church relations. Nonetheless, it became obvious that in this particular domain the encountered resistance was much stronger than in the case of liturgical questions. Now the matter at stake concerned not only the apparel of the clergy, the course of administering the Holy Sacraments, and, incomprehensible for the congregation, prayers at Holy Mass.[28] Intervention affecting the form of fasts and family rituals, the questioning of the position held by the archdeacon, and an attempted redistribution of Church revenues signified a threat to the social order.[29] The protest against the Jesuits and the Portuguese was, therefore, not so much religious as cultural. After all, deprived of their own cult traditions the Christians risked losing their caste.

Severance of ties also meant a split. The beginning of the seventeenth century initiated divisions within the community, first into those who rejected Rome and adhered to the Holy See, and subsequently further-going ones. This situation produced tension discernible in, i. a. a competition for churches. Division and rivalry lowered the status of the Christians in the eyes of the Hindus.

Only at first glance did the changes occurring under Portuguese impact pertain to elements of the cult, the endowment of the churches, and the use of liturgical books. Contrary to expectations, after 1599 the perspective of subjugating the community to external centres of power had to become distinct. This was a grave threat to the heretofore prevailing relations within caste society, and in practice it signified a loss of the held position.

It is too early to attempt a summary. Such a feat would call for a much more thorough familiarity with material from the eighteenth and nineteenth century. It is difficult to speak about an impact from the brief perspective of the sixteenth century, owing to the slight space of mutual influence. Also in the phase of intensified missionary activity during the last quarter of that century changes in the religious life of the *nazrani* were not structural. It is possible to consider some sort of a joint level only after 1599, i. e. the attempt at coexistence, which ended with a catastrophe. The direct effect of the union was an inner split and the onset of toppling the social status of the Christian community.

It was my intention to present a problem which I have been tackling for quite some time now. I have in mind a question concerning the character of the relations between two civilisations. I proposed a presupposition maintaining that during the stage of contacts between Portuguese expansion and the social system of sixteenth-century Kerala there could have taken place a situation described as an Encounter.[30] The existence in Kerala of a Christian community integrated within the caste system appeared to create a premise for reflecting on an exceptional situation, which I described initially as the occurrence of identical values and concepts among representatives of two totally different communities. The Hindus and the Europeans, the Malayalis and the Portuguese all proved to be Christians. The mentioned encounter is a form of relations between two cultures, two social systems, in which mutual impacts are counterbalanced and which generate a *sui generis* joint space deprived of all symptoms of domination and subjugation. A religious community which was not the outcome of expansion seemed to produce an exceptional chance for yielding precisely such a situation. A survey of pertinent problems appears to suggest that we may speak about a sixteenth-century Encounter only in reference to select fragments of reality. Actually, the college in Kodungallur or the seminary in Vaipinkotta imposed too great a burden upon those training for the priesthood, especially considering that the latter was conceived in Roman terms. The situation changed after the crisis of 1653, the elimination of Portuguese impact during the 1660s, and the appearance of Carmelite missionaries who, however, dealt already with a community rent apart.

The Portuguese impact upon the Malabar Christians actually existed mainly in the imagination of ambitious

Cristãos e Especiaria

missionaries. At the same time, it was precisely those endeavours which finally produced changes that, in a longer range, had essential consequences for transformations of the caste system in Kerala.

References:

1. The basic argument is the complete integration of Christians. A very important argument is the existance of *yogam*, X. Koodapuzha, *Eclesial Identity of the St. Thomas Christians* in: X. Koodapuzha ed., *Oriental Churches Theological Dimensions*, Vadavathoor, 1988, p.73-75. Cf. J. Aerthayil, *The Spiritual Heritage of The St. Thomas Christians*, Bangalore, 1982, V. J. Vithayathil, *The Origin and Progress of the Syro-Malabar Hierarchy*, Kottayam, 1980.

2. The form of building churches may be another good argument, see A. Monserrate, 12 I 1579 letter, DI XI, pp. 515, 518. A. Penteado was of different opinion, DHMPP, III, p. 545, also F. da Paz, Ibidem, VI, p. 247 (10 I 1557). I agree with opinion of J. Vellian, *The vicissitudes of the Syro-Malabar Liturgy down the Centuries* in: *The Malabar Church. Symposium in honour of Rev. Placid J. Podipara C.M.I.*, Roma, 1970, p. 12.

3. D. Barbosa, *Navegación de la India Portugal*, BNM, Mss 3016, f. 71-74.

4. *Relation Topographique, politique et religieuse de la Cote Malabare par Le P. Paulin de s. Barthelemie Carme Dachaussé Missionaire Apostolique de la meme Cote. L' année 1789*. BNR, Mss Fonti Minori, S. Maria della Scala 1, f. 160. Cf. J.M. Campori, Vaypicotta 1 I 1604, ARSI, Mss Goa 48, f. 92v.

5. A. Pacheco, Goa XI 1577, DI X, p. 969; A. Toscano, *Relaçao breve...*, 6 I 1600, ARSI, Mss Goa 48, f. 1.

6. This is the common opinion cf. J. Carcere, 2 I 1529, DHMPP, II, p. 175; F. Dionisius, 2 I 1578, DI, XI, p. 67; Captain of Cochin 9 II 1604, ARSI, Mss Goa 65, p. 278.

7. *Informaçao do que fez o padre mestre Melchior Carneiro em uns reinos que estao junto de Cochin pela terra dentro*, s.d., DHMPP VIII, p. 504.

8. J. Kieniewicz, *Faktoria i forteca. Handel pieprzem na Oceanie Indyjskim i ekspansja portugalska w XVI wieku*, Warszawa 1970 and J. Kieniewicz, *The Portuguese Factory and Trade in Pepper in Malabar during the 16th Century*, "The Indian Economic and Social History Review", VI,1, 1969.

9. Cf. Pius Malekandathil, "The Portuguese and the St. Thomas Christians: 1500-1570", A Paper presented in the International Seminar on *"The Portuguese and the Socio-Cultural Changes in India:1500-1800 A.D."*, held at St. Thomas College, Pala, 4-11 December 1999 (Forthcoming in the volume edited by K.S. Mathew, Teotonio R. de Souza and Pius Malekandathil, *The Portuguese and the Socio-Cultural Changes in India:1500-1800*, Fundação Oriente, 2001)

10. Cf. *Noticia do que obravao os frades de S. Francisco...* (18th C.), DHMPP, V, p. 406.

11. I have discussed the problem in *Faktoria i forteca...op.cit*, pp.250-259. Cf. J. Cabral 21 II 1550, DHMPP, IV, pp. 488-499.

12. I.a. J. Kieniewicz, *Pepper Gardens and Market in Precolonial Malabar*, "Moyen Orient & Océan Indien. XVIe-XIXe s.", 3, 1986, pp.5-8.

131

13 Cf. S. Halikowski-Smith, Ph.D. Thesis under K.N. Chaudhuri supervision, *Portugal and the European Spice Trade, 1480-1580*.

14 J. Kieniewicz, *Asian Merchants and European Expansion: Malabar Pepper Trade Routes in the Indian Ocean World-System in the Sixteenth Century* in: K. R. Haellquist ed., *Asian Trade Routes.*, pp. 80, 84 ff.

15 DUP III, pp. 320-323, 378, 379.

16 J. Kieniewicz, *Pepper Gardens...op.cit.*, pp. 22,23. Matyas de Cayanculao and his brother Bragaida Tequetome seems to me exceptions and Quilon not the main port for pepper trade in the begining of the 16th century, *Cartas do Affonso de Albuquerque seguidas de documentos que as elucidam...*, v. II, p. 268; III, p. 30. Of different opinion was K. S. Mathew, *Portuguese Trade with India in the sixteenth Century*, New Delhi, 1983, pp. 57-59.

17 M. Diaz 22 I 1550, DHMPP IV, p. 479.

18 DHMPP IV, p.495, VI, p. 169, 179.

19 I have not found arguments for change of opinion presented at length in my *Faktoria i forteca...*, pp.185-261, thirty years ago. Cf. J. Kieniewicz, *The Stationary System in Kerala*, "Hemispheres" 1, Warsaw, 1985, pp. 31 ff.

20 J.M. Campori, 1 I 1604, ARSI, Mss Goa 48, f. 92.

21 P. Dionisius, *Informaçao da cristiandade de S. Thomé*, 4 I 1578, DI XI, p. 133.

22 Several authors discussed the meaning of the ecene of Christians' deposition of the "rod of justice" to Vasco da Gama, T. Lopez, *Navegaçao as Indias Orientaes* in: *Colleçoao de noticias para a historia e geografia das nações ultramarinas que vivem nos dominios portuguezes...*, t. II, Lisboa, 1867, p.198. The opinion of A. M. Mundadan seems to me correct at the respect, *The St. Thomas Christians of Malabar under Mar Jacob (1498-1552)*, Bangalore, 1967, pp. 64-66.

23 A. do Porto 20 XI 1557, speaking about Mar Elias and Mar Joseph: "em nenhuma cousa ou palavra achei diferirem de nos", DHMPP VI, p. 323.

24 A project of how to dominate over St. Thomas Christians using George de Christo in P. Dionisius letter of 2 I 1578, DI XI, p. 69.

25 *Somaria relazione della christianitá della serra* (1654), ARSI,Mss Goa 68', ff. 58-63. Cf. J. Kolloparambil, *The St. Thomas Christians' Revolution in 1653*, Kottayam, 1981.

26 *Relation...op.cit, p. 160*.

27 *Informaçao...*, 1607, ARSI, Mss Goa 65, p. 45.

28 The question was of superiority of Goa over Angamalai, of territorial or personal character of the church power, *Informaçao...*, 1607, ARSI, Mss Goa 65, pp. 44-45.

29 ARSI, Mss Goa 68', pp. 12-15.

30 J. Kieniewicz, *Periphery and Backwardness: An Essay in the Interpretation of Colonialism* in: *17o Congreso Internacional de Ciencias Históricas*, Madrid 1992, vol. II, pp. 774,775. I develope the concept in my last book *Spotkania Wschodu*, Gdansk, 1999.

10

PARAVAS AND PORTUGUESE: A STUDY OF PORTUGUESE STRATEGY AND ITS IMPACT ON AN INDIAN SEAFARING COMMUNITY.

Kenneth McPherson

Introduction

In 1535, a delegation of leading members of the Hindu Parava fisher community of the Tirunelveli coast (at the southern extreme of the Coromandel Coast) approached the Portuguese in Cochin seeking an alliance. The Paravas were engaged in a bitter economic contest with the Muslim community of Kayal for control of the valuable Kayal pearl fisheries and the chank beds of the Palk Strait and the Gulf of Mannar. Perhaps because of the already evident anti-Muslim sentiment of the Portuguese the Paravas saw a chance to trounce the Muslims of Kayal. In return for assistance in driving the Kayalars[1] from the disputed pearl and chank fisheries the Paravas offered to convert to Roman Catholicism.

Eagerly seizing the Parava offer, the Portuguese began a series of seaborne attacks upon the Kayalar late in 1535 which were to make them dominant along the *Pescaria*, or Fishery Coast, until ousted by the Dutch in 1658. Control of the coast not only gave the Portuguese access to the proceeds of the pearl and chank fisheries, but even more importantly it strengthened their strategic position in southern India, facilitating their economic activities in Cochin, Sri Lanka and on the southern

Coromandel Coast. Access to ports on the Fishery Coast enabled the Portuguese, in theory at least, to better police the sea-lanes linking Cochin to Sri Lanka and the Coromandel Coast. In addition, control of the coast enabled the Portuguese to undermine a thriving Muslim seafaring community astride a sea lane vitally important to Portuguese economic and strategic interests in the Indian Ocean region, as well as providing new manpower resources to assist in the struggle to control Sri Lanka.[2]

Whatever the reasons for Portuguese involvement on the Fishery Coast it had a profound effect upon the fortunes and history of the Christian Parava community. A study of Portuguese-Parava relations is long overdue for, on at least two counts, it offers us new perspectives relating to Portuguese activity in the Indian Ocean region. Such a study can provide us with both a micro-view of Portuguese maritime strategy out of Cochin, and can help open up the largely unexplored territory of the reaction of South Asian societies to the intrusion of the Portuguese.

The idea for this paper came from reading Patrick Roche's study of the Parava, *Fishermen of the Coromandel*.[3] In this work Roche examines the internal structure of Parava society, but by extending his arguments it is possible to suggest further areas for study which will add to our knowledge of both the *Estado da India*, South Asia and the Indian Ocean region.

The Paravas

Whilst there has been a tendency amongst historians of the Portuguese in India to relegate the Paravas to the ranks of a low caste fisher community, Roche has challenged this generalisation.[4]

Roche[5] defines the Parava as a *jati* (caste) located mainly on the coast of the present-day Tirunelveli district, and to a lesser extent on the Ramnad coast - both in the modern Indian state of Tamil Nadu - and in Kerala. Traditionally the Paravas were fishermen and seafarers whose economic life centred upon a range of settlements located around thirteen major towns, *urs*, which before the advent of the Portuguese were functioning as ports. The most important of these settlements were seven major ports, *yelu urs*, the largest of which was Tuticorin. The *jati* had a variety of leaders ranked in accordance to the size and economic importance of the particular Parava settlement. Large settlements, specifically the seven *yelu urs*, were led by *patangatimo-mór* (or *jati talaivans*) (caste heads and their deputies), whilst less important settlements were under the leadership of headmen called *patangatims* (Tamil *pattankatti*). In the pre-Portuguese period the extent of the authority of these leaders is not clear. The positions do not appear to have been hereditary or clearly defined which would indicate a fairly loosely defined authority structure.[6]

The economic life of the *jati* was centred upon the sea. It would appear that most Paravas were involved in fishing and with the collection of pearls and chank shells. The majority of Paravas lived in small seaside hamlets and were poor fisher folk dependent upon the primitive *catamaran* constructed of two or three logs and manned by father and son crew. Within the larger Hindu community such Paravas would obviously have had low economic and ritual status. But the Parava *jati* was not confined to the economy of the *catamaran*. In the *yelu urs*, Paravas manned and sailed the *vellam*, a much more substantial plank built-vessel with sails and a crew of five or six. It was this vessel which was central to the exploitation of the pearl and chank fisheries. Were Paravas involved with the *vellam* held in the same low social and economic esteem as their fellow *jati* members dependent upon the *catamaran*? Roche does not tackle this question directly, but a brief consideration of the processes of pearl fishing would indicate a more complex social and economic life for the *jati* than the simple tag of fishermen would indicate.

Roche notes that the traditional involvement of the Parava with pearl and chank fishing defined the economic function of the *jati*. However, he does not note the very difficult and variable nature of pearl fishing. Pearl fishing seasons were extremely variable in timing and profit as the Portuguese, Dutch and British were to discover. There were long periods, from

135

1618 to 1634 for example, when the pearl banks failed, so it seems unlikely that the *vellam* was utilised solely in pursuit of the pearl.[7] The *vellam* was primarily a trading vessel, and *jati* history and the comments of travellers such as Marco Polo indicate that the ports on the Fishery Coast were centres of maritime trade as early as the thirteenth century. Whilst the *catamaran* was a symbol of low economic, and perhaps low social, status, the *vellam* indicates that some Paravas had much higher economic status based on substantial mercantile interests. Certainly Parava leaders laid claim to a proud mercantile past and *kshatriya* status, but the indications are that by the fifteenth century the economic base of the *jati* was under siege.

The problem for the Paravas was associated with the rise of Muslim mercantile and seafaring groups along the Coromandel Coast. From Nagapattinam to Tuticorin, groups of indigenous converts - Navayats, Marakayyars and Kayalars[8] - were, by the fifteenth century, links in the great chain of Indian Muslim mercantile groups which dominated sea lanes from the Arabian Sea to the Strait of Melaka. On the Tirunelveli coast, the Kayalar, Parava converts to Islam, and other Muslim groups were rapidly undermining the economic base of the Parava *jati* by intruding into their pearling and other maritime activities. The position of local Muslim groups was further strengthened by their links with Gujarati Muslim merchants and seafarers, which gave them access to a wide range of commodities eagerly sought by land-based powers such as the Hindu rulers of Madurai and Venad.

According to Roche, the Kayalar-Parava struggle centred upon the pearl and chank fisheries. Both pearls and chank shells were valuable commodities with regular markets in China and Bengal, but, given the variable nature of pearling and references to Kayalar "fleets", it would seem reasonable to argue further than Roche does. The Kayalar-Parava contest was in fact more broadly based and incorporated a struggle for the carrying trade along the Coromandel Coast and across the Palk Strait to Sri Lanka.

Certainly the contest was bitter enough to turn the Parava towards the Portuguese in Cochin in a desperate bid to preserve the corporate economy of their *jati*, just as Malabar Christian communities "had utilised religion and conversion as a crutch to win Portuguese support against Hindu and Mapilla traders".[9] The central figure in this move was Joao da Cruz, a Parava *patangatimo-mór* and merchant who had visited Lisbon. Upon his return, in the hope of getting a share of the lucrative Coromandel horse trade which was dominated by the Portuguese, da Cruz offered his services as a "spiritual broker" to bring his community into the Portuguese fold. Joao de Barros, writing in 1539-40, referred to a Parava delegation, which visited the Jesuit college in Lisbon some years previously, so the indications are that the Parava initiative was quite deliberate and well planned.[10]

Joao de Barros was bound to win widespread support within the Parava community if he could restore the *jati's* economic fortunes. In turn the Portuguese no doubt welcomed his overtures, as skirmishes between them and Coromandel Muslim seamen had escalated during the early 1500s as each side contested control of local sea lanes.

In 1535, da Cruz led a Parava delegation to Cochin to negotiate an agreement with the Portuguese. In return for a promise of conversion, a Portuguese fleet under Pero Vaz de Amaral arrived off the Fishery Coast in December 1535. De Amaral immediately launched an attack on Muslim shipping to remove the economic threat to the Parava. Early in the next year Parava leaders moved to keep their part of the bargain by leading thousands of their followers to mass baptisms at the various *yelu urs,* and within a few months some 20,000 baptisms had taken place.[11] In 1542 Admiral Martin crushed a large Muslim fleet, permanently removing the Muslim threat to Parava seafarers, and in the same year the Jesuits arrived on the Fishery Coast to confirm the nascent Christianity of the Paravas.

Portuguese Motivations and Rule

At one level it is easy to argue that the major concern of the Portuguese on the Fishery Coast was souls. The eagerness of the Portuguese to gain the accession of the Paravas to Christianity, the conscious introduction of the Jesuits after the first conversions had taken place, and the initial close liaison between Jesuits and the Portuguese authorities would indicate a concern for the souls of the Paravas. But is this interpretation too simplistic and does it mask a more complex series of objectives?

At the core of Portuguese interest in the Fishery Coast was a concern for the overall strategic interests of the *Estado da India*. Along the western coast of India the great commercial rivals of the Portuguese were the Gujaratis, Hindu and Muslim, and it was the Gujaratis who were involved in the Kayalar pearl trade as local Muslims edged the Paravas out. The horse trade was also particularly important along the Tirunelveli coast, where it appears that there was a business arrangement between the Hindu raja of Venad, local Muslims and Gujaratis.[12] Obviously, if the Portuguese were able to establish a presence on the Fishery Coast they would at least curtail the activities of Muslim traders and seafarers, their prime commercial rivals. But, as they had found along the coast of western India, there was in reality no substitute for the Hindu or Muslim merchant or sailor who was vital to the running of the Portuguese commercial empire. However, on the Fishery Coast they were presented with the opportunity of gaining a Christian mercantile and seafaring substitute for the detested Muslim.[13] In this sense the conversion of the Parava presented the Portuguese with a unique opportunity.

Given the chronic manpower shortage experienced by the Portuguese it was impossible for them to construct a purely Portuguese-run commercial empire in the Indian Ocean. Collaboration with non-Christians was forced upon them, but on the Fishery Coast they were presented with the opportunity to collaborate with a Christian community - indeed a Christian community that was Roman Catholic and not aligned to a suspect Christian sect as was the case on the Malabar coast.

The strategic importance of the Fishery Coast to the Portuguese was emphasised by their tenuous position further north along the Coromandel Coast at Sao Tomé de Maliapur. In 1521, the Portuguese built a church there around which a commercial settlement grew. Portuguese interest in Sao Tomé (or Mylapore as it was later known) centred upon the local cloth industry that provided valuable exports to Melaka, Pegu, Sumatra and China. Until the arrival of the Portuguese this trade had been in the hands of Hindu and Muslim groups, and if the Portuguese were to achieve their commercial objectives it was necessary for them to break into this trade. The Portuguese official position at Sao Tomé was never strong so it was imperative that the vital sea-lanes between Cochin and the Coromandel Coast be secured as best as possible.[14] To this end the Fishery Coast was central to any plans to promote the economic and political interests of the *Estado da India* eastward from Cochin.

Undoubtedly for some Portuguese there was a genuine concern for the souls of the Parava, and for the reputed wealth of the pearl and chank fisheries. However, it is difficult to argue that the desire to gain converts was the prime motive for the Portuguese, just as closer scrutiny of the pearl fisheries does not support the contention that they were a vital component in the Portuguese decision to intervene on the Fishery Coast.

Certainly, once in control of the Fishery Coast the Portuguese were concerned to raise revenue from the pearl and chank fisheries yet, as pointed out, returns from this source were notoriously unstable. In addition, as K.S. Mathew has noted, there is little evidence that pearls figured to any great extent in official Portuguese commercial statistics, although his figures relate to a period when the pearl fisheries were under the control of local Muslims and their Gujarati partners.[15]

The situation on the Fishery Coast was one where the interests of God and Mammon went hand in hand. On the one hand the introduction of the Jesuits in 1542 was a deliberate move to anchor the conversion of the Parava and to secure souls. On the other hand the interest of Mammon were served by a proposal seriously considered by the Jesuits, and to a lesser extent the Portuguese authorities, to establish a Christian Parava kingdom on the Fishery Coast, thus entrenching a client kingdom along a major line of Portuguese communication. But the Portuguese official presence on the coast was weak and soon the Jesuits began to work to achieve their own temporal goals. This led to conflict with both the *Estado da India* and local political authorities such as the Nayaka of Madurai. This tension was a constant factor in life on the coast until the Dutch took control in the mid-seventeenth century. A not dissimilar situation existed further to the north where private Portuguese enterprise at Sao Tomé, Nagapattinam and Porto Novo was often at odds with the power pretensions of Goa and local rulers.

Initially the Fishery Coast was vital to the Portuguese if they were to secure sea routes eastwards from Cochin. Throughout the sixteenth century, Cochin was a central cog in a network of sea lanes linking the major Portuguese commercial centres at Melaka and Colombo into the commercial structure of the *Estado da India*. But Cochin, Colombo and Melaka flourished not only on the ability of the Portuguese to control contiguous hinterlands - not evident in the case of Melaka - but, equally importantly, on the Portuguese ability to enter the trading world of the Indian Ocean region and to exercise some control over major seaways. In pursuit of these latter objectives, control of the Fishery Coast ideally permitted control of the Palk Strait and the Gulf of Mannar and kept access open to cloth exporting ports on the Coromandel Coast. But once Jaffna had been secured it would seem that direct control of the Fishery Coast was considered less important by Goa, and increasingly the Jesuits were left to their own devices.

In 1605, however, the Jesuits were expelled from the coast for 16 years by the authorities at Goa, due to suspicions over the declining returns from the pearls fisheries and disturbances caused by their interference in the affairs of local Catholics. Their return in the 1620s led to more social disturbances amongst the Paravas, and in the 1630s Goa made a last attempt to secure direct control over the coast and the more distant settlements at Sao Tomé, Nagapattinam and Porto Novo.

By the early seventeenth century the Portuguese on the Fishery Coast and in the more northerly settlements on the Coromandel Coast were under considerable pressure from other Europeans - the Dutch and the English - who were carving out a presence in the area. By the 1630s, Goa was determined to re-establish its authority over the Portuguese settlements from the Fishery Coast to Sao Tomé, but it was too late. They lacked sufficient resources and in 1658 Nagapattinam, the most important settlement on the Coromandel Coast, fell to the Dutch. In the same year the Dutch occupied the Fishery Coast and Sri Lanka, and in 1663 they took Cochin. The remaining Portuguese settlements at Sao Tomé and Porto Novo also passed out of the orbit of Goa altogether by the end of the 1660s.[16]

Paravas and Portuguese

The argument that strategic considerations were paramount for the Portuguese in their relationship with the Parava, is bolstered by the relationship that developed between the Portuguese and the Parava.

In the years immediately following the conversion of the Parava the Portuguese moved deliberately to consolidate the commercial and strategic position of the Parava. Because Portuguese power was so restricted on the Fishery Coast it was decided to relocate the Paravas into the seven *yelu urs* or major ports which were to function "as pivotal centres of security, trade [and] educational and religious activity and were fortified by the Portuguese."[17] Almost immediately after this, various schemes were mooted to achieve even greater security for the Paravas by removing them to offshore islands where a Parava Christian kingdom would be established.

Such immigration schemes foundered upon the strength of Parava attachment to their ancestral lands. The *yelu urs*, however, increased in population with the port of Tuticorin in particular benefiting from the consolidation of Parava settlement. In the 1620s, under the leadership of their Jesuit priests, some Parava communities were persuaded to settle on the west coast of Sri Lanka as part of the Portuguese scheme to secure the northernmost Sri Lanka port of Jaffna which came finally under their direct control in 1619. In this instance the Paravas were quite clearly being used to create a loyal community on a very sensitive flank of the Portuguese sphere of influence bounded by Cochin, Colombo and Jaffna.

Obviously the Paravas were being used as part of a continually evolving Portuguese strategy to protect and expand their commercial empire. To an extent they were pawns, but they were willing pawns and a functioning part of the administrative, defensive and commercial infrastructure of the *Estado da India*. Given the already noted chronic shortage of manpower amongst the Portuguese, they were not in a position to exercise close control over the Paravas on the Fishery Coast so they were forced to find surrogate means of binding the community to them.

One obvious avenue of influence and control was through religion. In the 1540s, the Portuguese authorities had worked closely with the Jesuits to entrench Christianity, and hence the authority of the parish priests, amongst the Paravas.

This move was enormously successful insofar as it wrought the Paravas into a model orthodox Roman Catholic community. Undoubtedly this was due immediately to the great skills of Jesuits such as St Francis Xavier. In the longer term, however, Parava converts such as Tomé da Cruz, who embraced the Portuguese language with such fervour, confirmed that in 1554 he translated the *Catechism* of Joao de Barros into Tamil.[18] The church militant on the Fishery Coast wove a Catholicism that bound the Parava initially very close to the interests of the *Estado da India*. But the Jesuits were not pawns of the Portuguese Crown and in the early seventeenth century they were expelled for some years from the Fishery Coast for helping their parishioners to avoid some of the more unreasonable pearl levies raised by the Portuguese authorities.[19] In addition, there is some evidence that "Jesuit interference in succession disputes to the posts of *patangatim* and *patangatim-mór*...exacerbated" tensions between the Jesuits and leaders of the Parava community.[20]

Central to the Portuguese plans for the Pescaria were the seven *yelu urs*, which they turned into fortified ports. Of necessity the Portuguese presence in these ports was limited, so the running of the ports depended upon Parava leadership. It was in this area that the impact of the Portuguese upon the structure of Parava society appears to have been greatest.

Prior to the coming of the Portuguese, the position of the *patangatim-mór* was far from clear in terms of authority over the *jati*. The *patangatim-mórs* and the *patangatims* were undoubtedly men of influence, but it appears that their formal authority was limited. However, the arrival of the Portuguese ushered in changes in the power structure within the Parava *jati*. Quite simply, the Portuguese needed to deal with a hierarchically structured group for they were forced to delegate authority to chosen partners within the Parava *jati*.

The obvious partners as far as the Portuguese were concerned were the presumed power brokers within the Parava *jati*, the *patangatim-mórs* and the *patangatims*. Their earliest contact with the Parava had been through a *patangatim-mór*, Joao da Cruz, the "spiritual broker" who had facilitated the conversion of the Parava. As his reward da Cruz had entered the commercial world of the *Estado da India*, and had been invested with the mantle of Portuguese authority within his *jati*. With the fortification of the *yelu urs* and the establishment of churches in lesser Parava settlements, Portuguese administrators and priests increasingly relied upon and bolstered the authority of the "natural leaders" of the *jati*. Such positions tended to become hereditary, office holders wore gold crosses and chains as symbols of their new religious status, and were called "Senhor Senhor Don" to emphasise their elevated social status.

At an obvious level the Portuguese were changing the power structure within the community. In later centuries the British were to do the same when they sought to impose a fiscal and social ordering on rural India. But the result of Portuguese activity upon the structure of indigenous society was markedly different from that of the British.

The Portuguese destruction of the commercial power of local Muslims reinforced the economic basis of sections of the Parava *jati*, not only in relation to the pearl and chank fisheries, but also in relation to the mercantile function of the *vellam*. In addition, the conversion of the Parava to Christianity re-emphasised *jati* boundaries in relation to the contiguous non-Christian population. Finally, the creation of a more powerful and hierarchical *jati* leadership provided yet another means for *jati* consolidation, and created a clearly defined group within the *jati* with an economic and power interest in maintaining a caste identity and solidarity. Ironically, the Portuguese intervention in the affairs of the Fishery Coast in the 1530s and 1540s probably saved the Parava *jati* from precipitous social and economic disintegration. Equally, the intervention created new divisions within the *jati*: at one end of the social and economic power spectrum were *vellam* owners (*champanottis*), "at the other the pearl divers, both of the same caste but with a vast social and economic gulf between them."[21]

As Arasaratnam noted, the end result of Portuguese intervention on the Fishery Coast was that the Parava "entrenched themselves in the trade of that region, separated themselves from Hindu Paravas and competed more strongly with the Muslims [and] in the seventeenth century...expanded from coastal trading to brokerage in the interior and became cloth merchants."[22]

After the Portuguese

In 1658, after they had expelled the Portuguese from Sri Lanka and before their seizure of Cochin, the Dutch captured the fortified *yelu urs* on the Fishery Coast. The Dutch entered into an agreement with the Nayaka of Madurai for exclusive rights over the pearl fisheries, but as these had not been profitable for years it is doubtful if they counted for much in Dutch considerations.[23] What the Dutch wanted was jurisdiction over the Fishery Coast to further wider commercial objectives. The Coromandel Coast was a major source of cloth for the country trade to the east, and a market for commodities from Sri Lanka and the Malabar coast. In strategic terms too, control of the Fishery Coast was vital to the protection of the recently acquired Dutch interests in Sri Lanka and elsewhere in southern India.

The *yelu urs* were occupied, the Parava settlers were expelled from Sri Lanka, and the Jesuits were banished from Dutch territory. Despite legal proscription, however, the Paravas proved obdurate in their Catholicism, which was central to their *jati* identity. The Dutch were in fact forced, like the Portuguese before them, to utilise the skills of the Paravas.

The Fishery Coast was in many ways more commercially important to the Dutch than to the Portuguese. In their economic exploitation of Sri Lanka and of the whole "country trade" system, the Dutch were more efficient than the Portuguese had been. But their efficiency was to a large extent posited upon the collaboration of indigenous commercial and maritime groups. Once their control over Sri Lanka and Cochin had been established, the Dutch began to actively trade a large range of commodities across and through the Palk Strait as well as exploiting the pearl and chank fisheries.

Elephants and areca nuts from Sri Lanka, pepper from Malabar and goods from the Indies were traded by the Dutch along the Coromandel Coast in return for textiles, and in this trade the Paravas found a niche. Pearling appears to have declined in importance for the Dutch,[24] but the Dutch shortage of manpower forced them to the same social and political compromises with the Paravas as the Portuguese. If the Dutch were to neutralise the Fishery Coast as a potential base for enemies and to utilise the wider commercial possibilities of the *yelu urs,* they needed Parava commercial and managerial skills.

This pragmatic approach in time allowed for the return of the Jesuits who were restored in 1714 to their churches in Dutch territory. Choosing between two evils: on the one hand the Catholic Paravas who were small-scale merchants, on the other the much more formidable Hindu Chetty merchants and Muslim Chulia shipowners, the Dutch absorbed the Parava into their system and concentrated upon attempting to exclude the Chettys and Chulias. Not only were the Paravas permitted to practice their religion, but in the 1740s the Dutch handed over complete control of the pearl fisheries to them and even offered protection from land-based powers. The social and economic dynamics of the Fishery Coast were such that it was logical for the Paravas "to preserve themselves into the eighteenth century as a 'Christian caste in Hindu society.'"[25]

In 1825, the Fishery Coast finally passed into the hands of the British. British commercial interests were going to place Anglo-Parava relations on much the same level initially as earlier relationships between Paravas and other Europeans. In the years that followed, the changes in the Parava *jati* that had been initiated by contact with the Portuguese were confirmed. The economic world in which the Paravas lived changed greatly in the nineteenth and twentieth centuries, but the seafaring and mercantile traditions of the Paravas enabled them to find a niche in the maritime economy of modern India when the *vellam* developed into the larger deep-sea sailing *dhoni* that continues to flourish out of ports such as Tuticorin.

Conclusion

A study of the Parava and the Portuguese has potentially much to tell us about two neglected aspects of Portuguese history in the Indian Ocean Region. At one level the Portuguese occupation of the Fishery Coast reveals the complexity of Portuguese motivation in the region, particularly Portuguese strategic motivations. At another level a study of Portuguese-Parava relations reveals the need for a multi-disciplinary approach to the study of the social history of the *Estado da India*.

Patrick Roche's study of the Paravas is historically and geographically restricted to the community itself. Nevertheless it suggests fascinating possibilities for new approaches to the history of the Portuguese in India: both from the angle of exploring the nature of Portuguese activity, and from the point of view of the indigenous peoples who came into contact with the Portuguese.

Portuguese intervention not only saved some sections of the Parava community from economic decline, but created a new caste with its own internal economic and social dynamics moulded by the economic forces unleashed by the processes of intervention.

A study of the Parava and of the Fishery Coast would also reveal more intimate detail of Portuguese strategy, with particular respect to the acquisition of fortified bases to sustain their commercial empire. Portuguese activity on the Fishery Coast, and indeed later Dutch activity on the coast, is often too readily explained by the attraction of the pearl fisheries. On closer examination the pearl fisheries were but one of a variety of commercial attractions, all of which were arguably less important than the strategic considerations of dominating the Palk Strait and the Gulf of Mannar.[26]

Although the author of this article does not possess the language skills necessary to research the large body of Portuguese and missionary material available for the sixteenth and seventeenth centuries, by using English-secondary sources a story and argument does however emerge. On the basis of this it is evident that historians with the appropriate language skills should focus their research more sharply on areas beyond the central points of the *Estado da India*. In doing so we would gain a more comprehensive view of the impact of the Portuguese upon indigenous peoples of the Indian Ocean region.

References:

1. The term Kayalar is somewhat ambiguous. The Tamil-speaking Muslim community comprised four main groups: Marakayars, Labbais, Rawther and Kayalar. The latter two groups were generally poor pedlars, whilst the other two groups were prosperous merchants with extensive shipping interests. In terms of Muslim-Portuguese conflict in the area during this period it is most likely that groups other than the Kayalar controlled the maritime Muslim interests that the Portuguese wished to curtail.
2. Sanjay Subrahmanyam, *The Portuguese Empire in Asia 1500-1700* (London, 1993), p. 263.
3. P. Roche, *Fishermen of the Coromandel. A Social Study of the Paravas of the Coromandel* (New Delhi, 1984).
4. M.N. Pearson, *The Portuguese in India* (Cambridge, 1987), p. 12.
5. All references in this article to the Paravas are taken from Roche unless otherwise stated.

6. See also Sanjay Subrahmanyam, *op. cit.*
7. C.R. de Silva, *The Portuguese in Ceylon 1617-1638* (Colombo, 1972), pp. 212-13, but note the textual contradiction where on p.48 the Portuguese conquest of Jaffna is attributed, in part at least to the need to control the pearl fisheries, but on p.212 the author notes that there had been no fishing for 15 years before the conquest of Jaffna in 1619. K.M. de Silva, *A History of Sri Lanka* (London, 1981), p. 117, uses the same "pearl" theory.
8. See K. McPherson, "Chulias and Klings: Indigenous Trade Diasporas and European Penetration of the Indian Ocean Littoral" in Giorgio Borsa (ed.) *Trade and Politics in the Indian Ocean* (New Delhi, 1990), pp. 33-46.
9. P. Roche *op.cit.*, p. 42.
10. C.R. Boxer, *João de Barros. Portuguese Humanist and Historian of Asia* (New Delhi, 1981), pp. 83, 94n.
11. Sanjay Subrahmanyam, *op.cit.*.
12. G. Bouchon, "Sixteenth Century Malabar and the Indian Ocean" in Ashin Das Gupta & M. N. Pearson (eds) *India and the Indian Ocean 1500-1800* (Calcutta, 1987), p. 3.
13. S. Arasaratnam, "India and the Indian Ocean in the Seventeenth Century" in Ashin Das Gupta & M.N. Pearson *op. cit.*, p. 105 refers to the Paravas as fishermen and coastal traders.
14. Kenneth McPherson, "Enemies or Friends? The Portuguese, the British and the Survival of Portuguese Commerce in the Bay of Bengal and Southeast Asia from the Late Seventeenth to the Late Nineteenth Century" in Francis A. Dutra & Joao dos Santos (eds) *The Portuguese and the Pacific* (Santa Barbara, 1995), pp. 211-37; L. Varadarajan "San Thome - Early European Activities and Aspirations" in *II Seminario International De Historia Indo-Portuguesa. Actas*, (Lisbon, IICT, 1985), pp. 436-438.
15. K.S. Mathew, *Portuguese Trade with India in the Sixteenth Century* (New Delhi, 1983), p. 134. See also reference 7.
16. For their later history see Kenneth McPherson, "Enemies or Friends?..."
17. P. Roche, *op.cit.*, p. 46.
18. C.R. Boxer, *op.cit.*, p. 85.
19. C.R. de Silva, *op.cit.*, p. 212.
20. Sanjay Subrahmanyam, *op.cit.*, p. 264.
21. *Ibid.*, p. 266.
22. S. Arasaratnam, *Merchants, Companies and Commerce on the Coromandel Coast 1650-1740* (New Delhi, 1986), p. 217.
23. C.R. de Silva, *op.cit.*, p. 214.
24. In the very voluminous *Memoir of Jan Schreuder, Governor of Ceylon, 1772*, published as No. 5 Selection from the Dutch Records of the Ceylon Govt (Colombo, 1946) there is only one very brief reference to seed pearls from the Mannar pearl fisheries.
25. S. B. Kaufmann quoted in Sanjay Subrahmanyam, *op.cit.*, p. 267.
26. For another approach to the historical problem of Portuguese-indigenous contacts see McPherson, K. "A Secret People of South Asia...", *Itinerario*, Vol. XI, No. 2, 1987, pp. 72-86.

11

NON - PORTUGUESE WESTERNERS TRIALED BY THE GOA INQUISITION (1563 - 1623)

John G. Everaert

Even from about 1540 onwards - still before the tribunal of the Holy office was definitively installed in Goa by royal decree (1560) - repressive actions were now and then taken by both episcopal and apostolic inquisitors. This campaign was mainly carried on against the Portuguese pseudo-converted Jews - called *conversos* or *cristaos-novos*-who had emigrated, clandestinely or not, to the *Estado da India*, attracted by the relative freedom, especially in outposts (Coromandel, Malacca, Ormuz) as well as allured by the commercial possibilities. Towards the end of the 1530's, the policy of religious integration was not only directed at the crypto-Jews, but also against the christian renegades, who often had joined the *mouros* (Moors=Muslims) or the *gentios* (pagans=Hindus) for economic motives, as well as against deviations of moral order, especially sodomy[1].

Around the middle of the 16th century, the missionaries - chiefly Jesuits - became clearly aware of those evangelisation problems, due to the extremely differing spiritual and material life-style. After having tried in vain to convert the "ritually conscious" Jews, Moors and heathens, they took measures of marginalisation and exclusion against the faithless. brahmans and yogis[2]. Nobody expressed better his indoctrinational frustrations than the Jesuit Gaspar Berse, from Zealand (Netherlands), who had to cope with Moors, Janitsars and mamelukes - from polish, Russian, Hungarian and Armenian descent -, New-Christians and "lutherans of different creeds"[3],in that small but extremely cosmopolitan community of the isle of Ormuz.

However, during his short stay (1549-51) in Ormuz, G. Berse, applying means of persuasion and pressure, succeeded in converting some eight heretics, holding "lutheran" beliefs. In Bassein, P[e] Melchior Nunez found some "lutheran" artillerists, spreading their heretical opinions. He ordered to capture them and hand them over to the bishop; one in particular was extremely keen and had caused much harm. We ignore if there has been any inquisitorial persecution. At the same time, the Jesuit strongly recommended to keep Flemish, English and Germans out of India, for many of them deserted as renegades to the Moors or were contaminated by "lutheran" heresies[4].

In 1557-59, another witch-hunt against the New-Christians was launched, even more vehement and on a larger scale than the previous one, first in Cochin and next in Goa. Roughly twenty *conversos* were deported to Portugal in order to be trialed by the inquisition of Lisbon in the course of 1560-61. The preliminary inquest by the ecclesiastical courts of both Cochin and Goa according to inquisitorial patterns, largely anticipated the inquisition-tribunal of Goa, which in 1560 had been effectively established, conducted by two inquisitors. Quite soon, not only crypto-Jews - with severe repression-, along with converted Hindus and Muslims, reverted into heathen creed - more gently dealt with -, but also other deviations of the true faith and violations of the moral code were fought[5].

Thanks to the inventory of the case-files of the Goa-inquisition over the period of 1561-1623, drawn up by João Delgado Figueira, the then *promotor-deputado* (prosecuting attorney-trainee) and subsequently co-inquisitor[6], we know with almost statistical accuracy the various sorts of charges/sentences:[7]

1561-1623 : ca. 3500 lawsuits (doubles deleted)

Infringements	%	Death-penalties (total : 3,66=100%)
Hinduism (apostates)	44	seldom
Islamism	18	7
Judaism	9	71
Protestantism	1.5	7
Doctrinal infractions	10	9
Moral behaviour	8	?
Obstruction Holy office	7	?

Our research is based upon the same source[8], though examined from another angle, i.e. searching for the non-Portuguese - all of them almost exclusively West-Europeans - put on trial by the Goa - inquisition during the course of some seventy years (1563-1623). Numerically, those account for hardly 1, 3% of all files, a very small number (about 50 of them) indeed, and comparatively a negligible proportion. However qualitatively spoken, this marginal group is of particular interest, when considering not only the nature of the charges, but also the nationality of the victims. Moreover, the chronological development points out the cyclical context of it all.

Trespasses, in order of importance, are to be subdivided into three main categories: heresies, infractions of the catholic doctrines and offence against public decency. As to overt heresy, by far and large protestantism takes the lead, a term embracing all the charges under the common denominator called *lutheranismo*, including all protestant varieties[9]. Besides, protestants form the largest group by far, counting for three fifths of all impeached. Then come the renegades prosecuted "*por culpa de mouro*", because they went over to Islam. Quite exceptionally in 1601, a Goanese - most probably of European origin - was punished "*por fazer sacrifizos aos pagodes*", i.e., for Hindu practices[10]. Among the non-Portuguese

Westerners, we do not trace a single *judaizante*. As a matter of fact, almost all victims in this category still happened to be Portuguese New Christians, of whom at least 84 people were executed in the course of the years 1561-90, covering a gamma from pedlars to wholesale traders[11]. Breaches of the church regulations, i.e., the second main group, only amounted to some 8%. Twice this concerned the possession of heretical or suspected books, an infraction adjacent to protestantism[12]. Both other cases refer to *"palabras malsoantes"* or blasphemy, as well as for not respecting the obligatory privation of meat. Two cases of *"peccado nefando"* (unmentionable/perverse sin) or sodomy were considered to be infringements upon proper moral conduct. Bigamy, however, was not referred to at all[13]. Finally we encounter some rare case of superstition[14].

Classified according to nationality, the French make up the main group, over half of them accused of protestantism and nearly one third of apostasy to the Islam. Next, the Germans come very close, with almost as many convicted for Lutheranism, a few islamic renegades and some sodomites. Then we meet the Flemish with so to speak as many protestant heretics and islamic apostates as the Germans. The Dutch were- as was to be expected - chiefly tackled because of their heretic convictions.

Most trials on protestantism took place in their initial years (1563-67: 13 sentences) of the Goa inquisition. The French especially were under fire: merely in 1563 five out of eight charged. Already in December 1562 some Frenchmen were imprisoned for alleged *"secta lutherana"*. Moreover it turned out that this kind of heresy was definitively rife among this nationality. Hence both the first inquisitors insisted upon strict application of the prohibitive rules concerning illegal immigration of foreigners under pain of death or perpetual exile to the galleys[15]. In 1563 a Jesuit missionary was sermonizing every sunday in the dungeon of the inquisition, in particular for the benefit of the *"luteranos"* who were locked up in jail[16]. Strangely enough, we even encounter a baptized Armenian who, after having been put to torture, admitted his "lutheran" error[17].

As for the English protestants, they are a case of their own. Antonio Gonzales "ingles" (sic), arrested on suspicion of heresy, died in 1577 in the course of his trial. Roberto Lapso, born in London from a Spanish father and a Portuguese mother and hence denominated "*cristão velho*", had deserted from the English vessels in Surat; as a "lutheran heretic" he begged for being re-adopted into the Roman-Catholic church and was granted conditional remission in 1616 ("*absoluto ad cautelam*") and on conditions of re-indoctrination. His fellow-townsman, the naval pilot Thomas Arot (alias Herod=Harrod) was caught with heretic writings, but nonetheless had to face only the minor abjuration. Finally, João Estampart had landed in India as a gunman and a trumpet-player on board the English ships. Since he had already been reconciled by the Sicilian inquisition, he was convicted to death in 1618 as a recidivist by the Goa inquisition and transferred to the secular justice[18].

A second wave of persecution, again mainly aiming at the protestants, flashed up between 1610-18. Along with the above-mentioned English, this time Germans, Dutchmen and even a Fleming were also tackled. This renewed chase of heretic Westerners undoubtedly fits in with the religious-military reaction by the Portuguese against the maritime-commercial infiltration by Dutch and Englishmen in the *Estado da India*. Still, also by overland route via the Near East and persia, "*muitos estrangeiros de diversas nações*" (Italian, French, German, Flemish) reached Portuguese-India, as was reported from Lisbon in 1606[19].

Indictments for islamism specially occurred in the early years (1563-67), namely two Flemings and a Frenchman. Quite notably, three Bretons - both of them, Francisco Capitão and Thomas Vimu, from Saint-Malo - gave themselves up together in 1609; Francisco Pinarte form Laval was arrested[20]. The two cases of sodomy were committed by Germans.

The correct nationality of the victims was not always with certainty to be discovered. Especially the appellations *flamenco* and *alemão* were sometimes erroneously used. As it was customary the Dutch were often identified as *framengos*.

153

Sometimes total confusion arose: for instance, Vicente Alemão, sounded very German indeed, and although he was originating from"Hacometis do estado de Holanda" nevertheless was registered as *"de nação flamengo"*[21]. The Germans Daniel Bibiquin (1588) and Francisco Roiz (1599) were also called *"flamengos"*, in spite of being respectively born in Lübeck and Hamburg[22]. Finally, João Carmini (1610), a native from Riga/ Latvia, in the same manner was booked as *"alemão"*, just like João Alemão (sic), although he came from Binova/Hungary[23].

As for the professions exercised in Portuguese-India, we are quite correctly informed for a little more than one third of cases. According to expectations, the majority (12 foreigners, primarily Germans and Flemings[24]) was active in the military-maritime branch: four *"bombardeiros"* - among whom Giraldo Redraemão (=Rademacher?) from Cologne, promoted "condestable" of the Goanese gallery-fleet[25] -, three soldiers[26], possibly two life -guards of the viceroy[27], two mariners and one naval pilot. The remaining occupations were rather divergent: two French hatters, a Breton carpenter, a turner from Aachen, a merchant from Antwerp and a certain *"mestre"* Bernardo (Gilabert) from the Cevennes.

In about twenty cases we have knowledge of the matrimonial status. There were as many bachelors as married men (11 in both categories, but as the last-mentioned come forward chiefly during the initial year 1563, the ratio supposedly is merely accidental in balance. Perhaps the high number of wedded persons is explicable by the policy of intermarriage, persued by the viceroys during the first half of the 16th century in order to encourage the ultimate settlement of Portuguese - and other foreigners in India? We came upon some indications in that direction, all of them registered in 1563. The Norman Francisco de Barnabel had already contracted no less than three marriages, the last time with a Portuguese orphan, surely brought over from the motherland. The Frenchmen Diogo de Roela and Martin Gigim got both married to *mestiza*, respectively Maria and Gracia Roiz, possibly sisters. Their compatriot Gaspar de Santamas preferred a Portuguese *"cristiana velha"* spouse.

German Francisco de Bomtempo was married in Goa to Maria Incuria, perhaps a member of the well-known German Imhoff family[28]. Some however had already married in Europe before emigrating: Frenchman Andre Piz (1563) in Bragança/Portugal; Thomas Arot (1619) in Papler/England; and German Martin Rot (1623) in Amersfoort/Holland[29].

The residence in India is seldom mentioned, hardly in one third of all cases. A dozen prosecuted perons were living in Goa, one was established in Cochin, while three stayed in "*nesto Estado*" without any further specification.

The investigation procedure followed by the Goa inquisition as well as the punitive measures were firstly noted in loose instructions, often inspired by "*Le Manuel des Inquisiteurs*" (Nicolau Eymerich, 1376/first print, 1503), but later on stated in an official regulation[30].

Those accused of protestantism were almost always convicted to the "*abjurção de apartado*", professed in a open auto-da-fe[31]. In most cases this abjuration in public was aggravated by punishment "*com carcere e habito* (penitencial) *perpetuo*". In real terms this perpetual incarceration was limited to some five years of imprisonment in a "*carcel de penitencia*" or a convent. The detainee was allowed to leave his cell during day-time in order to look for a job or to beg. However each time going out, he had to put on the penitential garment as well as the "*sambenito*" as marks of disgrace of this being convicted. The Latvian João Carmim (1610) and the German Martin Rot (1623) were not granted any reduction of sentence, for they had to serve their term "*sem remissão*", to the very end. Moreover the Dutchman Cornelio Bique (1563) and the Frenchman Diogo de Roela (1563) had to walk about wearing a rope around their neck. And on top of that, because of this suicidal attempt, the German Francisco de Bomtempo (1563) was flagellated as well[32].

Some of them, before pleading guilty, were submitted to torture ("*posto a tormento*"), this occurring mainly in the initial years. For the first time in 1612 the "Dutch" Armão Alberto, originating from the German border town of Emden, was already readmitted into the Roman-Catholic community (*"reconciliado"*) after a minor public abjuration (*"abjuração de leve"*). As a renegade lutheran, he was put again in the inquisition-gaol at the end of 1616. Since he kept denying, he was tortured, gave in and eventually ended up with a severe abjuration (*"abjuração de vehemente"*) in the auto-da-fe of 1618[33].

Other protestant heretics or suspects were granted mitigating circumstances. The Dutch seaman Adrião Cornel (1600) was only imposed religious tuition *"por não ser instruido"*. Strangely enough, his countryman, Alberto da Costa (1612) from Enkhuizen, formerly admitted into the christian church by the bishop of Malacca, got away with a mere reprimand *"por cometer dispois culpas de lutheranismo"*. The English deserter Roberto Lapso had turned himself in and asked for re-admittance; he obtained forgiveness at the tribunal (*"na mesa"*) on condition not to deviate again (*"absolvição ad cautelam"*) and was ordered religious instruction. Dutch "Vicente Alemão" (1569), who had already received the minor orders in Cochin, but was caught carrying a suspect treatise, was released on caution and his case dropped. Finally, Nicolão de Macedo (1623) from Paris, charged with fetisjism, was rebuked behind close doors in the audience-chamber[34].

For renegades who had adhered to the Islam, the heavy abjuration in a public act of faith was a regular punishment, even in the case of having given themselves up spontaneously, like did the German Francisco Ruiz (1599), the Hungarian João Alemão (1614), and both Bretons (1609) Francisco Capitão and Thomas Vimum[35], who brought offers to the Hindu-pagodes, like the Goa-born Andre Robert (1601), was condemned to the same degree of abjuration[36].

Breaking the religious rules in connection with privation of meat, cost the French "mestre" Bernardo (Gilabert), the minor abjuration and compulsary instruction (1563). The Flemish soldier João Gonzales (1613), denounced for blasphemy, proved to be innocent and thus was acquitted (*"absoluto ab instancia"*/sic)[37]

The most severe penalties consisted of banishment to the galleys and, of course, sentence to death. In this last case the execution was carried out after having handed over the victim to the secular authorities (*"relaxado a justicia secular"*). Obstinate heretics, recidivists, those who attempted to commit suicide and sodomites were almost always condemned to death.

The French protestant Gaspar de Santamas, a former catholic himself and married to a Portugese christian, was executed within an auto-da-fe (1563). The Dutch João de Volada, by birth a catholic, was also burned at the stake because of lutheranism (1610)[38].Supposedly, he is identical with the jeweller-diamond merchant, established at Goa for over 25years, very wealthy - having 30 to 40,000 *cruzados* of property - and married to an Indo-Portuguese half-caste. Denounced by his wife after matrimonial quarrels, his goods were confiscated and divided between accuser and inquisition. According to F. Pyrard de Laval, telling the tragedy, the man was put to death[39].

The French Janacointe, coming from Bulles (near Sens), had already been condemned to the heavy abjuration in 1569 by the inquisition of Lisbon for protestantism. Because of renewed heresy, he was executed in Goa in 1572. The English canonneer João Estampart as well, formerly reconciliated by the Sicily inquisition, was put to death in 1618 for protestant recidivism[40].

A horrifying drama was the fate of the cripple French hatter Martim Gigim, originating from La Rochelle and married in Goa to a half-blood. Accused of protestantism, he confessed on the rack, but afterwards hanged himself in jail. Therefore, considered a simulator without any remorse, his bones were burned in a public auto-da-fe(1563). The Flemish Nicolão Mont had run away just in time, but was nevertheless condemned in his absence as a incorrigible protestant; so in 1575 his portrait was symbolically executed (*"relaxada sua estatua"*). The Frenchman Andre Piz, married in Portugal at first admitted to profess the moorish religion, but afterwards revoked his confession, which, in 1563, caused him the death sentence[41].

Ultimately, sodomy was severely punished by the inquisiton. The German military man Alberto Homem, of lutheran origin and caught in the act of *"peccado nefando"*, was summarily executed in 1607 without trial at all. His compatriot Andre Maldar from Rostock, incriminated of sodomy, was banished to the galleys for ten years, a long term resulting in slow death[42].

By means of deterrence, the inquisition promotor J. Delgado Figueira ordered at the end of December 1622 to expose the images of the most repugnant cases of capital punishment - among them Nicolão Mont, Alberto Homem and João de Volada - in the Dominican cloister[43].

Just like against the New-Christians - by the most seriously afflicted victims - the Goa inquisition chased the heretic Westerners especially in the initial years (1563-75); protestants and, to a lesser degree, moorish renegades were the main target. During this period most of the executions also took place, against mainly "lutherans" in some six public auto-da-fes. After wards the persecution decreased, in such a manner that during the years 1587-96, not one single manifestation of any importance took place. In the early 17th century there was a revival of the inquisition activity, probably more for reasons of political hostility against Dutch and English, than out of religious necessity. Private auto-da-fes, organized in the Goa cathedral or some monastery church, as well as some three executions, are signs of this renewed zeal[44]. Apart from a couple of sentences for islamism and bigamy in the 1690-97 years, the Westerners will disappear from the horizon of the Goa inquisition, which almost exclusively applied herself to converted and pagan natives[43].

References:

1. A. Cannas da Cunha, *A Inquisição no Estado da India: Origens (1539-1560)*, Lisboa, 1995.pp. 25-28, 90-95, 127-59.
2. Idem, pp. 98-100.
3. J.Wicki, *Documenta Indica*, vol. 2 (1550-53), Roma,1950, pp.251,256-57. A good biography of "mestre Gaspar Barzaeus" is still lacking. Cfr.W. van Nieuwenhoff, *Gaspar Berse of the Nederlandsche Fr. Xaverius*, Rotterdam,1870.
4. A. da Silva Rego, *Documentação para a Historia das Missões do Padroado Portugues do Oriente- India*, vol. V, Lisboa 1993, pp. 243-44 & 261-62.

5. A. Cannas da Cunha, o.cit., pp. 132-39, 167-69, 146.
6. A. Baião, *A Inquisição de Goa*, vol. 1: *Tentativa de historia da sua origem, estabelecimento, evolução extinção*, Lisboa,1945, pp.214-18.
7. ch. Amiel & A.Lima (eds.), *L' Inquisition de Goa. La relation de charles Dellon (1687)*, Paris 1997. pp. 69,71-74.
8. Biblioteca Nacional Lisboa/*Secção Reservados* - codice 203 (microfilm 2545). Repertorio Geral de 3800 procesos que sam todos os despachados nesto sancto officio de Goa & mais partes da India do anno de 1561...ate 1623...feito pello Lic.loão Delgado Figueyra...(anno 1623), vol. 1 /651 folios. (henceforth cited as RGP).
9. The Englishman João Estampart (alias Stampar), originating from "Sahoxom" (county of Suffolk), persecuted in 1618 "*por hereje lutherano*", was arrested "por culpas de heresia da seita de Calvino". A. Baião, o.cit.,vol. III: *Correspondencia dos Inquisidores da 'India*,Lisboa 1930, p.554
10. Andre Robert, born in the parish of N.S. de Ajuda (Goa island), married and domicilied in Goa, RGP, f°s, 20ᵛᵒ,130ᵛᵒ.
11. J.C.Boyajiyan, "Goa Inquisition - a New Light on First 100 years (1561-1600)", in: *Purabhilekh-Paratava*, IV / 1986,pp.7-8.
12. Books imported from abroad were first examined in the Dominican convent and then eventually handed over to the inquisition. In 1587 the normative catalogue of forbidden literature, emended in portugal (1581) was reprinted in Goa. The pr-ecensorship aimed at the prohibitory lecture by "*soldados e gente dessas partes*". A. Baião, *Inquisição*...(o.c.) I/pp. 342, 268-69.
13. In the auto-da-fe, celebrated in the Goa cathedral in 1690, the Frenchman Henrique Trinchas, born and legally married in Saint-Malo, was sentenced to the light abjuration and deported for five years to the fortress of Mombasa because he had contracted a second marriage in Agacaim. Cfr. A.J. Moreira, *Colecção de listas de Autos da Fe, publicos e particulares, celabrados pela Inquisição de Goa*. Bibl. Nac. Lisboa, Cod. 866/film 5173 (ms a° 1863), f. 76v°.
14. In 1623, Nicolão de Macede, a bacheler from Paris living in Goa, was reprimanded("*reprehendida na mesa*") for having consulted "*fecheiros*" (*feiticeiros*=fetishists) in order to find out a theft. RGP, f° s 67 v°, 554r°..
15. A.Baião, *Inquisição*...(o.c.), I/p. 41.
16. A.da Silva Rego, *Documentação*...(o.c.), vol. IX, Lisboa 1995, p. 244 (carto geral do pᵉ L. Peres, Goa 17.12.1563).
17. Andre Jorjão (=gorgiano: Georgian?), born in Prim in Armenia (sic) RGP, f° 99v°. Already in 1562, the Goa inquisition sent two Armenians to Lisbon; one of them previously served in the Turkish army as a specialist in making gunpowder. A. Baião, *Inquisição*...(o.c.), I/p.43.
18. RGP, f°s 106v°, 599v°,634r°. A.Baião, *Inquisição*... (o.c.), I/p. 275 & II/554.
19. R.A.de Bulhão Pato, *Documentos remetidos da India*, vol. I/Lisboa 1880, p. 48.
20. RGP, f° s 332r°-v°.632v°.
21. RGP, f°s 76r°/639v°.
22. RGP, f°s 39r°/244v°; 46v°/321v°.

23. RGP, f°s 55v°/418v°; 56r°/423v°.
24. J. Everaert, "Soldiers", Diamonds and Jesuits: Flemings and Dutchmen in Portuguese India (1505-90), in : A. Disney & E. Boot (eds.), Vasco da Gama and the Linking of Europe and Asia, Delhi, 2000,pp. 85-91.
25. RGP, f°345r°.
26. Among them, probably also Martin Rot, alias(?) Matharem Rath, A German married in Amersfoort (Holland) and characterized as "suiço", which means elite-soldier. Cfr. A. Baião, Inquisição...(o.c) VI/p.579.
27. Daniel Bibiquin from Lübeck (RGP),f 244v). Possibly also João Carmim from Riga, who came to India in the retinue of the viceroy Martin Afonso de Castro, 1605-07 (RGP, f° 418v°).
28. RGP, f°s 302v°, 234r°, 480v°, 352v°, 303r°.
29. RGP, f° s 95r°, 634r°, 541v°.
30. R.Rego, O ultimo regimento (1778) e o regimento da economia da Inquisição de Goa, Lisboa, 1983.
31. Foreigners walked in the twice six "auto-da fes"organized between 1563-75 and again between 1600-18. RGP, passim. The long lists published by E.N. Adler, Auto de fe and Jews, London, 1908, pp. 139-40, 145, 147-48 are still incomplete.
32. RGP, f 418v°, 541v°, 212v°, 234v°, 303r°.
33 RGP, f°s 29 -30r°, 153v°, 161v°. A. Baião, Inquisição...(o.c.),II/pp. 547.554.
34. RGP,f°s 130r°, 152r°, 599v°,639v°,554r°.
35. RGP, f°s 321v°; 423v°, 632v°.
36. RGP f° 130v°.
37. RGP f°s 480, 421.
38. RGP, f°s 352, 419.
39. X. de Castro (ed), Voyage de Pyrard a Laval aux Indes Orientales (1601-1611), Paris 1998,pp.614-15
40. RGP f°s 483r, 484, 428.
41. RGP f° s 62, 480, 67, 545, 95.
42. RGP f° s 17, 144, 172.
43. RGPf°s 14-17: Lista das pessoas que se tem relaxado..., as quales mandou todas pintar e por novamente no convento de S. Domingos
44 A. Daião, Inquisição...(o.o.) I/pp. 269; 275-76
45. M. de J. dos Martires Lopes, "A Inquisição de Goa na primeira metade de Setecentos: una visita pelo seu interior", in: Mare Liberum, n. 15/1998, pp. 128-31.

GOA INQUISITION FILES
Charges & Sentences

Heresy | Doctrinal Violations

	Protestantism	Islamism	Hinduism	Blasphemy	Sacraments	Prohibited Books	Sodomy	Superstition	Unknown	Total
Nationalities										
French	7	4			1			1		13
German	7	2					2			11
Flemish	6	2		1						9
Dutch	6					1				7
English	3					1			1	5
Hungarian		1								1
Latvian	1									1
Armenian	1									1
Goanese			1							1
Total	31	9	1	1	1	2	2	1	1	49
Periodization										
1563-69	14	2			1	1				18
1570-79	3									3
1580-89	2	1								3
1590-99		2								2
1600-09	2	3	1				1			7
1610-19	9	1		1		1			1	13
1620-23	1						1	1		3
Total	31	9	1	1	1	2	2	1	1	49

GOA INQUISITION TRIALS
Chronological per Nationality

Doctrinal Violations

Year of Trial	France	Germany	Flanders	Holland	England	Hungary	Lativa	Armenia	Goa	Total
1563	7	1	1	1						10
1565			1							1
1566		1		1						2
1567			1	1				1		3
1569	1			1						2
1575			1							1
1577					1					1
1581			1							1
1588		1								1
1592		1								1
1599		1								1
1600				1						1
1601									1	1
1602			1							1
1607		1								1
1609	3									3
1610		1		1			1			3
1612		1	2	1						4
1614						1				1
1615					1					1
1616					1					1
1618		1			2					3
1623	1	2								3
Total	13	11	9	7	5	1	1	1	1	49

12

THE CONVENT OF SAINT MONICA AND ITS INHABITANTS IN THE EARLY DECADES OF THE SEVENTEENTH CENTURY

Carlos Alonso Vañes

In the beginnings of the seventeenth century, Fray Alejo de Meneses, the archbishop of Goa, founded the convent of Saint Monica in Goa. The convent still survives with all its structures and deserves further consideration especially regarding its origins.

From the very start of his taking charge of the diocese of Goa, Meneses felt the need of providing the capital city of his administration with some institutions dedicated to the service of women, whose social condition at that time was very delicate. Consequently he founded three houses, one for young orphan women in 1600, another for women religious in 1606 and a third for repentant women sinners in 1607. This was the chronological order in which the houses were founded, and Meneses always referred to them in the same order in all his letters and official communications. Already in one of the first letters after his arrival in India in 1595 addressed to his relative, the Augustinian archbishop of Braga Fray Agustín de Castro, Meneses reveals his intention of founding a house for the young orphan women. It was only after having put into operation the convent of Saint Monica in 1606 that Meneses would occupy himself with the third foundation.

In order to deal exclusively with the second, namely the convent of Saint Monica, we shall not occupy ourselves with the first and third foundations[1].

Already during the rule of the viceroy Aires de Saldanha, Meneses made the first moves to obtain permission for the foundation of this house, which was meant to provide accommodation for those who felt an inclination to religious life. For its construction he bought a large plot along the hillside near the city where already stood the Church of St. Antony (San Antonio), founded by the first Portuguese who arrived in India, and the monastery of Our Lady of Grace (Ntra. Sra. da Graça) and the People's college or the College of St. Augustin. Both these houses were of the Augustinian monks, the religious family of which the archbishop himself was a member.

In order to launch the project the archbishop required a person of confidence who would be the first superior, and finances sufficient enough to cover the needs of the future nuns. From the very start he could count for the superior on a Portuguese noble lady, Doña Felipa, native of Thana, whom Fr. Antonio de Gouvea received as an Augustinian tertiary during his stay in the monastery of that city in the beginnings of the seventeenth century. She was in charge of the reception of young orphan women from the very start of the orphanage, which as we mentioned, was the first house for women founded by Meneses.

For the sustenance of the future religious, Meneses could obtain from the city government an annual help of 2000 xerafins of the royal income proceeding from the one-percent tax which the government allotted for the defence of the State of India. In the future when the number of the religious would increase, the dowries brought by the new entrants of the convent would ensure the sustenance of the inhabitants, and consequently the state aid would become superfluous.

Intent on setting the project in motion, for which he took great interest, Meneses bought the plot for 3000 xerafins. Although his plans were ambitious, the first convent was quite a modest one. Meneses laid the foundation stone on 2nd July 1606 and entrusted the construction to an Augustinian priest by name Juan Pinto. The house was inaugurated two months later on 3rd September of the same year. For a short time the first religious had to live in the orphanage of Our Lady of the Mountains (Ntra. Senhora da Serra), from where they moved to the convent on the date given above. The change of residence took place during a solemn procession presided by the archbishop, who upon arrival at the convent gave each religious the Augustinian habit, starting with the first superior, the aforementioned Sister Felipa de la Trinidad[2].

The religious who took habit at that occasion were 21 whose social status was as following: excluding Doña Felipa, 3 were orphans coming from the orphanage, 15 were young women of normal middle-class families and 2 were widows.

One of these widows was certainly Doña Catalina de Lima, widow of Sancho de Vasconcelos, whose religious name was Sister Catalina de Sta. Monica. With her entered also three of her daughters, one of whom was Doña Antonia de Vasconcelos, known by the religious name Sister Ignacia das Chagas. We are informed of all these thanks to a letter of the king Philip III addressed to the viceroy of India D. Jerónimo de Azevedo, sent from Lisbon on 9th March 1613. It ordered the viceroy to concede to the above mentioned Sister Catalina, the widow, and to her children, and through them to the convent of St. Monica, all the money the public administration owed to D. Sancho de Vasconcelos for his services to the government. Further it also required the viceroy to grant a business trip to China to Antonia de Vasconcelos, one of the daughters, for which she already had obtained permission before entering the convent[3].

After the inauguration of the convent, as we have indicated, Meneses communicated the news with satisfaction both to Philip III, king of Spain and Portugal, and to Paul V, the Pope. The initial reaction of the king was negative, for he did not want to utilize any part of the amount (the one percent mentioned above) destined for the defence of his possessions in the East for other purposes, although he acknowledged the zeal of the archbishop and the positive results that might yield this new initiative. Two royal letters dated 17th and 27th of January 1607 testify clearly to this negative attitude[4].

But the king would end up by accepting the accomplished works. In one of his letters dated 11th December of the same year 1607 addressed to the viceroy, the king shows indignation towards the work done, but still accepts it. In consonance with his desire not to employ public funds for the maintenance of the convent, he asked the viceroy to watch over the convent that only women of well-to-do families enter there, so that luckily they with their dowries would make the public funding unnecessary. Moreover the cloister had to be kept in full sense. And the king did not approve the archbishop's proposal of allotting a tribute in favour of the convent on the customs office of Ormuz, for no public office should charge a toll for its services.

Following suit to the foundation of the convent of Goa, the Franciscans of that city as well as the cities of Cochin and Bassein attempted to erect similar houses. But the king ended definitely all such aspirations with his letter to the viceroy in India[5].

The foundation of this convent, as it has been accomplished by Meneses, did not comply with all the regulations and he was conscious of it. However he continued with the project; for he had no other alternative, given the fact that there existed in India no convent to provide him with a superior for the new foundation[6]. The main irregularity consisted in the fact that the prioress of the convent Doña Felipa had not completed the three years of profession canonically required to be elected as superior of the house. Consequently the vestition of the rest of the religious also resulted to be invalid. In order to correct both these irregularities Meneses wrote a letter in 1607 to the Apostolic Collector in Portugal requesting him to take care of the adequate papal dispensation. The Collector, Mons. Fabricio Caracciolo, did write to Rome on 8th December 1607 to this effect, but Cardinal Borghese, Paul V's Secretary of State, answered him on 5th February 1608 that the Pope did not want to take any decision on that matter without consulting with the Congregation of the Bishops and Regulars, which had not yet given its opinion on the issue. As soon as he would know their opinion, the Cardinal would send him the decision in time, so that the Collector could despatch it with the ships leaving for India in the same year from Lisbon[7]. On 4th March 1608 the Cardinal replied together with another communication. The request of the archbishop to clear all the irregularities associated with the erection of the convent of St. Monica seemed to be too generic to the Pope. And the archbishop was asked to specify the irregularities so that one would know if they were dispensable and if so, how. However, the Pope gave dispensation to the irregularity of the prioress of having only two years of profession, instead of the five years required by the Canon Law. Concerning the profession of the rest of the nuns, they were required to renew their commitment after the legitimation of the superior[8].

In a letter of 24th December 1609, addressed to his Augustinian superiors in Portugal, Meneses himself describes the actual situation of the convent of St. Monica during the end of the year. This is approximately a year before he would start his journey back to Portugal, where he would be entrusted with the archbishopric of Braga in 1612. After having narrated how he also erected the house for the repentant women sinners, Meneses writes in this letter on the convent of St. Monica as follows: "Many noble persons send their children to the sisters' convent which offers a great redress to this state [of Goa]. For since all wanted to get married, which was impossible, many got lost ..." In continuation he remarks that on All Saints Day they inhabited a quarter of the convent which was very spacious. He adds that they had all what they needed and offers details of the austere life they led in the convent by following the statutes given by him. These included mostly the prescriptions of the Augustinian Constitutions for women religious.

With regard to the number, Meneses states that there were 37 professed religious and some novices. The very same text leads us to conclude that besides the religious in the strict sense, there were also some maids or servants. Meneses states in the same letter that there were 60 young orphan women in the house which he erected for them[9].

Meneses returned to Europe in the summer of 1611. On occasion of his arrival at Portugal, the Apostolic Collector, sent among one of his briefings a positive evaluation of Meneses' activities in the Orient and anticipated the rumours that king Philip III was about to confer on him some important political mission. On this ground he also presented to Rome the archbishop's desire to have the statutes prepared by him for the convent of St. Monica approved by the Pope. Cardinal Borghese confirmed in a letter dated 13th September 1611 the receipt of the Collector's briefings, expressed his joy for the good news sent, but concerning the approval of the statutes wrote back as follows: "it is necessary to examine them, and for the time being sent them here"[10].

On 12th November of the same year 1611, Meneses himself wrote from Lisbon a letter in Latin to Paul V, in which he summarised the principal achievements of his 15 years of service as archbishop of Goa. One of the first issues treated in the letter was the foundation of the three houses for women in Goa; they were discussed in the same chronological order in which they were erected. In connection with the convent of St. Monica, Meneses emphasized the observance practised in the house[11].

During Meneses' passage to the peninsula, the municipal council of Goa took interest in the Convent of St. Monica and pleaded before the King of Spain and Portugal in its favour. Praising and acknowledging the great advantages it rendered to the city, the council stated that owing to insufficient funding and to the regulations which prohibited the nuns to utilize their heritage for the purchase of public real estate the convent was unable to admit all those who desired to enter. Consequently the council requested the king to grant the religious permission to buy public real estate for their sustenance, especially because no other property was available to them in India for this end.

In a letter dated 9th February 1611, the king ordered the viceroy D. Lorenzo de Tavora to allow the nuns, despite the existing regulations, to buy real estate for an amount not superior to 3000 xerafins with the exception of certain categories of public property. To this effect the viceroy was supposed to issue a corresponding document in virtue of the royal letter.

The letter resumes with the observation that the amount of 3000 xerafins, together with other income which certainly they would have, would be sufficient to maintain 40 religious. Hence the king informs the viceroy that he has already asked the Pope to limit the number of the nuns to 40 including both the professed and the novices. Further he has already given orders to instruct the archbishop of Goa, in whose authority laid the convent, that he should stick to this norm. But, since he knows that the founder of the convent, archbishop Meneses, was on his way to the peninsula, the viceroy should take the responsibility of instructing the successor of the archbishop to this effect[12].

Despite all these precautions, the convent grew incredibly, we anticipate, in the successive decades to such an extent as to become the abode of hundreds of religious and to end up with abundant possessions which ensured its normal development. We shall offer more concrete details below.

An issue which took a long time after Meneses' return to Europe was that of the approval by the Holy See of the statutes written by him to regulate the monastic life.

Meneses took charge of the dioceses of Braga in August 1612 and settled there. From here he wrote a letter to Paul V, which is of great importance for the matter we are concerned with. We know of this letter thanks to a copy of the original left with Mons. Juan Bautista Confalonieri, secretary of Fabio Biondi, chief of the Apostolic Palace and retired Apostolic Collector in Lisbon, with whom Meneses frequently corresponded during these years. He wrote a short letter of presentation to Confalonieri, dated 8th November 1612, requesting him to forward the enclosed letter through official channels to the Pope[13].

The letter addressed to the Pope offers a concise, complete and truthful description of how one lived the religious life in the convent of Goa. It begins with the foundation of the convent and its subjection to the local ordinary; but the Augustinians have assumed the task of providing confessors. The letter mentions also the statutes given to the convent which were based on the Constitutions of the Augustinian nuns and replete with strict observance. For instance, Meneses refers to the narrow iron grating in the parlour which separated the nuns from the external world; the prohibition to speak to all persons except parents, brothers, sisters and direct relatives; the presence of a nun in charge only of the young aspirants entering the convent and another exclusively of the novices; the perpetual adoration of the Blessed Sacrament facilitated by the great number of religious; the prohibition of accepting married women in the convent even if they possessed the pontifical permission; the recital of the holy office according to the Roman Calendar with the proper of the Augustinian Order; hours dedicated for daily meditation besides other prayers; the regular visit by the archbishop himself and not by delegated persons; and the possibility of re-electing the same superior for the first 20 years of the convent until others are prepared to fulfill the task.

Thus having described at large the life lived in St. Monica, Meneses requested the Pope for the approval of the statutes so that they should not be altered by other archbishops and that by the run of time the life of the convent should not deteriorate. At the same time he also asked the Pope to concede to the convent all favours and privileges which the Holy See used to yield to other Augustinian convents[14].

Two letters from the Congregation of Bishops and Regulars dated 18th January 1613 responded to Meneses' petitions. One of these was addressed to the archbishop of Braga, Alejo de Meneses and the other to the new archbishop of Goa. In the first letter[15] Meneses was told that he should first of all send the statutes of the convent of Goa, before he could get them approved. And in order that the life style of the convent be maintained, he was instructed to write to the new archbishop of

Goa to this effect. Together with the letter to Meneses was, in fact, enclosed another[16] addressed to D. Cristóbal de Sa or de Lisboa, a Jeronimite monk and bishop of Malacca (1604-1612), who succeeded Meneses to the archbishopric of Goa and continued to be in charge of the archdiocese till his death in 1622.

Meneses received both these letters before 6th April 1613 in Madrid where he was appointed by Philip III as president of the Council for Portugal. This was his first stay in the Spanish capital (1613-14), where he would return to later in 1615 and would die in May 1617. Fr. Luis Álvarez, whom Meneses took with him as his secretary to Madrid, alludes to the arrival of these documents in a letter addressed to the same Confalonieri, who has been and would be for a long time representing Meneses's interests before the Roman curia[17]. More explicit was the mention made by Meneses himself in a letter of the same day 6th April 1613, addressed to the same Confalonieri, where he observes that the letter from the Congregation of the Bishops and Regulars, asking the archbishop of Goa not to introduce any innovations in the convent of St. Monica, was very important. Concerning the statutes of the nuns which the Congregation required him to sent to Rome, Meneses writes that they were the same Constitutions of the Augustinian nuns, and the description he gave in the letter to the Pope contained the most important points, and it was enough that the Pope approved them. Further he explains which were the other two houses for women erected in Goa and specifies the names of each one.

Of special importance is a fragment of this letter where it alludes to a recently received papal breve sent to Goa conferring some favours, and of which we do not possess any other information. Meneses assures that he has already sent it to India, pointing out that the favours were granted only to the cloistered nuns, that is to say, to the Convent of St. Monica, and not to the other two houses[18].

As has been required by the Congregation of Bishops and Regulars, archbishop Menses had to submit through his representative Mons. Confalonieri, the text of the statutes which he wanted to be approved. By the end of May or the beginning of June, Mons. Confalonieri presented a petition requesting the approval of the text included with it[19]. This text comprised of 17 articles in which Confalonieri asked for all what Meneses had already petitioned for in his letter to the Pope[20].

On 25th June 1613 the Congregation of Bishops and Regulars approved the Statutes or Constitutions presented to it, but with two exceptions: first, the second part of the second chapter had to be omitted, where it was stated that the extraordinary confessor of the nuns, alike the ordinary confessor, also should be an Augustinian; second, chapter 10 had to be modified where it was stated that no [married] woman even with the permission of the Holy See could enter the convent. Further the Congregation obliged the archbishop not only to specify that no woman could enter unless this revision was clearly mentioned in the Constitutions but also to revoke explicitly the previous legislation[21].

As Confalonieri informed Meneses that there would be a breve of approval of the statutes with the aforesaid corrections, Meneses did express his satisfaction with a letter to Confalonieri dated 24th August 1613[22].

Since he initially has mentioned together with the convent of St. Monica two other houses, namely the orphanage for poor young women and the house for the repentant women sinners, wherein also the women were dressed in Augustinian habits without however taking the vows, Meneses requested the Pope in two letters dated 28th October and 5th November 1613 for the explicit approbation of these foundations exactly as they were erected and a copy of the approvance to be sent to Goa[23].

On 18th November 1613, responding to a letter of Confalonieri dated 8th October, Meneses expressed his agreement with the decisions of the Congregation of the Bishops and Regulars and advised Confalonieri not to trouble any more to insist on issues which were not of the liking of the Congregation. The issue in question amounted to Meneses's desire to obtain for the convent of St. Monica a breve conceding some indulgences and favours on the feast of the Holy African Virgins and Martyrs celebrated in the universal church on 6th December, for the Augustinians nuns of Goa had an altar dedicated to them in their church. There was also the petition for permission to recite the holy office *sub ritu duplici*. And all this was meant only for the professed nuns[24].

The papal breve approving the Statutes of the Convent of St. Monica was finally issued on 27th November 1613; it begins with the words: *"Ut ea quae pro religiosarum"*. As one would imagine, this documents brings together all the data which we hitherto examined in discussing its various stages of development[25]. Confalonieri sent this breve to the archbishop together with a letter of his own dated 3rd December 1613. The document gave the prelate great joy and he undertook all he could, to send it with the first ships that sailed to Goa. This is testified by a letter of Meneses to Confalonieri dated 12th January 1614[26].

There were no great problems in obtaining indulgences for the feast of the Holy African Martyrs. Mons. Confalonieri sent the letter of concession to Meneses on 2nd January 1614, together with the breve mentioned above. Meneses confirms the reception of all items with a letter addressed to Confalonieri on 13th February of the following year[27].

With regard to the celebration of the divine office *sub ritu duplici* for the same feast, Confalonieri presented on 22nd January 1614 a petition to the Congregation of Rites, in which he explained the grounds for his request already discussed above[28]. But the officials of the Congregation encountered certain problems which the documents available to us do not specify, as Confalonieri writes in his letter addressed to Meneses dated 29th January 1614. For this reason Meneses tells Confalonieri in a letter dated 13th of the following March that he needs not any more trouble himself with the issue, for the nuns would anyhow celebrate the feast though with less solemnity[29]. The same advice not to trouble himself anymore is expressed again in another letter dated 8th April 1614, which shows his admiration for the doubts harboured by the Congregation concerning the existence of the Holy Virgins, whom the Roman Martyrology mentions on 16th December[30].

But the continued interest of the archbishop Meneses, who as viceroy of Portugal resided in Lisbon from 1614 to mid 1615, and the repeated beseeching of Mons. Confalonieri before the Congregation of Rites were to be rewarded. On 11th November 1614 the Congregation of Rites issued a decree, signed by Cardinal prefect Galli and his secretary Mucanzio, which permitted the Augustinian nuns of St. Monica to celebrate the feast of the Holy African Virgins and Martyrs with the recital of the divine office *sub ritu duplici*[31].

Pope Paul V ratified this concession granted by the Congregation of Rites through a breve, "Domini nostri Iesu Christi", dated 2nd December 1614[32]. This must have filled the Augustinian prelate with joy, but we do not find any mention of its reception and dispatch to India among the archbishop's correspondence with his Roman agents.

On 3rd April 1613 Meneses wrote a letter to Mons. Confalonieri instructing him to request the Pope for certain favours, some of which were meant for his diocese of Braga and others for the Augustinian convent of Goa. The issue concerning the convent of Goa was related to its administration. He was told that except the founding members of the convent, all the others were young nuns and some were widows in mature age. Some of the founders were already dead. If the prioress were to die now, it would be impossible to elect anyone of the young nuns to succeed her, for none of them had reached the canonical age yet, and in case some were of the canonical age, the election would become obligatory and would be conducted without any possible secrecy. For this reason, he wished that the Pope, on the one hand take into consideration the impossibility of sending qualified women from Europe, who in the then given conditions would not dare to embark and to sail from the Cape of Good Hope, and on the other hand concede him that the election be conducted from among three widows nominated by him and three or four young women also designated by him, all with the age of 30. For no other solution was viable[33].

Among the documents found and published by us, we have not found any which indicates that such an authority has been conferred to the archbishop. But we encounter a list of all the superiors of the convent from its foundation to the end in an abridged history of the convent, included in a chronicle of the Augustinians in India, written during the suppression of the religious in Portugal in the 19th century. Referring to the first prioress, Sister Felipa de la Trinidad, it states that she has received a breve addressed to the founder archbishop[34] which authorizes her to continue as superior of the house for another seven years. It adds that on 5th February 1614, the archbishop of Goa Mons. Cristóbal de Sa or de Lisboa ordered to conduct a new election and that she being one of the candidates was unanimously re-elected against her will, but was absolved of her office on 15th August 1616 in consideration of her advanced age, decrepitude and dislike. Further the document states that she occupied the same post on two other occasions between 1621 and 1626 and died on 8th July 1626[35].

The discussion on the first prioress gives us the opportunity to make a few observations regarding the other superiors who were in charge of the house during the first decades of the century. The second superior was Sister María del Espíritu Santo, daughter of the former prioress. She administered the house as vicar prioress, nominated by the archbishop D. Cristóbal de Lisboa in 1614, till her mother recuperated the health. But since her mother disliked to continue in the office of the prioress, the archbishop saw to it that Sister Maria be canonically elected as superior of the house on 15th August 1616, "with all the votes in her favour except that of her mother", adds the chronicler. She finished her office in September 1618, and died on 15th August 1619.

The third superior, before Sister Felipa returned to occupy the post for the second and the third time, was Sister

Catalina de Santa Monica who had made her profession on 5th July 1609; she died in 1622[36]. We have already indicated that this was one of the widows who entered the convent during its foundation; she was accompanied by three of her daughters.

It has been mentioned above that the king ordered to restrict the number of religious to 40, including both the professed and the novices. As time passed, the life of the convent acquired quite a repute and more and more postulants wanted to join in. This forced the king to change his opinion, and in a letter dated 21st March 1615 he ordered the viceroy D. Jerónimo de Azevedo to permit the convent to accept as many candidates as it economically could afford. Further the viceroy was supposed to take care that no women of bad repute or separated from their husbands enter the convent. For it was necessary to maintain the life of the convent in the spirit and according to the rules one lived there hitherto[37].

Despite the death of some of the inhabitants, the convent of St. Monica must have been completely filled at the end of the second decade of 17th century; still there were numerous applicants seeking entrance. At a certain point the nuns considered it opportune to petition the Holy See to permit them to admit an additional number of 20 religious. Undoubtedly they thought that the dowries of the new comers would be sufficient enough to assure the subsistence of the house. In fact, we know of a breve, issued by Paul V, dated 2nd May 1620, approving the petition of the nuns and conceding them what they asked for[38].

Around this time, the convent, of which only a quarter was fit to be inhabited initially, was under construction to complete it. Huge sums of money were required to finance the project. It was on this occasion that the nuns sent a letter to Philip III asking him to instruct the State to pay them back the debts it incurred on various circumstances. The king assented to the request and ordered the viceroy, Count of Redondo, in a letter dated 10th March 1617, to check the documents of the nuns in the council of finances, and to pay them the amount owed, if the papers were in order. A minute of the viceroy's response, dated 29th December of the same year and copied in continuation of the royal letter, shows that the high functionary of Goa promised to act as required[39].

In order to construct the vast edifice that the Augustinian nuns of Goa were putting up, it was necessary also to buy a few private houses which the nuns wanted that their owners sell to them. So that the selling-price of the property be just, the nuns requested the king to nominate the archbishop of Goa or another qualified person as the assessor. The king acceded to this petition and sent a letter to this effect dated 20th March 1617 to the Count of Redondo[40]. According to a note at the end of the letter, the viceroy agreed to act as he has been ordered to do, but observed that the nuns later preferred to deal directly with the property owners which turned out to be the liking of both the parties concerned.

Remarks in the books of the acts of the conventual chapter of the monastery of Our Lady of Grace of Goa and the College of the People or of St. Augustin of Goa pertaining to the Augustinian friars, both buildings situated in the proximity of the Convent of St. Monica, confirm that the financial situation of the convent was at its peak. There were rumours that the nuns even travelled on business to China, and owned the village of Daince in the North which they later exchanged with the Augustinian monks for other possessions[41].

Great part of the merit for the progress of the house during the first two decades of the 17th century deserves Fr. Diego de Santa Ana, an influential Augustinian, who has been a missionary in Persia and was called to Goa to be nominated as ordinary confessor of the convent. He occupied this post for many years (1607-1644) and took great interest in the development of the convent. He was the one responsible for the re-edification of the convent after it was burned down to ashes in 1636. Also he obtained from Pope Gregory XV, in response to a letter of his own, the breve *"Alias a foelicis"*, dated 10th March 1622 which approved the mitigation of the austerity prescribed in the first Constitutions[42].

A crucifix which the nuns had kept in their church miraculously opened its eyes on various occasions for some days in 1636. The miracle was reported by the Dominican prelate who was then provisionally administering the diocese. The crucifix is still preserved to this day[43].

What has been discussed hitherto amounts to the central issues concerning the foundation and early development of the Convent of St. Monica in the first decades of its existence. But its history is large and continues till the suppression of the religious orders in Portugal and in its colonies in 1834.

Between 1606 and 1834, there were a total of 91 prioresses or superiors. The last one was elected in 1831[44]. The majority came from Goa, but there were many from other parts of the Portuguese oriental possessions such as the coast of Mombasa, Malacca and other cities. Even a Ceylonese, the daughter of a local king, was a prioress of the convent[45].

The total number of religious during the same period was 661, of whom 494 were of the superior rank or of black veil, and the rest 167 were lay sisters or of white veil[46].

The convent of St. Monica has survived to this day with its imposing, ancient architectonic structures; it is at present the seat of the Institute of Higher Studies for women religious of active life belonging to various congregations.

Translation: *P.G. Pandimakil*

References:

1 For a concise discussion of these three houses founded by Meneses in Goa, see our publication: Carlos Alonso, *Alejo de Meneses, O.S.A., Arzobispo de Goa (1595-1612). Estudio biografico.* Valladolid, 1992, pp. 207-215.

2 The first Augustinian chronicler, Fray Felix de Jesus, describes the ceremony of taking the habit and therewith ends his chronicle. See, Fray Felix de Jesús, "Chronica da Ordem de S. Augustinho nas Indias Orientais" (edited by Arnulf Hartmann), *Analecta Augustiniana* 30 (1967), p. 138.

3 See, *Documentos remettidos da India ou Livros das Monçoes*, vol II, Lisbon 1884, pp. 384-386.

4 *Ibid*, vol I, Lisbon 1880, pp. 86 & 126 respectively.

5 *Ibid*, pp. 155-156.

6   We have also discussed concisely these issues in the biography of the archbishop; see, C. Alonso, *Alejo de Meneses, O.S.A., Arzobispo de Goa* ..., pp. 231-233.
7   VATICAN ARCHIVES, *Nunz. Portogallo*, vol. 12, fol. 51v; fragment published by us, in: *Analecta Augustiniana* 27 (1964) 316, n. 50.
8   *Ibid*, pp. 316-317, n. 51.
9   See the extensive letter published in: *Analecta Augustiniana* 27 (1964) 378-393, especially pages 383-384 for what concerns the convent of Saint Monica.
10 *Analecta Augustiniana* 27 (1964) 326, n. 56.
11 *Ibid*, pp. 328-329, n. 59.
12 See, *Documentos remettidos da India ou Livros das Monções* ..., vol II, p. 23.
13 See, C. Alonso, "Alejo de Meneses, O.S.A. (1559-1617), Arzobispo de Braga, I Parte", *Archivo Augustiniano* 65 (1981) 41-74. The letter to Confalonieri is to be found on p. 66, note 14.
14 *Ibid.*, pp. 66-68, n. 15.
15 *Ibid.*, p. 72, n. 21.
16 *Ibid.*, p. 72, n. 22.
17 See, *Archivo Augustiniano* 66 (1982) p. 186, n. 26.
18 *Ibid.*, pp. 188-189, n. 28.
19 *Ibid.*, p. 205, n. 40.
20 *Ibid.*, pp. 205-207, n. 41.
21 *Ibid.*, p. 207, n. 42.
22 *Ibid.*, p. 209, n. 44.
23 *Ibid.*, pp. 218-219, nos. 51 & 52. Another petition with the same intention was sent on 11th December 1613, see: *Ibid.*, pp. 225-226. Further, on an undated petition, see: *Ibid.*, pp. 227-228, n. 62.
24 *Ibid.*, p. 220, n. 54.
25 *Ibid.*, pp. 223-225, n. 58. We have copied the text from the VATICAN ARCHIVES, *Segr. Brev. Registri*, vol. 498, fol. 135-140.
26 *Ibid.*, p. 230-231, n. 65.
27 *Ibid.*, p. 233, n. 70.
28 *Ibid.*, p. 231, n. 66.
29 *Ibid.*, p. 239, n. 77.
30 *Ibid.*, p. 242, n. 81.
31 See, *Archivo Augustiniano* 68 (1984) 162-163, n. 106.
32 *Ibid.*, pp. 165-166, n. 109. We have copied this breve from VATICAN ARCHIVES, *Segr. Brev. Registri*, vol. 516, fol. 284-286.
33 See, *Archivo Augustiniano* 69 (1985) 163: Appendix I.
34 This breve is unknown to us.
35 See, Manoel da Ave-Maria, OSA, "Manual Eremiítico da Congregação da Índia Oriental dos Eremitas de N. P. S. Agostino", in: António da Silva Rego, *Documentação para a História das Missões do Padroado Portugués do Oriente*, vol. XI, Lisbon 1995, pp. 95-833. The quotations referred to, are to be found on pp. 128-129.

36 On these prioresses, see the chronicle mentioned earlier: P. Manoel da Ave María, "Manual Eremítico ...", p. 129.

37 See, *Documentos remettidos da Índia ou Livros das Monções* ..., vol III, Lisbon 1885, pp. 330-331.

38 See, VATICAN ARCHIVES, *Segr. Brev. Registri*, vol. 585, fol. 341-346.

39 See, *Documentos remettidos da Índia ou Livros das Monções* ..., vol IV, Lisbon 1893, p. 24.

40 *Ibid.*, pp. 101-102.

41 See, "Libro de actas del convento de Ntra. Sra. de Gracia de Goa (India) (1604-1637)", *Analecta Augustiniana* 61 (1998) 171-282, esp. pp. 252-253; "Libro de actas del Colegio del Popolo de Goa (India) (1614-1636)", *Analecta Augustiniana* 62 (1999) 125-178, esp. pp. 142, 158, 171 & 175.

42 See, Casimiro Christovão de Nazareth, *Mitras Lusitanas no Oriente*, 2nd ed., Lisbon 1894, p. 99.

43 "Vera relazione del portentoso miraculo (che) segui nelle Indie Orientali di un Crocifisso che stava nel choro dell'Osservantissimo Monasterio di Monache di S. Monica di Goa dell'Ordine dell'Eremiti di S. Agostino all'8 Febbraro 1636 approvato nella forma del Sacro Concilio di Trento." In: *Analecta Augustiniana* 5 (1913-14) 66, 111-114.

44 See, A. da Silva Rego, *Documentação para a Historia das missões do Padroado Portugués do Oriente*, vo. XI, pp. 128-141.

45 This was Mother María de la Visitación, native of Colombo and daughter of king Jaffnapatão and Doña Clara de Austria; she made her profession in 1637 and died as prioress of the convent in 1682.

46 This detail is given by Casimiro Christovão de Nazareth, *Mitras Lusitanas no Oriente*, 2nd ed., p. 99; in note 45 the author offers an ample review of the historiography of this convent.

Deline of the Portuguese Naval Power : AStudy based on Portuguese documents.

13

INDIA OR BRAZIL? PRIORITY FOR IMPERIAL SURVIVAL IN THE WARS OF THE RESTAURAÇÃO

George D. Winius

For all the interest shown in the discovery and foundation of Portugal's Asian empire, far fewer writers have preoccupied themselves with its decline since the days of Diogo do Couto and the Venerable Brother Pedro de Basto over 300 years ago. Couto, the splendid curmudgeon whom Philip II (I of Portugal) appointed to continue João de Barros' unfinished *Décadas da Asia*, and Basto, a saintly Jesuit clairvoyant, typified the thinking of contemporaries when they cried out that Portuguese India had become so corrupt that God had seen fit to scourge it with the heretic Dutch, just as He had used the Babylonians to mortify the Children of Israel. This explanation occurred spontaneously to contemporaries steeped in the Old Testament; by the 1640's, even King João IV alluded to such divine chastisement in letters to his viceroys. And council minutes are full of phrases like 'for so God punishes our sins'

To the XXI century, the question of why the Portuguese failed to retain their Asian empire has ceased to hold much meaning. Rather than speculating why the empire fell, modern historians marvel that it held together so long in the face of native enemies and, once they arrived, of Dutch and English rivals. For there may never have been more than 10,000 native-born Portuguese in all the Orient at any one time.[1]

Roughly speaking, there were two distinct periods of Portuguese decline in Asia from the closing years of the XVI century to the middle years of the XVII. Through the time of the Spanish 'Captivity' (1580-1640) until the *Restauração* of December 1640, the Portuguese sustained heavy naval losses and were virtually deprived of access to the Malay archipelago. They also lost Ormuz, the stopper to the Gulf of Aden, and with it their monopoly on trade with Persia. But during this era, the empire had not yet suffered a fatal blow. Its core of armament and personnel had always been the chain of fortresses in India from Diu to Ceylon and these were still intact. While the Dutch of the VOC, or Dutch East India Company, had already landed in Ceylon two years before, they had got almost nowhere.

In the quarter century after the *Restauração,* the Asian empire virtually collapsed. By 1661, almost nothing remained in India save Goa, Diu, and Damão, and in the rest of the empire, only Timor and Macau. During this era, the Portuguese in Asia waged a desperate fight for survival that centered about the island of Ceylon, whose gems, valuable trained elephants, and status as sole producer of first quality cinnamon, made it the richest possession of Portugal's purely Indian empire. If Portugal could have held on there, it would have survived as an important power in India. It took the Dutch of the VOC twenty years to conquer Portuguese Ceylon and it was only after this conquest that the victorious Dutch could move on to assault and carry the Portuguese Malabar strongholds[2].

There were times in the battle for Ceylon when the Hollanders were on the run and when a few ships filled with Portuguese reinforcements might have convinced them that their invasion had been a failure. The Portuguese, after all, had already beaten off Dutch assaults on other colonial possessions, namely Mozambique, Macau, and Timor, and at a later time they had ejected the Dutch from Luanda and Pernambuco. But in Ceylon, the timely reinforcements never arrived. Anyone who has followed the course of the agonizing struggle for this island is bound to wonder why this was, for it often seems as if the destiny of empire could have been changed by the timely advent of a thousand sturdy troops from Beira or the Ribatejo.

The answer, or a substantial part of it, is suggested by some stray documents that exist only in copy from the councils of king Dom João IV that concern abortive truce negotiations with the Dutch in 1648. These papers show that when Portugal had to fight three simultaneous wars, one on its border with Spain, one in Brazil, and one in Ceylon, its government was forced to recognize that their limited resources could only be stretched, at the most, two ways. Only two councillors of D.João ever brought themselves to see the equation clearly enough to propose it directly, but from the king's own words and the actions of his Ultramarine Council, one can see that the royal government was forced to let India go when the war for Brazil reached its climactic stages.

Because the situation in which India's fate was decided grew out of the exceedingly complex wars and diplomacy of the *Restauração*, it is necessary to approach it through a review of that frantic epoch. Crises were the order of the day, and one would be tempted to use the metaphor of D.João hardly knowing which leak in the dyke to plug first with his finger-if, of course, the king had been of the nationality that was oppressing him.

One feels almost sorry for the Portuguese when they rose up so nobly against sixty years of Spanish oppression in December of 1640 and then failed to settle their differences with the Dutch which, after all, had only arisen because of their connection with Spain. If Tristão de Mendonça Furtado, the new Portuguese ambassador to their High Mightinesses of the States-General in The Hague was greeted with handshakes, alcohol, and noisy crowds, he still found that the imperial problem was all but unsolvable. For it seems that the Dutchmen, whenever they had swung at the Spanish empire overseas, had missed and hit their Portuguese captives. When Philip II of Spain had excluded the Dutch merchants from Lisbon who had come there to freight Asian goods on the final leg to Antwerp and other ports in the north of Europe, these had formed several India companies-in 1602 amalgamated into one United East India Company, or VOC-that sailed directly to the Far East. Soon the VOC had excluded the Portuguese from the Malay archipelago, and in 1636 invaded Ceylon. In the Atlantic, Philip embargoed growing Dutch participation in the Brazilian sugar industry. Although his prohibitions were not altogether effective, Portuguese merchants who had migrated to Antwerp and Amsterdam, nearly all of Sephardic origin, managed to conduct a good deal of trade in sugar and tobacco via their relatives and commercial contacts in Brazil. These clandestine, if peaceful, dealings had changed abruptly in 1621, upon the foundation of the *West-Indische Compagnie* (WIC), a warlike corporation inspired by the older VOC but chartered for the Atlantic region. It began by hijacking both Spanish and Portuguese vessels and convoys en route to and from the Iberian peninsula and the New World, but it soon developed territorial ambitions and attacked Pernambuco. By the time of the *Restauração,* it had taken over about half of Brazil's plantation coastline.

Naturally, their High Mightinesses of the States General were less than overjoyed when Mendonça Furtado proposed that Dutch conquests at Portuguese expense be given or sold back and invoked 'first possession' as a legal basis. Astounded, the Dutch invoked the 'right of conquest' instead. To complicate and worsen matters further still, the Portuguese were meanwhile frantically trying to fortify their frontiers with Spain for the invasions sure to come as soon as the Spaniards could gather enough of their troops presently engaged in putting down a revolt in Catalonia. This played into the negotiations when it became obvious that Mendonça Furtado had also come hat-in-hand to solicit aid from the same body to reinforce Portuguese armies awaiting the overland assaults.

Under the circumstances, the poor Portuguese diplomat was lucky to negotiate any kind of agreement at all. The VOC and WIC were not on any leash from the States-General; aside from periodic renewal of their charters and some informal pressures from relatives or friends who served in the two directorates, the companies were almost wholly independent and did not wish any hobbling of their expansionist ambitions. They were only willing to listen to some extent to arguments affecting the national welfare. In this case, the Prince of Orange and his party, more focused on European politics than the companies, saw a certain advantage in a Portuguese front as a useful impediment to Spain in the Thirty Years War. After much argument, the Orangist arguments prevailed in the States-General and Mendonça Furtado came home in June 1641 with a ten-year truce signed by the Dutch that at least seemed to protect the Portuguese possessions from further attacks during that period. No one in Lisbon was very happy with the treaty because it provided far less help than was wanted and because it left the whole question of the colonies in abeyance during a cease-fire. But it appears that no one perceived the danger in the treaty, either, namely that King D.João IV, chronically unable to make up his mind about most anything, would dawdle fatally before ratifying it, or that the virtually independent companies would do everything possible to keep from observing it.

In fact D.João waited six months before affixing his signature. According to its provisions, the treaty was to go into effect as soon as the ratified copy arrived in The Hague, but not until six months afterwards in Brazil and one year in Asia. And it was silent on the subject of automatic restitution of any territories captured even after those dates. If the king was confused over the possible consequences, the companies were acutely aware of the benefits to them of any delays. Abetted by D.João's hesitation, they set out to capture everything Portuguese in sight before the deadline. And when they were not satisfied with their gains, they merely ignored the cease-fire and continued hostilities. Wrote the Portuguese ambassador: 'I would rather be a slave in Algiers than an emissary to Holland, where there is neither goodfaith, nor justice, nor truth[3]'

The Portuguese directed their anger at the States-General, but as already suggested, they did not realize that this body had already given away too much of its sovereignty to the two India companies to exact much obedience from them. Hence it was that the chartered companies' aggression and the diplomatic protests continued until the Portuguese had lost all confidence in Dutch promises. Finally, in 1644, the truce did go into effect, but not until both companies had achieved the preponderance of their objectives and chose to defy the States-General no longer. By then the Dutch held not only the best parts of Ceylon and Brazil, but had wrested the choice slaving station of Luanda from the Portuguese as well.

The high command in Lisbon considered Portugal powerless to resist the Dutch onslaught abroad while dealing with the Spanish at home. If Portugal had so far beaten back Spanish assaults in the Alentejo, it was no secret that the margin of victory had been narrow: Lusitanian mistakes in supply and tactic had been offset only by Spanish blunders. Now that the colonial theatre was quiet, even though at great price, everybody wanted to keep it that way in the interests of securing the home front against Spain.

That is, everybody except the Brazilian colonists, whose revolt in 1645 against the WIC is well known. By then the India companies, who like all predators who have just brought down a great prey, wished to nourish themselves on it and recover their strength. The Dutch demanded restitution of King D.João IV, who professed innocence and even chided the colonists for their disobedience—with the predictable result that the Dutch did not believe and the colonists resented and ignored him. D.João, if he appeared spineless, was in a dreadful quandry. Not to aid the Brazilian colonists revolting in his name would almost certainly result in the loss of Brazilian territory still Portuguese and with it the vital sugar revenues needed for pursuit of the peninsular war[4]. But not to placate the Dutch might mean that the VOC might break the Asian truce with impunity[5]. For once D.João's indecision worked in his favor.

In 1643 he had found the perfect diplomat for his embassy to The Hague in Francisco de Sousa Coutinho, a nobleman part-Dutch himself who understood the Netherlanders and appeared to be liked by them. It was this man's inspired and tireless negotiations that convinced the States-General time after time

India or Brazil? Priority for Imperial Survival

that the king was working to bring about peace in Brazil and kept them from supporting the WIC with the drastic military action it threatened. Sousa Coutinho was still conciliating the Dutch two years after his monarch had begun sending clandestine aid to the insurgents.

The situation finally came to a head in 1648. First of all, it was thought certain that the treaties at Münster and Osnabrück ending the Thirty Years War would release hordes of Spaniards for fresh assaults on Portugal[6]. Then prospects in Brazil and the Atlantic were highly uncertain. Although the Portuguese had already sent a fleet under the Conde de Vila-Pouca to relieve Brazil and raised a separate one under Salvador de Sá to attempt recapture of Luanda, the Dutch were known to have sent across a large fleet of their own under Admiral Witte de With. For all the Portuguese knew, the Dutch would triumph with forces already in action, and if not with those, then surely with massive new expeditions sent out by the States-General. News of Salvador de Sá's recapture of Luanda did not reach Lisbon until November 25, and even then, some statesmen considered it more a lucky break than a sign that the tide was turning. Hence it was that with victory doubtful in every quarter, the Portuguese felt themselves on the precipice of disaster and willing to consider almost any conditions for peace the Dutch might propose.

On July 21, in The Netherlands, Ambassador Sousa Coutinho negotiated a provisional treaty based upon Dutch demands and forwarded it to Portugal. The States-General, who knew how desperate the Portuguese were, called for heavy reparations in cash and kind over a twenty-year period. But more than this, they required that the Portuguese cede Brazil from the Maranhão to Rio Real and all of Angola and São Tomé.[7]

The question was too important for the king to resolve unilaterally, involving as it did alienation of national territory. D.João had been crowned by his subjects; he was insecure and vascillating by nature, anyway. So he submitted the treaty for the advice of all his councils, high and low. One might gather that D.João himself was in favor of the treaty as it stood, but after much deliberation, his councillors voted overwhelmingly to reject it. As the parecer, or written opinion, of *Procurador da Fazenda* Dr.Paulo Fernandes de Monteiro showed, the councillors were fully aware of the great risks of not coming to terms.'If the peace is accepted, the crown will retain Bahia, Rio de Janeiro, Maranhão, India and the other places, but if it is not accepted, they will not only remain in peril, but so far as one can humanly gather, they will all be lost'. Nonetheless, he felt that without Angola to supply slaves for the part of Brazil still to remain Portuguese, "it would be impossible to sustain" and its revenues would dwindle. Then, Monteiro said, a Portugal without customs receipts from abroad could not face Spain. Moreover, he and the other councillors made it clear they did not trust the Dutch. And, above all, the crown would lose so much prestige by alientating territory and would so offend God by delivering Catholics to the heretic Dutch that the consequences might well be worse than a losing battle[8]. The only suggestion Monteiro, the Count of Odemira, and the other councillors could make was that the crown should offer once more to buy Angola back. This proposal had been made many times before and was almost certain to be rejected again[9].

Father António Vieira, D. Joáo's influential Jesuit confessor, took violent exception in his famous Papel Forte, as his rebuttal to Monteiro's opinion was called, because as he pointed out, Portugal could barely sustain one war, let alone three. But all his logic did not budge the majority. D. João was clearly as upset as Father Vieira by their stand. In a decree of December 24, 1648, he wrote: 'In my conformity with the opinion of the council(s), and because I consider the break with Holland to be certain in this case, I order you that you tell me by what means the kingdom can be defended against two so powerful enemies, it being so exhausted of personnel and capital that it has not even been possible, after examining every means, to find the wherewithal to pay 16,000 infantry-men and 4,000 cavalry......that are necessary to defend us against the King of Castile, whose power can only become greater now than it was before.' And he concludes: 'If this predicament necessitates withdrawing revenue from the customs houses, of which the greatest part must come from our territories overseas (*conquistas*), principally from India, then how will it be possible to reinforce [India] hereafter, just as it has not been reinforced to any considerable extent in years past?'[10] D. João had already notified Viceroy Felipe Mascarenhas at Goa on the previous April 3 that the outfitting of Vila-Pouca's expedition had precluded aid to India and asked him to be patient[11].

On March 11, 1649, D. João addressed a second query to his councils of State, War, and Finance, informing them that he had withheld making any decisions until he could learn whether the Dutch might accept the Portuguese counter-proposals. But they had instead all but broken off diplomacy with Portugal when they had heard of Salvador de Sá's recapture of Luanda. Now that war was assured, the king circulated his earlier decree and repeated his query as to how the exhausted Portugal could wage war against two so powerful enemies[12].

The only surviving replies are from the papers of the Council of War, for some reason not issued until September. Only two councillors could agree among themselves; the rest reflected varying degrees of timidity or bellicosity. But the Count of Serem and D. João da Costa proposed a solution that clearly diagnosed what the solution would have to be. 'To the Count of Serem and D. João da Costa,' the document read, 'it seems that by the greatest efforts the Kingdom might make, it cannot give Your Majesty the things necessary to defend itself at one time against both Castile and Holland; and thus it necessarily behooves Your Majesty to try to make peace; it perhaps being possible to attain this through means of purchase, which is the most fitting for [Your Majesty's] reputation and [the peace's] security. If this should be totally unacceptable, we should give up in Asia as much as we need to, in order to leave us free in Brazil, because whenever we are neighbors, the peace will never be too secure, nor our spices too valuable; besides which, Asia, by its distance and size is more difficult and costly and less useful to conserve[13].

No such deal over India was ever actually negotiated, but the king and his councils in effect voted for this solution by sending their men and supplies to Brazil and Angola and not to India. Between 1643, when the Ultramarine Council first met, and 1656, when Ceylon fell, there were 87 *consultas* dealing with the provision of relief expeditions to Brazil and only 19 to India[14]. It might be said that a great deal of the subsequent history of the two continents was framed by that decision.

References:

1. António Baião (ed.), *História da Expansão Portuguesa no Mundo*, Lisbon,1939, II, p. 89 (in Chapter by A.Botelho da Costa Veiga). Also, Charles Ralph Boxer, *Four Centuries of Portuguese Expansion, 1415-1825; A Succinct Survey*, Witwatersrand, 1965, pp. 19-20.
2. See K.W.Goonewardena, *The Foundation of Dutch Power in Ceylon, 1638-1658*, Amsterdam, 1958.
3. Quoted in Edgar Prestage, *The Diplomatic Relations of Portugal*, Watford, 1925, p.94.
4. Charles Ralph Boxer, *Salvador de Sá and the Struggle for Brazil and Angola*, London, 1952, pp. 213-214.
5. *Documentos Remetidos da India*, Arquivo Nacional da Torre do Tombo, Lisbon, fl. 270 & 352 (a duplicate). See also Gouverneur-General Johan Maetsuyker's reply to the Portuguese emissary, Padre Gonçalo de São Joseph, printed in W.van Goor, *De opkomst van het Nederlandsch Gezag over Ceilon*, Leiden, 1895, pp. 93-94.
6. Decree of King D.João IV to his council, Biblioteca Nacional de Lisboa, F.G. 1570, fl.143.
7. Prestage, Diplomatic Relations, 203-204.
8. The opinion of Monteiro regarding the proposed truce is in the afore-mentioned F.G. 1570, fls.173-174.
9. More fully voiced in Monteiro's parecer in idem, fl.123.
10. F.G.1570, fl.143.
11. *Documentos Remetidos da India*, Vol.58. fl.37.
12. F.G.1570, fls.144-145.
13. Papers of the *Conselho da Guerra*, Arquivo Nacional da Torre do Tombo, Lisbon, maço 9.
14. From a tabulation by title in the *Consultas Mixtas*, Arquivo Histórico Ultramarino, Codices 13-18.

14
A BRAZILIAN COMMERCIAL PRESENCE BEYOND THE CAPE OF GOOD HOPE, 16TH -19TH CENTURIES

A.J.R.Russell-Wood

European overseas empires (the so called "first" empires) share two historiographical characteristics. The first is bifurcation. Rarely do scholars of British mainland north America also study the British in India, nor do scholars of France's New World colonies(New France, the Antilles, Guyane) discuss the French presence in West Africa, in the Indian Ocean, or on the Indian subcontinent. There is a divide in the historiography on the Dutch commercial empire between the activities of the East and West India Companies. The Portuguese empire is no exception to these tendencies. With few exceptions, of which the most distinguished are Charles Boxer and Vitorino Magalhães Godinho, historiography on Portugal overseas is constrained territorially(Portuguese in India, in Ceylon, in Angola, in Brazil, in Thailand) or oceanically (The Atlantic; the Indian Ocean). But, already in a memorandum of 1735-36, Dom Luis da Cunha advocated that Dom João V should assume the title of emperor and reside in Rio de Janeiro[1]. He saw this as a critical step toward an integrated global Portuguese commercial empire with European, American, African and Asian components, and with an articulated commercial network of supply and demand involving the Atlantic Ocean, Arabian Sea, Indian Ocean, and seas of East Asia.

The historiography of the Portuguese empire reflects a second shared characteristic: namely a perspective which takes the metropolis as the point of reference. This reflects available documentation, linguistic shortcomings (*e.g.* knowledge of Persian, Arabic, Marathi, Tamil, Arabic Malayalam, *inter alia*) but also a mind-set of seeing colonies in a mercantilist and administrative framework with the metropolis at the centre and colonies on the periphery. In the case of Brazil, commercial history is often couched in the context of continental Portugal and/or where appropriate of Africa. Brazilian commercial initiatives and practices are invariably seen within the context of the Atlantic and of regions bordering the Atlantic.

My purpose is, first, to situate my discussion in the context of a history which will embrace both hemispheres of the Portuguese empire and examine a connection between them. Secondly, in an exercise in compensatory history, to consider this empire other than in the context of the metropolis. To see overseas history through a metropolitan prism has been to downplay intercolonial relations in general, and especially when a metropolitan component is absent. Thirdly, I shall be looking at Brazil other than in an Atlantic context. Fourthly, I shall be running literally against the current, in this case a historiography which has looked at the impact of Asia on Portugal, and to a modest degree on Brazil especially as regards the introduction of flora, possible oriental influence on painting in churches of colonial Bahia, on architecture, and the ill-fated introduction of some 300 Chinese and cuttings of tea plants into Rio de Janeiro in the early nineteenth century. In this historiography, Brazilian ports are reduced to mere way stations for outward and homeward-bound Indiamen. While it is undeniable that Indiamen homeward- bound (*torna-viagem*) from the 1660s through to the end of the eighteenth century were more likely to call at Brazilian ports than outward-bound, I hope to show that Brazilian ports, notably Salvador, and Brazilians played a proactive role and initiated trade to the Indian Ocean and that there was a Brazilian presence beyond the Cape of Good Hope[2].

The term *Estado da India* (lit: "State of India") refers to the web of trading posts, forts, settlements, and cities extending from Mozambique east to Nagasaki and the Moluccas, and which, with varying degrees of effectiveness, as of 1530 came under the jurisdiction of a viceroy or governor resident in Goa. Brazil was a Portuguese colony from 1500 until 1822 whose governor- general or viceroy resided in Salvador until 1763 and thereafter in Rio de Janeiro. Portuguese holdings in east and west were attacked by Europeans and, in the case of the *Estado da India*, by non-Europeans. The shift in emphasis from India to Brazil started in the mid seventeenth century and its consummation was noted by a Franciscan friar in Salvador in 1702[3]. Moreover, current and wind systems in the south Atlantic privileged Brazilian port cities with the opportunity to extend maritime links beyond the Atlantic[4]. In this regard, no other European colony in the Americas could compete with the port cities of Brazil.

The historiography has focussed on Brazilian commerce within the confines of the Atlantic, notably coastal trade, and oceanic trade to Portugal, the Azores and Madeira, West and Central Africa, and São Tomé and Principe. Ambrosio Fernandes Brandão, to whom is attributed the *Diálogos das Grandezas do Brasil*, stated that, from a Brazilian perspective, commerce with Angola was more important than that to the metropolis. One exception which has received scholarly attention were Brazilian ports, primarily Salvador, as waystations (*escalas*) for vessels of the India run (*carreira da India*)[5]. As such they were attractive to captains, officers, crews and passengers returning from India to Portugal who saw such landfalls as an opportunity to sell or barter oriental commodities for Brazilian sugar, tobacco, gold and other items. Such transactions were predominantly illegal and clandestine. In short, in the context of the *carreira da India* Brazilian ports were seen as ports for the discharge rather than the loading of goods and for clandestine rather than legal trade. Yet there is ample evidence to provide a corrective to this view and make Brazilian ports active participants in multi-oceanic trade.

This participation by Brazilian ports, essentially Salvador, to a lesser degree Rio de Janeiro, and others sporadically, took various forms. Let us examine four configurations which illustrate the degree to which Brazilians took advantage of the *carreira da India* actively to promote home grown products in Asian markets.

i) Bahian participation in legal commerce beyond the Atlantic was initially predominantly through the export to Lisbon of Brazilian products and their transshipment to vessels outward-bound to India. Tobacco, but only of the best quality, was the product most sought after in Asia. This reached its destination by two routes: transshipment in Lisbon and by direct passage from Salvador to Goa. Bahia was the major area of cultivation. Probably tobacco was being cultivated in Bahia in the 1570s. By the 1620s it was being exported regularly to Lisbon, where it was processed, and thence to India. Philip III established a monopoly on the sale of tobacco in Goa in 1624 and in Lisbon probably between 1624 and the early 1630s. These were highly lucrative. A *Junta da Administração do Tabaco* in Lisbon was created in 1674. In 1680 a *Junta da Administração do Estanco Real do Tabaco da India* was established in Goa to oversee all matters, notably fiscal, pertaining to tobacco. In Goa and neighbouring Bardes and Salsete the tobacco contract was "'farmed out" to local businessmen with triennial leases from the 1620s until the nineteenth century. This contract was highly contested. During the later seventeenth century, Bahian tobacco was the most profitable commodity of the export trade from Lisbon to Asia. After Bombay was ceded (1665) to England, the English bought tobacco in Lisbon for sale in India. Bahian tobacco was also transported to Macao, where an *Estanco do Tabaco* was established. This was despite efforts by the *Estanco* in Goa to destroy such trade by imposing exorbitant prices. From Macao, there was dispersal to China under the Qing (Manchu) dynasty. In China there was a preference for leaves (*folha aberta*) rather than rolls (*rolos*) of tobacco[6].

ii) During the latter part of the seventeenth century, and increasingly in the eighteenth century, homeward-bound Indiamen, put into Salvador. Royal decrees in 1672 and 1692 legalized, and even encouraged, stops in Salvador. A royal resolution of 1734 and a royal decree (*alvará*) of 1783 authorized the sale in Salvador of goods brought from Asia on payment of appropriate customs dues [7]. Goods of Asian provenance were sold in Salvador or transshipped for passage to the Costa da Mina and Angola in exchange for slaves or to Rio de la Plata in exchange for Spanish silver. Concurrently, but less frequently, outward-bound Indiamen from Lisbon also put into Salvador legally where they loaded tobacco (powder and leaf), sugar, cereals, *cachaça*, hides, manioc meal, food, woods, brazilwood, and gold bars. Goa was the primary destination although some goods were sent on to Macao, and Celsa Pinto has noted that Luso-Brazilian traders (Lisbon to Madras/Calcutta with stops outward-bound in Pernambuco/ Salvador/Rio de Janeiro were major suppliers of bullion to Coromandel and Bengal between 1798 and 1820[8]. This represented a new development: Salvador remained as a waystation, but Brazilian products were now being exported directly to Goa, albeit on vessels whose voyage originated in Lisbon. There was a further development before the century's close. The Portuguese monopoly on Brazilian tobacco was abolished in 1775, inaugurating a new era in direct trade between Brazil and India. During the 1760s and thereafter there was an increase in private trade to Goa of Bahian tobacco, especially of leaf. In the 1770s and 1780s especially, there are numerous references to consignments of tobacco in cords, powder, and leaf being loaded at Salvador on vessels from Lisbon whose destination was Goa. Sometimes the supply was inadequate, or deterioration leading to shortages, or some vessels put into Mozambique on the way to Goa. These vessels often carried troops to India. The *Mesa de Inspeção* in Salvador issued orders (*ofícios*) for loading tobacco on such vessels. In addition, governors in Salvador—especially the Marquis of Valença and Dom Rodrigo de Meneses—were kept busy by incessant requests from the secretary of state in Queluz to arrange for cargoes of tobacco leaves whose purchase and freight charges were met by the royal treasury and who instructed governors to act forcefully to diminish contraband. Detailed accounting of this trade was of great interest to metropolitan authorities. Dom Rodrigo de Meneses complied memoranda keeping Martinho de Melo e

Castro at Queluz abreast of details on exports of tobacco from Salvador to India. Governors in Salvador and in Goa were exhorted by the king to take every measure to avoid fraud and abuse, and the governor in Salvador had a special responsibility to control the quality of tobacco exported to India and to ensure this was adequately packaged[9].

iii) In the second half of the eighteenth century, the *carreira da India* assumed yet another configuration. This was direct trade between Brazil and Asia. This was an extraordinary saga involving the crown's senior representatives in Salvador and in Goa, metropolitan administrative and regulatory institutions, and merchants in Portugal, Brazil, and the *Estado da India*. In the 1690s, the merchant community in Salvador had taken the lead in placing pressure on the governor-general. The merchants pointed out that it was cheaper to send troops from Brazil to the *Estado da India* than from Portugal, and pledged that they would pay for vessels and the costs of clothing for soldiers and their upkeep if free trade were authorized between Brazil and the *Estado da India*. In 1699 the governor-general forwarded to Lisbon a proposal advocating that direct commerce be authorized between Salvador, Pernambuco and Rio de Janeiro in Brazil, to Mozambique, Goa and other ports of the *Estado da India*. The crown invited commentary and received conflicting views. The viceroy opined that Brazilian goods would find no market in Mozambique and such direct trade would have an adverse impact on India. Given such opposition, which doubtless found support from the merchant community in Lisbon which likewise saw its interests threatened, it came as no surprise that the Brazilian proposal was rejected in February 1700 by the *Junta de Tabaco*, which preferred that all trade to India be routed through Lisbon as previously, and by the *Casa da India* which dismissed commodities proposed by the Brazilian merchants for export to India—sugar, tobacco, rum, jacaranda wood, and Brazilian rosewood—as redundant or inappropriate. On the other hand, the notion of direct private trade from Brazil and even Angola to India was warmly received in Goa where it was felt this would breathe new life into the economy, increase the population, and provide customs dues. The king was opposed to having direct trade from Brazil to Mozambique but favored direct Brazil-India trade[10]. The merchants of Salvador did not desist. As the eighteenth century progressed, they developed into a community, their numbers grew, and they gained in terms of political power. That a Pombaline inititiave to create a trading company in Salvador was not implemented was attributable to their vociferous opposition. In other Brazilian ports there came into being by mid-eighteenth-century merchant communities whose members engaged in coastal, oceanic and multioceanic trade. In the second half of the century merchants of Rio de Janeiro especially had the financial resources and capital accumulation such as to be independent of metropolitan financial houses[11].

This direct trade between Brazilian ports and Asia took on two new forms in the eighteenth century. One took the form of vessels sailing from Asia to Brazil but returning to Asia instead of continuing on to Portugal. Their cargoes were either sold in Salvador or transshipped for transportation to Portugal or Africa. Products originating in Portugal and which had been unloaded in Salvador were transshipped onto vessels returning to Asia whose cargoes also included products of Brazil: sausages, cheese, marmalade, ginger and sugar. The end of the Portuguese *exclusif* on tobacco also led to greater private trade in this commodity from Brazilian ports to Goa, although the Indian historian Celsa Pinto notes that vessels leaving Salvador bound for Goa, made themselves liable to search and inspection in Rio de Janeiro before being authorized to resume the voyage to Goa [12]. But it must be emphasized that the vessels did not go beyond Salvador as their port of call in the Atlantic[13]. After 1808, direct trade of tobacco from Brazilian ports to Macao without stopping in Goa was authorized. Salvador thus took on a new role sanctioned by the crown: in addition to being the port of arrival and departure for vessels from Portugal, and for vessels engaged directly in the Bahia-Africa-Bahia trade, and as a port in the triangular trade Europe-Africa-Brazil, Salvador also became part of the commercial diaspora Asia-Brazil-Africa(Luanda, Benguela)-

Brazil-Asia. This situation changed with the transfer of the Portuguese court from Lisbon to Rio de Janeiro. In 1808 direct trade was authorized between Brazilian ports and India and Macao. Brazilian merchants, especially those of Rio de Janeiro, took advantage of this opportunity. The Chinese demand for Brazilian tobacco led Brazilian vessels to omit Goa as a waystation and instead to travel directly from Rio de Janeiro to Macao. Brazilian merchants in Asian waters were entering into direct competition not only with Portuguese merchants based in Lisbon but also with the British East India Company

Overlapping with this development was direct trade from Brazilian ports to the *Estado da India*. A quintessential component of such commerce were vessels and brief reference may be made to marine construction in Brazil. Bahian timbers were transported to Portugal for shipbuilding in the arsenal of Lisbon. In the seventeenth century, Dom João 1V promoted naval construction in Bahia, as too did his name sake in the eighteenth century. Clearly, there were available in Salvador qualified shiprights, labour, and suitable timber for shipbuilding. Galleons were built in Salvador in the 1650s, at least one of them of considerable size. During his viceroyalty (1735-49), the Count of Galveas was instructed to build on the *ribeira* of Salvador a *nau* with 60 artillery pieces for the *carreira da India*. This was to be at the cost of the royal treasury with funds from the *donativo real* and the fifths on gold production in Bahia. In February 1738 Galveas ordered the *provedor mor* of the treasury in Bahia to tell the master shipright Manuel de Araujo to start work. In 1738 he reported to the king about purchase of the wood for 60,000 *cruzados* and that the keel had been laid[14]. The Brazilian historian Amaral Lapa calculates that, in the period 1665-1822, at least 30 ocean-going vessels were built in Bahian shipyards, and opines that this production exceeded that of any other part of the Portuguese empire. Of these, at least 14 saw service on routes to Asia. Brazilian products, notably tobacco in the case of Salvador, were exported from Brazilian ports in Brazilian bottoms directly to Asia[15].

iv) Mozambique island provides the best example of a Brazilian commercial presence beyond the Atlantic. In the sixteenth and seventeenth centuries the Portuguese had dominated the city states of the Swahili coast, but 1698 signalled the end of an era with the Omani capture of Mombaça. Although briefly (1728-9), the Portuguese regained control of Mombaça, Mozambique was the key port of Portuguese East Africa. Sixteenth-century homeward-bound east Indiamen had carried slaves from East Africa to Salvador, but this was sporadic and the numbers few, in part because they were held in low regard in Brazil. Indeed, at that time probably larger numbers of slaves were carried from Mozambique by outward-bound Portuguese *naus* across the Arabian Sea to India. In the seventeenth- century the Dutch occupation of Mouri(1612), São Jorge da Mina (1638), Angola and Benguela (1641-48) provided a brief stimulus to trade in slaves from Mozambique and Quelimane to Rio de Janeiro, but crown policy saw Angola as the prime supplier for Brazil. This, and efforts by powerful pressure groups opposed to East African sources for slaves, halted further debate, although slaves from east Africa sporadically continued to be transported to Brazilian ports. In the eighteenth century, the potential of East Africa as a source of slaves was raised again but the combination of greater time and greater cost than from Central Africa, together with the poor reputation in which East African slaves were held in Brazil, led to the matter being shelved[16]. The situation changed in 1752 when Mozambique gained administrative autonomy and was no longer subordinate to the viceroy/ governor-general in Goa. A key component of Pombaline economic policy was enhancement of agricultural production in Brazil. This demanded more slaves, and creation of chartered companies for the Maranhão, Pará, Pernambuco and Paraiba. Pombal saw a Mozambique-Brazil slave trade as an instrument to carry more slaves to Brazil, to revitalize a moribund Mozambican economy, and integrate the two spheres of Portuguese activity. Abolition(19 September 1761) of slavery in Portugal and the Azores reinforced Brazil as the focus of the slave trade. Pombal favoured metropolitan merchants. A 1765 royal alvara permitted free trade from Lisbon to Asia. Portuguese merchants were authorized to send vessels and their cargoes to Mozambique island and adjacent mainland (*Terra firme*) ports, load slaves, and transport these to Brazil. In 1769 Brazilian vessels were authorized to trade freely in the ports of Mozambique, although during the previous decade vessels from Brazil had sporadically travelled to Mozambique. But a royal alvará of 1772 forbade Brazilians from entering the Indian Ocean to trade with Mozambique and this remained in effect until 1808 when decrees promulgated by the prince regent authorized Brazilian commercial initiatives beyond the Atlantic [17].

Captains-general in Mozambique played decisive roles in this initiative. During his long tenure (1765-79), Baltasar Manuel Pereira do Lago promoted commerce in slaves and ivory. His enthusiastic endorsement of a monopolistic company and proposals to open the ports of Mozambique to free trade outraged governors in Goa because of the pernicious impact this could have on merchants of Goa, Diu and Damão and on what had hitherto been an exclusive market for goods from India. The viceroy, the Conde da Ega, was vociferous in his protests, because such open trade would have undermined his policies to restore the fortunes of Portuguese India based on a guaranteed closed market. In 1768 King José I killed the idea of a company. This did not deter Pereira do Lago from encouraging the French to carry slaves from Mozambique to Ile de France and Ile de Bourbon, encouraging Portuguese and Brazilian traders to dispatch slaves to the Mascarene islands, and stimulating traders from Salvador and Rio de Janeiro to look to Mozambique as a source of slaves. In the 1790s, the governor-general of Portuguese East Africa, Dom Diogo de Sousa Coutinho, encountered no opposition when he endorsed a direct Mozambique-Brazil trade. Royal approval was granted in 1795. A decree of 1811 extended this to subordinate ports in Portuguese East Africa The transfer of the royal court to Brazil, British abolitionist pressures on Portugal and resulting constraints on the Atlantic trade, and Portuguese recognition (1825) of Brazilian independence, all favoured a shift from West and

Central Africa to East Africa as a source of slaves for Brazil where there was increasing demand for labour on coffee plantations [18].

Salvador, together with Rio de Janeiro, Pernambuco, Maranhão and Pará participated in this slave trade not only from Mozambique island but from Quelimane, the Querimba islands, and Inhambane. Numbers are difficult to ascertain overall. Aurelio Rocha suggests 10,000 slaves transported to Brazil annually between 1780 and 1800, increasing to 15,000 annually after 1800 and growing as Brazilian vessels extended the locations from which they took slaves. Rio de Janeiro was the major player. The shorter passage Mozambique-Rio, greater availability of merchant capital in Rio to invest in the trade, and the stimulant of the move of the royal court to Rio all contributed to *carioca* predominance[19]. But there was a place for Bahian participation. Indeed, in the 1680s a vessel from Salvador had made landfall in Quelimane but could find no market for its cargo and suffered financial losses. A royal order of 11 of February 1700 ordered the governor-general in Salvador, with the full knowledge of the viceroy in Goa, to send a vessel to Mozambique but the king insisted this was not to be regarded as setting a precedent for free trade but rather was to reposition the vessel should it be needed. In 1761 two vessels from Salvador travelled to Mozambique[20]. The revival of the sugar industry in the northeast increased the demand for slaves. Bahia was well positioned to provide sugar and *cachaça*, as well as timbers for ship construction and cordage (*cordame*) for this trade.

A 1773 memorandum refers to Bahian and *carioca* merchants participating in the Mozambican trade and establishing *casas de negócio* in Mozambique. Whereas there are seventeenth century references to Bahians trading to Central Africa and the islands of São Tome and Principe, splitting their time between the Costa da Mina and Salvador, and even constituting a Bahian community on the African mainland, this was the first time that there was actually a Brazilian community resident beyond the Atlantic and within the *Estado da India*. Brazilian vessels travelled to Mozambique with cargoes of sugar, foodstuffs, *cachaça*, timbers for boat construction, and firearms and powder and returned with cargoes of ivory, gold, and slaves of African provenance, and rosewood (*pau-preto*) and textiles from India and Bengal. Despite French opposition, Luso-Brazilian traders also dispatched vessels loaded with slaves from Mozambique to the Mascarenes and even to India with ivory, gold, and cowries[21].

This discussion of commerce has underlined the degree to which the paradigm of a *carreira da India* between Portugal and India, the longest non-stop run in the world before the age of steam, underwent considerable changes in the seventeenth and eighteenth centuries. All concerned a greater Brazilian presence in the trade. Let me summarise these developments: Brazilian ports became more prominent as waystations for vessels outward-bound from Portugal, affording opportunities for Brazilian goods to enter Asian markets; Brazil replaced Portugal as the final destination for some vessels from Asia which then returned to Asia, sometimes with a landfall in Angola; there was direct trade between Brazil and India and Macao; trade was initiated from Brazil to Mozambique as the final destination; and, finally, Mozambique became not only a point of destination but also the point of articulation for Brazilian trade to other ports of southeast Africa, to the Mascarenes, and even to India. This inter-colonial trade was accomplished without dependence on metropolitan capital or on Portuguese vessels. Revenues accruing to the metropolis were primarily of customs and other dues, the crown accepted this reality, and such trade was legal.

The commercial participation of Brazilian ports in trading diasporas has been discussed within the institutional framework of crown-sanctioned commerce. But in all Brazilian ports there was a well developed culture of evasion and local officials condoned or condemned illicit trade depending on the degree to which participants respected their control and authority[22]. This contraband was to destinations inside and outside the Portuguese empire. Brazilian gold and tobacco were major commodities. The very length of the Brazilian coastline, and the presence of navigable rivers reaching inland to mining regions, afforded ample opportunities for the smuggling of bullion from Brazil to

Portugal, to elsewhere in Europe, and especially to England either directly or on the Falmouth Packet from Lisbon, and to Costa da Mina and Central Africa. British vessels touching at Lisbon en route to Asia, loaded contraband American silver and gold. Contraband Brazilian gold and Spanish silver were also carried to India by Portuguese vessels and by French and British vessels touching at Salvador and Rio de Janeiro en route to Asia. As early as the seventeenth century there are indications of contraband tobacco being carried from Brazil to Goa, and these increased in the eighteenth century in Portuguese, French and British vessels[23] If more goods of Asian provenance were sold illegally in Salvador than vice versa, Salvador exported more contraband to Europe than it imported. Salvador was a port which saw the ingress and exit of commodities which should be studied in a global context: bullion, spices, tobacco. Salvador had major *carreiras* to and from Africa and Europe. These tied into broader trading diasporas involving Europe, Africa, North America and the Caribbean and extending beyond the Atlantic to the Arabian Sea, Indian Ocean and the numerous seas of Indonesia and East Asia.

Such commercial links had repercussions which included the impact of Brazilian commodities on mores and diet in the *Estado da India*. Sugar and tobacco were two of the prime exports from Brazil in the colonial period. It was the Jesuit Antonil (Giovanni Antonio Andreoni) who, in 1711, distinguished between them in terms of their impact beyond Brazil. A resident of 35 years in Salvador, he observed: "If sugar has made Brazil known in all the kingdoms and provinces of Europe, tabacco has made Brazil even more highly reputed in the four parts of the world". He referred specifically to the trade to the Indies[24]. Bahian-grown sugar cane provided a commodity which was exported to Europe primarily, but found its way as cargo on vessels bound from Salvador to Africa and Asia. The distribution of Bahian-grown tobacco to Central Africa especially and to Asia, via Lisbon and directly, has been discussed. Processed tobacco can take many forms: leaf, powder, and cords. It can be chewed, smoked, taken as snuff, or applied medicinally.

In powder form, Bahian tobacco was highly regarded in countries of western Europe, as too was leaf for smoking. My focus here is on the impact of Brazilian tobacco on mores in Asia.

By law, tobacco exported to Africa was of lesser quality. Often the leaves were so diseased, damaged and old that Bahian producers developed the technique of brushing the cords with molasses. This facilitated twisting and served as a cohesive. The result was a tobacco with a sweet aroma and taste. An unanticipated bonus was that this cord tobacco proved extraordinarily attractive to prevailing tastes precisely in that market from which Bahians imported the largest number of slaves: the Bight of Benin. In Asia there was a different spectrum of tastes: smoking and the taking of snuff were more common than in Africa, and the Asian consumer demanded high quality tobacco. There is debate as to the date and nature of the introduction of tobacco into India, but in the sixteenth century in the Deccan it was associated with the Portuguese. It provoked discussion by doctors and scholars at the Mughal court. Jahangir forbad its use and Aurangzeb (1659) forbad its cultivation. Imperial orders were ineffectual. It was widely cultivated by Indian farmers. The prime producers for the Goan market were in Balagate, Panani, Talecheri, and Calicut. Consumption was widespread: smoking either in a pipe or as a cheroot was common, but it was available as snuff and in small pieces for chewing. The smoke of a burning tobacco leaf was believed to be an effective remedy against convulsive attacks among children. Tobacco leaves were used externally in the cure of orchitis. A measure of its popularity was that three major vernacular languages of India had words for tobacco: *pan* or *dhunti* (Konkani); *tambacu* (Marathi), and *tambaku* or *surti* (Hindi). It was carried east to Malacca and China. Charles Boxer notes how Jesuits at the imperial court in Beijing stated that no present was more acceptable to the Manchu emperor and his mandarins than snuff from Brazil. In China tobacco was used for allegedly medicinal qualities and and treatment for eye problems. In Japan, its introduction met with official edicts banning its use, but men and women became addicted, smoking the leaf in metal pipes as depicted in namban screens[25]. On the North American continent, Indian peoples also had a liking for Brazilian tobacco which British and French merchants used as a medium for exchange for pelts. The Hudson Bay Company kept an agent in Lisbon to buy Brazilian tobacco for this market. In a 1780 memorandum, the ex-governor of Bahia, Manuel da Cunha Meneses, noted that tobacco found little market within Portugal but "in the three parts of the world where it circulates".

That Brazil was the point of dissemination of plants indigenous to America beyond the American continent is well known. As for dissemination to Europe, Brazil was largely preempted by Spanish America, but there is ample evidence that plants indigenous to Brazil in particul;ar and to the Americas in general were transported by the Portuguese in the sixteenth and seventeenth centuries to West, Central, and East Africa, to India, and to China: these included Indian corn (*milho*), manioc, sweet potatoes, peanuts, cashews, pineapples, and squashes. Manioc was probably introduced into Mozambique from Brazil, and thence spread to the *terra firma*, as too did other Brazilian foodstuffs. In the second half of the eighteenth century vessels from Brazilian ports carried a wide variety of foodstuffs to Mozambique: manioc, corn, sweet potatoes, beans, pumpkins, cashews, goiaba, papaya, pineapples, and vegetables of European origin. This Brazilian contribution to the diet of peoples of Africa, India, and China has been enduring: pineapples and cashews in India; sweet potatoes, corn and peanuts in southern China; and capsicums in India, Sri Lanka and China. But, as is always the case of what the Portuguese refer to as "the *aventura das plantas*" it is difficult to establish primacy, dates and routes for the introduction of plants. One dish in India is still referred to as being from Pernambuco and *feijoada* is served in Goa as well as Brazil[26].

In discussing this Brazilian presence in the *Estado da India*, reference could have been made to Portuguese-born who served as governors or governors-general of Brazil and subsequently as viceroys in Goa, to Brazilian-born magistrates serving on the high court in Goa, or to Brazilian-born Jesuits and others resident in Brazil who travelled to India and were missionaries and even martyrs. But such dignitaries of state and men of the cloth were few in number. Commerce provides a very different story with increasing ties between Brazilian ports and those of the State of India, with Brazilians playing an increasingly proactive role in direct trade between Brazil and Goa and Macao, and with Brazilians taking the opportunity presented by Pombal to trade beyond the Atlantic into the Indian Ocean and to India, probably in a manner not envisaged by the Marquis.

What did this mean in the context of empire? Much of what I have described underlines the shift in importance from the *Estado da India* to Brazil in the later seventeenth and eighteenth centuries. There is the emergence of an increasingly powerful merchant community who exerted political clout and had the assets to make them independent of metropolitan agency houses. The losers were metropolitan merchants who saw the erosion of their bargaining positions. Crown representatives in Brazil were compelled to compromise and even enact the wishes of such merchant groups. Moreover, whereas in the seventeenth century the viceroy in Goa could still defend the interests of Portuguese and other merchants in India and Mozambique, the following century saw erosion in his ability to curb inter-oceanic and inter-colonial trade in which there was a strong Brazilian presence. The Brazilian historian José Jobson de A. Arruda has pointed out the inherent paradox: to stimulate colonial production the metropolis was compelled to loosen restrictions on intercolonial trade with the resulting loss to the metropolis of certain sectors of overseas commerce and customs dues derived from it [27]. Above all there was the erosion in the effectiveness of pursuing a mercantilist policy when faced with increased intercolonial trade and a regulatory system which leaked like a sieve and was unenforceable. The metropolitan "exclusive" no longer existed and the Portuguese crown could count itself fortunate to derive revenues from dues and other taxes. In acordance with classic mercantilist doctrine, the crown imposed monopolies on selected sectors of colonial production, preferred

A Brazilian Commercial Presence Beyond Cape of Good Hope

metropolitan merchants over colonial competitors by granting them exemptions and privileges, and ensured that it was the metropolis which derived maximum benefits from taxes on production, commerce, and transportation. What I have described was indicative of the porosity of a monopolistic and mercantilistic system and its vulnerability to colonist-led challenges. The existence of what has been described as the "country trade",viz intra Asian trade came to have an Atlantic counterpart in the trade between Brazil and Angola without being part of the "triangular trade" and we find that Brazilians were active participants in another form of inter-colonial trade namely between Brazil and East Africa, India, and Macao.

Another dimension was the increasing internationalization of Brazilian port cities. The sometimes xenophobic policies of the Portuguese crown and its intransigence towards trade by Portuguese with non-Portuguese and reluctance to countenance non-Portuguese in Brazil had to yield in the face of reality. Commerce provided the context for Brazilians to come into contact with Europeans (English, French, Dutch), North Americans, and Spanish Americans. There often existed parallel trades: the legal and the illegal, as in the Azores and Madeira, the islands of São Tomé and Principe and ports of Central Africa. Mozambique, in a legally sanctioned and encouraged slave trade to Brazil, was where Brazilians met not only French, Spanish from Cuba and other Spanish American ports, and North American slavers, but here and on the Swahili coast they also came into contact with Muslim merchants and banians from Gujarat[28]. Vessels of the British East India Company introduced goods of European and Indian provenance into Salvador. French East Company vessels also put into Salvador. In 1724 a vessel under the command of captain Legat arrived in Salvador en route to Île de Bourbon and Pondicherry. Less frequent were vessels of the Ostend Company [29]. Salvador and Rio de Janeiro saw many foreign visitors, some on circumnavigations such as Le Gentil de las Barbinais, others such as François Pyrard de Laval in 1610 who took up temporary residence, and still others such as the Frenchman Gabriel Dellon who found himself (1676) accidentally in Salvador en route back to Lisbon from Goa. Brazil was also part of the global diaspora of New Christians and Jews forced out of Portugal. New Christians settled in Brazil and were part of a Jewish diaspora which extended to Portuguese Asia but whose members sometimes moved beyond the confines of the Portuguese empire and established themselves in cities of British India, in Dutch settlements in Indonesia, in cities of Spanish America, and in the Caribbean [30].

If the seventeenth century saw the beginning of the shift in the weight of empire from east to west, from the *Estado da India* to Brazil, the eighteenth century saw a reversal of roles between Portugal and what has been referred to by one commentator as "the jewel of your majesty's crown", namely Brazil. The exile of the Portuguese royal court to Brazil and subsequent residence in Rio de Janeiro in 1808, the declaration that Brazil be accorded the title of Empire in 1815, and the reality that Rio de Janeiro was the most important commercial emporium in the Lusofone world showed how far Brazil had moved from being on the periphery of such an empire in 1500 to being at its center three hundred years later. In 1794 José Joaquim de Azeredo Coutinho, the Brazilian-born bishop of Pernambuco, published an insightful essay on Brazilian commerce, in which he referred to Brazil as "looking towards Africa, with one foot on land and the other in the sea, and with its arms extended, one towards Europe and the other towards Asia". He placed Brazil at the centre of this world [31].

References:

1 *Instruções inéditas de D. Luis da Cunha a Marco António de Azevedo Coutinho.* Edited by Pedro de Azevedo and António Baião (Lisbon: Academia das Ciências de Lisboa, 1930).

2 For a partial lising of vessels calling at Salvador, see José Roberto do Amaral Lapa, *A Bahia e a Carreira da India* (São Paulo: Companhia Editora Nacional, 1968), pp. 327-43.

3 Fr. António do Rosário, *Frutas do Brasil numa Nova, Ascetica Monarchial* (Lisbon: António Pedroso Galrão, 1702) *apud* Diogo Ramada Curto, "As práticas de escrita" in *História da Expansão portuguesa*. Directed by Francisco Bethencourt and Kirti Chaudhuri. 5 volumes (Lisbon: Circulo de Leitores, 1998-99). Vol. 3 (1998), p. 421.

4   Russell-Wood, *The Portuguese Empire, 1415-1808* (Baltimore and London: Johns Hopkins University Press, 1998), pp. 30-37.

5   C.R. Boxer, "The Principal Ports of Call in the "Carreira da India"(16th-18th Centuries)", *Recueils de la Société Jean Bodin*, XXXIII. *Les grandes escales*, 2 ième partie: *Les temps modernes* (Brussels, 1972], pp. 29-65; and "Moçambique Island as a Way-station for Portuguese East-Indiamen", *The Mariner's Mirror*, 48 (1962), pp.3-18.

6   Carl A. Hanson, "Monopoly and Contraband in the Portuguese Tobacco Trade, 1624-1702", *Luso-Brazilian Review*, 19:2 (1982), pp. 149-68; Jean-Baptiste Nardi, "Le commerce du tabac vers l'Inde portugaise du xviie au début du xixe siécle",*Moyen Orient & Océan Indien/Middle East & Indian Ocean*, 6(1989), pp. 165-174; Roberto do Amaral Lapa, "Dimensões do comércio colonial entre o Brasil e o Oriente", *Studia*, 49(1989), pp. 394-96; Bonifacio Dias, "Impact of Tobacco on Goa (1620-1840)". in P. P. Shirodkar, organizer, *Goa: Cultural Trends* (Panaji-Goa: Directorate of Archives, Archaeology and Museum, Government of Goa, 1988), pp. 222-28; Celsa Pinto, *Trade and Finance in Portuguese Asia* (New Delhi: Concept Publishing Company, 1994) pp. 193-95.

7   Amaral Lapa, *A Bahia e a Carreira da India*, pp. 253-64, 272-77; Sanjay Subrahmanyam, *The Portuguese Empire in Asia, 1500-1700: A Political and Economic History* (Longman: London and New York, 1993), pp.183-85.

8   Amaral Lapa, "Dimensões do comércio colonial ", p. 395; Celsa Pinto, "Luso-Brazilian Commerce and the Eastern Littoral of India, 1780-1820," paper presented at the Tenth International Seminar on Indo-Portuguese History, Salvador, December 2000.

9   Amaral Lapa, *A Bahia e a Carreira da India*, pp. 292-97; Eduardo de Castro e Almeida, organizer, *Inventário dos documentos relativos ao Brasil existentes no Archivo de Marinha e Ultramar de Lisboa*. 8 volumes (Rio de Janeiro: Biblioteca Nacional, 1913-30). Vol. 2. *Bahia, 1763-1786* (1914),nos. 10.595-99; 10.601-5; 10.611-12; 11.005-7; 10.545; 10.849; 10.856-7; 10.860-66; 10.944; 11.011-12; 11.025-26; 11.238; 11.491; 10.494; 11.555; 11.625-9; 11.737; 11.754-6. See also Archana Kakodkar, "Source Material for Latin America in Goa(with Special Reference to Brazil)," in Teotonio R. de Souza, ed., *Essays in Goan History* (New Delhi: Concept Publishing Company, 1989), pp. 210-211; P. P. Shirodkar, "Brazil's Colonial Administration as Reflected in Goa Archives", *Purabhilekh-Puratatva*, 8: 1 (January-June 1990), especially pp. 34-37; Celsa Pinto, "Goa-Brazil Commercial Relations, 1770-1825", idem, pp. 43-51,58-61; Philomena Anthony,"Colonial Brazil and Goa", idem, pp. 73-75; Pinto, *Trade and Finance in Portuguese Asia* pp. 197-99.

10 Historical Archives of Goa(hereafter HAG), Livros das monções , vol. 63, fols. 418r-51r; vol 64, fols. 159-62, 164r-v, 166-67, 168r-v; 170r-173r.

11 A. J. R. Russell-Wood "Senhores de engenho e comerciantes" in *História da expansão portuguesa*. Vol. 3, especially pp. 205-209.

12 Celsa Pinto, "Goa-based Overseas and Coastal Trade. 18th-19th Centuries", in Teotónio R. de Souza, ed., *Goa through the Ages*. vol. 2. *An Economic History* (New Delhi: Concept Publishing Company, 1990), pp.180-81 and note 19.

13 Amaral Lapa, *A Bahia e a Carreira da India*, pp. 263-4.

14 Public Archive of the State of Bahia: Collection of Royal Orders (hereafter APBOR), vol. 57, fols.298-99; vol. 58, fol. 129r; and vol. 34, doc.24.

15 C. R. Boxer, *Salvador de Sá and the Struggle for Brazil and Angola, 1602*-1686 (London: The Athlone Press, 1952), pp. 308-9; Amaral Lapa, *A Bahia e a Carreira da India*, pp. 51-81 and appendix 1.

16 Aurélio Rocha, "Contribuição para o estudo das relações entre Moçambique e o Brasil—século xix", *Studia*, 51 (1992), pp. 64-68; Edward A. Alpers, *Ivory and Slaves. Changing Pattern of International Trade in East Central Africa to the Later Nineteenth Century* (Berkeley and Los Angeles: University of California Press, 1975), pp. 188-89.

17 Rocha, "Contribuição", pp. 70-72; Ernestina Carreira, "Os ultimos anos da Carreira da India". Separata from *A Carreira da India e as rutas dos Estreitos. Actas do viii seminário internacional de historia indo-portuguesa* (Angra do Heroismo, 1998), especially pp. 810-820.

18 Joaquim Romero Magalhães, "Os territórios africanos" in *História da expansão portuguesa*, vol. 3, pp. 71-73; Rocha, "Contribuição", pp. 75-85; Leslie Bethell, *The Abolition of the Brazilian Slave Trade:Britain,Brazil, and the Slave Trade Question, 1807-1869* (Cambridge: Cambridge University Press, 1970), chaps. 1-2. See also José Capela, *Escravatura. A empresa de saque. O abolicionismo, 1810-1875* (Porto: Afrontamento, 1974).

19 Alpers, *Ivory and Slaves*, pp. 211-17; Rocha, "Contribuição ", pp. 74-75; Mary C. Karasch, *Slave Life in Rio de Janeiro, 1808-1850* (Princeton: Princeton University Press, 1987), pp. 13-15, 21-25 *inter alia*; João Luis Fragoso, *Homens de grossa aventura: acumulação o e hierarquia na praça mercantil do Rio de Janeiro (1790-1830)* (Rio de Janeiro: Arquivo Nacional, 1992), pp. 179-182, 262-63.

20 HAG, Livros das monções do Reino, vol. 63, fols. 418r-23r; vol. 64, fols. 172r-173r; Rocha, "Contribuição, p.70.

21 Rocha, "Contribuição", pp. 71-73; Alpers, *Ivory and Slaves*, p.127; see also José Capela, *Donas, senhores, escravos na Zambésia* (Porto: Ed. Frontamento, 1990). I am indebted to Dom Marcos de Noronha Costa, Marquis of Subserra, for this reference which I have not been able to consult.

22 See the pioneering study of Ernst Pijning, "Controlling Contraband: Mentality, Economy and Society in Eighteenth-Century Rio de Janeiro" (Ph.D. dissertation: The Johns Hopkins University, 1997).

23 Sabugosa(Viceroy of Brazil) to the secretary of state, 18 November 1733 (APBOR, vol. 29, doc. 169); for an overview, see A.J.R. Russell-Wood, "Colonial Brazil: The Gold Cycle, c.1690-1750" in *The Cambridge History of Latin America*, vol. 2. *Colonial Latin America*. Edited by Leslie Bethell (Cambridge: Cambridge University Press, 1984), especially pp. 589-93; for tobacco, see Pinto, "Goa-based Overseas and Coastal Trade", p. 181 and note 18.

24 André João Antonil, *Cultura e opulência do Brasil por suas drogas e minas*. Commentaire critique par André Mansuy (Paris: Institut de Hautes Etudes de l'Amérique Latine, 1968), part 2, chapters 1 and 11.

25 Dias, "Impact of Tobacco on Goa", especially pp. 222-25; and also "Tobacco Trade in Goa, 1600-1850 A.D.", in B. S. Shastry, ed., *Goan Society through the Ages*. Goan University Publication Series No. 2 (New Delhi: Asian Publication Services, 1993), pp. 178-85; Irfan Habib, *The Agrarian System of Mughal India, 1556-1707* (New York: Asia Publishing House,1963), pp. 45-46 and notes, and p.94; C.R. Boxer, *Salvador de Sá*, p. 384, note 79; Maria Helena Mendes Pinto, *Biombos Namban/Namban Screens* (Lisbon: Museu Nacional de Arte Antiga, 1988), p.14 and illustrations.

26 Russell-Wood, *The Portuguese Empire*, especially pp. 164-70, 174.
27 Arruda, *O Brasil no comércio colonial*, p. 323.
28 Michael N. Pearson, *Port Cities and Intruders*. *The Swahili Coast, India, and Portugal in the Early Modern Era* (Baltimore: The Johns Hopkins University Press, 1998), pp. 129-54; and "Goa-based Seaborne Trade, 17th-18th Centuries", in Souza, *Goa Through the Ages*. Vol. 2, pp. 146-75; Celsa Pinto, "Goa-based Overseas and Coastal Trade", *idem*, pp. 186-91; and *Trade and Finance in Portuguese India*, pp. 111-117, 163-183; See also P.P. Shirodkar, "India and Mozambique: Centuries-Old Interaction", *Purabhilekh-Puratatva*, 6: 1 (January-June 1988). *Special Issue. India and Mozambique*, pp. 35-62.
29 APBOR, vol. 9, doc. 32; vol. 19, docs. 61, 78, 79; vol. 21, doc. 110; vol. 23, doc. 43.
30 Boxer, *Salvador de Sá*, p. 44; Russell-Wood, *The Portuguese Empire, 1415-1808*, pp. 107-109; James C. Boyajian, *Portuguese Trade in Asia under the Habsburgs, 1580-1640* (Baltimore: The Johns Hopkins University Press, 1993).
31 José Joaquim de Azeredo Coutinho, *Ensaio economico sobre o comércio de Portugal e as suas colonias*. 3rd.ed. (Lisbon: Academia Real das Ciências, 1828), part 2, chap. 7, 8.

15

THE NAYAKS OF TAMIL COUNTRY AND PORTUGUESE TRADE IN WAR-ANIMALS

S.Jeyaseela Stephen

The Tamil Coast and its hinterland had been famous for its export trade in rice and textiles. Among the imports, horses played a key role under the Pandya rulers since the Arabs introduced it in the Thirteenth Century. This animal trade in a large measure was encouraged by the Vijayanagara rulers in the Sixteenth Century. The Portuguese who established supremacy over the seas responded to it very much owing to the demand. It is a fact that the military requirements of the *nayaks* in Tamil country was an important feature in this direction of trade. Let us analyse how the trade in horses developed in Tamil Country and subsequently moved to trade in elephants. The active participation of both the *nayaks* and Portuguese may also be examined to understand the politics of trade.

Tamil Country in the Sixteenth Century was ruled by many *nayaks*[1]. Some of them such as the *nayaks* of Paramakudi, Madurai, Thanjavur and Gingee emerged as powerful rulers. Their territory included some portion of the Tamil coastal region and the Portuguese established their first settlement at Vedalai and subsequently settled down at Tuticorin, Nagapattinam and Devanampattinam inorder to secure profits of trade to the Portuguese Crown[2]. The overseas commerce of Portuguese depended mainly on the help extended by these *nayak* rulers. As the Tamil Coast had no pepper and spices to offer for the growth of Indo-European trade (mainly to Lisbon), the Portuguese began to undertake active trade within Asia and they found horses as one of the commodities of imports as needed by the *nayaks*.

Horses

Portuguese trade in horses from Ormuz to the ports of Goa and Chaul began in the second decade of the Sixteenth Century. In the Tamil Coast also it appeared around that time as noticed in the records. The Portuguese are reported to have sold horses as early as on 11 October 1512 to the *nayak* of Kanyakumari region[3]. When the Portuguese were planning to gain a foothold in the Pearl Fishery Coast, centred at the port of Kilakkarai, the opportunity to sell horses to the *nayak* of Paramakudi who was in dire need of horses for his army came in handy[4]. Therefore the Portuguese on the Pearl Fishery Coast requested the Portuguese Viceroy of India to arrange for the supply of horses which came from Ormuz to the ports of Goa, Chaul and Kannur. The viceroy in turn took special efforts to supply the requisite number of horses as per the demand placed by the captain of the Fishery Coast in order to supply them to Tumbichi Nayak (Chembeehe *nayak* as mentioned in Portuguese record). Later evidences suggest that some Portuguese private merchants who had sufficient capital to invest also participated in this lucrative horse trade with the *nayak* of Paramakudi. Privileges for the sale of horses were given to Andre Luis at Vedalai on 1 st February 1538. Orders were also issued from Lisbon in this regard on 2 August 1552[5]. João de Cruz, a horse trader in his letter written to Dom João III, the King of Portugal asked for the exclusive privilege of selling horses in the nayakdom of Thumbichi *nayak*[6]. Thus Portuguese at Vedalai could win over the patronage of this local ruler who allowed them to carry on their trade in the Kilakkaria region.

The trade in horses began to flourish in concrete shape during the period of Martim Affonso de Sousa (1542-1545) the Portuguese Viceroy of Goa. He issued instructions to the Portuguese Captain in Ormuz to send a minimum of twenty horses to the ports of Bay of Bengal as there was a lucrative trade on the East Coast of India[7]. Some Portuguese merchants like Pedro Alvarez de Mesquita and Diogo de Lisboa were stationed at Kanyakumari to know the arrival of horses from Arabia to West Coast and they took these horses in ships to the ports of Kayal and Punnaikayal where the Portuguese had settled down. Some *casados* (married settlers) in Kochi also evinced interest and they also took horses to the Coromandel Coast because of the profit derived from horse trade[8]. Cosme de Paiva who became the Captain of the Pearl Fishery Coast in 1542 resided at Tuticorin and he took interest in horse trade. During the year 1544 it is recorded that he sold horses for his personal gain[9].

Owing to the increasing demand for horses, the Portuguese Viceroy even encouraged the Portuguese on the Tamil Coast to purchase directly from Arabia. These imported horses were sold to various *nayaks* although its main sales was at the city of Vijayanagara where the emperor very much needed the swift moving horses for his army. The *nayak* rulers in Tamil Country also depended on the horses to carry on their warfare. Those horses brought to Cochin by the Portuguese were purchased by native merchants and then they were taken to Tamil country owing to its proximity. According to one record, as many as forty horses were brought to Cochin for resale at Kanyakumari[10]. Antonio Fernandes, a merchant had his base in Kanyakumari for horse trade[11]. So lucrative was the trade in horses that one Ruy Gonsalves de Caminha who became the Comptroller of Finance in 1547 was himself a horse dealer before he took up the post[12]. The horses that were brought from West Asia to the ports of the Western Coast initially were however allowed to be taken for resale only after paying taxes to the Portuguese[13]. Some of the Portuguese merchants who lived in Kanyakumari were constantly on the look out for information about the arrival of horses from Arabia to the ports of Kannur and Chaul so that they could go and buy them immediately and arrange for resale in the Tamil region[14]. In the course of time there emerged several brokers and horse trade agents in Chaul who supplied horses to the Tamil Coast[15].

Sevvappa *nayak* (1535-1563) of Thanjavur allowed the Portuguese to settle down at the port of Nagapattinam from the ports of the Western Coast which received supply from West Asia. Some Portuguese at Kanyakumari began to specialise in horse trade with the Coromandel Coast. They purchased horses when they received news about the arrival of horses from Arabia[16]. The *casados* in Cochin also engaged in the export of horses to Nagapattinam[17]. It is mentioned that the *nayak* of Thanjavur who was desperately in need of horses, used to send his men asking for horses from Portuguese at Nagapattinam [18]. According to Portuguese sources some of these horses became sick due to unfavourable climate even before they could be offered for sale at Nagapattinam. A Portuguese *casado* of Nagapattinam by name Marcos was appointed by the Portuguese Captain of the Coromandel Coast to treat the sick horses. He was paid four *paradaus* for rendering this special service [19]. Portuguese horse trade with the Tamil Coast declined in the second half of the Sixteenth Century. The possible reason may be attributed to the fall of the Vijayanagara kingdom at the battle of Tailkota in 1565.

Elephants

Vaiyappa Krishnappa *Nayak*, (1580-1593) of Gingee was keen to encourage the Portugueses to settle down at the port of Devanampattinam within his territory. On 13 March 1580, Damião Paes was appointed by the King of Portugal as the firsr resident captain of Devanampattinam [20]. The *nayak* of Gingee encouraged the Portuguese to supply elephants. Before the Portuguese could engage trade in elephants in the area, there were some natives who supplied elephants to the *nayak* of Gingee. The name of one Linganna of Telugu stock appears as a broker who is said to have once failed in his negotiations with the King of Kandy for the import of elephants to the port of Devanampattinam [21]. On another occasion he is reported to have brought elephants form Sri Lanka (one big and another small) but without anchoring at the Portuguese port of Devanampattinam sailed off to the port of Pulicat because he had a dispute with a servant of the port official of Devanampattinam when his ship was in Kandy.[22] The Portuguese at Devanampattinam found difficult to get elephants from Sri Lanka in the begginning to conduct trade.

In the meanwhile the Dutch were permitted to settle down at Davanampattinam in 1609 by Muthu Krishnappa *Nayak* (1597-1624). The Dutch took necessary steps to supply elephants to win favour from the *nayak* of Gingee. The Dutch had also sent costly presents to the King of Kandy to secure elephants from there. According to Dutch sources three elephants were expected to arrive at Thirupathiripuliyur (near Devanampattinam) by 1 May 1610. The Dutch resolved to supply ten or twelve elephants to the *nayak* of Gingee and he was happy.[23]

It was at this point of time that the Portuguese also took active steps to arrange for the supply of elephants to the *nayak* of Gingee in a bid to get the Dutch driven away from Devanampattinam and please the *nayak* thereby to restore the port to them. Therefore when the King of Ava(in Myanmar) who had sent his envoys to Ruis Dias Sampaio, the Potuguese Captain of Santhome of Mylapore, the king was asked to arrange for the early supply of elephants. An agreement was signed on 29 December 1616 with the King of Ava for the supply of elephants needed by the Portuguese to exchange for Coromandel textiles.[24] Elephants were successfully brought from Siam and Ava to the Coromandel Coast. In due course, the Portuguese in Sri Lanka also managed to hinder the import of elephants from Kandy by the Dutch[25]. The friendly relationship that existed between the *nayak* of Gingee and the Dutch did not permit the Portuguese either to sell the elephants or to obtain the port of Devanampattinam back. The Portuguese who contacted the King of Kandy and received elephants found it easy to sell the elephants to the *nayak* of Thanjavur[26].

Before the arrival of the Portuguese in Nagapattinam region, trade in elephants was conducted by the Marakkar traders as gleaned from Protuguese records. These Marakkars who owned large ships carried elephants from Sri Lanka. It is mentioned that there was always demand for these elephants. [27] We find one Chilay Marakkar had provided his ship for carrying elephants to Goa as requested by the Portuguese Viceory as the sailing vessel was found good.[28] It is recorded that the elephants of Sri Lanka were found to be more tameable. The best and the most throughly trained elephants were priced between 1000 and 1500 cruzados.[29] Achuthappa *nayak* (1563-1580) of Thanjavur requested the Portuguese to supply elephants. Sometimes the Portuguese also presented elephants as gifts and in one such case we find that as many as three elephants were presented to the *nayak* of Thanjavur.[30]

In fact it is evident from records that the *nayak* of Thanjavur was more interested in the purchase of elephants. The reasons for evincing interest in elephants by the *nayak* of Thanjavur are not explicitly stated in the documents. Antonio Vaz Perreira, the Portuguese Captain at Nagapattinam made special arrangements to sell all the elephants that were brought from Sri Lanka to Nagapattinam by the Portuguese to the nayak of Thanjavur in 1607 knowing his requirement.[31] In 1614 Jeronimo de Azevedo (1612-1617), the Portuguese Viceroy of Goa wrote in his letter that the *nayak* of Thanjavur alone enjoyed the exclusive right to buy all the elephants from the Portuguese.[32]

The *nayak* of Thanjavur always wanted the elephants to be delivered at Thanjavur and only then arranged payment for the elephants. The then ruler of Kandy allowed the Portuguese to hunt for elephants and engage in brisk trade. Elephants were sent from several ports of Sri Lanka for eventual delivery to the *nayak* of Thanjavur. This elephant trade continued upto 1620.[33]

The *naus* (cargo ships) that carried elephants were exceedingly strong and they carried fourteen to fifteen elephants.[34] The prow of the *naus* were built in such a way as to facilitate their movement in narrow channels and transport elephants safely from Sri Lanka to the Tamil Coast. Six Elephants were brought to Nagapattinam in 1622 and they were sold for a total amount of 3990 xerafins.[35] The *nayak* of Thanjavur is reported to have asked for elephants from Sri Lanka on 18 February 1630. This was agreed to by the Portuguese in order to ask for help from the *nayak* in their attempt to capture Pulicat, the chief settlement of the Dutch in the Coromandel. However (in 1631) the Portuguese decided to stop exchanging elephants with the *nayak* of Thanjavur since they attempted to buy saltpetre in exchange of elephants from Tirumalai *nayak* of Madurai.

The Portuguese with a view to entering into a contract for the purchase of saltpetre from Thirumalai *nayak* of Madurai (1627-1659) in 1633, agreed to sell elephants only to him. The king also in return agreed to make available saltpetre for sale to the Portuguese alone.[36] The agreement signed was opposed by Diogo de Mello de Castro, the Portuguese Captain of Sri Lanka who had to send elephants. His objection was that it caused financial loss to the Portuguese Crown, for the price fixed for saltpetre was found to be too high and that of the elephants too low. However a compromise was reached finally. Elephants were agreed to be sent by him to Madurai for exchange of saltpetre.[37]

In the year 1634, Miguel Noronha, the Viceroy of Goa concluded an agreement with the *nayak* of Madurai by which the ruler agreed to exchange Sri Lankan elephants for saltpetre.[38] This agreement was considered disadvantageous since the Portuguese did not obtain the exclusive right for saltpetre like the previous year as the *nayak* was also selling it to the Dutch. The Portuguese Captain of Sri Lanka therefore prevented the despatch of elephants to Madurai. He gave a flimsy reason that transporting elephants from Sri Lanka to Madurai was risky and difficult because of the famine and drought conditions prevailed at Tuticorin and Madurai.[39]

As per the agreement, the Portuguese had to supply the consignment of elephants at Tuticorin by November or December 1634 but it could not be delivered even by the end of January 1635. The price of each elephant was fixed at 620 *xerafins*.[40] However the Portuguese could not supply elephants and the contract fell through. The *nayak* was keen to accept elephants with a minimum size of three feet height alone as seen in a record dated 8 February 1635. The *nayak* also fixed the price of each feet at 120 *pardaus*. Further he wanted the elephants to be delivered at the port of Tuticorin and he would himself arrange for the transportation of elephants from Tuticorin to Madurai.[41] Elephants were continued to be supplied to the *nayak* between 1635 and 1638. In the year 1639, the *nayak* of Madurai preferred to have tusked elephants from Sri Lanka rather than elephants with stipulated minimum height. Diogo Mendez de Brito, the Portuguese captain of Sri Lanka was therefore instructed to make all possible arrangements to hunt for tusked elephants.[42] In the following years, the Portuguese were asked to offer military help by the *nayak* of Madurai in his expedition against the Sethupathi ruler. The Portuguese refused to help the *nayak* of Madurai as it would cause problems to their presence in Sri Lanka. Therefore the trade in elephants with the *nayak* of Madurai came to an end.

To conclude, we may say that the *nayaks* of Paramakudi and Thanjavur at first followed an open door policy in trade by inviting Portuguese merchants to supply horses required by them. In this phase the nature of trade was one that had been conducted by Portuguese merchants supplying horses for the purpose of profit. Eventually Portuguese diplomatic relations with this *nayak* of Paramakudi led to gain a foothold in the Kilakarai pearl fishery. When the trade in horses declined after the battle of Talikota in 1565, the trade in elephants was undertaken by the Portuguese with the *nayak* of Gingee and Thanjavur. This trade was motivated in a large measure by the Portuguese who wanted to drive the Dutch rivals in trade away from Devanampattinam and Pulicat seeking help from these two *nayaks*. Further the Portuguese also diverted the supply of elephants to the *nayak* of Madurai when they wanted to buy saltpetre. The *nayaks* always fixed the price of these war animals and paid the amounts on delivery in their capital city. The Portuguese motives engaging in elephant trade had been crystal clear to seek whatever was advantageous to them. They reacted quickly to the situation and instead of engaging in trade sometimes they even presented these elephants to win favours from the *nayaks* to gain control over the ports on the coast and influence at the royal courts in the hinterland. Portuguese Captains and the Viceroys of Goa took keen interest in purchasing elephants from Sri Lanka and Siam within South Asia. The horses were exported only from West Asia to the ports of Malabar and Canara on the Western Coast of India and they were brought for sale to the Tamil Coast. Thus trade within Asia was developed by Portuguese networks of overseas trade in this period. Transporting these animals might have been a difficult task from the ports to the courts, besides loading and unloading these animals in ships. As we find that a minimum of fifteen elephants had been brought in a sailing vessel, trade in war-animals definitely necessitated the building of huge cargo ships of high tonnage in this period. The military objectives of the *nayaks* and the commercial objectives of the Portuguese were determined more by circumstances than any other long term objective.

There has been significant changes introduced in the pattern of animal trade when compared to the previous period i.e., towards the end of the thirteenth century when horses were imported from the ports of West Asia such as Ormuz, Kis, Aden etc., to Kayal, the chief port of the Pandya kingdom. In this Pandya period, the demand for horses was always greater than the supply as a large number of horses died even while during transportation. Yet the importers had to pay the full amount and this money was paid from the Pandya treasury in accordance with the terms of contract. In the *nayak* period, death of these war animals are reported to be less and much care was taken by the Portuguese in transportation since doctors were appointed to treat sick horses and the animals that died before sale were not paid by the *nayaks* from their treasury. Several agents, brokers and merchants who were engaged in the horse trade under the Pandyas such as *kudirai chettis* mentioned in the medieval inscriptions were no more active in the *nayak* period. Similarly Marakkars engaged in elephant trade from Sri Lanka were also slowly replaced by Portuguese. The Pandyas followed a semi monoposonistic policy by allowing Muslims and Hindus to trade in horses at Nagore, Kundranarkovil, Tiruchitrambalam and supply animals to the Pandya rulers, while the Portuguese seems to have enjoyed a monopoly of trade in war animals under the *nayak* and supplied horses and elephants, although both the Pandya rulers and *nayaks* imported these war animals for their army.

1. S. Jeyaseela Stephen, *The Coromandel Coast and its Hinterland: Economy, Society and Political System, 1500-1600,* Delhi, 1997, pp.219-223.
2. S. Jeyaseela Stephen, *Portuguese in the Tamil Coast: Historical Explorations in Commerce and Culture, 1507-1749,* Pondicherry, 1998, pp.121-127.
3. Raymundo Antonio de Bulhão Pato (ed..), *Cartas de Affonso de Albuquerque,* 7 Vols, Lisboa, 1884-1935, Vo.I,pp.88-89.
4. Arquivo Nacional da Torre do Tombo, (hereafter ANTT), *Corpo Cronologico,* (hereafter CC) Part IIa, Maço 114, Document no.4.
5. ANTT, *Chancelaria de D.João III,* Privilegios, Livro I, fl.97v.
6. Letter of João da Cruz to the King of Portugal dated 20 December1553, in Georg Schurhammer,"Iniqitriberim and Bete Perumal: Chera and Pandya Kings in Southern India, 1534, in *Orientalia,* Rome, p.263.
7. Elaane Sanceau, *Colecçao de São Lourenço,* (hereafter CSL) 3 vols, Lisboa, 1973-83, Vo.II, p.120.
8. Ibid, CSL, Vol. II, pp. 335,364, and 372.
9. Letter of Francis Xavier to Mansillhas, 5 September 1544 written from Alandalai, in Hugues Dider, *Correspondance, 1535-1552: Lettres et Documents,* Paris, 1987, pp.132-133. See also Georg Schurhammer, op.cit,p. 263.
10. Armando Cortesão and Luis de Albuquerque, *Obras Completas de João de Castro,* III vols, Coimbra, 1976,Vol.II.p.215.
11. CSL,Vol.II, pp. 300,335.and 368.
12. Ibid, Vol,II, p.85.
13. Gaspar Correia, *Lendas da India,* 4vols, reprint, Porto, 1975, tomo,II,pp.65-66.
14. Armando Cortesão, op.cit, Vol.II,p.100; Vol. IV, p.50
15. Biblioteca da Ajuda, Lisboa, *Livro das Merces que fez Dom João de Castro,* Mss. Codice, 51-8-46, fl.92v.
16. Armando Cortesão, op.cit, Vol. III , p.100; Vol. IV, P.50.
17. Letter of Antonio Fernandes to Viceroy of Goa dated 2 August 1546 and letter of Manuel Lobato to Viceroy dated 25 August 1547 , in CSL , Vol.II, pp.335 and 364 - 372.
18. Samuel Purchas, *His Pilgrims,*Glasgow, 1905 , Vol. II pp. 227 - 228.
19. ANTT , CC , part - IIa, Maço 117 , document No.156.
20. ANTT, *Chancelaria de Dom Filippe I, 1580 - 1593* , Livro 17 , fl. 295v.
21. Om Prakash, *The Dutch Factories in India,* Delhi , 1980, p. 106.
22. T.I.Poonen, "Dutch Beginnings in India Proper" *Journal of the Madras University,* 1933, pp. 1-70, see , p.37.
23. Ibid, p. 28.
24. Historical Archives of Goa (herafter HAG), Mss.*Monções do Reino,* (hereafter MDR) Livro 99/1/3 fls. 301 - 302, letter no.123.

25. ANTT, *Documentos Remetidos da India* (herafter DRI), Livro6, fl.5.
26. ANTT, DRI. Livro 36, fl. 116.
27. Duarte Barbosa, *The Book of Duarte Barbosa*, 2 Vols, New Delhi, 1989, vol.II, p.113.
28. K.S. Mathew, *Indo-Portuguese Trade and the Fuggers of Germany*, New Delhi, 1997, p.211.
29. Duarte Barbosa. op.cit, p.117.
30. HAG, Mss. *Assentos do Conselho da Fazenda*, Codex 116, p.9. As per this record two elephants were given to the *nayak* of Madurai.
31. Bulhão Pato, *Documentos Remetidos da India*, Vols.1 - V, Lisboa, 1880 - 1935, Vol.III, pp.55-56.
32. ANTT, DRI, Livro 27, fl.116.
33. Tikiri Abyesinghe, *A Study of Portuguese Regimentos on Sri Lanka at the Goa Archives*, Colombo, n.d.p.9.
34. Duarte Barbosa, op. cit., vol. II. p.113.
35. Biblioteca Nacional de Lisboa, Codice 11410, fls.95 - 103v.
36. ANTT, DRI. Livro 36, fl.17.
37. Arquivo Historico Ultramarino, Mss.*India*, Caixa, 11, Document No. 44.
38. ANTT, DRI, Livro 36,fls.415 - 415v.
39. ANTT, DRI, Livro 36, fl.7; Livro 31, fl.227.
40. Biblioteca Universidade de Coimbra, Mss. 459, fl.7
41. ANTT, DRI, Livro 30, fl.59; Livro 31, fl.207, Livro 32, fl.156.
42. Tikiri Abyesinghe, op.cit, p. 79; HAG, Codex 1419, fl.79. Codex1420, fl.54v and 183.

16

THE SALSETTE CAMPAIGN OF 1658-1659: ISSUES OF WAR AND PEACE IN BIJAPURI-PORTUGUESE RELATIONS DURING THE MID-17TH CENTURY

Glenn J. Ames

By the year 1659, the Portuguese Crown and its servants in the *Estado da India* (State of India), an imperial edifice which stretched from Mozambique to Macau, had already maintained diplomatic relations with various indigenous kingdoms in Asia for more than a century and a half. During that time, the nature of these relationships had varied widely depending on time and place: open and aggressive bellicism, mutual peaceful respect, as well as diplomatic fawning in the quest for favorable trading concessions. Overall, however, open warfare had characterized a good deal of the history of the *Estado*. The Portuguese Crown, as a legacy of the *reconquista* against Islam and the cultural norms of the late medieval and early modern state in Europe had predictably embraced armed force as a crucial aspect of its foreign policy and economic system since the days of Afonso de Albuquerque, who began Bijapuri-Portuguese relations in earnest by twice besieging and eventually capturing the rich entrepôt city of Goa from that Muslim sultanate in 1510.[1] For the next century and a half, relations between the Portuguese *Estado da India* administered from the Viceroyal seat established at Goa and the Adil Shahi dynasty had predictably witnessed various cycles of "war and peace." Throughout this period, however, the geo-political and military structures of this relationship were intimately tied to the rise and fall of the other significant powers in the region: the Mughal empire, the Marathas, as well as the emerging European Companies of the English, Dutch, and French.[2] This chapter will examine some of the major elements of Bijapuri-Portuguese relations during the mid-17th century, with particular emphasis on the ill-fated Bijapuri invasion of the Portuguese "province" of Salsette in 1658-1659. While this campaign has been largely ignored in the historiography, it in fact constituted a notable episode in the long relationship between these two powers. The reasons for, and timing of, this invasion reveal much about the shifting structures and fortunes of these "Indian" powers and their neighboring rivals. Moreover, the fate of this armed incursion at least indirectly assisted the renaissance of one of these combatants during the 1660's and 1670's, while reflecting problems which would eventually result in the extinction of the other as an independent power by the late 1680's.

In 1489, Yusuf Adil Shah had founded an independent Bijapuri sultanate by exploiting the collapse of Bahmani power in the Deccan. The prosperity of the kingdom had continued for much of the sixteenth century and, based on this power and the lack of serious enemies, periodic attempts had been made by the Adil Shah dynasty to recapture Goa, Bardez, and Salsette until 1579. The rise of Mughal power to the north beginning with the reign of Akbar (1556-1605), and continuing with those of Jahangir (1605-1627), Shah Jahan (1627-1658) and Aurangzeb (1658-1707) posed an immediate threat to the sultanate. One result of this endemic threat of imperial invasion was the fact that relations had become generally more pacific with the Portuguese for a good deal of the seventeenth century. On Goa's part, the shift to more cordial relations was mainly due to the importance of Bijapur as a supply center for various products in great demand in the empire: cloth, precious stones from Golconda, saltpetre for the Royal Gunpowder Factory (*Casa da Polvora*)at Goa, as well as sailors for the coastal fleets. All these necessities were provided by or transshipped through Bijapur. A 1571 treaty recognized the importance of the kingdom by allowing the Adil Shah six free passes (*cartazes*) and the free importation of 25 horses each year; other duty free annual goods to the value of 6,000 gold *pardaus*, as well as a half share of all booty taken from ships without *cartazes* captured in the ports of the sultanate. In 1615, the Viceroy D. Jeronimo de Azevedo had even sought to utilize Ibrahim Adil Shah as an intermediary between the *Estado da India* and Nizam Shahi Sultan.[3]

There were, of course, exceptions to this rule of civility. As early as 1623, no doubt buoyed by the recent example of the joint Persian-English expulsion of the Portuguese from their vital entrepôt fortresses at Hurmuz, the Adil Shah had also sought an alliance with the English East India Company (EIC) with the goal of jointly expelling the Portuguese from his "domains." This offer, however, had been rejected based largely on Sir Thomas Roe's cautious imperial policy, designed to avoid open hostilities in India. Nevertheless, the 1620's and early 1630's had witnessed insults and reprisals by both sides. The Portuguese, seeking to enforce their "monopoly" *cartaz* system in the Indian Ocean trade, had captured two vessels belonging to the Adil Shah in 1629 and executed their crews. In turn, Ibrahim Adil Shah had detained a Portuguese ship with the revenue-comptroller of Mascat aboard in his port of Rajpur, after Bijapuri authorities had first given permission for the vessel to anchor there. Soon thereafter, the Portuguese had captured yet another Bijapuri ship and the Adil Shah had responded by withdrawing his ambassador from Goa, closing all his ports to Portuguese trade, stopping the flow of needed supplies across the Western Ghats to Goa, and threatening to invade Bardez and Salsette. At this point, the rise of Mughal power in the Deccan intervened to diffuse the situation, and focus the attention of the Adil Shah elsewhere. In April 1632, the joint forces of the Mughals and Ahmadnagar besieged Bijapur. It is interesting to note that in these grave circumstances, the erstwhile enemies each saw the benefits of mutual cooperation against this threat. Ibrahim Adil Shah requested gunners, powder, and ammunition from the count of Linhares, which the Portuguese Viceroy gladly supplied. This diplomatic *volte-face* for the Portuguese was based on the realization that ultimately it was much to their advantage to support the continued, yet enfeebled, Muslim enemy at Bijapur in favor of the appearance of Shah Jahan's forces in numbers so close to the Konkan coast. This practical observation would serve as the basis for Portuguese policies with respect to Bijapur for much of the remainder of the sultanate's history.[4]

Relations between the Adil Shah dynasty and the Mughals had been particularly strained since the accession of Shah Jahan to power in 1627. Thereafter, the Deccan policy of the Mughals became "more vigorous and purposeful". Above all, this imperialism in the south sought to destroy and absorb the Muslim sultanates of Ahmadnagar, Golconda, and Bijapur, with Shah Jahan demanding the formal submission of all three to his authority. The intrigues of Fath Khan and the machinations relating to the joint invasion of Bijapur had resulted in the destruction and absorption of the Nizam Shahi state by 1633. The shrewd Abdullah Qutb Shah in Golconda formally recognized the suzerainty of Shah Jahan in 1636. Only Ibrahmin Adil Shah sought to resist the Mughal emperor militarily. In fact, his staunch defense against Shah Jahan's armies in 1636 won him a more favorable peace settlement than the Qutb Shahis: recognizing the overlordship of the Mughal allowed him to retain his kingdom and to share the spoils of Ahmadnagar.[5]

The next two decades had witnessed relatively peaceful relations between the two Muslim powers. Yet, Aurangzeb's arrival as Subadar of the Deccan in 1653 and the latent imperialism of his father portended further difficulties. By 1657, following upon badly needed fiscal and agricultural reforms, Aurangzeb turned his attention to the conquest of Bijapur and Golconda. The death of Muhammad Adil Shah in November 1656 after a decade of poor health furnished the young prince with the excuse he needed. Challenging the legitimacy of Ali Adil Shah II to the throne, Aurangzeb received his father's permission to invade Bijapur with the assistance of the able Mir Jumla. Although Bidar and Kalyani fell in the spring of 1657, court intrigue in Delhi on behalf of Bijapur championed by Dárá Shukoh, resulted in Shah Jahan's orders to lift the siege and make peace, much to the chagrin of Aurangzeb. Moreover, the emperor's illness and the bloody succession struggle for the Peacock throne that ensued between his sons for the next few years furnished a much needed respite for Ali Adil Shah II and the circumstances for settling lingering scores with the *Estado da India*.[6]

Ironically, it was at precisely this point that the rising power of the Marathas further complicated matters in the Deccan and along the Konkan coast. The final three rulers in the Adil Shah dynasty: Sultan Muhammed Adil Shah (1627-56), Ali Adil Shah II (1656-1672) and Sikandar Adil Shah (1672-1686) all had to contend not only with the Mughal threat, but that of the rising power of Shivaji and the Marathas. The mercurial rise to prominence of Shivaji (1627-1680) had begun with the deeds of his father Shahji Bhonsla. Shahji had begun his own impressive career as a "small *jagirdar* under the Sultan of Ahmadnagar," who after the defeat and absorption of the Nizam Shahi dynasty in 1636 had become a powerful Hindu general for Muhammed Adil Shah and for a time governor of the Bijapuri Karnatak. "Imbued with an uncommon spirit of adventure and love of independence from his early life," and rejecting "the Indo-Muslim political culture defined by Bijapur," Shivaji had initially exploited the illness of the Adil Shah after 1646 to carve out an independent Hindu kingdom from the erstwhile territories of that sultanate, Ahmadnagar and beyond. Torna, Kondhana, Rohira, Chakan, Purandar and Supa, near Poona were all taken in this skillful campaign.[7]

Shivaji's capture of Javli in the Mahabaleswar range and the construction of the fort of Pratapgarh had then opened the way for further conquests in the north Konkan with Kalyan, Bhiwandi and the fort of Mahuli soon falling to him. In the meantime, the Mughal invasion of Bijapur orchestrated by Aurangzeb had allowed the Maratha leader to invade and plunder imperial districts of Ahmadnagar and Junnar. Yet, Aurangzeb had quickly responded to this threat and, at least for the moment, humbled him. In the 1657 peace with Bijapur, Shivaji had nominally submitted to the Mughals as well. Nevertheless, his campaign soon began anew and by 1659: "he had extended his dominions in the uplands or Desh to the southern limit of the Satara district, and in Konkan from Mahuli to near Mahad." These conquests had greatly perturbed Ali Adil Shah II and would force the new sultan to dispatch Afzal Khan in an ill-fated effort in 1659 to capture the Maratha leader.[8]

Despite chronic problems with both the Mughal and Maratha threats, Ali Adil Shah found himself in a favorable situation in the late 1650's for finally resolving the sultanate's long-standing geo-political and religious struggle with Portuguese Goa. Peace, at a cost, had recently been achieved with Shah Jahan. Moreover, the illness of the emperor and the escalating chaos engendered by the succession struggle for the Peacock throne promised a well- appreciated reprieve from Mughal harassment for the foreseeable future. The death of the strong sultan Muhammed Adil Shah followed by the accession of the young Ali Adil Shah anxious for glory and conquest in his own campaign to solidify his reign also favored the war party in Bijapur. Shivaji, while still marauding in nearby districts could either be dealt with by Afzal Khan or, failing that, most likely turn his attentions to the suddenly vulnerable territories of the Mughals. Finally, and perhaps most importantly, Ali Adil Shah's advisors almost certainly advised the young sultan that the time was also perfect for launching yet another attack on the *Estado da India* and Goa since that imperial European edifice was then in the throes of a chaotic period itself and could hardly be expected to withstand another Muslim invasion.

The late 1640's and 1650's indeed marked a clear nadir in that century for the fortunes of the once impressive *Estado*. During these decades, a renascent indigenous Portuguese Crown was forced to fight an independence struggle against Habsburg Spain in Europe and a vicious military and economic campaign in Brazil, Africa and Asia against the United Provinces of the Netherlands. Glory, conquests, and wealth had predictably given way to economic and military setbacks. The revival of the Levant trade after 1570 and competition from the Dutch (VOC) and

English (EIC) East India Companies slashed volume and profits in the spice trade around the Cape of Good Hope. Instead of sending 50,000-60,000 *quintals* of pepper from Goa each year, the Crown managed to import "little more than 12,000 *quintals*," as early as 1600, with the prices dropping as well.[9] Particularly hard hit in these disastrous years was the so-called *Carreira da India*, or the annual seaborne interchange between Lisbon and Goa carried on by the Crown's carracks, the very lifeblood of the empire. Between 1647 and 1649, the *Atalaia e Sacramento* sank off southeast Africa, over 1200 men and scores of vessels were lost in the Mandovi during a storm of April 1648, two carracks destined for India in 1647 were lost, as was the richly laden *Sao Lourenco* two years later off Mozambique. None of the five ships in the *frota* of the Viceroy Count of Aveiras (1640) reached India that year. Between 1658-1663 an average of one ship a year arrived in Goa, while not even that number made the return voyage successfully. In 1659, the Queen-Regent Dona Luisa de Gusmão told the French ambassador, in only slightly exaggerated terms, that no news had been received from India in three years![10]

These economic problems were exacerbated by military setbacks in Asia. Hormuz, key to the Persian Gulf trade, fell to an Anglo-Persian attack in 1622. Melaka, conquered by Afonso de Albuquerque in 1511 and long a major entrepôt in the Indonesian trade, was lost to the (VOC) in 1641. The rich island of Ceylon, after a long and bitter campaign had fallen to the Dutch by 1658. When the Count of Aveiras assumed the Viceregal office in 1640, the *Estado* still comprised some 26 coastal strongholds. By 1666, the deed of transfer to the Count of São Vicente would list only 16 places, and Goa's control over outlying areas like Mozambique and Macau was indeed tenuous.[11] As the Jesuit Manoel Godinho noted at this time on the *Estado*: "If it was a giant, it is now a pigmy; if it was great it was now nothing."[12] Exacerbating these problems were internal administrative and personal feuds in Goa within and between the ruling royal and ecclesiastical elites. The most glaring of these disputes had been the mutiny of D. Braz de Castro who had usurped the power of the Viceroy, the count of Obidos, and controlled Goa from 1653-1654![13]

Tensions between the two powers were indeed elevated at this time: the Portuguese were upset at Muhammed Adil Shah for trading concessions he had made to the Dutch and English on the Konkan coast, allowing factories to be established at Karwar, Rajapur, and Vingurla. Agents of the VOC had encouraged the sultan to invade Goa, an incursion they promised to support with their sizable fleet then cruising, and periodically blockading, the Mandovi and Goa. The losses that the *Estado* was then suffering in the south Konkan to the rising power of the Nayaks of the Keladi ruling family of Venkatappa Nayaka (1592-1629), Virabhadra Nayaka (1629-1645) and Shivappa Nayaka (1645-1660) had also no doubt encouraged Bijapur.[14] Meanwhile, Matheus de Castro Mahale, Vicar-Apostolic in Bijapur and subsequently confidential advisor to the *Propaganda Fide* in Rome was then resident in Bicholim. This Goan native and *Brahmene* had been refused ordination by the Archbishop of Goa. He had traveled to Rome and been consecrated as the bishop of Chrysopolis *in partibus infidelium*. An implacable enemy of the *Estado*, Castro Mahale had endeavored to insight an indigenous uprising against the Portuguese and had appealed to the sultan for support.[15]

Muhammed Adil Shah had indeed sought to exploit this seemingly favorable conjuncture of events in 1654. He began the year by offering to mediate a settlement between Shivappa Nayaka and the *Estado* then fighting over the remaining Portuguese fortress on the Kanara coast, Onor, utilizing his own ambassador and the Portuguese Jesuit Gonçalo Martins. The Adil Shah had then invaded the "old conquests" of Bardez and Salsette. In August 1654, an army of 4000-5000 troops evidently led by one of Shivappa Nayaka's erstwhile generals, Abdul Hakim (Abdala Aquimo?), had marched into Bardez. This force had encountered fierce resistance from a garrison at Tevim. On 14th August reinforcements from Panjim, some 300 in number, engaged the Bijapuris and, after a bloody encounter, forced the Muslim army to retire. In October 1654, Muhammed Adil Shah

The Salsette Campaign of 1658-1659

had ordered the invasion of Salsette with some 7000 infantry and 800 cavalry. This force captured Sarzora and Cutuly in fairly rapid fashion. Yet, news of a large Portuguese army forming at Rachol, based on resources from the abandoned fortress of Onor and some timely reinforcements from Lisbon, along with pressing problems in the Karnatak had resulted in the recalling of this invasion force.[16] A temporary peace had then been arranged with the *Estado da India*. Muhammed Adil Shah's ambassador, Melique Acute, had reached Goa in December 1654 with presents for D. Braz de Castro. By March 1655, a treaty had been arranged that reconfirmed peaceful trade between the powers and a commitment to keep the peace, goals originally promised in earlier treaties of 1582 and 1633.[17]

The period 1655-1659 had been dominated by continuing problems for both Bijapur and the *Estado da India*. The death of Muhammed Adil Shah, the ensuing power struggle relating to the accession of Ali Adil Shah II, and the Mughal invasion undertaken at the behest of Aurangzeb all served to retard further plans for a renewed offensive against Goa and its dependencies by the Muslim sultanate.[18] For the *Estado*, these same years had witnessed the arrival of the count of Sarzedos (August 1655), the prompt arrest of the D. Braz de Castro and the end of his usurpation of power in Goa. Yet, Sarzedos died abruptly, and somewhat mysteriously, in January 1656. He had been succeeded by the Governing Council of Manoel Mascarenhas Homem (d. September 1657), Francisco de Mello de Castro, and Antonio de Sousa Coutinho.[19] The Crown had appointed the count of Villa Pouca de Aguiar as the next Viceroy, but this talented noble had died on the voyage out from Lisbon.[20] Mello de Castro and Sousa Coutinho had thus been forced to deal with the plethora of administrative, economic, and military problems which between 1656-1658 had resulted most notably and damaging in the final losses in the long-standing struggle with the VOC for control of Ceylon.[21] The court of Ali Adil Shah emerged out of this panoply of problems of the late 1650's first and, as a result, was able to turn its attention to the seemingly easy target of Portuguese held Goa, still reeling from the losses to Shivappa

Nayaka and the continuing campaign of the VOC. For Ali Adil Shah and his advisors, an additional incentive for a renewed invasion was the fact that the Portuguese, perhaps as a *contrecoup* for the activities of Matheus de Castro, had also been harboring and encouraging renegade Bijapuri provincial officials (*desais*).[22]

By late 1658, the situation was indeed precarious for the two Governors of the *Estado da India*. The continuing threat from the Dutch fleet cruising the Konkan coast under Adriaen Roothaes and Rijkloff Van Goens, the growing VOC presence at Vingurla, and Dutch intrigue and payments at the Adil Shahi court combined to create an extremely dangerous conjuncture of events for the continuing Portuguese presence at Goa. Mello de Castro and Sousa Coutinho were forced to admit as much in a letter to the Queen Regent D. Luisa de Gusmão of December 1658. "If the Adil Shah [makes war upon us] it will be impossible for us to retain the lands of Salsette and Bardez given the paucity of resources that we have." Despite the meager results that previous ambassadors had obtained in their negotiations in Bijapur, the Governors had, nonetheless, decided to send D. Pedro de Henriques to present suitable "gifts" and to reconfirm the shaky peace arranged with Muhammed Adil Shah after the 1654 incursion. Problems with funding the embassy and the arrival of the Dutch fleet off the bar of Goa had delayed Henriques' departure until mid-December 1658 with the hope that "with God's help he will be able to re-ratify the peace [between us]."[23]

Unfortunately for the *Estado*, Henriques' mission was a failure, and in late 1658 the decision had been made to launch another invasion of Salsette with a sizable force of some 400 cavalry and 4000 infantry, again under the command of Abdul Hakim. This sizable force was ideally to act in league with the VOC fleet with an eye toward expelling the Portuguese from Salsette and eventually perhaps even Goa! The Adil Shahi army had entered Salsette on All Soul's Day (2 November) marched virtually unchallenged through the province capturing many villages and towns until it reached Margão, the largest town in the province. There, they besieged the Church of the Holy Spirit which was defended by the local population under the direction of Fr. Bento Ferreyra, later Provincial of Salsette, and Fr. Antonio Fernandez, the Vicar of Vernâ. Meanwhile, the Dutch fleet cruised off Murmugão, awaiting word of a convenient time to disembark. The only Portuguese force then in Salsette was some 250 men, "many of them very young," in Rachol, site of a Jesuit monastery and seminary school along the banks of the Zuari River. This force was under the command of Gaspar Carneiro Girão. In "Old" Goa, this news greatly alarmed the Mello de Castro and Sousa Coutinho, and prompted the dispatching of Mendonça Furtado as captain-general. Yet, a shortfall in customs receipts, prompted by periodic Dutch blockades of the Mandovi River, and other financial problems had ensured a dearth of capital in the Royal Treasury to meet these threats. The Governors, had accordingly been forced to borrow some 40,000 *xerafins* from local businessmen to pay for the salaries and foodstuffs for this force.[24]

The captain-general, Luis de Mendonça Furtado, at the outset of a glorious imperial career, was an exceedingly wise choice for this assignment. His father, Pedro de Mendonça, had been *alcaide-mor* of Mourão, *commendador* of Santiago de Cassem and Vila Franca, *senhor* of Seregeira, one of the principal acclaimers of D. João IV in the revolution against Madrid in December 1640, and later *guarda-mor* for the first Braganza king. Luis was the eldest child of Pedro's second marriage to D. Antonio de Mendonça, a *dama* of D. Luisa de Gusmão. He had begun his career in the late 1640's fighting in the war in Alentejo, where he performed with "reputation" and "distinction." Luis had first traveled to the *Estado* in 1651, as *capitão-mor* of the ships *San Thome, S. Antonio de Maragão*, and *Nossa Senhora do Socorro*. This *Carreira* fleet made a swift voyage to and from Goa in that year and 1652. In 1653, he had repeated this impressive feat in an epoch of general maritime disasters for the *Estado* by departing from Lisbon in late March with the ships *Sacramento da Trindade* and *S. Jozeph* and reaching Goa in October of that year. In 1657, Mendonça Furtado had returned to the *Estado* aboard the fleet carrying the *conde* of Vila Pouca, with the title of Admiral of the Indian Seas. Between January and March 1658, he had commanded the Portuguese fleet that unsuccessfully tried to break the Dutch blockade of the Mandovi, directed by Adriaen Roothaes, and relieve Jaffna, the remaining *Estado* outpost on Ceylon. Soon thereafter, he was informed of his selection as captain-general for Salsette.[25]

In a detailed letter from Mendonça Furtado to the Crown, the captain-general gave his impressions of the *Estado da India*, the policies of its Governors, and his views on the campaign against Bijapur. In his view, with the death of the count of Vila Pouca, "the hope of the restoration of India died for now, which his zeal had promised." Instead, Mendonça Furtado had found "in the Government, two old men (the third of which had died shortly before) so old that they not only lacked passion with their age, but also the direction of talent." The concentration of the Adil Shah's forces near Ponda under Abdul Hakim, "with the assistance of Rastu Mazama (sic) general of the king of Bijapur with 4000 cavalry and 5000 infantry in league with the Dutch" had prompted the Governors to appoint him captain-general to meet this threat. In his view, the mission of D. Pedro Henriques had been misguided: "spending 150,000 *xerafins* from His Majesty's treasury, without yielding any results..... I say that the expenses of this embassy would have been better spent on the galleys, because with this we would have been respected at sea and on land." Mendonça Furtado, accompanied by some of his most trusted officers and kinsmen like Manoel Furtado de Mendonça, had joined his forces, some 250 Portuguese troops, near Rachol and attempted to drill discipline into them since "by the lack of such discipline Your Majesty has lost many possessions of this empire, because the captains, and generals, that are empowered here live only for buying and selling."[26]

Outside Margão, Abdul Hakim's troops had deployed his infantry along a brook surrounded by tall grasses, while the Bijapuri cavalry waited along a nearby palmgrove. Mendonça Furtado, however, feared that the dry grasses might easily catch fire in the battle causing "disorder" among his troops. He thus chose to deploy his own troops in a more open location below the village of Arlî. The pitched battle of sorts that ensued did much to decide the fate of the invasion and by extension the continued viability of the *Estado da India*. In this encounter, the Portuguese inflicted a decisive defeat upon Abdul's army and obliged his forces to retreat from Salsette and back across the Western Ghats. According to the noted Jesuit chronicler Fernão de Queiroz, the most notable feat of *valor* performed on that day was in fact accomplished by Mendonça Furtado. As the armies deployed for battle, "one of his [Abula Aquimo's] higher officers who was considered the most valiant among them, took manifest pains to get a view of him [Mendonça Furtado]." The Portuguese general had "sallied out of the ranks to meet him with only the dress sword which he had at his side and a round target, which they had given him in Rachol by way of a shield, because the buckles were not large enough for his arms." Thus armed on foot, Mendonça Furtado had then engaged the mounted Muslim officer, "and when the Moor galloped at him at full speed, he got behind the hind quarters of the horse and with his left he made the Moor's horse stumble and from one side ran him through to the top of the opposite shoulder, the Moor dropping dead, a feat characteristic of his strength and daring."[27]

For Adil Shah II and Bijapur, the 1658-1659 expedition and its defeat was characteristic of the problems that would beset the sultanate for the remainder of its existence. The rather rash decision to take up the campaign again against the *Estado* largely at the behest of the VOC and its enticements was certainly ill-advised. After all, while the continued presence of the Christian Portuguese at Goa and its dependencies may have been galling, there was little danger that the *Estado* would seek to enlarge its holdings at the expense of Bijapur at this juncture of its history. There were, however, far more dangerous aggressors lurking nearby for the sultanate which should have received more attention: namely Aurangzeb and Shivaji. Both these rather ravenous powers no doubt received much satisfaction from the defeat that Mendonça Furtado inflicted upon the army of Abdula

Hakim in 1658-1659. If the beleaguered Portuguese could withstand this onslaught then perhaps the time was right for further aggression against Bijapur. The 1660's and 1670's in fact would witness renewed offensives by both Shivaji and the Mughals. Shivaji accompanied Jai Singh in the Mughal incursion into the sultanate in late 1665, and his own incursions into Bijapur, and especially the Konkan coast, continued in the early 1670's. The plunder and tribute which such raids yielded in conjunction with Shivaji's growing skepticism of Adil Shah's power certainly facilitated his decision to undertake his royal consecration (*abisheka*) ceremony in June 1674.[28]

Although Aurangzeb was seemingly secure on the Peacock throne by the mid-1670's, he continued to face the potential threat posed by his son Prince Muhammad Akbar acting in league with the Marathas, as well as the Deccan sultanates. The continued weakness of Bijapur exposed for all to see by the sultantate's failure to defeat the Portuguese, Shivaji's growing power, and the accession of the four year old Sikandar Adil Shah in 1672 all prompted the Mughal emperor to undertake renewed aggressive actions in the Deccan. Bahadur Khan, the Mughal viceroy of the Deccan, had been repulsed in his 1676 invasion. But in early 1685, Aurangzeb ordered an army of some 85,000 men under Princes Azam and Shah Alam against Bijapur. For over a year the 30,000 man garrison of Bijapur held out against the ensuing siege. By September 1686, however, Sikandar Adil Shah was forced to surrender. The sultanate was thereupon annexed to the Mughal empire. Sikandar was placed under house arrest while most of the Afghan and Indian Muslim nobles who remained alive were gradually assimilated into the Mughal power structure.[29] The weaknesses of the Adil Shah dynasty, heralded to all with the defeat of 1659, had definitively been exploited by its more powerful neighbors. Bijapur was no more.

Conversely, the significance of the 1659 victory for the *Estado da India*, won at a truly crucial juncture of its history, can hardly be overstated. As the Provincial of the Jesuits in Goa, Fr. Miguel de Almeida, informed the Crown in a letter of

November 1659 on this campaign: "The Moors had entered into Salsette with great power of cavalry and infantry, making themselves masters of a great part of it." But Mendonça Furtado's victory had obliged them to flee from the lands of His Majesty "with many losses." Almeida, a witness to these events, felt obliged to inform the Crown of this great triumph for Portuguese arms, noting that "the said Captain-general should be called liberator and restorer of Christianity in Salsette." On the same day in which Mendonça Furtado set foot in this province and engaged the enemy this threat was overcome by "his valor, zeal, and resolution" which, without doubt had saved Christianity in Salsette "from the tyranny of the Moors, and the rents that [this province] pays to Your Majesty would have been lost."[30]

The growing infirmity and preoccupations of Bijapur in the 1660's and 1670's also facilitated badly needed reforms within the *Estado*. These policies began with the assumption of power by Prince Regent Pedro of Braganza in late 1667 and culminated during the Viceroyalty of Luis de Mendonça Furtado from 1671-1677.[31] As the sultanate died its lingering death at the hands of its Sunnite and Hindu enemies, the Goa hierarchy could enact such reforms, including an impressive campaign against the Omani Arabs, without fear of further attacks from Bijapur.[32] Ironically, this campaign would yield impressive results by 1683. Yet, neither the Salsette campaign of 1659 nor the rehabilitation campaign of the 1660's and 1670's were free from problems and acrimony. As Mendonça Furtado's letters reveal personal jealousies, bickering, and worse beset the Goa hierarchy as much as court politics in Bijapur! In fact an abortive assassination plot against the captain-general upon his return from his victory at Arli and a subsequent investigation into that conspiracy would dominate much energy in Goa and Lisbon from 1659-1663.[33] Nevertheless, unlike in Bijapur, the Portuguese had achieved a buffer of protection from Indian political and military machinations in the Deccan during the next decade and a half which allowed them to reestablish effective rule in Goa and undertake reform. This was a seminal luxury that post-1659 Bijapur did not, unfortunately, enjoy and in the end it made all the difference in the respective destinies of these rival powers. For one a rebirth of sorts was achieved. For the other a funeral march was soon in store.

References:

1. On this tendency, among others, cf. C.R. Boxer, *The Portuguese Seaborne Empire, 1415-1825* (New York, 1969), pp. 40-50; M.N. Pearson, *The Portuguese in India* (Cambridge, 1987), pp. 29-35; and Sanjay Subrahmanyam, *The Portuguese Empire in Asia, 1500-1700* (London, 1993), pp. 55-79.

2. For a concise summary of this relationship, cf. T.R. De Souza, *Medieval Goa: A Socio-Economic History* (New Delhi, 1979), pp. 20-43.

3. Cf. De Souza, *Medieval Goa*, pp. 31-32; and P.S.S. Pissurlencar, *Assentos do Conselho do Estado*, (Henceforth ACE), 1618-1750 (5 vols., Bastora, 1953-57), I: pp. 237-39, 414-16.

4. De Souza, *Medieval Goa*, pp. 31-32; Pissurlencar, *ACE* I: pp. 237-39, 414-16 and A. Villiers, *The Indian Ocean* (London, 1952), p. 158.

5. On Mughal-Bijapuri relations during this period, among others, cf. S.R. Sharma, *Mughal Empire in India* (Agra, 1934, 1966), pp. 346-52; R.C. Majumdar (ed.), *The Mughal Empire* (Bombay, 1974), pp. 207-10; *The Cambridge History of India*, planned by Sir Wolseley Haig, edited by Sir Richard Burn, IV *The Mughal Period* (Cambridge, 1937), pp. 260-69; and J.F. Richards, *The New Cambridge History of India* I:5 *The Mughal Empire* (Cambridge, 1993), pp. 154-57.

6. For details on the relations between the powers in the 1650's cf., *Cambridge History* IV: pp. 268-72; Majumdar, *Mughal Empire* pp. 210-19; Sharma, *Mughal Empire* 346-53, 410-11; and Richards, *Mughal Empire*, pp. 156-63; 205-08.

7. On Shivaji's early life and career, among others, cf. Richards, *Mughal Empire* pp. 205-16; Majumdar, *Mughal Empire*, pp. 247-59; and *Cambridge History*, IV: pp. 260-80.

8. Richards, *Mughal Empire*, pp. 205-16; Majumdar, *Mughal Empire*, pp. 247-59; and *Cambridge History*, IV: 260-80

9. James C. Boyajian, *Portuguese Bankers at the Court of Spain, 1626-1650* (New Brunswick NJ, 1983), pp. 7 ff. For other estimates on the level of spice imports for this period, cf. F.C. Lane, "The Mediterranean Spice Trade and its Revival in the Sixteenth Century" *Venice and History: The Collected Papers of Frederic C. Lane* (Baltimore, 1966; V.M. Godinho, *L'Economie de l'Empire portugais aux XVe et XVIe siècles* (Paris, 1969), pp. 674-704; C.H.H. Wake "The Changing Pattern of Europe's Pepper and Spice Imports, ca. 1400-1700," *The Journal of European Economic History* 8 (1972), pp. 378-81; and Niels Steensgaard, "The Return Cargoes of the *Carreira* in the 16th and Early 17th Century" in TR. De Souza, ed., *Indo-Portuguese History: Old Issues, New Questions* (New Delhi, 1985), pp. 13-31.

10. On these problems for the Portuguese *Carreira da India*, cf. C.R.Boxer *A India Portuguesa em meados do seculo XVII* (Lisbon, 1980), pp. 39-49.

11. On the gradual diminution of the *fortalezas* listed in the deeds of transfer from 1640-1666, cf. Pissurlencar *ACE* II: pp. 410-12 and III: pp. 97-98.

The Salsette Campaign of 1658-1659

12 Quoted by C.R. Boxer, *The Portuguese Seaborne Empire, 1415-1825* (New York, 1969), pp. 128-29. Godinho made the trip back to Europe from Goa via the Levant in 1663. His manuscript was originally published as *Relação do novo caminho que fez por terra e mar, vindo da India para Portugal no anno do 1663* (Lisbon, 1665).

13 For details, among others, cf. F.C. Danvers, *The Portuguese in India* (2 vols., London, 1894), II: pp. 302-05; and G.D. Winius, *The Fatal History of Portuguese Ceylon* (Cambridge, MA, 1971), pp. 121-39.

14 For background on relations with Kanara, cf. De Souza, *Medieval Goa*, pp. 34-37.

15 On the background and role of Castro-Mahale, cf. De Souza, *Medieval Goa*, pp. 32-33; and "Matheus de Castro Mahale: An Unsung Hero" *Goa Today* (January 1975), pp. 18-28; and C.R. Boxer, *Seaborne Empire*, pp. 254-55.

16 For details on the 1654 incursion, cf. De Souza, *Medieval Goa* p. 33; Danvers, *Portuguese in India* II: pp. 308-10; and Winius, *Fatal History*, pp. 145-46.

17 On the 1655 peace treaty between the powers, cf. Danvers, *Portuguese in India* II: pp. 309-10; De Souza, *Medieval Goa*, p. 33; Pissurlencar, *ACE* III,pp. 366-67, 368-76; 382-86, 582-87; and J.F. Biker, *Collecção de tratados e concertos de pazes que o Estado da India Portuguesa fez com os Reis e Senhores com quem teve relaçoes nas partes da Asia e Africa Oriental desde o principio da conquista até o fim do seculo XVIII* (14 vols., Lisbon, 1881-87), II: pp. 232-39.

18 On these problems, cf. Richards, *Mughal Empire*, pp. 156-59; Sharma, *Mughal Empire*, pp. 346-48, 410; Majumdar, *Mughal Empire*, pp. 210-12; and Burn, *Cambridge History*, IV: pp. 270-72.

19 For details on the death of Sarzedos and the new Governing Council, cf. Winius, *Fatal History*, pp. 153-56; and Danvers, *Portuguese in India*, pp. 310-20.

20 Cf. Danvers, *Portuguese in India*, p. 320.

21 On the final debacle on Ceylon, cf. Winius, *Fatal History*, pp. 156-66; Danvers, *Portuguese in India*, pp. 310-20.

22 Cf. Danvers, *Portuguese in India*, II: pp. 324-25; Boxer, *A India Portuguesa*, pp. 59-60; and De Souza, *Medieval Goa*, pp. 33-34.

23 Cf. Historical Archive of Goa, Panaji [HAG] *Livros das monçoes do Reino* (Monsoon Books) [MR] 26B, fos. 337-41v., Governors of India to Queen Regent, 17/XII/1658. The contents of this letter were reviewed by the Overseas Council in Lisbon in October 1661, cf. Arquivo Historico Ultramarino, Lisbon, [AHU], Documentos avulsos relativos a India (Unbound documents relating to India) [DAI] Box 25, Document 36, *consulta* of Overseas Council, 11/X/1661.

24 For details on the initial stages of the incursion, cf. AHU, DAI/25 Document 36, *consulta* of Overseas Council, 11/X/1661; HAG/MR 26B fos. 337-341v., Governors of India to Queen Regent, 17/XII/1658; and AHU, DAI/24, Document 172, Mendonça Furtado to Queen Regent, 2/XII/1660.

25 On Mendonça Furtado's early career, cf. Gayo, *Nobiliario de Familias de Portugal* XX (Braga, 1939), pp. 53-56; Caetano de Sousa *Historia Genealogica* XI (Coimbra, 1953), pp. 260-61; Martins Zuquete *Nobreza de Portugal* II (Lisbon, 1960), p. 678; Braamcamp Freire *Brasões da Sala de Sintra* II (Coimbra, c. 1923), pp. 366-67; HAG Codex 650 fos. 9-10; Boxer *A India Portuguesa*, pp. 43-44, 59-61; Queiroz, *The Temporal and Spiritual Conquest of Ceylon*, trans. by S.G. Perera (Colombo, 1930), p. 990; and Glenn J. Ames, "A Noble Life: Luis de Mendonça Furtado and

239

the Quest for *Fama* in Baroque Portugal and her Empire" *Revista Portuguesa de História* XXXII (1997-1998), pp. 305-329.

26   Cf. AHU, DAI/24, Document 172, Mendonça Furtado to Queen Regent, 2/XII/1660.

27   Cf. Fernão de Queiroz, *The Temporal and Spiritual Conquest of Ceylon*, trans. by S.G. Perera, (Colombo, 1930), pp. 1000-1002. For additional details on the campaign, cf. AHU, DAI/24, Document 172, Mendonça Furtado to Queen Regent, 2/XII/1660; AHU, DAI/25 Document 36, *consulta* of Overseas Council on Salsette campaign, 11/X/1661; and Boxer, *A Índia Portuguesa* p. 60 and the sources cited therein.

28   On these renewed offensive, among others, cf. Majumdar, *Mughal Empire,* pp. 221-31, 242-65; *Cambridge History,* IV: pp.250-55; Sharma, *Mughal Empire,* pp. 410-13; and Richards, *Mughal Empire,* pp. 205-25.

29   Among others. cf. Richards, *Mughal Empire,* pp. 217-25.

30   Cf. AHU, DAI/24, Document 139, Miguel de Almeida to Queen Regent, 18/XI/1659.

31   Detailed in Glenn J. Ames, *Renascent Empire? The House of Braganza and the Quest for Stability in Portuguese Monsoon Asia, ca. 1640-83* (Amsterdam, 2000). Also, cf. Ames, "The *Estado da Índia,* 1663-1677: Priorities and Strategies in Europe and the East," *Revista Portuguesa de História* XXII (1987), pp. 31-46; The *Carreira da Índia,* 1668-1682: Maritime Enterprise and the Quest for Stability in Portugal's Asian Empire, *The Journal of European Economic History* XX (1991), pp. 7-27; "Spices and Sulphur: Some New Evidence on the Quest for Economic Stabilization in Portuguese Monsoon Asia, 1668-1682,": *The Journal of European Economic History* XXIV (1995), pp.465-87and Pedro II and the *Estado da Índia*: Braganzan Absolutism and Overseas Empire, 1668-1683," *Luso-Brazilian Review* XXXIV:II (1997), pp. 1-13.

32   Glenn J. Ames, "The Straits of Hurmuz Fleets: Omani-Portuguese Naval Rivalry and Encounters, c. 1660-1680," *The Mariner's Mirror,* LXXXIII (November, 1997), pp. 398-409.

33   Cf. AHU, DAI/24, Document 172, Mendonça Furtado to Queen Regent, 2/XII/1660; and the formal investigation report into this incident found in AHU DAI/24 Document 169, 21/VII/1660.

17

MERCHANTS, MARKETS AND COMMODITIES: SOME ASPECTS OF PORTUGUESE COMMERCE WITH MALABAR

Pius Malekandathil

Malabar was a commercial zone of prime importance for the Europeans who entered the Indian Ocean region even before the discovery of Cape route. However with the circumnavigation of the Cape of Good Hope, the Portuguese raised claim for an exclusive right to the new route, which gave an entirely new character to the trade of Asia including that of Malabar[1]. In fact the strategies of the Lusitanians to control Asian trade revolved round two modes of operations: on the one hand diverse mechanisms were evolved to prevent the flow of commodities from the Indian waters to the Levant. The elaborate system of *cartaz*-armada-fortress was introduced to severe the commercial links traditionally existing in the Indian Ocean region with Italian ports and thus to prevent the entry of oriental commodities into Mediterranean ports. On the other hand attempts were made to strengthen the Cape route commerce that started in Cochin or Goa (and fed by a number of politico-economic satellite units established along the west coast of India) and finally terminated in Lisbon. It was through the newly emerged Cochin-Goa-Lisbon commercial axis that the Portuguese tried to integrate the Indian Ocean World Economy with the Atlantic World Economy, which ultimately gave a new dimension to international trade. This takes us to the central problem of our investigation: How far did this re-orientation of Indo-European commerce, implemented by the Portuguese, affect the various mercantile groups and the market structure of Malabar. Were these impacts restricted to the exchange centers on the coast alone or did they permeate into inland markets? How did the Portuguese try to control the markets? What role did the Portuguese policies play in bringing about transformation processes among the merchant groups of Malabar? What were the responses of the diverse trading communities and market centers to the challenges raised by the re-structuring of trade both at regional and international levels? These questions are answered against the backdrop of the history of commerce carried out with Malabar by the Portuguese.

Commercial Scenario in Pre-Portuguese Malabar

Malabar, by the time the Portuguese traders stepped into its shores in 1498, had evolved a well-equipped market mechanism in its exchange centers. It in fact revoled round a port-hierarchy that evolved in the thirteenth century, in which Calicut held the superior economic and political position, while Quilon, Cochin and Cannanore were commercially confined to secondary roles[2]. The fourteenth and fifteenth centuries were a period in which the Zamorin consolidated his political and commercial position in Malabar with the help of Al-Karimi merchants linked with the Mamluks of Egypt[3]. Calicut became the rallying point for the traders from the Muslim world viz., Maghreb, Tunisia, Egypt, Yemen, Persia etc., who were eventually emerging as the principal mercantile group in the Indian Ocean region from the fourteenth century onwards[4]. By the end of the fifteenth century the developments in Cannanore were heading towards the direction of transforming it into a Muslim port[5]. It coincided with the Calicut's expansion to Cranganore, where the commercial hegemony of the Muslim traders was extended along with the political suzerainty of the Zamorin. Meanwhile the *Perumpadappu Swarupam*, looking for a place outside the orbit of the Zamorin's conquest, shifted its residence in 1405 from Cranganore (Mahodayapuram) to Cochin, which had by this time emerged as an important port

Merchants, Markets and Commodities

thanks to the great geo-physical changes that occurred because of the flood in the river Periyar in 1341A.D.[6] In fact the political expansion of the Zamorin and the commercial expansion of the Muslim traders went hand in hand to a great part of land-cum-sea–space, starting from north Kerala and stretching down to south, up to Cochin. These economic and political moves were taking almost a pan Kerala dimension, in which the Zamorin had the political agenda of expanding his territorial hegemony while the Muslim merchants had the commercial ambition of extending their trade networks.

The economic growth of Cochin, which depended greatly on the rich pepper producing hinterland located in the neighbouring areas, invited Zamorin's interference[7]. Towards the end of the fifteenth century the Zamorin, who attacked Cochin with the help of Arab merchants, demanded the conversion of this port into a Muslim trade center. One of the conditions imposed by the Zamorin upon the vanquished king of *Perumpadappu Swarupam* was that the Nazarenes (St.Thomas Christians) should be driven out from Cochin denying them right to participate in its trade, which in turn should be conferred upon the Muslim traders of Calicut.[8] However, even later the merchant guilds associated with these Christian traders seem to have continued to operate for some more time, as is evident from the existence of a merchant guild in Cochin called *Korran*, from which Francisco de Albuquerque bought 4000 *bhars* of well-dried pepper in 1503[9]. At the time of the arrival of the Portuguese, Quilon was the only port in Kerala, where Muslim presence was relatively less and where St.Thomas Christian traders (linked with the old Christian guilds) still retained some commercial predominance[10].

The Muslim traders who established their activities in the major markets of Malabar in the pre-Portuguese period were not a monolithic group; they included at least three main strands, which were held together by the commonality of religion and common *shafi'ite* tradition linked with Arab origin. The *paradesi* Muslims, among whom the al-Karimi merchants engaged in spice-trade with Mamluk's Egypt formed major component, appropriated the transoceanic trade emanating from the ports of Kerala and terminating in the ports of eastern Mediterranean, while the Marakkar Muslims, who were the natives of the coastal region between Kunimedu and Nagapattinam on the Coromandel coast, monopolistically held the coastal trade between the ports of Malabar and the Coromandel. As the *paradesis* from Red sea ports and the Marakkars from Coromandel appropriated the major chunk of Malabar commerce, the local Mappila Muslims, who were dwarfed by the two, were confined to peddling trade and stood commercially at the lowest strata[11]. While on the one hand the family networks and religious bonds helped the expansion of the Muslim traders, on the other hand, with the increasing capital accumulation, the frame of the merchant guild system was slowly disappearing from among the Jewish and Christian traders, who had by this time begun to resort to individual initiatives in commercial activities. Mathias of Kayamkulam[12] and Tarqe Tome (Tarakan Thomas) of Quilon[13] were the two frequently quoted merchants, who emerged into prominence in the first decade of the Sixteenth century, from the southern ports of Kerala.

The markets of Malabar were highly monetized with a variety of coins in circulation. Peter Holzschuher, who visited the exchange centers of Kerala in 1503 as an artillerist and a trader in the vessel of Afonso de Albuquerque, has given a detailed account of the market conditions of the land. There were three categories of native coins in circulation: a) The gold coin called *panam*, which was of light 15 carat gold. It was the main monetary medium used for exchanges in Calicut, Cannanore and Cochin, where 19 *panams* formed one Portuguese *cruzado*. However the value of *panam* was not uniform all through Malabar ports: in Quilon one *panam* had 19 carat gold and 12 *panams* of Quilon made one European ducat or *cruzado*. In fact the *panam* of Quilon was more valuable than that of Calicut and Cannanore. b) The silver coin called *Chare*, which was in circulation in all the port-towns of Malabar, where 16 *Chare* formed one *panam*. c) In Quilon there was also a copper coin called *Cashe* and 15 *Cashe* formed one *panam*[14]. The copper coin of Quilon seems to have had more intrinsic value than the silver coin *Chare*, as is well evidenced by the difference in constituting units. The high demand for copper for the manufacture of household utensils must have added considerable value to this metal, which in turn must also have been transferred to the coins made out of copper. As early as 1409 Ma Huan, who accompanied Cheng Ho (the famous Ming Admiral), has made reference to the use of gold coin called *panam* and the silver coin *Chare* (Ma Huan calls it *Ta-urh*) in the exchanges of Cochin. However, in 1409 the *Chare (Ta-urh)* had more value than the early sixteenth century *Chare*, as Ma Huan mentions that a *panam* was fifteen *Ta-urhs* only.[15]

Besides these typically Malabar coins, there were also other small silver coins like the silver *tangas* of Gujarat, of Bijapur, of Vijayanagara and the *larins* of Persia in circulation in the trade centers of Malabar.[16] Coins from the Mediterranean and Western trade centres also circulated in great number. The most important among them was the *Xerafins* of Cairo, which entered Malabar through the active commerce with the Mamluk Egypt. Along with them, the Venetian and the Genoan ducats also began to enter in large numbers through the Levant traders[17]. The gold coin called *pagoda* (which was called so because of the representation of *Varaha* or the Boar avatar of Vishnu on it) was referred to as *Pardao* (a corruption of the Sanskrit *pratapa*) *d'ouro* and was used all along the Western India including Malabar[18].

Thus on the eve of the Portuguese arrival in India, the markets and mercantile classes of Malabar operated as vital component parts of wider circuits of commerce linked with regional and international exchange systems: on the east the strands of this circuit extended up to South East Asia while on the west they reached up to the Mediterranean.

The Portuguese Attempts to Control Markets

Though Vasco da Gama's arrival in Calicut in 1498 via Cape route marked a new chapter in the history of commerce in Europe and Asia, da Gama and his men could impress neither the king nor the market of Calicut as traders and they found it difficult to sell the commodities, which they brought along with them in their first voyage. This was mainly because of the fact that the first Portuguese came not with any commercial preparation (but with the mission of finding a sea-route to India via Cape of Good Hope) and secondly because of the privileged position of the *paradesi* Muslim merchants in Calicut, who had better commercial links and political influence to engineer intrigues against the Portuguese and to keep them away from the Zamorin's market[19]. However the cargo, which Vasco da Gama got from the land of the Kolathiri, fetched for the Portuguese a profit worth sixty times the cost of expedition[20].

The first commercial fleet of the Portuguese consisting of 1200 men and 13 vessels, which also had the mercantile collaboration of Bartolomeo Marchioni and other Italian merchants, came to India under the command of Pedro Alvarez Cabral in 1500. However, the events followed by Cabral's demand for preferential treatment in the loading of the spices ushered in a belligerent atmosphere characterized by capturing of Arab ships, killing of the Portuguese factor and the destruction of the factory, massacring of innocents and massive destruction of the market and city of the Zamorin[21]. The commercial mission of Cabral became successful thanks to the timely help of the king of Cochin, from whom he obtained about 104920 kilograms of pepper, 20984 kilograms of ginger, 31476 kilograms of cinnamon for transshipment to Lisbon[22]. Besides cargo for Lisbon, he also won the friendship of the king of Cochin, who even gave a part of the port area for the establishment of a Portuguese factory[23]. Later the fleet of João da Nova that came in 1501 also procured majority of its cargo from Cochin alone, where, in the absence of sufficient capital for conducting trade, the local ruler even stood as surety for the Portuguese to buy spices. João da Nova took 52459 kilograms of pepper, 2623 kilograms of ginger and 23607 kilograms of cinnamon to Portugal from Cochin and Cannanore, of which the latter eventually was made the first and the last port of call in India for the vessels of *Carreira da India* [24].

However the entry of the Portuguese into the spice-market of Malabar made the prices shoot up and the merchants were reluctant to sell their commodities at the old price offered by the Portuguese. With the penetration into the markets of Cochin, Cannanore and finally Quilon in 1502, the Portuguese were compelled to evolve mechanisms to control markets to their favour. The price was shooting up all these years: In Calicut the price of pepper per quintal was 4.64 ducats in 1498, which increased to 5.96 ducats in 1500. In some markets of Malabar it rose to 14 ducats per quintal by 1502. The price of cloves per quintal increased from 9.88 ducats in 1498 to 26 ducats in 1502[25]. Vasco da Gama tried to check the rise in prices and to control the market mechanisms by dictating a fixed price for the spices. On 3rd January 1503, he entered into an agreement with the merchants of Cochin fixing the price of a *bhar* (166.3kgs) of pepper at 160 *panams* (8.3 *cruzados*). In Cannanore the price of a *bhar* (Cannanore *bhar* was worth 205.6kgs) of pepper was fixed at 210 *panams*.[26] . This price-fixation was, indeed, an under pricing of the commodities, as the price for the same quantity of pepper in Calicut in 1500 was 360 *panams* and the loss for the merchants of Cochin per *bhar* was almost 200 *panams*[27]. With the low price both in Cochin and Cannanore, only Calicut seemed to attract traders by keeping relatively a higher price. However, later in 1513, by enabling a pro-Portuguese candidate to occupy the throne of Calicut and by establishing peace treaty with him, the Portuguese tried to extend the same market-control mechanisms to Calicut as well. With this peace treaty, the price of Calicut was brought down, as a result of which one *bhar* of pepper in Calicut in 1516 cost only 10.17 *cruzados*[28] . It shows that the price of Calicut was reduced almost to the half and was brought near to that of Cochin. The price fixation, thus, was developed by the Portuguese into a mechanism to under-price the commodities of Malabar and to control its markets to their favour. The only alternative left to the Malabar traders to escape from this situation was to carry the commodities across the ghat to Tamilnadu and to transship them from the ports of Coromandel to the ports of Red sea and Mediterranean[29]. However this route, besides being risky, involved much expense and used to take away much of the possible profit.

While accepting the proposal of Vasco da Gama for price-fixation, the merchants of Malabar demanded that three-fourth of the payment should be made in cash and one-fourth in the form of copper[30]. In 1503 about ½ to 1/3 of the price of pepper in Cochin was paid in copper[31]. This mode of payment necessitated that a large quantity of copper was imported to Malabar from the copper mines of Alps region and upper Hungary through the German intermediaries till the beginning of copper crisis in Europe in 1570s. (After 1570s silver in the form of "Spanish *reals* of eight" and gold became the important commodities imported to Malabar). In the first decade of the sixteenth century 4000 quintals of copper were imported to the Portuguese trade centers of Malabar, which rose to 6000 quintals in the second decade[32]. The high demand for this metal from the social classes of copper-smiths and bronze-smiths, who were making household utensils for the aristocratic families of Kerala, played a vital role in making it the most important commodity imported to Malabar till 1570s. Cannanore had experienced the highest demand for copper where a *farasol* (8.31 kilograms) of copper was priced at 45 *panams*, where as in Quilon it was only 36 *panams*[33]. Materials like mercury, camphor etc., also used for the manufacture of copper and bronze vessels were imported to Malabar in considerable quantity. In Quilon mercury was available at 55 *panams* per *farasol*, where as its price in Cannanore was 80 *panams*. Camphor in Quilon was priced at 8½ *panams* per *farasol*[34]. This price situation in Quilon and Cannanore evidently points to the regional difference in their demands, which is also suggestive of the degree of the activities of artisan-groups of copper-smiths and bronze-smiths in the suburban areas adjacent to these markets.

Corresponding to price-fixation and market-control, attempts were also made to control the movement of commodities by monopolizing spice trade. After the initial experiments of allowing the participation of private merchants, the Portuguese crown declared pepper, cloves, ginger, cinnamon, mace nut-meg, silk, sealing wax etc as commodities reserved for the crown by the order issued in 1520[35]. The most valuable among these spices was cloves which was sold at 600 *panams* per *bhar* in Calicut, second place was occupied by nut-meg with 450 *panams*, mace 430 *panams*, long-pepper 400 *panams*, cinnamon 390 *panams* and brazil wood 160 *panams*. The cheapest spice was ginger, which cost 120 *panams* per *bhar* or 6 *panams* per *farasola*[36]. Cloves, nut-meg and mace, which were originally the products of South East Asia, entered Malabar ports regularly till the Dutch occupation of the sources of these spices in 1605. Cinnamon, coming from Ceylon, was also one among the highly priced spice item taken to Portugal. However, the merchants were prevented from conducting trade in these spices with the imposition of royal monopoly on them, which in fact turned out to be a control mechanism on free trade. Nevertheless, the Portuguese could not have a perfect and monopolistic control over the spice-trade for a long period in the Indian Ocean region, as spices were taken to the Red sea-Venice routes frequently after 1535. But, in spite of the failure in the control mechanisms of the Portuguese, the Cape-route, through which they carried out Indo-European commerce, was enviously preserved by them as a royal monopoly for about a century.

Collaboration with Indigenous Merchants

The Portuguese response to the Muslim merchants trading in Malabar ports was a mixed one. On the one hand they maintained a "crusading approach" against the *paradesi* Muslim traders, who formed the backbone of the Red-sea-Venice trade, while on the other hand the Portuguese were increasingly looking to the Mappila and Marakkar merchants as possible commercial partners for ensuring cargo for their Lisbon-bound vessels and as suppliers of food-materials for their factories and colonies established on the coast, cut off from the production centers. In fact the mercantile collaboration of the Marakkar and Mappila Muslims was incorporated by the Portuguese at the time of the price-fixation initiated by Vasco da Gama in 1502[37]. From 1503 onwards we find the Marakkar merchants actively cooperating with the Portuguese in procuring cargo for the *carreira* vessels. The first among these Muslim merchants to collaborate with the Portuguese was Charine Mecar(Karim Marakkar), who came to Francisco de Albuquerque on 7th October 1503 without the knowledge of Zamorin to supply pepper to the Portuguese vessels.[38] Later when the Zamorin tried to create an artificial famine in Cochin as a war-tactics by blocking rice supply to the city, Duarte Pacheco befriended Mame(Muhammad) Marakkar, the head of the Marakkar merchants in Cochin, to overcome this situation and to ensure regular supply of provisions in Cochin[39].

At a time when the Portuguese did not have strong base in India, the Marakkar merchants collaborated with them in many ways and above all helped them to procure spices from the various parts of Malabar for their Lisbon–bound vessels. In 1504 Cherina Marakkar and Mamale Marakkar supplied 3000 *bhars* of pepper for the fleet of Lopo Soares[40]; Nino Marakkar used to supply cinnamon from Ceylon to the Portuguese factory in Cochin[41] and he even supplied ships and fighting force consisting of 1500 soldiers to confront the forces of the Zamorin;[42] Chilay Marakkar gave his own ship to the Portuguese to take commodities to Goa[43]. Besides the Marakkar traders, the Mappila merchants of Edappilly like Ali Apule, Coje Mappila and Abraham Mappila also used to supply regularly pepper to the Portuguese in Cochin.[44] These Muslim traders, who co-operated with the Portuguese commercial system, were given considerable freedom to send vessels and commodities to Red sea ports, provided that they take *cartazes* or safe-conduct from the Portuguese[45].

The Portuguese expansion into the markets of Cannanore in 1501 and Quilon in 1502 was followed by the conversion of Cochin into the capital of the emerging *Estado da India* in 1505, which was the chief base of political and commercial operations for the Portuguese from the time of Cabral. This commercial expansion went hand in hand with the establishment of a chain of fortresses linking and monitoring the prime centers of exchange in Malabar viz., Cochin (the first fortress built in 1503, but later rebuilt in 1505), Cannanore (1508), Quilon (1519) and Cranganore (1536). Afonso de Albuquerque extended the chain of fortresses to Goa(1510), Malacca(1511) and Hormuz(1515), which, he believed, would check and control the movements of the vessels plying in the Indian Ocean and prevent the flow of commodities to Red sea- Venice route[46].

Meanwhile the Marakkar merchants emerged as prominent traders of Malabar with the mass exodus of the *paradesi* Muslims from Calicut thanks to the peace treaty, which Afonso de Albuquerque signed in 1513 with the new Zamorin on his ascension into the throne after poisoning his uncle and predecessor. This peace treaty, which appeared more detrimental to their existence than the several battles against the Portuguese, made the majority of the *paradesi* Muslims including the al-Karimis flee from Calicut to other safer ports of Gujarat, Vijayanagara, Hormuz and Red sea[47]. The favourable atmosphere that prevailed during the Albuquerquian period enabled the Marakkar traders to establish themselves as the principal mercantile community in South India and the exodus of the *paradesi* Muslims from Calicut accelerated this transformation process.

The Emergence of New Merchant Groups

By the beginning of 1520s, Portuguese *casado*(meaning family- men particularly the Portuguese citizens married to native women) traders emerged as a prominent mercantile class involved in the intra-Asian trade emanating from the exchange centers of Malabar. The married Portuguese citizens had begun to take up local trade as a means of their livelihood as early as 1510. Eventually the Portuguese with private interests got organized into a lobbying group in Cochin, known as the "Cochin group", and were demanding less state interference (which Afonso de Albuquerque had implemented by an elaborate system of fortresses) and more an atmosphere of free trade. In fact the nomination of Lopo Soares de Albergia as the new governor in 1515 was a victory to the private entrepreneurs among the *casados*, who made use of this favourable and liberal atmosphere for the extension of their commerce to the eastern space of Indian Ocean[48]. A major strand of the *casado* trade extended eastwards to the ports of Coromandel, Bengal, Malacca and South East Asia, while Cambay and Hormuz were also favoured navigational destinations of the *casados* of Cochin.

It is to be here specially noted that the abrupt emergence of the *casado* traders by 1520s coincided with the estrangement of Marakkar Muslim traders from Portuguese camp and their consequent shifting of loyalty to Zamorin. The frequent Portuguese attacks and confiscation of ships belonging to Marakkar traders, under the guise of checking *cartazes,* made many of them severe ties with the Portuguese and move over to Calicut. The prominent among them were Kunjali Marakkar, his brother Ahmad Marakkar, their uncle Muhammadali Marakkar and their dependents, who left Cochin in 1524 to settle down in Calicut. Coincidently, the Zamorin, whose relationship with the Portuguese had already strained by this time, was also eagerly looking for merchants and naval personalities to fill in the gap created by the exodus of Arab Muslims in 1513. However, with the migration of the Marakkar Muslim traders from Cochin to Calicut, there began a transition phase in the mercantile activities of Malabar in which the Portuguese *casados* of Cochin, who stepped into this commercial vacuum, eventually began to emerge as the principal traders of the Indian Ocean region, while the Marakkar merchants under Kunjali, who shifted base of operation to Calicut, began to develop "corsair activities" as an alternative arrangement of trade.[49]

Meanwhile new merchant classes emerged also from the natives of Malabar, whose conversion to Christianity enabled them to operate under the commercial umbrella of the Portuguese. The most prominent among such traders was a relative of the Zamorin who got converted into Christianity and took the name D.João da Cruz. In 1513 the Zamorin after having concluded peace-treaty with the Portuguese sent a young relation of his (only 15 years old) to see".....Portugal, its king and his things". On reaching Lisbon he learned to read and write Portuguese and lived at the court of king Manuel for a considerable period of time. Later he embraced Catholic faith and was given the name Dom João da Cruz (Gaspar Correia calls him the young Nair João da Cruz) and was accorded the habit of the famous Order of Christ on 12th March 1515[50]. By becoming a *fidalgo* (noble man) of the royal house and a knight of the Order of Christ he secured a grant for his entire life.[51] On returning to Calicut in 1516 he built a church there for his use.[52] Occupying a privileged position as a knight of the Order of Christ, he got licences to send a certain amount of pepper and ginger to Portugal for three years till the crown officially monopolized spice trade in 1520. Another privilege he got was that he secured a loan of 7400 *pardaos* from the Portuguese factory of Calicut to conduct trade and earn his livelihood. João da Cruz stepped into commercial activities at a time when private trade was thriving in the Portuguese settlements. However, soon in 1521 he lost all his merchandise because of the drowning of the ship, in which he was carrying the cargo, and was hence unable to repay his loans[53]. Even in this crisis phase as well, he was given permission (in 1525) by the crown to send 100 quintals of pepper and 30 quintals of ginger to Cambay[54].

Nevertheless by 1525 João da Cruz shifted his residence from Calicut to Cochin probably against the background of the strained relationship between the Portuguese and the Zamorin, who had already by this time extracted an amount of 35,000 *pardaos* from João da Cruz for becoming a Christian in Portugal.[55] But in Cochin he was arrested and imprisoned by the Portuguese for not having paid back the loan, which then came about 4000 *pardaos*. In his letter of 1533, he says that with his imprisonment he lost much of his credibility with the kings of the land and with the people, who wanted to embrace Christianity. He further says that about a thousand of them, who earlier had showed willingness to embrace Christian faith, were reluctant to do so because of the ill treatment meted out to him. However he still hopefully places certain requests before the crown that would safeguard his entrepreneurial activities, which ultimately would help him to improve his financial position. In his letter he expresses a variety of desires: (a) the post of captain and factor of Quilon, which, if conferred upon him, would enable him to prevent pepper-smuggling to Vijayanagara kingdom; (b) the monopoly right of selling horses to Rey Grande(king of Cape Comorin), to the king of Travancore, to the kingdom of Chymbechenaque (Tumbichchi Nayak) and to the kingdom of Beteperemal (Vettumperumal who resided in Kayattar) and the neighbouring principalities which were involved in wars with Bisnaga(Vijayanagara) and Idalcao(Bijapur); (c) the office for collecting the tribute of the Pearl Fishery Coast which was lying in the territory of Rey Grande[56].

João da Cruz then turned his attention to Pearl Fishery coast, where he supplied horses from Cochin (imported from Hormuz) for the war needs of the local kings and combined the activities of trade in horses and evangelization into one unit of operation. He persuaded the people to embrace Christianity through the king of Cape Comorin, to whom he was selling horses. In 1537 he spoke with the king of Travancore on the advantages of being a Christian and pointed out to him how the king would get horses regularly from the Portuguese for his wars against the king of Cape Comorin, provided that the king and his men would become Christians. Due to the persuasion of João da Cruz, who was assisted by Vicar General Miguel Vaz, about 50,000 people were already converted and by 1537 the number increased to 80,000[57]. St.Francis Xavier writes in 1542 that the Paravas were baptized 8 years before[58] and the Jesuit priest Manuel Teixeira attributes the evangelization work among the Paravas to João da Cruz, who then used to take horses to that coast.[59] Thus a new category of merchants was evolving in Malabar, who were carving out commercial privileges in exchange for their service in the spread of Christianity. Nevertheless the mass conversion of Pearl Fishery coast into Christianity undertaken by João da Cruz eventually led to the clashes of commercial interests between the Portuguese and the Marakkar merchants of Calicut on the question of conducting pearl trade.

Corresponding to the emergence of various new trading classes, diverse trade-routes linking the exchange centers of

Malabar also evolved: some operated within the commercial system of the Portuguese, while some others ran parallel to the Lusitanian networks and functioned as channels for the diversion of spices to the ports of Red sea. João da Cruz refers to a parallel network of markets and exchange centers running through the hinterland part of Malabar and finally terminating at Cape Comorin. They started from the land of the pepper (Vadakkenkur) king called Chempenecoy (Chempene koyil or king of Chembe). The land route for the diversion of pepper to Cape Comorin passed through the lands of Lerta Morte Treberery (Ilayidathu Mutha Tiruvadi, whose kingdom was in Arthinkal near Shertalai), Teque Cute Nayre(Thekkumkutti Nayari or the king of Thekkenkur), Cherabacoy (Chiravay Koyil or the king of Chiravay family) Yreme Treberery , Yrama Trebery(may be Rama Tiruvadi or Iravi Varma Tiruvadi)[60], Unyque Trebery(Unni Kerala Tiruvadi)[61], Ylamana Lambeatry(Lambratry?). It finally terminated in the kingdom of Rey Grande (*Valiya Tampuran* or senior Tiruvadi of Tiruppapur)[62], which was the title of the king of Cape Comorin.

Meanwhile, by 1540s the Kunjali's men, who were by this time ousted from their trading bases in Coromandel, began to increasingly resort to dual modes of operations: on the one hand to patrol the west coast with tacit or explicit consent of the Zamorin, blockading and plundering the vessels of the Portuguese and on the other hand to integrate the native trade net-works for sending spices regularly to Red Sea-Venice route. The first mode of operation provided them wealth for continued resistance and space for the movement of the vessels destined for Red sea ports. Most of the anti-Portuguese factors seem to have co-operated with these corsair endeavours, which appeared as both political and economic outlets for exercising freedom. The corsair activity developed by Kunjali's men turned out to be an alternative arrangement of trade, where plundering and confiscation of enemy vessels went hand in hand with parallel shipment of commodities to the destination of their choice[63].

Coincidently the Muslim merchants of Cannanore had also by this time developed a parallel commercial network outside the Lusitanian control systems by keeping Maldives as the base for diversion of merchandise to the Levant. The commodities of South East Asia began to move to Red sea through the straits of Karaidu and Haddumati(opposite the ports of Sumatra)via Maldives, a route which bypassed all the control mechanisms of the Portuguese[64]. By exercising control over this route, Mamale and later other *regedors* including Ali raja succeeded in generating wealth from its commerce for their state-building ventures at Cannanore.

Monetary Rewards to the Native Rulers

With the establishment of rigid and elaborate system of trade-control on the west coast of India, which the Portuguese implemented through the instruments of *cartaz*, armada and fortresses, the private traders began to increasingly use the diverse traditional inland-trade-routes starting from the spice-hinterland of Kerala and terminating in the seaports of Coromandel for diversion of commodities to the destinations of their choice. As the Portuguese used to give only low price for the spices, which was fixed in 1502 and continued to remain the same till 1620s, the producers and the traders preferred the inland-trade-routes, which offered relatively higher price. The most prominent among these routes ran across the Western Ghats, although the land-route running parallel to the sea-route and terminating in Cape Comorin was also very active. However, the Portuguese, whose power depended more on the sea and influence restricted to the littoral, had little control over the far-flung spice-producing centers and over the inland routes used by the private traders. In order to overcome this handicap and to ensure continuous supply of spices at the Portuguese factories on the coast, the Lusitanians began to pay regular annuities and subsidies to various kings ruling in the hinterland[65].

The monetary rewards to the native rulers varied on the basis of the supply of pepper cargo from their kingdoms to the Portuguese factory and on the basis of how their markets were facilitated to feed the Portuguese commercial centers. The highest monetary reward was given to the king of Cochin, who used to get annually 640 *cruzados* from the Portuguese[66]. The principal region from which the Portuguese used to get pepper for their Lisbon-bound vessels was the kingdom of Vadakkenkur, which they used to call pepper kingdom (*reino da pimenta*). Correspondingly the members of the royal family were given special monetary rewards. The share of the ruling king of Vadakkenkur was 240 *pardaos* per year[67], while the *Amma Rani*(mother of the king of Vadakkenkur) used to get annually 100 *pardaos* more as her share, which was raised to 220 *xerafins* in 1600[68]. The smaller kingdoms of Alengad, Parur, Diamper and Porcad were located in the vicinity of Cochin and were always looked upon as the satellite feeding units for the politico-commercial ventures of the Portuguese. The rulers of each of these principalities were given annually 240 *pardaos* each in recognition of their service for the trading activities of the Portuguese in Malabar[69]. From 1560s onwards, two kings were reigning in the kingdom of Thekkenkur; probably one residing at Kottayam and the other at Kanjirappilly. Each of them used to get 100 *pardaos* each.[70] The Karta of Alwaye was given an annual amount of 140 *pardaos* [71] for enabling the spices coming through the river Periyar to flow to the Portuguese factory in Cochin. In 1600 the king of Thodupuzha (differently written as Turuguly or Turubuli) became the king of Vadakkenkur and transferred the seat of the combined kingdom to Caricotty (Karikode near Thodupuzha). Fracisco da Costa writes in 1605 that only the king of Thodupuzha and Vadakkenkur used to supply pepper regularly to the Portuguese in Cochin, for which he received an annual reward of 240 *xerafins* [72]

In principle these monetary rewards were given to the native rulers to keep their production centers and markets integrated with the Portuguese commercial structure. However it did not bring out the desired result, even though these regions continued to feed the Portuguese factories occasionally, if not regularly. In fact the native kings, who used to receive monetary rewards from the Portuguese, did not resort to force or any coercive measure over the producers and merchants to supply spices only to the Portuguese. The price-factor did play the vital role: both the cultivators and the traders in the interior region preferred to sell commodities to those who offered the highest price, rather than taking them to the distant Portuguese centers only to sell at already quoted lower price, which deprived them of all incentives. As Caesar Frederick says, the better quality pepper was highly priced and it went to inland-routes, which finally found way to Mecca[73].

The intensification of the movement of commodities through the inland regions of Kerala led to the revitalization of the already existing markets, besides the emergence of new ones in the various nodal points. The important markets thus formed in the inland part of Kerala were Erimamoly (Erumely), Canharapely (Kanjirappilly), Iratepely (Erattupetta), Turubuly (Thodupuzha), Zaruquly (Chalakudy), Corgeira (Kodakara) and Paleacate Cheri (Palakkad Churam).[74] These places became important exchange centers because of their junctional position between the trade routes to Tamilnadu and because of their vicinity to the principal production centers of Kerala. It was chiefly through these places that spices were taken across the ghat to Tamilnadu, which ultimately moved to the ports of Coromandel for further transshipment to the ports of Red sea or to those of Bengal and China. As Ferdinand Cron (who reached Cochin in 1587 as the agent of the Fuggers and the Welsers) testifies, the powerful merchants involved in the ghat-route trade were taking pepper to the Coromandel coast regularly with the help of a large caravan of 800 to 1000 oxen [75]. The volume of pepper taken from the markets of Kerala to Tamilnadu was as follows: from Erumely 3000 *bhars*, from Kanjirappilly and Tecanqutes(the kingdom of Thekkenkur) 4000 *bhars*, from Erattupetta 1000 *bhars*, from Chalakudy 5000 *bhars*, from Kodakara 3000 *bhars* and from Palakkad 3000 *bhars*[76] In fact the distribution of pepper cultivation, the territorial topography, the political system and above all the demand-factor played vital role in shaping the routes of pepper trade in Malabar[77].

The Changing Trends in Commerce

As the inland markets and merchant groups were developing a trend towards Coromandel-oriented economic activities, the *casado* traders engaged in the sea-borne trade were increasingly turning out to be pro-Asian in their operations. In fact the flow of people (including the *Cristãos novos* or New Christians converted from Judaism) from the mother country to the Portuguese settlements in Malabar increased unprecedentedly by 1530s, as a result of which the number of *casados* involved in private trade also swelled[78]. These *casado* traders eventually began to bag huge profit from their trade with the ports of Bay of Bengal and South East Asia, which was the most lucrative among the destinations in Asia. However a good many of the *casado* traders were against the official trading system of the Portuguese, which they found as an obstacle for the free development of their entrepreneurial talents. Some of them even joined hands with Muslim traders and corsairs to attack the fleet of the Portuguese Government. In 1537, the Portuguese *casados* residing in Culimute(?) used to make ships and armaments for Kunjali's men and were helping the latter to enlarge their fleet. The reason for the association of the Portuguese *casados* with the Muslim corsairs and traders was explained by one Diogo Fernandes as due to the Muslim origin of the wives of the *casados*[79].

By 1550s the rift between the *casado* traders and the official Portuguese structure took wider and serious dimensions: the *casados* entered into a phase of conflict with the mother-country-born-*fidalgos*(nobles), whom the crown preferred in distributing concessions and public offices. The *casados*, who opposed the hegemony of nobles in Portuguese India, even developed a system almost parallel to and relatively independent of mother-country arrangements. By 1559, even a rumour spread that the *Estado da India* (obviously assisted by the *casados*), taking advantage of the presence of Dom Constantino de Braganza, a noble of royal blood as viceroy, had cut ties with Lisbon. The Lisbon administration, being alarmed of the situation, tried to appease the *casados* by reserving some navigational lines for them to conduct regional trade[80]. Later with the liberalization of Indo-European commerce in 1570, the Portuguese *casados* got more freedom and opportunity to extend their empire of private trade. In fact the Portuguese private traders carved out more space for operation when the Indo-European trade was handed over to the German and Italian contractors during the period between 1570 and 1598.

Interestingly this period also coincided with the phase of state-building activities, which Kunjali Marakkar initiated in Pudupattanam. Kunjali's assumption of the titles "Lord of the Indian Seas" and "King of the Malabar Moors" was only imitation of the title of *"regedor do mar"*, which the leader of Cannanore Muslims used to bear in the transformation phase from mercantile stature to kingly stature. A good many of the Muslim merchants took part in the state-building ventures of Kunjali, in which a great share of the mercantile capital, which should have been invested for further commerce and productive ventures, became frozen by diverting it for the establishment of diverse instruments and machineries of state as well as for meeting the expenses of the recurring wars. With the destruction of Pudupattanam by the Luso-Zamorin force, it was, in fact, the surplus accumulated nearly for a century and transplanted into various state-structures that got shattered. The tragic aspect of this transformation process was that a great many of the Muslim traders, linked with the state-building ventures, turned out to be economically poor by the beginning of the seventeenth century and were incapable of undertaking any large-scale commercial activity that involved substantial capital. However, the Portuguese *casado* traders, on their part, made use of this situation to intensify their private trading activities and to penetrate into regions, which had so far been monopolistically held by the Muslim traders[81].

By this time the flow of spices through the ghat-route to Coromandel ports increased unprecedentedly with the estrangement of the spice-cultivating-cum-mercantile group of St.Thomas Christians from the Portuguese, following the developments after the synod of Diamper in 1599. As we have already seen above, about 19,000 *bhars* of pepper were moving in 1605 to the exchange centers of Tamilnadu from Erumely, Kanjirappilly, Erattupetta (through Kumaly pass), Chalakudy (through Peringalkuthu), Kodakara (through Kormala) and

Palakkad (through Palakkad pass). As a result during the period between 1600 and 1609 the Portuguese did not get spices in Cochin for transshipment to Lisbon. Since this phenomenon of dearth of spices in Cochin continued for a long time, the vessels of *Carreira da India* stopped coming to Cochin to take pepper directly from there from 1611 onwards. With the diminishing supply of pepper in Cochin and with the increasing flow of spices from the hinterland to Coromandel coast through the mountain passes, there commenced a mass exodus of *casados* from 1612 onwards, from Cochin to Nagapattanam, Mylapore and other parts of eastern coast including Bengal, Pegu and Ceylon, to take advantage of the changed situation[82]. As a result of the flow of Portuguese *casados* to the prospective destinations in the eastern space of Indian Ocean from Cochin, the city experienced depopulation and decline of trade. The viceroy D.Jeronimo de Azevedo writes in 1617 that the city-population of Cochin was reduced to one-third[83]. The second and the third decades of the seventeenth century present a contrasting situation: while many of the middle class and lower middle class *casado* traders of the city of Cochin shifted their commercial bases to the Coromandel coast, the rich Portuguese *casados* of Cochin were supporting the tottered structure of the *Estado* by providing huge loans. By 1616 the loan given by them increased to 60,000 *cruzados*, an amount which the Portuguese Exchequer could not repay in the future[84]. Some of these bourgeoisie *casados* were even invited to send *navetas* (ships) carrying a cargo of 2000 quintals of pepper to Portugal every year starting from 1627 onwards[85].

Thus we find that different mechanisms developed in Malabar as responses to the challenges raised by the entry of the Portuguese into local markets. The Portuguese wanted to keep only the Indo-European trade as a royal monopoly, while the intra-Asian commerce by the *casados* as well as the Malabar traders was allowed to operate in a system, which acknowledged Portuguese commercial hegemony. Both the indigenous traders and the Portuguese private traders used to join hands frequently to expand commercial networks and to open up new markets.

Even in the diversion of commodities from the production centers of Kerala across the ghat to the ports of Coromandel, the hands of the indigenous merchants were active at the starting centers, and those of the *casados* at the terminal points. The merchants and the markets of Malabar reacted differently to the mercantilist means (both coercive and peaceful), which the Portuguese used to control and influence both the producers and the trading partners. The Portuguese attempts to monopolize the trade in spices and other wares, highly valued in Europe, undermined the existing atmosphere of free trade and liberal movement of commodities from Malabar, as a result of which alternative passages, running outside the control system of the Lusitanians, were evolved for the flow of commodities to traditional Red sea-Venice route. In short, though the mercantilist policy of the Portuguese to control the principal markets and their mechanisms through price-fixation and regular payment of protection rent to the rulers of the hinterlands helped the Indo-European commerce of the Portuguese to a great extent, the alternative market-arrangements and trade networks, developed and fed in the inland regions as well as outside by the indigenous traders and often assisted by *casados*, were also operating in a remarkably considerable measure in the frame of intra-Asian trade.

References:

1   K.N.Chaudhuri, *The Trading World of Asia and the English East India Company, 1660-1760*, London, 1978,p.1

2   Pius Malekandathil, *Portuguese Cochin and the Maritime Trade of India:1500-1663*,Unpublished Ph.D.Thesis submitted at Pondicherry Central University, 1998(Forthcoming as a volume in the South Asian Study Series of Heidelberg University, Germany),pp.47-48;101.See also Pius Malekandathil, *Urban Growth of Cochin in the Sixteenth and Seventeenth Centuries*, Unpublished M. Phil. Thesis submitted at Pondicherry Central University, Pondicherry, 1992,pp.24-37

3   For details about Al-Karimi merchants, see Walter J.Fischel, "The Spice Trade in Mamluke Egypt", in the *Journal of the Economic and Social History of the Orient*, vol. I, Leiden, 1958, p.165; Eliyahu Ashtor, "The Venetian Supremacy in Levantine Trade: Monopoly of Pre-colonialism", in the *Journal of European Economic History*, vol.III, Rome, 1974, p.27; Genevieve Bouchon, "Calicut at the Turn of the Sixteenth Century", in *The Asian Seas 1550-1800: Local Societies, European Expansion and the Portuguese, Revista de Cultura*, vol. I, Ano V, 1987, p.42

4   Ibn Batuta, *Die Reise des Arabers Ibn Batuta durch Indien und China*, ed.by Hanz von Mzik, Hamburg, 1911,pp.302-308; Genevieve Bouchon, "Les Musulmans du Kerala à l'Époque de la Découverte Portugaise", in *Mare Luso-Indicum*, 2, 1973, p.20

5   Genevieve Bouchon, *Regent of the Sea:Cannanore's Response to Portuguese Expansion, 1507-1528*, tran.by Louise Shackley, Delhi, 1988,pp.23-24;44

6   Pius Malekandathil, *Portuguese Cochin*,pp.41-43

7   Ibid.,pp.50-52

8   O.K.Nambiar, *The Kunjalis:Admirals of Calicut*, London, 1963,p.40; Pius Malekandathil, "The Portuguese and the St.Thomas Christians:1500-1570", A Paper presented in the International Seminar on *"The Portuguese and the Socio-Cultural Changes in India:1500-1800 AD"*, held at St. Thomas College, Pala, 4-11 December 1999,p.1.Forthcoming in the volume edited by K.S. Mathew, Teotonio de Souza and Pius Malekandathil, *The Portuguese and the Socio-Cultural Changes in India:1500-1800*, Fundação Oriente, 2001.

9   Reisebericht des Franciscus Dalbuquerque vom 27.December 1503, in B.Greiff, *Tagebuch des Lucas Rem aus den Jahren 1494-1541:Ein Beitrag zur Handelsgeschichte der Stadt Augsburg*, Augsburg, 1861,p.146. Both Jean Aubin and Genevieve Bouchon refer to Korran as a Christian merchant guild. See Jean Aubin, "L'apprentissage de l'Inde Cochin 1503-1504", in *Moyen Oriente et Ocean Indien*, 1988; Genevieve Bouchon, "Calicut at the Turn of the Sixteenth Century,p.44

10 In the Commentaries of Afonso Albuquerque we read that there was neither a single native Moor in Quilon in 1504 nor any foreigner there except the brother of Cherina Marakkar. See Walter de Gray Birch (ed.), *The Commentaries of the Great Afonso Dalboqerque, Second Viceroy of India*, New York, 1875,p.11. At the same time we find that the St.Thomas Christian traders as emissaries of the queen of Quilon inviting Vasco da Gama in 1502 for trading with Quilon. Nationalbibliothek in Wien, Nr.6948; Christine von Rohr, *Neue Quellen zur zweiten Indienfahrt Vasco da Gamas*, Leipzig, 1939, p.51. For details on the prominent St.Thomas Christian traders of the port of Quilon, see Raymundo Antonio de Bulhão Pato(ed.), *Cartas de Affonso de Albuquerque seguidas de documentos que as elucidam*,Lisboa,1884, tom.III,pp.30; 258-259

11 For details see Pius Malekandathil, "From Merchant Capitalists to Corsairs: The Role of Muslim Merchants in the Maritime Trade of the Portuguese", A Paper presented at the International Seminar on *The Maritime Activities in India with Special Reference to the Portuguese:1500-1800*, held at Department of History, Goa University, 25-28 April, 2001,pp.2-5

12 ANTT, Cartas dos Vice-Reis, Maço unico, No.2.Letter of Mathias to the king of Portugal dated 18-12-1504

13 Raymundo Antonio de Bulhão Pato(ed.), *Cartas de Affonso de Albuquerque*, tom.III,pp.30;258-259

14 Karl Otto Müller(ed.), *Welthandelsbräuche(1480-1540)(Deutsche Handelsakten des Mittelalters und der neu Zeit, Band V)*, Berlin, 1934,pp.118,210-213. The original of Peter Holzschuher's letter is preserved in "Paumgartnerschen Usancenbuch" in Fürstlich-Zeilsches Archiv of Leutkirch. For further details see Pius Malekandathil, *The Germans, the Portuguese and India*, Münster, 1999, pp. 45-46.

Pius Malekandathil

15 Ma Huan, Ying Yai Sheng Ian 12-"Kochih", as translated by W.W.Rockhill, "Notes on the Relations and Trade of China with Eastern Archipelago and the Coast of the Indian Ocean during the Fourteenth Century", T'oung Pao, vol.XVI,1915,Leiden, p.451

16 Gabriel Fernand, "Les poids, mesures et monnaies des Mers du Sud aux XVI et XVII siecles", in *Journal Asiatique*, (July-December:1920),Paris, 1921; Henry Yule and A.C.Burnell, *Hobson-Jobson: A Glossary of Colloquial Anglo-Indian Words and Phrases, and of Kindred Terms, Etymological, Historical, Geographical and Discursive*, ed.by William Crooke, London, 1903, p.506

17 Ibn Taghri Birdi, *History of Egypt, 1382-1469*,translated from the Arabic Annals, by William Popper, Los Angeles, 1954-1960, 7 vol.,part 4, p.30; Henry Yule and A.C.Burnell, *Hobson-Jobson*,pp.974-976

18 Ludovico di Varthema, *The Travels of Ludovico di Varthema in Egypt, Syria, Arabia Deserta and Arabia Felix, in Persia, India and Ethiopia, AD.1503-1508*, ed.by George Percy Badger, New York, 1863,pp.115-116; Henry Yule and A.C.Burnell, *Hobson-Jobson*,pp.653-657;673

19 Gernot Giertz, *Vasco da Gama, die Entdeckung des Seewegs nach Indien:ein Augenzeugenbericht 1497-1499*,Tübingen, 1980,pp.92-98

20 For a list of the spices brought by Vasco da Gama see "King Manuel's Letter to the King and Queen of Castile, July 1499" in E.G.Ravenstein(ed.), *A Journal of the First Voyage of Vasco da Gama, 1497-1499*, 1898,London, p.113

21 William Brooks Greenlee, *The Voyage of Pedro Alvares Cabral to Brazil and India from Contemporary Documents and Narratives*, London, 1938,pp.56; 83-84; 147-148; 169;

22 Rinaldo Fulin, *Diarii e diaristi Veneziani*, Venice, 1881, pp.157-164; Girolarro Priuli, *I Diarii di Girolamo Priuli:1494-1512*, vol.II,Bologna, 1933,p.174

23 William Brooks Greenlee, op. cit. ,p. 143

24 João da Nova, who came first to Cannanore visited it again on his way back from Cochin to Portugal to complete his cargo. Fernão Lopes de Castanheda, *Historia do descobrimento e conquista da India pelos Portugueses*, tom.I,cap.43, Coimbra, 1924,pp.93-96:Genevieve Bouchon, *Regent of the Sea*, pp.57,62; Marino Sanuto, *I Diarii de Marino Sanuto:1496-1533*, ed.by G.Berechet R.Fulin and Alii, Venice, 1897, vol.IV,p.544

25 Pius Malekandathil, *Portuguese Cochin*, pp. 249-250

26 Thome Lopes,"Navegação as Indias Orientales escrita em Portugues por Thome Lopes", in *Collecção de noticias para a historia e geografia das nações ultramarinas que vivem nos dominios Portugueses ou ilhes são vizinhas*, tom.II,nos.1&2, Lisbon,pp.181;193;200; Mateo da Bergamo in P. Peragallo(ed.), *Cenni intorno alla colonia italiana in Portogallo nei secoli XIV,XV e XVI*, Genoa, 1907,pp.119-120; Genevieve Bouchon, *Regent of the Sea*,p.72;Pius Malekandathil, *Portuguese Cochin*, pp.248,261; K.S.Mathew, *Portuguese Trade with India in the Sixteenth Century*, Delhi,1983,pp.187-188

27 For the price in Calicut see "The Anonymous Narrative", in William Brooks Greenlee, op.cit.,p.92

28 Duarte Barbosa, *The Book of Duarte Barbosa:An Account of the Countries Bordering on the Indian Ocean and their Inhabitants*, tran,by Mansel Longworth Dames, vol.II, pp. 226 ff.

29 R. A.de Bulhão Pato(ed.), *Cartas de Affonso de Albuquerque*,tom.IV,p.175

30 Thome Lopes,op.cit.,p.200; K.S.Mathew, *Portuguese Trade with India*, p.192

31 Karl Otto Müller(ed.), *Welthandelsbräuche*,p.117

32 Vitorino Magalhães Godinho,*Os Descobrimentos e a Economia Mundial*, vol.III,Lisboa,1982, p.9;The Portuguese king needed 5000-6000 quintals of copper every year to be taken to India. ANTT, Corpo Chronologico,I,Maço 12, doc.77;For further details see H.Kellenbenz, *Die Fugger in spanien und Portugal*, vol.I, , München,1990, pp.53-54; Pius Malekandathil *The Germans, the Portuguese and India*, pp.45-46.

33 Karl Otto Müller(ed.), *Welthandelsbräuche*,pp.211-213.

34 Ibid.,p.212

35 HAG, *Regimentos, Provisões e Alvaras*, No.52027, fol.4ff; J.H.da Cunha Rivara (ed.), *Archivo Portuguez Oriental*, Fasciculo 5, parte 1, New Delhi, 1992,p.48

36 William B.Greenlee, op.cit.,pp.190-193; Karl Otto Müller(ed.), *Welthandelsbräuche*,pp.115-122

37 Pius Malekandathil, From Merchant Capitalists to Corsairs, pp. 6-7

38 Reisebericht des Franciscus Dalberquerque vom 27.December 1503, in B.Greiff(ed.),op.cit.,p.148

39 Fernão Lopes Castanheda, op.cit.,tom.I,p.74;Gaspar Correia, *Lendas da India*, tom.I, Lisboa, 1921, pp. 430 - 431; See also Ludovico di Varthema, op.cit, p.106

40 *As Gavetas da Torre do Tombo*, tom.IV,Lisboa, 1964,p.132; See also R.A. de Bulhão Pato(ed.), *Cartas*, tom.I,p.320;tom.II, p.361

41 K.S.Mathew, "Indian merchants and the Portuguese Trade on the Malabar Coast during the Sixteenth Century", in Teotonio de Souza(ed.), *Indo-Portuguese History: Old Issues- New Questions*, New Delhi, 1985,pp.6-7

42 R.A. de Bulhão Pato(ed.), *Cartas*, tom.II,pp.377-378

43 Ibid. tom.VI,p.31

44 Ibid.,tom.V,pp.503-504; K.S.Mathew, "Indian merchants and the Portuguese Trade", 6-7; K.S.Mathew, *Portuguese Trade with India in the Sixteenth Century*, New Delhi, 1983,p.102.Eventhough the kingdom of Edappilly was an enemy of Cochin and the Portuguese , the latter succeeded in penetrating into its production centers with the help of the Mapilla merchants.

45 For details see Pius Malekandathil, *Portuguese Cochin*, pp. 219-221; 394-396; Luis Filipe Thomaz, "Portuguese Control on the Arabian Sea and the Bay of Begal : A Comparative Study, A Paper presented in the Conference on *Bay of Bengal*, held in Delhi, December 1994

46 Pius Malekandathil, *Portuguese Cochin*, pp. 67; 236-239

47 ANTT, *Chancelaria de Manuel I*, liv.II, fol.83"Capitulos de pazes entre Afonso de Albuquerque e o Samorin de Calicut", Lisboa, 26de Fevreiro de 1515; Genevieve Bouchon, "Calicut at the Turn of the Sixteenth Century", p.46; R.A. de Bulhão Pato(ed.), *Cartas*, tom.I,p.126

48 For more details see Vitor Luis Gaspar Rodrigues, "O Grupo de Cochim e a Oposição a Afonso de Albuquerque", in *Studia*, 51, Lisboa, 1992, pp.119-144; Sanjay Subrahmanyam, *The Portuguese Empire in Asia 1500-1700: A Political and Economic History*, London, 1993, p.97

49 Faria y Souza, *Asia Portuguesa: The History of the Discovery and Conquest of India by the Portuguese*, tran.by John Stevens, vol.I, London, 1695,p.284; Shaykh Zaynuddin, *Tuhfat-ul-Mujahidin*, tran.by S.Muhammad Husain Nainar, Madras, 1942, pp.66; 89-91; A.P.Ibrahim Kunju, *Studies in Medieval Kerala*, Trivandrum, 1975,p.60; Pius Malekandathil,"Portuguese *Casados* and the Intra-Asian Trade:1500-1663", A Paper presented in the 61st Session of the *Indian History Congress*, Calcutta, 2-4 January, 2001, pp.3-4

50 ANTT, Ms.B.Pimenta de Avellar, *Livro dos Cavalleiros de Cristo*, fol.213v; R.A. de Bulhão Pato(ed.), *Cartas*, tom.III, pp.208-209; Gaspar Correia, *Lendas da India*,tom.II,pp.331;556-558

51 ANTT, *Corpo Cronologico*, I,Maço 23, doc.7

52 ANTT, *Corpo Cronologico*,I, Maço 19, doc.75

53 ANTT, *Corpo Cronologico*, I,Maço 27, doc.78

54 ANTT, *Corpo Cronologico*, I,Maço 52, doc.25

55 Gaspar Correia says that it was because of the health problems that D. João da Cruz shifted from Calicut to Cochin. Gaspar Correia, *Lendas da India*, tom.II,p.895. However it seems that the increasing anti-Portuguese mood prevailing in Calicut made him move to Cochin. See also ANTT, *Corpo Cronologico*, I,Maço 60, doc.44

56 ANTT, *Corpo Cronologico*, I,Maço 52, doc.25;For identification of these place names, see Georg Schurhammer, "Some Malayalam Words and Their Identification ", in *Kerala Society Papers*, ed.by T.K.Joseph, vol.I&II, Thiruvananthapuram, 1997, p.221; See also Georg Schurhammer, "Letters of João da Cruz in the National Archives of Lisbon", in in *Kerala Society Papers*, p.304-307

57 ANTT, *Corpo Cronologico*, I,Maço 60, doc.44

58 Georg Schurhammer, "Letters of João da Cruz ",p.306; *Monumenta Xaveriana*, Matriti, vol.I,p.273

59 Ibid.,vol.II,p.847

60 During the period 1536-37(M.E.712) there was a Ravi Varma of the Quilon family. See Georg Schurhammer, "Some Malayalam Words..", p.221 and also the Notes given by T.K.Joseph, p.223

61 T.K.Joseph says that no Unni Kerala of 1533-1544 is known to epigraphy so far. In 1544 as head of the Chiravay family Aditya Varma was the king of Travancore. However Georg Schurhammer mentions him to be Unni Kerala Varma whom S.Francis Xavier used to call as "Iniquitribirin"(Inikketrempriyan), meaning my dearest friend. This king, who was miraculously saved by St.Francis Xavier from the Badagas, is referred to by the saint as his dearest friend. Georg Schurhammer , "Some Malayalam Words..",p.221 and also the Notes given by T.K.Joseph, p.223

62 The king of Travancore occupied the kingdom of Cape Comorin on the death of Rey Grande or Valya Tampuran in 1543. Gaspar Correia, *Lendas da India*, tom.IV, p.304; For details see ANTT, *Corpo Cronologico*, I,Maço 52, doc.25

63 Pius Malekandathil, *Portuguese Cochin*, p.232

64 For details about this route, see Genevieve Bouchon, *Regent of the Sea*, pp.118;161; Pius Malekandathil, "The Maritime Trade of Cannanore and the Global Commercial Revolution in the 16th and the 17th Centuries", A Paper presented in the National Seminar on "*Cannanore in the Maritime History of India*" at Kannur University, 8-9th March, 2001,p.5

65 Pius Malekandathil, "The Portuguese and the Ghat-Route Trade:1500-1663", in *Pondicherry University Journal of Social Sciences and Humanities*, Pondicherry, vol.I, no.1&2, 2000,pp.129-154

66 Simão Botelho, "Tombo do Estado da India(1554)", in *Subsidios para a Historia da India Portugueza*, ed. R.J.de Lima Felner, 1868, Lisboa, p.25; Paduronga S.S.Pissurlencar, *Regimentos das Fortalezas da India*, Bastora, 1951,pp.217-219;Vitorino Magalhães Godinho, *Les Finances de L'etat Portugais des Indes Orientales(1517-1635):Materiaux pour une Etude Structuralle et Conjoncturelle*, Paris, 1982,pp.306-308;Francisco da Costa in Antonio da Silva Rego, *Docuentação Ultramarina Portuguesa*, vol.III, Lisboa, 1963,p.310

67 Simão Botelho, op.cit.,p.25. From 1564 onwards he was given 200 *pardaos*. See for details Paduronga S.S.Pissurlencar,op.cit.,pp.217-219; Vitorino Magalhães Godinho, Les Finances, pp.306-308

68 From 1564 onwards she was given 100 *pardaos* as annuity. See for details Paduronga S.S.Pissurlencar, op.cit.,pp.217-219; Vitorino Magalhães Godinho, Les Finances, pp.306-308. However Francisco da Costa says that in 1605 the amount given to her was 220 *xerafins*, which must have been her annual share after the transfer of the seat of Vadakkenkur kingdom from Kaduthuruthy to Thodupuzha in 1600. Francisco da Costa, op.cit.,p.310

69 Simão Botelho, op.cit.,p.25. From 1564 onwards they were given 200 *pardaos* each. See Paduronga S.S.Pissurlencar,op.cit.,pp.217-219; Vitorino Magalhães Godinho, Les Finances, pp.306-308; However in 1605 the amount given to them was 240 *xerafins*. Francisco da Costa, op.cit.,p.310

70 Paduronga S.S.Pissurlencar,op.cit.,pp.217-219; Vitorino Magalhães Godinho, Les Finances, pp.306-308; In 1605 the amount given to each of them was 120 *xerafins* each. Francisco da Costa, op.cit.,p.310

71 Simão Botelho, op.cit.,p.25;Paduronga S.S.Pissurlencar,op.cit.,pp.217-219;Vitorino Magalhães Godinho, Les Finances, pp.306-308; Francisco da Costa, op.cit.,p.310

72 Francisco da Costa, op.cit.,pp.310;312

73 See Caesar Frederick in Richard Hakluyt, *The Principal Navigations, Voyages, Trafiques and Discoveries of the English Nation*,vol.V, Glasgow, 1905, p.392

74 Francisco da Costa, op.cit.,p.315

75 Fürstlich und Gräflich Fuggersches Familien und Stiftungs Archiv, Dillingen/Donau, 46.I, The Letter of Ferdinand Cron sent from Cochin, dated 2-12-1587; Pius Malekandathil, *The Germans, the Portuguese and India*, p.89

76 Francisco da Costa, op.cit.,p.315

77 Jan Kieniewicz, "Asian Merchants and European Expansion: Malabar Pepper Trade Routes in the Indian ocean World System in the Sixteenth Century", in Karl Reinhold Haellquist(ed), *Asian Trade Routes: Continental and Maritime* (Studies on Asian Topics No.13), London, 1991,p.79

78 Pius Malekandathil, "Portuguese *Casados* and the Intra-Asian Trade", pp.4-6; For the details on the flow of new Christians from Portugal to India to escape from inquisitorial trial see Jose Alberto Rodrigues da Silva Tavim, "Outras Gentes em outras Rotas: Judeus e Cristãos novos de Cochim- entre Santa Cruz de Cochim e Mattancherry , entre o Imperio Portuguese e o Medio Oriente", A Paper presented in *VIII Seminario Internacional de Historia Indo-Portuguesa*, Angra de Heroismo , 7-11 June, 1996,pp.4-9

79 Gaspar Correia, Lendas da India, tom.II,p.830;tom.III,p.712. The exact geographical location of Culimute could not be identified. It could be Calmutão which Georg Schurhammer identified as Muttamtura in Travancore. See Georg Schurhammer, *Die Zeitgenössischen Quellen zur Geschichte Portugiesisch- Asiens und seiner Nachbarländer zur Zeit des hl.Franz Xaver,1539-1552*,vol.I,Leipzig,, 1962, nr.6147,pp.461 and 540; ANTT, *Corpo Cronologico*, II, Maço 211, doc.65, fols.5-6. The Letter of Diogo Fernandes to D.John III dated 1-6-1537; See also Jorge Manuel Costa da Silva Flores, *Os Portugueses e o Mar de Ceilão 1498-1543:Trato, Diplomacia, e Guerra*, Dissertação de Mestrado em Historia dos Descobrimentos e da Expansão Portuguesa presented to the Faculdade de Ciencias Sociais e Humanas da Universidade Nova de Lisboa, 1991,pp.200-205

80 Luis Filipe Thomaz, "A Crise de 1565-1575 na Historia do Estado da India ", in *Mare Liberum*, No.9, July 1995,pp.503-508; Pius Malekandathil," Portuguese Casados and Intra-Asian Trade", pp.8-9

81 Pius Malekandathil, From Merchant Capitalists to Corsairs, pp.17- 23

82 AHU, Caixas da India, Caixa 2, doc.107. The Letter of the municipal council of Cochin sent to Philip II(Philip III of Spain) giving account of the economic condition of Cochin, dated 21-12-1613; Pius Malekandathil, "Portuguese Casados and Intra-Asian Trade",pp.13-115; For the volume of pepper going through mountain passes from the inland markets to Coromandel coast see Supra no.76

83 HAG, Livro das Monções , no.12(1613-1617), fols.254-280, dated March 1617.See also AHU, Caixas da India, Caixa 3, doc.29 dated 25-1-1615; Caixa 3, doc.31, dated 25-1-1615.

84 AHU, Caixas da India, Caixa 2, doc.89, fols.1-4;11-15, dated 27-1-1613; Caixa 3, doc.174, dated 2-1-1616 ; Sanjay Subrahmanyam,"Cochin in Decline, 1600-1650: Myth and Manipulation in the *Estado da India*", in Roderich Ptak(ed.), *Portuguese Asia: Aspects in History and Economic History*, Stuttgart, 1987, pp.65-79

85 BNL, Cod.No.11410, fols.173-178.Contract to send *navetas* from Cochin to Lisbon.

18
HUNTING RICHES: GOA'S GEM TRADE IN THE EARLY MODERN AGE.

João Teles e Cunha

"Moreover, if thou seek for Marchandize
Produc't by the Auriferous LEVANT;
"*Cloves, Cinnamon*", and other burnig *Spyce*;
Or any good and salutiferous *Plant*;
Or if thou seek *Stones* of endless price;
The flaming *Ruby*, and hard *Adamant*:
Hence the may'st *All* in such abundance beare,
That thou may'st bound thy wish and *Voyage*
Here."
Camões, *Lusiads*, II,4.

The message of Mombassa's King to Vasco da Gama reminded his crew of the proverbial fame of Asia's riches, fed during the preceding centuries by a flow of spices, drugs, textiles, gemstones and pearls to Europe; and also by the travelogues of real and imaginary travellers. Europe lacked mines of precious and semi-precious stones and pearl fisheries, with the exception for the garnet mines in Bohemia, coral fishing in the Mediterranean Sea, and river pearls in Scotland and Ireland. Thus, the European continent depended entirely from Asian supply until the discovery of new sources in America: emerald mines and pearl banks in Spanish America explored since the sixteenth century, and later, in the eighteenth century, the output of Brazilian diamond mines. So European demand was always higher than Asian supply, making transcontinental trade in precious stones and pearls very lucrative since Hellenistic and Roman days. But the majority of Asian production ended up in local markets and in its ruler's treasure-houses.

Hoarding and lavish display of wealth was not an Eastern monopoly, because it could be seen in Europe from the Classical age. Medieval Europe faced only a change in their clientele, since the Church became one of its most eager consumers. The Europeans got their supply from the Muslim *entrepôts* in the Mediterranean, where Italian merchants, mainly Venetian and Genoese, bought and distributed them throughout Europe. Northern European courts, especially the French and the Burgundian, were great consumers of Asian precious goods, to an extent that diamond lapidaries formed a separate guild in Paris and Bruges[1].

Only part of the Asian production in diamonds, rubies (real, spinel and balas), pearls and seed-pearls, sapphires, amethysts, jacinths and the semi-precious stones[2], arrived in Europe. Some stones like jade had no demand in Europe, but were eagerly sought by the Chinese due to a cultural tradition attached to it. Others like seed-pearls had medicinal applications known in the West through Arab medical science, and were widely used by European pharmacology until the eighteenth century[3].

Long before the discovery of a sea route to Asia, precious stones were a commodity traded on international level, on account of their rarity and price. Their size attracted investment, because they were easily concealed from marauders attacking sea and land convoys, besides representing a capital readily available in case of emergency, and were less conspicuous than coins to customs officials. Smallness was also priced by investors, because traders could easily smuggle them, thus increasing their profit. In what would became a traditional topic, Chao Ju-Kua complained in 1225 against foreign merchants smuggling pearls into China in their clothes' linings and in umbrellas' handles[4].

No wonder that rulers tried to control both production

and trade, since revenues from its commerce were high. In India, for instance, diamonds of great size belonged to the ruler of the area where they were found. Twenty eight years before the arrival of Vasco da Gama at Calicut, D. Afonso V (r. 1438-1481) established in 1470 a royal monopoly over several priced commodities, including precious stones, in all his newly discovered territories[5].

By the time the Portuguese reached India, the royal exclusive was forgotten, but the interest in gems and pearls remained, as seen in the list of countries and their natural riches written in the end of the journal of Vasco da Gama's voyage. That information was provided by Gaspar da Gama or da Índia, and though most of it was false politically, there was some veracity regarding the commodities mentioned, like the pearls from *Caell* (Kayal), sapphires and rubies from *Ceylam* (Sri Lanka), and rubies from *Peguo* (Pegu)[6].

For the next two and half centuries, precious stones would constitute an important branch of the international trade carried out by the Portuguese in three continents, changing old patterns and establishing new routes on a more global level.

Mines and Fisheries.

Excepting the pearl banks on the Persian Gulf, Gulf of Oman and Fishery Coast, Portuguese power in Asia never had any direct or indirect interference in the production of precious stones in India or elsewhere. Even the access to the fisheries eluded Portuguese authorities from time to time, before their final fall into the hands of the competitors in the 1640's in the Persian Gulf, and a little later in the Fishery Coast. In the early 1500's, Portuguese and their commercial associates, trading in Asia and with Europe, bought stones at Indian ports.

In the beginning of the sixteenth century part of the Indian, Singalese and Burmese production in gems was acquired in Calicut, which by then became the leading emporium in Southern India. Kerala had no significant gems, excepting a soft stone found in beaches named wrongly "sapphires", along with jacinths, garnets and cats'-eyes. Calicut attracted Singalese rubies and sapphires, and pearls collected in the Fishery Coast, besides being a major market for Indian false stones. The best diamonds, beryl and amethysts came from the Deccan and Vijayanagara, as reported, among others, by Duarte Barbosa[7].

The other major mining centres, Sri Lanka and Pegu, were also out of direct reach to the Portuguese merchants in the beginning, even if rubies were the most traded stones in Cochin during the first decade of the sixteenth century[8]. But the newly arrived Westerners knew already the difference between the real ruby[9], coming from Pegu, more priced than the ones coming from Sri Lanka, not so red, the *Espinellas* (spinels[10]) and the *Balaches* (balach or balass[11]).

Barbosa acknowledged the preference for the ruby in his book, since he wrote first about it, and then on other gems, including topazes and jacinths from Sri Lanka, turquoises from Persia, and emeralds from Middle and Near East[12].

Diamonds, although handled by Europeans in Cochin, came in the second place, due to the difficulty to get good supply routes, because Calicut still held them and Indian markets consumed most of the production. It was only in the 1510's, when ports along the Coromandel Coast were open to them, that the Portuguese got a new supply route to their Malabar factories. Pulicat was the main re-distributing centre for precious stones in the Bay of Bengal, keeping a role played since medieval times. Pulicat received rubies from Pegu, and diamonds coming from the recently discovered mine in Vijayanagara. The Florentine *"tratante"* Piero Strozzi bought from there in 1515, a large stone with 23 carats. It would be the first of a series of exchanges made by him in the Coromandel Coast before his appointment in 1519 as royal factor for the region, by governor Diogo Lopes de Sequeira (1519-1522)[13].

According to Barbosa, Pulicat was the greatest emporium for gem commerce in the Bay of Bengal, where Chetties and Mappilas dominated the exchanges. They were fierce competitors, as the Portuguese and Italian traders discovered soon[14]. News over diamond mines were still vague. Their existence was acknowledged in the Deccan, in the Muslim Sultanate nominally under the suzerainty of Bahmani epigones. Those were the oldest mines in operation, though a new one had been recently discovered in Vijayanagara. As the Portuguese traveled to the interior of India, either on political or trade missions, sometimes both, they got more information about mines and their location. Two gem-cutters, Francisco Pereira and Mestre Pedro named only three mines for Vijayanagara in 1548, the "new mine" Carul (Kollur ?), *Comdepelym* (Condapilly) the "old mine", and *Pempay*, in the outskirts of the former. To the North, in Berar, was another, supplying the coveted *"roca velha"* diamonds[15].

In the beginning of the seventeenth century the mine list was bigger, showing that mining activity increased over half century. Jacques de Coutre, a Flemish gem-cutter and jeweller based in Goa, mentioned Canaveli (Mallavelly), Condapoli (Condapilly), Costagonda, Duaneguti, Gostual (Nandial), Langapur (Cuddapah), Marmur, Mina Nova, Poli and Ramanacota (Ramalcottah)[16]. The mines were in Golconda and in the Nayaka kingdoms, located along the belt of the Krishna river and its tributaries. Mine discovery was common, like the one found in Golconda c. 1619, whose enormous output diminished carat price, besides supplying the market with flawless stones of great quality and size[17].

Coutre referred to more than eight mines in Golconda alone, which took him more than a year and a half to visit in 1616. Despite the new ones in activity, a few closed in the course of time[18]. Some were closed because the diamonds ended, others were locked temporarily to avoid exhaustion and due to technical difficulties, since there was no adequate machinery to pump out the water flooding the galleries. Others, in a capitalistic approach, were closed-down by its owners and farmers to fight over-mining and low prices. For example, the "mine of the Portuguese" in Marmur, owned by Tima Nayaka, was closed and heavily guarded to prevent illegal mining[19].

Indian rulers controlled closely the mines, though they were explored in different ways. In Vijayanagara, and later on in Golconda, all the stones above a certain weight were to be handed over to the sovereign, though it varied from the sixteenth until the eighteenth centuries. In 1535 diamonds over 20 *mangelins*[20] belonged to Vijayanagara's emperor, in 1563 the weight reached 30 mangelins, to descent to 25 in the 1580's. The figure diminished in the seventeenth and the eighteenth centuries[21]. In the early 1620's, William Methwold stated that the Sultan of Golconda, Muhammad Qutb Shah (r. 1612-1626), reserved to himself all diamonds above 10 carats produced in his mines, although some large ones were smuggled. But according to the V.O.C. governor in Coromandel, Andries Soury, all diamonds over 7 carats coming out of Bannaganapalli mine, discovered c. 1619, belonged to the Qutb Shah. This low figures remained constant for the seventeenth and the eighteenth centuries [22].

Miners worked in open pits, like in Ramalcottah, or in galleries, as in Poli; but techniques were rudimentary in both cases and employed a large labour force. Francisco Pereira described in 1548 the open pit mine of Carul, explored since 1513, where 2,000 miners worked in twenty teams of a hundred men each, supervised by a head-man. The plot given to each team was cleaned and the miners dug up a layer of land called "*mormo*", i. e. alluvium soil, several inches thick. Workers carried the land in baskets to a sort of threshing-floor, where women pounded it with rocks. Then two men came and winnowed the land in a flat basket under the scrutiny of watchers, who picked up every diamond and took it to the mine's farmer, trying not to look at it[23].

The scenery was the same in Ramalcottah in 1611, according to the testimony of Jacques de Coutre. There some 50,000 men, women and children tried to get rich in the pursuit of the glittering diamonds. But each day they got poorer and more dependent on financiers and farmers, until slavery became their final condition; although they sacrificed a goat daily to propitiate their good luck. In Kollur, in the early 1620's, the system was the same for a ragged crowd of 30.000 souls.

Techniques had not improved over the years, though economic method of mining had[24].

Working conditions in galleries were more appalling than in the pits, because, unlike in Europe, they were not supported by beams; and so disasters were not uncommon. Sliding was recurrent in the pit, and the miners' fate ended often under a large lay of land. Galleries were very narrow, like the ones in Poli visited by Coutre, and ran into large cavities. There, more than a thousand miners worked almost nude covered in mud and sweat, caused, among other things, by running water and poor ventilation, thus accumulating natural heat and the smoke of the torches and lanterns. Workers used iron pikes to break the rock in order to find gems. Coutre entered Poli dressed only in his white breeches, and left the mine completely wet and soiled, but with a 30 carat diamond bought illegally for 700 pagodas[25].

Mines belonged to rulers, who looked carefully for production and commerce, though they did not handle them directly. According to Fernão Nunes (c. 1535), Achyutadevaraya (r. 1529-1542) had a treasurer for precious stones called Narvara and a counsellor Adapanayque (Adaiyappâ Nayaka), who farmed the diamond mines in the Empire paying annually 40,000 *pardaus* to the monarch[26]. Farming mines was frequent, like Kollur in 1548 and in the 1620's, when the Qutb Shah farmed it to a Hindu merchant. The farmer could explore it directly, as in 1548, or lease it to others, as he did in the 1620's. In the Nayaka kingdoms, ownership was sometimes in hands of members of the royal family, like Ramalcottah handled by Gopal Raya, nephew of Madurai's nayaka, or Nandial explored by a brother of the nayaka of Vellur[27].

Ramalcottah was also explored by free miners, generally a family, leasing a plot from Gopal Raya and paying a monthly capitation of half pagoda. Part of the capital came from local merchants. They delivered to the owner all stones above 7 carats, selling the remaining production to ransom their debt from the financier. As production was fortuitous, miners became progressively indebted to money lenders, ending up as slaves.

Very seldom miners attained fortune, and so they tried to make quick money with illegal sales to traders visiting the mines[28].

The attempt often ended sadly. Coutre gave to Krishna Raya, Poli's owner, the diamond bought illegally from a miner and smuggled to his brother in Goa. But he was lucky enough to receive back his 700 pagodas. The miner was not so fortunate and the mine guards beat him to death. The owner-explorer guarded directly the mine and maintained a large network of informants to stop diamond smuggling. Punishment for transgressors meant the seizure of their property and the scaffold. The financier's task was simpler, since the debt worked in its way and the burden was laid on the shoulders of the free miners[29].

But the spell of diamond was greater than difficulties. A multitude of people rushed to a mine soon after its discovery, trying to make fortune. The new urban centres attracted rapidly a crowd of poor miners, who spent their lives in miserable huts and in the pits or galleries, attempting to improve their lives. The new town attracted merchants lured by profit to trade in diamonds and finance mining, and still visiting jewellers from distant places in search for cheap and good gems. The owner or farmer received 4% for each transaction, half paid by the seller and the other half by the buyer. The carat price remained competitive, due to the cheapness of the abundant labour force. Coutre valued in the 1610's the daily expenditure of Ramalcottah miner in 8 *maravedis*, while in Spain 6 *reales* were insufficient[30]. According to him, carat price would fetch over 500 *escudos* if diamonds were mined in Spain. Even so, Indian mines closed and production stopped to drain the market surplus and prevent fall in prices. Coutre mentioned Marmur's shut down in the 1610's, and the same thing happened in Mughal conquered Golconda during the last quarter of the century, when Aurangzeb (r. 1666-1707) ordered the closing of all mines for ten years (1687-1697)[31].

The diamonds varied according to their origin, and had different consumers. The Portuguese showed a keen interest in the gems called *roca velha* (old rock), coming from the mines of the 'Idmad Shahis' in the Deccan. Orta mentioned them as the most priced gems in 1563, and half a century later, they were still in demand by the Portuguese, although by then those diamonds were perhaps coming from new mines in Golconda. The viceroy Rui Lourenço de Távora (1609-1612) told his son-in-law, the former viceroy Count of Vidigueira, about the shipment of three *bizalhos* of diamonds *roca velha* in 1609, which was considered to be the best stones sent that year to Portugal[32].

If Portuguese market liked *roca velha* diamonds, South India preferred uncut gems called *naifes* by Garcia da Orta. On the other hand, Muslim India preferred stones polished or set in jewels. Georges Roques noticed Aurangzeb's preference for lapidated diamonds. South Indian market sought eagerly other stones which had little or no demand in Portuguese and European markets, like topazes and cat's-eyes. When *Estado da India* forces captured the treasure of king Bhuvanekabahu VII (r. 1521-1551) of Kotte, viceroy D. Afonso de Noronha (1550-1554) sent Álvaro Mendes, a goldsmith, to sell part of it in Vijayanagara, the best market for uncut gems, and invest the return in diamonds for queen D. Catarina, wife of D. João III (r. 1521-1557)[33].

As for pearls, the best came from the Persian Gulf and had the preference of the Asian and European markets. Then came the banks along the Fishery Coast, followed by less important fisheries in Borneo and China. In the Persian Gulf the great pearl banks were in the Arab side, Qatar, Bahrain and Julfar. Bandar Nakhilu was the only major bank in the Persian shore. Besides these, there were minor banks in the Gulf of Oman, near Mascat, Ra's al-Hadd, Taiwa and the islets of Suwadi, near Suhar. The former had annual fisheries, while diving in the latter was done intermittently for biological reasons, as they would reach the verge of extinction if explored yearly. Even some major banks faced the same problem. For instance, Qays' intense exploration from the fifteenth century onwards led to its exhaustion by the end of the sixteenth century. Pedro Teixeira made no mention of it in the beginning of the 1600's[34].

Qatar was the most important bank in Teixeira's time. Fishery started in July, though sometimes a month earlier, and ended in August. In September, ships and men moved to the banks of Bahrain, Julfar and Bandar Nakhilu, and also to the Gulf of Oman every other year. In the 1600's, the pearl fleet had over 200 *terradas*, of which Bahrain had half, and Julfar and Bandar Nakhilu had 50 sails each. These ships returned to their home-port for a second season after August, and Bahrain's fleet took Qatari sailors and divers to work in the island's bank. Over the years there was a steady rise in the number of ships employed. After the figures given by Pedro Teixeira c. 1604, António Bocarro mentioned 600 sails in Qatar's bank thirty years later (1634)[35].

Pearl fishery in the Persian Gulf suffered several halts, occasioned mainly by war. Ottoman presence in the region since the late 1530's, with the conquest of Basrah and the recognition of the Porte's suzerainty by Arab Sheiks, disturbed the fisheries. Even so, pearls and seed-pearls continued to flow to Hormuz. The first major blow to Portuguese circuits came in 1602, when Shah Abbas conquered Bahrain, though supply was quickly re-established through Julfar. Banks in the Gulf of Oman still provided pearls to Portuguese networks until the fall of Mascat in 1649, taken by the Imam of Nizwa's men. Although a joint Anglo-Persian fleet took Hormuz in 1622, the fruit of *Meleagrina margaritifera*, L., changed its course to the main Portuguese base in the area, Mascat, either by smuggling or by the looting of the pearl fleet. Rui Freire de Andrade and his ally, the Pasha of Qatif, raided frequently Qatar's ships and Bahrain's banks in the 1620's and early 1630's[36].

Trading Networks.

There were records of commercial transactions in precious stones since the beginning of Portuguese settlement in India. Gems and pearls sold in Malabar factories came from Sri Lanka, Fishery Coast and the Deccan, and the new-comers competed with Asian demand. *Pedraria* traded through Cochin's factory was already considerable in the early 1500's, since the commerce was not bound by a royal monopoly, like spices and drugs. Legislation from the time of D. Afonso V onwards had not attempted to monopolize their trade, and D. Manuel (r. 1495-1521) opened it to everyone, and investors paid taxes ranging from 20% to 25% over the stone value, and registered in a separate ledger-book. Precious stones composed a great part of the *liberdades* and *quintaladas* aboard the home-bound carracks from an early stage[37].

Gems, pearls and seed-pearls became increasingly important in Portuguese private trade, not only in the Cochin-Lisbon run, but also in the Asian trade. Other European merchants using Portuguese routes and ships also engaged in their commerce. Stones, unlike money or other bulky commodities, were easily smuggled to Europe, thus escaping registration and taxation. Florentine merchants like Giovanni Buonagrazia, Giovanni da Empoli and Piero Strozzi, engaged intensively in this trade, and amassed a rich spoil of gems and jewels. Their untimely death prevented them from sending to Europe their accumulated treasure, and the hoarded stones and jewels were transformed into money[38].

The glitter of the precious stones also haunted the royal family. D. Manuel and his successors commanded the viceroys and governors to purchase precious stones to satisfy their wishes of magnificence and piety, besides the gifts given to their relatives in other European ruling houses, especially the House of Austria, with whom the Avis dynasty was closely connected by marriage. Supply was the main problem in the beginning, because the Malabar factories were secondary markets for gems and they had no direct access to production and redistribution centres. In a letter to D. Manuel written in 1508, viceroy D. Francisco de Almeida (1505-1509) associated the non-availability of pearls in Cochin to the lack of direct supply routes to the fisheries in Sri Lanka and Kayal, then dominated by the Mappilas. Much to his distress, D. Francisco could not comply with his king's request[39].

But the Crown had alternative ways for securing precious commodities, especially through tributes. Rulers, like the king of Hormuz, settled their payment partly in precious goods, pearls in the Hormuzian case[40]. Supply improved as the Portuguese entered into the trading world of Asia, visiting the main redistribution markets, like Elichpura in the Deccan, Vijayanagara, Pulicat, the Fishery Coast and Hormuz. Those circuits were well known and visited in the middle of the sixteenth century, since Portuguese demand for gems increased incessantly. Though Elichpura was the most important diamond fair, and remained so until Garcia da Orta's times (1563), Portuguese private and official traders preferred Vijayanagara, a preference maintained until the downfall of the capital and the dislocation of the Empire's core to the South after the battle of Talikota in 1565. Large transactions took place in Vijayanagara, including the sale of Singalese stones from the treasure of Bhuvanekabahu VII, and the purchase of a single diamond to set in a ring offered by D. João III to Pope Julius III (1550-1555). *Vedor da Fazenda* Cosme Anes bought the stone by 10,000 gold *pardaus*, under command of governor Jorge Cabral (1549-1550). The royal officials in Lisbon priced the diamond in 30,000 *cruzados*, and it fetched 100,000 *cruzados* in Rome. There, two jewellers offered 70,000 gold *scuddi* for it, but Julius III declined the offer and decided to give it to his family and not to St. Peter's treasure. Members of the Portuguese diplomatic mission in Rome advised D. João III to send more diamonds if he wanted to get his way in the lengthy negotiations held in the Curia on the Inquisition and the New-Christians[41].

Part of the stones went to Goa through Banyan and Gujarati networks. They tracked Deccani routes to buy diamonds in Elichpura, and sold them in Goa and Vijayanagara. Portuguese merchants bought and sold gems, uncut or set in jewels, in the Southern markets, although they tended to include Deccani and Mughal courts in their commercial circuits from the last quarter of the sixteenth century. Circuits and routes were the same for diamonds, jewels, textiles, dyes and horses, and it was not uncommon to see merchants trading in several of these commodities simultaneously. Before the end of the first half of the sixteenth century, Portuguese merchants were moving from Vijayanagara's redistributive markets to the major mining centres in the Empire. Although they were private merchants, they also took royal commands and the Crown displayed interest in the location of those mining centres. The Portuguese traders became deeply involved in the diamond business in Southern India, and some even farmed mines. Jacques de Coutre mentioned Álvaro Mendes, a farmer of the mine near Mallavelly during D. Sebastião's reign (r.1557-1578), known thereafter as *"mina dos portugueses"* (mine of the Portuguese)[42].

Trade in precious stones grew steadily during the sixteenth century, since it was a free commodity. Merchants working in Portuguese routes paid only a meagre 4.5% income tax at Goa's customs, and then they could take them to Asian or European markets free of charge. Royal officials knew too well the difficulty faced in the control of gem commerce, since they were easily smuggled, and preferred free-trade during the sixteenth century, though minds changed in the early 1600's. New-Christians became the more important merchant community dealing with stones and jewels, and their ascendancy came from family networks scattered all around the world. Using Lisbon as their major turn-table, at least until the 1630-40's, they drained uncut Indian stones to the main European markets, and in return dispatched lapidated gems and jewels to Asia, besides supplying the Asian market with American stones.

The liberalization of commerce in Portuguese Asia under D. Sebastião, introduced a new cycle in the spice and drugs trade, and strengthened the dissemination of New-Christian networks across *Estado da India*. The last pepper contract signed with a New-Christian syndicate made them the masters of gem and textile trade. By the 1590's, a revolution occurred in the commodities transported through *Carreira da India*. The bulk was no longer pepper but textiles and, in a smaller scale, precious stones. The importance of these goods grew to Portuguese private trade as the Dutch cut the access to pepper producing areas and flooded the European market with cheap pepper, thus curtailing any chance of recovery of the former bulk commodity. According to a New-Christian *arbitrista*, Duarte Gomes Solis, gem trade was the only reason behind private investment in the India Run in 1622[43].

Although Solis overstated its importance, he knew it well, because he made and remade his fortune in precious stones[44]. Its trade attracted other Europeans. Some lived in Portuguese India, mainly in Goa, like the Augsburger Ferdinand Cron and the Flemish brothers Coutre. Others, especially Venetians, traded and traveled in overland routes. Cron went to India aboard the ships of *Carreira da India*, to serve as factor for the Welsers and the Fuggers in the pepper contract of 1586. Others, like Frans Coningh, who met a tragic death described in Linschoten *"Itinerario"*, came through land route to buy precious stones in Aleppo, a major re-distributive market in Syria. There, Frans Coningh lost his uncle's money and moved to Basrah, thence to Hormuz until he finally reached Goa. The Venetian gem merchants used constantly the overland route stretching from Alexandretta to Hormuz, and from there to India via Sind or Dabhol. They avoided calling centres of Portuguese power, excluding Hormuz, but had no problem with private traders. Jacques de Coutre met Bernardo di Nardona while buying diamonds in Ramalcottah in 1616. Land route was also widely used by traders from the Eastern Mediterranean, during the seventeenth century, like the Jew found by Coutre in the Deccan in 1616. But the bulk of the stones carried through caravans went to the Mediterranean area, and only a small part arrived in the European markets, mainly the Italian[45].

New-Christians based in Goa dominated the maritime traffic, and they continued in business during the second half of the seventeenth century, though on a smaller scale. In the early part of this century, Jacques de Coutre mentioned two brothers of the Silveira family, Fernão Jorge and Francisco da Silveira, trading intensively with relatives in Portugal. Even c. 1681, the greatest diamond dealers in Goa, the Martins brothers, were New-Christians. But the Holy Office ravaged the ranks of New-Christians in Portugal and in her Empire from the 1630's onwards. Their families left Portugal to safer places in Holland and England, where they recentred their networks and know-how. The attack inflicted by the Dutch on Portuguese maritime traffic in the Indian Ocean and Goa's blockade, severed regular sailing to Portugal and brought things to a stand-still from 1634 until 1662. When Portugal and the V.O.C. signed a peace treaty in 1662, it was already too late to recover *Estado da India* to its former self, including private trade. New-Christian families restarted business in Amsterdam and London, restoring old networks and cornering the Indian and European markets once again. Goa still played a singular role, even if it were through English ships visiting the port. According to the Government Council (1668-1671), in a letter to the regent D. Pedro (1667-1683), English ships anchored in Goa's harbour and smuggled most of the gem trade carried out in Portuguese India. Around 1680 John Fryer complained against this ascendancy and connected it to the revival of the Middle East overland route, mentioning the French jewel trader Jean Baptiste Tavernier as one of the adventurers who visited India recently coming from Aleppo and Basrah[46].

By then the Maratha expansion had already disturbed Deccani routes, and broke regular supply, thus diverting traders and investments to Golconda and the ports in the Bay of Bengal. After Santhome's conquest in 1662 by 'Abd Allah Qutb Shah (r. 1626-1672), Portuguese settlers moved to other ports, especially Madras, and supplied diamonds to the English and to Goa. The English dominated progressively the market of precious stones through the private trade carried out by East India Company agents, even if Goa kept some importance in their international trade. Portuguese merchants settled in the Tamil Coast maintained their networks within Asia during the eighteenth century, and looked forward to other markets, trying to escape from Goa's key redistributive role in *Estado da India*, especially in Portugal and China. Despite the discovery of diamond mines in Brazil in the late 1720's, Goa kept sending gems through Indian merchants acting as commissioners for traders based in Lisbon, along with some minor parcels sent by Portuguese residing in India, including religious orders, to their relatives, friends and fellow priests. The two Indiaman bound to

Lisbon in 1750, *Nossa Senhora do Monte Alegre* and *São Francisco Xavier*, had a legal diamond cargo evaluated in 349,995-2-14 *xerafins* (104,998$634)[47].

Gem and pearl trade rapidly developed into a complex business. Traders could buy diamonds, rubies, etc., with money, lapidated gems and jewels. The latter were not so conspicuous and heavy as money, an important factor in roads plagued with robbers. Some merchants also invested in horses, textiles and dyes, because it supplied the ideal cover to avert robberies, besides deceiving Goa's customs officials from registering incoming gems. Such a commercial association had its economic compensations, because it saved the traders from unknown factors in their business-trip, like the scarcity of good stones and their price. And the merchants often invested surplus capital in commodities available locally, mainly textiles and dyes, thus making a good profit back in Goa. They traveled frequently with fellow-traders, sometimes old acquaintances from Goa, and almost always with an armed escort, since assaults in the Deccan were frequent[48].

Pearl supply from the Persian Gulf and the Fishery Coast suffered from similar upheavals. The latter could be reached through Quilon in the early 1600's, when Fr. Antonio de Gouveia evaluated in 800,000 *cruzados* the pearls and other goods stocked there. But Mappila action eroded the supply channels to Portuguese factories in Malabar, helped incidentally by the nayaka of Madurai. Portuguese authorities tried to revive the route by farming the fisheries in two year terms, but no one showed up in the auctions held in 1603 and 1605, leaving its exploration to *Estado da India*. The fishery renewed in 1612, but its centre shifted to Tuticorin by Jesuit action. Their involvement in the fisheries came from the previous century, with mass conversion of the Paravas by Francis Xavier. After the 1620's the supply routes were diverted once again, and the Malabar factories no longer engaged in the trade of pearls produced in the Fishery Coast. According to António Bocarro, Quilon had no activity connected with its trade in 1634. In the following decades, Goa's supply relied integrally on Portuguese merchants operating in Madurai, and later in Santhome and Madras[49].

The bulk of pearl production in the Persian Gulf went to Hormuz, because the kings of that Thalassocracy received it as a tribute paid by their Arab vassals. Bahrain's conquest in 1602, inflicted a major blow in Hormuzian supply routes. Although part of the production went to the Safavid's treasure house, the Persian vizier made an annual income of 500,000 ducats from pearls in 1604, and the captains of Hormuz received a share, evaluated in 100,000 ducats, smuggled through the fishing fleet of Julfar and Qatif's divers. The latter port also supplied Hormuz with Arab horses[50].

Mir Fahruddin Shah, king of Hormuz (r. 1602-1609), also collected pearl tributes from Julfar. Though Bahrain pearls ceased to appear in Hormuz around 1610, the local market was well supplied by Julfar's production, the most important center in the Gulf during the 1610's. Notwithstanding the new route, Hormuz captains rigged yearly two *terradas* to buy pearls illegally in Bahrain and Julfar until 1615, under the pretext of patrolling the Gulf. Meanwhile other changes occurred in Hormuz. Its captains began to intercept quietly the tribute paid to Muhammad Shah III (r. 1609-1622), and also the pearls brought to Hormuz by Julfar merchants, using force in the latter case[51].

As the battle over the control of the Strait of Hormuz approached its climax in the early 1620's, pearl-fishing was no longer possible in the near-by banks, especially since Rui Freire de Andrade raided and destroyed part of the pearl fleet; because ships were crucial for Anglo-Persian objectives, mainly to blockade and siege Hormuz. Bahrain was the only bank undisturbed by Portuguese raids, and had no match until 1622-1623[52]. After the conquest of Hormuz in 1622, *Estado da India* centred its presence in Mascat and revived the trade routes to Julfar. Mascat was also supplied by the banks in the Gulf of Oman with the looting and raid of Bahrain and Qatar *terradas*, by Rui Freire de Andrade and his Qatif's allies since 1624. The precarious agreement signed between Rui Freire and Bandar

Abbas's governor in the early 1630's, granted a six month truce in the Persian Gulf, thus enabling merchants to buy pearls in Bahrain and Qatar through Mascat[53].

Acting as a negotiator for Safi Shah I (r. 1629-1642), Kung's governor offered a permanent settlement to Portuguese authorities in Mascat in 1634. He opened four Persian ports to the merchants trading in Portuguese commercial networks, thus providing free access to the fishery banks in the Gulf, in exchange for a permanent peace settlement. *Estado da India* accepted Safavid proposals, because the Imam of Nizwa had begun to threaten seriously Mascat. Portuguese garrisons were abandoning a series of small fortress along Oman's coast to strengthen Mascat, and Julfar's bank was lost to the Imam's forces in 1633-1634[54].

The shift of Portuguese power to Mascat led to a change in commercial circuits. Basrah became an important port to buy pearls and redistribute them to India or to Mediterranean ports and thence to Europe. Caravans linked Basrah to Aleppo and Alexandretta, maintaining the traditional overland route used by Venetians, despite the contemporary Persian-Ottoman war. In 1634, viceroy Count of Linhares (1629-1635) received a letter from Prospero Benedetto offering the services of Luigi Sagredo, his broker residing in Aleppo, to serve as a courier. Benedetto had close contacts with a known Goan New-Christian, Manuel Correia, possibly his commercial associate in overland trade with Europe[55].

Goa's Role in the Commerce of Precious Stones.

Goa became progressively the greatest Indian centre for commerce in precious stones with Asia and Europe, through the Cape Route or the Levant. Goan-based merchants benefited from its redistributive role within *Estado da India*, and the town held its ascendancy from the first half of the sixteenth century until the early 1640's. Even officials of the East India Company acknowledged its importance in the 1610's, stating that it was the principal trade centre made by Portuguese in India[56].

Gem and jewel trade grew in quantity and specialization, and in the late sixteenth century its complexity reached the peak. There were lapidaries with workshops full of Indian craftsmen cutting gems to the Indian market and to European customers. One of them was Domingos Nunes, who worked regular for viceroy D. Francisco da Gama, Earl of Vidigueira (1622-1628). Others, like João Rodrigues de Lisboa, acted as valuer and middleman between gem traders and buyers.The Earl of Vidigueira resorted often to the skills of Vicente Ribeiro in these crafty negotiations. Others still, acted independently as financiers, buying and setting stones without command, though they had regular clients. For instance, Ferdinand Cron besides engaging freely in the commerce of stones and jewels to Europe and in Asia, worked for D. Francisco da Gama and his father-in-law Rui Lourenço de Távora, since the tenure of viceregal office of the former (1597-1600)[57].

Indian traders competed side by side with New-Christian and European merchants, matching them in sophistication and specialization, though Indian craftsmen never reached the quality of European cutting. Goldsmiths like Langi Soni, son of Narna Soni, had business with D. Francisco da Gama during his second term as viceroy. He acted many times as the broker of the viceroy buying un-cut stones, like the one bought from a Balaghaut Brahmin, Sancarsa, weighing 36 *mangelins* for 10,800 *patacões*. Others, like Ragozi Devi and Sivigissa, were official *pedraria* brokers during the 1620's. Banyan financiers were also involved in diamond trade, especially as guarantors in the transactions of large stones[58].

Despite the participation of several merchant communities in this trade, New-Christians played an important part in it, and were responsible for the operation of the Goa-Lisbon-Antwerp axis. Their family connections in the major markets of Europe, Asia and America made their rise easier. The pepper contract of 1592 confirmed their ascendancy, in spite of the complains of the Goan municipality about it to the Lisbon authorities during the first quarter of the seventeenth century. But New-Christians networks enjoyed a dominant position until the 1640's[59].

New-Christian families traded between Goa and Lisbon, buying stones in India and dispatching them through carracks, through relatives residing in Asia also engaged independently in private commerce with Europe. In return, they received from Europe cut gems of Asian and American origin for sale in the Indian market. Diamonds, rubies, sapphires and pearls used to be a safe way to accumulate fortune in Asia, since they were a relatively free commodity until the early 1600's. Duarte Gomes Solis invested in precious stones the capital made in India, and sent them to Lisbon or sold them in Goa and received the money in Lisbon through a bill of exchange. He had experienced shipwrecks twice and the English took him prisoner once, but he always managed to have money on arrival in Europe. Others, like Jacques de Coutre, carried stones as ready cash in their hazardous overland travels to Europe and throughout India. Private trade in the *Carreira* thrived during this period, and people often sent diamonds to Lisbon already secured in the capital's market, like the six diamonds, weighing 61 *mangelins*, dispatched by a Goan lapidary in 1628[60].

The sale of "liberties" was common since the beginning in *Carreira da India*, and textiles, gems, jewels and drugs constituted the bulk of free cargo. The liberalization of commerce and the establishment of the pepper contracts under D. Sebastião, boosted private trade to its zenith from the late sixteenth century until the first quarter of the seventeenth century. Viceroy Earl of Vidigueira engaged intensively in private trade, sending diamonds, textiles and furniture to Lisbon during his second term in office (1622-1628), and he was not alone. Sailors, pilots and officials sold their "liberties" assuring the delivery of the purchaser's goods in Lisbon. Some crewmen shared their "liberties" with merchants, receiving part of the cargo's value after they hand over it to its receiver in Portugal. In the latter case, the receiver took all the risk. For instance, D. Francisco da Gama dispatched to Portugal 157 diamonds in 1624, in Manuel dos Anjos, "liberties" aboard *São Tomé*. D. Francisco shared them with António da Costa, a New-Christian associated with Vicente Ribeiro, with whom the viceroy had several commercial ventures. The same trade association reappeared in 1626, when Manuel dos Anjos, then *São Bartolomeu's* pilot, received from António da Costa a diamond *bisalho* to deliver to the Countess of Vidigueira upon his arrival in Lisbon[61].

Orders were another form of transcontinental sale, and came from private and institutional figures. Filipe I (r. 1580-1598) gave an order in 1597 to João Simões a *tratante em pedraria nestas partes da Jndia ha vinte e sete annos* (gem dealer in India for 27 years)for having 282 diamonds, an affair priced in 10,000 *xerafins*. The king made a new order in 1598 after receiving two Singalese rubies sent by viceroy D. Francisco da Gama. Others kept dealing in precious stones after returning home, through mercantile and financial contacts left in Goa. Count of Vidigueira continued his diamond business after returning to Portugal in 1600, using in his transactions Ferdinand Cron and later his father-in-law, Rui Lourenço de Távora, through a correspondence exchanged between them[62].

Viceroys often engaged in the profitable gem trade carried between India and Portugal. Vasco da Gama's descendant, the fourth Count of Vidigueira (1565-1632), traded in diamonds during his second viceregal term. He sent to Portugal stones evaluated in 24,531 *xerafins* under a commercial pseudonym, Francisco da Cruz, from 1624 to 1626. Details of his commercial transactions came into daylight in the course of a judicial inquiry held after his removal from office and incarceration. The judges found that he sent diamonds to Portugal priced in 32,383 *xerafins* through one of his commercial associates, António da Costa, received in Lisbon, by the brother of the latter, Álvaro Fernandes da Costa. D. Francisco had profit of 300% in his diamond business in 1626, receiving back a handsome net-profit of 24,000 *xerafins*. He resorted to extreme coercive measures to get gems, imprisonment and torture were not uncommon. The Coutre brothers complained bitterly against their incarceration in Goa's gaol, the *Tronco*, on D. Francisco's command. The viceroy's only desire was to get cheaply some diamonds which were in Coutre's possession. But nobody came under the viceroy's cupidity if he had good gems. D. Francisco was too eager to get diamonds from anyone, and according to the inquiry three banyans, Panipal, Andradi and Viraça, sold him a diamond weighing 15 *mangelins* after a short period in prison. Count of Vidigueira was not the only one to venture in the trade of diamond and jewels; his successors also engaged in its commerce as soon as they arrived at Goa[63].

Indian and Asian markets acquired large part of the precious stones and jewels traded through Goa, until Surat and Madras replaced the role of the former in the late 1600's and in the 1700's. Though Goan based merchants, gem-cutters and jewellers visited Indian Courts with large supplies of stones and jewels, the ambassadors of Indian sovereigns visiting Goa acquired them for their masters and themselves. Mir Musa Maluco (Amir Musa/Muzaffar al-Mulk ?), Jahangir's ambassador to viceroy Count of Redondo (1617-1619) in 1619, bought several gems and jewels from Ferdinand Cron and the Coutre brothers, leaving behind a debt of 12,000 *xerafins*. But generally traders visited Indian courts for sale purpose, like the visits by Jacques de Coutre to Golconda, Bijapur and Agra. Agents of the English East India Company wrote to their masters in 1617 that Portuguese traders appeared at the Mughal court to sell jewels, investing the return in indigo, textiles and carpets. The Deccan and South Indian courts were also visited by these travelling traders. Besides Coutre, officials like Vicente Ribeiro, the *corretor-mor da pedraria* during the time of Linhares' governace, had substantial connections in Deccani courts, mainly in Bijapur[64].

Organization and Evolution of the Goan Market in the Early Modern Age.

Transactions in precious stones grew considerably during the sixteenth century, which reached its zenith during the period from 1600 to c. 1635. Goan market, though the greatest in India, still had some difficulties in coping with the ever-increasing demand in the end of the sixteenth century. João Simões provided only a third of Filipe I's command of 282 diamonds for 1597.

Hunting Riches: Goa's Gem Trade in the Early Modern Age.

The lapidary warned that it would take him two years and cost him 50,000 *xerafins* to comply with the king's order[65].

Two decades later, the annual business of D. Francisco da Gama in gems was greater in capital and carat-weight than his sovereign's in 1597. This was due to the new mines discovered in India, associated closely with the development of trading networks centred in Goa. The volume revealed itself in the illegal cargo seized aboard the carrack *São João* in 1625, before she sailed to Europe. Royal officials evaluated a third of the cargo in 58,354 *xerafins*. The stone's auction held in Goa paid 62,346 *xerafins*, and the money went to the extraordinary contribution of 1626, being the second more significant levy (15,7%) after the one given by the Asian Houses of Mercy (51,8%)[66].

Throughout the sixteenth century its trade was free, but Goan market became tightly regulated in the beginning of the seventeenth century. The changes occurred at a time of diminishing customs income for *Estado da India*. This movement coincided with the control introduced by Goan authorities in the export of capital to buy textiles, dyes and gems. Regulations changed from 1605 onwards, moving from free trade to a controlled market, returning to open commerce. A less restrictive regime introduced in the 1620's prevailed until the 1700's, with minor alterations. Those changes revealed the closely-knit fabric between textiles, dyes and gems trade.

In 1605 viceroy D. Martim Afonso de Castro (1603-1607) levied money to furnish the *armada* set to sail against the Dutch in the Malay Archipelago. He devised a plan to tax a profitable commerce still free, and created the office *corretor-mor da pedraria* (gem's chief broker) to register and tax all the gems and jewels sent from India to Europe through the sea route and *vice versa*. He appointed Baltasar de Vasconcelos to the post, but the newly elected broker attracted the criticism of Goa's Municipal Council. Goan city officials accused him of accepting a per centage from traders with European contacts as he stopped registering stones sent and received through the Cape Route. The Municipal Council members complained to the king against the new office in 1605 and 1606, and asked for its abolition, since they connected its creation with the rising price of gems and jewels in Goa.

Filipe II (r. 1598-1621) complied with the wish of municipal council in 1607, and abolished the office and forbade new legislation in the matter without consulting him. Meanwhile in India, governor D. Fr. Aleixo de Meneses (1607-1609) was still unaware of the monarch's decision. So he appointed Domingos Soares to the office in 1607, and restricted further the commerce of precious stones. The new law limited gem's sale from 25 November until ships left to Portugal, in an attempt to divert investments to other commodities available in Goa and drop their prices, especially gems, highly inflated recently. Although the archbishop's main concern was to gather all money he could, to send to the viceroy in Malacca, he also tried to fight against New-Christian preponderance in its commerce, thus pleasing a group of supporters in the Goan Municipality[67].

The laws affected gem and jewel trade in double ways, as they paid export and import duties in Goa. Though during the sixteenth century Goa exported Indian stones, a new trend appeared in the 1580's or 1590's. In those decades, Goa started to receive in return precious stones and jewels from Lisbon. Some of them were Indian stones cut in Europe, mainly in Antwerp, and dispatched to Goa with American emeralds and baroque pearls. The novel trade rendered a profit of 200% to 300% to the merchants engaged in transcontinental traffic, besides a profit of 50% received in the export of *reales* to buy textiles, gems and dyes, which boosted the economic preponderance of the New-Christian mercantile community residing in Goa. Their *respondentes* (brokers) increased during the first quarter of the seventeenth century. From five or six declared in its beginning they rose to sixteen in 1617. They rapidly took over Goa's trade in precious stone with their commercial skills, controlling supply through a network of agents buying uncut gems in mines and selling lapidated stones and jewels in Indian courts. Some of them, like Vicente Ribeiro, even lived near mining centres and royal seats. They bought and drained to

Goa diamonds, rubies, sapphires and pearls. As masters of the supply routes, New-Christians fixed prices in Goa and dispatched the bigger and best gems to Europe through Portuguese ships, besides giving them to goldsmith and cutter-workshops in India. In return, they received cut stones and jewels, and took them to Indian courts in sale voyages, along with silver *reales*. The circuit began once again with the investment of the return money in new stones, textiles and dyes[68].

The suppression of the office of *corretor-mor da pedraria* in 1607-1608, and the providential oblivion of 1607 provision, led to a commercial boom, as seen in the diamond-trade by viceroy Rui Lourenço de Távora and his son-in-law D. Francisco da Gama, through the services rendered by Ferdinand Cron. The recovered trade freedom led to a price fall in the Goan market until 1613-1614. During this period everyone invested in precious stones, including the Crown. But prices rose once again in 1614, at least for institutional buyers. That year, viceroy D. Jerónimo de Azevedo (1612-1617) and counsellors of *Conselho da Fazenda* (Finance Council) denied permission to the queen's agents to invest the returns from the sale of two voyages to Japan in gems[69].

A royal charter promulgated in 1611 made price rise inevitable, since it restricted the export of pieces of eight from Goa to Gujarat and Balaghaut. The legislation had collateral effects in Cochin, an important port for the invoice of stones and pearls coming from Sri Lanka and the Bay of Bengal. The charter aimed almost exclusively at the non-Portuguese traders operating in *Estado da Índia* circuits and networks, leaving New-Christian merchants untouched and free to export silver *reales* from Goa. The circuits remained, though apparently their agents changed[70].

Meanwhile Portuguese administrative circles discussed further reforms in the control and tax of the gem trade, without informing the Crown representative in Goa, viceroy Rui Lourenço de Távora. He intervened in the developments following the royal charter, probably due to his private trade in diamonds and the pressure received from his commercial associates, like Ferdinand Cron. The viceroy modified existing conditions and gave extraordinary licences to export pieces of eight from Goa. His policy displeased strongly Crown officials in Lisbon, and Filipe II forbade his successor, D. Jerónimo de Azevedo, to grant more special permits to export silver coins from 1613 onwards. But prices kept rising, especially that of diamonds, caused by the registration of all gems sent from India to Lisbon, enforced since the promulgation of new legislation in 1613. In accordance with the law, a judge of Goa's *Relação* (Court of Appeal) registered the stones and sent the ledger-book to Portugal, thus enabling cargo check and taxation by officials of *Casa da Índia* (India House) in Lisbon[71].

But things turned up differently from the Crown's expectations, since customs officials discovered a gap between India's register and the cargo checked in Lisbon. The gems declared were inferior to those loaded aboard the carracks. The shipwreck of *Nossa Senhora da Luz* near Fayal island in 1615, revealed the amplitude of smuggling carried out through Indiaman. Royal officials responsible for the recovery and inventory of all goods saved from the wreckage, evaluated in 1,000,000 *cruzados* the value of the diamond cargo. It became obvious to the Crown that legislation was ineffective in Goa. So Filipe II revived the provision issued by D. Fr. Aleixo de Meneses in 1607, and tried to improve the register of precious stones shipped to Portugal, in order to make prices fall in the Goan market[72].

Once again the outcome was different from what the Crown hoped for, due to New-Christian ascendancy in Goa, especially in the commerce of textiles, dyes and precious stones. They cornered Goan market since the promulgation of the royal charters, regulating capital export and the registration of gems, issued in 1611, in 1613 and in 1615. This legislation diverted the attention of Balaghaut merchants temporarily from Goa, thus stopping supply of textiles, and the situation worsened with the war between *Estado da India* and the Mughals, because it disrupted traditional trade routes to Gujarat. The situation gave a virtual monopoly in the supply of textiles and precious stones to Goa's New-Christian traders. Besides controlling the supply routes from Deccan and South India to Goa, they also commanded sales and prices in the latter market, and similarly they dominated transcontinental trade with Europe. Goan market acted as a turn-table connecting trade networks in Asia, Europe and America, and New-Christians played a major role in the distribution of key commodities, leaving to others a secondary position. The renewal of trade routes with Gujarat after 1615 maintained New-Christian supremacy in supplying textiles and dyes to Portuguese India. Despite the revival of the overland route to the Ottoman Empire and the Mediterranean by 1613, the bulk of gem trade went to Europe in Portuguese ships, even if they were preys for Dutch, English and Moorish privateers. Indian demand and prices maintained the return route for cut stones and jewels[73].

A royal charter in 1616 forbade the trade carried through the Hormuz Strait, and another in 1618 diminished the entry rights levied in Lisbon to 0,5%, to those who volunteered to register the stones. Though it tried to divert overland trade to maritime routes, its outcome was unsuccessful. But cut gems and jewels were still returning to India, even if Goan workshops renewed its importance since 1619. Crown official Lopo Álvares Pereira in a letter to Filipe II reported the change witnessed in 1619, when New-Christian merchants restarted cutting diamonds in Goa instead of sending all to Lisbon[74].

Although market organization suffered several innovations in Goa in the 1620's, no major change occurred in gem trade, excepting the expulsion of all foreigners living and trading in Portuguese India. After the reorganization of Goa's market in that decade, two brokers elected yearly by their peers registered the transactions, under the scrutiny of a judge of the court of Appeal. Goa remained the greatest exchange port for precious stones in Asia, and many Indian merchants traded intensively in this secure and solid market. For instance, the two *pedraria* brokers in 1626, Ragozi Devi and Sivigissa, were

Indians. The Indian goldsmiths were accounted as a different socio-economic group in Goa, as seen in the extraordinary contribution given in 1626[75].

Gem registration was far from being fully recorded, even with the innovation introduced in the 1620's. New-Christian ascendancy in the market made the control difficult, since they conducted most of their business a few days before carracks sailed to Lisbon. Those late sales obstructed the work carried out by the *pedraria* brokers and the judge, because they could not record all transactions in the ledger-book, and verify the cargo. On the other hand, as the brokers were also dealers, they did not list all business made in Goa. Lisbon authorities became aware of New-Christian manipulation in Goa's market towards the end of the 1620's, and Filipe III (r. 1621-1640) commanded viceroy count of Vidigueira to enforce legislation, especially the archbishop's provision of 1607. Furthermore, the king ordered an annual inquiry into the *pedraria* broker's activity, and the invoice to Portugal of a copy of the ledger-book. But royal orders were not applied in 1627 and 1628[76].

Though Goan market underwent dramatic disturbances in 1629-30, the laws introduced in 1627 had little to do with it. Tumult came from the regulations enforcing textile trade and its new routes, thus dragging associated commodities, like gems, into the turmoil. Shortage in the supply of gems and textiles led to a price rise in Goa in 1629-30. This happened before the occurence of drought and famine in Western India which caused a deeper crisis in 1630-31, affecting particularly the weaving and production centers of Gujarat. The Portuguese trading in the textile markets of Cambay, Surat and Dabhul were competing hard with European joint-stock companies. But Goan traders received another blow when Balaghaut merchants diverted part of the Deccani textiles to other ports, thus reducing the offer available in Goa. The New-Christians were almost the only traders to have independent supply routes to Gujarat and the Deccan, thus the situation made them the masters of Goan market and revived the commercial circuits of 1615-1619. In the expression of the Judge of Appeal Court, Paulo Rebelo, *Cristãos*

Velhos (Old-Christians) were once again in the hands of *Cristãos Novos* (New-Christians). The crisis of 1630-31 and the following economic depression, made Goan traders more dependent on New-Christian suppliers. But viceroy D. Miguel de Noronha tried to maintain Goa well supplied with every commodity, including precious stones, and reorganized the market in a different pattern. Linhares revived the office of *corretor-mor da pedraria* in 1630, and appointed Vicente Ribeiro, a merchant with many Deccani contacts, especially in Bijapur's court[77]. Anyhow viceregal measures were ineffective and kept the leading position of the New-Christians, to the despair of other merchants and the top bureaucrats of *Estado da India*. Despite Linhares' action, prices rose in those years, leaving out all small traders from transcontinental commerce.

Pressed by the Crown, Linhares introduced changes in Goan market in 1632, dividing *pro-rata* all commodities coming from the Deccan. To the New-Christians it meant the end of a profitable virtual monopoly. Among their ranks discontentment grew, because they were unwilling to take all risks while others, mainly Old-Christians, stayed in Goa and received merchandise without sharing hazards. In 1633 they were unwilling to continue with the plan of Linhares issued in 1632, and pressed the viceroy to re-open trade routes to Balaghaut on a free basis. D. Miguel de Noronha complied with their request, because he had close mercantile ties with them and supported their activity. The abrogation of the provision infuriated the highly conservative members of *Estado da India*'s administration, Goan Municipal Council and Inquisition. Francisco de Lucena, a municipal official, wrote angrily to Filipe III in 1633 stating: *"(...), de sorte senhor que os Homens da Nasção neste Estado sam peores em terra que os olandeses no mar."*[78]

Aftermath.

Dutch blockade of Goa from 1635 to 1662, meant the slow asphyxy of institutional and private trade, and the disruption of regular maritime traffic from India to Portugal. Although a new regime emerged in Portugal after the Restauration in 1640, and the new monarch D. João IV (r. 1640-1656) signed a truce with the Dutch Republic, the old inquisitorial practices prevailed. They hindered the already frail New-Christian networks in Portugal and in her overseas Empire from recovery, by incarcerating its leading members around 1644. All these strokes proved fatal to their relatives in India, though some, like the Martin brothers, remained active in Goa until 1680's. Most of the New-Christian capital and expertise fled from Lisbon, first to Madrid, then to Holland and England. The remnants in Portugal diverted their capital to Brazil during the 1660's and 1670's, since India was no longer a zone for profitable investment.

But gem trade in India carried out by Portuguese subsisted, because it was all done through private merchants, and their networks survived, especially in centres far away from official presence, like in the port-towns in the Bay of Bengal. And Goa still retained some traffic, though on a smaller scale, well into the eighteenth century. Niccolao Manucci mentioned the wrong doings of Fr. Gonçalo Martins S. J. in 1654-1655, and his dispute with Muhammad 'Adil Shah (r. 1626-1656) over a large balas[79]. Though gem trade subsisted, traders begun to change. Portuguese born and their descendants prevailed in the commerce with Portugal until the end of the seventeenth century, but Indiaman crews and Indian merchants took their place slowly, and the latter emerged as the real force moving trade in *Carreira da India* in the eighteenth century.

Precious stones, mainly diamonds, were traded during this period, and Goa remained central to its traffic, though in a smaller degree. Traces of its survival were in their presence in the cargo captured by pirates aboard the *Nossa Senhora do Cabo* in 1721, or in the expertise of D. Lourenço de Almeida, one of the "discoverers" of Brazil's diamonds in 1726-1729, acquired during his long residence in Goa[80]. And its volume was still important in 1753, when Sebastião José de Carvalho e Melo, later known as Marquis of Pombal, reorganized the production and trade of Brazil's diamonds under a monopoly, leaving free those coming from India[81].

References:

1. W. Heyd, *Histoire du commerce du Levant au Moyen Âge*, (reprint of Leipzig's edition of 1885-1886), (Amsterdan-1983), vol. II, pp. 648-658. Eliyahu Ashtor, *Storia economica e sociale del Vicino Oriente nel Medioevo*, (Turin-1982), pp. 278-279.

2. Even if not all are minerals, like pearls and the coral, nor have the same classification according to their hardness, they are treated in the same category.

3. Vide Garcia da Orta, *Colóquio dos Simples e drogas da Índia*, "colloquy 35th", (reprint of Lisbon's edition of 1891-1895), (Lisbon-1987), vol. II, pp. 119-132.

4. Chao Ju—Kua, *Chu Fan Chih*, "On the Chinese and Arab Trade", (edited and translated by Fr. Hirth and W. W. Rockhill), (reprint of St Petersburg 's edition of 1911), (Amsterdam-1966), pp. 229-230.

5. *Portugaliæ Monumenta Africana*, (Lisbon-1993) vol. I, doc. 67, "Royal Letter," Alenquer, October 19th, 1470, pp. 161-162.

6. *Diário da viagem de Vasco da Gama*, (introduction by Damião Peres, paleographic reading by António Baião and A. de Magalhães Basto, and modernization of the text by A. de Magalhães Basto), (O'Porto-1945), vol. I, p. 82, 84.

7. *The Book of Duarte Barbosa*, (edited by Mansell Longworth Dames), (reprint of the Hakluyt Society edition of 1918-1921), (New Delhi-1989), vol. II, p. 202.

8. Artur Teodoro de Matos, "Some Aspects of the Portuguese Trade in the Malabar Coast: Cochin and the «Mercadorias Meudas» (1506-1508)", in *Indica*, vol. 26, 1 & 2, March-September 1989, p. 97.

9. The red transparent variety of corundum, or crystallized alumina, whose blue counterpart is the saphyre.

10. A magnesium aluminate.

11. Also a magnesium aluminate, whose name derives from the place where it was mined, Badakhshân, thence *badakhshî* or the more commom form *Balakhshî*,"from Badakhshân", corrupted into "Balache" by Barbosa, who wrongly puts it into the interior of Bengal and Pegu, and not in the Upper Oxus, nowadays divided between Afghanistan and Tadjikistan; cf H. Yule and A. C. Burnell, *Hobson.Jobson*, s.v.

12. Duarte Barbosa *op. cit.*, vol. II, pp. 217-226.

13. Marco Spallanzani, *Mercanti Fiorentini nell'Asia Portoghese*, (Florence-1997), pp. 195-197.

14. Duarte Barbosa, *op. cit.*, vol. II, pp. 124-126, 129-132.

15. Garcia da Orta, *op. cit*, vol. II, p. 198; Municipal Library of Elvas (Portugal), mss. nº 5/381, fls. 37-38, "Information of Francisco Pereira and Master Pedro gem-cutters on the diamond mines of Vijayanagara", published by S. Jayaseela Stephen, in *Revue Historique de Pondichéry*, vol. XVIII (1995), pp. 111-112.

16. Jaques de Coutre, *Andanzas Asiáticas*, (edited by Eddy Stols, B. Teensma and J. Werberckmoes), (Madrid-1990), book II, chap. XVI, pp. 258-263, book III, chap. III, pp. 280-281.

17. Duarte Gomes de Solis, *Discurso sobre los comercios de las dos Indias*, (Lisbon-1943), p. 16; António Bocarro, *O livro das plantas de todas as fortalezas, cidades e povoações do Estado da Índia Oriental*, (Lisbon-1992), vol. II, p. 170.

18 Jacques de Coutre, *op. cit.*, book. III, chap. III p. 280.

19 *idem*, book II, chap. XVI, pp. 262-263.

20 A weight corresponding generally to the carat (in fact only two thirds of the latter) and used in South India and Sri Lanka. A Telegu word *manjali, manjadi* in Tamil, from the Sanskrit *manju*, "beautiful", applied to the seeds of *Adenanthera pavonina*, L., employed as weight for small commodities. Cf. Henry Yule and A.C. Burnell, *Hobson-Jobson*, s.v.

21 Dalgado, *Glossário Luso Oriental*, (reprint of Coimbra's 1921 edition), (New Delhi-1988), "mangelim"; Garcia da Orta, *idem*, vol. II, p. 198; Jan Huighen van Linschoten, *The Voyage of John Huyghen van Linschoten to the East Indies*, (reprint of the Hukluyt Society edition of 1885), (New Delhi-1988), vol. II, p. 137; Kanakalatha Mukund, "Mining in South India in the 17th and 18th Centuries", in *Indica*, vol. 28-1, March 1991, pp. 15-16. After the discovery of diamonds in Brazil, the Crown declared the mines its property, and all gems found above 24 carats belonged to the sovereign. If a black slave found one with 20 carats or more, he was automatically free. In "Law", December 24, 1734, in Manoel Fernandes Thomaz, *Reportorio geral ou indice alphabetico das leis extravagentes do Reino de Portugal, publicadas depois das Ordenações, comprehendendo tambem algumas anteriores, que se achão em observancia*, (Coimbra-1843), vol. I, p. 212.

22 *Relations of Golconda in the Early Seventeenth Century*, (edited by W. H. Moreland), (London-1931), pp. 32-33.; Om Prakash [Ed.], *The Dutch Factories in India 1617-1623*, (New Delhi-1984), doc. 117, "Letter of Andries Soury to the Directors in Amsterdam", Masulipatam, 29 January 1621, p. 147.

23 S. Jeyaseela Stephan, *art. cit.*, pp. 111-112.

24 Jacques de Coutre, *idem*, book II, chap. XV, pp. 254-256; Moreland [Ed.], *op. cit.*, p. 31.

25 Jaques de Coutre, *ibid.*, chap. XVI, pp. 261-262.

26 David Lopes [Ed.], *Chronica dos reis de Bisnaga. Manuscripto inedito do seculo XVI*, (Lisbon-1897), pp. 73-74.

27 S. Jeyaseela Stephan, *idem*, pp. 111-112; Jacques de Coutre, *ibid*, book II, chaps. XV, XVI, pp. 260, 262; W. H. Moreland, *op. cit.*, p. 32.

28 Jacques de Coutre, *ibid.*, book II, chap. XV, pp. 254-255.

29 *ibidem*, book. II, chap. XVI, p. 262. Ludovico de Varthema noticed in the beginning of the sixteenth century, that the Bahmanis surronded their diamond mine with a wall and guarded it heavilly, cf. *aut. cit.*, *Itinerário*, (translation, preface and notes by Vincenzo Spinelli), (Lisbon-1949), p. 132.

30 To have a notion of the difference 1 real worth 34 maravedis, cf. Adrian Room, *Dictionary of Coin Names*, (London-1987), s.v.

31 Coutre, *idem*, book II, chap. XV, p. 256; Moreland, *idem*, p. 31; Georges Roques, *La manière de négocier aux Indes 1676-1691. La compagnie des Indes et l'art du commerce*, (edited with notes by Valérie Béristain), (Paris-1996), pp. 158-159. For o comprehensive overview on the matter see H. Fukazawa, "Non-Agrucultural Production: Maharashtra and the Deccan" and L. Alaev, "Non-Agricultural Production: South India", both in Tapan Raychaudhuri and Irfan Habib [Eds.], *The Cambridge Economic History of India*, vol. I, *c.1200-c.1750*, (New Delhi-1982), pp. 314, 323; Kanakalatha Mukund, *art. cit.*, pp. 13-20; and the pioneer article by George Winius, "Jewel Trading in Portuguese India in the XVI and XVII Centuries", in *Indica*, vol. 25-1, March 1988, pp. 15-34.

32 Garia da Orta, op. cit., vol. II, p. 198; Biblioteca Nacional de Lisboa-Fundo Geral (thenceforth BNL-FG) cod. 1975, "Viceroy to count of Vidigueira", Goa, January 10th, 1609, fls. 305-305v.

33 Garia da Orta, idem, ibidem, pp. 198-199; "Viceroy to Queen", Cochin, January 27th, 1552, in Georg Schurhammer and E. V. Voretzsch, Ceylon zur zeite des Königs Bhuvaneka Bâhu und Franz Xavers 1539-1552, (Leipzig-1928), vol. II, p. 605; "Simão Botelho to King", Cochin, January 30th, 1552, in Rodrigo José da Lima Felner, Subsidios para a História da Índia Portuguesa, (Lisbon-1868), p. 39; Georges Roques, op. cit., p. 159; Jorge Flores, Os portugueses e o mar de Ceilão. Trato, diplomacia e guerra (1498-1543), (Lisbon-1998), p. 62.

34 Pedro Teixeira, The Travels of Pedro Teixeira with his "Kings of Harmuz", and extracts from his "Kings of Persia", (reprint of the Hukluyt Society edition of 1902), (Nendelm-Liechtenstein-1967), pp. 175-177; António Bocarro, op. cit., vol. II, p. 56, 64; Jean Aubin, "Le royaume d'Ormuz au début du XVIe siècle", in Mare Luso-Indicum, 2-1973, pp. 97, 100.

35 Pedro Teixeira, op. cit., pp. 176-177; António Bocarro, idem, p. 64.

36 Ibidem supra; Comentários do grande capitão Rui Freire de Andrade, (Lisbon-1940), p. 255; Jean Aubin, art. cit., p. 116. For an overview on the pearl fishery in South India see Vitorino Magalhães Godinho, Les Finances de l'État Portugais des Indes Orientales (1517-1635). Matériaux pour une étude structurale et conjoncturelle, (Paris-1982), pp. 109-110 and S. Jeyaseela Stephen, Portuguese in the Tamil Coast. Historical Explorations in Commerce and Culture 1507-1749, (Pondicherry-1998), pp. 60-91.

37 Artur Teodoro de Matos, art. cit., pp. 94-95.

38 Marco Spallanzani, op. cit., pp. 27, 194-197, 208, 210; Marco Spallanzani, Giovanni da Empoli. Mercanti navigatore fiorentino, (Florence-1984), pp. 68, 74-75.

39 Gaspar Correia, Lendas da Índia, I-ii, (Coimbra-1921), pp. 908-909.

40 Simão Botelho, "Tombo do Estado da India", in Rodrigo José da Lima Felner, op. cit., p. 82.

41 Georg Schurhammer, Die zeitgenössischen quellen zur geschichte Portugiesisch-Asiens und seiner nachbarländer zur zeit des Hl. Franz Xaver (1538-1552), (Rome-1962), nº 2750, nº 4237, nº 4677; As Gavetas da Torre do Tombo, vol. I, do. 413, "D. Afonso de Lencastre to King", Rome, August 18th, 1551, pp. 614-615.

42 Garcia da Orta, op. cit., vol. II, p. 198; Jacques de Coutre, op. cit., book II, chap. XVI, pp. 262-263.

43 Duarte Gomes de Solis, op. cit., p. 16; Simão Botelho, "Tombo do Estado da India", in Rodrigo José de Lima Felner, op. cit., pp. 47-48; J. Gentil da Silva, Stratégie des Affaires à Lisbonne entre 1595-1607. Lettres marchandes des Rodrigues d'Evora et Veiga, (Paris-1956), pp. 25, 27, 97.

44 The best overview of Solis's life is by António Borges Coelho, "O mercantilista português Duarte Gomes Solis (1561/2-c. 1630), in Portugaliæ Historica, second series, vol. I-1991, pp. 183-257.

45 Jacques de Coutre, idem, book II, chap. XV, p. 252, book III, chap. III, pp. 281, 284-285.; Jan Huighen van Linschoten, op. cit., vol. II, pp. 204-205; Herman Kallenbenz, "Le front hispano-portugais contre l'Inde et le rôle d'une agence de renseignements au service de marchands allemands et flamands", in Studia, nº 11, January-1963, p. 265; Sanjay Subrahmanyam, "An Augsburger in Ásia

301

João Teles e Cunha

Portuguesa: Further Light on the Commercial World of Ferdinand Cron, 1587-1624", in Roderich Ptak and Dietmar Rothermund [Eds.], *Emporia, Commodities and Entrepreneurs in Asia Maritime Trade*, c. 1400-1750, (Stuttgart-1991), pp. 401-425.

46 Arquivo Histórico Ultramarino (thenceforth AHU), India, caixa 50, doc. 108, "Governors to Regent", Goa, January 30th, 1670; Jacques de Coutre, *idem*, book II, chap. XV, p. 253; James C. Boyajian, *Portuguese Bankers at the Court of Spain 1626-1650*, (New Brunswick N. J.-1983), p. 8; John Fryer, *A New Account of East India and Persia, Being Nine Years Travels 1672-1681*, (reprint of the Hakluyt Society edition of 1909-1915), (Milwood N.Y.-1967), vol. I, pp. 225-226; vol. II, p. 87; Georges Roques, *op. cit.*, pp. 158-159.

47 BNL-FG, cod. 4179, "Register of gems sent to Lisbon in 1750", (un-foliated codex); John Fryer, *idem*, vol. II, p. 25; C. R. Boxer, *The Golden Age of Brazil. Growing Pains of a Colonial Society 1695-1750*, (second edition), (Manchaster-1995), pp. 205-206; Om Prakash, *European commercial Enterprise in Pre-Colonial India*, in *The New Cambridge History of India*, vol. II-5, (Cambridge-1998), pp. 241-242; S. Jeyaseela Stephen, *op. cit.*, pp. 187-188.

48 Jacques de Coutre, *op. cit.*, book II, chap. XIII, pp. 237, 242-243, book III, chap. I, pp. 268-270, chap. II, p. 275.

49 Fr. António de Gouveia, *Jornada do Arcebispo*, (Lisbon-1988), book II, chap. VII, p. 93; Jacques de Coutre, *idem*, book II, chap. XIII, pp. 242-243; António Bocarro, *op. cit.*, vol. II, pp. 207-211; Vitorino Magalhães Godinho, *op. cit.*, pp. 109-11.

50 Pedro Teixeira, *op. cit*, p. 176.

51 AHU, India, caixa 3, doc. 3, "Proceeding of captain D. Henrique de Noronha", Hormuz, January 20, 1615; José Inácio de Abranches Garcia, *Archivo da Relação de Goa, contendo documentos dos séculos XVII, XVIII e XIX até à organização da nova Relação pelo decreto de 7 de Dezembro de 1836*, vol. I, (1607-1640), "Proceeding of November 26th 1614", pp. 172-173.

52 Rui Freire de Andrade did not destroy all the pearl fleet, since 400 sails were hidden ashore and were later used in the Anglo-Persian attack to Hormuz; cf. "Part of a Letter Written to Sir Hohn Westenholme by T. Wilson Chyrurgion", in Samuel Purchas, *Hakluytus Posthumus or Purchas His Pilgrimes. Containing a History of the World in Sea Voyages and Lande Travells by Englishmen and Others*, (Glasgow-1905-1907), vol. X, pp. 335-336.

53 *Comentários de Rui Freire de Andrade*, pp. 240-249, 255-258, António Bocarro, *op. cit.*, vol. II, pp. 63-64.

54 Panduronga S. S Pissurlencar, *Assentos do Conselho do Estado*, vol. I *(1618 1633)*, (Bastorá/Goa-1953), "Proceeding of September 21st, 1633", pp. 487-488; *Diário do 3ª conde de Linhares, vice-rei da Índia*, vol. I, (Lisbon-1937), "Register of February 18th, 1634", p. 10, vol. II, (Lisbon-1943), "Register of September 22nd, 1634, pp. 179-180.

55 *Diário do 3º conde de Linhares, vice-rei da Índia*, "Register of September 8th, 1634, p. 168.

56 William Foster, *The English Factories in India*, vol. I *1618-1621*, (Oxford-1906), "William Biddulph to the East India Company", February 15, 1618, p. 21; George Winius, *art. cit.*, pp. 15-16; James C. Boyajian, *Portuguese Trade in Asia under the Habsburgs 1580-1640*, (Baltimore/London-1993), p. 135.

57 BNL-FG, cod. 1975, "Rui Lourenço de Távora to earl of Vidigueira", Goa, January 10th, 1609, fls. 305-305v.; BNL-FG, cod. 1986, fls. 129-132v., 134v.135v., 154v-155; Jacques de Coutre, *idem*, book III, chap. V, p. 293.

58 BNL-FG, cod. 1981, fls. 103-105; BNL-FG, cod. 1986, fls. 122v.-123.

59 AHU, caixa 10, doc. 105, "Francisco de Lucena to King", December 30th, 1633; Arquivo Nacional da Torre do Tombo (thenceforth TT), Corpo Cronológico, I-116-77, "Goa's Municipality to King", December 30th, 1617, and "Royal letter-patent", Lisbon, March 16th, 1616; José Gentil da Silva, *op. cit., inter alia* letters 54, "Manuel Veiga and brothers to Ruiz family", Lisbon January 10th, 1598, p. 175, and 56, "Manuel da Veiga and brothers to Cosme Ruiz", Lisbon, January 17th, 1598, p. 178; James C. Boyajian, *op. cit.*, p. 135.

60 BNL-FG, cod. 1986, fl. 154v.; Duarte Gomes Solis, *op. cit.*, p. 16; Jacques de Coutre, *op. cit.*, book III, chap. XI, p. 328.

61 See *inter alia* in BNL-FG 1981, fls. 74-75v., 91-94v.

62 TT-Miscelâneas Manuscritas do Convento da Graça, caixa 6-2º E, "Miguel de Moura to viceroy", Lisbon, March 31st, 1598, fls. 565-570; "Ferdinand Cron to count of Vidigueira", Goa, December 20th, 1616; BNL-FG, cod. 1975, "Rui Lourenço de Távora to count of Vidigueira", Goa, January 15th 1612, fl. 206, Goa, December 30th, 1610, fls. 212-216, Goa, January 10th, 1609, fls. 305-305v., Goa, December 8th, 1609, fls. 319-325; BNL-FG cod. 1977, "Certificate of João Simões", Goa, October 2nd, 1597, fl. 209.

63 BNL-FG, cod. 1981, fls. 74-75v., 102-105; BNL-FG 1986, fls. 34-35v., 127-129v., 153-155v.; Jacques de Coutre, *idem, ibidem*, pp. 340-341. Starting with his successor count of Linhares. For his business see A. R. Disney, "The Viceroy as Entrepreneur: The Count of Linhares at Goa in the 1630's" in Roderich Ptak & Dietmar Rothermund [Eds.], *Emporia, Commodities and Entrepreneurs in Asian Maritime Trade, c. 1400-1750*, (Stuttgard-1991), pp. 439-441.

64 AHU, India, cx. 10, doc. 105, "Francisco de Lucena to King", Lisbon, December 30th, 1633, "Report of Paulo Rebelo", Lisbon, February 3rd, 1635; William Foster [Ed.], *Letters received by the East India Company from its Servants in the East. Transcribed from the "Original Correspondence" Series in the India Office Records*, vol. VI, (*1617*), (London-1902), "Francis Fetiplace and Robert Hughes to the EIC", Agra, December 20th, 1617, pp. 250-251; Coutre, *idem*, book II, chap. XVI, p. 259, book III, chap. I, p. 268, chap. II, pp. 274-276, chap. V, pp. 293 *passim*.

65 BNL-FG cod. 1977, "Certificate of João Simões", Goa, October 2nd, 1597, fl. 209.

66 BNL-FG cod. 1784, fls. 280-282, BNL-FG cod. 1986, fls. 145v-146v.; BNL-FG cod. 1983, "Viceregal charter", Goa, August 19th, 1625; fls. 73-76.

67 AHU, India, caixa 10, doc. 105, "Report of Paulo Rebelo", Lisbon, February 3rd, 1635; J. H. da Cunha Rivara [Ed.], *Archivo Portuguez Oriental*, (reprint of the Goan edition of 1876), (New Delhi-1992), fasc. 1, part 2, doc. 26, "Goan Municipality to King", Goa, 1606, p. 187; *Documentos Remettidos da India ou Livros das Monções*, (thenceforth DRI), (from the series kept in the Lisbon Archive published in 10 volumes from 1880 to 1982), vol. I, doc. 26, "King to viceroy", Lisbon, January 18th, 1607, p. 107; DRI, vol. III, doc. 514, "King to viceroy", Lisbon, February 14th, 1615, p. 215.

68 AHU, caixa 4, doc. 138, "António Galvão to King", Goa, January 6th, 1617; AHU, caixa 6, doc. 32, "Lopo Álvares Pereira to King", Goa, February 14th, 1619; TT, Corpo Cronológio, I-116-77, "Goan Municipality to King", Goa, December 30th,

1617; Duarte Gomes Solis, *op. cit.*, pp. 16, 82; Jacques de Coutre, *idem*, book. III, chap. III, p. 284; Vitorino Magalhães Godinho, *Os Descobrimentos e a economia mundial*, vol. III, (second edition), (Lisbon-1987), p. 77.

69 Filipe II offered to his wife, D. Margarida of Austria, two voyages to Japan. In V. T. Gune [Ed.], *Assentos do Conselho da Fazenda. (Preceedings of the Revenue Council at Goa)*, vol. I, part 1, (1613-1617), doc. 12, "Preceeding of November 27th, 1614", p. 14, and doc. 18, "Preceeding of January 20th, 1615", pp. 18-19.

70 DRI, vol. II, doc. 170, "Royal charter", Lisbon, February 12nd, 1611, pp. 31-33; vol. II, doc. 173, "King to viceroy", Lisbon, February 17th, 1611, pp. 35-36.

71 DRI, vol. II, doc. 305, "King to viceroy", Lisbon, January 29th, 1613, p. 296; vol. II, doc. 374, "King to viceroy", Lisbon, March 27th, 1613, pp. 429-430.

72 DRI, vol. III, doc. 514, "King to viceroy", Lisbon, February 14th, 1615, p. 214; vol. III, doc. 685, "King to viceroy", Lisbon, March 5th, 1616; James C. Boyajian, *op. cit.*, p. 137.

73 AHU, Índia, caixa 4, doc. 138, "António Galvão to King", Goa, January 6th, 1617; TT, Corpo Cronológico, I-116-77, "Goan Municipality to King", Goa, December 30th, 1617; DRI, vol. III, doc. 765; "Royal charter", Lisbon, March 16th, 1616, pp. 495-496.

74 AHU, India, caixa 6, doc. 36, "Lopo Álvares Pereira to King", Goa, February 14th, 1619.

75 TT, Miscelâneas Manuscritas do Convento da Graça, cx. 6, 2º-E, "Certificate of Pêro Moniz", Goa, January 27th, 1628, fls. 107-108; BNL-FG, cod. 1983, "Viceregal charter", Goa, August 19th, 1625, fls. 73-76; BNL-FG, cod. 1986, fls. 122v-123; DRI, vol. IX, doc. 114, "King to viceroy", Lisbon, February 3rd, 1623, p. 401.

76 TT, Livros das Monções 24, "King to viceroy", Lisbon, March 6th, 1627, fl. 285.

77 Vicente Ribeiro's appointment was unclear. Though Linhares informed Filipe III on the adjournment of Ribeiro's appointment, the viceroy was negotiating it with him. A Goan municipal official, Francisco de Lucena, and a former judge of the Appeal Court, Paulo Rebelo, stated clearly that Linhares made the assignment despite the existing royal orders. Cf. *Boletim da Filmoteca Ultramarina Portuguesa* nº 7, 294, "Viceroy to King", Goa, December 6th, 1630, p. 557 with documents cited in note *infra*. On Vicente Ribeiro's activities in Deccani courts see *Boletim da Filmoteca Ultramarina Portuguesa*, nº 7, nº 310, "Viceroy to King", Goa, January 6th, 1631, pp. 567-569.

78 "(...) *in a way Sir, the Men of the Nation* (i.e. New-Christians) *are, in Portuguese India, a worse evil overland than the Dutch on sea.*", in AHU, India, cx. 10, doc. 105, "Franciso de Lucena to King", Goa, December 30th, 1633, "Report by Paulo Rebelo", Lisbon, February 3rd, 1635.

79 Niccolao Manucci, *Mogul India or Storia do Mogor*, (reprint of William Irvine edition), (New-Delhi-1989), vol. III, pp. 157-159.

80 G. V. Scammell, "European Exiles, Renegades and Outlaws and the Maritime Economy of Asia c. 1500-1750", in K. S. Mathew [Ed.], *Mariners, Merchants and Oceans. Studies in Maritime History*, (New-Delhi-1995), p. 133; Charles. R. Boxer, *op. cit.*, p. 206.

81 "Royal Charter", August 11, 1753, in Manuel Fernandes Thomaz, *op. cit.*, vol. I, p. 212.

19

THE PORTUGUESE AND ASPECTS OF TRADE IN PORTS OF SOUTH KANARA[1]

Nagendra Rao

The arrival of Portuguese led to long-lasting impact on the economy of South Kanara. The Portuguese were first European traders to arrive at the ports of South Kanara. On the eve of the arrival of the Portuguese, South Kanara comprised of large number of major and minor ports. There existed trade with Malabar, Maldives and ports of the Red Sea. There also existed the trading communities like the Arabs, Jews, Saraswats, Telugu Komatis, Navayats and others. International trade was not new to the traders of South Kanara. The traders dealt with commodities like rice, pepper, ginger and other spices. The arrival of Portuguese helped in enhancing the volume of trade in the ports of South Kanara. In this paper we analyse the trends in trade in the different ports of South Kanara, which are being studied on the basis of their relative importance. Inscriptions, Portuguese records and foreign accounts constitute the major source for this study.

The arrival of the Portuguese was noticed through inscriptions. In South Kanara only one inscription in Portuguese has been discovered.[2] The content of the inscription does not help us much in writing about the trade contacts. But the significance of this inscription lies in the fact that this symbolised the settlement of the Portuguese in South Kanara. One hero stone inscription found in Trasi (Kundapur taluk) dated A.D. 1546 describes the combat between a woman leader called

Nayakti and the Portuguese. The woman died in the fight.[3] The evolution of Portuguese trade in South Kanara was a gradual process. The early Portuguese records give more reference to the presence of the Portuguese in Malabar. But after 1620 the Portuguese had to depend on the ports of South Kanara for the supply of rice, pepper and other items of trade. This was because the Portuguese relation with kings of Malabar did not remain cordial. There was great demand for the rice and pepper of Kanara in the factories and various settlements of the Portuguese. In spite of the fact that pepper of South Kanara was costlier than the Malabar pepper, the Portuguese, due to certain political developments and compulsions, had to depend on the pepper supply from ports of South Kanara. The demand for pepper was also due to the presence of Arab and Gujarati traders in these ports. The rise of Surat too helped in augmenting this demand.[4]

Mangalore

The port of Mangalore was situated on the confluence of two rivers, Netravati and Gurupur. The structure of the river formed backwater, which increased the navigability of Mangalore port and facilitated the entry of ships in the port. The hinterland of port of Mangalore produced pepper, betelnut, coconut, sandalwood, cardamom and different varieties of rice.[5] Among them rice was the major item of export from the port of Mangalore.

In 1502 the Portuguese scholar Thome Lopez mentioned Mangalore as the home of some Christians who sent a deputation to Vasco da Gama on his second voyage.[6] Tome Pires described Mangalore as an attractive port for ships and merchants, who traded with Cambay and with the kingdoms of Goa, Deccan and Ormuz, taking products of the country and bringing others. Further Pires says that there were garrisons in this port under a Captain. The king derived huge revenues from seaports.[7] Duarte Barbosa described Mangalore as a great town "wherein dwell both Moors and Heathen of the aforesaid kingdom of Narsinga, named Mangalor, where many ships take cargoes of black rice, which is better and more wholesome than the white, to sell in the land of Malabar, and it can be got good cheap".[8] During the first decade of 16th century Mangalore was described as a port which participated in coastal trade net work on the western coast. Eventually the Portuguese tried to get into the trade of Mangalore. In 1522 the king of Portugal freed the merchants of Mangalore from the entrance duty of 4.5 per cent which other traders continued to pay at Goa.[9]

The Portuguese pursued a consistent policy of excluding Arabs from the maritime trade.[10] In the treaties that they signed with Vijayanagar rulers and petty chieftains like the Bangas, they insisted on exclusion of Arabs. However this policy of the Portuguese does not seem to have been commercially productive. Their hostility with Arabs led to conflict not only with Arab traders but also with local kings and traders who maintained contact with the Arabs.

The Portuguese maintained friendly relationship with the Vijayanagar kings who had to depend on the former for the purchase of horses. This horse trade obviously fetched handsome profit for the Portuguese traders. Krishnadeva Raya, the most powerful of the Vijayanagar monarchs, gave permission to the Portuguese to build fortress in Mangalore.[11] The initial policy of the Portuguese was to use force, which led to few bloody wars and destruction of urban structures in Mangalore. During the period from 1520 to 1590 the Portuguese tried to maintain control over trade by using military power. In Cannanore the Portuguese attempts to dominate by using their military power led to exodus of Muslim chiefs from Cannanore to Mangalore. These Muslim chiefs on their turn began to organise pepper trade and supply rice to Calicut from Mangalore. Though the Portuguese protested against the Islamisation of Mangalore trade, the Vijayanagar governors ignored them. D.Simao de Menezes and Fernao Gomes de Lemos spotted seventy *paroas* off Mangalore.[12] Many a time the local chiefs were castigated for allowing the rivals to trade in the Kanarese ports. In 1513 Afonso de Albuquerque sent some of his Captains to Mangalore to take possession of some of Calicut ships which were on their way to Red Sea strait. The local chiefs knew very well that if they had not co-operated with the Captains by allowing them to take the ships, the trade of the ports would be hindered. The chiefs did not resist and the Captains took the ships with goods. Later in 1525 the Portuguese destroyed few of the ships which were trading at Mangalore.[13]

The Portuguese in 16th and 17th centuries faced resistance from a local principality called Chautas of Ullal. As early as 1530 the Portuguese under the command of Nuno de Cunha crossed the river of Mangalore, which flowed through the Ullal territory. They devastated the barricade and the fortified positions. The purpose of this offensive was to penalise a rich merchant of Mangalore, who surreptitiously maintained trade contacts with Muslim traders of Calicut.[14] In 1538 Alvaro de Noronha, son of the Viceroy, chased near Mangalore 25 ships belonging to Calicut. He massacred many of the adversaries and burnt their ships.[15] In the year 1556 Dom Alvaro de Silveyra was sent at the head of several vessels against the Queen of Ullal for refusing to pay the ordinary tribute. The city of Mangalore was pillaged and a Hindu temple was destroyed.[16] In 1567 the Portuguese assaulted the city. They set fire on the city. Besides, they cut down the grove of palm trees.[17] These attacks led to a process of de-urbanisation in Mangalore. However in 1568 a fortress named Sao Sebastiao was constructed with a church and other buildings.[18] The construction of these buildings and the settlement of *casados* and other Christian population eventually led to urbanisation of Mangalore on European patterns. The Christians introduced new crops like papaya, pineapple, etc. They participated both in agriculture and trade. In 1656 there existed a settlement of about 35 families of *casados*.[19]

The Italian traveller Pietro Della Valle gave a description of Mangalore. According to him, the port was in the mouth of two rivers,

> "one more Northern runs from the Lands of Banghel; the other more southern from those of Olala, which stands beyond the river southwards, or rather beyond the bay of saltwater, which is formed round and large, like a great Haven by the two rivers before their

entrance into the Sea, whose flowing fills the same with the salt water. Mangalore stands between Olala and Banghel and in the middle of the bay right against the Mouth of the Harbor, into which the Fort extends itself, being almost encompassed with water on three sides. It is but small, the worst built of any I have seen in India, and, as the Captain told me one day... may rather be termed the House of a Gentleman than a Fort. The City is but little neither, contiguous to the Fort and encompassed with weak walls; within which the houses of inhabitants are enclosed. In Mangalore there are three churches..."[20]

The above description shows that the port was not well maintained. Thus when the enemies attacked the fort it was an arduous task for the Portuguese to defend it. Pietro Della Valle also mentioned the existence of market place (*bazaar*) in Banghel and Ullal,[21] where areca, cloth, gold knives and other merchandise were available for sale. In the interior regions the merchants had to pay toll to the officials of Venkatappa Nayaka, the Keladi king.[22] Venkatappa Nayaka comprehended the importance of Portuguese for the economy of his kingdom. Pietro Della Valle states that Venkatappa Nayaka did not capture the Portuguese fort of Mangalore to "let those Portugals in that small place, in respect of the Traffick and Wares which they brought to the benefit of their countries".[23]

The Portuguese factory at Mangalore was looked after by a factor. The factory was a centre of trade, a military post and a centre of missionary activities. The Portuguese merchants loaded rice, saltpetre, sandalwood, timber, pepper and other articles of trade at Mangalore. Merchants sailing from Goa to China, Macao and Bengal anchored at Mangalore for supplies of merchandise, marines and convoys. The Portuguese supplied ammunitions, salt, mirrors, etc. to the people in the port of Mangalore. A Muslim from Goa Ismail Khan, was in the pay of Portuguese at Mangalore. He had a fleet at his command, fought, and traded on behalf of the Portuguese. The factory was also used to recruit mariners to Bengal and far off ports. *Cartazes* were issued at Mangalore to local merchants.[24]

According to the English traveller Alexander Hamilton Mangalore was the premium port on the Kanara coast. He says "the Portuguese have a Factory for rice here, and a pretty large church, because great numbers of black Christians, reside there." Hamilton further says that, "the fields here bear two crops of corn yearly in the plains; and the higher grounds produce pepper, bettlenut, sandal wood, iron and steel, which make Mangulore a place of pretty good trade. The town is poorly built along the sides of the rivers, and has no defence against an enemy, but two small forts, one on each side of the river's mouth."[25] Here Hamilton repeated the statement of Pietro Della Valle that the town of Mangalore was not well defended. In 1695 the Arabs attacked and plundered Mangalore and carried a large booty.[26] In 1720 the Marathas under Kanoji Angria attacked Mangalore.[27] In 1749 again the Maratha leader Tulaji Angria attacked Mangalore and plundered the Portuguese factory.[28]

The various Portuguese settlements depended on the rice exports from Mangalore and other ports of Kanara coast. In 1630 2,77,985 kilograms of high quality rice was exported from Mangalore.[29] In the year 1631, about 83, 920 kilograms rice was exported from Mangalore to Ceylon.[30] Saltpetre was another item exported from Mangalore. In 1632, the agent of the Portuguese sent their men to Mangalore to procure saltpetre from Mangalore.[31]

The trading community of Mangalore consisted of Muslims, Saraswats, Komatis, Virashaiva traders of Karnataka, Christians, Gujaratis, traders from Kerala and foreign traders belonging to Red Sea ports. According to the *Livro do Cartazes,* during the period from 1705 to 1724 about 8600 *khandis* were exported to different markets.[32] The destinations of Mangalore trade were Malabar, Goa, Surat, Bengal, Malacca, Maldives, Mecca, Aden, Congo, Hormuz and Ceylon.

Basrur

Basrur was another important port of South Kanara. Tome Pires mentioned Basrur as an important port town on the Kanara coast.[33] In Basrur there existed the production of myrobalans.³⁴ Duarte Barbosa stated that Basrur belonged to Vijayanagar kingdom. ³⁵ Here the Portuguese followed the usual mode of building a fortress some distance below the Hindu town so as to command the river approaches. According Bocarro, government archivist at Goa, Portuguese Basrur was a thriving trade centre exporting rice, textiles, saltpetre and iron from the hinterland and importing corals, exotic piece goods, horses and elephants.³⁶

In 1514 the Vijayanagar emperor sent a legation at the head of which was one Retelim Cherim (Cheti), Governor of Basrur, who offered the Viceroy £20,000 for the exclusive right of buying 1000 horses. Albuquerque courteously declined the offer on the ground that such a privilege would destroy trade.³⁷ In 1546 a treaty was signed between the Portuguese and the king of Vijayanagar. According to this treaty the king of Vijayanagar had to coerce all merchants in his kingdom trading with the coast, to send their goods through Honnavar and Basrur. These goods had to be purchased by the Portuguese factors. This would compel the governors of India to send their merchants to buy those goods. At the same time the king of Vijayanagar had to ban export of iron and saltpetre to the kingdom of Adil Shah (Bijapur) from his port towns and his merchants were compelled to bring this merchandise to the harbours of the kingdom of Vijayanagar, where they would be quickly purchased by the Governors of India, not to cause them any loss.³⁸

By the end of 16ᵗʰ century the Portuguese were able to subjugate the local chiefs and merchants of Basrur. They levied a grain tribute on the merchants of Basrur. They had to pay annually 500 loads of rice.³⁹ In the Portuguese fortress of Basrur, a church, and houses for the Captain, various civil and ecclesiastical functionaries and thirty salaried Portuguese *casados* were located. Another thirty-five *casados* with their families lived in a Portuguese settlement, encircled by mud walls, a musket's shot from the fort.⁴⁰ Most of the *casados* possessed rice fields outside the settlement. They enjoyed the yield without any predicament as long as there was accord with the local merchants and their chief. The *casados* owned 7 or 8 *gallivats* of 300 *khandis* each. Loaded with merchandise these *gallivats* used to sail amidst the convoy of a Portuguese armed fleet, for security. The *casados* recruited the required number of mariners from among the local people.[41] In Basrur the Portuguese practice was to arrange contracts with individual merchants and Syndicates, whether Portuguese, Eurasian or Indian, or Christian or Hindu. In 1602 Antonio Mendes de Tomar and Antonio Fernandes de Sampaio were contracted to supply the Portuguese with pepper. In 1603 an Indian goldsmith and his nephew agreed to supply 1500 quintals at Honnavar and Basrur.[42]

Pietro Della Valle gives the following description regarding Basrur:

> Thence we came by a short cut to Barselor, called the Higher i.e. within Land, belonging to the Indians and subject to Venkatapa Naieka, to distinguish it from the Lower Barselor on the sea coast belonging to the Portugals. For in almost all Territories of India near the sea coast there happen to be two places of the same name, one called Higher, or In-land, belonging to the natives, the other the Lower, near the sea, to the Portugals, wherever they have footing. Entering the Higher Barselor on this side, I came into a fair, long, broad and straight street, having abundance of Palmetos and Gardens on either hand.
>
> ...I took boat and rowed down the more southern stream; for little below the said town is divided into many branches and forms divers little fruitful islands. ...The fort of Portugals is very small, built almost in form of a star, having not bad walls, but wanting ditches, in a plain and much exposed to all sorts of assaults. Such Portugals as are married have Houses without the Fort in the Town, which is pretty large and hath good buildings.[43]

Della Valle mentions the existence of houses of Portuguese officials in Basrur. He went and stayed with Antonio Borges.[44] He also went to dine with Ascentio Veira, a Notary of the city. He was given an empty house belonging to Paolo Sodrino, who was married in Mangalore.[45] The details given above demonstrate that ports in South Kanara consisted of different settlements of Portuguese and the natives.

The Portuguese settlement consisted of houses of both civil and military officials.

Alexander Hamilton noticed the port of Basrur standing on the banks of a broad river, about four miles from the sea. He says that the country abounded in rice, having in many places two crops in a year, by the advantage they had of some lakes at the feet of the Mountains of *Gatti* (ghat). The water from these lakes was let out at convenient times to water the rice fields. Hamilton mentioned that in Basrur the Dutch had a factory to procure rice to garrisons on the Malabar Coast. The Dutch factory stood about a mile from the river's mouth, which possessed a bar of 13 or 14 foot water on it at spring tides. The Dutch factory had a castle on its north side for its guard. Further Hamilton says that the Portuguese also got supplies of rice for Goa and that they had six or eight ships belonging to Basrur. Those ships carried cargoes of rice to Muscat and brought back in return horses, dates, pearl, and other merchandise of Arabia. Hamilton described the road from Basrur to Mangalore. He says that on a plain road that led to Mangalore, were planted four rows of trees. They served as umbrellas to the passengers. On several places huts were built where some old people stayed in the daytime, with jars of fine clear water for the passengers to drink at the charge of the state.[46]

The coercion by Portuguese created problems for indigenous traders. It was common for them to forcibly take articles of trade from the local merchants. Francisco de Mello de Sampaio, who became Captain of Basrur in 1583 damaged the trade of that port so much by forcibly taking goods at a lower price that the local merchants endeavoured to drive the Portuguese away from there. But this attempt made by local merchants failed. There were also instances of Captains who levied and collected illegal imposts from merchants at Basrur. Sometimes the Portuguese confiscated Kanarese ships and sold their goods for sheer profit.[47]

In the seventeenth century Portuguese Basrur was a thriving trading centre exporting rice, textiles, saltpetre as well as iron and importing corals, exotic piece goods, horses and elephants.[48] Ships of the merchants were frequently employed in the fetching of rice or for sending the cash for rice. In 1630, an amout of 4,000 Sao Tomes in gold were sent to Basrur in a ship belonging to a Muslim merchant accompanied by another ship owned by Antonio Carreira Salema. In return they were supposed to bring rice from there. In 1629 about 4,99,481 kilograms of *girasol* rice (high quality rice) was sent from Basrur to Goa. In 1630, vessels carrying 2,80,607 kilograms of rice were sent to Goa. During the period between 1629 to 1633, the volume of rice exported to Muscat was 27,39,671 kilograms.[49]

The merchants of the port were referred to by the Portuguese collectively as the *'chatins de Barselor'* (Settis of Basrur). It is said that the settlers of Basrur governed themselves like a Republic, and paid some tribute to the King. The power in the city is described as being in the hands of a collective of *'governadores'* or *'regedores'*, who on specific occasions appointed agents from the merchant community to prosecute negotiations. The port was *terra franca* governed like a Republic, without having any other subjection nor recognising any form of overlordship save for a small tribute that is paid to the Vijayanagar kings.[50] This description leads us to study the internal set up of the port town of Basrur. In Basrur, as in Barkur, there existed *keris* or streets of merchants where there existed the settlement of merchants. They had their own temples in their respective streets. During the medieval period the merchants were given important responsibilities in society. The merchants were appointed as heads of port towns, who were called *pattanasetti* or *pattanaswami*. They were supposed to maintain administration of the towns. Whenever grants were made to certain temples, money was deposited with the merchants and with the interest amount they were supposed to maintain the temples. The merchants had their corporations and they assembled in their meetings. There existed merchant guilds like *halarus, settikaras, nakharas* and *hanjamanas*. Thus when the Portuguese chroniclers mentioned the existence of a republican form of administration, they were referring to this kind of a system, operating among the merchant groups.

From the inscriptions it is known that the Vijayanagara governor at Barkur controlled the activities of the traders of Basrur. The Basrur inscription belonging to A.D. 1465 records a grant made by Mahapradhana Ramachandra Dannayaka Odeya through his subordinate Pandarideva Odeya, the Governor of Barkur, to the temple of Paduvakeri at Basrur of some taxes due to the king from the *hanjamana* (trade guild which traded in horses) of the place.[51] Another inscription from Basrur dated A.D. 1465 refers to *senabova* (accountant) attending the ports to collect the taxes from loaded ships leaving the port of Basrur.[52] This practice of interference in the activities of the traders continued in the sixteenth and seventeenth centuries. At least we know that prior to the arrival of the Portuguese the traders of Basrur did not enjoy position of autonomy. However, during the period of transfer of power from the Vijayanagar to Keladi rulers, it is possible that some element of autonomy was granted to the traders of Basrur. But even then the king of Tolar tried to control Basrur and Gangolli. The king of Tolar even fought a war with the Portuguese to capture Basrur from them.[53]

It is said that in Basrur there existed four doors to enter the city, two for those coming by road and two for those coming by river or water transport. Mudukeri and Paduvakeri were important streets of Basrur. There also existed various other streets like Mandikeri, Vilasakeri and Ravutakeri. The traders and the merchandise reached through Mandikeri where there was facility to stockpile the goods in huge pots. *Mandi* was the place where there was the wholesale trade of goods. These *keris* had doors that were to be closed in the night and opened in the morning. In the Vilasakeri, the traders used to relax with the dancing girls and inebriating drinks.[54]

In *Livro do Cartazes*[55] (book of passports) there is large number of reference to passports issued to traders of Basrur. The ships can be divided into those owned by private traders and state owned ones. The ships owned by the private traders were small compared to the ones owned by the king of Kanara. The largest ship that was owned by the private trader Vishnudas of Gujarat had the capacity to carry 800 *khandis*. The ships of king of Kanara usually carried 600 to 700 and even 1300 *khandis* of cargo. According to *Livro do Cartazes* the total volume of commodities sent from Basrur to different destinations during the period from 1707 to 1724 was 13,441 *khandis*. Considering the fact that all the ships did not take *cartazes*, this number was only a part of total export. The destinations of Basrur trade were Congo, Serdefar, Surat, Barra Araba, Mecca, Ormuz, Bassora, Aden, Sind, and Bengal. The important traders mentioned are Custa Paddiar, Sidy Basavayya, Sedua Naique, Vattadas Guzerate, Babu Hegado, Rama Poy, Ranganna Bagata, Amadax Mouso and Abdul Rahiman. There were Saraswats, Muslims, Gujaratis, Telugu Komatis and Kannada Banajigas.

Barkur

Before the arrival of the Portuguese, Barkur was a flourishing trading centre. Its importance was signified by the presence of the Vijayanagara governor at Barkur. On the eve of the arrival of the Portuguese Barkur consisted of ten *keris* where different traders had their commercial establishments. In the 15th century there existed certain trade guilds like *hanjamana, nakhara, settikaras* etc. The importance of Barkur as a trade centre is revealed by the fact that there was a road called *Barakanura ghatta* (ghat of Barkur) linked with ghats. Tome Pires has seen in Barkur ships and merchants trading with Cambay and with the kingdoms of Goa, Deccan and Ormuz, taking the products of the country and bringing others in exchange.[56] Duarte Barbosa says that, " Here is much good rice, which grows in the lands thereby, and many ships from abroad, and many as well of Malabar, take in cargoes thereof, and take it away".[57] The Portuguese forced the king of Barkur to pay 1000 loads of rice per year as tribute.[58] By A.D. 1515 the Portuguese had established contacts with merchants of Barkur. In that year the Portuguese commanders Gomes Martines de Lemos and Antonia da Silva attacked Barkur. The reason for this attack was that the traders had sold the goods to traders other than

Portuguese against a previous contract. It is said that the Vijayanagara governor Ratnappa Odeya organised a defence and in the naval warfare the Portuguese were defeated.[59] In A.D. 1524 the Portuguese sent the forces to defeat the Muslim traders of Calicut, who used to come to Barkur. A fierce battle was fought near Barkur and the Muslims were vanquished. It is said that sometime before this incident Vasco da Gama, who had embarked for Cochin, had ordered his men to take possession of the bars of Barkur and Mangalore rivers where the *paraos* of Calicut were frequenting for rice in exchange for Malabar wares. Vasco da Gama placed here Jeronymo de Souza and Manuel de Machado with vessels for the purpose of clearing these places of pirates. After defeating Zamorin's fleet in Barkur River, the Portuguese could develop their trade with Barkur without any problem. During the reign of Vitharasa Odeya the Portuguese contact with Barkur increased considerably,[60] where a Portuguese factory was later established, as Domingo Paes testifies.[61]

Barkur continued to have commercial relations with the West in the 17th century. From the writings of Jean Baptiste Tavernier we come to know that ships used to bring silk from Persia in return for rice from Barkur. But Tavernier says that ships used to anchor far away from the capital city. He states that the ship in which he was sailing reached Barkur on 18th April 1648. But the Captain of the ship had to take permission to purchase and load rice on ship. Hence he had to sail three leagues on boat in a river to reach Barkur City. Tavernier also describes that the Captain obtained the permission to purchase rice from Barkur and the governor of Barkur treated them well.[62] But during the later part of 17th century, Barkur lost its political and commercial importance. Basrur superseded Barkur as an important supply centre for rice and pepper.

Gangolli

Gangolli was situated on the mouth of Pancha Gangavali River. It was an agrarian trade centre of rice, sugarcane, coconut, betelnuts, cashewnut and pepper. By the end of 17th century the

Portuguese used to purchase from here 1500 *khandis* of pepper.[63] In the Portuguese records Gangolli is mentioned as Cambolim. In 1569 the Tolar chief and the ruler of Gangolli tried to attack Portuguese but they were unsuccessful in their venture.[64] It was in Gangolli that the Portuguese built their last fortress in the Kanara coast. The port of Gangolli was located in a peninsula formed by the sea and the river Gangolli and was just opposite to their fortress of Basrur. With the construction of this fortress the Portuguese were able to gain control over the island of Gangolli. The island yielded 30,000 bags of rice with which the fortress could be sustained as also other fortresses of Kanara. The fortress could receive relief by sea as well as by river any time of the year.[65] The idea of the Portuguese was to develop this port with a view to replacing Basrur.[66] In Gangolli there was cheap supply of workers to run the Portuguese ships. But due to policy the Nayakas of Ikkeri the Portuguese were not able to achieve success in their mission of converting Gangolli as a major port. However, with the advent of the Portuguese, the hinterland of Gangolli experienced increased production of coconut, pepper, black rice, and also the cultivation of pineapple, tobacco and different varieties of mangoes.[67] The Kodladi copper plate inscription belonging to A.D.1681 mentions the coconut plants in Gangolli seashore. Increased demand for coconut resulted in increased coconut production. Even the lands like *bele*, which were not useful for raising any other crops, were brought under coconut cultivation. This inscription reveals that the state used to take initiative in planting coconuts because it could bring more income to the state treasury. This is a clear example of impact of foreign trade on the pattern of agricultural production.[68]

Apart from the above ports there existed other ports like Baindur, Mulki, Manjeshwar and Kumbla. Baindur was adjacent to the port of Bhatkal. Duarte Barbosa referred to this town as Majandur. He says that Baindur supplied rice to Bhatkal. Here different varieties of rice like, *giracal, acal, quavagas* and *pachary*, were produced. It is said that the Portuguese collected 300 *fardos* of rice from this port.[69] During the rule of Keladi kings, Baindur was an important place where custom duty was collected. The Sirur copper plate inscription dated A.D.1610[70] states that Keladi Venkatappa Nayaka conferred on Keriya Sankanna Senabhova alias Narana the office of *sthalasenabhovike* (office to collect custom duties). The *stalasenabhova* was entitled to collect custom duties from five places: Ulanadu, Hammaranadu, Bidarnadu, Baiduru (Baindur) and Haligere. This inscription testifies the hectic external contacts that developed as a result of increased demand through Portuguese trade and the constant contacts between port and hinterland.

The port of Mulki or Karnad situated on shores of Shambhavi river. The Portuguese identified a group of islands in 1580, which were fertile and well cultivated. The Keladi rulers used to collect substantial amount of custom duty from here. In 1705 a treaty was signed between the Portuguese and the Keladi ruler Basvappa Nayaka. According to this treaty the Portuguese obtained the right to collect custom duty from here. Mulki was known chiefly for the export of rice.[71]

The port of Kumbla exported rice, pepper and coconut to Malabar, Gujarat and Arabia. Duarte Barbosa stated that "Here is garnered great abundance of very bad black rice, which the Malabares come hither to purchase, and to take away in their *zambuquos*, to sell to the lower sort of people, who buy it readily, as it is good cheap, and by it they make more than by the good rice. They also take much thereof to the Maldive islands, which lie over against Malabar, as the inhabitants are poor Moors, who, by reason of its lower price, would rather have black than white rice. They gave it to them in exchange for *cairo* (coir), which is a thread used for making cables and ropes; it is made out of the husks of coconut, and much of it is made here."[72] The soil of Kumbla was suited for production of black rice. However, we may note that black rice was consumed in Malabar not only by poor class of people but also by the upper class. The king of Kumbla gave 800 loads of rice to the Portuguese per annum as tribute.[73]

The growth of coastal trade and overseas trade led to dilated contact between ports and the hinterland. *Sunkathanes* (custom stations) were established in the trade routes. An inscription belonging to A.D 1606 mentions the collection of custom duties at Sagara, Kumbhasi, Pombucha, Agumbe, Belare, Kalasa and Kiga.[74] An inscription belonging to A.D.1673 mentions the transport of commodities on pack bullocks. This inscription mentions the items like arecanut, pepper, tassels, silk, coconut kernels, wood, rice, paddy, ragi, oil, ghee, fruits, jaggery and rattan. In the custom stations the colour and age of bullocks were registered.[75] Another inscription belonging to A.D.1711 mentions the commodities like arecanut, pepper, tassels, silk, wood, rice, paddy, ragi, salt, acid, rattan, grain, oil, ghee, pulse, jaggery, fruit, cutch, coconut kernels, clothes, iron, dates, tobacco, asafoetida, cumin seed, mustard, fenugreek, onion, garlic and turmeric.[76]

The above references connote that arteries of trade were well connected. The traders participated in both coastal trade and overseas trade. The arrival of the Portuguese led to acceleration in volume of export of different commodities, which in turn led to increased agricultural production. The Portuguese operations in South Kanara did not remain constant, monotonous. There were different phases in their interaction with native traders. In the initial phase the Portuguese were able to dictate terms since they were powerful on the sea. There was supply of essential commodities from Malabar. However, with the antagonism with the kings and traders of Kerala, the Portuguese increasingly found it difficult to gain access to Malabar ports. In Kanara also there was a transition in the political power. The Vijayanagara rulers were succeeded by the Keladi rulers, who due to their political power were able to dictate terms to the Portuguese. In the 18th century the Portuguese competed with English and the Dutch. The arrival of these Europeans in the ports of South Kanara led to urbanisation of port complexes. There was settlement of different community of traders in these ports. The traders participated in both coastal trade and overseas trade. The study exhibits that the pre-colonial economy of South Kanara displayed symptoms of expansion and led to capital accumulation. This study also shows the transition of an agrarian zone into a maritime zone. The contact of the traders of South Kanara with the Portuguese helped them in participating in the international trade.

References:

1. South Kanara was a coastal district of Karnataka. At present two separate districts, Udupi and Dakshina Kannada have been created out of this district. For our academic purpose we consider South Kanara as a single historical unit.
2. Annual Report of South Indian Epigraphy, (henceforth ARSIE), 1926-27, No. 367. The translation of this inscription is following: "He who put me in this place put also his own figure. If there be anyone to enter it, his wretchedness will turn out a great boon". Also see, J.J.Cotton, Inscriptions of Tombs, p. 168.
3. K.G.Vasanthamadhava, 'A Note on Trasi Hero Stone dated Saka 1468 = A.D.1546', Journal of Institute of Asian Studies. The inscription mentions parangadavara kapitaru, which meant invasion of Portuguese army. This shows that the Portuguese ventured to establish their supremacy not only on sea, but even in the inland territories. In this hero stone, weapons like big sword, shield, dagger and rifle are engraved.
4. S. Arasaratnam, Maritime India in the Seventeenth Century, Delhi, 1991, p. 93ff.
5. K.G. Vasanthamadhava, Western Karnataka Its Agrarian Relations 1500-1800, New Delhi, 1991, p. 242.
6. Thome Lopez, Navegação as Indias Orientães, Chapter 19, quoted in Manual Longworth Dames(Ed.), The Book of Duarte Barbosa , Vol. I, Reprint, Madras, 1989. p. 196. Vasco da Gama was aware of some ports of South Kanara. This is evident by the attempt made by Vasco da Gama to sell some commodities to native fisher folk of an island of South Kanara identified as St. Maries island near the port of Malpe. Also see Sanjay Subrahmanyam, Vasco da Gama, Cambridge, 1997, p. 145; Sturrock, Madras District Manuals South Kanara, Vol. I, Madras, 1894, p. 67.
7. Armando Cortesão (Ed.), The Suma Oriental of Tom Pires, Vol. I, New Delhi, 1990, pp. 60-63
8. Ibid, p. 195.
9. B.S. Shastry, 'Commercial Policy of the Portuguese in Coastal Karnataka',H.V.Shrinivasa Murthy et. al., (Ed.), Essays in Indian History and Culture, New Delhi, 1990, p. 116.
10. K.S.Mathew, 'Indian Merchants and the Portuguese Trade on the Malabar Coast during the Sixteenth Century', Teotonio R de Souza(Ed.), Indo-Portuguese History Old Issues, New Questions, New Delhi, 1985, p. 1. ; Teotonio R de Souza, Medieval Goa, New Delhi, 1979, p. 38.
11. Sturrock, op. cit., p. 68.
12. Genevive Bouchon, 'Regent of the Sea' Cannnore's Response to Portuguese Expansion, 1507-1528, (Tr. Louise Shackley), Delhi, 1988, p. 168.
13. B.S.Shastry, Studies in Indo-Portuguese History, Bangalore, 1981, pp. 209-210.
14. H. Heras, The Aravidu Dynasty, Vol. I, Madras, 1927, p. 188.

15. B.S.Shastry, "The Portuguese in Kanara 1498-1763", Unpublished Ph.D. Thesis, Bombay University, 1969, p. 91.
16. H. Heras, *op. cit.*, p. 189.
17. *Ibid*, p. 190.
18. *Ibid.*
19. K.G.Vasanthamadhava, *Trends in Karnataka Historical Research*, Mangalore, 1996, p. 117.
20. Edward Gray(Ed.), *The Travels of Pietro Della Valle in India*, Vol. II, New Delhi, 1991, p. 301.
21. *Ibid*, pp. 302-303.
22. *Ibid*, pp. 304-306.
23. *Ibid*, pp. 314-315.
24. B.S.Shastry, "The Book of Correspondence concerning Kanara: A Note", *Indica*, Vol. 15, September, 1978, No. 2, pp. 121-126.
25. Alexander Hamilton, *A New Account of the East Indies 1688-1723*, Vol. I, London, 1739, Madras, 1995, pp. 282-283.
26. *Ibid*, p. 283.
27. *Ibid.*
28. B.S. Shastry, "Portuguese Relations with Tulaji Angria and Basavappa Nayaka II 1747-1750", in, G.S.Dikshit, *Studies in Keladi History*, Bangalore, 1981, p. 62. The Maratha raids on the ports of South Kanara began with the attack of Basrur by Shivaji.
29. Afzal Ahmad, *Indo-Portuguese Trade in Seventeenth Century (1600-1663)*, New Delhi, 1991, p. 119.
30. *Ibid*, p. 121.
31. *Ibid*, p. 129.
32. Historical Archives of Goa, *Livro do Cartazes*, MS. No. 1363.
33. Armando Cortesão, *op. cit.*, pp. 60-63.
34. Armando Cortesão,(Ed.), *The Suma Oriental of Tom Pires*, Vol. II, p. 514.
35. Mansel Longworth Dames (Ed), *op. cit.*, p. 193.
36. A.R.Disney, *Twilight of the Pepper Empire, Portuguese Trade in South West India in the Early Seventeenth Century*, London, 1978.
37. H. Heras, *op. cit.*, p. 59.
38. *Ibid*, p. 62.
39. Sturrock, *op. cit.*, p. 68.
40. A.R.Disney, *op. cit.*, p. 5.
41. B.S.Shastry, 'A Glimpse of the Socio-Economic conditions of the Port-Towns of Coastal Karnataka in the Sixteenth and Seventeenth Centuries as Described in some Condemporary (sic) Portuguese Sources', Dr.K.Veeratappa(Ed)., *Studies in Karnataka History and Culture*, Mysore, 1987, p. 98.
42. A.R.Disney, *op. cit.*, pp. 36-37.
43. Edward Gray, *op. cit.*, pp. 296-298.
44. *Ibid*, pp. 298-299.

45 *Ibid*, pp. 301-302.
46 Alexander Hamilton, *op. cit.*, p. 281.
47 B.S.Shastry, "The Portuguese in Kanara 1498-1763", *op. cit.*, p. 305 f.
48 Afzal Ahmad, *op. cit.*, p. 13.
49 *Ibid*, 118-119.
50 Sanjay Subrahmanyam, 'The Portuguese, the Port of Basrur, and the rice trade 1600-1650', Sanjay Subrahmanyam(Ed), *Merchants Markets and State in Early Modern India*, Delhi, 1990, pp. 30-31.
51 *ARSIE* 1927-28, No. 406.
52 *South Indian Inscriptions*(henceforth *SII*), Vol. IX, Part II, No. 459.
53 H. Heras, *op. cit.*, pp. 296-297.
54 B. Laxminarayana Upadhya, 'Pravasigara tana Basaruru nagara noda banni', in, *Hesarada Pattana Basaruru Ondu Adhyayana*(in Kannada), Basrur, 1997, p. 10.
55 HAG, *Livro do Cartazes*, *op. cit.*
56 Armando Cortesão, *op. cit.*, pp. 60-63.
57 Mansel Longworth Dames, *op. cit.*, pp. 193-194.
58 Sturrock, *op. cit.*, p. 68.
59 B. Vasanth Shetty, "Barkaruru – A Metropolitan City of Antiquity", Unpublished Ph.D. Thesis, Mysore University, 1985,pp. 216-217.
60 *Ibid*, pp. 218-219.
61 Vasundhara Filliozat (Ed.), *The Vijayanagara Empire As Seen by Domingo Paes and Fernao Nuniz*, Delhi, 1977, p. 18.
62 H.L.Nage Gowda (Ed.), *Pravasi Kanda India,*(in Kannada), Vol. V, Mysore, 1975, pp. 489-490.
63 K.G.Vasanthamadhava, *Western Karnataka Its Agrarian Relations A.D. 1500-1800*, *op. cit.*, p. 238.
64 H. Heras, *op. cit.*,pp. 296-297.
65 B.S. Shastry, "The Portuguese in Kanara 1498-1763", *op. cit.*,pp. 107 ff.
66 P.S.S. Pissurlencar(Ed.), *Assentos Do Conselho do Estado, I*, Bastora, 1953, p. 249; Braganza Pereira (Ed.), *Archivo Portuguese Oriental*, Tomo IV, Vol. II, pp. 311-313.
67 K.G.Vasanthamadhava, *op. cit.*
68 B. Vasanth Shetty, 'A Keladi Copper plate from Kodladi (Kundapur Tq.)' *Quarterly Journal of Mythic Society*, Vol. LXXVIII, & Issue No. 3-4, pp. 1-5.
69 Mansel Longworth Dames, *op. cit.*,p. 192.
70 K.G.Vasanthamadhava, *op. cit.*,p. 200.
71 *Ibid*, pp. 13-14.
72 Mansel Longworth Dames, *op. cit.*,pp. 196-197.
73 Sturrock, *op. cit.*, p. 68.
74 *Epigraphia Carnatica*, Vol. VIII, Sagar No. 123.
75 *Ibid*, Tirthahalli, No. 68.
76 *Ibid*, Tirthahalli, No. 72.

20

DECLINE OF THE PORTUGUESE NAVAL POWER : A STUDY BASED ON PORTUGUESE DOCUMENTS

K. M. Mathew

Portugal was the spearhead of European expansion. It was the Portuguese who inagurated the age of renaissance-discovery and thus initiated the maritime era of world history. There is hardly any period in world history as romantic in its appeal as this ' Age of Discovery ' and hence it is of perennial interest. The Portuguese achievement in that age is a success story which has few parallels. That they achieved what they set forth - "possessing the sources of the spice-trade and its diversion to European markets" -is a great feat for a country of her size, population and resources. If the Portuguese had not evolved the great *'nau'* which could withstand the buffeting of the mysterious Atlantic tides and carry materials for the long, unknown and perilous voyages, Columbus' historic voyage might have been a mere dream.

The discovery of the sea-route in 1498 was one of the greatest events for a small but enterprising nation. Vasco da Gama's voyage was the longest on the high-seas to that date. The total distance from Lisbon to Calicut and back was approximately 22000 miles. His voyage was the climax of a century of determined navigation and exploration by Portugal, masterninded by one of the greatest seafarers and statesman of the sea , Prince Henry , appropriately surnamed as Navigator. Da Gama's feat of navigation with his hostile crew sailing at the mercy of winds and storms, fired the imagination of the Portuguese poet Luis de Camoens who wove the tale of the Lusitanian seafarers in the narrative of a historic voyage. Da Gamas's arrival at Kappat near Calicut in May 1498 marks a unique watershed and opening of a new chapter in Indian history. It became the harbinger of modern organised naval power in Indian waters and da Gama became the first discoverer of the true means of utilizing sea - power as the foundation of colonial power.

From the point of view of the results that followed, this voyage had far-reaching consequences. It inaugurated what Sardar K.M. Panikkar called the 'Vasco da Gama epoch of Asian History', which down to the emergence of America and Japan as major naval powers at the end of the 19th century, was an age of maritime power, of authority, based on the control of the seas by the nations of Western Europe. The discovery made radical changes in the economic balance of the world and placed Portugal in a unique position. Portugal became the mistress of the Eastern Sea-route and they looked upon the sea as their own. Lisbon became the emporium of world-trade with the East.

The Portuguese were the first to have understood the concept of sea-power and evolved a naval strategy for the effective control of the Indian sea. Their aim was to break the monopoly of Muslim trade and to reach the source of the lucrative spices. However, the Portuguese hold on the Indian mainland was confined to coastal areas, within the range of the guns of their ships and their fortresses. Strangely enough, they held the smallest areas in India. Viewed from this angle, there is a peculiar interest to the story of the Portuguese in India. The mastery of the Indian sea passed to them in 1504, when they gained a decisive victory of great importance over the Zamorin of Calicut. Since then, their naval supremacy enabled them to dominate the high-seas and to deny free navigation to others by their own concept of sovereignty of the sea. They forced others to purchase their security passports- *'Cartazes'*. Though their political control remained restricted to scattered coastal areas, it did attempt, if not necessarily achieve, some political and maritime unity, which had a very significant consequence.

Afonso de Albuquerque consolidated the Portuguese rule in the early 16th century and selected Goa in 1510 as the main base on the Western coast. Since then the Portuguese dominated the coast. However it is surprising that this domination did not continue beyond 1570, by which time they began declining.

If the 16th century had made the Portuguese the wealthiest, the same century also saw the Portuguese sink into an insignificant power. In fact the seeds of this decline were sown much earlier. The position of Portugal deteriorated under King John III when he introduced the ill-famous Inquisition and from the mid-16th century there began a period of quick and profound decline[1]. King Sebastian tried to save the situation by undertaking an expedition to Africa, but his death in the battlefield was a great blow, out of which the Portuguese never recovered. In view of this tragic event, we notice a weak naval activity since 1578[2]. The Portuguese met opposition from all sides, found their trade return on the decrease and thus they were not able to maintain a naval establishment in the East. By the beginning of the 17th century, the Portuguese power began to show definite signs of decline and their navy, once superb and splendid, became the glory of the past. A number of factors seems to have contributed to the decline of the Portuguese power in the East. An attempt is made in this paper to critically study the source materials available in the Archives of Goa, Portugal and France etc. An analysis of the factors reveals the many-sided degeneration of the Portuguese domination in the Indian waters.

Union of Portugal with Spain(1580-1640) and its Echo in the distant Indian Waters.

The amalgamation of Portugal under the Spanish domination had its echo and serious repercussions in the Indian waters. What happened in 1580 was that the fate of the Portuguese was tied with the Spaniards. When the Spanish ruler prohibited the protestant merchants of Amsterdam (Holland) and England from purchasing Asiatic goods at Lisbon, the latter were naturally resented and turned to India not only to punish the Spanish King, but also to collect the Eastern commodities now under the Spanish protection. "The capture of India seemed to Holland a continuation of the just revolt against Portugal"[3]. The Dutch also wanted to try their hand and propagate a new religion. They collected a good deal of nautical information and charts and even got published the Portuguese *roteiros* on navigation. In 1595, when three Dutch ships also rounded the Cape of Good Hope and broke forth into the Indian waters, the Portuguese, whose power depended on the absence of a rival naval power, were unable to check the new-comers and were destined to collapse. The Spanish ruler Philip II was preoccupied with domestic problems and could not help in the maintenance of Portuguese power in India. He could not even send enough men to India to defend the Portuguese possessions against the increasing attack of their enemies. The Portuguese were neither strong nor numerous enough and therefore they had to yield. The *Estado da India* suffered from indecision and delay. During the 60 years of the Portuguese union with Spain, the Portuguese power received a hard blow from the enemies of Spain and it left a scar which had never been fully healed[4]. The destruction of the Spanish Armada at the hands of the English meant a great setback to the Spanish naval supremacy, under which the Portuguese were now only a part. Many of the Portuguese fleets were also destroyed in the action.

The arrival of the Dutch in Indian waters in 1596 was followed by a long struggle between them and the Portuguese and altogether the Portuguese lost 1429 men, 155 ships and property worth 7500,000 *xerafins*[5]. In 1603, the Dutch blocked Goa and even though abortive, it marked the beginning of a struggle which in the next 70 years shattered the Portuguese power in India[6]. The Portuguese began to loose their possessions one after another to the Dutch. "The take over of Cranganore by the Dutch was the beginning of the end of the Portuguese power in Malabar, if not of their Eastern empire itself[7]". During 1611 and 1615, the Portuguese suffered defeats of Cambay and Surat. Ormuz was lost in 1622 and Emperor Shah Jahan took

Hughli in 1629. Malacca and Jafnapatanam (Sri Lanka) were lost in 1640 and 1658 respectively. In 1656 Cannanore was taken by the Dutch and that was followed by Nagapatanam, Kayamkulam and Quilon in 1661. Bombay had to be ceded to the English in 1661 as part of the dowry of Catherine of Bragança. In fact, it was a face-saving measure and by it the Portuguese were purchasing safety from the English at a high price. In 1670, the Arabs plundered the Portuguese Diu which had earlier resisted the greatest onslaught of the Muslim forces in 1538 and 1546 by Governor João de Castro. The Marathas took back Bassein in 1739 and even stormed the very wall of Goa. All what remained after these conquest were captured by the rulers of Ikkeri in South Kanara who captured the Portuguese forts of Mangalore, Bhatkal and Honawar and thus effectively cut off the supply line of rice to Goa[8].

Weak Rulers and Reversal of Policies.

The successors of King Manuel I were men of mediocre talent and they selected Viceroys/Governors of the same type who being not good diplomats contributed only to the ruin of the Portuguese in the East. "Truely the Portuguese have bred heroes in place of diplomats and poets in place of capitalists[9]". The wise policy of Afonso de Albuquerque visualized a vast Portuguese empire in the East based on imperial notions. But his successors were only inferiors and they set aside the policy as impracticable and changed the role of the Portuguese as traders and took up a career of conquest not backed by enough resources. This proved fatal in the long run[10]. João de Castro was really the last great Portuguese Governor in India and with his death in 1548, the Portuguese naval power declined definitely in the Eastern Seas. Finding it impossible to hold the Indian Ocean-supremacy the Portuguese had turned their attention to Brazil, which was nearer to Portugal[11]. It was difficult to find the heroism of the Portuguese of the times of Afonso de Albuquerque. But they still survived with their remaining pockets of Goa, Daman and Diu. Professor Plumb has rightly said that, "the Portuguese were the first to come and the last to go"[12].

The Role of the Native Rulers.

Tired of the Portuguese yoke and anxious to shake off their rule in India, the native rulers of the Indian coast sought support and alliances of the enemies of Spain and therefore of the Portuguese. They further weakened the Portuguese by sea and land[13]. The native troops also participated and added only confusion to the Portuguese. These troops who were earlier trained for the war by the Portuguese became masters of the situation. Mutiny and revolt became common.

Poor Resources.

The costly naval wars fought during 1580-1640 against the various powers had crippled the Portuguese economy completely and the ever decreasing and meagre revenues of India were fully absorbed in the continental wars of Europe fought by the Spanish rulers. The Portuguese who had become rich suddenly due to outside resources had nothing to fall back in the economic race which was won by her rivals with greater resources than her own.[14]. The fall of Vijayanagara in 1565 was a death-blow to the Portuguese commerce because since then the lucrative horse-trade between Goa and Vijayanagara declined[15]. Some amount of this trade continued with other native states like Bijapur and Ahmednagar and this helped the Portuguese economy to a certain extent.

Corruption, Negligence and Piracy.

Corruption, embezzlement and dishonesty prevailed everywhere. In one particular year, the officals of the *Casa da India* showed 17,000 names on the pay-roll when actually 4000 men were only sent to India[16]. The officials in India got poor salary, if at all they got regularly and hence they began to organise their own private expedition and trade. Everyone desired to make fast fortune by all means. The sudden acquisition of wealth dazzled and blinded the Portuguese and prevented them from seeing the real problems and they became slaves of their own glory. Vanity was the cause of her ruin. A letter from Goa to the King of Portugal dated 25/11/1552 said that "each one considered only himself in India.... and there is no justice. The object is getting together of money by all means. Help us Senhor, help us Senhor, for we are sinking"[17] The Viceroys, Governors and Captains of forts were traders and not rulers and they came to India to amass wealth. They neglected the *armadas* in India for which they had no money. It was not surprising that a Viceroy could collect 1 million *Cruzados* in his three-years term when his salary was hardly 30,000 *Cruzados*![18] Piracy was practised in the Eastern seas. One of the main assignments of the Portuguese fleets in India was to chase the Muslim pilgrim-ships in the Red Sea on their way back from Mecca. This not only led to a moral decline but was disastrous to the royal trade leading to great political weakness[19].

Insufficiency of Manpower

Afonso de Albuquerque encouraged the policy of mixed marriage-the Portuguese men to marry native women so that the forts in India could be manned by honest men in India itself. He created a race of half-caste Portuguese by encouraging the Portuguese to marry the wives of Muslims who had been killed in the conquest of Goa. He also encouraged the Portuguese artisans like shipbuilders, rope-makers, gunners and other workers in the arsenal and dockyard to marry from Goa. His basic aim was to form a population who should be at once loyal to Portugal and would remain in India for life[20]. This colonizing policy was carried out by Albuquerque for moral and political reasons[21]. It was one of his favourite schemes and was well suited to the inclinations of Portuguese people. But the success of this system depended on several factors. However this policy was ignored by his successors[22]. Year after year, Portugal sent fleets to India consisting of 3000 to 4000 men of which a few only returned to Portugal. Many perished in battles, shipwrecks and in bad weather[23]. Thus Portugal had been drained of men and she had neither enough men nor resources to protect her Eastern possessions and naturally the Portuguese Eastern empire entered into degeneration and decadence. Their forts and factories deteriorated for want of men to guard them from the attack of their enemies.

Lack of Artillery and Ammunitions

The Portuguese naval forts on the coast were ill-equipped for want of money and neglect by their Captains. There was not enough artillery and the existing ones were insufficient. The gun powder and ammunitions were of inferior quality. The Captains of the forts pilfered artillery from the forts and supplied to private traders. In 1587 the Portuguese King tried to check these abuses by issuing necessary regulations which were often repeated, but of no avail[24]. In 1596, when the new Viceroy D Francisco da Gama reached India and found that the artillery was in extreme short supply, he soon acquired some copper and ordered the manufacture of some artillery. In that year itself, the King had asked him to stop issuing of artillery to private persons as it was reported that a good quantity of artillery was stolen and even sold to the Muslims. No wonder that in 1596,when the Dutch entered the Indian waters with 11 ships, they could easily seize some Portuguese ships. Again in 1603, when the Dutch had blockaded Goa, the forts of Bardez and Gaspar Dias were unable to face them due to lack of weapons, even though the King had been advising the authorities in Goa to manufacture artillery in sufficient quantity.

Increasing Cost of Construction and Repair of Ships

By the end of the 16th century, the cost of shipbuilding and repair work in Goa rose sharply. One reason for this was that the Captains of the fortresses whose perquisites included falling and selling of local timber, always charged exhorbitant prices. The Captains of Bassein and Daman sold the timber to the shipyard at 40 Xerafins per khandi, even though it cost them only 5 Xerafins[25]. A letter from Goa in 1629 to the Portuguese East Indian Company reported that "there was no longer (in Goa) contractors who used to repair and refit Carracks. Nowadays, it is clear contrary, because they all went bankrupt and have no capital." By the beginning of the 17th century, the cost of repairing, caulking and careening of ships at Goa shipyard had almost doubled!

Shipwrecks and Lack of Ships

There was lack of ships of big tonnage and there were not enough ships to be sent to the help of a threatened spot. In fact, Portugal did not possess more than 300 ships at the height of her maritime glory (around 1536) and this was insufficient for supporting a far-flung sea-borne and trading empire with world- wide ramifications[26]. As early as 1534 (15.11.1534) Admiral Martim Afonso de Souza wrote to the King of Portugal a confidential letter in which he discounted the affairs of the Portuguese navy in India in the 16th century. He felt that the Portuguese navy was not in a position to maintain warfare, "even for three years as no person wished to serve in the *armada*." He gave a graphic account of overall decline and suggested immediate remedial measures. He advised that if the ships were laid up and repaired, "they would last ten thousand years."[27] Again Governor Castro wrote to King John III on 16.12.1546 giving a detailed report about the conditions of the Portuguese fleets in India. It throws light on the miserable state of the decline of the navy in India. The ruin was so much that the Governor had" no words to describe". "The ships were all rotten and eaten by a variety of worms (*buzano*)". He was sure that unless repair work was commernced very soon, "within three months, the entire fleet would perish". He felt that "since our fleet constituted the wall of our India, timely repair work was required".[28]

By the end of the 16th century, the size of the annual fleets, which in the early days was 12 to 14 sails, was now reduced to five to six and sometimes even three. A large number of "abortive" voyages and maritime mishaps had reduced the Portuguese navy to the barest minimum. One of the causes for the loss of so many ships was the system of contract construction and repair of ships adopted by King Sebastian and Philip II. The Contractors used inferior materials for shipbuilding and the whole work was not at all done carefully and perfectly. The result was that during 1585-1597, ie during the first two contract periods, out of the 66 ships that sailed for India, only 34 returned safely[29]. Ambitious naval construction made 'floating castles' with excessive and improper size. This ruined the construction of ships. Most of these ships could not withstand the long voyages and wrecked on the way. "Not one Portuguese ship out of three returns safe from the voyage". The cup of Portuguese maritime disasters was full.

At the end of the 16th century, a *nau* of India-voyage could hardly make two voyages while the old *naus* had done ten to twelve round-voyages. To remedy this evil, it was ordered in 1570 that *naus* of India-voyages were not to exceed 450 tonnes, but the effect of this order was nullified by increasing the number of storeys of the ships as the capacity of the hold was not allowed to be increased[31]. When the Dutch and the English came to India to dispute the Portuguese naval supremacy, the Portuguese vessels were about a century behind in shipbuilding, naval equipments and tactics. The Portuguese ships were rotten and broken and this shook the very confidence of their navigation in India. On 3.11.1571 orders were issued for convoying of ships and election of Captains of the fleets; but all these belated measures could not arrest the progressive dismantlement of the Portuguese in the East.

On the basis of India House records, it was computed that during 1497-1612 (115 years) out of 806 ships that left for India, 620 ships (ie 75 ships per year) were during the initial period, 1497-1597. During the next period (1580-1612), 186 ships (ie 58 ships per year) came to India. During the period 1500-1579 (80 years) 31 ships were wrecked, but during the next 30 years, 35 ships were wrecked[32]. The total loss of ships during one century (1550-1650) was 130. During 1580-1592, ship-wreck was alarmingly high. Within a period of 12 years 1585-1597, out of 60 ships which left Portugal, 18 were wrecked, i.e 27.4% against 7.7% of the earlier period[33]. During 1590-1592, out of 7 the ships that left Lisbon for Goa only 2 ships returned safely. By 1650, shipwrecks reached an alarmingly disastrous level[34]. The loss of so many ships must have been a great strain on the Portuguese economy. During 1521-1551 itself, 31 *naus* were wrecked which cost about 33,52,150 *Cruzados*[35].

333

The particulars of movements of ships and shipwrecks etc, for the period 1585-1597 (hardly 12 years under Spanish domination) show that 22 ships (18 wrecked or lost and 4 burnt) were wrecked, 2 ships were seized by the enemies as against 66 wrecked, 6 brunt and 4 seized during the whole period. Thus it can be clearly seen that the cause of the decline and ruin of the Portuguese naval supremacy in India was internal and not completely external.

The main reasons for the loss of so many home-bound ships on the return voyage were the use of old ships for long voyages, willful, reckless and ambitious overloading, superficial and inadquate careening of ships, careless caulking work at Goa, greed of profiting and easy money by building cheap and unsafe vessels, abuse of overcrowding and untimely departure of ships. Among the other factors were the structural crankiness of the ships, shortage of trained and experienced sea-men, late leaving of the fleet (which were forced to abort the voyage and winter at Mocambique) and the stubborn behaviour of the Captains of the ship[36].

There were all kinds of allegations of inefficiency in the fitting of *armadas*. An enquiry held in Goa in 1630 revealed that the pilots and gunners were incompetent and they had infact purchased their positions rather than secure them on merit and expertise. This fact was admitted by the King himself earlier in 1597[37]. Lack of discipline on board the ships led to disagreement between the Captain and crew. The behavioural attitudes of the Captains also added to the problems. There were occasions when the pilot was not speaking with his colleagues! Hence the Royal Orders prescribed that they were to be punished seriously if they failed to consult each other amicably[38]. There were all kinds of allegations which included that the ships were not properly equipped for war during the voyage and because of which they were the victims of plunder and enemy attack. There were not enough provisions of all types for long voyages and sometimes there were not even a spare set of sails[39]. The rigging and tackles of ships were deficient and rotten.

It was the decadence in the art of shipbuilding and the art of navigation that caused the Portuguese decline in the East. Historian Oliveira Martin had very appropriately commented that "the Portuguese navy was lost even before the loss of national independence (1580), because the ships construction was bad, navigation was worse and because the ships were overloaded and the ignorants arrogated themselves as pilots. It was the sea which devoured the Portuguese ships and not the Dutch and the English"[40].

References:

1. Herculano, Alexandro, *Historia da Portugal*, Livraria Tavares Cardoso, Lisbon, 1901, Vol.I.p.6.
2. Britto, Naugeria de, *Caravelas, Naus e Gales de Portugal*, Livraria Lello, Port, n.d.a.pp. 46-57
3. Poonen, T.I, *Dutch Beginnings in India Proper 1580-1615*, Univ.of Madras, 1933,pl
4. Poonen,T.I., British Survey'(BS), British Society for International understanding, London, 1954.no 61, p. 4
5. Poonen,T.I., 'Journal of Bombay Historical Society', (JBHS) Bombay, 1928, vol 5. no 2, p. 26
6. Rao, R.P, *Portuguese Rule in Goa 1510-1961*, Asia Publishing House, Bombay, p. 37
7. Menon.K.P.P., *History of Kerala* (MHK), Cochin Govt.Press, Eranakulam, 1924, vol I. p. 316
8. JBHS (1928), op. cit. p. 28
9. Campos, J.J.A, *History of the Portuguese in Bengal*, Butterworth and Co., Calcutta, 1919,p. 10
10. Campos, J.J.A, 'Indo-Portuguese Review', Indo-Portuguese Association, Calcutta, 1928, p. 1
11. Singh, R, *Politics of the India Ocean*, Thomson Press, Delhi, 1974, p. 10
12. Boxer, C.R, *The Tragic History of the Sea 1589-1612*, Haklyut Society, Camb. Uni Press, 1959, p. 20
13. Souza, A.B, *Subsidios para a Historia Militar e Maritima da India 1585-1612* (SSHMM), Lisbon, 1930, vol I, pp. 223-225.
14. B S, op.cit. 1954, p. 4
15. JBHS, op.cit. 1928, p. 36
16. Hunter, W.W, *A History of British India*, Turner & Co; London, 1885, vol.I, p. 178
17. MHK, op. cit vol.I.pp.184-185
18. SSHMMI, op.cit., vol. I. pp. 8-13
19. Costa, Marechal Gomes, *Descobrimentos e Conquistas*, Imprenca Nacional, Lisbon, 1929, vol. I.p. 94
20. Morse Stephens, H, *Rulers of India : Albuquerque* (MRIA), Clarendon Press, Oxford, 1892,p. 45

21. Albuquerque, Aofonso de, *Commentarios de Grande Afonso de Albuquerque* Imprenca Universidade, Lisbon, 1942.vol.III.pp. 41-42
22. Correa, Francisco A, *Consequencias Economicas dos Descobrimentos*, Lisbon, 1937, pp. 68-69.
23. MRIA, Op.cit p. 201
24. SSHMMI, Op.cit.vol. I, pp. 8-38
25. 'Separata do Centro de Estudo Historicus Ultramarinas e as Comemorações, Coimbra', 1961, p. 38
26. Boxer, C.R, *The Portuguese Sea-borne Empire, 1415-1825*, Hutchinson & Co. London, 1969, p. 58
27. Document. Letter dated Diu 15/11/1534 from Martim Afonso de Souza to D. Antonio de Athiade, from the collection of S. Lourenco, Tombo. Vol.I.pp 438-441
28. Document. Letter dated Diu 16/02/1546 from Governor Joao de Castro. From Elaine Sanceu's Cartas de D Joao de Castro, pp 303-305.
29. SSHMMI, op.cit. Vol I pp 58-59
30. Flecknoe, Richard, *A Relation of Ten Years Travels in Europe, Asia and Africa*, London, 1656, p. 101
31. Oliveira, J.de Braz, *Influencia de Infante D. Henrique no progressos da Marinha, Portuguesa : Navios e Armamentos*, Imprenca Nacional, Lisbon, 1894, pp. 83-84
32. Falcao, Luis F. de, *Livro em que se contem toda a Fazenda da real patrimonia (1612)*, Lisbon, 1859, p. 203
33. Martin, Oliveira de, *Portuguese nos Mares*, Lisbon, 1902, Vol I, pp. 41-45
34. Games de Sohs, *Discursos sobre los Comercios de las dos India*, Lisbon, 1934, p. 152
35. Marjay, F.P, *Portuguese India : A Historical Study*, Livraria Bertandl, Lisbon, 1959, p. 125
36. Boxer, C.R, *An Introduction to the Historia Tragico Maritimo*, Lisbon, 1957, pp 49-50
37. SSHMMI, op.cit., vol. I, p. 57
38. Fonseca, Querino de, *Diario de Navegações de Carriera de India nos annos 1595, 1596, 1597, 1600 & 1603*, Lisbon, 1938, pp. 47-48
39. 'Harward University Library Bulletin'. Vol IV No 1. 1957, pp. 47-48
40. MPI, op.cit pp. 41-45

21

JOSÉ CUSTÓDIO DE FARIA IN THE HISTORY OF THE WORLD OF PSYCHOLOGY:

A DIALOGUE BETWEEN INDIAN AND EUROPEAN PSYCHOLOGIES.

Hannes Stubbe

Introduction : On the Current Interest about Faria:

The present paper had its origin on the set-up of an ongoing research project which is entitled "Culture and Psychology in the Lusophone countries"[1] and is devoted to the cultural relations between India and Europe.

In the history of modern sciences of the Western countries and of the economic-cultural centres, the scientific sources which do not originate in Europe or in the United States are still ignored. Here one can see the ethnocentrism, Eurocentrism and Anglo-Americanism in the sciences, which in the era of so-called globalisation, seems to me not adequate. A remarkable example of this type of vision is the significance of Abade Faria (31-05-1756 to 20-09-1819)for the development of psychology and psychoanalysis (he was born exactly a hundred years before Sigmund Freud!).

In the compendiums and handbooks of the history of psychoanalysis are mentioned normally only the European sources and roots. They quote the Greek and Roman past (compare the complex of Oedipus), the German Romanticism (compare the dreams and the role of the unconscious), the Judaism (compare the Psychology of religion in the texts of Freud)[2], the European Philosophy and Psychology (compare Fechner, Brentano, Schopenhauer, Nietzsche, Carus, Wundt, etc.), the researches on sexuality, European poetry (Goethe, Heine, Shakespeare etc.), among other things. On the other hand, the non-European sources and influences are not generally quoted, outside the frame of Portuguese literature. Among the diverse basis of Psychoanalysis and of the study of the unconscious, there is also the research of hypnotic phenomena, on which Robert Heiss[3] wrote as follows in the fifties. "The knowledge of hypnotic processes and especially of processes of auto-suggestion and auto-hypnotising extend over a large amplitude outside our cultural set-up. A great part of these phenomena, which are known as yoga techniques and which originate in the Indian culture are some of them."

Hippolyte Bernheim (1837 - 1919), the important researcher of hypnosis, wrote in the year 1892: "This is already being done by the fakirs and yogies in India for more than 2400 years; they fix for forty-five minutes the point of the nose, they reduce or stop the breathing and they concentrate their attention until the point when somebody, tells them that a blue flame is coming out of his nose. There at that moment they take the extraordinary position of the cataleptic form[4]. Especially as regards the research of hypnotic phenomena, we have to draw the attention to the significant role - until our days - of the Goan Abbé Faria as the mediator between the Indian and European thought in the beginning of nineteenth century.

Whereas Faria's father is seen as one of many intellectual parents of the initial political movements for the liberation of colonial regions during the phase of Enlightenment and the French Revolution (1789), Abbé Faria may be characterised as a precursor of Psychology as a modern science of Psychoanalysis, of Psychotherapy and of dynamic Psychiatry and because of this fact he became famous as one of the first researchers in Psychology, Hypnotherapeutics and the theory of Psychology. Here lies, exactly, in my opinion, the current interest in him.

As a result, I will concentrate in the following paper on these scientific aspects.

In the modern literature of Germany, France and in the Anglo-American and Portuguese literature on the history of hypnosis, Faria holds frequently a distinguished place. The Protuguese psychoanalyst Pedro Luzes allots to him, in his collection *"Hundred Years of Psychoanalysis"* published in 1997 a complete chapter and characterises him as "an important precursor of Psychoanalysis"[5]. Already the Portuguese doctor who won the Nobel prize of 1949, Egas Moniz (1874 - 1995), devoted to Faria in the year 1925 an essay of profound knowledge. He classifies the work of Faria as follows: "His book, except the philosophical part, is even today a compendium of precious indications on hypnotism. It is time for us to do justice to the great majority of contemporary French authors who give today to Faria the place which he deserves as creator of the doctrine of suggestion in hypnotism which we all profess today"[6]. Also in the work on the history of medicine titled *"Histoire de l'hypnose en France"* of Barrucand (1967), Faria is dealt with in detail as the initiator of psychological currents (courant 'psychologiste') between 1819 and 1884 in the French movements of hypnosis. Barrucand certifies that "Abbé Faria is the first to propose a Psychological system to explain the *"someil lucide"*[7]

Faria as a Pioneer of Hypnotherapy and Psychological Researcher:

Abbé Faria occupied himself in Paris, probably ever since 1802 (until 1811) with hypnotic experiments and cures.[8] After his appointment as Professor of Philosophy at the Academy in Marseilles in the year 1811 (where he remained for only one year) he also worked as a magnetiser. After his transfer to Nimes, he organised in his house a consulting room for magnetization in the style of Mesmer, that is, with a magnetic "baquet". This he did until the police banned his therapeutic practice.

In the year 1813, the Abbé Faria returned to Paris and started on August 11, 1813, at the Rue de Clichy No. 48 a public class on magnetism, a class which was repeated on all Thursdays and whose entry fee was five franks. In his lectures Faria criticized both the hypothesis of physical fluid (Mesmer) and the will power of the hypnotiser (Puységur). To Faria, the hypnotic state (magnetic sleep) represented - in tune with the spirit of European Enlightenment - a phenomenon which is totally natural and can be explained rationally. In addition, he used to affirm that the essential in the process of magnetization could be hardly connected with the magnetiser, but actually to the person who would be magnetised. He also taught in these lectures that some fixed groups of people (as for example anaemic, hysterical and women) are specifically more predisposed for magnetism.

Faria called the magnetiser a concentrator (*"concentrateur"*). The magnetised or the *sonambulo* of the concentrated (*"concentré"*) and the magnetic state of concentration (*"concentration"*).[9]

The Abbé was the first to postulate the theory of suggestion in hypnosis.[10] Here the hypnotiser does not possess the "fluid" as Mesmer was postulating or any other form of will power (*volunté externe*) as Puységur was affirming. The hypnotised himself represents only the active part of the hypnotic process. The innovative techniques of magnetism postulated by Faria[11], consisted among other things, of the procedure in which he kept his patients to sit on a sofa-cum-bed, comfortable, and asked them to fix their attention on the palm of his raised hand and then he would order loudly: "Sleep!" (*dormez*) and then they fell into a "*sommeil lucide*" (hypnosis, *sonambulismo*)[12].

Faria experimented for the first time in the history of hypnotism not only with therapeutic suggestion with psychosomatic patients, but also with the post-hypnotic suggestion, as witnessed by his student General Noizet.

In his work "*De La Cause De Sommeil Lucide, ou Etude De La Nature De L' Homme...*"(1819) which originally was conceived in various volumes, of which only the first volume was published, he exposed his psychological experiments and his theoretical knowledge. This work Faria dedicated - in spite of his critical position before him - to the Marquiz of Puységur.

The Theory of "Sommeil Lucide" of Faria as a Result of a Dialogue of the Indian and European Psychologies.

We have already drawn the attention to the fact that the Goan Faria - a complete outsider in the movement of the European hypnotism of that time - was the first to develop the theory of suggestion or the psychological theory of hypnosis. The "*Sommeil Lucide*" which since 1843 was called "hypnosis" on the basis of the English Ophthalmologist Braid (1795 - 1860) was for Faria a totally natural phenomenon: firstly for being the result of a special receptibility of a person, secondly, for being the result of concentration in the imagination of sleep, which means, in the fixation of an object [13] and thirdly, for being the result of a suggestion of somnolence through the hypnotiser.

At this point I arrive to my main question: Did this practice and psychological concepts, original and innovative, of the hypnosis which Abbé Faria practiced and postulated, have the (ethno-) psychological practices of the Indians as a fundamental influencing factor?

Faria called himself often a Brahmin, as for example on the cover of his work of the year 1819 (see above). Besides this, we know today that his family, on the paternal side, comes from Brahmins Antü Shenoy.[14] That Faria could have brought with himself this knowledge on hypnotic phenomena from India, was already hypothetized by various authors, without any way providing any proofs to certify it. Crocq (1900) writes, as for example, in his general work on scientific hypnotism. "*C'est en 1815 que commence l'ere de l'hypnotisme tel qu'on le conçoit aujourdhui: son fondateur fut l'abbé Faria, pretreportugais, dont les théories different totalment de celles de Mesmer.Faria, grand vieillard efflanqué, au teint cuivré, avait habité longtemps les Indes, on t'il avait étudi, les mysteres de Brahma*"[15]. The Hungarian hypnotherapeutist and historian of hypnosis Franz Völgyesi also drew the attention to the following[16]: "The proximate steps for the development of hypnotism was given by the Portuguese of Indian origin Abbé Faria(1819). He brought with him the knowledge of eastern hypnotism to Paris. With a fine capacity of observation and with a vision beyond his times, he draws the attention and demonstrates the surging of hypnotism (of magnetism) corresponding to the actual knowledge of the theory of suggestion. Manuel Anaquim stresses in the same way in his work *"The Modern Question of Hypnotism"* (Coimbra 1895) that the ideas of Faria on the "magnetic sleep" were brought from India, where he had also learnt the mysteries of the Brahmins.

These quotes show that the Goan Faria must have had deep knowledge of Indian Psychologies and religions. We also found various statements in his work which are directly related with Brahmanism and with India (Goa).[17] Séance of his work (*Des différents procédés employés en tout temps pour soulager les malades et pour endormir*") he dsescribes various therapaeutic techniques of massage and somnolence in ancient India, which he knew personally even from Goa and which he places in direct relation with the religious practices of Brahmin priests as a source for the development of his concept of *"sommeil lucide"*. He writes in this connection: *"D'apres la conduite mystérieuse que tiennent ces pretres, il est difficile de déterminer la maniére dont ils provoquent dans leur époptes le sommeil lucide. Mais je suis certain qu'ils n'emploient aucun de ces efforts pénibles dont on fait usage en France et en Prusse.....Je présume meme que ces pretres conaissent le secret de perpétuer chez leurs époptes l'aptitude a cette concentration occasionelle"* [18]. He also refers to direct links with Goa:" A la suite de ces *témoignages, je puis ajouter l'usage que j'ai fait moimeme a Goa, de l'action de masser des l'enfance jusque' a l'age de quinze ans"*.[19] With all the reason Faria mentions here the knowledge and practices of (ethno-)Psychology of India, for the knowledge of hypnotic and suggestive phenomena are very old in India.

The psychological knowledge in India was mostly perpetuated orally and some elements of this knowledge only were passed on to groups of specific initiates (compare *"épopte"* in Faria), as for example, the Brahmins. Besides this fact, the daily psychological knowledge, transmitted in the socialisation of an Indian, encounter an ample spectrum of psychological wisdom which are passed on in the so-called oral literature as proverbs, prayers (mantras), fables, chants, dramas, legends, etc. Also in the Hindu scriptures (compare Upanishads ca. 800 B.C.), for example in the Atharva Veda, one finds various passages which refer to suggestion and hypnosis.[20] In the second century A.D., we find in the Yoga systems, especially in the meditative Yoga, the practice of concentration, the disconnection of unwanted and involuntary thoughts, the keeping at a distance of the emotional activity from the domination of external objects, and the active concentration of the attention for a specific conscious object (*pratyahara*), as also the trance as the experience of a unity with oneself, with other persons and with nature (*samadhi*).[21]

The trance, which is practised in India for centuries is a state similar to the hypnotic, with narrowing of the field of consciousness and reduction of the freedom of action, but at the same time, with the development of new capacities, especially of the perception of experience and strange desires. This state can also be observed in the so-called cults of trance in Africa, Asia and Latin America on which many European magnetisers have written.

The capacity of many yogis to paralyse their vital functions through auto-hypnosis must also be mentioned in this context. In Hinduism just as in the Western hypnosis, the trust between the guru and the disciple have a fundamental role to play. The disciple has to remain prepared for acceptance and obedience before his guru.

The fact of Faria having been born in Goa, of his having characterised himself as a Brahmin, of his having made in his work a direct relation with the ethnopsychological Indian practices and of there being a deep connection (theoretical) between his conception of "*sommeil lucide*" and of the conceptions and practices above mentioned of (auto)hypnosis, shows concretely the dialogue between the European and Indian Psychologies. In relation to my initial hypothesis it seems to me, through what has beeen shown above, that the European hypnotic movement received impulses of great significance from India through Abbé Faria

The pioneering empirical contribution of Abbé Faria for the theory of suggestion in hypnosis allows us to include it in the scientific research on India, which intensified in Europe from the end of the eighteenth Century.

The knowledge of psychological concepts and hypnotic techniques of Abbé Faria were also known deeply to Sigmund Freud, through their translations of Bernheim.

Faria, The School of Nancy and Sigmund Freud:

When Sigmund Freud opened his consulting room in Vienna, on the Easter Sunday, April 25, 1886, he perceived rapidly that with neurology, as he learnt it at the university, it would almost be impossible to help his patients.

The large part of his patients were not suffering from organic neurological ailments, but rather from "nerves" or, as we would diagnose today, they were neurotic. "My therapeutical arsenal consists only of two weapons, the electric therapy and the hypnosis" writes Freud later, in his "Self Presentation = *Selbstdarstellung.*"[22] Sigmund Freud applies in the ever more frequent form the hypnosis (first application of hypnotic suggestion in December 1887). During his stay in Paris (13-10-1885 to 28-02-1886) he could see how Charcot (1825 - 1893) was taking hysterical patients to provoke symptoms and to make these symptoms again to disappear with the help of hypnosis. Freud uses hypnosis from the beginning just like Charcot. He places the patient in a trance and suggests to her the disappearance of the symptoms while returning to the conscious normal state. He will soon be utilizing other methods, which will have great importance in the development of his work. The patient was asked to remember when her symptoms appeared for the first time and to describe with the maximum details the conditions in which the symptoms appeared"[23].

Towards the end of the nineteenth century there arose in Vienna an enormous interest in hypnosis, provoked, among other things, by the publications of Obersteiner (1885, 1893) as also by the publications of Sigmund Freud in 1888, 1891 and 1892/93. Freud was therefore seen for a long time, as a specialist of hypnosis.

Freud took notice then of the School of Nancy which used the hypnotic suggestion, with or without hypnosis as a therapeutic medium. As he could not attain with his patients the required hypnotic depth, he decided, in the summer of 1889, to make a voyage to Nancy for some weeks to improve his hypnotic techniques.

"I saw the old and active Liébault carrying on his practice with women and children of the poor working class; I have witnessed the wonderful experiments of Bernheim with the patients of his hospital and I had the strongest impressions of the possibility of the powerful psychic process which remain hidden from human consciousness"[24]

The outcome of his "various exciting conversations" with Bernheim is the decision to translate two works of Bernhein from French to German: Bernheim, Hippolyte :Neue Studien über Hypnotismus, Suggestion und Psychotherapie, übersetzt von Dr.Sigmund Freud, Leipzig:Franz Deuticke, 1892.Bernheim, Hippolyte:Die Suggestion und ihre Heilwirkung. Autorisierte deutsche Ausgabe von d. Sigmund Freud, Leipzig: Franz Deuticke, 1888(1896, 2, Auflage). In these two works of Bernheim, Sigmund Freud finds probably for the first time the Abbé Faria, for they deal in detail with the concepts of Abbé Faria.

On Faria is discussed in the translation of Freud in *"Vierte Vorlesung* = Fourth Lecture "(*Entdeckung der Suggestion durch Faria* = Discovery of suggestion by Faria): "In reality it was Abbé Faria who approximately in 1811 gives us the first correct and true description of the hypnotic phenomenon, which he called *"lucid sleep"*. According to him, the cause of this sleep is the will of the person. There is neither a magnetic fluid nor any other influence of this type which the magnetiser can exercise on the magnetised. The cause of the changes which take place in the organism have their cause solely in the brain of the person, in his imagination". "The remarkable report of Husson, which was read at the Academy of Medicine in 1831, confirms the real existence of almost all the phenomenon which the Abbé Faria describes "[25]

And in "*Fünfte Vorlesung* = Fifth Lecture (The suggestive Method of Abbé Faria), Freud translates the following: "Anyway the correct path of hypnosis had been already discovered by Abbé Faria since 1814. He asked the persons to sit comfortably, ordered them to think of sleep and to look at him (to the Abade); he would stare at them from afar with big eyes and would show them the back of his hand which was raised, would take some steps in their direction and then would suddenly lower his arm in front of the person and would ask them to sleep. On some rare occasions he would go quite close to the person and placing the finger on the forehead of the magnetised he would repeat the order: "Sleep!"... "At least 3 to five times", says General Noizet.... I saw him attain his objective in less than a minute"....... Without doubt, to Faria goes the credit of having been the first to state the theory and method of hypnosis through suggestion and to free the same from strange and superfluous processes which it possessed and which was hiding the truth"[26]. In the translation of Freud, (The Suggestion and its Therapeutic Effect", 1888) is also found in similar form in the Seventh Chapter (p. 101.f) reference to Abbé Faria and the hypnosis through suggestion.

Thus, we can confirm a direct line in the history of sciences which has a connection of Abbé Faria upto the School of Nancy and thence to Sigmund Freud.

The Canadian Historian of Sciences, Henry Ellenberger (1973) mentions, in his basic work on the history of dynamic Psychiatry, Faria as one of the founders of modern dynamic psychiatry and writes: "Pierre Janet (1859-1947) showed later that Faria, through the path of Noizet and Liébault was the true father in the geneaology of the School of Nancy"[27]. Even in his rejection in the hypothesis of the fluid of Anton Mesmer, Faria was a precursor of Hippolyte M. Bernheim (1840 - 1919) from whom Sigmund Freud in the summer of 1889 learnt the technique of hypnosis. I even want to add that the School of Nancy had a very important role in the development of psychoanalysis.[28]

The Psychoanalysis in India:

On the road of expansion of psychoanalysis from Vienna to the world, was formed after the "*History on the Psychoanalytic Movement*" (Sustaz 1923 = Supplement 1923) in British India (Calcutta) a wall of special protection of analysis[29] to which Havelock called the attention already in the year 1911. Fundamental in this process was Dr. Girindrasekhar Bose (1887-1953), who also was interested in hypnosis and started in Calcutta in 1912 the attempts of psychoanalytic treatment. He presented with his thesis in Medicine "the concept of repression" (1921) a study on psychoanalytical lines, which he sent to Freud, a new moment in the history of Psychology in India. It was also Bose who drew the attention in the article "The Psychological outlook in Hindu Philosophy" (1930) to the parallels and similarities existing between psychoanalysis and the Indian Philosophical concepts (compare Bose, 1930). Bose maintained also a correspondence with Sigmund Freud[30] and he was President of Indian Psychoanalytic Society which was founded in 1922.

Thus gets completed the circle between the Indian Ethnopsychology and Faria through the School of Nancy and Sigmund Freud in return to India!.

I tried to visualise in Chart I which follows the relations within the scope of the history of sciences between the Indian Ethnopsychology and Faria, followed by the School of Nancy and Sigmund Freud to finally return to Indian Psychoanalysis.

Translation: *Remigio Botelho*

References:

1. Hannes Stubbe, *Geschichte der Psychologie in Brasilien. Von den indianischen und afrobrasilianischen Kulturen bis in die Gegenwart.* Berlin: Reimer, 1987;Hannes Stubbe, Sigmund Freud in den Tropen. Zur Frühgeschichte der psychoanalyse in Brasilien", in *Kölner Beitrage zur Ethnopsychologie und Transkulturellen Psychologie*, No 3, 1997; Hannes Stubbe, *Der Goaner Jose Custodio de Faria (31.5.1756 - 20.9.1819) und die Hypnose Ein Dialog indischer und europaischer*

Psychologie? In: H. Siepmann(Hrsg.), Indien-Portugal - Deutschland (In press); Hannes Stubbe, "Jose Custodio de Faria, the school of Nancy and Sigmund Freud. An unknown Goan Source for Psychoanalysis", in Charles Borges, O. Pereira & H.Stubbe(eds.), *Goa and Portugal: History and Development*. New Delhi: Concept Publishing, 2000,pp. 326-335

2. P.J.Harry Stroeken, *Der Einfluß von Freuds Judentum auf sein leben und die Psychoanalyse*, Forum Psychoanayse, 7, 1991,pp.323-335; Peters, 1992,pp.105-116

3. Robert Heiss,*Allgemeine Tiefenpsychologie*, 2 Aufl, Bern :Huber, 1964, p.53

4. Hippolyte Bernheim, *Neue Studien über Hypnotismus , Suggestion und Psychotherapie*, Uebersetzt von Dr.Sigmund Freud, Leipzig:Franz Deuticke, 1892, p.43

5. Pedro Luzes, *Cem anos de psicoanalise*. Lisboa, ISPA,1997,pp.4ff;35-50

6. Egas Moniz, *O Padre Faria na historia do hipnotismo*, Lisboa:Faculdade de Medicina de Lisboa,1925, pp.86;88

7. D.Barrucand, *Histoire de hypnose en France*, Paris: Presses Universitaires de France, 1967, p.69

8. Egas Moniz, op.cit;,pp.61ff

9. L'Abbé de Faria, *De La Cause Du Someil Lucide, ou Etude de La Nature de l'Homme*. Tome premier. A Paris Chez Mme Horiac, rue de Chlichy, no.17,novembre,1819,p. 39f

10. Egas Moniz,op.cit., p.77; D. Barrucand, op.cit., p.76

11. Compare Egas Moniz,op.cit., p.87;D.Barrucand,op.cit., pp.74ff;Pedro Luzes, op.cit., p.6

12. L'Abbé de Faria Faria, op.cit.,pp. 192ff

13. Ibid., pp.52ff

14. Compare Egas Moniz,op.cit.,p.36

15. Crocq, *L'hypnotisme scientifique*(1895),Paris: Societe d'Editions scientifiques,1900,p.9

16. Franz Völgyesi, 1948, p.313

17. L'Abbé de Faria Faria, op.cit., pp.129,169

18. Ibid.,p.176

19. Ibid., p.171

20. For example Otto Stoll, Suggestion und Hypnotismus in der Völkerpsychologie, Leipzig:K.F. Koehler's Antiquarium, 1894, pp.54ff

21. Compare Edward Conze, *Eine kurze Geschichte des Budhismus*, Frankfurt/M:Suhrkamp, 1986, pp.23ff; Margret Stutley, *Was ist Hinduismus Eine Einführung in die grosse Weltreligion*.München,: O.W.Barth Verlag1994, pp.70ff

22. Sigmund Freud, *Gesammelte Werke*, Bd.XVIII, Gesamtregister, Frankfurt/M: Fischer, 1972 (Obras completas)XIV,pp.39-40

23. W. Ronald Clark,*Sigmund Freud*, Frankfurt/M:Fischer, 1985, p.119

24. Sigmund Freud, Gesammelte Werke(Obras completas), XIV, p.41

25. Hippolyte Bernheim , op.cit., p.45

26. Ibid., p.56

José Custódio de Faria in the History of the World of Psychology:

27. F.Henry Ellenberger, *Die Entdeckung des Unbewußten*, 2 Bde, Bern: Huber,1973,p.122
28. Compare Heinz Schott," Fluidum- Suggestion-Übertragung .Zum Verhältnis von Mesmerismus , Hypnose und Psychoanalyse" , in *Wunderblock:Eine Geschichte der Modernen Seele*, Wien: Lücker Verlag, 1989, pp.83-95
29. Sigmund Freud, "Zur Geschichte der psychoanalytischen Bewegung(1914)", in Sigmund Freud, *Selbstdarstellung*, Frankfurt/M:Fischer, 1971,pp.165, 169
30. Sinha,"T.C.Development of Psychoanalysis in India", in International Journal of Psychology, 47, 1966, 427-439; M.Petzold, *Indische Psychologie:Eine Einführung in traditionelle Ansätze und moderne Forschung*, München:Psychologie Verlags Union, 1986,pp.155ff; Psychoanalysis International, 1992

CHART - I
ABBE' FARIA, HYPNOSIS AND PSYCHOANALYSIS

Psychoanalysis In India

- *Freud*: (1914 : 165, 169) : References on Psychoanalysis in India.
- *Bose:* (1921, 1930) : The first Psychoanalytic attempt in India and correspondence with S. Freud. 1992 Indian Psychoanalytic Society.
- *Sinha:* (1966) : Psychoanalysis in India.
- *Petzold:* (1986 : 155 ff) : History of Psychoanalysis in India.
- *Kakar*(1992) : Psychoanalysis in India.

⇑

Sigmund Freud (1856 - 1939) and the Hypnosis:

- From October 13, 1885 to February 23, 1886, S. Freud at Salpetrieri, in Paris, with Jean-Martin Charcot (1825 - 1893), whose hypnotic experiments with hysterical girls he could observe.
- *December 1887 :* First application of hypnotic suggestion:
- 1888 : Freud S., *Hypnose durch Suggestion*. *Wiener Medizinische Wochen Zeitschrift*, 38.
- 1888 : 898 - 900 (presents without critical notes the fundamentals of the technique of hypnosis of Bernheim.
- 1889 : Freud visits Bernheim at Nancy, translates two of Bernheim's works ("Hypnotisme, Suggestion, Psychotherapie etudes nouvelles, 1891" and " De la suggestion et ses applications a la Therapeutique, 1886".
- 1891: Freud S. Hypnose - In a Bum(Hrsg), *Therapeutisches Lexikon* Wien: Urban and Schwarzenberg. 1891, 724 - 734 (basic medical work of that time, new editions 1893 and 1900, not included in the complete work of S. Freud!).
- 1892: Freud S : Ueber Hypnose und Suggestion. Aerzte Centre Anz 4

- 1892/93. Freud S. Ein Fall von-hypnotischer Heilung - nebst Bemerkungen ueber die Entstehung hysterischer Symptome durch den "Gegenwillen" Zeitschrift fuer Hypnotismus, 1, 1892/93 : 102-107, 123-129, 258-272.
- 1918: He draws the attention, in a letter to Simmel, to the usefulness of hypnosis in the treatment of neurotics of war (Clark, 1985 : 139).

⇑

The School of Nancy (Liebault, Bernheim Etc.)

- Ambroise A Liebault (1823 - 1904) : Takes up again the method of simple suggestion of Faria (Liebault, 1889, Bernhein, 1892 : 59).
- *Hippolyte Bernheim* (1837 - 1919): "The School of Nancy (Bernheim, 1896 : 117)
- 1886: "De la suggestion et ses applications a' la therapeutique".
- 1891: "Hypnotisme, Suggestion, Psychotherapie, etude nouvelles".

⇑

Abbe Faria (1756-1819) ⟵   ⟶ European Psychology.

- Hypnosis through suggestion:
- Meaning of concentration
- Post hypnotic suggestion
- Refutation of the hypothesis of the fluid:
- Hipnotic Anesthesia
- *Sonambulismo = Sommeil Lucide*
- Brahmin
- Goan influence

- Mesmerism (Anton Mesmer, 1734-1815).

- Sonambulism (M.De Puysegur, 1751 - 1825).

- Christian Wolff (1679 - 1754)
- Psychology of Enlightenment

⇑

Indian Ethnopsychology

- Meditation Techniques.
- Auto hypnotic techniques.
- Yoga System : relaxation position (*asana*); retraction of the senses (*Pratyahara*) from all the external reactions, concentration (*dharana*) on a specific object, consequent interruption of meditation (*dhyana*), total immersion into fire, in god or in a specific object, until the point when individual consciousness merges totally with it and can no longer perceive it (compare Stutley, 1994 : 70f).
- Vedas, as for example, Atharvaveda (Ethnopsychology).

José Custódio de Faria in the History of the World of Psychology:

◆ *Sources:* Freud, 1914, Bernheim, 1888, 1892, 1896, Stutley, 1994, Petzold, 1986, Conze, 1986, Stubbe, 1998, 1999, 2000 Hartnack, 1990, Clark 1985, Ellenberger, 1973, Barrucan 1967.

Bibliography

1 Ackerknecht, Erwin H.: *Kurze Geschichte der Psychiatrie,* Stuttgart: Enke, 1967, 2.Aufl.
2 Ackerknecht, Erwin H.: *Geschichte der Medizin,* Stuttgart: Enke, 1979, 4.Aufl.
3 Barrucand,D.: *Histoire de hypnose en France,* Paris:Presses Universitaires de France, 1967
4 Bernheim, Hippolyte: *Die Suggestion und ihre Heilwirkung. Autorisierte deutsche Ausgabe von Dr. Sigmund Freud.* Leipzig und Wien: Franz Deuticke, 1888 (enthält ein Nachwort des Uebersetzers von 1889!)
5 Bernheim, Hippolyte: *Neue Studien ueber Hypnotismus, Suggestion und Psychotherapie,* Uebersetzt von Dr. Sigm. Freud. Leipzig: Franz Deuticke, 1892
6 Bernheim, Hippolyte: *Die Suggestion und ihre Heilwirkung. Autorisierte deutsche Ausgabe von Dr. Sigmund Freud,* Leipzig: Franz Deuticke, 1896, 2.Auflage
7 Borges;Charles S.J.(ed.):*Goa and the Revolt of 1787,* New Delhi: Concept Publishing Company, 1996
8 Bose,G.:"The psychological outlook in Hindu Philosophy", in *Indian Journal of Psychology,*5, 1930:119-146
9 Boss, M.: *Indienfahrt eines Psychiaters,* Freiburg, 1966
10 Cabral e Sa,Mario & Nou, Jean Louis: *Goa,* New Delhi:Lustre Press, 1993
11 Cabral e Sa, Mario & Rodrigues, Lourdes Bravo da Costa: *Great Goans,* Pune(India):Kirloskar Press, 1985
12 Clark,Ronald W.: *Sigmund Freud,* Frankfurt/M.:Fischer,1985
13 Conze, Edward: *Eine kurze Geschichte des Buddhismus,* Frankfurt/M.: Suhrkamp, 1986
14 Crocq:*L'hypnotisme scientifique (1895),* Paris:Societé d'Éditions Scientifiques, 1900, 2.ed.
15 Eliade, Mircea: *Yoga-Unsterblichkeit und Freiheit,* Zürich: Rascher, 1960
16 Eliade, Mircea: *Die Religionen und das Heilige,* Darmstadt: Wissenschaftliche Buchgesellschaft, 1976
17 Ellenberger, Henry F.: *Die Entdeckung des Unbewußten,* 2 Bde., Bern: Huber, 1973
18 Faria,L'Abbé de, (Bramine, docteur en Théologie et en Philosophie, Ex-Professeur de Philosophie A L'Universit, de France, Membre de la Societ, M,dicale de Marseille, etc.etc.etc.): *De La Cause Du Someil Lucide, ou Etude De La Nature De L'Homme. Tome premier,* A Paris Chez Mme Horiac, rue de Chlichy, n°17, novembre 1819
19 Freud, Sigmund: «Selbstdarstellung», *Schriften zur Geschichte der Psychoanalyse,* Frankfurt/M.: Fischer, 1971
20 Freud, Sigmund:"Hypnose durch Suggestion"in *Wiener Medizinische Wochenschrift,* 38,1888:898-900
21 Freud, Sigmund:" Hypnose", in A. Bum(Hrsg.), *Therapeutisches Lexikon.* Wien: Urban & Schwarzenberg, 1891:724-734

22 Freud, Sigmund: Ein Fall von hypnotischer Heilung: nebst Bemerkungen über die Entstehung hysterischer Symptome durch den „Gegenwillen", Zeitschrift für Hypnotismus, 1, 1892/93:102-107, 123-129, 258-272

23 Freud, Sigmund: Ueber Hypnose und Suggestion, Aerzte Centr. Anz., 4, 1892

24 Freud, Sigmund:" Zur Geschichte der psychoanalytischen Bewegung(1914)", in Sigmund Freud, Selbstdarstellung, Frankfurt/M.: Fischer, 1971:141-201

25 Freud, Sigmund: Gesammelte Werke, Bd. XVIII. Gesamtregister. Frankfurt/M.: Fischer, 1972

26 Hartnack, Christiane:"Indische Psychologie", in Siegfried Grubitsch & Günter Rexilius (Hg.), Psychologische Grundbegriffe, Reinbek: RoRoRo, 1990:478-484

27 Heiss, Robert: Allgemeine Tiefenpsychologie, Bern: Huber, 1964, 2.Aufl.

28 Kakar, Sudhir: Die Gewalt der Frommen. Zur Psychologie religiöser und ethnischer Konflikte, München: Beck, 1997

29 Luzes,Pedro: Cem anos de psicanálise, Lisboa: ISPA, 1997

30 Mesmer, Franz Anton: Abhandlung über die Entdeckung des thierischen Magnetismus(1781), Tübingen: Edition Diskord, 1985

31 Moniz,Egas:O padre Faria na história do hipnotismo, Lisboa: Faculdade de Medicina de Lisboa, 1925

32 Neitzert, Lutz: Franz Anton Mesmer. Der "animalische Magnetismus", das "therapeutische Theater" und die Glasharmonika. Südwestrundfunk (SR2) Musikfeuilleton vom 20.4.2000

33 Neues Lexikon der Musik; Bd.2 , Tübingen: Metzler, 1996

34 Obersteiner, H.: Der Hypnotismus, Wien,1885

35 Obersteiner, H.: Die Lehre vom Hypnotismus. Eine kurzgefaßte Darstellung, Wien: Breitenstein, 1893

36 Pattie, Frank A.: Mesmer and Animal Magnetism: A Chapter in the History of Medicine, 1994

37 Pereira, Oscar: "Goa in Vergangenheit und Gegenwart", ABP,Zeitschrift zur portugiesischsprachigen Welt, 1, 1994:131-147

38 Petzold, M.: Indische Psychologie. Eine Einführung in traditionelle Ansätze und moderne Forschung, München: Psychologie Verlags Union,1986

39 Pitres,A.:Leçons clinique sur l'hysterie et l'hypnotisme faites ... l'hôpital Saint Andr, de Bordeaux, Préface de M. le Professeur J.M.Charcot. Paris, vol.2, 1891

40 Psychoanalysis International. A Guide to Psychoanalysis throughout the World. Ed. Peter Kutter. vol.2. India by S. Kakar. Stuttgart:Frommann-Holzboog, 1992

41 Santos-Stubbe,Chirly dos & Stubbe,Hannes: "Quem foi "Katharina"? História familiar e ambiente psico-social do caso de Sigmund Freud (1895)", Psicologia Clínica(PUC-Rio de Janeiro), ano II, 1987:17-29

42 Santos-Stubbe, Chirly: "O abade Faria na literatura e ciência", Palestra no Internat. Symposium "Goa and History" vom 6.9. - 9.9.1999 em Panjim/India

43 Schott, Heinz:" Fluidum - Suggestion - Übertragung. Zum Verhältnis von Mesmerismus, Hypnose und Psychoanalyse", in Wunderblock. Eine Geschichte der modernen Seele. Wien: Lücker Verlag, 1989:83-95

44 Sinha,T.C."Development of Psychoanalysis in India", International Journal of Psychoanalysis, 47, 1966:427-439

45 Sinha,D.: "Psychology in the context of Third World Development", *International Journal of Psychology*,19,1984:17-29

46 Sloterdijk, Peter: *Der Zauberbaum. Die Entstehung der Psychoanalyse im Jahr 1785: Ein epischer Versuch zur Philosophie der Psychologie*. Frankfurt/M.: Suhrkamp, 1987

47 Stoll, Otto: *Suggestion und Hypnotismus in der Völkerpsychologie*. Leipzig: K.F.Koehler's Antiquarium, 1894

48 Stroeken, Harry P.J.: *Der Einfluß von Freuds Judentum auf sein Leben und die Psychoanalyse*. Forum Psychoanalyse, 7, 1991:323-335

49 Stubbe, Hannes: *Geschichte der Psychologie in Brasilien. Von den indianischen und afrobrasilianischen Kulturen bis in die Gegenwart*. Berlin: Reimer, 1987

50 Stubbe, Hannes: *Experimentalpsychologie in den Tropen. Psychologie und Geschichte*, Heft 3/4, 1993:278-299

51 Stubbe, Hannes:"Sigmund Freud in den Tropen. Zur Frühgeschichte der Psychoanalyse in Brasilien," *Kölner Beiträge zur Ethnopsychologie und Transkulturellen Psychologie*, N° 3, 1997

52 Stubbe, Hannes: „Der Goaner José Custodio de Faria(31.5.1756 - 20.9.1819) und die Hypnose. Ein Dialog indischer und europäischer Psychologie?" In: H. Siepmann(Hrsg.), *Indien – Portugal –Deutschland*. In press

53 Stubbe, Hannes: "José Custódio de Faria, the School of Nancy and Sigmund Freud: An unknown Goan source for psychoanalysis", In: Charles Borges, O.Pereira & H.Stubbe(eds.), *Goa and Portugal: History and Development*, New Delhi: Concept Publishing, 2000:326-335

54 Stutley, Margaret: *Was ist Hinduismus ? Eine Einführung in die große Weltreligion*, München: O.W. Barth Verlag, 1994

55 Vaz, J.Clement:*Profiles of eminent Goans. Past and Present*, New Delhi: Concept Publishing Company,1997

56 Wolf,M.:*Psychologie ou trait, sur l'âme, contenant les connoissances, que nous en donne l'expérience*, Amsterdam: Pierre Moutier, 1745 (Reprint: Hildesheim: Georg Olms AG, 1998)

57. Wundt, Wilhelm: *Hypnotismus und Suggestion*, Philosophische Studien, 8.Bd., 1893:1-85

22

HINDUISM IN THE QUOTIDIAN OF THE CHRISTIANS OF GOA IN THE 18TH CENTURY

Maria de Jesus dos Martires Lopes

The ideas concerning the world, future life and God, mould mentalities and guide the course of civilizations. The "Greek miracle" bloomed in the Greece and not in another region of the globe because certain ideas, which were decisive for this cultural development, had become important there. In this context, the importance of the religious conceptions in the individual as well as in the community, is well known. They stipulate, in many ways, man's attitude towards life and death, towards what is material and what is eternal

These aspects are very evident in India where religion is blended with life. Every human activity is, thus marked by rites[1]. The natives of Goa who were converted to the Chrisrian faith, emerged from this religious past. Their ancestors undertook with the same rigidity, generation after generation, the *puja* (or sacrifice) and recited meticulously the *mantras*. Many Christian natives, however, were Hindu for the major part of their lives. The purpose of this paper is to analyse their views concerning Hinduism after their conversion.

It is nevertheless important to ponder over the religious situation in Goa at the 18th century. There are two surveys regarding the first half of this century: one, on the 28th of August 1722, *"Lista do Povo Catholico das Freguesias de cidade de Goa, suas Ilhas, Salcete Bardez"* which comprised 1,81,430 inhabitants and the other one in 1745 concerning the lists of gentiles from the Ilhas who were made to pay the *sendi* or *xenddi* pension in 1744 and in 1745[2]. It's a well-konwn fact that in the second half of the 18th century the number of Christian people in the *Velhas Conquistas* were always higher than the number of gentiles. Owing to emigration, only in the second half of the 19th century, Christians were surpassed by gentiles in Bardez and in Ilhad[3]. It becomes more difficult to enquire on the true meaning of these numbers, that is, to what extent or, above all, how the new Christians had understood as well as issue opinions on this subject from the edict of the Inquisition of Goa on the 14th of April 1736 as, while it mentions the gentile customs forbidden to Christians, it confirms the practice of these customs among them[4]. Therefore, one may, for instance, assume that some natives celebrated every Wednesday, the days of the new moon and those of the full moon, the elevenths of the moon; they fasted during the eclipse of the moon and had the sacred plant of the Hindu, the *tullos,* in their gardens. It must be mentioned that even some *reinois* had grown this plant[5].

While specifying with detail the sins that were committed, the lists of the condemned people by the Inquisition of Goa in the 18th century are another important source for the study of the religious customs[6]. These sources mention that several baptised natives had reverted to Hinduism thus going over to heathen countries, wearing heathen clothes and the *sendi* on their heads (a pigtail characteristic of the Hindu people). Although more seldom, other Christians got involved with a number of societies in order to perform gentile ceremonies or profess idolatry in their villages, often summoning Christians to pray on hills, in private houses or in temples[7]. However, these Hindu activists maintained an outward appearance of true Christians while performing certain religious rites or even receiving a sacrament. In addition, some native Christians after having lived many years as gentiles, returned to Goa with the intention of going back into the catholic practices. Later on, we will come back to this subject[8].

It may be said concerning the directives of the religious policy in Goa during the 18th century, that public performances of the *Divali, Ganesh* and *Shigmo* festivities as well as marriages and "lines" were not allowed in order to avoid scandal in Santa Maria and the religious contamination of Christians. In fact, several gentiles having acted against the established rules, fell under the sphere of influence of the Inquisition[9]. The Hindu could perform their religious ceremonies inside their home, without the presence of Christians and before a religious authority pertaining to the Holy Office. This directives took however different gradations during 18th century with more or less tolerance, allowing or forbidding, for instance, the use of gentile musical instruments, gentile dances performed by female dancers, the presence of Hindu priests (*botto*), and so on[10].

In the context of this religious policy, the Court of the Inquisition of Goa intervened aiming to eliminate every evidence of paganism in the lives of the Christian natives. These Christians had kept several gentile habits which were allowed to them "as they seemed practical and civil"[11]. The edict of the Inquisition of 1736 was aware of the inconveniences of this policy considering that the similarity and the identity of these customs furthered the spread of idolatry. They had therefore to be suppressed. The measures that were then taken were very explanatory.

Thus, the arrival of Hindu priests in Goa and the practice of professions such as *botto, iogui, mully, paraui, jossi,* etc. were banned; it was also forbidden for Christians to be engaged in the building of pagan temples; the use of gentile musical instruments in Christian marriages; the distribution of *viddo* (cylinder) of betel and areca; the use of gentile names, gentile colthing by Christians (the *puddvem* for men and the chole for women) and gentile songs in native language (*vovio*) during marriage ceremonies. These interdictions aimed at suppressing any similarity between Christian and Hindu clothing and to bring the baptised natives closer to the Portuguese from whom they had received the benefit of the conversion[12].

Had the Inquisition been able to reach this important purpose? Could it contribute to cleanse the Christian cult from Hindu influences? In order to answer these questions, first of all, we must analyse the aspects of the religious practice of the native Christians in Goa during the 18th century. From the list of the condemned persons of this century, one may presume that the daily life of the baptised natives of Goa was supplied with invocations, offerings and sacrifices to their idols as they always appealed to them on every occasion of their lives. There were sailors giving away coconuts and asking the sea for a good fishing, farmers sacrificing a cock or *bagatas* in order to have "good news" on their land, tavern's innkeepers asking the gods to help them get enough sura, and so on. However, besides the attainment of success in their daily activites, the native Christians had a great variety of reasons that made them perform gentile ceremonies such as their children's marriages, their wife's labour, the health of the patients, the relief of a bull with a broken leg, the cure of sick cattle, a wide spread disease in the village,the discovery of a treasure or of a theft, the birth of a son after three daughters and so on. Reasons as strange as causing the death of a woman or as seducing others, had also been in the origin of gentile ceremonies[13].

In this religious quotidian, deceitful ceremonies and superstitious cures were very frequent. Here, also, the reasons were very different: to provide harmony among relatives, to foretell the future, to cure women's aversion to married life, to gain a game, to discover a treasure, to find a missing jewel and so on[14].

Among the charges fastened upon these convicts, there were also those of "invoker and supplicant of the devil", the offerings and sacrifices to the devil in order to cure patients, to discover a thief or to inquire into the cause of a death[15]. In fact, it seems that the cult of the devil was largely spread among the native people who believed in his evil sortileges and tried to placate them in order to obtain their solicitations. These artifices were often used to cure by gentile doctors to whom the native

Christians had recourse, thus disobeying the rules of the Inquisition[16].

In 1783 and 1784 a number of Christians were punished by the Holy Office for having participated in pagan ceremonies; they believed in the transmigration of the soul, another fundamental aspect of Hinduism[17]. There was indeed a contamination of this religion in Christain ceremonies. We have found baptised natives performing their daily ablutions, creating superstitious figures made of rice and flour, calling forth the idols and presenting them with offerings [18].

The constancy of Hinduism in Christian ceremonies was even more evident when it concerned the cycles of life such as in birth, marriage, death etc. Thus, when a married woman had her first menstruation, according to the gentile tradition, a banquet was held and she would receive gifts and flowers. We must remember that many girls would marry at 12 (or a little more) years old[19]. At child-birth, gods were called forth and very often the midwives, themselves, performed pagan ceremonies[20]. Certain rites were also held on the 4th, the 8th and the 30th day after the delivery. The place where child-birth had taken place was covered with cow dung. We must not forget that cow dung was considered sacred and therefore it was used on floors for sanitary as well as for purifying reasons[21]. The new born child was placed over rice and on the 6th day a banquet was given in order to remove the devil who wanted to enter his body. That is why mother and child were constantly visited. Some *reinois* however celebrated this date with many festivities[22].

Concerning death, the tradition of holding a banquet for the dead was very trivial. According to pagan beliefs, food was given to the poor in order to satiate the dead people's souls these poor people should look as much as possible like the dead ones[23]. There was also the custom of throwing laundry and sometimes the dead person's bed to the sea as well as of covering with cow dung the house where he died in order to be inhabited again[24]. The comparison between Hindu and Christian marriages allows us to imply that there is a certain parallelism of habits and, also, an adaptation of former practices. Let us exemplify: as it happened with Hindu people, some Christian couples performed pagan and superstitious ceremonies on the eve of their marriage. In 1791, two girls did that same thing in the morning of their marriage before going to confession and receiving the communion[25]. They did "lavatory" and worshipped certain delicacies. On certain days, it was customary for the engaged couple to anoint themselves with pounded saffron, milk, coconut milk, rice flour and powder made from certain leaves[26].

The edict of 1736 refers to a number of other Hindu traiditions present in Christian marriages such as bringing flowers, *betel* and *areca*, and *fugueus* from the groom's to the bride's home and vice-versa; *viddos* of betel and areca were distributed during the marriage ceremonies and were placed under the bed of the enewlyweds; native songs, the *vovio*, were also sung in the native language as a display of happiness; the *daigi* or *gotri* (the most important people of each family) served up the meal with no shoes on.

On certain days, before the wedding, rice was peeled, temples were pounded and *fugueus* were fried either in the groom's or in the bride's home. It was a *pitans* ceremony which followed a certain ritual such as to give priority, on this occasion, to the *daigis* and *gotris*. After returning from church the groom wore the costume given by the bride and vice-versa and people touched the wedded couple's forehead with grains of rice possibly as a sign of fertility. It was customary to give a present to the person who was serving the *mully* in the village (the most important person in the village) and even to attend the marriage ceremony.

From the edible ingredients, something was reserved which was guarded in certain recipients and places in order to be cooked and eaten on certain days[27]. Hindu influences on Christian marriages were indeed very strong. Even today, the number of the festivities, the splendour and the ostentation of this ceremony remind us of the grandeur and the sumptuosity of the gentile marriages.

The convicts of the Inquisition of Goa in the 18th century were mostly from inferior castes(*Shudras, kunnbi, colle, gaudde*) and were farmers, "labourers", fishermen, masons and so on[28]. We may therefore infer that the influences of Hinduism were stronger in the lower classes of society. The new Christians of this social provenance maintained the Hindu traditions of their gentile ancestors after their conversion to Christianity.

The accusations laid on the condemned by the Inquisition during the second half of the 18th century allows us to infer that the main objective of the edict of 1736 which was to erase the pagan practices in the lives of the Christian, was never achieved. We have noticed that the daily life of the Goanese Christians was full of pagan acts performed on different cirucumstances of their lives. There were many acts of religious syncretism: superstitious prophecies while making the sign of the Cross and praying the Credo; "false "medications" mixed up with sacred things of our religion"; pagan invocations at the Cross; pagan ceremonies before confession....[29].

There were also a curious adaptation of ancient habits of paganism: the case of the songs sang during the marriage ceremonies which remained but under a new form(the romantic *mandde* for instance) followed in some case by the reciting of the *Laudate* or the *Te-Deum* at the altar of their houses[30].

In order to escape the Inquisition, Christian people replaced some articles usually offered by Hindus to the couple's families but they maintained the offering's tradition[31].

The interpenetrating of religious elements in both religions is very strong in Goa; it created harmonious synthesis. That is why the continuous efforts of the Inquisition and the ecclesiastical authorities could not dismantle the system. The increasing access of native priests to diocesan offices may also have favoured this interpenetration while contributing to a certain "indianisation" of the religious usage.

References:

1. On this subject see Abbe J.A. Dubois, *Hindu Manners, Customs and Ceremonies* by (....), Translated from the author's Later French Ms. And edited with notes, corrections and biography by Henry K. Beauchamp, C.I.E., 3rd ed.., Oxford, 1906, pp. 150 and following.

2. The survey of 1722 was made according to the lists of confessants and communicants of the Ecclesiastical Court of Goa. It comprised men, women and slaves from the Ilhas' churches (including Angediva) Bardez and Salsete (Ilhas, 58430; Bardez, 52118 and Salsete, 71017). The survey of 1745 is the *"Lista de todos os Gentios, Moradores na cidade de Goa, e em todas as suas Ilhas, que são obrigados a pagar pensão de Sendi de dous annos de 1744, cuja cobrança se ha de fazer na Feitoria de Sua Magestade"* (B.P.A.D.E., cod. CV 2-6, p. 182 from the 1st Series and CXv 1-33). We are grateful to Dr. João Pedro Ferro for the information he has given to us.

3. See the tables of the Christian and gentile population from Ilhas, Bardez and Salsete 1853, 1778, 1785, 1791 and 1797 included in our work, *Goa setecentista: Tradição e Modernidade*, 2nd ed., Lisbon, Centro de Estudos dos Povos e Culturas. de Expressão Portuguesa, Universidade Catolica Portuguesa. 1999, pp.83-85.

4. Edict of the Inquisition of Goa in Arquivo da Curia Patriarcal de Goa, *Livros dos Conventos e Igrejas,* n°6 (Church of Saint Joseph Daugim) In the future we'll mention this archive as A.C.P.G.. The edict was edited by A. Lopes Mendes, *A India Portugueza*(...), vol. I, Lisboa, 1886, and reedit. by Asian Educational Services, N. Delhi, Madras, 1989, pp.250-260 and by A. B. de Bragança Pereira, *Etnografia da India Portuguesa*, vol.II, Bastora, 1940, pp. 289-293 (only the part concerning marriage).

5. Edict of the Inquisition, already mentioned, in A.C.P.G. *Livros dos Conventos e Igrejas*, n°6 (Church of Saint Joseph Daugim), pp.125v.-126.

6. B.N., cod.201 and 202, A.N.T.T. *Conselho Geral do Santo Oficio*, bd. 32, doc.49, bds. 33 and 38. doc.6.

7. Leandro, a 31 years old kunnbi, lived many years as a gentile in the lands of the infidels wearing a *sendy* on his head; afterwards returning from these lands, he was once again baptised and was named Manuel(list of the convicts of the 22nd of November 1711, A.N.T.T., *Conselho Geral do Santo Oficio*, bd.38, doc.6. Gaspar de Sousa, a 20 years old bachelor living in Daman, reverted to idolatry and lived as such, after having been baptised; Pedro de Sa a 20 years old *faraz* living in Trapor and Antonio 30 years old, Maratha and living in Tana acted the same way (List of the convicts of the 5th of September 1734, B.N., cod. 201, p.165v) Rosa Cristina, an unmarried girl of 14, living in Pangim, fell under the sphere of the Inquisition "for having gone to the land of the infidels and, while remaining in thier service, wore the gentile costume" (list of the convicts of 1782, B.N. cod. 202, p.47) See also in this codex, the n°1 of the list of convicts of 1768, p.20 and n°1 of the list the 7th of Feburary of 1773, p.34.

8. Pascoal de Souza Xavier was accused of being one of the main partisans of idolatry which was fostered in his village with the acceptance of the *gancars* (list of condemned of 1794, cod. 202, p. 109v.) In 1799, 5 native Christians were sentenced for summoning gatherings of many Christians at night in order to invoke idols (List of 1794, cod.202, pages 131 and 131v.); 23 native people were condemned for very similar reasons and for their militancy of the gentile idolatry, in 1800(List of

convicts of that same year, p. 132-132v, 136-137v) Pascoal de Araujo, 75 years old, professed the pagan faith for 39 years and, encouraged by a mendicant friar, he returned to his country showing signs of repentance(codex 202, p.124-125). Domingos Mergulhão, a Kunnbi and 13 more Christians of the same caste and profession "were militants of the pagan idolatry, living many years astray from the gentile faith with a false appearance of Christian and abuse of sacraments" (B.N., cod. 202,ps. 136v-137, already mentioned)

9. The list of convicts of the 16th of March 1721 show 4 hindus who were punished for having celebrated publicly the *Divali* festival in Gao(A.N.T.T. *Conselho Geral do Santo Oficio*, bd.32. doc.49).

10. The traveller Innigo de Biervillas, during his visit to India noticed that pagans had freedom of religion but they could not have temples in the city of Goa (Cf. Souvenir de Beaumont(pseudonym). *Voyage de Innigo de Biervillas, Portugais, a la cote de Malabar, Goa, Batavia, outres dieux des Indes Orientales*, Paris, 1736. See letter of the 12th of April 1731 from king John V to viceroy João Saldanha da Gama forbidding the celebration of the *sigmo* as it coincided with the Lent (A.C.P.G. *Copia de Varios Documents*, ps.32-32v., in F.U.P. , in *Livros dos Conventos e Igrejas*, n°6 already mentioned, p.122.

11. Edict of the Inquisition in 1736, in *Livros dos Conventos e Igrejas*, n°6, already mentioned p.122.

12. ibidem, p.122, 122v, 126. In fact, the edict allowed the singing of songs in marriages provided they were not similar to the *vovio*.

13. In 1799, Rita Afonso, a tavern keeper, was accused of having attached to her dress a piece of paper given to her by an infidel in order to make her husband treat her well. (B.N.,cod. 202, p.130). Francisco de Araujo performed pagan ceremonies and made offerings in order to obtain the fertility of a grove of cahew-trees (List of 1798, cod.202, p.128); Remedio Caetano de Figueiredo asked a gentile minister to throw in, the fundamental stone of a new building in order to be successful (list of 1786, cod.202, p.62v) The kunnbi Bernardo kept inside his house a coconut with coins nailed to its shell; he was told to do these things by the invoker in order atain happiness(list of the condemned of 1793, cod.202, p.105) see cod.202, ps.120, 121v-122v, 124, 166v, 54, 60v, 109.

14. B.N.cod. 202, p.56, 61v, 114, 62v, 74.

15. Jacinto and Caetano Fernandes, tillers of palm-tree groves, put a horse frame on their farm to thank the devil because their palm trees produced may sura(list of 1785, cod.202, p.62); see also cod.201, p.128, 72; cod,.202, p.50,51 and 51v. Father Manuel Caetano de Figueiredo, had recourse to infidels in order to know things of the occult through invocations and offerings to the devil (list of 1784, cod. 202, p.54v. Cf.cod.202, p.55. 59v, 60, 60v, 62, 97v, 103, 122, 122v.).

16. Lourenço Coutinho, a farmer, accompanied the carrier of a covered vase and, advised by a gentile, he buried it in a lagoon. This deceptive doctor assured him that he had captured the devil who had caused the sickness upon his relative(List of the condemned of 1794, cod.202,p.108v.).

17. Cf. cod.202, p.49,52.

18. Cf.cod. 202, p.112, 73v

19. A.C.P.G., *Livros de Conventos e Igrejas*, n[os]6, already mentioned, p.125.

20. Cf. cod.202, p.95, 79,75. 75v, 76,84v, 90, 90v, 91,52, 41v, 58v, 78, 78v.

21. A.C.P.G. *Livros de Conventos e Igrejas*, n°6, already mentioned, p.125.
22. Ibidem, p.124v-125 and cod.202, p.23. See also the letter from viceroy Caetano de Melo e Castro on the 20th of April 1701 where he put an end to the existing excesses. Punishments were established for the *reinois* and the native Christiàns who violated the law. Cf. J.H. Cunha Rivara, *Arquivo Portugues Oriental*, 6th fasc., suppl. 1st and 2nd. Nova Goa, 1876, reedited by Asian Educational Services, N.Delhi, Madras, 1992, pp.198-201(doc.59).
23. Tome Fernandes gave supper to a poor man who looked like his father (List of the condemned on the 9th of January 1752, B.N.cod.202,p.62v). Arcangela Henriques gave a banquet for the poor on account of her husband's souls (List of 1782, B.N.code.202, p.44v.). Valentim Teles was condemned because he had feigned that certain dead people's souls had entered his body(List of the condemned of the 3rd of February 1794, cod.202, p.36). Ana Quiteria was punished for having accepted an invitation to supper from someone for the sake of her dead sister(List of the condemned of 1785, p.63) Antonia Martins was present at a superstitious banquet held for the relief of the souls of dead relatives at all soul's day(List of condemned of 1792, B.N.code.202, p.105v). Isabel de Sousa was punished for performing pagan food ceremonies before sunrise for the sake of the dead people's souls (List of the condemned 1793, B.N.code.202, p.105v). See also codex 201, page 140; codex 202, pages 59,89,90v, 101 and 103.
24. Edict already mentioned, in A.C.P.G. *Livros dos Conventors e Igrejas*, n°6, p.125.
25. Cod.202, p.44, 72v, 73v, 77v, 86,87,91,95, 95v,96,96v,97,97v and 100.
26. Edict, already mentioned, in A.C.P.G., *Livros dos Conventos e Igrejas*, n°6,p.123.
27. Ibidem, p.122-124v.
28. For the first half of the 18th century, only the social provenance of 52% of the convicts was known; their profession is only indicated in 17% of them. For the second part of this century, only the social provenance of 57% of the convicts is known and their profession is only mentioned in 10% of the cases. These conclusions should therefore be taken as a suggestion.
29. Cod.202, p.91, 101v, 111, 114v.
30. A.L. Mendes, op.cit., vol.I, p.42 and A.B.de Braganca Pereira, op.cit., vol.II, pp.298-299.
31. A.L.Mendes, op.cit., vol. I, p.150-151 and A.B. Braganca Pereira, op.cit., vol.II, pp.290.

23

GOAN WOMEN IN OTHER LANDS

Fatima da Silva Gracias

Goan women have been migrating for a long time to other places either to settle permanently or for a period of time. We may classify Goan women's migration into three main phases: The early initial migration to the neighbouring kingdoms, migration to the British India and Africa in the first fifty years of the twentieth century and the postcolonial migration to the Middle East, West (Europe and America), Australia and New Zealand.

There is reference to sporadic migration of women to the neighbouring kingdoms during the pre-Portuguese period. This migration was mainly restricted to dancing girls and a few others. The first recorded wave of Goan women's migration can be traced back to the XVI century— the first century of the Portuguese rule in Goa.

Large number of Hindu women along with their families left their homes and fled from Portuguese areas of Goa to the neighbouring kingdoms in order to escape conversion. Migration of Hindu women was followed by the migration of new convert women who fled to escape the zeal of the Holy Inquisition established by the Portuguese in the sixteenth century. In the early centuries of Portuguese rule in Goa, Goan women also migrated along with their families due to insecurity caused by the Dutch blockade, threats from neighbouring rulers and repeated attacks of epidemics.[1] These women settled outside the Portuguese territories of Goa as well as in areas such as Mangalore and Kanara.

Historical evidence also reveals that in the second half of the eighteenth century, Goan women from *Recolhimento de Maria Magdalena* (Goa) were sent overseas.[2] They were sent in *naus da Carreira da India* to other parts of the Portuguese Empire such as Brazil, Pegu and Malaca.[3] In some instances they were sent as prospective brides for Portuguese soldiers working in overseas Portuguese territories as in the case of Ceylon. The same *naus* brought from Lisbon *orfas del Rei*-orphan girls who were sent to Goa to be married to Portuguese men in India. Slaves from Goa were also taken to the mother country and other parts of the globe including Brazil in the early centuries of the Portuguese rule in India. This limited migration of Goan women overseas was confined to those of Christian community.

In the nineteenth century economic necessity forced Goans to migrate in large number. However, there is no evidence available that points to women's migration in significant number at this point of time.

The second wave of Goan women's migration began at the dawn of the 20th century. It was of socio-economic nature. High cost of living, poverty, unemployment of the male members of the family, monotony of the village life, the negative attitude of the Goan society to some social problems are some of the factors responsible for migration. To add to these factors there were some others such as the possibility of social freedom, better standard of living outside Goa and marriage alliance could have compelled women's migration to other parts of the globe. Improved means of communication and transport between Goa and the rest of India from the end of the nineteenth century made travel easy and fast.[4] A very small number also migrated to British India to improve their educational qualifications.[5]

It is said that one third of those who migrated in the early twentieth century were women. However, we do not have statistics about the feminine migration during the Portuguese period. The various Census reports for example only give the number of those absent from their homes but it does not provide any break based on sex. We know for instance that by 1910 about 48,000 Goans had migrated to different parts of India, Africa, Middle East and Brazil. In 1935 around 38,788 Catholics were absent from their homes in Ilhas, Salcete and New Conquests.[6] But we do not know exactly how many of these were women.

In the first half of the twentieth century, Goan women migrated in two directions to far away British and Portuguese colonies of Africa and closer home to British India mainly to metropolitan cities of Bombay (Mumbai), Calcutta (Kolkata), Poona (Pune) and Karachi.[7] There were two types of migration—independent migration and associational migration, the later type was mainly to Africa and British India including Burma. These were the wives and daughters of men working in Africa and British India or prospective wives. Large number of Goans of Christian community was involved in pioneering work in the fields of medicine, teaching and other fields.[8] Many also worked as musicians, tailors and cooks.

Goan women living in Africa particularly in British Africa returned home every few years to visit their parents, at the time of some family events such as weddings, illness, death, religious feasts, exposition of St. Francis Xavier, to settle their daughters or property matters. Migration of Goan women to Africa was not permanent migration, these women eventually returned home to imbibe their children with Goan culture or after the retirement of their husbands or to take care of their old parents.

In the first fifty years of the twentieth century independent migration of Goan women usually took place to British India especially to Bombay. They were predominantly from lower strata of the society, between the age of 18-45 and belonged to both Christian and non-Christian communities. Majority of them were not literate. Independent migration during this period was confined mainly to women who were menial workers and artists such as the dancing girls. These belonged to both Hindu and Christian communities. Women of upper and middle classes did

Goan Women in other Lands

not migrate on their own but if they did so, it was along with their families

Independent migration of unmarried women to Africa was limited either to those who went to work in Portuguese Africa or those who migrated to both Portuguese and British Africa as prospective brides.. Women from the two retirement homes namely *Recolhimento de Nossa Senhora de Serra* and *Recolhimento de Maria Magdalena* managed by *Santa Casa da Misericordia* and daughters and sisters of the brothers of *Misericordia* were sometimes given monetary grants to migrate to Portuguese Africa for better prospects.[9]. Goan women in Africa took up jobs in offices as typists, clerks, nurses in the hospitals or teachers in schools. The standard of living for these women in Africa was better than in Goa.

A sizeable number of women who migrated to places such as Bombay were unmarried or widowed. Among these, widows were significant in number. How does one explain this situation? As in the rest of India the conditions of the Goan widows were miserable. Several restrictions were imposed on their behaviour, movement, dress and even food. They were considered inauspicious. Therefore, women of lower class preferred to migrate away from their milieu in order to improve their economic conditions and enjoy some degree of freedom which big cities could afford.

Another group of women who migrated to British India in the early decades of the twentieth century was *bailadeiras* (dancing girls). They migrated to British India in order to improve their standard of living. Majority of these women settled in Bombay, where they accumulated much wealth. Some of them became the mistresses of rajas, nawabs, rich traders and British officials.[10] There were times when they had children out of these relationships. Accumulated wealth enabled them to provide their children with better education and better standard of living. In 1930 the state banned the ceremony of Xens in Goa.[11] At this time a number of *bailadeiras* left Goa and settled elsewhere in India.

The early women migrants to British India worked in offices, factories, hospitals as nurses, helpers and as domestic staff in the houses of well to do families. The conditions of domestic staff in Goa left much to be desired. They were paid poor wages or many times no wages at all except for food and some clothing. The weekly magazine *Mascote* published in Goa in the 1930's describes in some of its issues the plight of domestic staff in Goa. Orlando da Costa in his *O Signo da Ira* also describes the plight of the women of this class.

Consequently, many women migrated to British India to work for British and Parsi families.[12] The service conditions for instance in Bombay was far better than in Goa. Goan maids were in great demand in Bombay, as they were known for their good work and loyal service. Many of them at the end of their service were even pensioned off. These women were responsible in spreading Goan culture including the Konkani language, Goan values and even some religious teaching among the young children they helped to bring up in their employers' family.

Goan women in Bombay who worked as domestic maids lived normally in the home of their employers. Those working in other sectors lived with relatives, hostels or in the *kudds* of Goan clubs. Majority of villages of Goa, particularly of Salcete and Bardez had their own clubs in Bombay that provided accommodation in *kudds* to the people of their villages.

Some women migrated to Bombay and other big cities of India without any definite jobs. As a result a certain number of them were involved in vices. The plight of these women as well as the conditions of other Goan women in British India was of great concern to the Church in Goa and the Goan society. In early decades of the twentieth century, the Church through the parish priests cautioned Goan women about dangers of migration. Goan women were discouraged from migrating to British India but despite these warnings the out migration of women continued.

In the early 1930's many Goans living in Bombay showed their concern about the distressing conditions of some Goan women in Bombay and other cities in British India. Through the newspapers and other agencies they tried to draw the attention of the authorities in Goa about the plight of the migrant women. Goans living in Bombay sent several appeals to the Government in Goa requesting to take some steps in this direction.

Newspapers published in Goa and by Goans in Bombay also brought to the notice of the government in Goa, the conditions of Goan migrant women in British India and Africa. The weekly *Mascote* asked the Goa government to introduce measures to improve the conditions of migrants in British India.[13]

Various Congressos Provinciais held in Goa, in the early decades of the twentieth century discussed also the problem of migration and in special the problems of feminine migration to British India. During the seventh *Congresso Provincial*, Dr. Socrates Noronha proposed the establishment of a *"Liga de Saude e Moral Publica "* in British India. Several suggestions were made to prevent out migration of Goan women. Participants of some of these *Congresos* were of the opinion that unmarried women should be prevented from migrating to British India. They also discussed the need to keep vigilance on unmarried women living in Bombay and other cities of British India. However, some prominent Goans including A. Braganca Pereira objected to this suggestion on the grounds that such measure would violate human rights.

In 1930's as a result of various appeals made by the people, the Portuguese Government in Goa, appointed a standing committee known as *Comissão dos Emigrantes Goeses*, the office of this *Comissão* was at Dhobitalao, Bombay. *Comissão dos Emigrantes* was established with a fund of Rs. 45,000 to provide help to Goan women in Bombay. The organisation was subsidised by the State and institutions of social welfare such as *Santa Casa da Misericordia de Goa* and *Hospicio do Sagrado Coração de Margao*. Similar committees were set up in other cities of British India namely in Pune, Calcuta and Karachi.[14] Efforts were also made to start a similar committee in British East Africa to help Goan women there.

Comissão dos Emigrantes in the above-mentioned cities of British India conducted regular inspection of the premises where the migrant women lived. In order to help the unemployed Goan migrant women in Bombay a few courses were started by the committee. Among these were courses in typing, short hand and sewing. Women were also taught to write in Konkani and Poruguese to enable them to correspond with their families in Goa. Widows and orphans in places such as Karachi were provided with financial help to tide over their difficulties. Women of easy life who had repented were given shelter at *Casa de Refugio de S. Catarina*, Kandivli, Bombay, learnt the art of weaving, cooking, sewing, soap making and gardening. During the years 1936-1937 the same committee paid for the lodging 26 Goan girls at Catholic Women's Hostel, Vila Theresa, and Bombay. These girls were provided training in nursing, baby care, embroidery and sewing. Young women were advised and provided financial help to return home to Goa. The *Comissão* requested missionary sisters from Catholic Women's Hostel, Vila Theresa –Bombay to visit regularly *kudds* of Goan Clubs where the young Goan women lived

In 1937, the above-mentioned committee started a club for working class women in Bombay. The Club provided accommodation to domestic maids. The unemployed among them was provided free meals until they could find employment.

Another organisation the Gomantak Maratha Samaj helped Hindu women in Bombay and neighbouring areas. Members of the Samaj paid regular visits to places were Hindu Goan women lived. The Samaj conducted a census to find out the number of Goan women living in Bombay, their marital status and occupation. The census also provided information on the number of unemployed. The Samaj financed education of some Hindu girls and arranged marriages of *devadasi* girls. It tried to help girls who led immoral life. A home was set up o provide accommodation to Goan working in Bombay particularly for domestic servants.

The Portuguese did not discourage out migration of Goan women even though the Church and large number of Goans in Goa and Bombay were opposed to this migration. It appears that the State favoured migration due to lack of employment opportunities in Goa and scarcity of essential commodities, mainly during the two world wars. Portuguese institutions such as *Misericordia de Goa* helped women to migrate to Angola and Mozambique.

Post colonial times has seen a spurt in feminine out migration. Sheer economic conditions, a better life in foreign land, better educational facilities, possibility of more freedom and some other social problems have prompted Goan women to migrate in present times. Goan women have migrated in different directions to Middle East(Gulf countries), Australia, Canada, Europe, USA and Brazil for further studies, to improve their economic conditions or as wives to Goans and others living overseas. Some Goan women from East Africa have migrated to Canada, Europe and Brazil after the independence of East African colonies. These women belong to different classes of the society and include both married and unmarried. Others who have migrated are widows or women estranged from their husbands. This group of women have mainly migrated to Middle East. Unmarried women migrate to the Gulf countries also to earn and save for their dowry. Others go there to supplement family income or even to support a large family, particularly when the husband is unemployed or drunkard. [15]. For some Goans, it is an obsession as well as status symbol to secure jobs in the Middle East.

A significant number of Goan women who migrate to Middle East go there to work as maids at the home of Arab and European families. Some take up white-collar jobs and others accompany their husbands. In countries such as Saudi Arabia women are not permitted to take up certain types of jobs and they have to observe some local custom. There are instances when a few Goan women in the Middle East have married natives and converted to Islam.

Today, practically every other family has or had a member or a relative in the Gulf countries. In some villages in Goa, a sizeable number of women folk both married and unmarried are working today as housemaids in the Gulf. Since mid 1990's migration to the middle east suffered a set back for several reasons. The Kuwait-Iraq crisis and more recently the new migration laws passed in UAE has affected Indian migration. Nevertheless, there is still demand for Goan women as domestic staff in the homes of Arab, European and Indian families.

Migration of Goan women especially migration of married women has both negative and positive impact on their families and the society. These women particularly from the Gulf countries send home regular remittances which have helped the families to improve their standard of living, impart education to children and even to build houses. However, absence of mother from the home has created many problems in the family and at times have contributed to the break of the family.

Goan women have strived to preserve their culture outside their land. They strive to maintain some traditions and food habits, although they are also influenced by new ideas, other cultures and restrictions imposed by the "host" countries as in the case of Gulf countries. Women migrants when they return home bring along with them new ideas from the host countries..

References:

1. Teotonio R. de Souza, *Medieval Goa*, New Delhi, 1979,p.116.
2. Fatima da Silva Gracias,*Beyond the Self-Santa Casa da Misericordia de Goa*,Panjim,2000,p.97.
3. Fatima da Silva Gracias, *Kaleidoscope of Women in Goa*, New Delhi, 1996, p.1
4. Avertano C. Fernandes,Emigração Indo -Portuguesa, Separata do Boletim nos.708 da Sociedade de Geografia de Lisboa, Lisboa 1938 As result of Anglo-Portuguese Treaty 1878, the British took the responsibility of building railways linking Goa with rest of India.
5. Lack of institutions of higher education forced many Goan parents to send their children for higher studies to Bombay,Bangalore,Belgaum and Poona.(*Congresso Provincial da India Portuguesa—Segundo Congresso* ,vol..I,Nova Goa,Casa Luso Francesa Editora,1924,p.203.
6. *Alguns Aspectos demograficos de Goa,Daman and Diu,* Goa,1965,p.188.
7. J. B. Pinto, *Goan Imigration*, Panjim, Goa; Raffat Khan Haward"*An Urban Minority:The Goan Christian Community in Karachi*" in *The City in South Asia— Pre-Modern and Modern*, ed. Kenneth Ballhatchet and John Harrison, London, 1980,pp.299-318.

Goan Women in other Lands

8 Fatima Da Silva Gracias, *Health and Hygiene in Colonial Goa 1510-1961*, New Delhi, 1994, p.186. In Africa the graduates of Goa Medical school made important contribution in the field of medicine including the eradication of several epidemics: General Encyclopedia Portuguesa Brasileira,vol VII,Lisboa; Aleixo Manuel da Costa,Literatura Goesa—*Apontamentos bibliograficos para sua historia*, Lisboa,1967; P.J. Peregrino da Costa, *A Escola Medica de Goa e sua projeção na India Portuesa e no Ultramar:*P.J. Peregrino da Costa, *Medicos da Escola de Goa nos Quadros de Saude das Colonias(1842-1942),Bastora,1944.*

9 *Santa Casa da Misericordia de Goa—Relatorio e Contas da Gerencia da Pia Mesa*, 1924- 1925, Nova Goa, 1926

10 *O Oriente Portugues*,vol.3 de 1906,Nova Goa,1906.

11 Xens was a ceremony performed to initiate a girl as dancing girl. The ceremony was like a marriage. However, the girl was married to an object, a flower usually a hibiscus or another girl dressed as a men.

12 Propercia Correia Afonso Figueiredo says that large number of women migrated to Bombay in late 1920's and early 1930's.(Propercia Correia Afonso Figueiredo, *A Mulher na India Portuguesa*, Nova Goa,1933,p.134.

13 Mascote (weekly),Nova Goa, 9th August 19360.pp.1 and 2.

14 Comissão Adminstrativa do fundo dos Emigrantes-Relatorio anual dos trabalhos realizados pela Comissão durante ano findo de 31 de Agosto 1936, Nova Goa,1937.

15 Fatima da Silva Gracias,"Goans away from Goa-Migration to Middle East", in Lusotopie,A French based Academic Journal (in Print).

II

INDIAN OCEAN AND MARITIME ACTIVITIES

24

INDIAN TRADITIONS OF BOAT-BUILDING

B. Arunachalam

Dr. K.S.Mathew has rendered great service to the study of Indian maritime history of the 16th and 17th centuries through his studies of Protuguese sources in archives at Goa and Portugal. Valuable in themselves, these studies need argumentation of Indian source materials. The present paper in the felicitation volume in his honour highlights the richness of the indigenous sources in our understanding of the Indian sea-craft building of the same period.

When the Portuguese first arrived on the west coast of India, early in the Sixteenth century, they were surprised to observe a brisk overseas maritime trade, and the relatively large size of the sea-going vessels on the ports, in comparison to their own. Even earlier in the fifteenth century, a number of European travellers who visited ports like Cochin had noted the sewing traditions prevalent all along the shores of the Arabian Sea from Arabia to India. Though a number of Europeans have remarked on what appears to them to be striking features of the Indian timber-built vessels and their building, there is no comprehensive account of the same.

On the other hand, in spite of a long period of sea-going traditions, there is very little written by the Indian seafarers themselves. This is primarily because the practicing sailing and boat building coastal communities were mostly illiterate and had not rendered in writing about the boat-technology and the associated skills. Yet, a few scrappy details are available from the limited writing of some sea-farers in the form of ship/boat

Indian Traditions of Boat-Building

songs, ballads and astrological verses. More significantly, traditions have been carried from generations to generations as hereditary heritage by word of mouth, and by giving training to younger ones by the elders. This living practice enriched by later day additions and refinements is however on a critical phase of total eradication, due to the decline of sailing craft usage. Field work and discussions with elder boat-men, tandels and boat carpenters (*achan*) in a number of traditional country-craft building centers still surviving on both the west and east coasts of India reveal a rich tradition of boat building methods, customs and practices, beliefs and tools. The present paper summarises in brief such traditions obtained from folk wisdom.

There exists an eleventh century sanskrit text, the *Yukti kalpa taru* that talks of different boat-forms, both river and sea going, their sizes and sailing qualities. It also adopts a caste-classification of boat timber and advises against mixing them in usage. Much of what is said in the text appears elitist and debatable and not acceptable in terms of folk practices. There also exists a mutilated Tamil palm leaf manuscript, by name '*Navoi Sastram*', which is essentially astrological in character. This text, of early sixteenth century, however provides glimpses of technical knowledge concerning the laying of the keel, timber-quality for boats etc. A later, mid-eighteenth century Tamil manuscript, *Kappal Sastram*, written in the Danish port of Tarangambadi (Tranqebar) on the east coast, is also astrological, but perhaps is the only known text to provide technical measurement data for building a boat, plank by plank from hull upwards. A Malayalam work, also of eighteenth century, the *Kappal Pattu*, written by Kunjali Musaliar, is an allegory, but is useful in providing technical terminology in Malayalam of the boat components and their relative importance. A Tamil-grantha ballad of late eighteenth century from old Travancore state provides a vivid description of practices of boat building at contemporary times and its maiden voyage in the waters of the Arabian Sea and Bay of Bengal.

Most ship and boat songs are social in character. However, a few give technical details of the boat or sailing characteristics. A Muslim *cala-vattu(Jal vahatuk) pattu* of Nagore and Hindu *Kappal-pattu* of Vedaranyam are of this nature.

Along the Gujarat coast, some boat-builders have hand drawn visuals or designs of boats in sections and profile, worked out from their hereditary wisdom and own experiences. Mostly the traditional boat carpenters have a mental vision of the boat form and properties of component details, which they can readily reproduce on the coastal sands. They have a keen eye for meticulous details. Template usage, by and large, is very recent.

Sea-going vessels are generally built on banks of river mouths or coastal beaches, well above tide-level. but can be readily dragged by pulling or dragging. The site is open, flat or gently sloping to the waterside, and at times provided with a thatched weather shelter.

Contrary to the popular beliefs, and the treatise, *Yukti kalpa taru,* discussions with boat builders, indicate that the timber required for different boat components demand varying qualities of specifications and hence are drawn from different species. No doubt economic considerations are of paramount importance but stability, sea-worthiness and durability, apart from capabilities to sail in rough tropical weather logically outweigh cost considerations. Proximity to the timber-yielding forests in nearby accessible areas also influence location of boat-yards. Thus, traditional boat-building at Beypur near Calicut draws upon the Nilambur frorests: Bombay draws upon the Thana forests: Billimora, Dahanu from Dangs: Veraval from Gir forest: Cuddalore from the Kolli hills: Baleshwar, Midnapur from Chotanagapur. Quality timber for specific components now-a-days is imported to the extent necessary, local and regional timber being used for less exacting and demanding components to the maximum extent possible to reduce costs.

While at present timber marts located in forest margins and interiors supply the required timber, that is nowadays transported by trucks and rail, the procurement of timber traditionally was a laborious time-consuming process, demanding timber expertise of master-carpenters. Invariably, the timber procurement was not a commercial market purchase, but a process of selection by search in accessible forest areas of a specific tree or trees with the desired quality of timber-log, followed by the purchase of the whole tree. A late eighteenth century Tamil ballad, called the *'Kulathurayyan kappal Pattu'* speaks of such a search in the southern Travancore forests, inspection on spot of the *in situ* timber potential of a variety of timber species like *iluppai, karimaruthu, tekku, aini, kongu* and others, till the right timber tree is chosen. On an auspicious *muhurta* and day, the tree is felled with a ceremonial saw, dragged to a nearby flowing river by male elephants, and floated down stream to the boat-yard. This choice of the forest tree is to ensure required timber species of quality, free from physical defects. Specific boat-component requirements like right angularity of natural growth curvature is also ensured. Such traditions of transportation by elephants through specially cleared forest tracks and floatation of logs on *bamboo-tarappams* have existed in Kerala and Karnataka coastal areas till recently. However, in the East Coast, transportation of forest logs from the hills of Eastern Ghats was through specially designed bullock carts with wheels larger than normal diameter.

The master carpenter looks for specific timber species for a particular boat component, that has proved by past experience to be the most desirable; then he looks for the required specifications of length, girth and other qualities in relation to the craft of planking and joinery he intends using; and freedom from physical and growth defects in the tree, specially in sections intended for logging. Knots, knuckles, bores and cavities in the lower trunks or above, running through the sapwood to the heartwood are weakening defects, visible on surface. Knots may be round, spiked, tight or loose, decayed, inter-grown encased not firm or even hollow. The knot weakens the timber due to its effect of cross-grain on the wood adjoining it. They are most detrimental in the compression face. Cut sections of branching locations are also potentially weak in an otherwise strong and hard timber. Decay defects that destroy the heart of the timber are not visible on surface and may be seen only in a cut section, though decay may be caused on surface by injuries such as axe cuts. A hollow heart, a cavity in the hard wood running through the length of the log is a distinct decay effect. Decay increases susceptibility to fire. Any dicolouration or stain other than natural fire is also symptomatic. Warps and twist produce uneven stress levels. A radical split or check seen in a cut section is a major defect that results in failures of many beams. Cross-grain is also a treacherous defect. In tropical hard-wood, brashness often leads the wood to break suddenly in bending.

A Tamil palm leaf manuscript in complete and mutilated, called the *Navoi Sastram*, has a couple of stanzas each relating to the *vastu* or architecture relating to timber felling, *muhurta* or auspicious time of intiating timber vesel building, (to lay the keel). This work goes into details of timber-quality, especially its physical defects, colour appearance of a fresh-cut section of the log, and doscolouring stains. The type of knots, their configuration and position on a keel-timber are commented upon in terms of their adverse impacts. A Muslim Tamil *Cala-Vattu-Pattu (Jalavahatuk* or Sea-transport) of Nagapattinam-Nagore shores classifies timber as masculine, feminine and eunuch, based on log girth, and further states that the best timber for keel of a vessel is eunuch timber, namely, a log, straight and of uniform girth right through its length.

Of the different boat components, the keel and keelson, the stem and stem posts, the lower ribs, the side-planks permanently below the water-level, the cross-beams, the masts and spars are the most exacting in terms of timber-quality specifications. Upper level side planks above water-level, the inner decks, cabins and platforms permit a much greater degree of flexibility in the use of timber, though sophistication, finish and appearance may lead to some choice. The popular notion of a teak built boat arises from the inner planking.

The keel is the vital key timber of a vessel that gives it its strength and stability. It is the backbone of the vessel and single massive timber of a boat. In most small/medium vessels, with a keel length of 5m or less the keel timber is a single log, but there are traditions of larger sea-going vessels, with keel length of 30 to 40m having been built on Indian shores. With a square cross section of 0.3 to 0.4 m, a single keel log about 30 m long and straight is not only difficult to procure, and to transport to the yard, but woefully expensive-many times the cost per sq. ft. in comparison to a log 10 m or less in length. Such a length free from physical defects of weakness is another problem. The elastic tensile strength of such single long logs to resist stress under pressure due to sag is also debatable. Yet there are rare cases of such single log keel of length having been used in the past timber-vessels. More often, in case of such long keels, three timber pieces of the same timber species of comparable dimensions are used by joining the planks together. The keel planks are joined by ineterfingering tongue and groove joining and fastened with wooden pegs.

According to the *Kappal Sastram* a 17th century Tamil text, the ideal timber for keel are *vembu, iluppai, punnai* and naval if the required length is available. The *Kulathurayyan Kappal pattu* mentions in addition *karimaruthu, sirutekku, sirunangu, aini, karu-nelli kongu* and *vengai*. Field investigations all over the coast show that the *karimaruthu* is the most preferred for keel, and in its absence *punnai, iluppai* and rearely, for smaller keel length, *seerani (puvarasu)* or *vembu. Siris, sal* and *sundry* are in use in Bengal, but mostly in relation to river boats. The usage of teak for keel is not in vogue.

The choice and special preference of *karimaruthu* appears to be related to its inherent qualities; high density and compressibility, its capacity to last under saline water, and freedom from attack of wood-borers. With its heaviness an load-bearing capacity, it ensures a low centre of gravity for the vessel as a whole, and hence stability, and sea-worthiness even in a rolling sea. Its ready availability in West Coast forest and lesser costs than teak are also contributory factors. Its erect trunk and branching at a height from the ground ensure logs of medium length about 20m, and occasionally even greater lengths. *Punnai* and *iluppai* are second level preferences where the keel length is less than 20m, because of their ability to be durable under water and freedom from attack of wood-borers, toredos and termites, because of their disinfectant oil content

The stem-post timber as compared to the keel is long and slender, fixed on the keel at a high angle to provide the cutwater. Its most vulnerable segment is the angular curve through which it is perfectly fitted into the fore or the keel. It has to be quite resistant to water pressure, and should not split, crack, or bend readily. Though the required curvature at the keel end of the stem can be carved, and the stem carefully fitted through knee joints into the special grooves prepared in the keel, and fastened by wooden pegs and wedges, a natural curve in the log at the required angle is preferred as the grain texture of the timber will be sustained to give strength. The stem-post has similar specifications, but less exacting, and does not have the angularity of the stem even in double-ended boats. *Babul, Khair, harra, illuppai, sissoo* and *shiwan* are all used as stem and sterm timber because they are readily available in local jungles and can provide logs at various desired angular curves. In the last two centuries, when the boat timber is purchased in timber marts, the search for natural curvature as the lost sight of. Instead, the timber is bent through a process of fire-curing.

In most Indian boat building traditions, once the keel and the wider keelson above it are laid, the bottom-most three planks of the hull on either side of the hull are carefully fitted into and fastened with the keel, mostly by pegging and ribetting. The skelton is then built by adding the ribs (*vanku-manikkal*) at the hull base from stem end to stem end, and then adding rib extensions as the plank frame is built upwards. These ribs, thought inside the boat, have to be sturdy and load bearing. Rib timber is never straight; it is of U shape of sharply angular. In most vessels rib logs are crude, retaining their original rough form. Timber for ribs is preferred in their natural state of grain and curvature; many shorts to medium sized tropical hard-woods provide such timber cheap; *babul, khair, bendi* or *puvarasu* are ideally used, since they are relatively cheap and transportable in bulk quantity from closeby areas.

Side planking is done row by row bottom upwards and each row from end to end. Side fittings of planks is done row to row by perfect plank-fit. A highly labour-intensive methodology of such a perfect fit is the *vadhera system* of joinery as practised by South Gujarat boat-builders. The plank edges are grooved in a tongue and groove manner to achieve the perfect fit. Such a joint does not require caulking for hydrodynamic reasons; where the fit is not perfect, caulking with cotton fibre of fine cloth or coir using viscous *kalafat* (a tree resin-lime mixture) ensures leak-proof fitting. The caulking mixture has a composition of lime, tree-resin (*Kundurga* or *Kunkulyam,* an incense of myrrh tree), in oil boiled to a semiviscous liquid condition. Side planks are *carvel* (flush fit) joined or clinker fitted (with overlap of planks). Most Indian boats are *carvel* fitted. Individual timber planks are sawn, planed to a good finish and are generally 3 m by 0.3 m and 2 to 3 cm thick. The side planks below water level and load line that remain submerged under water except when beached for repairs are carefully chosen looking to their durability under water and resistance to insects and wood borers. The timber invariably used is *iluppai (mahuva), benteak, jarul* or *arjuna, sag, kindal, ain* and *aini,* depending upon local availability. A much greater freedom is available in the choice of the upper side planks, well above water level; *jack* (phanas), mango, tamarind, *bhendi, sisso, babul* and *khair* all find a wide use.

For the main corss-beams amidst the vessel, very hard, sturdy, load-bearing timber is used. *Anjan, tekku(sag), karimaruthu,* and *punnai* are in use. The inner planking stem and stern platforms, holds, decks, cabins all permit a wide range of timber usage depending on cost economy and nature of cargo holds. Where passenger decks and cabins are to be built in, timber with a good carving and finishing and present smooth surface are chosen. The so-called teak-built vessels of the post-colonial period make a good use of teak timber, but jack, mango, *neem, aini* are good substitutes.

Masts and spars need ideally pole-timbers of considerable straight length, not susceptible to brashing, splitting and cracking.

Small masts, slender spars and yards invariablu make use of casuarina and now a days eucalyptus. But for masts of substantial heights and girths of uniform size, the traditional usage is of *punnai, aini* and even jack.

Rudder posts are not only under water but liable to water-pressure while turning. *Punnai, aini, benteak, iluppai* and *teak* are in use. In the by-gone-days when *cini* or wooden anchor was in use, very hard and highly compressed wood was used for such anchors. *Anjan, tamarind, karimaruthu, ilupai* and some of the mangrove species like *sundri* were in use.

The traditionally built timber vessles were mostly sewn or stitched over most of the west coast, south of Mumbai and the East coast as far as lake Chilka. The Sewn form was common in the vessels of Oman, Arabia and Persian Gulf, probably because they were dependent on Malabar labour and in most cases built on the Malabar coast. In Gujarat, the boat planks were lashed together using *vadhera* joints, wooden pegs and over time with copper or brass nails. It is only in Bengal coast, with a South East Asian tradition, boats were nailed for a longer past. Sewing holes are bored with hand drills at close distances close to the rims of the planks and the sewing coir is taken through them for fastening through a cross-stitching method. A combination of pegging, use of wooden wedges and stitches enhances the overall strength of the stitched boat, imparting it a quality of resilence that stands the vessel if grounded, crashes and wrecks. However, European boat-builders have argued that sewing makes these vessels weak.

With the increasing usage of nail-joints in boats, and steady replacement of the earlier techniques of plank joiner, the timber usage had undergone remarkable changes. The efficiency of structural nail joints depends upon a number of factors such as type of joints, size, spacing, and depth of penetration of the nails, methods of driving the nail; and shape and choice of nail-points. All these factors impinge on the timber itself: the species and its physical, mechanical properties, position of the timber in the log (i.e. from pitch, bottom, middle or tip of plank), timber moisture seasoning behaviour (split,warp,twist,crack), the grain and cross grain of timber. Since many varieties of timber used in traditional boat-building are not ideally suited for nailed joints, post 17th -18th century boat-building has brought about a shift in timber specifications as boat-material. It is this fact that *babul, khair,teak, kindal* and *aini* are good timber for nail-joins that brought their usage as boat timber into prominence while many others, fomerly used, are going out of vogue or are confined to traditionally built vessels. Also new timber species like Malaysian Kongoo is gaining strong footholds, especially on the East Coast boat-yards.

In the more recent decades, direct nailing is getting replaced in the boat-yards of Kutch and Saurashtra by a bolt and nut technology through well-spaced drill holes on the planks

Cross-beams are fixed inside the boat to give strength to this vessel. Holds, platforms on stem or stem ends, decks and cabins are the last to be added internally before the boat finished. Rudder at the stem end with a tiller is also an end fixture. The timber for rudder is also carefully chosen, as the blade and lower part lie within the salt-water and is subject to constant water-pressure.

Traditionally, the exterior of the boat is given a coating with fish or vegetable oil. *Punna, iluppai,* groundnut or even *neem* oil is used, since these oils carry a strong disinfectant flavour.

Once the boat is ready for launch, it is dragged on cylindrical coconut or log-rollers from the building site to the water edge and floated in water. Two methods are in use; either by pulling with thick ropes from the stem end or by shifting it on the side of the boat laterally. Only after the boat is floated, the mast or masts are fixed in the mast hole carved in hull through one of the cross-beams.

Boat-building traditions are intimately associated with superstitions and religious beliefs. Invariably, initiation of every major phase of the activity-main timber felling in the forest, keel-laying, mast-fixing - is associated with rituals. Before the boat is let into the water, a major ritual is the "opening of the eye" cut into the boat-side at the stem end of the prow on both sides by the master-carpenter accompanied by a midnight animal sacrifice to ward off evil spirits. The maiden voyage is itself done with much pomp and gaiety, with substantial rewards to the carpenters.

Though steeped in beliefs and rituals, traditional boat building in Indian coastal waters by the commumnity of *acharis* (boat-carpenters) used to be an exercise in implemen-tation of inherited skills and wisdom of centuries essentially through 'an eye for precision and details', visualised mentally and not through any design drawings.

Appendix

Botanical Names of Timber used in Indian Boats.

Babul	Acacia Arabica
Khair	Acacia Sundra
Aini or Angeli or Ramphanas	Artocarpus Integra
Neem	Azadirachta Indica
Iluppai	Bassia Latifolia
Undi or Punna	Calophylum Inophylum
Sundri	Heritiera Littwalis
Benteak	Lagerstromia Lanceolata
Arjuna	Legerstromia speciosa
Mango	Mangifera Indica
Teak (Sag, Tekku)	Tectona grandis
Karimaruthu	Terminalia Tomentosa
Bhendi or Seerani Or Puvarasu	Thespesia Populnea

Note: The references used in this paper are in Indian vernacular languages, mostly unpublished, and in cases quoted by the traditional boat builders on Indian coasts.

25

HISTORICAL CONTACTS BETWEEN QUILON AND CHINA

Haraprasad Ray

1. Quilon (Kollam) - The Early Phase

The early Chinese rendering of Kollam was corrupted into Gulin. Kollam was later changed into Quilon by the Europeans. The teriitory was roughly equivalent to the former princely state of Travancore (Thiruvananthapuram) on the west coast of India. The port of Quilon (8°53'N, 76° 35E) is situated in the present day state of Kerala.

It was in the 9th century AD that Quilon (Kollam) emerged from oblivion as a great political and commercial centre. The town was the capital of the Venad who were the subordinates of the Kulasekharas of Mahodayapuram (AD800-1102). It carried on an extensive trade with China and Arabia, and its port was one of the largest in the world at that time. Several writers have associated the town of Quilon with the origin of the Kollam Era which began in AD 825.[1]

When Cosmas referred to the city of Male during the sixth century AD., he was in fact, referring to Quilon. A century later Xuanzang calls this area *Mo-luo-ju-zha* (Malaya-or Malakuta) also called *Zhimoluo* (Kumara, Kumarika) by which the entire west coast is implied. The form *Mo-lo-ye* also occurs at about the same time.The Arabs used the form Kulam-Male. In the Song period it was called by the Chinese *Gu-lin* and in the Yuan period *Ju-lan* (Hirth and Rockhill write *Ku-lan*)[2].

While Indian and Sri Lankan (Ceylon) ships dominated in merchant navigation in the Indian Ocean till the 5th - 6th centuries, the vessels of K'unlun took over in the 7th century AD. These were the vessels in which Chams, Khmers, Sumatrans and Javanese sailed and which called at Chinese ports more frequently than other foreigners. Beginning with the 8th century Persian and later the Arabs took their place. The Chinese also traded with foreign countries, but their ships normally sailed to the Malabar coast, and sometimes also sailed to the Persian Gulf in the late 8th and the mid - 9th centuries[3].

Jia Dan's reference (between 785 and 805) is to the sea way from Guangzhon into the Persian Gulf via the Singapore straits, Kalah (Keddah, Kadaram) and *Molai* (Malaya), the old name of the Kerala region. The itinerary of Jia Dan takes us to Fustat (old name of Cairo), entire journey requiring about 205 days in the sea, not taking the intervening period of midway stop, etc.[4]

By Zhou Qufei's (1178) time, it had become a very busy and well known entrepot deserving a separate notice on Quilon (*Gu-lin*). He states "The ships took forty days form Guang - zhou to lambri (*Lan-li*) where the Chinese spent the winter and resumed journey next sailing season to reach Quilon in about a month. From here, those Chinese traders who wished to go to the Arab countries embarked on small boats. With a fair wind the entire journey from China to the Arab lands and back took two years".[5]

Most of the western scholars and Chinese authorities like Wang Gungwu opine that the Chinese did not sail beyond Quilon till the 12th century in their voyages to the Arab countries through ports of Siraf, Oman, Ubullah and Basra. However, the evidence of at-Tabari (AD 839-923) and al-Masudi (956) raise doubt about the contention of such scholars as Rockhill and Velgus.[6] However, as Wang Gungwu has been forced to admit the Chinese ships did sail to the Persian Gulf in the late 8th and the mid-9th centuries.[7] Needham has always insisted on the basis of other strong arguments that the Chinese sailed to this area as early as 8th century AD.[8]

As regards Quilon appearing in Chinese notices, till 12th century Chinese concept of the sub-continent is limited to "Five Indies" - the North, South, Central, West and East India only. The configuration of the south becomes clearer with the appearance of the Cholas on the east coast of peninsular India. Even then the king is generally indentified as belonging to South India.[9] It is only in the 12th century that the independent existence of Quilon is acknowledged by the Chinese historians and the first author to do so is Zhou Qufei who as already noted provides a separate chapter to Quilon under the name *Gulin*.[10]

Zhao Rugua who draws upon Zhou's work says it was a dependency of the *Nanpi*[11] country (Nambi or Nambutiri) which meant Calicut of the early period. With the Mongol period (Yuan dynasty) the name is transcribed as *Julan* (*Yuanshi*) whereas *Daoyi Zhilue* renders the name as *Xiao Junan* (*nan* is obviously South Chinese tonal mis-representation of the sound *lan*). The Ming travelogues and Mingshi write *Xiao Gelan*. *Xingcha Shenglan* of Fei Xin mentions Da Gelan in addition to *Xiao Gelan*.[12] The latter name obviously point to Quilon (Kollam) the famous port north of Trivandrum (Thiruvananthapuram).

Rockhill locates *Xiao Gelan* at Kayam Kollam, north of Quilon (Kollan) on the authority of Yule.[13] Some scholars equate *Xiao Ge-lan* of Yuan dynasty with Fandaraina. This hypothesis has been proved wrong because the latter place is listed separately under this very name in *Dade Nanhaizhi*, a historical workof Yuan dynasty which also has, *Da Gelan*, but does not have Xiao Gelan.[14] Wang Dayuan's *Ban-da-li* is also identical with Fandaraina. According to Pelliot *Xiao Junan*, *Xiao Gelan* and *Julan* stand for the same place i.e. Quilon, while *Da Junan* or *Da Gelan* are fabrications. This is wrong since not only Fei Xin includes *Da Gelan* in his travelogue, *Dade Nanhai Zhi* also gives this name. The latter work does not have *Xiao Gelan*.

Xiao Gelan is the more wellknown of the two and has been mentioned more often especially during the Ming and its status corresponds with that of Quilon.[15] All descriptions mention that the place is surrounded by sea on all three sides. This

389

description tallies with Quilon on the Malabar coast. Side by side with *Xiao Gelan,* we have for the same place, the Chinese rendering *Julan* (Yuanshi, j.12,14,16,210), *Ge-lan* (YS, 18), *Ke-lan* (Songshi, j.490), *Gu-lin* and *Jia-ling Ma-lai* (Kulam-Malai),[16] the last one being the nomenclature given by the Arabs during the 9th century AD. The local name remains to be Kollam.

The name *Xiao* (Small) *Ge-lan* suggests that there was another place named *Da*(Bigger)-*Ge lan.* Rockhill, as pointed out earlier, identifies the Bigger *Gelan* with Quilon proper while equating the Small (or Minor) Gelan with Kay kulam (Kayam Kollam). Pelliot thinks *Da-Ge-lan* to be non-existant; Su Jiquing identifies *Da-Ge-lan* with Atingal which lies on a bay on the coast between Trivandrum and Quilon, not far from Anjengo where the English had a factory around 1684.[17] But this identification does not seem to be covincing as the, name in no way conveys any sound similar to Kollam. It is in all probability Kayam Kulam north of Quilon. As the name is longer than Quilon the Chinese migt have added *Da* (big) in place of *Kayam.* Being not so wellknown as harbour it was not in much use and was overshadowed by the more thriving port of Quilon (Kollam).

Wang Dayuan's account places Quilon near *Dulan* rocks which Su Jiqing identifies with Chirayankil near Anjengo (8°40'N) while Feng Chengjun identifies it with a place near *Chitu* and *Xiali.*[19] *Chitu,* a table land is about 6.5 km north of Anjengo on the west coast while *Xiali* or *Xie-li* (Hili) is identified with Mount Delly (12°02'N) on the same coast.[20] Looking at the map of Kerala one can at once realise that Xie-li is wrongly included as a neighbouring place to Quilon. The *Jilu Huibian* version of *Xingcha Shenglan* mentions Cochin as conterminous with Quilon which seems to be the correct description.[21]

Ma Huan's description which is more detailed says, "Setting sail from the port named *Bie-Io-li* (Beruwala, Barberyn) in the country of *Xilan* (Sri Lanka), you go northwest, and after travelling with a fair wind for six days and nights you can reach the place (Quilon). The country abuts the sea; on the east it adjoins large mountains; on the west is the great sea, on the south and north the territory is narrow; and beyond it is the great sea again[22].

The Western Connection

Duarte Barbosa's description of the Kerala ports helps us to identify these ports. He says that the kingdom of Kollam commences from Porca which lies between Cochin and Kollam. Having passed Porca, the first town he reached was called "Caymcolan (Kayam Kolam) in which dwell many Gentiles, Moors and Indian Christians...... There is much pepper in this place, of which there is much exported. Farther on along the same coast towards the south is a great city and good sea-port, which is named Coulam (Kollam), in which dwell many Moors and Gentiles and Christians. They are great merchants and very rich, and own many ships with which they trade to Cholmendel (Coromandel), the Island of Ceylon, Bengal, Malacca, Samatara and Pegu; these do not trade with Cambay." [23]

Kayamkulam also called Kall or Kulli Quilon was a wellknown port, and now forms an important town. Situated on a shallow sheet of backwater, the place is very productive in pepper, its port for shipment being Porcade about ten miles south of Allepey.[24] It is quite possible it thrived for some time but later was abandoned in favour of Kollam because of the dashing bellows and wind which prevented the ships from finding a good anchorage before the change of the monsoon.[25]

It is significant that the Dutch captain Nieuhoff, in noticing Quilon, speaks of two Quilons, "the Upper or Malabar Koulang (Kollam), the other the Lower Koulang; in the first the king and queen kept their ordinary residence; the last was formerly in the possession of the Portuguese, as lying near to the sea-side."[26] Speaking of Lower Quilon he says that its suburbs are large and stately and is called Coulang China by the Portuguese, probably because that was the portion where the Chinese frequented and had their settlement. That the Lower Koulang i.e. *Xiao Gelan* was the same as Quilon is beyond any doubt, while Upper Coulang, the normal residence of the

391

kingdom known as Odanad, remained an important centre even beyond 15th century.[27]

Venad, of which Quilon was the headquarter enjoyed prosperity under the Kulasekharas. But during the reign of Bhaskara Ravi Varman I (AD 962-1019), the great Chola ruler Rajaraja (AD 985-1016) followed an aggressive policy towards Kerala which continued during his successor Rajendra Chola's time (AD 1012-1044).[28] During this period of Chola-Chera war, Venad suffered havoc at the hands of the Chola invaders. In 1096 AD the city of Quilon itself was destroyed by Kulottunga's army. The Venad king submitted finally around 1182.[29] The record of Jatavarman Sundara Pandya and his successor Maravarman Kulasekhara (1268-1310) testify to the establishment of Pandyan hegemony over the region including Quilon.[30]

Under Ravi Varma Kulasekhara (AD 1299-1314), Venad attained a high degree of economic prosperity and social progress. Quilon retained its position of commercial prominence and developed into the premier port on the west coast. There was brisk trade at this port between Kerala and the countries abroad, particularly China. Ravi Varma paid special attention to the improvement of Quilon town. It was a fabulous city provided with all amenities of civilised life. The brisk trade carried on through the port is testified to in the works of foreign travelers who visited the coast and in Malayalam poems like *Unniachi Charitam* and *Unnunili Sandesam*.[31]

Benjamin of Tudela (12th Century) praises the integrity of the King's officers who supervised the commercial transactions of Quilon port. Whenever foreign merchants entered the port, three secretaries of the king immediatly repaired on board their vessels, wrote down their names and reported them to the king. The king there upon, granted them security for their property which they could even leave in the open fields without any guard. Pepper, cinnamon and ginger were the most important spices transacted at Quilon.[32]

Al Kazwini (1263-75) refers to Kulam (Quilon) as a large city in India.[33] Marco Polo who visited Quilon towards the end of the 13th century throws light on the prosperous pepper trade of Quilon, particularly with China. He says, "The merchants from Manzi (Machin = *maha china*) (China) and from the Levant come there with their ships and their merchandise and make great profits both by what they import and by what they export". The Venetian traveler was greatly impressed by the high degree of economic prosperity that prevailed in the Kingdom.[34] Friar Odoric (1321-2) calls this city by the name of Polumbum in which "is grown better ginger than anywhere else in the world. And the variety and abundance of wares for sale in that city is so great that it would seem past belief to many folk."[35]

Kollam city (Quilon) founded probably around 825 AD was from the very beginning a trade centre. The Chera king welcomed the foreigners and granted their petition to settle down there. One such foreigner was *Mar Sapir Iso*, the Syrian Christian missionary, who has been described as the founder of the *Nagaram*, the mercantile corporation of Kollam.[36] This Syrian founded the church of *Tarsa*, invited the *Anchuvannam* and *Manikkiramam* corporations of the jews and Christians respectively, to have their branches there, and step by step rose to the position of a local aristocrat by receiving the confidence and good will of the rulers and the people. The church was given the custodianship of weights and measures and was permitted to enjoy the weighing fee.[37] Even as late as 1348 AD. John de Marignoli who came to India on his return journey from China and stayed at Kollam has recorded that the Christians of St. Thomas i.e. the Syrian Christians were the masters of the public weighing office.[38] This privilege was earlier enjoyed exclusively by the Hindu temple-corporations in the normal course. This trust placed in the church seems to have been lost after the Arab influx into the Indian and India-China trade, because by the time of Alfonso d'Albuquerque (1504 AD) the church had lost the privilege of keeping the seal and the standard weight of the city.[39]

The demand for Kerala goods must have received impetus with the rise of Islam in West Asia. The Syrian guilds included the Arabs also.[40] As early as 825 AD. merchant

Sulayman describe the Arab trade to India. Commodities were brought from Basra and Uman to Siraf and then to Muscat, from where it took a full month to reach Kollam Mali (Elimala). From here the ships sailed for China. At Kollam there was a dock for ship-building and repairs.[41] Abu Zayd (or Zaid) in 851 AD speaks of great exchange of merchants between Al-Iraq and China and India. The important town in Malabar, he says are Shaliyat (Chaliyam), Shinkili (Kodungallur) and Kulam (Kollam), the last one being the last town in the pepper country in the east.[42] Ibn Battuta who was on the West coast between AD 1342-44, described the journey from Sandabur (Goa) to Kulam as extending over a length of two months journey, the latter port being the nearest of the "Mulabar (Malabar) towns to China and most of the merchants (from China) come there.[43]

Diplomatic and Trade Relation with China

By comparing the accounts of Ibn Battuta with those of the Portuguese, it is possible to place the growth of Muslim power and influence between the 14th and 16th centuries.[44] But, there is no doubt that ascendancy of the Muslims in the trading world of the west coast led to the gradual eclipse of the Christian guilds and finally left no trace of these traders except their churches and the converted Christian community.[45]

Chinese were late comers in this area of the Indian Ocean. However, heavy commitment of the court in the revenue accruing from maritime trade and tremendous expansion in shipping and nautical science encouraged both the Yuan and Ming emperors to take keen interest in trade. Exchange of official missions had increased, sumptuous largesses were bestowed by both sides, and official historiography took great care to record each event.

The Arab ascendancy to power also coincided with the decay of Kollam (Quilon) as an entrepot. This is also reflected in the Chinese records. The last mission from Quilon during Yuan dynasty is dated around September 1291, whereas the return mission from China was in October 1294, while in case of Malabar the last mission was in 1296. In 1314 a Mabar mission was sent to China. After this, thirty years had elapsed before a

Chinese envoy was sent to Kollam in 1344.[46] It will be natural to presume that both the above missions from China were sequels to visits from Mabar and Quilon respectively.

But it would be interesting to probe the background of the gap between these years. Drainage of China's metallic currency,compelled China to take measures from time to time to preserve the metals from flowing out. For example, as early as 1282 and 1283 use of cash was restricted;only iron was allowed to be used as a medium of exchange, private trading in gold, silver, satins,copper cash, etc., was strictly prohibited (YS, 104, 4a).[47] In 1296 the exportation of gold and silver was again prohibited, and the government tried to limit the trade with Mabar, Kollam(Quilon, wrongly written as *Bainan*) and Fandaraina to the meagre amount of 50,000 *ding* (1*ding* =50 ch. ounce).[48]

The attempts to stem the trend of private trading and flow of metals continued into early fourteenth century(specifically till 1329 AD). Influx of Muslim and Uighur officials into imperial service and constant inflow of Muslim traders affected various services especially the courier service which was pressed into service for carrying the strange animals (obviously for the Chinese) and valuable objects, and the entire exercise would also have caused pressure on state finance.[49]

In the year 1292 the Mongol emperor sent punitive expedition against the northeastern state of Java called *Gelang*. The expedition afforded the leader of the expedition, *Yi-hei-mi--shi*,the opportunity to open friendly ties with some South East Asian states like Lambri, Samudra (Semudera), etc.(YS, 131). Sea trade had been banned, and the sea-going junks were requisitioned for transportation. Although the expedition to Java proved abortive, it led to the establishment of profitable trade and official intercourse between China and Java.[50] The South East Asian states had their own compulsion, while for China the trade was profitable in comparison with South Asia and the Gulf countries. It is pertinent to state here that a regulation promulgated in 1293 was intended to prevent Buddhist priests,

Christian teachers and Muslim mullahs, most of whom were from India and further west, from smuggling into China free of duty Chinese traders and their goods. This abuse must have become quite common and caused serious loss to the treasury.[51] That is why we find such a long silence in their relation during this period.

Yuan dynasty (1279-1368)
Mission from China to Quilon (Kollam)[52]

1280 (January, 12th Month, 16th year of Kalblai Khan rule)	-	Yang Tingbi, the *Daroga* of Pacification office(Commander-in-Chief), Ordered to proceed to Quilon (YS j.210).
1280 (3rd month)	-	Yang reaches Quilon. The king was *Bi-na-di* (Pandya?) (ibid)
(10th Month)	-	*Ha-sa-er-hai*, elevated to ambassador's rank to accompany Yang (but the mission strayed to the Mabar coasts).
1282 (1st month)[53]	-	The mission reached Quilon during the 2nd month of 1282 (ibid). They came from Mabar.
1283 (1st month)[54]	-	Sent Yang Tingbi with presents of bows, arrows, (horse) saddles and straps.
1283 (2nd month)	-	The Chinese emperor presented *Wa-ni*, the king of Quilon, gold seal (ibid,j.12)
1291 (9th month)[55]	-	Tie- li, Minister of Rites and *A-lao-wa-ding* (Alauddin) and *Bu-la-bing* as attending officers carried matching tiger-seats to Quilon (ibid,j.16)
1294 (9th month)	-	*Tu-gu-tie-mu-er* (Temur) and others dispatched as envoys.

Quilon Mission to China[56]

1280 (11th month)	-	Hanlin Academy Chancellor reports about the arrival of embassies from Quilon (*Ju-lan*), Maba (er), Java (*shi-bo*),

	Jiao-zhi (Annam, Vietnam) for presentation of memorial. The Emperor proclaimed Quilon's return to allegiance. (This seems to be the first Quilon mission, and the envoy came independent of Mabar). (YS, j.11)
1282 (9th month) -	The envoy memorialised and presented costly merchandise and one black ape (libid,j.12)
1287 (1st month) -	*Bui-liu-wen-nai* and others came as envoys.
1291 (8th month) -	*Ma-bu-la-han-ding*, (Md.Burhanuddin or Mahavardhana?) presented letter written in gold, black lion (?), cotton cloth made in Quilon and medicines.

Quilon (Kollam) - The last Phase

Inspite of the historical importance of Quilon only very few relics of old palaces and forts are found in the district. Relics of old buildings were discovered from the premises of the Quilon railway station near Iravipuram which may be remnant of Panamkavil or some other place. Similarly ruins of old stone walls in several rows in the ocean at some distance from the Quilon coast are believed to be of ancient forts and palaces. The new Puthampalli church also conceal beneath it remains of old buildings, and so also are numerous relics here.[57] The mystery of the two Quilons falls in the same category. However, John Nieuhoff who was the Chief Director of the Dutch company at Quilon in 1664 gives in his *Voyages and Travels* a short description of the Upper and Lower Coulang China(Quilon). The Chinese names *Da Gelan* and *Xiao (Hsiao)-Gelan* are the exact translation of the Quilons of Nieuhoff's description. In that case we have to look for small or Lower Quilon at the present site while the Upper one will be the one more exposed to the bellows and adverse winds of the coast.

John of Montecorvino, the first Roman Catholic missionary to China and the first Archbishop of Peking (Beijing) spent thirteen months in India between 1291 and 1292 visiting both the Malabar and Coromandel coasts. At the time of his visit to Quilon he noticed that the Chinese, Christian and Jewish traders of Quilon were being gradually ousted from the position of commercial prominence by the Muslims who had begun to settle there in large numbers. Friar Odoric refers to the existence of a Jewish community in 1322. John de Marignoli of Florence was in Quilon in 1347 AD.[58] He mentions about his receiving payments for fourteen months from the Thomas Christians who were the keepers of the public pepper weighing office (Steelyard).[59] The Muslim traders had established themselves by fourteenth century in the entire Malabar coast and even as far north as Tana(Thane) near Bombay, as the massacre of the Franciscans by the *Oadi* (Kaji) and the Muslim inhabitants show.[60]

John of Montecorvino's statement about the Christians being ousted from the Quilon trade may be correct but in case of the Chinese it is a little different. The Chinese drainage of metallic currency, etc. had led to restriction on Chinese trade with the entire Malabar region. The situation improved with the establishment of the Mongol power, as we have seen earlier. But the fate of Quilon did not improve. The Chinese interest had waned to such an extent that during the thirty years when Zheng He sailed the waters of the Arabian Sea between 1405 and 1433, the voyages came to Quilon only thrice although this excellent port falls on the way to its neighbouring countries like Cochin and Calicut where the Chinese ships anchored whenever they came to India.

The inventory of commodities traded between China and Quilon is available for 14th and early 15th centuries. It shows that as a result of strict enforcement of trade regulations and encouragement by Kublai Khan, China had profitable trade with Quilon, and pepper was the only substantial item which the Chinese cared for and which was available as easily at Cochin and Calicut. During 15th century the Zheng He entourage were still using this port to their advantage though it had a lower priority in the eyes of the Chinese. The list of traded commodities stand proof to that if we compare it with that of Calicut. The balance of trade was in China's favour as the list very clearly demonstrates.

Kollam i.e. Quilon had already yielded place to Calicut to which the Chinese clientale was being lured by the Muslim traders. This is evident from the table of missions. The Zheng He missions did not show the interest that Quilon deserved with its glorious past as the traders' rendezvous.

Ming dynasty (1368-1644)
Chinese Missions to Kollam (Quilon)

1407[61]	Under the name *Xiao Gelan*	Visit by a branch fleet attached to Zheng He's first Voyage(return Voyage)
1409[62]	Under the name *Xiao Junan*	during the third voyage, Fei Xin accompanied Zheng He.
1431-33[63]	Under the name *Xiao Gelan*	during the seventh voyage Gong Zhen was a member of the entourage.

Kollam (Quilon) Missions to China

1368-78[65]	(Early Hongwu period)[64] Under the name *Da* (the Bigger) *Junan*	
1407[65]	Under the name *Xiao Gelan* Envoy = *Bi-zhe-ya-man-hei-di* (Vijaya Mannadi?)	came with Samudra and Calicut mission, may be in their boat.

Inventory of Chinese Imports and Exports
14th century.

Import(into China)	Export (to Quilon)	Remarks
Pepper, coconut, betel-nut, *Li*, fish[67] (dried fish of the Maldive Island) Jewelled Umbrella, White velvety (mien) cloth[69]	Gold, Iron, blue and white porcelain-ware, Ba-dan cloth(?)[68] satins of various colours, iron ware and the like colours, cardamom, sapan wood, coloured satin, musk, silver, copper ware, iron wires, black tassels.[70]	Cash and exchange of goods both used.

References:

1. For its early history and foreign contacts see, A Sreedhara Menon, *A Survey of Kerala History,* Kottayam, 1967 pp.52-111, For Kollam era, see, pp.112-20, for Kulasekhara of Mahodayapuram, see pp.121-55.

2. Ji Xianlin, et.al, eds. *DaTang Xiyu Ji Jiaozhu* (Journey to the Western Region annotated 5, pp.857-8; Hirth and Rockhill consider it to be the Quilon coast. op.cit., p.12, n.5.

3. Wang Gungwu, "The Nanhai Trade, A study of the Early History of Chinese Trade in the China Sea", *Journal of the Malayan Branch of Royal Asiatic Society* (JMBRAS), 31, No.182, 1958, p.106 and note 65.

4. For Jia Dan's itinerary, see Xin Tangshu (New History of Tang dynasty), j. 43 B, Geng, op.cit., pp.648-9; Feng Chengjun, *Zhongguo Nanyang Jiatong Shi (History of the Contacts of China with the South sea Regions),* Shangai, 1937 pp.42-44. According to the account the journey to Quilon and the west coast required around 70 to 80 days.

5. Lingwai Diada (In Response to Queries on Regions beyond the Mountain pass), j.s, Congshu Jichang Chubian edn. book, 3118, p.23.

6. Hirth and Rockhill, *Chao Ju-kua,* 1911, Paragon reprint, New York, 1966. pp. 15,18;n Wang Gungwu, op.cit. 9.105.

7. Wang, ibid, p.106, For a detailed discussion of this question see, V.A.Velgus, "Some Problems of the History of Navigation in the Indian and Pacific Oceans", in D.A.Olderogge, e-in-chief, *The Countries and Peoples of the East,* USSR Academy of Sciences, Moscow, 1974, pp.45-90; for reference to at Tabaric see, p.46.

8. J. Needham, *Science and Civilisation in China,* Vol. I, Cambridge 1954 p.179, note no.C and K.

9. For five Indies see *Jiu Tang Shi* (JTS) j. 198, Geng, op.cit., p.361; for the generic term *Nan Tian* (South India), see for examples, Geng, op.cit. p.347, 348-361,363, 364, etc.

10. See n.5. However as already noted it is during this period (Song dynasty) that the Cholas also figure prominently in Chinese notices.

11. Hirth and Rockhill, op.cit. p.88

12. For *Yuanshi* (YS) see Geng, op.cit., pp.829-32, 841 for Daoyizhilue(DYZL), see Su Jiqing, ed., *Daoyi Zhilue Jiaoshi* (Record of the Foreign Island, by Wang Dayuan) Annotated (1350), 1965, reprinted, Beijing, 1981, pp321, for Ma Huan see, Feng Chengjun, ed.Ying Yai Shenglan Jiaozhu (The overall survey of the Oceans shores (Annotated) 1433, 1937, reprinted, Taipei, 1070, pp.37-8, For Fei Xin see, Feng Chengjun, ed., *Xingcha Shenglan Jiao Zhu (The overall Survey of the Star Raft Annotated),* 1936, reprinted Taipei, 1970, I, p.31, II (Houji), 16, (Da Junan); for Gong Zhen see, Xiang Da, ed. *Xiyang Fanguo Zhi (Record of Foreign Countries in the Western Ocean),* Beijing, 1961, p.24, also Xie Fang, ed, *Xiyang Chaogong Dianlu* (Ming) Huang Shengceng Zhu (Record of Tributes from the Western Ocean Countries by Huang Shengceng of Ming dynasty) Beijing, 1982, p.92.

13. W.W. Rockhill, TP, 1915, op.cit., pp. 445-6.

14. Geng, op.cit. p.709

15. See n.12,

16. For Jia-ling Ma-lai, see, su, op.cit. p.323

17. Ibid, pp.323-4
18. Su, Ibid, 324; Feng Chengjun, ed., Xingcha, II, p.16.
19. Ibid, p.31
20. J.V.G. Mills, ed., *Ma Huan, Yingyai Shenglan*, Hakluyt Society, London, 1970, 99.190,197.
21. Feng, ed., *Xingcha*, p.32.
22. Feng, ed., *Yingyai*, p.37.
23. Quoted in Rockhill, 1915, op.cit., p.446.
24. K.P.P. Menon, *History of Kerala*, Vol. I, Ernakulam 1924, pp.293-4.
25. Feng, ed, Xingcha, II, p.16
26. D. Ferroli, op.cit.
27. A. Sreedhara Menon, op.cit. p.188, see also H. Yule and H. Cordier, *Cathay and the Way thither*, republished, Taipei, 1966, Vol. III, pp.203,249, and K.P.P. Menon, op.cit. p. 278.
28. A. Sreedhara Menon, op.cit., pp. 112-55.
29. Ibid, p. 157, K.A. Nilakanta Sastri, A *History of South India*, 4th edn. O.U.P Delhi, Bombay, etc. 1991, pp. 157, 196.
30. Ibid., p. 161, N. Sastri, op.cit., p.216.
31. Sreedhara Menon, op.cit. pp. 163-4.
32. K.A. Nilakanta Sastri, *Foreign Notices of South India from Megasthenes to Ma Huan*, 1939, reprinted, Madras, 1972, 99.134-5.
33. Sreedhara Menon, op.cit. p.165.
34. R. Latham, tr., *The Travels of Marco Polo*, Penguin Books, New York, 1958, pp.287-8.
35. N. Sastri, *Foreign Notices*, p. 194. For other foreign notices see, p.211(Jordanus, AD 1323-1330) p. 214, (Abulfeda, 1273-1331), pp 221, 245-7 (Ibn Battuta, 1333-45, pp 286-7 Marignolli, 1347-AD.
36. M.G.S. Narayanan, "Mar Sapir Iso, founder of the Church of Tarsa", in his *Cultural Symbiosis in Kerala*, Trivandrum, 1972, p.32.
37. Ibid, pp. 35, 37.
38. D. Ferroli, *The Jesuits of Malabar*, I, p.66.
39. Quoted in T.K. Joseph, " The Malabar Christian Copper-plates", *Kerala Society Papers*, 4, p.20, f.n. 13.
40. Narayanan, op.cit. p.33.
41. A.P. Ibrahim Kunju, *Studies in Medieval Kerala History*, Trivandrum, 1975, pp.8-9.
42. Ibid, p.10.
43. H.A.R. Gibb, *Ibn Battuta : Travels in Asia and African 1325-54*, London, 1924, pp. 234, 238.
44. G. Bouchon, "Some Aspects on Islamisation in the Coastal Regions of India during the Medieval period, (in French), *Purusartha* 9, 1986, p.29 (translation by courtesy, Mr. Nangia, Centre for French Studies, JNU)
45. Bouchon, "The Muslims of Kerala", *Mare Luso-Indicum* (in French) 2, 1973, p.49, (translation by courtesy, colleagues in C.F.S., JNU)

46. Yuanshi(YS) j. 41, p.5a, cited in Rockhill, "Notes on the relations and trade of China with the Eastern Archipelago and the coast of the Indian Ocean during the fourteenth century, pt. 1, *T'oung Pao*, 15,1914, p.443.
47. Quoted in Rockhill, ibid, p.425, n.1.
48. YS, j. 94, Geng, op.cit. p.833.
49. Rockhill, op.cit. pp.426-8.
50. Ibid, pp. 442-7.
51. Ibid, pp. 425-6, n.2.
52. Geng, op.cit., pp. 841-2. The references to the related reference from Yuanshi (YS) are also given at the end of our text itself.
53. Ibid., p. 842.
54. Ibid., p. 829.
55. Ibid., p. 831. (for both 1291 and 1294)
56. Ibid., pp. 828-31.
57. A. Sreedhara Menon, *Quilon District Gazetteer*, (Trivandrum, 1964), p.69.
58. Idem., *A Survey of Kerala History*, (Kottayam, 1967), pp. 25-6.
59. John D. Ryan, "European Travellers before Columbus: the Fourteenth Century's discovery of India", *The Catholic Historical Review*, 79, 4, 1993, p. 667.
60. Ibid., pp.656-8.
61. Jin Yunming, "Zheng He qici Xia Xiyang nianyue kaozheng" (a textual study of the dates of the seven voyages of Zheng He), *Fujian Wenhua (Journal of the Fujian University)*, 26, 1937, pp. 6-1; J.J.L. Duyavendak, "The True dates of the Chinese Maritime Expeditions in the early Fifteenth century, " *T'oung Pao*, 34, 1938, p. 360; JV.G. Mills, *Ma Huan*, Hakluyt Society, 1970, p.10; Haraprasad Ray, *Trade and Diplomacy in India China Relations*; New Delhi, 1993, p.37.
62. Luo Richong, *Xianbin Lu (Record of all the Guests)* (1590), j. 6. Zhonghua Shuju edn, Beijing, 1983, p. 159, (Under the name Xiao Junan); Ray, op.cit. p.36, Feng Chengjun ed. Xiangcha, 1, preface. p.1.
63. Xiang Da, ed., *Gong Zhen: Xiyang Fanguozhi (Gong Zhen: Records of the Foreign Countries in the Western Ocean, (1434)*, Beijing 1961, pp 24-5; Mills, op.cit., p.19; Ray op.cit., p.40.
64. Luo Richong, op. cit.
65. MTZSL j.71, p. 987 (also called TZSL); Mao Ruizheng, *Huang Ming Xiangxu Lu* (1629), in Geng, op.cit. p.1037 *Mingshi*, j. 326, Zhonghua Shuju edn. Beijing, 1974 p.8443; *Da Ming Huidian*, j. 1599, Mingshi Gao (Draft History of Mingshi); j.200, Wenhai Chuban she edn. p. 1599, MSG, j.200, Wenhai Chuban she edn., p.285.
66. Su Jiging, op.cit., p. 321.
67. Ibid., p. 264.
68. Ibid., p. 321; alternative reading is *bazhou* (ibid) : the identity of this cotton cloth is uncertain.
69. Feng, *Xingcha*, I, p.32.
70. Xie Fang, ed., *Xiyang*, p. 93. Ma Huan only mentions sapanwood and pepper as local products, but it seems the demand for sapanwood could not be met locally.

26

MARITIME TRADE AND CULTURAL INTERACTIONS IN THE INDIAN OCEAN (1500 - 1800)

T. Jamal Mohammed

The destiny of India was changed by the Indian Ocean. Even before the European contacts with India during the 15th Century, traders from Arabian countries had already established their commercial contacts. Though sea travel at that time was a hazardous task it did not prevent the merchants from different parts of the world to seek their fortunes in the land of spices. India was engaged in maritime trade and navigaton from ancient times. Egyptians, Arabs, Romans and Chinese were the early traders who had established trade relations with this subcontinent. From 9th to 12 th century, Chola kingdom had long standing trade relations with Ceylon, Bengal, Burma and South East Asian countries. After the decline of Chola empire no Indian ruler came forward with maritime ambitions. This opportunity was successfully taken up by the Arabs and the maritme trade with the Indian Ocean became their monopoly. They continued to be the masters in the field till the arrival of the Portuguese.

The Indian merchants were prevented by religious taboos from crossing the sea. Inspite of this, the Indian merchants did not hesitate to establish their commercial contacts with countries across the sea. The Portuguese merchants had met the Indian navigators on the East African coast in 1498. The Indian merchants had founded a colony in Massua in Abyssinia at the close of the Middle Ages.[1] Indians were also found on the Persian

Gulf area, Red Sea regions and various parts of the South East Asian Countries during this period. It is to be noted that they had managed to reach these places by sea in the period much prior to the arrival of the Europeans.

Commercial interests were definitely the prime motivation behind the adventurous navigations undertaken by the Indian and European merchants. But once the contacts with the people of different locations were established it was bound to create interactions and the consequent cultural diffusion. The Indian merchants had already established wide ranging contacts with coastal regions of various parts of the world, even before the 15th century. Wherever they had established these contacts they had their own cultural impacts. Zansibar of East African coast is an excellent example of cultural contributions made by the Gujarati merchants, during this period. The trading communities form India like the Gujaratis, Chetties, and Klings had made great cultural contributions in the social life of the Malay Peninsula. The religious and cultural contributions of the Indian communities in the countries of South East Asia and the West Asia are well known. The strong bondage of cultural relationship between India and these countries were made possible only through oceanic trade and commerce.

During the ancient period the Indo-China relations were not based on trade alone. It was the spiritual hegemony enjoyed by India that attracted the Chinese towards the country. Buddhism fired the imagination of the Chinese who were longing for a spiritual salvation. This continued for a few centuries till the arrival of the Europeans. It completed the transformation from spiritual attainments to material advantages. The South Indian merchants who traded with the Chinese successfully followed a middle path mingling both spiritual and material aspects in their dealings. But with the arrival of the European merchants they too had to change the policy due to the tough competition they had to face from the Europeans. By the beginning of 15th century this process was complete. The atmosphere was completely filled with commercial activities. The ruling class who required material prosperity of their countries because more concerned about trade than spiritual activities. But still religious influence continued to remain a powerful factor in the relationship between India and China. A lot of research and excavations are still necessary to find out the real history behind the remains of temples and stone slabs discovered in the Chinese province, Quanzhou. It may throw sufficient light on the existence of an Indian cultural heritage in the Chincse land.

The relationship between India and China especially during the Pre-colonial era cannot be confined to the trade conducted between these two countries through land routes alone. The evidence gathered from the travelogues of the 15th century and the contemporary histories have proved that the brisk trade going on was due to maritime activities in the Indian Ocean. The discoveries of Chinese ceramics on the coasts of India have established beyond doubt the maritime trade going on between the two countries much before the arrival of the Europeans in India. The areas near Gangaikonda Cholapuram and Periyapattinam in Tamilnadu have also yielded a lot of Chinese and Islamic procelain wares[2]. These discoveries confirm the existence of maritime trade between China and important coastal cities of Tamilnadu. Similarly the coastal towns of Quilon, Cochin and Calicut also yielded Chinese potsherds in large number belonging to the 15th century.

The existence of an ancient Indian social structure in South East Asia has been proved by the accounts given by Chinese sources. There are ancient remains of Indian civilisation in countries like Thailand, Kampuchea, Indonesia and Quanzhou in China. They are supposed to be the remains of a culture that flourished during the period of the Chola invasion around 11th century.

Apart from the Buddhist influence there is sufficient evidence to show that Hinduism with its different aspects flourished in the kingdom of Java. A number of temples with Siva as the deity were constructed there to propagate Saivism. The predominant characteristics of the social life in these areas were south Indian because the traders were mainly from Tamilnadu. The Tamil traders had complete control over the economy of the area. Even the Tamil commercial organisations like *Manigramam and Ainnurruvar* were found in these places.

Another spot in the Indian Ocean which developed into a multi-cultural centre was a small uninhabited island which was later known as Mauritius. It was a practically unknown, uninhabited and insignificant island in the 15th century[3]. The Portuguese navigator Mascarenhas discovered the island in 1505. Though it was known to the Arab merchants much earlier, it was not given any importance since it was found unworthy of human habitaton. In 1598 the Dutch navigators under the leadership of Admiral Wybrandt van Warwyn reached the island and they gave it the name Mauritius after the name of their Prince Maurice. But even the Dutch did not have the patience to remain there for long. It was left to the French to occupy the island and converted it into a prosperous colony. The basis for the future development of the island which was later known as "the star and key of the Indian Ocean", was laid down by the French administration from 1733 to 1746.

The social formation of Mauritius is a typical example of cross cultural relations between different nationalities. The society is mainly composed of the Asian communities like Indian, Chinese and Arabs in addition to the European Communities mainly the French. Due to the close inter relations and interactions going on for centuries a composite culture evolved there consisting of the characteristic features of diverse races having black, brown, yellow and white complexions. The African people reached there as slaves to be employed in the plantations. Large number of Indian labourers migrated to Mauritius from South Indian regions like Madras, Tanjore and Deccan. Trading Communites from Gujarat monopolised the business scene.

Mauritius society is distinctive with its multi-religious character. It has three major religions, Christianity, Hinduism and Islam. With in the limited population all these religions flourished with all their sects and sub sects. English and French are the major languages taught in the School. Thus Mauritius today is a plural society with the combined characteristics of Asian, African and European Cultures.

The Portuguese policy of establishing their supremacy in India cannot be confined to trade alone. They have a strong conviction that they were carrying out a mission of expanding Christianity. They even considered themselves to be carrying out the mission of St. Thomas[4]. But further developments show that they were just exploiting the natives for the attainment of commercial objectives. They never treated the converted Christians on par with the European Christians. They were forced to work hard without proper remuneration and were often subjected to ill treament[5].

Once the Portuguese got themselves settled down in Indian provinces, their attitude changed. They considered the new land full of opportunities and unlimited profits. It offered them good life satisfying many of their needs both religious, financial and sensual. Even the official administration and the church found it impossible to bring them under control[6]. Many Portuguese men who had their own family and children got married in India. Even the request sent to the king by priest to control the Portuguese settlers in India was not given proper attention by the concerned authorities[7]. Their activities continued unabated creating administrative problems for the authorities. The ultimate result of the unlicensed and uncontrolled life of the Portuguese men in the coastal cities was the creation of an illegitimate society which had no moral values at all. It was this society that created a great headache to the Portuguese authorities in India. It had a far reaching adverse effect on the history of Portuguese settlements in India.

When conversions into Christianity took place it created social developments incompatible with the social stigma of the Indian caste system. Apart from the social implications it created some changes in the languages prevailing there. As a result of translation of ideas of the new faith into the regional languages it began to create a new prescription of colonial culture and to produce the contingent transaction of radically distinct languages, bodies and objects between the colonisers and the colonised. The vernacular languages of religious converts began to develop conflict of interests.

When conversions took place resentment grew up within the native clergy against the discriminatory methods of the Portuguese people. Even though Christianity preached equality they tried to retain the caste system. In the beginning only Brahmins were admitted to priesthood. This was done in order to avoid down grading the excellence of priesthood in the eyes of the lower caste. The non Brahminical clergy was kept at the bottom of the Catholic hierarchy. Several old Hindu practices are allowed to continue. This policy of keeping up old traditions inspite of the change of religion was a technique adopted by the Portuguese at the time.

In Kerala the Hindus and Christians used to have a cordial relationship and they used to live in the same area. The Portuguese took steps to avoid this by issuing orders that the Hindus should not live among the Christians and they should have separate places for their residences[8]. The new Christians were not allowed to continue any contacts with their Hindu relatives. When the Portuguese assumed political power they issued orders regarding the social life of the people above whom they had control. The local women were asked to dress themselves in such a way that they could easily be distinguished from the Christians. The Hindus were also prevented from riding horses using palanquins or exhibit any signs which added preeminence to them in the society. They even tried to control the elaborate ceremonies of Hindu marriage.

The Portuguese influence in Indian life began to go deep into the social life of the people when they started to interfere in the social practises of the Hindus. The life of a Hindu widow in India irrespective of her age and health was much inferior to that of a slave. The Portuguese encouraged the widow marriage and removed the difficulties that prevented it. They legislated against the practice of "Sati" by intorducing strict laws against it and punished those who worked for it.

The Portuguese Christians were asked to keep up a separate identity of their own. They were kept away from all the possible contact with the HIndus. They even instructed the newly formed Christian community to wear a particular dress that could distinguish them from the non-Christian groups.

The areas of coastal regions in Malabar had witnessed the emergence of many religious groups both local and foreign. But the social harmony among the different Communities was not broken. The Portuguese were the first European community who took deliberate steps to destroy the harmonious relationships that existed among communities of different faith. They restricted the Christians from participating in the socio-cultural events of the land.

The general trend of the Portuguese in their interaction with the society in Malabar during the sixteenth and seventeenth centuries was characterised by the attempts to do away with the existing social customs and manners for the sake of replacing them with those of Europe especially of Portugal[9]. They managed to keep the Christians under their control and persuaded them to follow European pattern of life.

The Portuguese considered the local trading communities especially the Muslims as their number one enemy. They even encouraged the Christians and the Hindus to indulge in trade and commerce in order to remove the Muslims from the field. They wanted to replace the Muslim merchants from Malabar and put in their place other loyal merchants belonging to other communities including Hindus.

The Portuguese policy of utilising religion as a weapon of psychological domination to complete their military domination was causing an increasingly acute dissatisfaction among the local people both Hindus and Christians.

The local languages had to undergo changes due to the foreign influences. The activities of the European missionaries were the major factor responsible for these changes. The *modus operandi* of the missionaries was to become experts in the local languages and thus enter into the minds of the people. As expected the policy was a great success. The vernacular languages were not only learned by the missionaries alone but also by most of the Europeans who settled down on the western coast for commercial and administrative purposes. Learning of the local languages was the best way to get the support and sympathy of the people. The introduction of printing press was the next development of far reaching consequences. Printing machines were introduced in India for the first time by the Europeans during the 16th century. The essential pre-requisites for the growth of a language are a systematic grammar and dictionaries. Herman Gundert in the case of Malayalam and Father Beschi in the case of Tamil were able to make great contributions in their respective fields. Printing media helped the origins of journalism in these languages.

Colonial expansion in India during the 16th century went side by side with the cultural interactions between the colonial power and the colonised.[10] This is a process which nobody can deny inspite of pretensions of patriotism. This is not something particular to India alone. It cannot be explained and interpreted in such a way that the superior culture alone can impose its characteristics on the inferior one. It is a matter of cultural diffusion and policy of give and take and cannot be explained away as one sided. No country for that matter can claim to be unicultural and if any country claim so it is an illogical argument. In the process of colonial domination it is quite possible that certain elements of compulsion and inhuman cruelty could have been exercised. The colonised people would have been subjected to untold miseries. Their native culture could have been totally destroyed. But it is something which happend in India from the time of Indus valley civilisation and cannot be attributed to one group of people alone. The attempt to erase the prevailing symptoms and signs of a bygone culture is a meaningless approach to de-culturisation.

References:

1. K.S.Mathew, *Indian Ocean and Cultural Interaction (AD1400-1800)*, Pondicherry, 1996,p.16(Introduction).
2. Haraprasad Ray, "India Settlements in China", in K.S.Mathew, op.cit.,p.53
3. Jeanethe Pinto, *"Mauritius-A Confluence of Myriad Cultures"*, K.S.Mathew, op.cit.,p.82
4. E.G.Ravenstein, *A Journal of the first Voyage of Vascoda Gama,1497-1499*, NewDelhi, Reprint,1995,p.48
5. Teotonio R.de Souza, "The Religious Policy of the Portuguese in Goa 1510-1800", Paper presented in the International Seminar on the *Portuguese and Socio Cultural Changes in India*, Dec, 1999,Palai(Kerala)
6. Ibid, p.4
7. Ibid,
8. K.S.Mathew, "Provincial Councils of Goa and Cultural changes in India"(paper presented) in the *International Seminar on the Portuguese and Socio Cultural Changes India*, Dec,1999,Palai(Kerala,India)
9. Ibid
10. Anthony de Silva, "The Discoveries versus the Discovered Psychological Persepectives on Portuguese-Goan Prejudices in the 16th and 18th Centuries" in *Discoveries, Missionary Expansion and Asian Cultures* Ed. by Teotonio de Souza, New Delhi, 1994, pp.45-54.

27

SANSKRIT IN MAGINDANAON: IMPLICATIONS ON PRE-ISLAMIC TRADE AND TRAFFIC

Juan R. Francisco

In a number of works on the influx of Indian cultural elements into the Philippines (vide Francisco, in Selected References), there has been no specific, or more appropriately, detailed discussion on the presence of such elements in Magindanaon. Some references were made in 1964 and 1988 pieces, particularly referring to language, but no further discussions were made. Nonetheless, these provided impetus to concentrate on the present subject of this paper.

Like the gulu Archipelago, which in early times was an ideal trade and traffic entrepot, coastal Magindanao, particularly the area where the Pulangi River empties into the Illanun Bay, provided an equally ideal port of entry of trade and traffic, indeed, being perhaps the end of the maritime route from across the high seas, and the beginning of the riverine trade and commercial routes into the hinterlands.

The trade and traffic routes shown in Reynaldo C. Ileto[1] (vide maps, attached) which is dated 17th century, and identified as Illanun/Magindanao navigational patterns only serve to indicate the sea routes that the traders of this period used. In fact such trade and traffic routes seem to be replicated in another work that somehow was drawn from direct experience by Thomas Forest[2], who voyaged through the Magindanao Island in 1775 (front map). I am certain that these routes used in the 17th, and replicated in the late 18th centuries must have been the same routes used by traders of earlier centuries, i.e., the earliest period of the inroads of Islam in the Southern Philippines, and goes back even to the trade and traffic to the periods of Madjapahit (middle 13th-14th centuries) and of Sri Vijaya (7th-early 13th centuries). And, indeed it is quite possible to speculate that trade and traffic through these regions followed the same route, providing easy access to the phenomenon that occurred in the area, the "Indianization" of the region. The phenomenon does not, however, indicate that the Indian elements as they are known in India were transmitted without their having undergone some changes in the process of acceptance by the host culture.[3]

It must not be forgotten at this point that trade and traffic in the past, as in the present was not without the medium of language. It is not just assumed that use of a language in the conduct of trade was evident; it is a fact of interchanges or more appropriately exchanges precipitated the entry of new ideas, concepts, ideologies and values as well as symbols in each of the media of communications. On a broader perspective, it is perhaps interesting to take special note of D. Devahuti's perception of the ancient cultural encounter between India and South East Asia. She wrote in part, "cultural exchanges and the synthesis of the original and the local is the overriding characteristic, and an ever-present theme in the story of India's relations with South East Asia, and the relations with each other, of the various countries in this vast region[4].

Considering that Magindanao was at the farthest end of the maritime trade and traffic routes in the South East Asian region (in that direction) and at the same time through various entrepots, we have here what we have just referred to as massive exchanges resulting from the dynamism of the cultures that came into "confirmation" yet enriching each other's experiences. We have, therefore, not merely contemporary witness of that encounter, but also beneficiaries of that enriching experience of our ancestors. We owe them a lasting debt of gratitude. It must not be forgotten, however, that these exchanges were both literal and symbolic in nature.

Sanskrit in Magindanaon

In very general terms, I discussed the role of trade and traffic in the movement of cultures, and among such cultural elements are language and literature[5] and art and iconography.[6] In this paper I would like to focus on a Philippine language, i.e., the Magindanaon. This is predicated on the recognition of the extent to which the Indian language could have penetrated into one which we can consider to be at the end of the route followed by the trade and traffic in the light of the extensive exchanges in the region (vide supra).

The wordlist gives a view of the extent of that incursion into the Magindanaon culture and society. It is not just a wordlist, but a comparative one, also to give further understanding of the extent of that trading of cultural goods in pre-colonial times.

Antecedent to discussing the words in the list, particularly some principles having to do with language borrowing especially the internal linguistic developments, I would like to devote a few lines on the possible date of the entry of Sanskrit words into Mangindanaon. The date of the influx of Indian culture into the Philippines had been more or less set on the basis of datable evidence[7]. These are images of significant religious works discovered in various sites in the country, and they belong to the period ranging from the 10th through the 13th centuries A.D. These had been corroborated by those adduced to be of the date of the introduction of the systems of writing in the country, i.e. from the 10th to the 13 th centuries A.D. These dates taken from archaeological as well as palaeographic data, if we could use the term by the discovery of an inscribed copper plate from Laguna, with date Saka era 822, which would fall within the first millennium in the Christian Era, i.e., 900 A.D[8]. Francisco (1995) subjected the inscription to a very close study. He analysed the inscription's social- political and legal implications in Philippines society and culture in the 10th century[9]. The language of the inscription is very much infused with Sanskrit. We are led to the view that Sanskrit, as seen through the intervening cultures, ie., Malay and Javanese, appeared to be the language by which these structures were understood.

These dates though very general in coverage could certainly encompass that of the influx into the Magindanao region, and indeed into Magindanaon culture and society, in this instance, and more specifically, Magindanaon language.

In examining the list which we have identified to be of Sanskrit provenance through the intervening old Malay and old Javanese, there is a recognizable pattern of exchange, if there be any, in terms of the phonological as well as in the semantic dimensions. These changes had been established by Jan Gonda in his magnum opus, *Sanskrit in Indonesia*.[10]

This was further revised in the 1973 edition. Juan R. Francisco (1964) presented more revisions in his study of Sanskrit in Philippine languages, and on to his works in 1973 and 1988.[11] These two later works, however, were primarily focused on Sanskrit words as they are identified in Maranaw and Tausog languages. There seems to have been significant changes from the patterns established in the 1964 work, where both phonological and semantic changes of Sanskrit words as they found themselves in Philippine languages were discussed extensively with chapter 1 forming the classification of Sanskrit words in Philippine languages. These are effectively illustrated if we examine the wordlist more closely in which all the principles of change, phonetic and semantic are discerned.[12]

Some Reflections on Pre-Islamic Trade and Traffic vis-à-vis the Presence of Sanskrit in Magindanaon

In a paper I presented before second International Symposium on Maritime Studes held at Pondicherry University, South India, in 1991[13] (later published in 1995), I had the occasion to write under the sub-title *Sri Vijaya and the Philippines*, particularly with reference to trade and traffic:

> The view that Sri Vijaya had political control over the Philippines at the height of its power between the 7th and 13th centuries A.D. has been the work of H.O. Beyer (1929)[14] and others who had dominated the Philippine history book writing industry in pre-1941 years to

the present time (Agoncillo and Alfonso 1948 and Agoncillo and Guerrero 1968)[15]. This view had been rejected in a paper, I published in 1961, but it still persisted in current textbooks on the subject.[16]

It is not however the purpose of this section of the present paper to devote on this very controversial view. Rather, Sri Vijaya is brought into the discussion in view of its role in the process of Indianization of South East Asia, in general and of the Philippines in particular.

While the view of Sri Vijaya Political control over the Philippines has been rejected with very strong evidences, the influx of Indian cultural elements certainly occurred at the height of Sri Vijaya's power, and such elements reached the Philippines via trade and traffic. In other words, the filtering of Indian elements at a period it is believed to have occurred was during the height of maritime interchanges between the peoples of South East Asia. The goods that were exchanged were not just material goods, but also the intellectual goods, like concepts having to do with the universe, belief systems, etc. The kind of power that Sri Vijaya was believed to have wielded at that time generated trade which expanded as far west as India [17] and as far north as China, with the Philippines providing the 'entrepot facilities' particularly between its capital in Palembang and the Southern Chinese ports. It must be understood, however, that Sri Vijaya was the entrepot, par excellence, between China and India.[18] Hence it may not be ill-considered to advance the view that the influx of Indian cultural elements into the Philippines was generated by the trade and traffic that emanated from/ through Sri Vijaya.

Our citation is rather long but this was done in view of our attempt at more clarity vis-a-vis the discussions on trade and traffic in the context of Magindanaon having been the recipient of language influx in pre-colonial times. As such, it cannot be ignored that one of the most important goods exchanged or adopted by a given locality in the process of trade and traffic was language. Sri Vijaya being highly Indianised certainly had the access to the language of the elite, that is Sanskrit...may have used it in various activities ritual as well as secular, including its main source of power, economic power, that is namely trade and traffic.[19]

It is inevitable that Sri Vijaya figures in our discussions here because it had a very important role in the trade and traffic between India and the point beyond, i.e., to the east and north to the Sulu Sea and to the western coast of Mindanao, and on through the South China sea towards Southern China. But in the context of that trading and commercial movements through the Sulu Sea to the Gulf of Mindanao on to the mouth of the Cotabato (Pulangi) River, brings us to the recognition that the role of the Magindanaon was certainly crucial to the commercial trading interchange on the coastal and along the riverine areas up to the headwaters of the river.

Sanskrit in Magindanaon is evidence to the pre-colonial trading and commercial movements. Of course, I do not argue that it is only the Sanskrit language that played an important role in the enrichment of Magindanaon. There are others like Arabic and Spanish, but I am looking at the period earlier than their advent in Mindanao. At this point in time the present generation is witness to that cultural as well as social enrichment of the Magindanaon language. Evident in this very important phenomenon in Magindanao history and culture is the fact that Sanskrit had contributed to the enrichment of other languages in the area, i.; Tausog and Maranaw, both of which had also been recipients of the enriching power of Sanskrit in all aspects including intellectual and social dimensions as well as religio-philosophical life.[20]

Concluding Remarks

This paper does not have a conclusion, because I recognize the fact that the search for the cultural identity and roots of the Philippines is a continuing activity; and that our attempt to discover elements of culture that had enriched Magindanao language is never ending. In terms of that recognition of the implications that such an influence in the Philippine languages, in general, and Magindanaon, in particular, "it is ..... acceptable that the period in Philippine pre-history as an age of emerging commercial interchanges between every active economies within the region and equally viable economies beyond the western seas, that is, beyond Mindanao Gulf and on to the straits of Malacca. I would not agree for a static Philippine economy during pre-colonial times. Rather, Philippine society was dynamic and pulsating contrary to the vew so successfully put forward by other students of Philippine society and culture.[21]

Magindanao as a part of the (Philippine) society was a direct participant in the state of dynamism and continuing pulsation contributing to the enrichment of equally dynamic and pulsating societies, generated by trade and traffic, in practically all aspects of its cultural and social history, in which language played a crucial role in that enrichment.

References:

1. Reynaldo C. Ileto, *Maguindanao, 1860-1888: The Career of Dato Uto of Buayan.* Data paper No. 82, South East Asia Programme, Department of Asian studies, Cornell University, Ithaca, N.Y., December, 1971, XI.

2. Thomas Forest, *A Voyage to new Guinea and the Moluccas, 1774-1776.* Kuala Lumpur: Oxford University Press. (Vocabulary of the Magindanao Tongue, 1969, pp. 389-400).

3. Juan R. Francisco, *Selected Essays in Mindanao Art and Culture,* Marawi City: Mindanao State University. (Mindanao Journal, vol. XIV, nos. 1-4), 1988, pp. 136-151; V. Raghavan, *The Ramayana in Greater India,* Surat: South Gujarat University, 1975

4. D. Devahuti, "India, Malaya and Borneo: Two Millennia of Contacts and Cultural Synthesis," *India's Contribution to world thought and Culture,* Madras: Vivekananda Rock Memorial Committee. 1970, pp. 509-532.,

5. Juan R. Francisco, "Tamil and Sanskrit in Philippine Languages: Reflections on Pre-Colonial Trade and Traffic", 2nd International symposium on Maritime Studies, December 15-20, Pondicherry University South India, 1991; Juan R. Francisco, *Maharadia Lawana,* Quezon City: Philippine Folklore Society., 1969.

6. Juan R. Francisco, *The Rama-Hanuman Bronze Piece from Manila, Philippines,* 12th Conference of the International Association of Historians of Asia, University of Hong Kong, June 24-28. (Unpublished, under revision), 1991.

7. Juan R. Francisco, "Tamil and Sanskrit", 1991.

8. Anton Postma, "The Laguna Copper Plate Inscription," *National Museum Papers* Vol. 2, No.1 Manila. Cf. Francisco, 1995, supra, 1991.

9. Juan R. Francisco, "Tenth Century Trade/Settlement Area in South East Asia: Epigraphic and Language Evidence in the Philippines," *National Museum Papers,* vol. V, No.2 (Manila), pp 10-33, 1995.

10 J. Gonda, *Sanskrit in Indonesia*, New Delhi : International Academy of Indian Culture. 2nd Edition (1973), 1952/1953.

11 Juan R. Francisco, *Selected Essays in Mindanao Art and Culture*, Marawi City: Mindanao State University. (Mindanao Journal, vol. XIV, nos. 1-4), 1988; *Philippine Palaeography*, Quezon City: Philippines Linguistic Society, 1973

12 Juan R. Francisco, *Indian Influences in the Philippines*, Quezon City: University of the Philippines., 1964.

13 Juan R. Francisco, "Tamil and Sanskrit in Philippine Languages: Reflections on Pre-Colonial Trade and Traffic", 2nd *International Symposium on Maritime Studies*, December 15-20, Pondicherry University, South India, 1991; K.S. Mathew, Editor, *Mariners, Merchants and Oceans; Studies in Maritime History*, New Delhi: Manohar, vide pp. 43-56, 1995.

14 Otley Beyer, *History of the Orient*. (with G. N. Steiger and C. Benitez). Boston: Ginn and Company, 1929.

15 Teodoro A. Agoncillo and Oscar Alfonso, *A Short History of the Filipino People*. Quezon City: University of the Philippines, 1958; Teodoro A. Agoncillo and Milagros Guerrero, *A Short History of the Filipino People*, (rev. ed.) Quezon City: University of the Philippines, 1968.

16 Juan R. Francisco, "Sri Vijaya and the Philippines: A Review," Philippine Social Sciences and Humanities Review, vol. xxvi, part 1 (March), Quezon City: University of the Philippines, 1961.

17 H. Otley Beyer and Jaime C. de Veyra, *The Philippine Saga*, Manila: Capital Publishing Company, 1952.

18 George Coedes, *Les 'Etats Hindouise d' Indonesie et d' Indochine*, Paris: Histoire du Monde. Tome VIII (An English Translation of this work had been published in 1968, Honolulu, Hawai), 1948.

19 Juan R. Francisco, *The Rama-Hanuman Bronze Piece*; 12th Conference of the International Association of Historians of Asia, University of Hong Kong, June 24-28. (Unpublished, under revision), 1991

20 Juan R. Francisco, "Sanskrit in Philippine Language and Literature," Studies in Indo-Asian Art and Culture, Vol. 2, New Delhi: International Sanskrit Conference, March 27-31, 1972.; Juan R. Francisco, "Sanskrit in Maranaw Language and Literature," Mindanao Journal, vol. I, No. 1, July - December, Mawawi City: Mindanao State University., 1974; Juan R. Francisco, *Selected Essays in Mindanao Art and Culture*, Marawi City: Mindanao State University (Mindanao Journal, vol. XIV, Nos. 1-4), 1988

21. Juan R. Francisco, "Tamil and Sanskrit in Philippine Languages: Reflections on Pre-Colonial Trade and Traffic", 2nd International Symposium on Maritime Studies, December 15-20, Pondicherry University South India, 1991; Juan R. Francisco, *Maharadia Lawana*, Quezon City: Philippine Folklore Society, 1969; Ibidem, *The Philippines and India: Essays in Ancient Cultural Relations*, Manila: National Book Store., 1971; Ibidem, "Indian Culture in the Philippines; Views and Reviews", Fourth Sri Lanka Endowment Lecture, Kuala Lumper: University of Malaya, October 18. (Reprinted in the Philippines in 1987), 1985.

A. Comparative Wordlist

MAGINDANAON	OTHER PHILIPPINE LANGUAGES	SANSKRIT	MALAY / OLD MALAY	JAVANES / OLD JAVANESE
ALAGA n.	price, cost, value, recompense, current value of a commodity	Mar. ARGA, price, cost. Tau. HALGA, Tag, ceb, HALAGA, price, cost, value, change	ARGHA, value, price	HARGA, value, price	HARGA, value, price
ANYAYA v.	to usurp, tc take Tau. possession by favour or without right	Tau. ANYAYA, persecute, grab, Tag. ANYAYA, to harm, destroy indolence	ANYAYA, unjust or harmful action	ANIYAYA, ANLAYA oppression, injustice, tyranny	
ATAWA	or		ATHAVA, either- or, rather	ATAU-ATAWA, either-or	ATAWA, UTAMA either-or rather
BAGI n.	share, portion, part	Mar. BAGI; Tau., Tag. BAHAGI, Share, allotment, section, portion, division, fraction	BHAGA (/bhaj), divide, distribute, allotment	BAHAGI, share, part, portion	BAGI, share, part, portion
BASHA BASA n.	sayings, idioms, way of speaking, language	Tau. BAHASA, Mar. BASA speech, language, dialect	BHASA, speech, language, any of the Prakrtic Languages	BHASA, language	BHASA, language

A. Comparative Wordlist

MAGINDANAON	OTHER PHILIPPINE LANGUAGES	SANSKRIT	MALAY / OLD MALAY	JAVANES / OLD JAVANESE
(BALA) BANSA — noble, or royal lineage, or distinguished family	Tau. Mar. BANGSA Tag. BANSA, people race, nation	VAMSA, lineage, race	BANGSA, BANSA race, nation	WONGSA race, nation
(BALA) DUSA adj. — sinful	Tau. DUSA, also Tag. Bik., Ilk., sin, crime, guilt, fault; mourning, grief suffering	DOSA, fault, sin, vice, guilt, crime	DOSA, sin, a crime	DOSA, sin
(BALA) GUNA adj. — beneficial, worthwhile worthy	GUNA, usefulness utility, worth value, use, applicability; Ilk. GUN GUNA, profit, benefit	GUNA, good quality merit, virtue	GUNA, benefit	GUNA, profit, benefit
A BLAHALA n. — idols, images regarded as god	Tag., BATHALA, supreme god	BHATTARA, lord applied to gods and to great learned men	BATARA, deity, divine ruler	BETARA, deity, divine ruler
(BALA) PUASA n., adj. — one who fasts, every fasting day, regularly fasting	Tau., Mar., PUASA to fast, to keep a religious fast, abstinence	UPAVASA, abiding in the state of abstinence	PUASA, fast	PUASA, fast

A. Comparative Wordlist

MAGINDANAON	OTHER PHILIPPINE LANGUAGES	SANSKRIT	MALAY / OLD MALAY	JAVANES / OLD JAVANESE
BANGSA BANSA, nationality, nation, tribe	vide supra under (BALA) BANSA	VAMSA, ibid.	BANGSA, ibid	BANSA, ibid.
BANIAGA, slave, alien	Tau. BANYAGA, chattel, slave, Tag., Ilk., BANYAGA, foreigner, Ceb. BALIGYA, commerce, trade & traffic, merchant	VANIJA, traffic, trade, commerce; VANIJIKA, merchant	BENIYAGA, BERNIAGA, WANIYAS, merchant, trader	BANYAGA, merchant, trader
BASA, BAHASA, syn. vide supra	ibid	ibid.	ibid.	ibid.
BENDAHARA, treasurer	Tau. BANDAHARA, title given by the Sultan to one of his worthy followers; Mar. BANDARA title of nobility	BHANDAGARA, treasurer; BHANDAGARIKA, treasury	BENDAHARA, royal treasurer, prime	BENDARA, master, chief, commandant captain

A. Comparative Wordlist

MAGINDANAON	OTHER PHILIPPINE LANGUAGES	SANSKRIT	MALAY / OLD MALAY	JAVANES / OLD JAVANESE
BIDADALI BIYADALI — fairy, angel, a female given by god to man who in his earthly life committed no sins.	Tau. BIRADALI, fairies beautiful human beings with wings; Mar. BIDARIA, MIDADARI, hour, angel, lady of God, beautiful lady in heaven	VIDYADHARI, a female of the class above supernatural beings, fairy, sylph	BIDIADARI, BIDADARI celestial nymph	WIDADAR, celestial nymph
BILANGGU — prisoner	Tag. BILANGGO, IIk BILANGGU, prison, fetters	Tamil, VILANGU, fetters, chains	BELENGGU, fetters, chains	
BINASA V. — to destroy, to lay waste, to render desolate, perish		VINASA, annihilation, decay	BINASA, ruination, ruined	BINASA, destroyed lost
BISA — potency, effect, the effectiveness of something, esp. medicine, poison	Tau. BISA, sharpness or sting, effectivity of medicine; deadly, poisonous, noxious; Tag., Mar., Ceb. BISA, poison, effective	VISA, poison, venom, anything active	BISA, venom, venomous	WISA, venom, venomous

A. Comparative Wordlist

MAGINDANAON	OTHER PHILIPPINE LANGUAGES	SANSKRIT	MALAY / OLD MALAY	JAVANES / OLD JAVANESE
BITIALA — conversion, speech, settlement of dispute	Tau. BICHARA, speech talk, discuss; Mar. BITIARA, speech dialogue	VICARA, deliberation, reflection	BICARA, deliberations	WICARA, deliberation, reasoning, speaking
DALUWAKA — evil doer/person, wicked, one who frequently does evil of any kind	Tau. JAHULAKA, cruel, unkind, pitiless, malicious, also DRAKHA, DAHULAKA, to give false testimony, treachery, betrayed	DROHAKA, injury, perfidy, treachery	DURHAKA, treachery, treason agaist a ruler or state; DERHAKA, disobedience to lawful authority	DORAKA, crime, sin offense, disloyalty
DEWA DIWATA DEWATA — spirit, god	Tag. DIWATA, spirits, goddess, nymph; Mar. DIWATA, water spirits, Ceb. DIWATA, godhead	DEVATA, divine beings, divinity	DEWATA, minor or mythological godhead	DEWA, minor or mythological godhead

A. Comparative Wordlist

MAGINDANAON	OTHER PHILIPPINE LANGUAGES	SANSKRIT	MALAY / OLD MALAY	JAVANES / OLD JAVANESE
DUSA	sin	Tau. DUSA, sin, crime, guilt, fault, Tag, Bik., Ilk, DUSA, mourning, grief, suffering	DOSA, fault, vice, sin, guilt, crime	DOSA, sin, a crime	DOSA, sin
GADYA, GAGYA	elephant	Ilk, Tag., GADIA, (could be) elephant; Mar. GADIA, bishop in the chess game; Ceb., Tau., GAJAH, elephant	GAJA, elephant	GAJAH, elephant	
GALAGALA	resin, mixture of resin, oil and lime to fill cracks of small boats, pitch for roofing	Tau. GULA, thick sweet syrupy substance extracted from sugarcane; Mar. GOLA, SUGAR; Ceb., Tag., Ilk. GULAMAN, Sweet jelly	GULA, raw, unrefined sugar		GULA, sugar
GALAHANA GALANA	eclipse	Mar. GARAHANA, BARAHANA eclipse, seizure of the moon	GRAHANA, seizure of the moon, eclipse of the sun or moon	GERHANA, eclipse of the sun or moon	GRAHANA, eclipse of the sun or moon

A. Comparative Wordlist

MAGINDANAON	OTHER PHILIPPINE LANGUAGES	SANSKRIT	MALAY / OLD MALAY	JAVANES / OLD JAVANESE
GULO, teacher	Tag. GURO, Tau, GURU, teacher of esoteric knowledge, teacher	GURU, spiritual teacher or preceptor	GURU, teacher	GURU, teacher of Islamic studies.
GUNA, beneficial profit	Tau. GUNA, usefulness, utility, value, worth; Ilk., GUN-GUNA, profit	GUNA, good quality, merit, value	GUNA, benefit	GUNA, benefit, profit
CUNSI, key, lock	Tag. KUNSI, bolt, latch; Mar. GUSNI, key	KUNCI (KA), key	KUNCHI, key-hole, lock	
(KA) BINASA, destruction, perishing to perish		VINASA, annihilation, decay	BINASA, ruination, ruined	BINASA, destroyed, lost
KALUNIA, grace	Tag. KALUNIYA, mistress compassionate	KARUNA, pitiables; KARUNYA, compassion, kindness		KARUNA, distress, weeping
KAMUDI, steersman, one who guides the boat	Tau. KAMUDI, guide	KAUMUDI, a guide	KEMUDI, KAMUDI, rudder	KAMUDI, rudder

A. Comparative Wordlist

MAGINDANAON	OTHER PHILIPPINE LANGUAGES	SANSKRIT	MALAY / OLD MALAY	JAVANES / OLD JAVANESE
KAPALA	head	Tau. KAPALA, master, leader, head, as head of an organization	KAPALA, skull, head	KAPALA, KEPALA head	KAPALA, head
(KA) SULGAN	glory, heaven	Tau. SURGA, SHAGRA, Mar. SURGA, heaven, glory	SVARGA, the abode of light, and the gods of heaven	SURGA, heaven	SWARGA, SWARGI, SUWARGA, heaven
KUTIAPI	a two-stringed lute	Tag. KUDYAPI, Ilk. KODIAPI, Ceb. KUDYAPI Blk. KODIAPE, lute	KACCHAPI, lute		KACCHAPI, lute
KUTIKA, KATIKA	time	Mar. KOTIKA, time	GHATIKA, Indian clock, time	KETIKA, KOTIKA, time, season	
LAGYA	king	Tag., Ceb., RAJA, Mar. RADIA, king	RAJA, king	RAJA, king	RAJA, king
LAKSA, LAKSAN	million, one million	Tag. LAKSHA, ten thousand; also Tau., Hil., LAKSHA	LAKSA, one hundred thousand	LAKSA, ten thousand	LAKSA, ten thousand

A. Comparative Wordlist

MAGINDANAON		OTHER PHILIPPINE LANGUAGES	SANSKRIT	MALAY / OLD MALAY	JAVANES / OLD JAVANESE
LANSUNA	onion	Tag. LASONA, Ilk. LASUNA, Tagb. KESUNA, LANSUNA, onion	LASUNA, RASUNA one of the ten kinds of onions		
LASA	sense	Tag. LASA, taste, savour Ceb. LASA, to season, spice	RASA, taste, flavour, lust for flesh, sentiment, feeling		RASA, taste, meaning, feeling
LISA	nit, eggs of the lice	Tag. LISA; Ilk LIS-A; Ceb. LOSA, nit	LIKSA, louse		LINSA, nit
(MA) BISA	effective	Tag., Tau., Ilk. Mar. BISA, deadly poisonous, noxious	VISA, poisonous, venom, anything active	BISA, venom, venomous	WISA, venom, venomous
MA(HA) LADIA	Maharajah, title of the 3rd ranking official in the sultanate of Sulu; also subordinate ruler	Tag..., Tau., Ilk. Mar. MAHARDIA, MAHARADIA, RAJA, RADYA, LADYA, king, monarch	MAHARAJA, great king; RAJA, king	RAJA, king	RAJA, MAHARAJA king

A. Comparative Wordlist

MAGINDANAON		OTHER PHILIPPINE LANGUAGES	SANSKRIT	MALAY/OLD MALAY	JAVANES/OLD JAVANESE
MALISA	black pepper	Mar. MARISA, pepper, black pepper; Ceb. MALISA, pepper	MARICA, pepper, kind of occinum	MERICA, pepper, shrub	
MANIKAM	jewel, garnet, also egg cell	Tag. MANIK, glass beads	MANIKA, gem, jewel, precious stone, pearl	MANIKA, precious stone; also MANEX, MANIK	MANIK, precious stone
MANTELI Also MANTIRI	adviser of the datu, minister of the state	Tau. MANTILI, MANTIRI minister of state	MANTRI, minister	MENTERI, hereditary minister of state	MANTRI, minister
MANSULA	man, the human being	Tau. MANUSIYA, human being, mankind; Tag. MANUSIA, idol, spirit	MANUSYA, human, mainly, human being	MANOSIA, human, mankind, person	MANOSA, human being
MARDIKA	free	Tau., Mar. MAHARDIKA, free as a people, country; TAG. MAHARLIKA, a free man, noble	MAHARDDHIKA, rich, he who, has talent or knowledge; freeman	MARDAHIKA, free, liberated	MAHARDIKA, priest, learned man; MARDIKA, free, freeman

429

A. Comparative Wordlist

MAGINDANAON		OTHER PHILIPPINE LANGUAGES	SANSKRIT	MALAY/OLD MALAY	JAVANES/OLD JAVANESE
MUNTIA also MUTYA	an amulet, pebbles, stone that causes an enchanting effect for the owner, charm, pearl	Tag., Ceb. MUTYA, Ilk. MUTIA, pearl, gem precious stone, Mar. MONTIA, Jewel, gem; Tau.MUCHA, pearl	MUTYA, MUKTA, MUKTIKA, pearl	MUTIYA, MUTTA pearl, mother of pearl	MUTIARA, pearl
NAGA	dragon	Ceb., Mar., NAGA, serpent, dragon	NAGA, serpent	NAGA, dragon mythical serpent	NAGA, large serpent, dragon
NARAKA	hell	Tag. NERAKA, Mar. NARAKA, hell, sinner	NARAKA, hell	NARAKA, hell, infernal regions	NARAKA, hell
PAHALA	reward, merit	Mar. PAHALA, use, value	PHALA, benefit, enjoyment, compensation, reward, fruit	PAHALA, reward, merit	PAHALA, id.
PALIHARA	to govern, to keep in order, to take charge, manage	Tag. PALIHARA, to protect	PARIHARA, defending protecting, preserving	PELIHARA, to attend, to take care of	

Sanskrit in Magindanaon: Implications on Pre-Islamic Trade and Traffic

A. Comparative Wordlist

MAGINDANAON		OTHER PHILIPPINE LANGUAGES	SANSKRIT	MALAY / OLD MALAY	JAVANES / OLD JAVANESE
PALIK(E) SA, also PALISA	enquiry, examine	Tag. PARIKSA, PREKSA, Mar. PERIKSA, Tag. PALIGSA, examine, enquire, to probe, competition between contestants	PARIKSA, scrutinize, examine, inspect	PEREKSA, PARESA, enquiry, investigations	
PANA	bow for shooting arrows	Tag.; Bik.' Ilk., Mar., Ceb., PANA, bow and arrow	BANA, arrow	PANAH, arrow archer's bow	
PANDAY	workman, craftsman	Tau, PANSAY, one who has special skill or talent, PANDET apt, clever, skillful; Tag., Ilk., Bik., Ceb., PANDAY, blacksmith, mason, carpenter.	PANDITA, wise, learned	PANDEY, PANDEI, skillfull, learned	PANDE, skillfull learned
PANDITA	religious person, leader, scholar	Mar, Tau. PANDITA scholar, priest	PANDITA, wise learned	PANDITA, sage, doctor of laws	

431

A. Comparative Wordlist

MAGINDANAON	OTHER PHILIPPINE LANGUAGES	SANSKRIT	MALAY / OLD MALAY	JAVANESE / OLD JAVANESE
PUASA, day of fasting, fast	Tau., Mar., Ceb. PUASA, fast, religious fast, abstinence,	UPAVASA, abiding in the state of abstinence	PUASA, fast	PUASA, fast
PUGI, eulogy, praise, appreciation admiration	Tau. PUDJI, glorify, praise, honour; Tag. PURI, praise, honour, fame	PUJA, honour, worship, adoration	PUJI, praise, honour, adoration	PUJI, honour, praise
PUTELI PUTLI PUTERI, A name always used to address a queen, princess	Tau. PUTLI, princess, feminine name; Mar. FOTRI, queen, princess; Ceb., FUTLI, maiden, virgin	PUTRI, daughter	PUTERI, princess	PUTRI, daughter of a prince
SALSI, witness	Tau., Tag., Ilk., Bik., SAKSI, witness, testimony, evidence	SAKSI, the office of any legal witness, testimony, attestation	SAKSI, witness	SAKSI, witness

A. Comparative Wordlist

MAGINDANAON	OTHER PHILIPPINE LANGUAGES	SANSKRIT	MALAY / OLD MALAY	JAVANES / OLD JAVANESE
SALAKSA	ten thousand	Cf. LAKSA, LAKSAN, supra.	id.	id.
SALIPADA	title of a pandita	Tau. SIRIPADA, king of Sulu (pigafetta)	SRIPADA, holy feet, honourific title	SERIPADA, royal feet, a royal form of address	SERIPADA, id.
SANDALA	a low caste, a low condition of life.		CHANDALA, class of outcaste; CANDALA, son of a sudra by a brahman mother		CANDALA, impure
SANDIATA	weapon, arms, pertaining to evil	Tau. SANJATA, SINJATA, firearms, deadly weapons; Mar. SANDIATA, weapons, arms of any kind; Tag. SANDATA, id.	SANYATTA, prepared, ready	SENDYATA, SENJATA, weapons of war of any kind	SENJATA, ready, armed; weapon, esp. rifle
SASANA	to instruct	Mar. SASANA, to have confidence on, to rely	SASANA, religious or scientific instruction; charter, royal edict, any written book, scripture for teaching or instruction		

A. Comparative Wordlist

MAGINDANAON	OTHER PHILIPPINE LANGUAGES	SANSKRIT	MALAY / OLD MALAY	JAVANES / OLD JAVANESE
SATUL SATULAN — to play chess, a game called chess	Mar. SATORAN, chess game; SATARI, game, chessman; SATUR, chess, chess play	CATURANGA, the limbs of the army: elephants, chariots, cavalry, infantry; a kind of chess, the game of chess.	SATUR, chess or chess-like game	CATUR, id.
SAUDALA — a form of address used by a datu to another datu; brother	Mar. SAUDARA, friend, chum, pal, sweetheart, brother	SODARA, brother, born of the same womb	SUDARA, SAUDARA brother, sister	SAUDARA, id.
SIKSA — to punish, punishment	Mar. SIKSA, chastisement; Tau. SIKSA, to punish physically or mentally, pertaining primarily to punishment by God.	SIKSA, punishment, chastisement	SEKSA, SIKSA agony, punishment, torment	SIKSA, punishment, tormment, agony
SIPA — a kind of a game using a ball made of woven rattan and kicked to hit the manggis (prize); kick	Bik., Mar., Tag., SIPA, to kick, a game using a ball made of rattan	KSIPA, throw, cast away; to kick	KSEPA, football made of woven rattan	KSEPA, id.

A. Comparative Wordlist

MAGINDANAON	OTHER PHILIPPINE LANGUAGES	SANSKRIT	MALAY/OLD MALAY	JAVANES/OLD JAVANESE
SUALA, voice	Tau. SUWARA, sound of voice. word message; Mar. SUARA, heavenly voice	SVARA, voice	SUWARA, SUARA, voice, sound	SUARA, sound, voice
SUTLA SUTRA, silk, thread used by Muslim to weave fine cloth	Tag. SUTLA, Ceb. SUKLA, silk, silk thread	SUTRA, thread, string, silk	SUTERA, silk	SUTRA, silk
SUTLI, holy	Tau. SUCHI, clean, undefiled, chaste; Tag., pamp. SUSI, clean, neat, pure. Of. Ilk. SUDI, holy, clean	SUCI, clean, pure, undefiled	SUCHI, pure, neat innocent	
UTALA, wind, air from land or mountains, land breeze, north east wind	Tau. UTTARA, north, strong north wind, north monsoon season; Mar. OTARA, north east monsoon.	UTTARA, higher, upper, northern	UTARA, month	UTARA, wind northeast

435

3. SUSPECTED SANSKRIT WORDS IN MAGINDANAON

ANGKA,	estimation	LALAWA,	spider
ANTAL,	to something far by chance, to hit by a projectile	LAWALAWA,	sap, resin
		LITA,	guide
BIDAK,	pawn, a piece in chess game	PADUMAN,	
BINASAKTI,	the milky way, constellation	PAMALITIALA,	believer
BUTA,	blind	PAMITIALA,	to convince, to persuade
DARANGEN,	a chanted story, epic song	SAMAYA,	promise
KUDA (Tamil),	horse	SUPAMA,	
KASAPAKAT,	friendliness	UPAMA,	if, for example
KASUMBA,	pink	TUMBAGA,	copper
LAGA,	young woman, virgin	SIWAKA,	special category of bride price in a wedding
LAGIA,	the seven starts which are said to effect the 24 hours of the day, i.e., sun, moon, venus, mercury, earth.		

BIK — Bikol
Ceb. — Cebuano
Ilk. — Iloko
Mar. — Maranaw

Pamp. — Pampango
Tag. — Tagalog
Tagb. — Tagabili
Tau. — Tausog

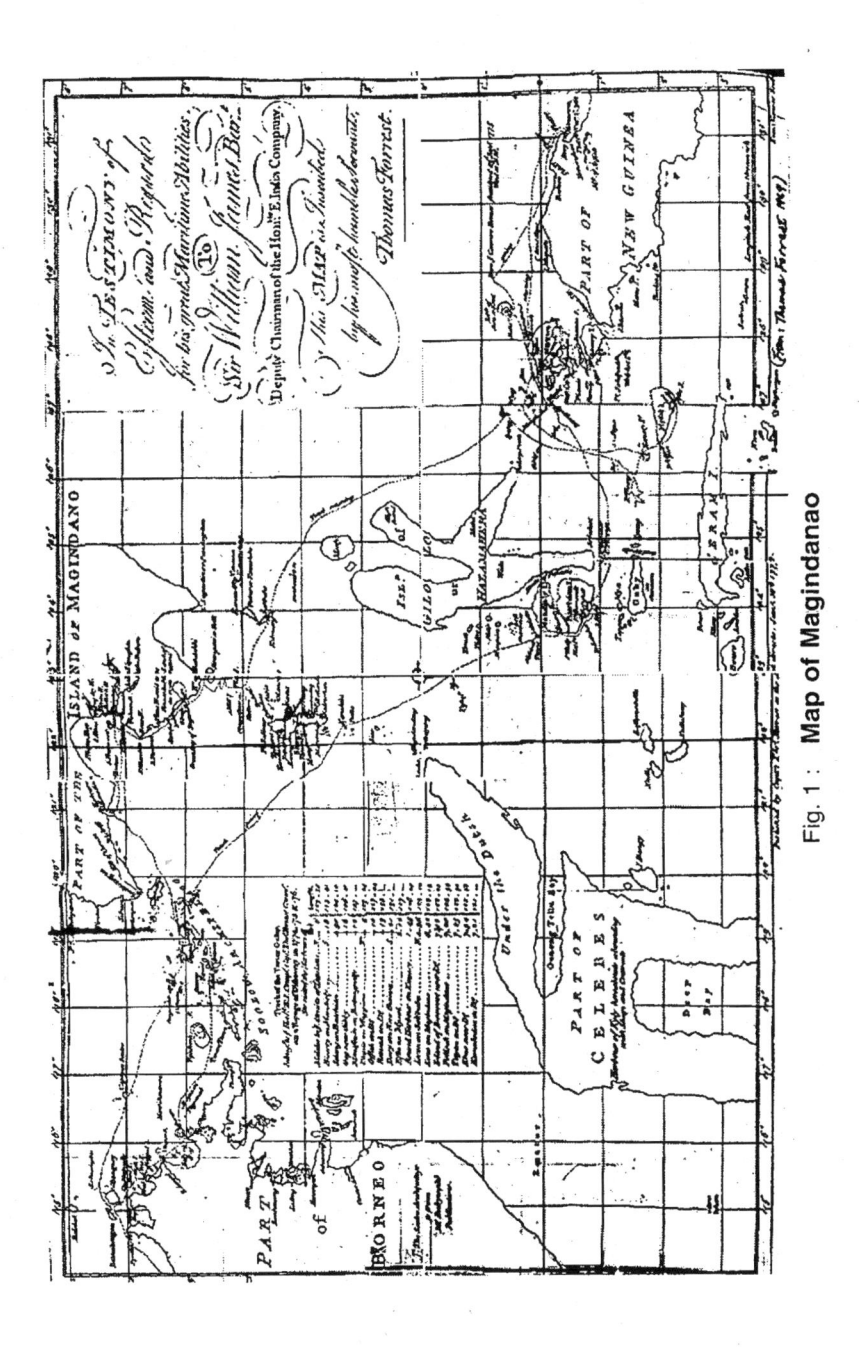

Fig. 1: Map of Magindanao

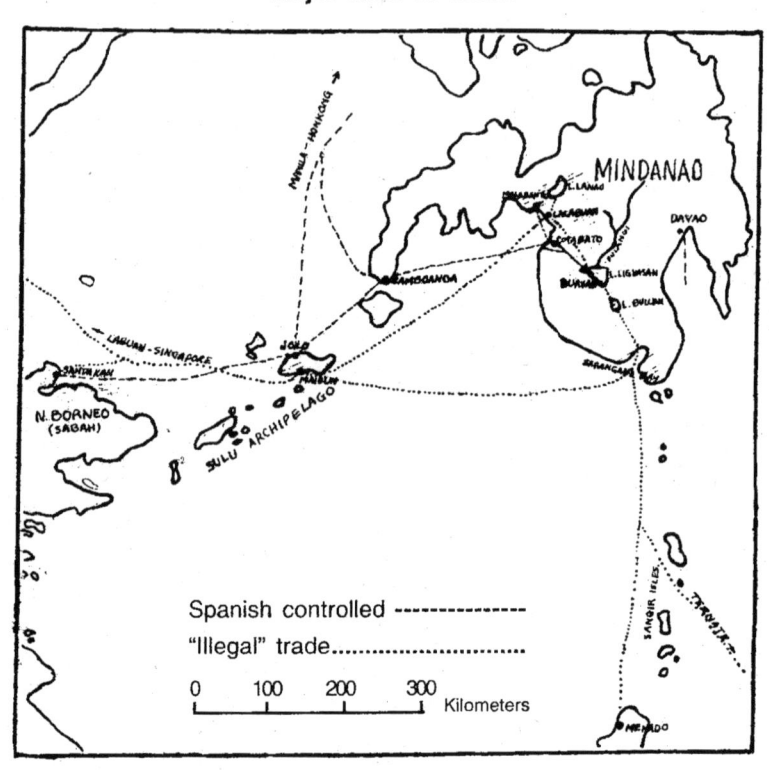

Fig. 2 :
Major lines of trade.

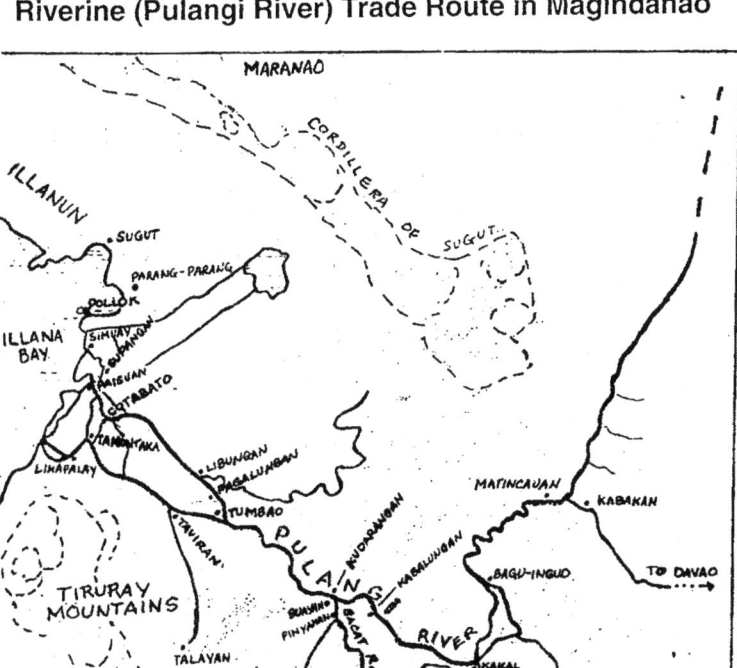

Fig. 3:
Riverine (Pulangi River) Trade Route in Magindanao

(Ileto 1971: Map II, p. xii)

28

INDIA AND GREECE : A CULTURAL, HISTORICAL AND LINGUISTIC SYMPHONY

Francis Arakal

The attempt in this paper is only to suggest that the two cultures, civilisations and philosophies of India and Greece are not as independent of each other as many Indians and Greeks seem to assume. The suggestion here is that the kinship between the Indian and Greek peoples is both ancient and deep. Those who look upon the Greek culture as the matrix of Western civilisation and also those who try to understand Indian culture as of purely Eastern origin should do further exploration to see to what extent the Greek civilisation had been shaped by Indian elements that came into contact with it, as well as how the classical cultural development of India at its best in the seven centuries from 330 B.C to 350 A.D. had been triggered by contact with Greek civilisation and culture. This paper attempts to provide fresh thought and to help see new relations. These aspects are highlighted in order to encourage Indians and Greeks to take a greater interest in each other.

The contact between India and Greece seems to have begun even before the invasions of Alexander (B.C. 4th Cent). There was a royal road from Magadha to Taxila from where it got bifurcated to China and Europe. Alaxander got the information about India through the mercenary communities. This cultural interaction between India and Greece increased during the period of Chandraguptha, Bindusara and Asoka.

B.A. Salatore in his historical work '*Pracina Karnataka*' refers to the Kannada dialogue mentioned in a Greek drama of papyrus scroll (of A.D. 2nd cent) found from Oxyrhynus in Egypt. The plot is based on a shipwreck on the western coast of India wherein was a Greek lady being rescued by her brother. Nevertheless the fact that the interaction between India and Greece during the beginning centuries of Christian era is beyond doubt.

There are ever so many references to the Greeks in the puranas. A good example for this mingling and symphony can be seen in the field of astronomy. In fact the Rasi division is closely related to Greek system. Each Rasi was named on the basis of its form and shape eg. the Rasi 'Aries' which is so called due to its shape of 'goat' - (Erraos).

Mesa	Erraos	Aries
Rsabha	Tauros	Taurus
Mithuna	Didimos	Gemini
Karkataka	Karkinos	Cancer
Simha	Leon	Leo
Kanya	Parthenos	Virgo
Tula	Zigon	Libra
Vrscika	Scorpios	Scorpios
Dhanus	Toxotes	Sagittarius
Makara	Aigokeros	Capricornus
Kumbha	Udrokos	Acquarius
Mina	Ixtis	Pisces

Varahamihira in his '*Horasastra*' (of 5th Cent A.D) describes the synonyms of the Rasis which were all taken from the Greeks. " Kriya - Tauru - Jithuma- Kulira - Leya - Parthona - Juka - Korpyakhya: Tauksika - Akokora - Hudroga - Certhasi - Kramasah " (*Horasastra* 1-8)

Sanskrit (Skt.)   **Greek (Gk.)**

Kriya   Krios

Tauru   Tauros

Jithuma	Didimos
Kulira	Kolouros
Leya	Leon
Parthona	Parthenos
Juka	Zugon
Korpi	Skorpios
Tauksika	Toxotes
Akokera	Aigokeros
Hudroka	Hidroxoos
Irthasi	Ixthis

Apart from these, there are other terms like 'Hora' (Gk. *Hore*) (interpreters say that it was shortened form of A-hora-tra), Kendra (Gk. *Kendron*), drekanam (Gk. *drekanos*), Lipta (Gk. *lipte*), Anabha (Gk. *anaphe*), sunabha (Gk. *Sunaphe*), dhurudhura (Gk. *dorythoria*), Kema druma (Gk. *Khrema thismos*), Vesi (Gk. *Phases*), Panaparam (Gk. *epanaphora*), apoklima (Gk. *apoklima*), Trikonam (Gk. *Trigonos*), Mesuranam (Gk. *Mesuranama*) - all these terms might closely be linked with and borrowed from Greek system.

The cultural similarities between Indians and Greeks in Homer reflect the common heritage of our peoples. Though Homer had heard the name of India, he confused it with eastern Ethiopia. Certain gods in Homer bear names derived from the same roots as their Indian counterparts: the Greek Ouranous is the Sankrit Varuna, Zeus is Dyaus 'Sky'. The similarities in their names and in some of the myths about them bear witness to a period when the Indian and Hellenic peoples had not yet separated. Homer mentions several items which come from India, particularly tin and ivory. The Greek names for these articles are similar to Indian ones. The availability of Indian luxuries produced economy-draining enhancement in the life style of the wealthy classes.

While appreciating the fragrance of the cultural heritage of India and Greece, the affinity of their roots, the sharing of the fragments of commonality - one has to look into the phase of intervention made by the Byzantine emperor, Justinian I. The emperor spoke Greek with a bad accent. He was called 'the Great', because many of his laws were directed against Pagans who were forbidden to teach any subject whatsoever. Justinian expelled pagan teachers from the once famous schools of philosophy at Athens. Along with other pagan schools, in 529 he closed the Academy at Athens which was founded by Plato in 387 B.C. The whole period between the end of Classical civilization and the revival of learning in the 15th century, came to be termed 'the Dark Ages'. The use of the term implied an exclusive respect for Classical standards in literature and art and a corresponding disparagement of all that was achieved between the decline of ancient culture and the work of Renaissance scholars, writers and artists.

The Greek revival in the 18th century roused a desire to reappropriate the whole abandoned provinces of mundane energy, and a hope to emulate antiquity in works of living loveliness and vigour. For a generation nursed in scholasticism and stereotyped theological formulas it was the fountain of renascent youth, beauty and freedom, the shape in which the Helen of art and poetry appeared to the ravished eyes of medieval Faustus. The rise of the Romantic movement coincided with the discovery of the kinship of Sanskrit, Greek and Latin. In the words of Sir William Jones: "The Sanskrit language, whatever be its antiquity, is of a wonderful structure; more perfect than the Greek, more copious than the Latin, and more exquisitely refined than either, yet bearing to both of them a stronger affinity, both in the roots of verbs and in the forms of grammar, than could possibly have been produced by accident."

The inflexions of Greek with the categories of number, case, person, tense, and aspect, mood, voice have their closest equivalents in Sanskrit. Indo-Iranian and Greek inflexions together with an extensive cognate vocabulary justified a reconstruction of Indo-European (EB. 10852). Sanskrit 'dadhami' is Greek '*tithemi*' (*Tionmi*), '*epheron*' (*eoepov*) = Sanskrit '*abharam*'. The Greek '*patrasi*' (dative plural of *pater*) corresponds to the Sanskrit locative *pitrsu*, even in respect of the accent (EB. 10.855). Nouns and adjectives of the type "*dusmenes*" "ill-affected" = Sanskrit *durmanah dispirited* exist only in Greek and Sanskrit (Wright 1912, 208). The suffix 'ti' was almost as productive in Greek as in Sanskrit compare : Gk. *dosis*. Sanskrit *datih*, Gk. *stasis*: Skt. *sthitih*.

The discovery of the genetic affinity of Sanskrit and Greek was the opening up of the voices of ancient minds at their noblest, the magnificence of the depths of the Indo-European soul, transparent and intoxicating in its purity and maturity. The vast gamut of the development of languages gave rise to the idea of evolution without any necessity for miraculous interposition or supernatural interference with the laws of nature. In 1816 Franz Bopp compared the conjugation system of Sanskrit, Greek and others *Ueber das Conjugations-system der Sanskrit-Sprache in Vergleichung mit jenem der griechischen, lateinischen, persischen and germanischen Sprache*. Thirty-six years later, in 1852 appeared the Sanskrit Woerterbuch, which interpreted the entire linguistic inheritance of Sanskrit, and established the concept of development in human speech. It was followed in 1859 by the monumental work of Charles Darwin (1809-1882) who soundly established the theory of organic evolution in his *Origin of Species*. Comparative philology of Sanskrit, Greek and other languages thus gave birth to a new scientific *Weltanschauung* of organic evolution wherein slow first steps led to a critical threshold that opened new ways in human thought.

In the fourth century B.C. the Greek philosopher Euhemerus propounded that all myths were of historical origin and that the gods were men who had performed great exploits. The Euhemeristic view was limited because of its extreme position, till the discovery of Sanskrit, Greek mythology as a fragment of metaphors and dreams, pages torn from the album of Cleo. With the rise of Comparative Philology and Comparative Mythology it became possible to sift and interpret the several strands that wove the magnificent fabric of Greek myths: natural phenomena, origins of the universe, gods, men and animals, heroic legends and historical events, demons and monsters, the mystical and allegorical elements, the artistic and ethical parameters that gave rise to creative symbolisation in a galaxy of mythologies. The collective Greek appellation of the gods was Vedic deva. The Sanskrit word clarified the conception of the gods as light (root div 'to shine') and their connection with heaven (div). The omnipresent Greek god Zeus was Vedic 'Dyaus' ('sky'). "What was at first only an appellative of the sky has here become the supreme ruler of the gods dwelling in the serene heights of heaven, who gathers the clouds, who wields the thunderbolt, and whose will is law." (Macdonell 27 - 28). (The concept of Earth as mother and of Heaven as father (Skt. Dyaus pitar, Gk. Zeus Pater, Latin Jupiter) was common to Vedic and Greek mythology. The name of Ushas 'dawn' is derived from the root *vas* 'to shine' and is cognant to Gk. *Eos*. The Gk. Helios is allied to the Vedic. Surya to whom ten entire hymns are devoted in the Rg Veda trita, who is impelled by Indra to slay the demon in the Rg Veda phonetically corresponds to Gk. *Tritos*. The Gk. *pheguai* is identified with the ancient tribe of *Brgus* as fire priests (Weber, ZDMG. 9. 242). The *Brgus, Angirases* and Atharvans are spoken of together in the Rgveda. The Angirases were higher beings intermediate between gods and men, attendants of Agni, who is so often described as a messenger between heaven and earth. They may possibly have been personifications of the flames of fire as messengers to heaven. This view is borne out by the etymological connection of *angiras* with the Greek angelos 'messenger'. They are the angels of English.

Dionysius was one of the most important deities of Olympus. He was the son of Zeus and the Theban princess Semele. He discovered the vine and became the god of wine and also that of ivy, that plant whose perennial hardiness may be taken as a symbol for the continuity of life. He is said to have travelled as far as India, in the midst of a triumphant procession. He was a god who loved joy and merry tumult. The maenads danced to the sound of his flute. The maenads were maid servants of Dionysius and followed him in procession or else accompanied him dancing, intoxicated by mystical passion. (Devambez 1966: 163, 277). That Dionysius travelled to India is an ancient Greek indication of his links with our country. The maenads dancing to the tune of Dionysius remind of the Gopis indicated with mystic passion on hearing the flute of Krishna.

Synthesis of Indian and Greek forms occured in the Gandhara statues of the Buddha. The statues were drawn to Classic proportions following Hellenic models for physiognomy, gestures and drapery.

A relief depicting the Descent of the Buddha from the Trayastrimsa Heaven has stylistic parallels to the Arch of Galerius in Thessalonika (Ackerman 1975:12-13).

Access to India

Classical Greece gained direct access to India through the Persian Achaemenid empire. Greeks served in the Indian province of the Achaemenid dominions. The two Greek authors, Skylax and Ktesias, were Achaemenid servants. Meanwhile Indians in the army of Xerxes were on Greek soil, as well. Greeks came into contact with Buddhism in the reign of emperor Ashoka (3rd century B.C.) Eusebios (4th century A.D.) reports that an Indian discussed philosophy with Socrates in Athens. The generalised resemblance between the Brahman of the Upanishads and the arche of the Greek is striking. The doctrine of metempsychosis seems to have been derived by the Greek Orphics, Pherekydes, Pythagoras, Empedokles from India. The casual link between a person's current social status and his good or evil deeds in previous existences is found only in India and Hellas. "According to Diogenes Laertios, Pythagoras (6th century B.C.) was the first person in Greece to teach metempsychosis as a metaphysical idea." (Sedlar 1980: 270)

Orpheos is believed to have lived before Homer. By the 4th century B.C. Plato could refer to the doctrine of metempsychosis as "ancient tradition". The practice of abstention from meat-eating was imported from India. Like the Indians, Plato claimed that animals and human beings possess the same soul.

The Greek sceptic philosopher Pyrrhon, who is said to have accompanied Alexander to India found Indian ascetic practices instructive. Reminiscences of the physical endurance of the Indian ascetics circulated widely in the Hellenistic world. The legend of Alexander and the Brahmins testifies favourable Greek disposition towards Indian ascetics and their wisdom. "India served as an object upon which educated Greeks projected their own demoralization, namely their loss of confidence in contemporary Greek culture and institutions. Thus India became an idealized country, abundantly fruitful, while Indian philosophers came to possess a wisdom superior to that of the Greeks." (Sedllar 1980 : 302)

With the invasion of India by Alexander, cultural interflow began. The memory of the historic horse of Alexander lives on in Punjab. Local peasants still venerate a Buddhist stupa near Rawalpindi as its tomb where Alexander founded a city named Bucephala in his charger's honour. Nearchos (about 312 B.C., as quoted by Strabo born c. 50 B.C) refers to the use of writing material in India from well-beaten cotton cloth. It is the earliest reference to rag-paper in India. Megasthenes, the Greek amabasador at the court of the Maurya emperor, Chandragupta, wrote an extensive account of the life and customs of India. The town of Sirkap near Taxila had a typical Greek layout. Ai Khanum was a genuine Greek city. Menandros, the Greek king of Bactria, appears in the Budhist scripture, Milinda-panha 'Questions of Milinda', as a devout Budhist.

Numerous coins inscribed in Greek are found all over north west India, while Greek inscriptions have been discovered in Bactria which have been discussed by Louis Robert in his paper 'De Delphes a l'Oxus'.

The ethnical term *Yavana*, or *Yona* in Middle India, occurs for the first time in the Rock Inscriptions of Ashoka, II, V, XIII. The *Yonas* comprise here evidently the peoples of the five kings: Antiochos, Ptolemaios, Antigonos, Magas and Alexander, i.e. Syria, Egypt, Macedonia, Cyrene, Epirus or Corinth respectively. Inscriptions of Ashoka written in Greek and Aramaic have been discovered at Kandahar. They are the easternmost locations where Greek inscriptions are found.

The Besnager Inscriptions datable to the first century B.C. was dedicated by Heliodoros, the son of Dion, who was the ambassador of Antialkidas of Kashipura Bhagabhadra. A number of inscriptions from the caitya-hall of Karli (Ist cent. B.C.) contain the ethnicon *Yavana*. These *Yavanas* donated pillars, cisterns, dining halls and other items to the Buddhist community. The *Yavanars* are mentioned in the early Tamil literature. The oldest testimony is in *Pura 50. 16-21* which describes the *Yavanas* as importers of wine. *Pura 343, 1-10* explains the import of western gold. (Zvelebil 1956: 401 - 410)

The Periplus of the Erythraen Sea of the first century A.D. describes the ports and specific products imported from India into the Classical world. It speaks of Proklais (from Pukkhalavati, Puskalavati) as a great trade emporium of Gandhara and as famous for its steel. The Pahlavi *polavaten* as well as New Persian *pulad* for steel is an adjectival noun from Middle Indian *pokkhalavata* from the name of the town of Pokkhalavati (mod. Charsadda). Like the Silk Route, a steel Route must have linked India and Greece via Iranian lands. The Gypsies must have taken this Steel Route as itinerant iron - smiths in continuation of age-long traditions.

In a list of articles for which there was a ready market at Barygaza, the Periplus says that the king would buy "good looking virgins for concubines" and the way it is put indicates a 'standing order' in that market (Tarn 1951:374). Kalidasa represents the king as accompanied by Yavana women. Poseidonius says that Eudoxus shipped 'flute-girls' for his attempted voyage to India round the Cape in the end of the second century B.C. "In the third century Ptolemy II was importing Indian girls into Egypt along with Indian dogs and cattle". (Callixenus in Athen. 5.20 Ia) The name of an Indian courtesan of sensual beauty at Alexandria is preserved as: *Jalantas-candra-capala*, that is, "shimmering as the reflection of the moon upon the waters", a name as rapturous as must have been her figure. So I leave you in this rapture, in liquid silence, and let the hymns go to sleep.

Conclusions

The symphony of art, literature, culture, architecture, myths, languages, philosophy etc, between India and Greece is marvellous. Grousset calls India: *l'Inde, cette Greece excessive*. In Greece everything tends to harmony. Greek mathematics and geometry concentrate on the finite and the measurable. With India it is different. Everything is immense, sublime and infinite. Counterparts to the Iliad and the Odyssey are to be found in the form of poetic continents, with tens of thousands of verses. In Greece, the world is always brought back to the measure of man. In India, man strives to adapt himself to a phantasmagoria of universes beyond the horizons of the mind. Its intention is to provide fresh thought and help see new relations and to encourage Indians and Greeks to take greater interest in each other in the Indo-European studies.

Select Books

1 John Marshall, *The Buddhist Art of Gandhara, The Story of the Early School, its Birth, Growth and Decline*, Cambridge (The University Press), 1960.
2 Jean W.Sedlar, *India and the Greek World, A Study in the Transmission of Culture*, Totowa, N.J (Rowman and Littlefield), 1980.
3 O.Stein, *Yavanas in Early Indian Inscriptions*, Indian Culture 1(3), Culcutta.
4 N.W. Tarn, *The Greeks in Bactria and India*, Cambridge (University Press), 1951.
5 Balasubramaniam (ed), *Freedom Progress and Society*, MLBD, Delhi 1986.
6. Joseph Wright, *Comparative Grammar of the Greek Language*, Oxford, 1912.

III

INDIA AND ASPECTS OF EUROPEAN EXPANSION

29

ORIENTALISM, OCCIDENTOSIS AND OTHER VIRAL STRAINS: HISTORICAL OBJECTIVITY AND SOCIAL RESPONSIBILITIES

Teotónio R. de Souza[*]

In Defence of Multicultural Diasynchrony

This essay was originally prepared for a manual of "contemporary thought" of a Portuguese University where I head a Department of History. This is to explain why the footnote references are so very often to Portuguese editions of the works that could have been cited in their English versions. I beg therefore the understanding of the readers of this English version of the essay, which may also suffer from some "lusitanized" syntax! The aim of the essay is to call attention to the multicultural diasynchrony, and to express my sympathy for those who are worried about the more visible consequences of the western "modern" thought pattern which is proving itself increasingly destructive to the Western society, as it is witnessed by the growing male infertility, more mad cows, cloven-hoofed victims of foot-and-mouth disease, and the more casualties of the uranium-based explosives in Serbia and Kosovo! This is my note of protest against the hard believers in the "progressiveness" of the "western thought" that is taught in the West simply as "contemporary thought", while it is no more than *euro-american* occidentalism with Greco-Roman roots, but proclaimed as world heritage. It leaves us with the impression that the West retains the monopoly of thinking and representing the rest of the humanity. It could well be true, but a sad distortion of reality for those who are aware of the perceptions and priorities of the Eastern world. For the East the rational "thinking" hardly allows to reach the "reality". Few in the West would doubt about the *universal* validity of their rational skills that serve them well to justify their biases. I will not be surprised if these biases would consider this essay as a "romantic" defence of the "oriental" wisdom!

I wish to call the attention of the readers to what I mean by multicultural *diasynchrony* of the human mind. I wish to do it with references to the challenges posed by the Eastern cultures. To begin, I have chosen to deal with a present day problem concerning the dialectic heterogeneity and the western unwillingness or inability to dialogue. The Eastern cultures tend to value more the *intemporality* of the unconscious and hardly display much interest in the synchrony or diasynchrony, because they are wary of them all, looking upon them as variants of the *avidya* of the thinking "I".[1] It is so with the Indian Buddhism, which later passed on to China and to Japan, transforming *Jnana* into *Ch'an* and *Zen* respectively. It is this Eastern wisdom, and not the rational "thought" of the West that sustains more than half of the humankind in the East, despite the repeated thought aggressions of the West in the recent history of the East.[2]

Besides the affirmation that there exist other polarities of human thought and with their own characteristic qualities, the East has its reasons and experiences to question the usefulness of the western thought as a "surplus value" that the West has to offer. Does it not lead rather to an impoverishment of cultures that value more the *totality of their lived experience,* possible only through *nirvana* ou *satori*, or through the freeing of the conscious "I" and his thoughts, which are responsible for the "scientific" fragmentation of the unity of the reality, perpetuating thereby the *maya* and the illusions of ego-centrism? This profound difference is illustrated well by the fact that the western psychology limits itself to distinguishing normal mind from the

453

neurotic mind, measuring the normality in terms of the capacity of the individual to *adjust itself to the society* and by its *productive capacity* in the world. There is no great concern about the adjustment of the individual to himself or herself, within a wider cosmic harmonization, that is seen as essential for the well-being of a person in the East.[3]

It is not possible for me in this short essay to list or to describe all, or even the more important diachronic synchronies or synchronic diachronies that have accompanied the evolution of the peoples and nations along history. What I wish to repeat is that the contemporary thought is essentially "diasynchronic". It is a complex philosophical heritage, a co-existence of various philosophies of various times and cultures, whose background and origin is not always sufficiently known to us. Little is known, for instance, about the importation of *sidhantas* or the mathematical and astronomical knowledge from India to Europe as a result of the Islamic expansion, allowing Europe to correct the Roman calendar and to measure time with a greater precision. Aryabhata (Fifth century A.D.) is a better known figure of ancient India for his treatise *Aryabhatiya,* written in 499 A.D.)[4], wherin he collected information previously known in India about mathematics (*ganita*), measurement of time (*kalakriya*) and geography (*gola*), calculated the solar year as consisting of 365.358 days, differing from our year by only 7 seconds. Aryabhata had no doubts that the earth was spherical and his calculations of earth's diameter as 8,316 miles was almost correct. The Chinese mathematician Ch'ung Chi (430-501), who gave us a more precise reading of *pi* before the European renaissance studies, was a contemporary of Aryabhata. The concepts of fractions, algebra and geometry seem to have originated in Mesopotamia and reached India quite early through commercial contacts. But the Indians went further and invented "zero" (*shunya* = emptyness)[5], represented initially by a dot, in order to convey with brevity the millions of years of their creation myths.[6] It was through the Arabs, specially the more famous Abu Jafar Mohammed ibn Musa al-Khwarizimi (780-850), whose name remains linked to *algorythm,* that Europe came to know the Indian numbering style and the decimal system, which reduced enormously the *Latinorum penuria* (poverty of the Latins) at the close of the first millenium.[7] India seems to have recovered today its traditional talent to play maths! This is becoming evident from its recent technological advances, and particularly the international admiration and demand for Indian software programmers in the Sillicon Valley of U.S.A. More recently even Germany, China and Japan have been alluring Indian collaboration in computer programming. In Germany the interest of its Government in modifying its immigration policy to invite several thousand Indian software programmers raised the hackles of the political opposition and trade unionists, leading to an almost racist campaign in German media against the Indians. It only revealed the inability of many Germans to accept that kind of assistance from India without feeling humiliated. It is precisely this kind of situations that will denounce in the near future in an increasingly ugly manner the crisis of multiculturalism in the West.

2. *Orientalism and Occidentosis*

This is the problematic of the dialectic heterogeneity with little capacity to dialogue. The East has always lived multiculturalism with a manifest reciprocity,[8] while the colonial habits of the West to limit its capacity to engage in cultural reciprocity based upon mutual respect.[9]

We could not turn to another aspect of diasynchrony. It concerns Time as methaphor of History. It can help us to clarify little better the prejudices of the "orientalist" constructions. James Mill (1773-1836), Scottish philosopher, historian and economist, was a pioneer of the English Utilitarianism. He wrote a History of British India, wherein he makes no secret of his lack of regard for the Indian notion of time and chronology. He denounced the concept of cyclical time as characteristic of primitive people who were unable to distinguish between history and myth.[10] Obviously, such a concept of time would not serve to glorify the English intervention as a radical rupture in the history of the subcontinent. However, those who are familiar with the *jyotishastra* literature and know of the importance given in Ancient India to horoscopes to determine the *muhurta* (propitious moment) for important decisions of personal, social or political nature, will hardly consider Hindu *yugas* as a creation of ingenuity as Mill did. Ancient India utilized a variety of concepts of time: *kalpa, mahayuga,* e *manavantaras* were categories of cosmological time in *Dharmashastras* and corresponded to some extent of modern geological eras with a very extended notion of time. But already in the epic *Mhahabharata* and in the mythological and dynastic accounts of *Puranas* we come across the use of other variants of time, such as genealogical and dynastic categories. Various eras were created, such as *Vikrama* or *Samvatasara* (58 a.C.), *Shaka* (78 d.C.), *Kalachuri* (247 d.C.), *Gupta* (319 d.C.), etc. corresponding to the emergence of States and the need of registering their major events with greater precision. But all these continued to utilize the wider context of the cosmological time. The utilization of linear historical time with greater consciousness of dates was promoted by the Buddhist *sanghas,* which gave much importance to *Mahaparininirvana* or to the death of Budha.[11] We may conclude that different concepts of time have nothing to do with "primitivism" of a society, but only with the complexity of their time perceptions. In the West, the so-called "New History" of the mid-twentieth century started paying attention to the "diasynchrony" of structures, conjunctures and phenomena, as well as to the existence of various types of time cycles![12]

Leaving aside the cultural dialogues of the past and its continuity in the contemporary diasynchrony, we will restrict our analysis to the relationships of power and of dominance that emerged from the European expansion of the XVI century, of the so-called "Discoveries." They gave rise in the West to the "complex" of superiority and paternalism in relation to "other" peoples.[13] It is almost impossible nowadays to accompany any analysis of the society without taking into account these relationships of the colonial past. This happens, because the structures of power, created during the colonial times are still in place, although hidden by the international organizations and cultural relationships controlled subtly by the neo-liberal capitalism. Are we in the era of globalization, or in an era of "hidden" agendas?

It should not surprise my readers if the nature and limitations of my training and experiences, I concentrate predominantly upon the Asian concerns, inviting the reader to confront them with the manifestations of the western thought and praxis. Happily, there are some points of convergence and cases of cultural dialogue. I have mentioned the eminent western psychoanalyst C.G. Jung, but there was also another western psychoanalyst of great fame, born in India, namely Wilfred R Bion (1897-1979), whose familiarity with the oriental wisdom led him to develop his theory and pschoanalytic practice of contact with "O", (Hindu OM) that can only be *lived* and never sufficiently *known*.[14]

Not to claim too much originality for my considerations about cultural diasynchrony, I wish to refer to some Asian voices that had some echo in the West since the middle of the last century, or rather, since Asia entered in the era of decolonization and claimed the right to say to its former colonizers what it thought about their ways. The main intention of the Asian reactions was to help its own people to reflect upon their new responsibilities, in order to avoid the mistakes of the past, particularly the mistakes that had made them easy victims of colonial manipulation. Among such voices we have the Indian, K.M.Panikkar (1895-1963), an Iranian, Jalal Al-i Ahmad (1923-1969) and a Palestinian Professor at Columbia University in USA, Edward Said (1935 -).

K.M. Panikkar, studied at Oxford, was a trained historian, and occupied the chairs of Vice-Chancellor of various Indian Universities till the end of his life. As a statesman he was Minister of Foreign Affairs of the Princely States of Patiala and Bikaner before India's independence. He was a close collaborator of Jawaharlal Nehru in shaping India's foreign policy and became an architect of India's relations with the Republic of China. He published many historical works, but the book that earned him international fame was *Asia and Western Dominance* (London: George Allen & Unwin Ltd., 1953), which provoked the academic world and caused heartburns among several former colonial powers.[15] The author was conscious of the pioneering nature of his analysis. He stated in the concluding lines of his Introduction: "This is perhaps the first attempt by an Asian student to see and understand European activities in Asia for 450 years".[16] Panikkar pointed out two chief factors of the European success in Asia, namely, its technological and naval superiority, and its strategy of cultural penetration through the missionary agencies, chiefly through the Society of Jesus.[17] His final evaluation gave credit to the Asiatic peoples for their capacity to resist the cultural assaults of the West and advised them to improve their technical means and defences.

Jalal Al-i Ahmad was a teacher from the countryside. He was a militant of the Tudeh party, and acted as its political analyst and propagandist. However, his publications were not always of political nature. His vast literary output includes fiction and anthropological studies. He abandoned politics in protest against the incapacity of the Tudeh party to criticise the policy of the Soviets regarding Azerbaijan at a time when the autonomous government of that republic was forced out of power by the armed forces of Iran. He was not very systematic in his thinking, but compensated for it with originality and with his pungent style – and with his *hadisaju'i* – or his permanent search for change. The University of Tehran had invited him to coordinate a project of anthropological studies, but he left after publishing 5 volumes. He disagreed with the criteria of research that were dictated and which he considered as Western. He had discovered *gharbazadagi* or "occidentosis", a perspective that distinguished him from the rest of the Iranian intelligentsia, with a sole exception perhaps of the Iranian sociologist and writer Ali Shari'ati (1933-1977). Owing to State censorship, only a part of his *Gharbazadagi* was published in a monthly magazine. His complete analysis of the historical conflict between Islam and the West was circulating in manuscript versions and was published only in 1978, that is, after the fall of the Shah regime[18].

His analysis is not confined to Iran, but covers the whole of Asia and Africa under the Western capitalist domination.

Here follow some samples of his understanding of "occidentosis":[19]

I speak of "occidentosis" as of tuberculosis. But perhaps it more closely resembles an infestation of weevils. Have you seen how they attack wheat? From the inside. The bran remains intact, but it is just a shell, like a cocoon left behind on a tree. At any rate, I am speaking of a disease: an accident from without, spreading in an environment rendered susceptible to it. Let us seek a diagnosis for this complaint and its causes — and, if possible, its cure.

"Occidentosis has two poles or extremes – two ends of one continuum. One pole is the Occident, by which I mean all of Europe, Soviet Russia, and North America, the developed and industrialized nations that can use machines to turn raw materials into more complex forms that can be marketed as goods. These raw materials are not only iron ore and oil, or gut, cotton, and gum tragacanth; they are also myths, dogmas, music, and the higher worlds. The other pole is Asia and Africa, or the backward, developing or non-industrial nations that have been made into consumers of Western goods. However, the raw materials for these goods come from the developing nation: oils from the shores of the Gulf, hemp and spices from India, jazz from Africa, silk and opium from China, anthropology from Oceania, sociology from Africa. These last two come from Latin America as well: from the Aztec and Inca peoples, sacrificed by the onslaught of Christianity" (p. 27)

"And we know that the vanguard of colonialism is the Christian missionary. Beside every trade mission around the world they built a church, and by every sort of chicanery they drew the indigenous people into that church". (p. 32)

"To follow the West – the Western states and the oil companies – is the supreme manifestation of occidentosis in our time. This is how Western industry plunders us, how it rules us, how it holds our destiny. Once you have given economic and

459

political control of your country to foreign concerns, they know what to sell you, or at least what not to sell you. Because they naturally seek to sell you their manufactures in perpetuity, it is best that you remain forever in need of them, and God save the oil reserves. They take away the oil and give you whatever you want in return – from soup to nuts, even grain. This enforced trade even extends to cultural matters, to letters, to discourse." (pp. 62-63)

"Most of our intellectuals, those who have made their way into the leadership apparatus of the country, see it as their moral duty to serve ultimately as interpreters for the Western advisors, as administrators and executers of their decisions and goals." (p. 90)

Some other Asian intellectuals also proved their capacity to analyse critically the social and political situations of their peoples. *Batililasma Ihaneti* (A Treason called Westernization), is comparable to *Gharbazadagi*. Its author, a Turkish intellectual, Mehmet Dogan, brought out several editions since 1975, but none is known outside Turkey. The reason is not difficult to gauge. Jalal Al-i Ahmad was lucky for having participated in the VII International Congress of Anthropology and for being invited by Harvard to lecture in 1965. The vision of Jalal Ali-i Ahmad is today represented in Iran by its President Khatami, who seems to have pacified the West with his opposition to fundamentalist extremists and by defending freedom of the press, but he also raises many questions in the Western minds by his appeals to "Asian convergence" and to new ways of dialogue between the living cultures of Asia and the West with a view to put an end to a unipolar domination and hegemony of the West.[20]

Edward Said is better known in the West for his vigorous denunciations of "Orientalism", by which he seeks to explain how Europe constructed the image of the East in order to legitimise its imperial activities and global domination. His starting point is that European orientalisms convey more about Europe than about the East in itself. These constructions of the West are based on methods of field observations and tools of analysis developed as colonial praxis.[21]

Many will be convinced that nothing much has changed since the declared end of colonialism: The European hegemony has not ended with the lowering of the imperial flags. The mechanisms of colonial exploitation continue operating, though without the same visible forms of the past. We need to admit however that the conditions in which we now live are substantially different from those of the last century. In the West itself we see the currents of counter-illuminism and postmodernism that reject the basic concepts of the Lights of the modernism which constituted the foundation of the "orientalist" project. But despite the dissident voices,[22] the new postmodernist and neo-pragmatic trends, as represented Rorty, S. Fish, J. F. Lyotard, or J. Baudrillard, offer to the hegemonic forces an open field for creating a "reality of consensus" by manipulating public opinion.[23] Despite the recent economic crisis of Asiatic "tigers", Asia continues to advance and proclaim ever more challengingly its strategies for economic development against the objections of the western liberal democrats. The Asian powers keep reminding the West of the economic strategies that led them to power during the colonial era, particularly in the initial phases of their industrialisation and modernization. They do not seem to be overly concerned with the Western cries of urgency about the environmental dangers. They prefer to remind the West of its responsibility for the damage done by it to the environment during centuries of its industrial growth and the on-going damage of consumerist behaviour. The Asian powers see the Western concern as eco-colonialism.[24]

The Asian people wish to work out their modernization on the basis of their own analysis of Westernization that was forced upon them during the colonial rule and continues to be forced through new mechanisms of globalization. The Asian powers tend to reject the European model of globalization as unhelpful for their development. They manifest their increasing disillusionment with the impoverishment to which the Western model of development subjects the cherished cultural values of Asia.[25] If the West exploited the East as the "Other" for constructing its own modern cultural identity, as emphasized by

Edward Said, the East too claims the right to do the same for defending and recovering its own cultural heritage. There is a tendency to view the West as a decadent society, characterized by Christian individualism, disintegrating family bonds, decline of social solidarity and exploitation of democratic discourse under covers of the "civil society" and the role of "NGOs" to continue its control and manipulations of the "periphery". Against this, the Asian leaders talk about the "Asian Values", implying respect for the family and community, which they look upon as a guarantee of good functioning of political power, dispensing from the Euro-American models of democratic participation with eyewash elections and manipulations of mass media.[26]

What the western critics point out as political authoritarianism and as a violation of human rights in Asia, is explained and justified by the leaders of Asian countries as a way to guarantee the pace and rhythm of their technological modernization, without subverting their traditional cultural values. The capacity of the Asian leaders to influence their masses utilizing emotional appeals to cultural values seems to irritate the political and economic interests of the West, whose "democratic" rationalizations and categories of "thought" are strange to the cultural experiences of Asia and do not have the same mass appeal. That is why the West sees ghosts of "fundamentalism" everywhere, while failing to see the "market fundamentalism" at home. Obviously it is not on its list of definitions of fundamentalism.

The process of globalization seems to be escaping from the control of its own initiators. This certainly worries the West and forces it to seek a more agreeable and mutually profitable alliance with select Asian countries. It does not happen with Africa in general. The West recognizes Asian capacity to demand a new type of relationship based on cultural reciprocity and free from the past Orientalist tendencies. Globalization could be more positive and less discriminatory for the Asian countries if cultural pluralism and the values thereof were respected worldwide. It needs to be an interactive pluralism which respects the traditional identities and loyalties, going beyond any strategic tolerance and displaying ability to learn from the "Other".[27] Is it generally accepted that in the past centuries Asia has not experienced only a negative treatment. It is admitted with some reluctance by both sides that there have been mutual benefits. On the Asian side this reluctance is caused by its awareness of the inequality of such benefits and by the cultural disruptions caused by the Western missionary activities in the Asian social fabric, which has always been regarded as profoundly religious and deeply philosophical.[28]

3. Cultural Multiversity: A World Heritage

What are concretely the post-Orientalist challenges? In the new global world order inaugurated at the end of the Cold War, we can observe the rise of new nationalisms, a resurgence of the extreme right-wing politics in the West and a religious fundamentalism, "a rather curious development, which none of the sharpest social thinkers of the 19th century had predicted".[29] The emergence of China as a regional power, the attempts to India, with its nuclear capabilities and other resources to claim what it considers its rightful place in the Indian Ocean,[30] leave open the door for many possibilities. In the meantime, the European Union, the U.S.A. and other rich countries of the West are worried with increasingly low rates of population growth, leaving them increasingly more dependent upon immigrant labour. The former colonial powers face difficulties of economic, social and cultural integration of the immigrant ethnic groups coming from their former colonies and elsewhere.[31] Racist tensions and xenophobic reactions are becoming ever more common in the West. What could be a solution? A capitalist management of the crisis tends to opt for quick solutions and with least compromises. According to the Egyptian economist Samir Amin (1931-), what the capitalist management proposes presently is "Latin-americanization" of East Europe and the creation of more active peripheries (China, Southeast Asia, India and Latin America), but always subservient to the advanced capitalism of the West.[32]

It is very important and urgent for the society to engage itself in a calm and critical reflection upon the nature and implications of multiculturalism, including its long-term benefits. It is a duty of the philosophers to help preparing the public opinion for an inter-cultural dialogue and to present an alternative to the capitalist management of the crisis of multiculturalism. The capitalist monocultural solutions only propose fictitious dialogues in their policies of integration.[33] It is a challenge to the philosophers and they should take it up with enthusiasm, not only to prove the relevance of their profession, but even to ensure its survival. The illuminist project of modernism sought to convince people that there were rational solutions for every problem, but we are realizing ever more that in human affairs, and this is particularly clear in the context of cultural conflicts.

It is within the competence of philosophy to clarify the meaning of culture, including its ongoing struggle to determine its goals and its values in changing historical contexts. It is also a task of philosophy to assist individuals in their "intra-cultural protests", namely, in their *critical appropriation* of the traditional vision of their culture, making an allowance to the possibility, and at times even the necessity of mutual exchanges among cultures. It would be a mission of a philosophy of interculturalism to formulate ethical principles for the practice of intercultural exchange, for recognizing the *true* value of a culture with its specific vision of the world in its specific *material environment*. It would be important also to place the intercultural dialogue in the context of the human rights, such as the right for cultural *multiversity*, a parallel to the natural biodiversity as heritage of mankind.[34] The fulfilment of this philosophical mission would create anti-bodies of resistance to neo-liberal market philosophy, reducing thereby the violations of the rights of cultures to preserve their material environment to ensure the quality of life of the majority of their people.

It is also important to make it clear that the tradition of Human Rights is not a monopoly of the West. We have well known cases of the western capacity to violate human rights on a big scale, both numerically and in terms of brutality. The tradition of human rights belongs to *human* history which presents innumerable cases of persons who struggled and sacrificed their lives to fight oppression and injustice in different parts of the world and in different world communities. All these communities have their perception of injustice and their *memory* of liberation. It is on this basis of a *pan-human identity* that we need to recall those who fight for the survival of the great masses of peoples in their respective cultures and against the atrocities of the monoculturazing trends that the philisophy of interculturality should formulate its project of solidarity with cultures.[35]

Western Pluralism falls short of Multiculturalism

There have been efforts to find solution to the differences between the East and the West. But unlike what I wish to propose as a *practical* philosophy of interest (*inter-esse* = to be with, in solidarity with) in promoting an intercultural dialogue of solidarity, the past attempts to have rarely left the academic cocoon or the professorial chairs. Leibniz sought to create a philosophy that would include what was essential for all the major religions and philosophies of the world as a way to reduce the religious wars that were destroying Europe. He thought that he could link Europe and China which he admired greatly. The French encyclopaedists and Quesnay also laboured in the same direction.[36] In the mid-20th century (1939), in an international conference of Philosophy at Hawaii, G.E. Moore proposed in his inaugural address a "universal philosophical synthesis", expressing an urgency to create a world vision of a world order in which the cultures of the West and of the East could get along harmoniously.[37]

Another version of universalism was in vogue in the middle of last century, and one could find its definition in the works of F.S.C. Northrop[38] and C.G. Jung.[39] Both defended "complementarity" as the key for mutual understanding between the West and the East. There is no question of fusion of the differences, but what is considered vital is the recognition of specificities of each side, particularly the spirituality as characterizing the East and the scientific rationalism as characterizing the West.

This model of complementarity has been criticised by the deconstructionists who have regarded it as a simplistic and naive "essentialization" of the East and the West, as well as a discriminatory binary discourse, unfavourable to the Asian thought and reflecting a polarization of the gender discourse which tends to look down upon the female gender. The East is characterized as having the qualities generally associated with the female gender, such as intuition and passivity, in contrast with the rationality and dynamism of the male West.

More recently, there has been a new variant of the universality model as presented by Francis Fukuyama in his book "The End of History". The liberal democracy of the West and the market economy are presented as the only viable alternatives for the modern society anywhere in the world. He defends that the new technologies of information do not permit self-isolation of any country; new trends fly rapidly to every nook and corner of the globe and are adopted rapidly at thousands of kilometres away from the source of their origin. These changes are seen as providing autonomy to individuals and as powerful democratizing forces.[40] Ten years after having defended this thesis, and after having observed the economic crises of Asia and Russia, as well as the conflicts in former Jugoslavia, in Ruanda, in Somalia and other spots in the world, Francis Fukuyama remains convinced of his thesis, excepting the new challenges in the area of biotechnology. He admits that the new tools of social engineering could lead to the end of human beings, initiating a new post-Human era.[41]

Some Eastern visions

Despite criticisms, the universalist model of dialogue had its admirers among the Eastern intellectuals. One of them was the Indian philosopher and statesman S. Radhakrishnan. He proposed his neo-Hindu version of universalism. Hinduism is known for its tolerance and eclectic vision. Radhakrishnan preached spiritual unity of mankind. He wished nothing less than a truly cosmopolitan philosophical and religious discourse, which could help bringing about a cross-fertilization of ideas and intuitions, and could bring about a global society with a global religion in which individual beliefs and religious traditions would be respected as multiples branches.[42] In his conferences at Oxford in 1927, Radhakrishnan alerted to the dangers of conflicts provoked by dislocation of peoples, caused by the imperialist and racist policies of some countries. Radhakrishnan proposed a "Hindu solution" which consisted in recognizing the entire humanity as one extended family in which all ethnic groups had their right to live and mix, safeguarding their identity and right for self-development. In this context, and without ignoring the need of reforming the abuses that keep creeping into the social structures, Radhakrishnan tried to explain how India invented the system of castes, in which every new social group could be integrated and still preserve its identity and continue to contribute to the well-being of the others. This system avoided the need of ethnic cleansings.[43] Radhakrishnan was not the first Indian to come out with a universalist discourse in the recent times.

The first Indian Nobel prize winner in 1913, Rabindranath Tagore (1861-1941), the *gurudev* (just like Gandhi their *mahatma*), was a staunch defender of universalism and a harsh critic of narrow nationalisms, which he regarded as a plague of the humanity. At a time when the Indian nationalist radicals were becoming to gain the upper hand and were threatening the colonial authorities with violence, the message of Rabindranath Tagore must have come as a music to the colonial ears! It is not surprising therefore if the British proposed and supported his candidature for Nobel prize. It was also a historical context which gladdened the British hearts to see Gandhi arriving on the Indian political scene with a model of non-violent struggle. Only the personal talents of Gandhi without the strategic collaboration of the British, would not have sufficed to transform him into a national leader. It suited the British interests to prefer Gandhi to the radicalism of Savarkar and Tilak, and to catapult him as a representative of all Indians![44]

The philosophy of Rabindranath Tagore evoked much international interest at a time when the world was under clouds of global conflict of the World Wars. He founded a University with a peculiar pedagogy which sought to alert the young people against the cult of nationalism. In his book of short stories *The Home and the World* [*A Casa e o Mundo*], Nikhil represents the genius of the Poet, and Sandip, a fanatic nationalist and member of *Swadeshi* movement, is made to realize the following as the only real way out of dangers: "The history of mankind is made up of united efforts of many races of the world. Forgetting this for narrow political gains can only lead the country to a dangerous situation. I know that Europe, deep within itself does not admit it, but it has no right to teach us. Those who die for Truth become immortal, and if the whole people would die for the Truth, it too will achieve immortality in the history of mankind."[45]

Tagore travelled widely, till U.S.A. and Japan, crossing the European continent and Asia, and left a "diary of a westward journey" and reflections on "nationalism". I shall cite here only a few passages that reveal the capacity of the poet and the mystic to observe critically and to express his reflections on multicultural differences, without beating about the bush. He lashes out particularly against the Western gift of "Nation", as a source of all modern conflicts and mass sufferings:

"We have to consider that the West is necessary to the East. We are complimentary to each other because of our different outlooks upon life which have given us different aspects of truth. Therefore if it be true that the spirit of the West has come upon our fields in the guise of a storm it is all the same scattering living seeds that are immortal. And when in India we shall be able to assimilate in our life what is permanent in Western civilization we shall be in the position to bring about a reconciliation of these two great worlds. Then will come to an end the one-sided dominance which is galling."

"When I was in America, I had felt like one imprisoned in the stone fortress of its extreme efficiency, of its bleak maturity. That day I saw clearly there was nothing so deplorable as the business of accumulation. The business magnate thinks he can defy the ever-moving quality of the universe, but nothing can last, if not to-day, tomorrow everything will be swept away.

The current that has in a whirlpool caused solid heaps to accumulate in places, is the same current, which in its incessant flow will finally set them afloat and draw them into the blue ocean; the hearth of the earth will become healthy. The creative strength that is at play on earth is greedless, it is detached, and is not miserly; it does not allow accumulation, its path to creation is obstructed by hoarding; it wants to keep its leisure free of all impurities to express eternally the ever new. The greedy man turns up with his paraphernalia, and in order to guard them he engages millions of fettered slaves to build up colossal store houses.... Imprisoned within these blind material hoardings, and faced with the colossal belchings of the machine, I spent some time, feeling suffocated in the poison-ridden atmosphere of suspicion that lacked hospitality. It was then that I heard on the path outside these dark, dense walls, the footsteps of the eternal traveller. The rythmic beat of these footsteps struck a chord in my blood, it echoed in my meditation. I knew clearly that day, that I was a comrade of that traveller."

"It is the continual and stupendous dead pressure of this inhuman upon the living human under which the modern world is groaning. Not merely the subject races, but you who live under the delusion that you are free, are every day sacrificing your freedom and humanity to this fetish of nationalism, living in the dense poisonous atmosphere of world-wide suspicion and greed and panic. I have seen in Japan the voluntary submission of the whole people to the trimming of their minds and clipping of their freedom by their government, which through various educational agencies regulates their thoughts, manufactures their feelings, becomes suspiciously watchful when they should show signs of inclining toward the spiritual, leading them through a narrow path for the complete welding of them into one uniform mass according to its own recipe. The people accept this all pervading mental slavery with cheerfulness and pride because of their nervous desire to turn themselves into a machine of power, called the Nation, and emulated other machines in their collective worldliness.

"You, the people of the West, who have manufactured this abnor-mality, can you imagine the desolating despair of this haunted world of suffering man possessed by the ghastly abstraction of the organizing man? Can you put yourself into the position of the peoples, who seem to have been doomed to an eternal damnation of their own humanity, who not only must suffer continual curtailment of their manhood, but even raise their voices in paeans of praise for the benignity of a mechanical apparatus in its interminal parody of providence? Have you not seen, since the commencement of the existence of the Nation, that the dread it has been the one goblin-dread with which the whole world has been trembling?.... The Nation, with all its paraphernalia of power and prosperity, its flags and pious hymns, its blasphemous prayers in the churches, and the literary mock thunders of its patriotic bragging, cannot hide the fact that the Nation is the greatest evil for the Nation, that all its precautions are against it, and any new birth of its fellow in the world is always followed in its mind by the dread of a new peril."

"The political civilization which has sprung up from the soil of Europe and is over-running the whole world, like some prolific weed, is based upon exclusiveness. It is always watchful to keep at bay the aliens or to exterminate them. It is carnivorous and cannibalistic in its tendencies, it feeds upon the resources of other peoples and tries to swallow their whole future. It is always afraid of other races achieving eminence, naming it as a peril, and tries to thwart all symptoms of greatness outside its own boundaries, forcing down races of men who are weaker, to be eternally fixed in their weakness.... This political civilization is scientific, not human.

"The charge brought against us is that the ideals we cherish in the East are static, that they have no impetus in them to move, to open out new vistas of knowledge and power, that the systems of philosophy which are the mainstays of the time-worn civilizations of the East despise all outward proofs, remaining stolidly satisfied in their subjective certainty. This proves that when our knowledge is vague, we are apt to accuse of vagueness our object of knowledge itself. To á Western observer our civilization appears as all metaphysics, as to a deaf man piano playing appears to be mere movement of figures and no music. He cannot think that we have found some deep basis of reality upon which we have built our institutions. ... The East with her ideals, in whose bosom are stored the ages of sunlight and silence of stars, can patiently wait till the West, hurrying after the expedient, loses breath and stops."[46]

A Globalizing Monoculturalism: Shock, Dialogue and Pragmatic Balancing

The contemporary "western" thought has also some pluralist models. But just as it happens with its universalist model, multiculturalism is treated as a source of conflict and intolerance. There have been pluralist theories wrapped in sophisticated right-wing jargon. Samuel Huntington has been of such theoreticians who rejects the idea of a single world civilization, but prefers to believe in an unavoidable "clash of civilizations" for the evolution of a post-modern world order under the western hegemony. In a conference in Lisbon, at the Mario Foundation Conference Series on "The invention of democracy" in 1997, he stated:

"The great world civilizations differ much among themselves as to their degree of closeness to the West or Westernization. Latin America is closely related to the West, and some believe that it should be regarded as belonging to the western family. The orthodox world is a distant relation and difficult to deal with. In Africa, the western rule was short and its impact was limited, except the case of South Africa. The western influence in the Muslim countries has varied, but has been short in the Arab countries. The same could be said of China. In general terms, the degree of acceptance of democracy by non-western societies varies according to the degree of their Westernization."

"For the leaders of China and many other Asiatic societies the liberal democracy is of new use. Some Western intellectuals have even defended that Asia has been the cradle of "liberal democracy", resulting from a cultural inheritance that emphasizes the protective and disciplinary role of the State, which is regarded as a guide for the behaviour of the citizens and not an instrument for the protection of the individual rights of its citizens. (...) The suspicion and the competition are rejected in favour of social harmony and cooperation, while the maintenance of order and respect for hierarchy are regarded as basic cultural values.."[47]

This is a neo-liberal stand which the Asian defenders of "Asiatic values" tend to identify with the Huntington disease which affects the nervous system and has no known cure as yet! The main symptom of the disease is the difficulty the patient feels to swallow![48] The arrogance of the neo-liberal thinkers of the West makes it also hard for them to swallow the cultural and economic resistance of the Asian societies confronted by the challenges of the West-controlled globalization.[49]

Yet another pluralist version is related to Hermeneutics and with the idea of dialogue. Dialogue is referred to as a great rupture, particularly in the context of inter-religious dialogue. Hans-Georg Gadamer (1900-) conceives hermeneutical dialogue as different from a pleasant conversation. He defines it as clash of traditions, a clash of historical prejudices. He defends a true dialogue which does not ignore the differences or seeks to wash them away, but tends to recognize them and integrate them into the process of mutual understanding. The difference of perspective is thus seen as an indispensable condition for true understanding of the dialogue partners. It is a process marked by a creative tension, with willingness to listen to the discordant views and to try to share them.[50]

Gadamer has been criticized for not taking into account more seriously the political interests, the racist attitudes, the ideological manipulations and the social discriminations that often seek cover beneath the strategy of "dialogue". It is also my personal view that it is difficult to believe in the success of an "hermeneutical dialogue" that owes so much to the philosophical thought of Husserl and Heidegger, who championed the western values to such an extent that the "regeneration of the being" was possible only through the western thought and not through eastern or any other thought.[51] Heidegger's sympathy for the

Nazis is a known fact.[52] It is curious how the great majority of the "thinking" westerners do not see that the so-called horizon of "intentionality" phenomenology and ontological temporality of these philosophers does not provide place for the non-Western cultural "being" that makes a great part of the mankind. It is a serious negation of what the phenomenology "intended", namely, to fight against alienation that results from the thought that hides its source. Would it not be relevant here to ask how the time-space "curvature" of the general theory of relativity [53] is explained by a phenomenology that wishes to do justice to these categories of existence as fundamental thoughts? An answer could help to confirm the diasynchronic nature of the human thought, denouncing the shallowness of the claims of the western *particularities* as "universal" thought. It would satisfy at least the claim of the "western thought" for scientific criteria![54]

I shall give the last word to Isaiah Berlin (1909-1997) who defends a thesis of pragmatic balance and has been a zealous defender of the pluralism of cultural values. He admits the limits for dialogue and for solutions for cultural misunderstandings, but sees no other easy way out. He rules out the idea of resorting to a single system of thought and methodology as an invitation for renewal of tyrannies. Isaiah Berlin admired G. Vico and J. G. Herder as champions of pluralism of values in an extended horizon of human existence [55] and defends that a meeting of West and East in a *post-orientalist* and globalized world could be positive only on the basis of a creative dialogue between various centres of cultures and their specific thought-patterns and values, and never by seeking to impose uniformity or through paternalism of one group over the others by dictating what would be good for the others. [56]

Conclusion

As a concession for those who know only the western philosophies, the intercultural dialogue could perhaps begin with the "*cogito*" of Descartes, but it could never end there without getting stuck in the mire of equally adamant "*sum*" + "*sum*". I wish to end by citing Jung, who visited India and discovered the depth of its wisdom. He discovered "other ways" for the civilized human beings to organize their lives without a slavish depending upon "thinking". This is what Jung recorded in an essay entitled "What India can teach us":

"We should thank God that there is still a man who has not learned to think, but has the ability to perceive the thoughts as visions or live things.....It is true that the logic of India is interesting and it is fantastic to see how pieces of western science co-exist with what we would call superstition. The Indians are not bothered by the contradictions that are apparently unacceptable. If they exist, it is the thinking that produces them, and a person may not be considered responsible for them. The person does not create the thoughts, they just appear. An Indian is not interested in the minute details of the universe. He is interested in understanding the whole. He does not know yet that the world can be captured firmly through concepts. Have you ever thought how much of the conqueror (to avoid saying thief or aggressor) is conveyed by the word "concept"? It is derived from Latin *concipere*, 'to grasp something by force'. This characterizes our attitude towards the world. The Indian 'thought' is a widening of vision and not an assault to capture what remains untapped in the nature." [57]

References

* Head of the Department of History, Universidade Lusófona de Humanidades e Tecnologias, Lisboa; Fellow of the Portuguese Academy of History; Fellow of the Geographical Society of Lisbon.

* Other writings of the author may be consulted at the following website: http://www.geocities.com/Athens/Forum/1503/teo_publ.html

1 J.L. Brockington, *The Sacred Thread: Hinduism in its continuity and diversity*, Edinburgh, University press, 1996, pp.108-111.

2 C.G. Jung, *Psicologia e Religião Oriental*, Petrópolis, Vozes, 1991, *passim*. Referring to Yoga from India (also applicable to tantric yoga of lamaism, as well as to taoist yoga of China), he writes: "In the East, where these ideas and practices had their origin and where four thousand years of uninterrupted tradition has created the basis and the necessary spiritual prerequisites, yoga, as its can be easily imagined, became the most adequate expression and the most appropriate methodology to merge the body and the spirit into a unity that can be hardly denied, generating thereby a psychological predisposition which enables the surge of feelings and intuitions which transcend the level of consciousness. The historic mentality of India, does not have basically any difficulty in working with analogical

concepts, such as *prâna*. But the West, with its bad philosophical habit of wanting to believe, and at the same time to be philosophically and scientifically critical, falls prey to the belief and swallows concepts and terms like *prâna, âtman, châcra, samâdhi,* etc. [...] The rupture in the western mind makes it impossible from the start an adequate realization of the objectives of yoga. [...] A Hindu does not forget either his body or his spirit. An European, on the contrary, always forgets one or the other. It is due to this quality that he could conquer the world. That was not possible for a Hindu, because he knows his *nature,* and also till what extent he himself is part of that nature. The European, on the contrary, has a *science* of the nature and knows fantastically little about the nature in himself." (pp. 55-56). Cf. Heinrich Zimmer, *Mitos e Símbolos na Arte e Civilização Indianas,* Lisboa, Assírio & Alvim, 1996. C.G. Jung, *op.cit.,* p. 82: Jung thanks H. Zimmer for deepening his understanding of India and Yoga and regretted his premature death in 1943.

3   *Ibid.,* p. 57: "The western man does not *need* to prove his superiority over the nature, neither inside nor outside of himself, because he handles both with a diabolical perfection. What he lacks is the consciousness of his own *inferiority* in relation to the nature, both around him and within him. What he needs to know is that he cannot have it as he wishes. Without this consciousness he will end up destroying the nature. He does not know his own soul in rebellion against him in a suicidal manner."

4   The fame of this astronomer-mathematician led many other mathematicians to assume his name, and more recently, India decided to give his name to its first satellite placed in space in 1975.

5   The designation "zero" is derived from Arabic *sifr,* and evolved into *zephirum* in Latin. Contrary to the Indian use of 9 digits and the consequent need of *shunya,* the Greeks utilized 10 digits without zero. It is said that Aristotle rejected zero, considering it as "non-number", because it could not divide nor was divisible. Cf. David Ewing Duncan, *The Calendar,* London, Fourth Estate, 1998, p. 166.

6   David Ewing Duncan, *The Calendar,* London, Fourth Estate, 1998, p. 157.

7   David Ewing Duncan, *op.cit.,* p. 192; Stephen Jay Gould *et al., O Fim dos Tempos,* Lisboa, Terramar, 1999, p. 17: "The western mathematics during this period (of Dyonisius Exigus) had not yet developed the operative concept of zero. The Egyptians had used it, but sporadically. The Chinese knew the concept, but not the number. The Mayas knew it, but did not use it. As to our present day zero actual, it was invented by the Hindu mathematicians and by the Arabs between the 8th and the 9th centuries". Cf. also Robert Kaplan, *The Nothing that Is: A natural history of zero,* London, Penguin Books, 1999.

8   It is true of the Indian caste system. It was a way of integrating new social groups without recourse to ethnic cleansings. The castes based on division of labour allowed the society to benefit from the talents of the new groups without threatening the dominant position of the ruling hierarchies. S. Radhakrishnan, *The Hindu View of Life,* New Delhi, Harper Collins Publishers India, 3rd ed., 1996, pp. 85-105. In his conferences at Manchester College, at Oxford in 1926, Radhakrishnan defended that the caste system made sense within the spiritual vision and the organization of the Hindu society of the times. He doubts if the individualist vision of the society will have the last word in social theory, and rejects the idea of a democracy that seeks to obliterate peculiarities and diversities- "We cannot put our souls in uniform", states the Indian philosopher-President, and calls it a democratic dictatorship. Radhakrishnan presents the conservative and progressive social movements in

ancient Indian history as represented by Vashishta and Vishvamitra respectively, and regards the philosophy of *Upanishadas* as profoundly democratic. Cf. Adeodato Barreto, *Civilização Hindu*, Lisboa, Seara Nova, 1935, pp. 142-143: "O próprio sistema das castas – que tão odioso se apresenta modernamente – tivera a sua origem num largo espírito de coordenação e de harmonia. 'É preciso fazermos justiça aos conquistadores arianos – escreve o professor Sylvain Levi, *L'Inde et le Monde*, p. 88 – e reconhecer que eles nunca procuraram suprimir a dificuldade (de colonizar a Índia), *aniquilando* as raças indígenas; eles ensaiaram, sim, métodos de colaboração capazes de lhes assegurar a sua própria salvaguarda sem privar as outras comunidades dos meios indispensáveis de subsistência. A formação das castas, a hierarquia das castas, foram meios de defesa contra a absorção que ameaçava (a pequena minoria ariana)". A reprint of this work of the Goan author, including also his poetic production *Livro da Vida*, has been recently released in Lisbon. It carries my introductory essay, entitled "Um missionário da civilização hindu em Portugal"[A missionary of hindu civilization in Portugal], *Civilização Hindu*, Lisboa, Hugin Editores, 2000, pp. 47-56.

9   Ashwan Raman, "Deutschland? Bloss nicht!" *Berliner Tageszeitung*, 27 Março, 2000; http://www.rediff.com/money/2000/jul/20shang.htm (20 Julho, 2000); http://www.rediff.com/money/2000/aug/05japan.htm (5 Agosto 2000).

10 James Mill, *The History of British India*, Vol.I, London, 1958 (5ª edição), p. 107.

11 Romila Thapar, *Time as a metaphor of History: Early India*, New Delhi, Oxford University Press, 1996.

12 J.M. Amado Mendes, *História Económica e Social dos Séculos XV a XX*, Lisboa, Calouste Gulbenkian Foundation, 1993, p. 35; Fernand Braudel, *História e Ciências Sociais*, Lisboa, Ed. Presença, pp. 18-22.

13 G.V. Scammell, "Essay and Reflection: On Discovery of the Americas and the Spread of Intolerance, Absolutism, and Racism in Early Modern Europe", *The International History Review*, XIII, 3, August 1991, pp. 441-660; Jack Goody, *O Oriente no Ocidente*, Lisboa, Ed. Difel, 2000, p. 336: "Only the ethnocentrism could have invented the western singularity, benefiting for this purpose from the uncontested western successes of the last five centuries, and of the 19th century in a special way.." [English translation is mine]

14 Pedro Nuno Pereira, *O Espaço e o Tempo: Intraligações*, Lisboa, Fim de Século Edições, 1998, pp. 132-133. Cf. W.R. Bion, *Transformations*, London, Karnac, 1984, ch. 11; http://www.sivananda.org/vedanta.htm

15 I had the privilege to contribute, jointly with Claude Alvares, a Preface to the re-edition of this work by The Other Press, Kuala Lumpur, 1993.

16 *Ibid.*, p. 17.

17 As it could be expected, the Society of Jesus did not resist the provocations of Panikkar, and a leading Indian Jesuit, Jerome D'Souza, who was a member of the Constituent Assembly of India for debating and approving the Indian Constitution, published *Sardar Panikkar and Christian Missions*, Trichinopoly, 1957. There was a reaction in Portugal. Cf. Júlio Gonçalves, "Also sprach... Assim falou Sardar K.M. Panikkar", Offprint of the *Boletim da Sociedade de Geografia de Lisboa*, October-December, 1956.

18 The first English edition is entitled *Occidentosis: A Plague from the West*, trans. R. Campbell, Berkeley, Mizan Press, 1984.

19 Jalal Al-i-Ahmad, *op.cit.*, pp. 27, 32, 62-63, 90.

20   President Khatami's address at the University of Beijing (Beida) last year was one illustration of his discourses on this issue.

21   Edward W. Said, *Orientalism: Western Conceptions of the Orient*, London, Penguin Books, 1995. Cf. António Manuel Hespanha, "O Orientalismo em Portugal (Séculos XVI-XX), *O Orientalismo em Portugal*, Lisboa, CNCDP, 1999, pp. 15-37;

22   Noam Chomsky, *Discurso da Dissidência*, Lisboa, Ed. Dinossauro, 2000; Christopher Norris, *Uncritical Theory*, Amherst, The University of Massachussetts Press, 1992, pp. 100-115.

23   Christopher Norris, *op. cit.*, pp. 159- 191; Peter Sloterdijk, *Critique of Cynical Reason*, London, Verso, 1988, pp. 5-6; Richard Rorty, *Contingency, Irony, and Solidarity*, Cambridge, Cambridge University Press, 1989; Stanley Fish, *Doing What Comes Naturally: change, rhetoric and the practice of theory in literary and legal studies*, Oxford, Clarendon Press, 1989; Jean-François Lyotard, *The Differend: phrases in dispute*, Manchester, Manchester University Press, 1988; Jean Baudrillard, *Simulacros e Simulação*, Lisboa, Relógio d'Água, 1991; Jean Baudrillard, *O Crime Perfeito*, Lisboa, Relógio d'Água, 1996.

24   Helmut Buchholt, "Southeast Asia: The Way to Modernity", in Maria Johanna Schouten, *A Ásia do Sudeste: História, Cultura e Desenvolvimento*, Lisboa, Vega, 1998, pp. 97-104; Abraham George, "From colonialism to eco-colonialism", *International Conference on Europe and South Asia: 500 Years* (Abstracts), Calicut & Cochin, 16-20 May 1998, pp. 210-211.

25   Walter Fernandes & Anupama Dutta (eds.), *Colonialism to Globalisation: Five Centuries after Vasco da Gama*, Vol. I: Main issues around Colonialism and Globalisation, Delhi, Indian Social Institute, 1999.

26   Helmut Buchholt, *op. cit.*, pp. 100-101; S. Huntington, "The clash of civilizations", *Foreign Affairs*, Vol. 72, n.3, Summer 1993, pp. 22-49; Yeo Lay Hwee & Asad Latif (eds), *Asia and Europe: Essays and Speeches by Tommy Koh*, Singapore, Asia-Europe Foundation, 2000. For a balanced and critical assessment of the debate on "Asian Values", one may profitably consult the text of a Conference by Amartya Sen at the Carnegie Foundation in 1997: htt://www. mtholyoke.edu/acad/intrel/sen.htm

27   Raúl Fornet-Betancourt, *Interculturalidad y Globalización: Ejercícios de crítica filosófica intercultural en el contexto de la globalización neoliberal*, Frankfurt, IKO, 2000.

28   Gaudencio Rosales & C.G. Arévalo (eds.) *For all the Peoples of Asia: Federation of Asian Bishops' Conference – Documents from 1970-1991*, N. York, Orbis Books, 1992, p. 337: In the conclusions of the Consultation of the Theologians who met at Hua Hin (Thailandi) on 10 November 1991, the Federation of the Bishops of Asia admitted that: "As a social institution the Church is perceived as a foreign body in its colonial origins while other world religions are not. The lingering colonial image survives in its traditional ecclesiastical structures and economic dependence on the west. This gives ground for suspicion. The Church is even sometimes seen as an obstacle or threat to national integration and to religious and cultural identity. Alignments between the Church and socio-political elites often legitimize and preserve the socio-political *status quo* and do not succeed in obviating this image. The Church remains foreign in its lifestyle, in its institutional structure, in its worship, in its western-trained leadership and in its theology. Christian rituals often remain formal, neither spontaneous nor particularly Asian."

Teotónio R. de Souza

29 Isaiah Berlin, *A Busca do Ideal*, Lisboa, Editorial Bizâncio, 1998, p. 43.

30 Here is what an important Portuguese daily in Lisbon had to say about the Indian IITs: "O exemplo indiano", no *Jornal PÙBLICO*, Lisboa, 15 de Maio de 2000: "Os *Indian Institute of Technology* encontram-se entre as escolas de engenharia com mais prestígio ao nível mundial pela extraordinária qualidade das pessoas formadas e pelo seu impacto na criação de uma indústria de alta tecnologia, desde o"software" à microelectrónica mais avançada, de grande competitividade a nível mundial. (...) Hoje, as histórias de sucesso dos *Indian Institute of Technology* são objecto de cobertura jornalística nas revistas e jornais de maior prestígio mundial, desde a "Time" ao "International Herald Tribune". (...) Não surpreende que os jovens licenciados dos *Indian Institute of Technology* sejam avidamente procurados a nível internacional, quer por empresas mundiais líderes de alta tecnologia quer pelos centros de ciência e tecnologia de maior prestígio mundial. São, sem dúvida, um bom exemplo que se poderia dar a conhecer em Portugal."

31 Alfredo Bruto da Costa, *Exclusões Sociais*, Lisboa, Fundação Mário Soares / Ed. Gradiva, 1998; José Gabriel Pereira Bastos & Susana Pereira Bastos, *Portugal Multicultural*, Lisboa, Ed. Fim de Século, 1999; Jorge Vala *et al.*, *Expressões dos racismos em Portugal*, Lisboa, ICS, 1999.

32 Samir Amin, "For a progressive and democratic new world order", paper presented at an International Conference on "Colonialism and Globalization – Five Centuries after Vasco da Gama" (2-6 Feb. 1998) organized by the Indian Social Institute, New Delhi to commemorate 500 years of the arrival of Vasco da Gama in India. Samir Amin's analysis of the novelties of the capitalist system and of possible alternatives to it is clear as regards five areas which the Capitalism holds as its closely guarded monopolies: globalized finances, technological innovation, access to planetary resources, means of communication, arms of mass destruction. His analysis of the role of Germany and Japan is also thought provoking. Both recovered after World War II with massive inputs of the Marshall Plan, and are utilized as the bases of the capitalists expansion, dependent upon the American hegemonic interests in Europe and in the East. His analysis of the capitalist strategy to control and reduce the anti-systemic forces, or to promote sub-nationality movements, so as to create more Slovenias, Kosovos e Chechnyas. Cf. Also Boaventura de Sousa Santos, *Pela Mão de Alice*, Porto, Ed. Afrontamento, 1997, pp. 130-132.

33 Raúl Fornet-Betancourt, *op. cit.*, pp. 9-34, 42.

34 *Ibid.*, pp. 85-97.

35 *Ibid.*, pp. 92-94.

36 K.M. Panikkar, *Asia and Western Dominance*, Kuala Lumpur, The Other Press, 1993, p. 308.

37 Citado por John Clarke, "Beyond Orientalism", *IAAS Newsletter*, Leiden, February 1999, pp. 4, 14.

38 F.S.C Northrop, *Meeting of East and West: An Inquiry Concerning World*, Woodbridge CT, Ox Bow Press, 1979; *The Taming of the Nations: A study of the cultural bases of international policy*, Woodbridge, CT, Ox Bow Press, 1987.

39 C.G. Jung, *Jung and Eastern Thought: A Dialogue with the Orient*, ed. J. Clarke, London, Routledge, 1994; *The Psychology & Religion: West & East*, Princeton University Press, 1972; C.G. Jung, *Civilização em Transição*, Petrópolis, Vozes, 1993, pp. 213-230: These are chapters entitled "A Índia – Um mundo de sonhos"

40 [India: A world of dreams" and "O que a Índia nos pode ensinar" [What India can teach us]

40 Francis Fukuyama, *O Fim da História e o Último Homem*, Lisboa, Gradiva, 1992.

41 Francis Fukuyama, *A Grande Ruptura: A natureza humana e a reconstituição da ordem social*, Lisboa, Quetzal Editores, 2000; "Reflectindo sobre o fim da História dez anos depois", *PÚBLICO*, Lisboa, 17-7-99, p. 12.

42 S. Radhakrishnan, *The Hindu View of Life*, New Delhi, Harper Collins Publishers, 1996, pp. 41-44. Cf. Debiprasad Chattopadhyaya (ed), *Radhakrishnan: The Centenary Volume*, Oxford University Press, 1990.

43 S. Radhakrishnan, *The Hindu View of Life*, pp. 84-86.

44 B.R. Nanda, (ed.) *Essays in Modern Indian History*, Delhi, Oxford University Press, 1983, pp. 58-61.

45 Due to difficulty of access to an English version, I have paraphrased the Portuguese version of the book. Rabindranath Tagore, *A Casa e o Mundo*, Lisboa, Ed. Presença, 1986, pp. 125-126. Cf. E. Tudela de Castro, *Shantiniketan (O Asilo da Paz)*, Lisboa, Tip. Simões M. Santos, 1925. Text of a Conference organized on 11 May 1923 by the Theosophical Society of Portugal.

46 Rabindranath Tagore, *Nationalism*, New York, The Macmillan Company, 1917; *The Diary of a Westward Voyage*, English translation of Indu Dutt, Bombay, Times of India press, 1962.

47 João Carlos Espada (coord.), *A Invenção Democrática*, Lisboa, Fundação Mário Soares, 2000, p. 25-26.

48 There exists in Portugal an Association of the Patients of Huntington disease. Cf. *Diário de Notícias*, Lisboa, 23-06-2000.

49 João Carlos Espada, *op. cit.*, p.203: Ralf Dahrendorf defends the same theory and criticizes the Asian countries for utilizing State machineries for ensuring social harmony. But he has nothing to say about the monopolies of mass media which do the same in the western liberal democracies.

50 Hans-George Gadamer, *O Problema da Consciência Histórica*, Lisboa, Estratégias Criativas, 1998, pp. 69-89.

51 John Clarke, *op. cit.*, p.14. Vide *British Encyclopaedia*, s.v. Martin Heidegger.

52 Catherine Clément, *O Último Encontro*, Lisboa, Ed. ASA, 2000. É uma história do relacionamento amoroso de Heidegger com Hannah Arendt.

53 *TIME*, Vol. 154, Nº 27, December 31, 1999 – Person of the Century: Albert Einstein, p. 41.

54 Emanuel Lévinas, *Descobrindo a existência com Husserl e Heidegger*, Lisboa, Instituto Piaget, 1997, pp. 72-77, 109-111, 183-189.

55 Isaiah Berlin, *A Busca do Ideal*, Lisboa, Ed. Bizâncio, 1998, pp. 31, 50-52.

56 *Ibid.*, p. 294; John Clarke, *op. cit.*, p. 14.

57 C.G. Jung, *Civilização em Transição*, Petrópolis, Vozes, 19993, pp. 226-227. The original version was published as "What India can teach us", *Ásia* XXXIX, New York, 1939, pp. 97-98. I am sorry for having to make a retroversion from a Portuguese translation.

A CRITICAL EVALUATION OF THE POLITICAL AND ADMINISTRATIVE POLICIES OF THE DUTCH EAST INDIA COMPANY IN KERALA

M.O. Koshy

The Dutch East India Company was a trading company[1]. It was a sovereign body with an elaborate and efficient system of administration. The administrative head quarters of the Dutch East India Company in the East was at Batavia[2] in Java. The government of the company was invested with a governor-general and council. After the conquest of Cochin and Cannanore in 1663, Kerala was placed in charge of a commander. The administrative set up of the Malabar command of the Dutch East India Company was sound. The states general granted vast powers to the company taking into account the long distance between the Netherlands and the Eastern Countries. The company was empowered to enter into treaties with the rulers east of the Cape of Good Hope, 'to build fortresses there, and to establish governors, garrisons and officers of justice and police; but the treaties are concluded in the name of the states, - in whose name all officers, both military and civil take their oaths'.[3] In fact the company was entrusted with powers to make war and peace and formulate its own rules and policies to suit the circumstances of the country and time.

The Dutch East India Company concentrated on trade in the early years of its contacts with the countries in the East. The policy was to buy cheap and sell dear[4]. But soon the company

An Evaluation of the Political and Administrative Policies of the Dutch

ascertained that it could not deal with the traders directly without their governments. Moreover, the political conditions in the Est was not conducive to peaceful trade. These problems compelled the company to support trade through negotiations, treaties and war. But the authorities of the Dutch East India Company at home did not support war to promote trade. The successive governors-general were directed to avoid war as far as possible and maintain peace.[5]

The officials of the company found themselves in an uncertain and unpredictable situation in the East. They advocated war to carry on trade. In 1614, governor general Coen wrote that 'trade in India must be conducted and maintained under protection and favour of your weapons, and that weapons must be supplied from the profits enjoyed by the trade, so that trade cannot be maintained without war, or war without trade.'[6] Coen was convinced of the fact that only through the force of arms, the company could gain favourable terms of trade. In 1619 he wrote that 'without war you will never in the world attain a good peace.[7] This policy forced the company to remain in arms to protect and preserve its trade.

Besides the directors of the Dutch East India Company were ignorant of trade, geography and politics of the Eastern countries. They had to depend upon the officials of the company in the East for information to take resolutions to guide the course of the political and commercial policies. When governor general Van Diemen was criticised for his policy of extension of trade through war, he retorted 'we have said, and we repeat, that affairs in India must be left to us, and we cannot wait orders about them if we are to do the company's service. Your Honours know the reason, namely that the times will not suffer it.'[8] The force of circumstances made the directors of the company in the Netherlands to grant freedom to its officials in the East to adopt measures that they considered necessary to preserve its interests in places that came under their sway.

The supreme government at Batavia framed policies for their factories and settlements. The pressure of circumstances and changes in the pattern of trade influenced the policy of the company. These policies differed from country to country.[9] The Dutch policy in Kerala was governed by the single consideration of maximum pepper trade at minimum expense.'[10] The policy of the Dutch East India Company towards Kerala falls into six different periods: (1) from 1604 to 1657, (2) from 1657 to 1663, (3) from 1663 to 1697, (4) from 1697 to 1717, (5) from 1717 to 1753 and (6) from 1753 to 1795. A study of the political and administrative policies of the Dutch East India Company reveals and exposes the Dutch statesmanship and diplomacy to shape their policies according to the changing events and times.

1. The Dutch envinced interest to win the goodwill of the rulers in the early years of their contacts with Kerala. They entered into treaties with the Zamorins of Calicut and the ruler of Kayamkulam. They gained trade privileges in return for protection from the Portuguese.[11] The ships of the Dutch East India Company visited many ports of Kerala and traded through mercantile means.[12] During these earlier contacts with Kerala the Dutch 'posed as liberators of the Indian people from the tyrannies of the Portuguese; and were hailed by the people and princes alike for developing industrial and financial resources'.[13] The Dutch found the commercial contracts profitable. During 1604-1657, the Dutch operated as a trading company championing the cause of the local rulers supporting them against the Portuguese.

2. The Dutch policy towards Kerala underwent drastic change after their conquest of Ceylon in 1658. The proximity to the pepper markets and the strategic importance of Kerala tempted the Dutch to plan for the conquest of the land. The Dutch obtained the alliance of the Zamorin of Calicut in their grand design to conquer Kerala.[14] Besides, the Dutch extended their support to the Mutha Tavazhi branch in the disputed succession to the throne of Cochin which strengthened them to assault the Portuguese in Cochin.[15] The Dutch undertook three expeditions to Kerala with the aim of conquering the land. On

29 December 1658, the Dutch conquered the Portuguese stronghold of Quilon.[16] But the Dutch gave up the conquest and withdrew their forces in 1659. The Dutch expeditions of 1660[17] and 1661[18] also ended in failure. The final stage of the siege of Cochin began in November 1662 and it was capitulated on 7 January 1663.[19] This was followed by the conquest of Cannanore on 15 February 1663.[20] During 1657-1663 the Dutch policy was motivated by aggressive designs to conquer Kerala and expel Portuguese with the support of the local rulers.

3. The policy of the Malabar Command from 1663 to 1697 was to consolidate and extend its power enforcing monopoly of trade in Kerala. The conquest of Cochin found the Dutch in a strong position. The political condition was also favourable to them. They became kingmakers in the Kingdom of Cochin after the expulsion of the Portuguese.[21] The Dutch reduced the power of the ruler and forced him to depend on them. They took advantage of the helplessness of the king and interfered in the affairs of the royal family and government. Besides, the company was able to collect the customs in the rivers, the royal rents, taxes and fines, judgements and executions, monopolies and tobacco, salt, wheat, etc. throughout the country.[22] The Dutch also interfered in the affairs of other states. They became arbiters in the affairs of Kerala.

The Dutch adopted different strategies to gain monopoly of trade in the contracts with the rulers on the coast. Van Rheede recorded that the Dutch East India Company entered into agreements with the rulers of Quilon, Karthikapally, Purakkad, Calicut and Kolathunad through pressure of arms. The agreements of peace signed with Travancore, Kayamkulam, Cochin feudatories, Cochin, Tekkumkur etc., were voluntary.[23] Strict alliance with the rulers on the coast secured them exclusive rights of commerce.

General Ryckloff Van Goens was the author of the policy of enforcement of monopoly of trade after assuming political power in Kerala. In the supreme council at Batavia he discussed and resolved to procure all the pepper of Deccan and the Malabar coast. The general prosecuted the plan,

> vigorously at prodigious charge, and had fair hopes of effecting it, so long as the war continued; for what he could not engross in a mercantile way, he brought about by arms, entering by force into several Rajahs' country and constraining them to agree to his imperious articles, one where of was certain and undeniable, to witt, the exclusion of the English[24].

The Dutch East India Company kept large military establishments to enforce monopoly of trade and to maintain hegemony in Kerala. The monopoly of trade deprived the rulers of the coast their economic freedom. They ascertained that their alliance with the Dutch curtailed their political power and shattered their prestige. With the progress of years, the Dutch found that it was difficult for them to enforce monopoly of trade. Van Rheede observed that so long as the fear of the Company's arms remained fresh in their minds, the rulers kept up their promises; but 'when they got accustomed to the withdrawal of those arms and enjoyments of peace, they began to evade their promises.'[25] Some of the rulers on the coast sold pepper to others for higher price instead of supplying it to the company at lower rate. The ruler of Kayamkulam openly sold pepper to William Kidd, a notorious pirate. Thus the

> experience of thirty years had already pointed out the injurious tendency of the former expensive establishment, with no adequate benefit. The ostentation of a great power, which cost the company such large sums of money, had not the effect of producing in the native princes that degree of awe and apprehension, which is indispensably necessary for carrying on an exclusive trade. [26]

4. The Dutch became conscious of their error in seeking to expand trade at the point of the sword by the end of the seventeenth century.[27] They found to their shock and surprise that whatever profits accrued to them through trade had to be expended for the purpose of maintaining garrisons for the protection of various settlements. The experience of the few years of the Dutch existence in Kerala proved that the commercial

system skilfully woven by them was crumbling. At the same time the expenses on the military establishments were mounting and burdensome without adequate profits of trade. On 19 August, 1687, the Supreme government at Batavia resolved the following.

1. As the fortifications of the city of Cochin were too large, they required a huge force for their defence. The extensive walls required continuous reparations. The Dutch East India Company spent huge sum of money to maintain these establishments. Therefore, it was resolved to reduce it to one half of its size.

2. The company resolved to preserve the Portuguese tower in the fort of Cannanore. The garrison was to be reduced to twenty or at the most twenty five.

3. In the ancient fort of Cannanore the company decided to preserve the interior works and maintain a small force of twenty European soldiers.

4. In Quilon it was judged necessary to preserve the old Portuguese tower and certain important parts of the fort. The military establishment was to be reduced to fifteen or twenty men. It was resolved to destroy the remaining parts of the above mentioned forts.[28]

The Dutch resolved to reduce the forts and withdraw all military out posts on the coast of Kerala except Pappinivattam, Purakkad and Kayamkulam. They decided to retain these as factories or residencies in order to watch the developments all along the region. The company considered the employment of 530 Europeans and 370 local people sufficient for its service in Kerala. All artillery and naval establishments of the company came under the purview of reduction. The strength of the artillery was fixed at ninety five pieces of iron, six pieces of brass ordnance with two mortars. The vessels of all descriptions were to be cut down to one small yacht, two sloops and three row boats. It was also decided not to obstruct the navigation and trade of Kerala.[29] The Dutch policy from 1697 to 1717 was to reduce military establishments because the military system framed to enforce monopoly of trade in Kerala was unsuccessful and unrewarding. Another reason for the decision was the proximity of a large fleet maintained in Colombo. The fleet could be deployed against enemies in times of emergency. The readiness of the fleet for action would defend Dutch interests and help them to save a huge amount that they were spending for the preservation of commerce in Kerala.

The Dutch could not implement their decision to reduce military establishments in Kerala due to the out break of a war between the company and the Zamorin in 1701. Though the war ended by the conclusion of a treaty of peace on 8 January 1710,[30] hostilities began again in 1715. The Dutch engaged a large force of 4000 men both Europeans and local people in the campaign to win the war. A peace was concluded between them once again on 17 December 1717.[31] The policy of the company to reduce the military establishments in Kerala was not implemented owing to the war with the Zamorin. On the contrary the company increased the military strength on the coast and spent huge amounts of money to win the war.

5. The prestige of the Dutch shot up in Kerala after the conclusion of peace the Zamorin in 1717. The position thus gained made them believe that they were arbiters in the affairs of Kerala. A period of intervention of the Dutch in the affairs of the rulers of Kerala was inaugurated from 1717 to 1753. The Dutch policy of intervention generated the hostility of the rulers on the coast. The balance of power maintained by the Dutch in Kerala was totally titled in the South with the rise and expansion of Travancore under Marthanda Varma in 1729. When Gustaaf Willem Baron Van Imhoff, governor of Ceylon visited Kerala in 1739,[32] he found that the conquests of Travancore upset the balance of power that prevailed in Kerala for more than a century. In his report of 6 July 1739, Van Imhoff recorded his opinion that

> If it were requisite for the company to maintain a balance of power amongst the chiefs of the Malabar coast, it could never be made to preponderate more to the prejudice or danger of the company, than

in favour of that prince, who was almost wholly attached to their competitors, and whose increase of power could not but be pregnant with the most alarming consequences to their interests, whilest he, at the same time merited some chastisement for his insolence towards them, independent of primary consideration of maintaining a due balance among the native powers of the Malabar.[33]

The governor asserted in another place that the interests of the Dutch East India Company could be best served 'in the right of exclusive occupation and in the peaceful possession of such territory as is necessary for obtaining the profits which the country yields.[34] He also ascertained that the Dutch East India Company could not remain in peaceful possession of Kerala and gain maximum profits of trade because 'the king of Travancore, [sic] with whom we had formerly but little to do, must in the present circumstances be also considered when speaking of our peaceful occupation of territory, because it seems that he intends to destroy it'.[35]

The critical state of affairs of Kerala, made Van Imhoff to propose two lines of action. The first proposition was to follow the market price to purchase pepepr and the second was to force the rulers on the coast to fulfil their contracts with the Dutch East India Company. Punitive expedition was recommended if the rulers remained refractory. He rejected the first stating that it was dangerous and unprofitable to the interests of the company. Hence he strongly approved the second course of action.[36] The recommendation of the governor of Ceylon was acceptable to the Malabar command and war was declared on Travancore without waiting for reinforcements from Batavia.[37]

In the first stage of the struggle, fortune favoured the Malabar command. But the campaign went against them in the second phase. The Dutch received a setback when their forces at Colachel surrendered to the Marthanda Varma without a fight for want of provisions.[38] Stein Van Gollenesse recorded that 'at first the Honourable Company was pretty successful against him [Marthanda Varma], but later on for want of men and other necessaries had to leave him master of the field.'[39] The failure of the Dutch to check the expansion of Travancore shattered their prestige and prominence in Kerala.[40] Yet the Dutch did not give up their hope of re-establishing their hegemony in Kerala. They sent fervent appeals to the governments of Ceylon and Batavia to despatch reinforcements for deployment against Travancore. Gollenesse noted that 'should the Honourable Company have a great force at any time in India and occasion permit us to push the matter energetically my opinion would be that it would suffice to make ourselves completely masters of the states of Peritally and Berkencur.'[41]

The grand scheme of the Malabar command to hold its sway over Kerala waned 'because of the heavy financial drain which the war in Java involved, and the Dutch were also willing to treat with Travancore and reserve their grandiose schemes for a future which never arrived.'[42] Therefore the Dutch adopted a new strategy to open peace negotiations with the king of Travancore.[43] Another factor that prompted the Dutch to negotiate for an accord with Travancore was the mounting expenses the company incurred to maintain military establishments in times of peace and the heavy expenditure to carry on the war.

Besides these two reasons, the Dutch ascertained that Kerala turned out to be an unprofitable settlement of the Dutch East India Company from the time of its conquest. The Company incurred loss every time they reviewed commerce as could be seen from the following table.

The loss incurred by the Dutch East India Company from 1663 to 1744.[44]

From the year	Including	Light money (in Guilders)
1663	1669	838120
1670	1679	1452980
1680	1689	224410
1690	1698/99	1622730

1699/1700	1708/1709	919080
1709/1710	1718/1719	2809830
1719/1720	1728/1729	2331360
1729/1730	1738/1739	2118570
1739/1740	1743/1744	2866952

The loss incurred in trade all through those years from the time of the conquest of Kerala alarmed the Malabar Command. The sharp rise in the price of pepper and the decline of its procurement every year caused considerable anxiety to the Dutch East India Company. These factors necessitated the Malabar Command to reasses its policy in Kerala. The Company had two options before them. It had either to follow the market price or compel the rulers to supply the stipulated measures of pepper. Gollenesse was of the opinion that both the plans involved great difficulties. If the Company adopted the first plan to follow the market, like other merchants, it would be a sheer waste to have conquered Kerala. The Company spent enormous amounts of money and lost many lives to secure monopoly contracts of commerce. Moreover, it was impossible for the Dutch Company to accept market price because the merchants did not incur any expenditure of importance, while the Dutch East India Company had to spend huge amounts of money to maintain their establishments on the coast. The alternative plan - to force the rulers to observe the monopoly contracts - was risky because the Company had to bear the burdens of war which was certain while the result was uncertain. Even if the Company came out victorious, it was doubtful whether the rulers would keep their promises without the use of the Company's force against them. The Company found that it was difficult for them to remain in arms continuously on the coast.[45]

The critical state of affairs of Kerala in December 1749 awoke the Malabar Command to find itself in the land beset with thousands of internal problems and disputes. The Malabar Council discerned that it could easily lose the track in the intricating web if it too got involved in it. This was especially so with regard to the kingdom of Cochin at the time of the conquest of Kerala. The Company expected its ally to grow into a prosperous and efficiently administered kingdom with the passage of the time. But contrary to their expectations, the Company found the rulers corrupt, inefficient and disinterested in the matters of administration. Often the Dutch found the rulers creating problems for the Company instead of supporting them. The confused state of affairs in Cochin shattered the faith of the Company on the rulers of Cochin.[46]

These developments forced the Company to review its policy with Cochin and other kingdoms of Kerala. Frederik Cunes, the Dutch Commander of Cochin reviewed the policy of the Company from the time of the conquest of Kerala. The Company maintained several fortifications and settlements in Kerala and looked for means to preserve these conquests by making treaties with the local rulers. It obtained the exclusive privilege of buying pepper and other products, which it enjoyed for a few years. In the course of years the supply of pepper declined owing to smuggling and competition of other European powers. The main trade in pepper was lost to the Malabar Command. At the same time the Company protected the rulers and their subjects in times of need and dangers and maintained them. It waged costly and bloody wars to save its allies from their enemies, for which service it did not get the expected acknowledgement. In the days of peace and prosperity, these rulers defied the Company and denied the right of profit it could have gained according to the terms of contract. The continuous reproaches, recommendations of the Malabar Command had no effect on the rulers of the coast. All these developments forced the Malabar Command to choose a course of action whether it should follow the market price or force the rulers of Kerala to keep the agreement.[47] Thus the policy of involvement of the Company in the affairs of the rulers of Kerala during 1717-1753 discredited the Malabar command and ruined its trade on the coast.

6. The experience of the Company all through the years of its existence in Kerala forced it to alter its policy in Kerala in 1753.

The new policy during 1753-1795 was to preserve the commercial interests of the Company by detaching itself from the rulers of the coast. The upkeep of the forts and military establishments did not permit the Company to follow the market price. The Company was not prepared to force the rulers to observe the terms of contract entered into between them since it would incur heavy expenditure. The Company was cornered in a critical position. As the main aim of the Company was trade, it resolved to preserve it at any cost. In the meanwhile, the Malabar Command was able to promote trade in Travancore even while it was at war with the kingdom. The Malabar Command and the king of Travancore found the transactions profitable. The profitable trade brought them closer and they signed the treaty of Mavelikara on 15 August 1753 which clearly revealed the policy of the Company.[48]

'By the treaty', observed Moens, 'the old system was discarded and the chief rule of Malabar administration became, as still is, keep friends with Travancore.'[49] The treaty was an admission of the fact that the policy of the Company enforcing monopoly of trade had failed in Kerala.[50] The Dutch tried their best to place Cochin under their protection. But they could not include the clause due to the pressure of the king of Travancore not to insist on that term. Besides the Dutch felt by this time that the kingdom had become a liability instead of an asset to the company.

The Malabar Command was upset by the course of events after the treaty of Mavelikara in 1753. As the Company's affairs in the East Indies required its close attention, it could not tighten its grip on Kerala. The Company's interest and trade on the coast diminished. It was to keep peace with the native kings and to be economic as far as possible.[51] The decision of the Dutch to detach themselves from all engagements continued until Kerala passed under the British rule in 1795.

On the whole the political and administrative policies of the Dutch East India Company were directed by the objectives of maximising profits from the Eastern trade. As a trading corporation, their main aim was commerce and not colonisation. Hence, they devised ways and means to earn large profits from trade. They did not commit atrocities to maintain their power on the coast, unlike the Portuguese. As the settlements of the Dutch East India Company were located along the coast of Kerala, their sway and influence were not extended into the interior. The Dutch did not identify themselves as agents of a state or advocates of a religion. They were tolerant towards other religions and they strictly kept away from forcible conversion of people to Christianity. They did not enforce their religion or customs on the people who came under their sway or contact with them for commerce. Evaluating the Dutch contact with Kerala, it is to be noted that their policy in Kerala is free from rancor and bitterness.

References:-

1. The Dutch East India Company was formed in 1602.
2. The Modern name of Batavia is Jakarta in Indonesia.
3. John Henry Grose, *A Voyage to the East Indies* (London, 1766), I. p.304.
4. J.K.J De Jonge, *De Opkomst Van Het Nederlandsch Gezag in Oost-Indie* (s' Gravenhage, 1864), p.448.
5. Clive Day, *The Dutch in Java* (Kuala Lumpur, 1975), p.46.
6. J.K.J De Jonge, *De Opkomst Van Het Nederlandsch Gezag in Oost-Indie* (s' Gravenhage, 1869), IV, p.15.
7. Ibid., p.132.
8. J.K.J. De Jonge, *De Opkomst Van Het Nederlandsch Geag in Oost-Indie* (s' Gravenhage, 1980), V. p.249.
9. In Ceylon the Dutch changed their policy to suit the need of the changing times, Vide, Memoirs and Instructions of Dutch Governors, Commandeurs & C. Memoir left by Gustaaf William Baron Van Imhoff, Governor and Director of Ceylon, to his ouoooooor willom Maurits Bruynik, 1740, irans., Sophia Pieters (Colombo, 1911) p.p.5-6, 84-85.
10. K.M. Panikkar, *Malabar and the Dutch* (Bombay, 1931), p.112.
11. Record of the Dutch Commercial Transactions in India, English 1569-1688, Dutch MSS Records No. 23375, pp.121-122, 129, 205-206.
12. H.K.S' Jacob, *De Nederlanders in Kerala 1663-1701* (s' Gravenhage, 1976) p.XL.
13. Balakrishna, 'The Rise and Fall of the Dutch in India', *Proceedings of the Indian Historical Records Commission*, (1939),XI, p.38.
14. J.A. Van Der Chijs, *The Dagh-Register gehouden in Cassteel Batavia, Anno 1661* (s' Hage, 1839), pp.100-101, 116-118.

15. Kerala Archives Department Publication No.1, *A Translation of a Record-Grandhavari* (Trivandrum, 1973), pp.1-6; C. Achyuta Menon, *The Cochin State Manuel* (Ernakulam, 1911),pp.87-88, 96-97.
16. J.A. Van Der Chijs, *The Dagh-Register gehouden in Casteel Batavia, Anno 1659* (s' Hage, 1889), p.43.
17. Selections from the Records of the Madras Government: Dutch Records No. 13, *Dutch in Malabar* by A. Galletti, Rev. A.J. Van Der Burg, Rev. P. Groot (Madras, 1911) p.9.
18. John Nieuhoff, *Voyages and Travels into Brazil and East Indies* (London, 1703), II, pp.253-254.
19. A.J. Churchil, *A Collection of Voyages and Travels* (London, 1732), III, p.570.
20. Dutch MSS Records No. 23375, p.331.
21. Jean Baptiste Tavernier, *Travels in India*, ed., and trans., V. Ball (London, 1925), I, p.193.
22. Purakkad to Surat, 17 November 1663, William Foster, *The English Factories in India 1661-1664* (London, 1923), p.218.
23. Selections from the Records of the Madras Government: Dutch Record No.14, *Memoir written in the Year 1677* A.D. by Hendrick Adriaan Van Rheede (Madras, 1911), p.10.
24. William Foster, *The English Factories in India 1668-1669* (London, 1927), p.273.
25. Van Rheede, loc.cit.
26. John Splinter Stavorinus, *Voyages to the East Indies* (London, 1798), III, p.237.
27. William Logan, *Malabar* (Madras, 1951), I, p.341.
28. Stavorinus, op.cit., pp.234-236.
29. Ibid., pp.236-237.
30. Ibid., p.238
31. Ibid., p.238-239.
32. *The Diary of Van Imhoff*, January to March 1739, Dutch MSS, Record No. 281.
33. Stavorinus, op.cit. pp.240-241.
34. Memoirs and Instructions of Dutch Governors, Commandeurs and C., Memoir left by Gustaff Willem Baron Van Imhoff, Governor and Director of Ceylon to his successor Willem Maurits Bruyrunk, 1740, trans., Sophia Pieters (Colombo, 1911), p.6.
35. Ibid., p.15
36. Stavorinus, op.cit., III, pp.241-242.
37. Galletti, op. cit., p.23.
38. The English factors at Tellicherry recorded the news that 'the Dutch at Colethy [Colachel] surrendered to the king of Travancore for want of provision'. Anjengo to Tellicherry, 8 August 1741. Letters received 1741-46, VI, p.4. See also A.P. Ibrahim Kunju. 'The Battle of Kulaccai [1741] and Debacle of the Dutch on the Malabar coast', *Journal of Kerala Studies* (September, 1975), II Part III, pp. 375-385.
39. Selections from the Records of the Madras Governments: Dutch Record No. 1, *Memoir on the Malabar Coast by J.V. Stein Van Gollenesse* (Madras, 1908), p.4.

40. Stavorinus, op.cit., III, p.243.
41. Gollenesse, op. cit., p.19.
42. T.I. Poonen, *Dutch Hegemony in Malabar and its Collapse A.D. 1663-1795* (Trivandrum, 1978), p.99.
43. Gollenesse, op. cit., p.36.
44. Batavia to Cochin, 10 August 1745, Dutch MSS. Record No. 308, p.356.
45. Gollenesse, opp.cit., p.19.
46. Cochin to Colombo, 31 December 1749, Dutch MSS. Record No. 468, p.75.
47. Selections from the Records of the Madras Government: Dutch Record No.3, *Memoir of Commander Fredrik Cunes* (Madras, 1908), pp.2-3.
48. J.E. Heeres and F.W. Stapel, *Corpus Diplomaticum Neerlando-Indicum* (The Hague, 1919), GI, pp.38; T.K. Velupillai, *The Travancore State Manuel* (Trivandrum, 1940), II, Appendix, pp.137-142. (Malayalam Version).
49. Selection from the Records of the Madras Government: Dutch Record No.2, *Memoir written in the year 1781 A.D. by Adriaan Moens* (Madras, 1908). p.4.
50. Ashin Das Gupta, *Malabar in Asian Trade 1740-1800* (London, 1967), p.43.
51. Selections from the Records of the Madras Government: Dutch Record No.4, *Memoir of Johan Gerard Van Angelbeek* (Madras, 1908),p.1.

31

THE TRADE IN INDIAN TEXTILES AND THE INDUSTRIAL REVOLUTION IN ENGLAND

Dietmar Rothermund

Since ancient times India has produced excellent cotton textiles on fairly simple looms. The ingenuity of the weavers and textile printers enabled them to make wonderful fabrics which were in great demand both at home and abroad. There is evidence that even the traders of the Indus civilisation were able to sell Indian textiles in distant Mesopotamia. In ancient and medieval times, Indian textiles found a ready market in the countries surrounding the Indian Ocean. When European traders cut in on that trade, they soon discovered that this was a profitable business. The Portuguese concentrated on the spice trade, but when the Dutch appeared on the scene, they made so much money in the intra-Asian textile trade, that they could buy the wares which they sent to Europe from the profits of that textile trade.

The Dutch East India Company conducted auctions in Amsterdam. This was a very flexible system of serving the European market. The volume of the goods to be auctioned could be controlled so as to maintain the stability of prices. At the same time the auctions provided a good instrument for gauging the demand for all types of goods. Introducing new items such as Indian textiles in this way was very easy. After a few experimental consignments in the first half of the 17th century, this textile trade made up about 15 per cent around the middle of the century and then increased to about 45 per cent by the end of the century while pepper had receded to about 25 per cent. The total value of Dutch imports from Asia amounted to about 1.2 mill. Pound Sterling around 1700. Nearly half of this must have been due to the import of Indian textiles.

The East India Company which held its auctions in London was a keen competitor of the Dutch East India Company, but the value of its trade at the end of the 17th century was only about half of that carried by the Dutch. However, Indian textiles made up about 70 per cent of British imports. Their value amounted to 367,000 Pound Sterling. If one adds to this the Dutch textile imports which must have been worth about 600,000 Pound Sterling, Europe received Indian textiles worth approximately 1 mill. Pound Sterling around 1700. The total British export of woollens was worth about 3 mill. Pound Sterling at that time. This shows that Indian textiles had attained a considerable share of the European textile market. For the future development of trade in this commodity this was of great importance. If this trade would have only been a marginal affair it could not have served as a base for the industrial revolution. But in addition to a large market this revolution required further preconditions which emerged after 1700.

The Rise of the London Cotton Printers

The Dutch trade in Indian textiles peaked around 1700 and then rapidly receded in the first quarter of the 18th century. The recession of this trade which had expanded so vigorously in the previous decades was caused by the phenomenal rise of the London cotton printers who were the vanguard of the industrial revolution in England. They owed this rise to a particular historical constellation. The growing import of printed Indian piecegoods had affected the economic interests of established textile traders such as the producers of woollens or the linen drapers. Finally a very mercantilist type of legislation was passed by Parliament in 1700 which prohibited the import of printed piecegoods. This also affected the Dutch re-export of this commodity to England. The import of white cotton piecegoods was not prohibited and this was the material which the London cotton printers needed for their lucrative trade which soon increased to an amazing extent. They did not only produce for the home market, but also for the export trade and thus competed with the Dutch in this respect who continued to import Indian printed goods freely and supplied them to the European continental market.

The London cotton printers had a decisive advantage - they could adjust their production to European fashions and even create new fashions by introducing designs of their own. Indian designs were of a traditional type. British attempts to persuade Indian weavers and printers to introduce new designs had invariably failed. Moreover, the London printers were closer to the European market and were therefore able to react to changes in demand much more quickly. Their workshops were of an impressive size. Some of them employed about 400 workers. Only about one fifth of these workers would be skilled ones such as designers, cutters, printers, the rest would perform routine operations as there was a great deal of mechanical work to be done. The cotton printers would also have their apparatus for preparing dyes on the premises as the quality and fastness of colours was essential for their trade. In fact, this is where trade secrets were kept which the master printer would not divulge to his apprentices. (Aiolfi 1987:168) Unlike weaving, this line of production did not lend itself to the establishment of a putting out system. Production had to be concentrated and the plants required a relatively large amount of capital. The owners of such plants would often take up money from third parties. There is no evidence that the East India Company invested capital in this line of business, but the wealthy linen-drapers probably did participate in it. (Aiolfi 1987:176) They did not restrict their trade to linen but were actively involved in procuring white cotton cloth for the printers and selling printed cloth to the public. The alliance with the linen - drapers also helped the cotton printers to keep the producers of woollens at bay who were always clamouring for the prohibition of cotton cloth imports and cotton printing. In fact, these people were crying wolf although they were doing very well in this period. In order to compete with light cottons they had learned how to produce light worsteds which sold very well. Exports of British woollens increased in terms of value from about three to four Mill. Pounds from the 1720s to the 1750s. (Rothermund 1981:91) The only problem was that woollens were not fit for printing and that is why the wool lobby wanted to stop the printers altogether. Fortunately they did not succeed in this, otherwise they would have done great harm to British economic growth.

The Procurement of Intermediate Goods in India

The cotton printers were faced by a crucial constraint - they depended on the supply of the right quality of white cotton cloth from India. A consignment of cotton cloth which was not properly bleached would be a complete loss. Its defect would only show up during the printing when the pattern was smudged. The East India Company which had to adjust its operations to the new industrial demand of the cotton printers rose to the occasion. But in order to do so it had to adopt new methods of production control for such intermediate goods. The servants of the company in India had to supervise such difficult technical processes as proper bleaching according to industrial specifications. For this they had to rely on skilled Indian bleachers. The best method would have been to hire these people, pay them good wages and supervise them closely in workshops established in the British factories in India. But the Board of Directors in London was averse to this kind of direct employment; they could not conceive of a company of traders as an industrial employer hiring labour. (Aiolfi 1987:317) On the other hand, the directors were well aware of the need to supply quality products to the cotton printers in London.

The servants of the company in India were thus caught on the horns of a dilemma. They had to guarantee specific performance without getting involved in long term labour contracts. But whether the directors liked it or not, the servants of the company in India actually ventured into the field of production in different ways which closely approximated direct employment and entrepreneurial investment as distinct from investment in trade. This did not apply to weaving in which British interference only related to such things as the adaptation of Indian looms to the size of cloth demanded at home. Initially the weavers had resisted this, because European demand accounted only for a minor part of their production, but when that demand grew they did make the required changes. Dyeing and bleaching, however, were lines of production in which the servants of the company had taken a more active interest even before industrial demand at home made itself felt. The quality of the finished goods depended very much on those processes and there was also an important constraint as far as the timing of the shipments to London was concerned. Unlike the Dutch company which built and maintained its own ships the British leased them from private shipowners. This enabled their company to invest all of its capital in trade, but it also meant high freight rates and enormous costs for demurrage if a ship could not return to London in time because it had missed the North-East monsoon. The British ships had to leave India in October. But the bleaching of cloth was a seasonal activity which could start only at the end of the rainy season because it depended both on an ample supply of fresh water and on intensive sunshine for the drying of the cloth. For proper bleaching the cloth had to be repeatedly soaked, steamed and dried - a procedure which would take about two weeks for one lot. (Aiolfi 1987:309) The few weeks between the end of the rainy season and the deadline for the return of the ships to London were therefore a very busy time for the bleachers. The company settled them in some of their important factories such as Madras, invested money in their workshops and equipment and in the maintenance of their wells. They also supplied rice to them and saw to it that they would not starve. Often this type of investment was given as credit to begin with but then had to be written off as "bad debt", because the bleachers certainly did not become rich while working for the company. Hiring them as regular labourers was difficult not only because it was incompatible with the policy laid down by the directors in London, but also because the work was seasonal. But just short of actually employing them the factors did everything to attach them to the service of the company and to make them do their work under their close supervision. (Aiofi 1987:319 ff.)

Factors and "writers" were trained for commercial work, but not for technical inspection. The company had actually sent out quite a few British artisans who could do this kind of work. The directors had even issued an order that each bale of cloth had to be marked with the initials of the inspector so that he could be held responsible for his quality control. This was done even before the rapid expansion of the trade in white bleached cloth which is under consideration here. With that expansion the number of the inspectors had to increae, too. But it is not very easy to document this because most of these people were sent out as soldiers in the company's service. This made sense as their inspection work was also seasonal and for the rest of the time they could do their "soldiering". The lists of passengers going out to India as soldiers fortunately contain some information about their background. There were quite a few artisans and people with other skills among them. Of the 500 soldiers whose destination was Madras in the years from 1718 to 1738 there were only 71 professional soldiers, but there were at least 68 "soldiers" who had worked in some textile trade or the other, including weavers, dyers etc. (Aiolfi 1987:381) This kind of people represented the new directions of the company's activity. They could help to intensify the control of production and - as soldiers - contribute to the expansion of terrtorial control which went hand in hand with it.

The type of cloth required as intermediate product for supply to the London cotton printers was not always easy to get. The staff of the East India Company in India actually showed great ingenuity in coping with this new demand for the right type of white cotton cloth. Bengal was the main source of supply for this cloth, whereas the Madras Presidency had supplied mostly printed piecegoods. The trade with Bengal accordingly expanded very vigorously in the first half of the 18th century. In the 1720s the import of white cloth from Bengal doubled and was worth 400,000 Pound Sterling by the end of the decade. It then remained at that level for some time and then peaked at 500,000 Pound

Sterling in the early 1740s. (Rothermund 1981:92) But in the middle of this century there was a great deal of political instability in the areas of production which were located in the interior of the country. The servants of the company penetrated into Bengal in search of the proper kind of cloth and were very good at tapping sources of supply unaffected by Maratha raids and other turmoil. An analysis of the statistics of cotton cloth sent to London from 1701 to 1757 shows this very clearly. Certain types of cloth were associated with specific areas of Bengal, e.g. *"gurrahs"* were mainly from Kasimbazar and Malda, *"cossaehs"* from Dhaka etc. The Marathas had raided the first region in 1742 and it did not recover from it for some time, but they had not reached Dhaka from which *"cossaehs"* were exported in greater numbers from 1743 to 1744. (Rothermund 1999:283) Such regional shifts in supply reflect the impact of political events, but they also are a testimony to the quick adjustment of the East India Company to this situation. However, after 1750 there was a steady decline in this trade. (Rothermund 1981:92) This was certainly not caused by a decreasing demand for the output of the London cotton printers. They were forced to think of import substitution, i.e. the spinning of cotton and the weaving of cotton cloth in England.

Import Substitution: The Spinning and Weaving of Cotton Cloth in England

This kind of import substitution was a major problem, because labour was scarce and therefore expensive in England. The British Isles had a population of about 5 mill. at that time whereas India had probably about 150 mill. Spinning was the most labour-intensive part of this work as one weaver required the yarn of about six spinners for his production. This induced inventors to apply their minds to the task of enhancing the productivity of labour with mechanical devices. The first of a line of such creative men was James Hargrave who invented a spinning machine in 1764, which he named after his daughter Jenny. This spinning-jenny could spin several threads at once. Spinners had the tricks of their trade literally at their fingertips. Hargrave's major achievement was the invention of a mechanism which could replace this work of nimble fingers. But the thread produced by his "jenny" was a soft one, more suitable for the weft than for the warp. Five years later Richard Arkwright invented an improved spinning machine which he then provided with a waterframe in 1775. This gave rise to the establishment of spinning mills driven by water power. Arkwright's machine produced a strong thread suitable for the warp. In 1790 he made further progress by attaching a steam engine to this machinery. In the meantime Samuel Crompton had invented the "mule-jenny" around 1780. This machine could produce finer and stronger yarn suitable for mechanical looms, and in 1784 Edmund Cartwright promptly invented such a loom.

The relentless progress of the industrial revolution by means of newly invented machinery seems to be demonstrated by this quick sequence. But whereas the spinning machines were soon put into operation as labour-saving devices, the mechanical loom took a much longer time to swing into action. For quite some time handloom weavers with improved shuttle looms were still getting better results than the mechanical loom. Thus the number of handloom weavers increased in England from about 100,000 in 1788 to 240,000 in 1830. It was only by 1860 that their number dwindled to 10,000. (Paulinyi/Troitzsch 1997:307) It is, therefore, wrong to assume that the weavers "whose bones bleached in the plains of Bengal" were the victims of industrial powerlooms. They had been outproduced by British handloom weavers working with improved looms and industrial yarn.

Cartwright's powerloom was initially a slow and cumbersome machine. He and his brother were the only entrepreneurs who invested their money in weaving mills equipped with this machinery. But both failed by about 1793. It took a number of further improvements to make powerlooms a paying proposition. But by 1830 about 100,000 had been installed in British mills. (Paulinyi/Troitzsch 977:310) The rise of the powerloom depended on advances in the production of machine tools which enabled mechanics to work on metal parts with great precision. The legendary Henry Maudslay who established his workshop in 1797 was a pioneer in this field. He invented the industrial turning lathe, followed by numerous other machine tools. He did not apply for patents, but concentrated on expanding his production which made him the leading industrialist in this field. (Paulinyi/Troitzsch 1997:332) The synergies of all these inventions speeded up the industrial revolution.

Economic historians have been puzzled by the fact that this revolution was sparked off by the British cotton industry which was smaller than the contemporary French one and which even in the British context was initially a minor industry. (Davis 1973: 311-312) The solution of this puzzle may be that due to the trade in Indian textiles the scope for import substitution as well as the export market were enormous in this field. Therefore this industry could forge ahead at a rapid rate. Unfortunately this sealed the fate of Indian weavers in the export business. The mechanical devices which have been described above did not require much capital investment and could have been easily reproduced in India. But as they were invented in order to save labour, nobody felt the need for them in India. The debate on the crucial question why India did not make the transition to capitalism has usually centred on "capital" rather than on "labour". It was the surfeit of labour which prevented the transition to capitalism in India, whereas the sarcity of labour in England challenged the ingenuity of inventors and ushered in the industrial revolution.

But in conclusion we must stress once more that the trade with Indian textiles was the precondition for this development. This trade had created an enormous demand and generated a great deal of income for the merchants participating in it. This trading network could then take up the products of the London cotton printers. A printer who was assured of a ready sale of his products could easily raise the capital required for his workshop. Presumably he would start it on a small scale and then reinvest some of his income in order to expand his operations. It is very likely that the printers did not buy the cotton cloth directly from the East India Company but from the linen drapers who also might provide some capital to such printers.

The printers. The printers, however, did not emerge from the ranks of the linen drapers. They were technocrat-entrepreneurs who combined mechanical skills with a special knowledge of dyes and designs. Initially they worked with flat printing presses, but later on they installed rotating presses when the weavers were able to supply them with longer pieces of cloth.

The "External Arena", the "Plunder of Bengal" and the Industrial Revolution

The research presented here permits a revision of theories dealing with India, the capitalist world system and the industrial revolution. The first theory which we wish to take up here is Immanuel Wallerstein's world-system theory. According to this theory the world- system consists of a core and a periphery and has only very tenuous relations with an "external arena". (Wallerstein 1980:273 f.) The system evolves by "peripheralising" more and more regions of the world and thus finally eliminating the "external arena". As long as the "external arena" still exists, its links with the world system are characterised by trade relations which are not essential for the maintenance of the system and could cut off without any loss. The trade in small quantities of luxury goods would be a case in point. Wallerstein postulates that India remained a part of the "external arena" until the 1750s and was perpheralised when the British established their territorial rule in Bengal. The supply of intermediate goods to the cotton printers of London in the first half of the 18th century obviously does not fit into this pattern. But one may even contend that the massive trade in Indian textiles of the late 17th century which created an important European market for this commodity does not seem to conform to the characteristics of tenuous trade links with an "external arena".

As Wallerstein's world- system expands continuously, he cannot tolerate "revolutions" which imply discontinuities. The readers of his "The Modern World-System III" will notice this with great surprise, the more so as his volumes were published in a series entitled "Studies in Social Discontinuities". He obviously reacted to theories which tended to portray the industrial revolution as a rather sudden dynamic upsurge. The developments discussed in this paper show that the industrial revolution was a rather long process if we date its beginning with the work of the London cotton printers in the early 18th century and its final stage with the replacement of the work of British handloom weavers by powerlooms in the 1830s. But it was a revolution nevertheless, because it was characterised by the replacement of the artisan by the industrial worker and the substitution of capital for labour. Moreover, it witnessed a major shift of the centre of cotton textile production from India to Great Britain.

Another prominent theory propounded by British Marxist writers is that the "Plunder of Bengal" financed the British industrial revolution. Wallerstein has not joined that chorus for obvious reasons, because he does not believe in the "industrial revolution". But many other authors have referred to this theory again and again. Bengal undoubtedly did contribute to the rise of the industrial revolution, but rather by means of the supply of intermediate goods described in this paper. The "Plunder of Bengal" was a much later affair, it refers to the activities of the East India Company and its servants after the assumption of the Diwani of Bengal in 1765. Robert Clive did want the British crown to take over the territorial administration of Bengal, but William Pitt who feared that King George III would use the revenue of Bengal so as to bypass the powers of Parliament refused to sanction this and clearly said that he much rather wished that the wealth of Bengal would flow into private pockets. This decision led to the rise of the "Nabobs" as the rich men were called who returned to Great Britain after serving in India. The "Plunder of Bengal" did take place, but its links with the rise of the industrial revolution were at the most rather indirect. The "Nabobs" did not invest their money in industry for the simple reason that the early investment in this field could be easily taken care of by the producers themselves as long as they were sure of a brisk trade in their products. The indirect link was the general rise of liquidity in Great Britain which faciliated all kinds of economic transactions. The "Nabobs" contributed to this liquidity, but so did the thriving British export trade in which printed cotton textiles played a major role.

References:

1. Aiolfi, Sergio (1987), *Calicos und gedrucktes Zeug. Die Entwicklung der englischen Textilveredelung und der Tuchhandel der East India Company, 1650-1750,* Stuttgart
2. Davis, Ralph (1973), *The Rise of the Atlantic Economies,* London
3. Paulinyi, Akos and Ulrich Troitzsch (1997), *Mechanisierung und Maschinisierung, 1600 bis 1840* (Propylaen Technikgeschichte Bd. 3), Berlin
4. Rothermund, Dietmar (1981), *Asian Trade and European in the Age of Mercantilism,* New Delhi
5. Rothermund, Dietmar (1999), "The Changing Pattern of British Trade in Indian Textiles, 1701-1757", in: Sushil Chaudhuri and Michel Morineau, eds. (1999), *Merchants Companies and Trade. Europe and Asia in the Early Modern Era,* Cambridge.
6. Wallerstein, Immanuel (1980), *The Modern World-System II: Mercantilism and the Consolidation of the European World-Economy, 1600-1750,* New York

32

ANGLO-CARNATIC RELATIONS OF THE EIGHTEENTH CENTURY

B. Sobhanan

The Anglo - Carnatic relations of the eighteenth century forms a significant chapter in the history of moderen India. The Carnatic kingdom which extended from the Bay of Bengal in the east to the Western Ghats and Mysore in the west and from Kanyakumari in the south to Gundalakama river in the north occupied a preeminent status among the local powers of South India. This fertile territorial unit formed an integral part of ancient Tamilakam with its abundant supply of spices, cloves, pepper, indigo, pearls, silk, calico and a variety of other valuable goods. As a result of the political vicissitudes under the Mughals, the Marathas, the Nizam of Hyderabad and the European powers like the English the French, the Duch and the Danes, the Carnatic kingdom lost its identity and ultimately became a victim to the machinations of the British.

After a series of trials and tribulations in 1749 the Carnatic kingdom went under the Nawabship of Muhammad Ali, the third son of Award-ud-din, the founder of the Wallajah dynasty. In the course of his long reign from 1749 to 1795 he was called upon to face severe challenges both from the internal and external powers. As far as the French and the English were concerned the Carnatic kingdom of Muhammad Ali was the venue to decide who should control the fortunes of South India. In the course of the crisis Muhammad Ali submitted himself to the aid and assistance of the English. The English who strictly confined themselves to commercial pursuits, tried to keep aloof from the political disputes in the beginning. When the French tried to emerge themselves as the greatest imperial and commercial power in the south, the English gave up the policy of strict isolation and began to deal with the political disputes of the local rulers.

The Carnatic kingdom of Muhammad Ali provided the most suitable base to commence the imperial designs of the English in the south. In the course of the expansion of the English spheres of influence Muhammad Ali became the most effective instrument to realise the political ambitions of the English. While adhering total subservience to the English, Muhammad Ali fought a number of battles against the neighbouring powers like the rulers of Mysore, Marathas, the Nizam of Hyderabad, and the Raja of Thanjavur. The dynastic struggles against the Nevayats and the auxiliary chieftains further ruined the resources of the kingdoms. Though Muhammad Ali fought such battles mostly with his men and money the ultimate benefits and credit went over to the English. In the name of such battles the English continued to collect huge amounts from the Nawab. When a series of such exactions came one after the other, the Nawab became a huge debtor. The English prevailed upon the Nawab to sign a number of arbitrary treaties, which ultimately eroded the independent status of the kingdom. Without considering the past services the English proceeded to assume the civil and military administration at first and finally to annex the kingdom.

The defeat of the Carnatic forces in the battle of Adayar at the hands of the French in 1746 made the Nawab to seek the support of the English. The combined forces of the English and the Nawab offered a potent resistance to the French. Besieged by the Nawab's forces from the land and attacked by the English troops from the sea, the French withdrew from Fort St.David and retreated to Pondicherry.[2]

The French soon got ready for the next round of the trial of strength by exposing the cause of Chanda Sahib, the

Nevayat chief who remained a traditional rival to Anwar-ud-din. the Wallajah chief. Similarly in Hyderabad, following the death of Nizam-ul-mulk Asaf Jah, the founder of Asaf Jah dynasty in 1748, Nasir Jung, his second son became the Nizam of Hyderabad. Muzaffar Jung, the grand son of Asaf Jah, staked a claim to the throne producing a will of his grandfather. The French identified themselves with the cause of Muzaffir Jung and Chanda Sahib and then formed a formidable hostile alliance against the English.

In an attempt to counter the French support to Chanda Sahib, Anwar-ud-din sought the help of the British to strengthen his artillery in particular[3]. Even after repeated requests the English kept mum. At the crucial hour, unsupported by the English, the Nawab and his sons fought a major battle against the hostile forces of Chanda Sahib, Muzzaffar Jung and the French at Ambur. In the course of the battle Anwar ud-din was defeated and killed[4]. His elder son Maphuz Khan became a prisoner and the younger son Muhammad Ali fled to Tiruchirappalli.

Muhammad Ali in his attempts to defend Tiruchirappalli and restore the lost territories, continued the request for English assistance. In July 1750 Charles Floyer, the Governor of Madras despatched an army of 200 Europeans and 1500 sepoys under the command of Major Lawrence to assist Muhammad Ali at his own expenses[5]. Failure of Muhammad Ali to meet the expenses of the English forces resulted in its withdrawal in the same year. Though in the midst of troubles, Muhammad Ali continued to identify the English as a true friend, helper and protector[6].

The mounting financial crisis made Muhammad Ali to seek an aid of two lakhs of rupees for his private expenses and one and a half lakhs of rupees every month for the maintenance of the army. In lieu of it he agreed to mortgage the territories of his kingdom, including Tiruchirappalli, Madurai and Tirunelveli[7]. Again, at the difficult situation, the English failed to respond. When Muhammad Ali proceeded to settle the problem through a compromise with Chanda Sahib, Thomas Saunders who succeeded Charles Floyer as Governor of Madras agreed to reopen the correspondence.

When Chanda Sahib was preoccupied with the annexation of Tiruchirapalli, as per the suggestion of Muhammad Ali, the English led 200 Europeans and 300 sepoys under the command of Robert Clive to annex Arcot through a surprise attack. Clive successfully carried out the missions and thus "the Anglo-Indian army received its baptism of victory"[8]. Immediately after the occupation of Arcot the Nawab contributed an amount of 1,50,000 pagodas for the assistance given by the English[9]. No doubt the occupation of Arcot became a turning point in the history of South India which decided the course of events in favour of the English.

The combined forces of Chanda Sahib continued to tighten their grip both upon Tiruchirapalli and Arcot with added strength and determination. Surrounded by hostile forces Muhammad Ali searched for allies. At that critical juncture in September, 1751 Nanja Raja, the Wodeyar king of Mysore, led an expedition of 5000 cavalry, 10,000 infantry and 1000 wall piece bearers and came to the rescue of Muhammad Ali [10]. In retun he agreed the cession of Madurai region with all its dependencies[11].

It marked the beginning of a steady supply of forces from other local powers which included 6000 cavalrymen under Murari Rao, the Maratha Chief, 3000 horses and 2000 soldiers from Thanjavur[12] and 500 horses and 3000 soldiers from Pudukkottai [13]. The combined army subjugated the forces of Chanda Sahib and wrested the control of all the areas including Arcot and Tiruchirapalli. After the termination of hostilities the English claimed large amounts as military expenditure from the Nawab. But the Nawab continously evaded the promises given to Nanja Raja which made the Mysoreans revengeful.

The prolonged struggle for the occupation of Tiruchirapalli increased the arrears due to the English to an amount of one million rupees. In order to settle the arrears the English suggested that if the whole district of Arcot were mortgaged to the Company and left to their management it would be attended with great advantages both of the English and the Nawab. When the debt to the English was cleared, the districts would be returned to the Nawab under a better regulation than they had hitherto been [14]. In lieu of the entire Arcot Subah the Nawab mortgaged the revenue of Chingelpet for two years at 28,500 pagodas per annum, Covelong at 8000 pagodas for one year, Manamangalam at 13,000 pagodas for one year and Kanchipuram and eighty four villages of Tripassore for one year[15].

The third Carnatic battle, the echo of the seven years' war (1756-1763) in Europe also brought further liabilities upon Muhammad Ali. The friendship between the English and the Nawab made the French forces to embark upon the Carnatic soon after the ourtbreak of the seven years war [16]. Though he could get the English protection at his own expenses Lally, the French General, defeated the English forces and occupied Arcot on 4 October, 1758 which made Muhammad Ali find shelter at Fort St. George, Madras[17]. When forces rushed to madras the Nawab and his family members were sent back to Tiruchirapalli through Thanjavur[18]. On the arrival of fresh reinforcements the English recaptured all the occupied places one by one and brought back Muhammad Ali in March, 1761 to his capital at Arcot. The treaty of Paris signed on 10 January, 1763 put an end to the third Carnatic battle by going back to previous positions. But at the end of the war Muhammad Ali was overburdened with debts to the extent of 25,98,801 pagodas[19].

Following the third Anglo-French battle in the Carnatic the English emerged as the paramount imperial and colonial power in the south. Thus having entered the imperial fray, the English required provisions and funds to sustain its war machine and military operations. In Muhammad Ali the English found the needed resources and necessary base of operations.

The letters which Muhammad Ali wrote to the English clearly manifest the frame of his mind. For instance in one of the letters he wrote: "I value the friendhip and regard the English company and nation, superior to being master of the whole world and that I esteemed good as included, in theirs. I told you that it was not in the power of the universe to break my friendship with the company, or their friendship with me... The Nawab and the company have even been invariably united like too much milk and sugar and our correspondence also has been conducted on the same footing."[20] Guided by such a strong affinity to the English, the Nawab earned the displeasure of the local powers who tried to assert their independence. Among them Haidar Ali, the Sultan of Mysore became the most inveterate enemy.

With the assistance of the English he carried out a prolonged battle against Murtaz Ali, the Governor of Vellore, Tuckia Sahib, the Governor of Wandiwash, Nazeabulla Khan, the Governor of Nellore, the Rajah of Ongole, the poligars of the Madurai region, Maphuz Khan and Yusf Khan. It further made an additional debt of 19,77,041 pagodas to the English. The Nawab was obliged to assign the districts of Nellore, Tirupati, Kalahasti and Venkatagiri which yielded an annual revenue of fifty-one lakhs of pagodas to the English for a period of three years.[21] Thus the expeditions which Muhammad Ali carried out against the Nevayats and the auxiliary chieftains brought more treasures to the English and expanded their possessions in the South.

After the consolidation of his influence in Arcot and Madurai, Muhammad Ali proceeded to annex the kingdom of Thanjavur and the Marava states of Sivaganga and Ramanathapuram. He sought the assistance of the English for the conquest of Thanjavur. He agreed to meet all the expenses of the expedition and also to remit thirty-five lakhs of rupees.[22] The combined forces invaded Thanjavur in 1771 and again in 1773[23]. In the second phase of the aggression he agreed to remit two lakhs and sixty-five thousand pagodas for the support of three battalions of the Company's troops.[24] After a minor resistance, Tuljaji, the king of Thanjavur, surrendered on 16 September, 1773.[25] Thus the Wallajah rule was extended to Thanjavur. In return for the English assistance the Nawab paid ten lakhs of rupees as present and six lakhs and seventy-five thousand rupees as prize money to the English troops.[26] In the same year the combined forces of the Nawab and the English annexed the Dutch settlement at Nagore.[27].

Intoxicated by the victories Muhammed Ali proceeded to assert his equality with the king of England as recognised by the treaty of Paris,[28] and claimed his sovereignty as acknowledged by the Mughals.[29] Further he tried to establish direct relations with the French, the Dutch and Danes in total disregrd to the British interests. He prevented the attempts of the English to garrison the fort of Thanjavur for the Hindus were afraid of the Europeans killing cows.[30] Further he declared that he was the absolute Lord of the country and the best judge of his own affairs.[31] It made the Court of Directors to issue immediate orders to carry out the restoration of Thanjavur to the former Raja of Thanjavur as early as possible. The Madras Government under Lord Pigot carried out the restoration of Thanjavur. It wounded the feelings of the Nawab and it was totally against his expectations.

The restoration of Thanjavur further weakened the Nawab and earned the wrath of all anti-British forces. It made him to lament: "Such are passengers on the sea, who after a long and dangerous voyage have the happy prospect of their Harbour, but in the midst of their joy are overtaken by a sudden and dreadful storm and driven again on the troubled ocean."[32] It was almost like a slip between the cup and the lip. At a time when the Nawab was eager to enjoy his victory, the English denied it.

Muhammad Ali became a victim to the fury of Haidar Ali and Tipu Sultan, the rulers of Mysore, for his total approval to the machinations of the English. The so called 'perpetual friendship' existed between the English and the Nawab dragged the Carnatic kingdom into the vortex of the Anglo-Mysore battles. Both Haidar Ali and Tipu Sultan concentrated their attention on the Carnatic to cause the maximum depredations. In the course of battles they occupied the pivotal places and caused total dissolution. At the crucial hours of warfare the English troops stood as mere spectators. To the great agony of the Nawab, quite against the laws of men and god, the English continued to demand exorbitant amount to meet the expenses of war. When Muhammad Ali found it impossible to meet the arbitrary demands of the English in September 1780 he was forced to assign the revenue of Tiruchirapalli and Tirunelveli to settle the expenses of second Anglo-Mysore war.[33] The agreement provided that the revenue of the Circar territories should be transferred to the Company for a period of five years and one-sixth of the annual collections should be assigned for private expenses of the Nawab.[34] George Proctor and George Andrew Ram were appointed as the receivers of assigned revenue in Tirunelveli and Tiruchirapalli respectively. Further the government constituted a Committee of Assigned Revenue for revenue administration. They supervised the conduct of revenue servants and sought to check fraud and embezzlement.[35]

The Madras Government exercised the right to appoint its own nominees in the place of corrupt renters. It restricted the number of revenue servants to the bare minimum.[36] The committee introduced a number of measures to improve the administration of revenue. In order to enhance the revenue, the committee divided the districts into many farms and were let for lease. They followed a conciliatory attitude to the poligars. They preferred the system of renting, mainly to restrict the possibilities of intrigue, oppression and extortion from the side of the local servants.[37] It turned the waste lands into cultivable lands. It regularized the collection of taxes from the people. It repaired water course ruined by the invaders, gave loans for cultivation and distributed paddy seeds in *gratis*. Thus through the assumption, the Madras Government thought that "they may be gradually able to free the country from oppression, to recover the lands and manufactures from their present most deplorable state greatly to improve the revenue and finally to establish wealth, credit and prosperity throughout the country".[38]

But in practice the Nawab's amuldars disregarded the orders of the receivers and refused to furnish the accounts of collection.[39] The Nawab also continued to collect revenue from poligars for his own expenditure. Thus the proper working of the assignment became rather difficult.[40] No doubt the system of assigned revenue reduced the Nawab to the status of a titular sovereign and the English emerged as the de facto sovereign. The Nawab continued to record his protest and wanted the immediate restoration of the administration. He represented his grievances both in Madras and in London. Ultimately it paved the way for the treaty of 1787 in tune with the imperial ambitions of the English.

On 24 February 1787 Muhammad Ali, the Nawab of the Carnatic and Sir Archibald Campbell, the Governor of Madras signed a comprehensive treaty. The treaty conferred upon the English significant advantages at the expense of the Nawab's authority. It was intended to establish a scheme of joint defence for the Carnatic and the Northern Circar to finance the defense-establishment and to entrust with the Company the right to apply the finances intended for defense, the conduct of war together with the command of the army, magazines of stores and provisions with full power to occupy or dismantle such forts as it deemed essential for the security of the country. It asserted that the friends and enemies of either party were the friends and enemies of both the powers. The English secured the right to establish its system of defense in the Carnatic. To meet the expenses of the English forces the Nawab was required to pay nine lakhs of star pagodas in two instalments of three lakhs and six lakhs on the 30th November and 31st March respectively to the English every year beginning from the date 12 July 1787. In case of failure in the punctual payment of the said amount within a month after due date the company was permitted to collect revenue from the districts of Palnad, Ongole, Madurai and Tiruchirapalli in the Southern Carnatic. If these provinces were insufficient to the full discharge of the arrears within a year, the Nawab was bound to assign other territories in order to make up the deficiency. The Company secured the right to appoint superintendents or receivers, to collect and receive from the Nawab's amuldars all the rents, revenues, duties, customs and *peshcush* of the assumed Circar territories and to exercise all the necessary authority for collecting such rents and revenues.

But it had to resotre the assumed provinces on the complete liquidation of the war debts. Further it should not infringe upon the dignity of the Nawab.[41] It was only a formal statement.

In case any war broke out in the Carnatic or on the coast of Coromandel the Company undertook the responsibility for the conduct and direction of war. The Nawab and the English pledged to apply four-fifths of the revenues of their territories in the coast and the Northern Circars for the expenses of war.[42] It did not mention anything about the sharing of gains ot the Nawab. Similarly there was no compensation in case of failure to the Nawab. It represented another distinct step in the transformation of the English from the status of commercial agents to that of imperial masters.

The third Anglo-Mysore War (1789-1792) once again dragged the Nawab to the whirlpool of warfare. As per the provisions of the treaty of 1787 the Nawab was bound to help the English. In order to revenge against the English intimacy of the Nawab, Tipu Sultan led an expedition to the Carnatic in November, 1790 and carried out depradations.[43] In the course of desolation of the country by the forces of Mysore, Medows, Governor of Madras, in consultation with the Court of Directors, London,[44] proceeded to assume the administration of the Carnatic. The Governor General stated that they decided to assume the revenue of the Carnatic, guided by the strongest considerations of humanity, justice and public necessity.[45]

The Board of Assumed Revenue which virtually became a separate department of the Board of Revenue appointed the Company servants as collectors in the districts and gave them individual responsibility for effective administration.[46] The districts were further divided into small units and farmed them out for one year period in the interests of efficiency in collection. The district of Madurai was divided into seven taluks and Tirunelveli into twenty-two farms.[47] The collectors were directed to take measures for increasing the original offers without infringing upon justice, which was due to the people. They were directed to take measures for retrieving the former flourishing state of the districts as well as the increase of the customs.[48]

It marked yet another step in the erosion of Muhammad Ali's suzerainty and in the establishment of British ascendancy in the Carnatic. When the very existence of the Nawab as an independent power was threatened, the Nawab called upon the Madras Council to send no servants to make collections. He directed his amuldars never to submit to the British authority.[49] The resentment of the Nawab received no attention. Further when the war continued against Tipu Sultan with added strength,the English collectors extracted the maximum amount through all means. With the active assistance of the Nawab the third Anglo-Mysore war came to an end through the treaty of Srirangapatanam. In the course of the negotiations the representatives of the Nawab as well as the Raja of Travancore were kept outside. The territory surrendered by Tipu was divided among the Marathas, the Nizam and the English. On the other hand the Nawab was overburdened with additional collections and a fresh treaty to legalise the same.

The new treaty declared that the whole country should be garrisoned by the British troops, for the expenses of which the Nawab was required to pay nine lakhs of pagodas and for the liquidation of his debts a further sum of 6,21,103 star pagodas. In the event of war the Company was to take the entire management of the affairs of the country into its own hands except that of the private jagirs of the Nawab estimated to yield annually 2,13,911 star pagodas and that of charities calculated to yield annually 21,366 star pagodas and to retain it under its administration for the better prosecution of the war. In that case the Company was to pay one fifth of the net revenue to the Nawab and to restore the management at the end of hostilities. In times of peace the Nawab was permitted to collect the *peshcush* or tribute of the poligars in the Nawab's name estimated 2,64,704 star pagodas, 20 fanams, 26 cash and to give him credit for it against his contribution.

The Nawab was required to pay every year 12,56,400 star pagodas 15 panams and 54 cash, being the amount after deducting the poligar *peshcush* from the aggregate in ten instalments and that after the discharge of the debt in full, a proportionate deduction from each instalment would take place. In case the Nawab failed to pay any instalment before the expiration of fifteen days from the stipulated date, the Company had the right to assume the revenue of any or all of the provinces of Tirunelveli, Madurai, Tiruchirapalli, Nellore, North Arcot, Palnad and Ongole - altogether estimated to yield an annual revenue of 13,41,770 star pagodas. These territories would be held by the Company till the discharge of the debts. In case of a second default in payment, the Company would assume the territories permanently.

The Company agreed to furnish its troops to the Nawab if he required them for the support of his authority and the good order and government of his country. In that case he had to pay the additional expenses of the forces employed. The Nawab was instructed not to enter into any negotiation or political correspondence with any European or native power, without the consent of the Company.

The treaty of 1792 almost crippled the very existence of the Nawab and established the English control with added strength. The arbitrary measures of the English which came in rapid succession gave severe mental agony and it even reduced the span of his life. The attitude of the English came quite against his expectations. The English who once depended on the goodwill of the Nawab when emerged as an imperial power gave scant regard to the feelings of the Nawab. The appeals of the Nawab went without any response. Further he was forced to remit huge amounts which was beyond his capacity. He lost his control upon his subordinate chiefs and other revenue servants. The English continued their attempts to annex the Carnatic kingdom and modify the treaty of 1792 for the same. At that context he breathed his last with a heavy heart on 13 October, 1795 at the age of seventyfive with a parting advice to his son and successor Umdul-ul-Umara that "don't forget one word of mine, that is to do not make the deviation of a hair's breadth in the late treaty of 1792 which is the remover of all evils. If any one should tell you that he would alter the treaty for your good, don't agree to it."[50]

Anglo-Carnatic Relations of the Eighteenth Century

The advent of Marquess Wellesley, as the Governor General of India activated the forces of assumption and annexation of the Carnatic like the other princely states of India. He apprised the English Officers to bestow full attention to establish the English paramountcy at the earliest. The Carnatic kingdom which already came under the imperial grip of the English only rquired the formal acceptance of the subsidiary alliance. The English resorted to different measures like creation of succession dispute, threat to annex the kingdom in the name of violation of treaties, instigation of internal feuds and finally they attempted to poison the Nawab.

Nawab Umdul-ul-Umara, the son and successor of Muhammad Ali followed an uncompromising policy against the English. Considering the attitude of Umdul-ul-Umara, Wellesley cautioned Lord Clive, the Governor of Madras, "it is very necessary that we should be prepared to decide the eventual question of the succession to the Nawabship in the probable event of His Highness' early death, your Lordship will have goodness to ascertain the respective pretensions of those who might lay claim to the land. Upon such information as I shall receive from you, we may be enabled to anticipate the mischiefs of a disputed succession and to avoid the disgrace of adopting a premature decision, which we might be compelled to revoke."[51]

The outbreak of the last Anglo-Mysore battle in 1799 diverted the attention of the English from the creation of a succession dispute to the enforcement of the 3rd article of the Carnatic treaty of 1792 viz., the English assumption of the entire management of the Carnatic except the jagirs and charities. But the successful termination of the war within two months missed the claim to assume the administration under the pretext of warfare. Then the Madras Government proceeded to annex in the name of mal-administration of the servants as per the provisions of the treaty. With a heavy heart the young Nawab wrote to the Governor of Madras: "the frightened deer flies at the approach of danger and finds shelter in the recess of impenetrable forests but for me there is no retreat. Against an enemy I might have defended myself or avoided his snares but it is the

519

arm of friendship which is raised against me, that draws the hostile arrow of destructions... crushed are all my hopes and prospects of happiness vanish from my sight. The rose has fallen and the stalk with all its thorns alone remains in my hand... O my lord, I complain! I complain! I complain !"[52]

The discovery of certain friendly letters written by the Nawabs and the Sultans from the Palace Archives of Srirangpattanam after the fourth Anglo-Mysore war, was soon advanced as a valid evidence to establish the violations of another article of the treaty. In the midst of all such serious charges, Umdul-ul-Umara continued to defend his stand and opposed the proposed move towards annexation. At last when Wellesley inisisted on the Madras Government to carry out the annexation without any more delay the Nawab died on 15 July, 1801. Before his death he succeeded to nominate his eighteen year old son Ali Hussian as his successor. Though he was very young he also followed an unparalleled uncompromising stand against the annexation of his kingdom. When the commission led by Webbe and Close failed to settle the problem Lord Clive, the Governor in person met the young Nawab and warned him of the bitter consequences in case of refusal. His continued hostility made the English to administer poison to his life too. Simultaneously the English created a succession problem also. They brought forward Azim ul Doula, son of Amir ul-Umara, and the grandson of Muhammed Ali. Immediately after the tragic demise of the Ali Hussain, Azim ul Doula ascended the throne as the Nawab of Carnatic and submitted himself to the subsidiary treaty which ultimately established the paramountcy in the Carnatic.

References:

1. Military Sundries, 1793, pp. 290-292.
2. Military Country Correspondence, Vol.I, 1749, p.2.
3. H.H. Dodwell (ed.), *The Diary of Ananda Ranga Pillai*, Vol.IV, pp.219-211.
4. James Mill, *History of British India*, Vol,2,p.178.
5. H.H. Dodwell, *The Cambridge History of India*, Vol.V.p.125.
6. Military Country Correspondence, 1751, Vol.I,p.89.
7. Public Country Correspondence, 1751, Vol. IV, p.47

8. G.B. Malleson, *Dupleix*, p.100
9. Public Country Correspondence, Vol. IV,p.57
10. K.Rajayyan, *History of Tamilnadu*, p.114
11. Military Country Correspondence, 1751, Vol.I., p.48
12. Ibid, Vo.IV,p.72
13. Military Consultations, 1751, Vol.I.,p.13
14. Diary and Proceedings,1755,pp.142-143
15. Military Despatches to England, Vol.I, 1756,p.73
16. C.S.Srinivasachari, *AnandaRanga Pillai*, p.64
17. Military Despatches to England, Vol.III, p.14
18. Military Consultations, Vol.X, 1759, p.404
19. Ibid., Vol.XII, 1761, p.332
20. Military Country Correspondence, Vol.XXI, 1172,pp. 16-17
21. Diary and Proceedings, 1755,p.142
22. Military Country Correspondence, Vol.19, 1771, pp.218-222
23. Tanjore Records, Vol.III, p.1108
24. Military Country Correspondence, Vol.26,1775,p.106
25. Military Consultations, Vol.48,1773, p.883
26. Military Country Correspondence, Vo;.23, 1773, p.106
27. Ibid., Vol.25,1773, p.12
28. Mark Wilks, Historical Sketches of the South of India, Part I, p.427
29. Military Consultations, Vol.46, 1772, p.59
30. Ibid, Vol.46, 1773, p.909
31. Ibid., Vol.51, 1773,p.596
32. Military Country Correspondence, Vol.26, 1777,p.283
33. Military Consultations, Vol.71, pp.1470-1477
34. C.U.Aitchison (ed.) *A Collection of Treaties, Engagements Sannads*, etc., Vol.V,p.181
35. Proceedings of the Committee of Assigned Revenue, Revenue Department, 1780-85, Vol.I,pp.2-3
36. Ibid, Vol.II, pp.243-244
37. Revenue Consultations, Vol.40,pp.458-490
38. R. Caldwell, History of Tinnevelly, p.144
39. Proceedings of the Committee of Assigned Revenue, Vol.II, p.243
40. Military Consultations, Vol.74, p.1187
41. C.U. Aitchison,op.cit., Vol.X, pp.60-62
42. Ibid
43. Military Miscellaneous, Vol.XXV, 179, p.427
44. Papers relating to the Nawabs of Carnatic, p.61

45. Ibid., p.62
46. Proceedings of the Board of Assumed Revenue, Revenue Department 1790-1792, Vol.I, p.36
47. Ibid., p.570
48. Ibid., Vol.II, p.637
49. Military Consultations, Vol.137, p.2357
50. Military Country Correspondence, Vol.16, 1795, pp.188-206
51. Marquess Wellesley's Despatches, Vol.II, pp.226-228
52. Military Consultations, Vol.268, 1800, pp.2996-3027

33

ASIAN STATES AND MERCANTILISM IN THE INDIAN OCEAN ECONOMY: BENGAL NIZAMAT AND THE ENGLISH COMPANY IN 18TH CENTURY.

Ujjayan Bhattacharya

East India Company and the Mercantilist Doctrine and Practice.

The chartered Companies of Europe, like the VOC and the English East India Company, and their activities in Asia, understood from perspectives that followed the very definition of "mercantilism" has posed certain problems for the historians. About two and a half decades ago K.N.Chaudhuri pointed towards the limitations of the theoretical approach of formal systems or economic models in understanding the realities of international trade.[1] Such theoretical models would invariably interpret mercantilism in a limited sense, as it would take into account mainly facts which could be located within the boundary and parameters set by the data, or arranged on, a time-series of exports and imports, or the balance-sheet of profits and dividends showing the continuous logic of development. This interpretation was further based on the premise that the discourse of commerce pursued by the overseas chartered companies was, that, wealth increased *only* if price differentials could be successfully worked upon, and led to further expansion of investments and markets. This was virtually a corollary to the basic bullionist doctrine that wealth of nations increased with inflow and retention of treasure or precious metals and decreased with its outflow.

This notion was widened or given more amplitude, later, when national wealth was not treated synonymously with treasure or precious metals only, but with indicators of the economy that secured the sovereign position of the national state.[2] With this began an attempt to understand a more aggregate entity and a process, that is accumulation of capital. However the quest for glory and power overseas, through trade, navigation and if possible, conquests, had to be matched by an export surplus in the balance of trade. That was the main thrust of the mercantilist argument, which in moments of crisis of the national economy turned out to be a critic of Company trade.[3] However, as Chaudhuri argued, that contemporaneous polemics of the seventeenth century, on the alleged economic effects of the East India trade was apt to overlook the long term structural changes taking place in English overseas trade particularly in the area of re-export. Thus it would not be an exaggeration to state that, the growing and accumulating discourse on national wealth and power which goes by the name of "mercantilism" had a few gaps to be filled in, occasionally by the experience from realities. But, still, even for the writers of the eighteenth century with a mercantilist slant, equation of wealth with money remained the basic idea. Though for some mercantilists the reason for scarcity of money was in the decline of trade and not the other way round.[4]

Thus to draw upon Chaudhuri's arguments regarding unreality of models in explaining realities of international trade it is necessary to locate the gaps in the mercantilist arguments. This is to be located in the gap between the explanation provided by formal theoretical models of international trade and the ideology and practices of the corporate body, the East India Company in enhancing and consolidating it's gains in Asia. Trade was of essence in any mercantile situation, but according to the mercantilist doctrine national power resting to a great deal on the export surplus obtainable through commerce, could not be a function of trade simply. It is in this context that Chaudhuri's description of the Company as a "perfect example of what we today understand as the spirit of mercantilism", particularly "in it's policy of harnessing political power and privileges to commercial purpose", becomes apt as a characterization of the corporate entity, a state within a state. In Chaudhuri's view successful trading strategy meant "location and establishment of the sources of supply, construction of ships, the appointment of able men, a regular exchange of correspondence, and above all an operational plan that took into account the spatial demarcation of economic regions and temporal constraints of long-distance commerce".[5]

Further, the Company could rely on the diplomatic support of the Crown and its ministers to bring pressure on foreign European governments to subdue small rival companies on the Continent. In India and elsewhere in Asia, it had established a number of trading settlements which possessed semi-sovereign status, distinguished by an elaborate procedure of government, courts of law, a municipal system, and a military force. In this circumstances it is not surprising to discover that the Company's organisational structure and bureaucratic apparatus shared many of the attributes of a great department of state.[6]

Moreover, though, along with the possession of a legal monopoly, joint-stock capital structure of the Company gave it an essential continuity in Asian trade, that cannot be taken as sole criteria for Company's success in Asia. In fact there is strong case for arguing that its performance should be judged against the success obtained by those who traded without these trappings. As Chaudhuri pointed out that already by the end of the end of the 17th century the monopoly of the Company had been diluted, and many individual trading voyages were successful.[7] Therefore what mattered in the trading world of Asia, was not only successful business ethics and acumen, but a vast number of other factors.

All the elements of strategy were influenced by three other factors of great importance: nature of demand in the European markets, the attitude of and relation with Asian states and merchants, and, supply of bullion for procuring Asian

525

commodities. Relation with Asian states and merchants was of vital importance so far as the presence and activities of the Company on the coastal and the hinterland trading stations were concerned. So also was the question of granting tariff concessions or exemptions on a preferential basis. The question of demanding tariff concessions, or making semi-sovereign claims in settlements, or armed trading instead of peaceful trade were issues on which the position of the neither the chartered companies nor the Asian states were very unambiguous. There was also a very remarkable difference between Indian and European perceptions regarding important questions of international relations. Those questions that were considered important in contemporary European polemics and debates, were hardly of any importance in India. Thus the response of the Indian rulers hardly conformed to any pattern. On the other hand the questions were never categorically settled by the European Companies either. If for Sir Thomas Roe trading in peace could be most profitable, the argument in favour of obtaining the 'price' of protection from Asian traders was equally strong, as it could fetch high profits. At the same time acts of war could well be economically unprofitable for the Company.[8]

Mercantilism and the Asian States

Having reviewed the notion and practice of mercantilism from the angle of European chartered Companies, it is necessary to join the issue from the other angle, that is of the Asian states, too. In the case of former we have drawn upon the arguments of K.N.Chaudhuri mainly. Mercantilism in the context of the Asian states, has been conceptualised in a different sense by Sanjay Subrahmanyam. This understanding is derived mainly from observations of the behaviour of Asian states, and the European experience of it. "Mercantilism" here "is an ideology wherein the comportment of the state is conceived of as analogous to that of a merchant: the state for the mercantilists must behave *like a merchant*."[9] However this does not mean that state would withdraw itself from trading and economic activities in the society. On the contrary the state would be required to conduct itself through coercion, control and influence on trading partners and producers.[10]

Thus the notion of mercantilism and free-trade does not follow the stereotypical incompatibility or contradictoriness as in the western discourse. Rather quite paradoxically, the idea of free and unfettered trade within Asiatic kingdoms was advanced by European Company servants[11] - who one would presume to be guided by the mercantilist mind-set. This is much in evidence in the records of the East India Company of late 17th and 18th centuries.[12] By the time the Company took over power in the mid-eighteenth century this demand for free-trade, particularly in the domain of private trading, had its resonance in the corridors of power of the official establishment of the East India Company.

However the comportment of all states in their attitude to traders in the Asiatic littoral was not so "mercantilist". One ought to note that rulers of stretches of the western coastline, that were rather infertile, often extorted a share of commodities which passed by the coast.[13] Then again, there were factions in the courts of rulers - as in Bengal in 1521 - who confronted each other on the question of state policy towards trade and overseas traders. There is definite evidence to suggest that in 1521, that there was a distinct ideologically oriented group that urged assertion of state power over the Portuguese - for ideological reasons - at the expense of trade.[14] However in Bengal the faction favouring trade and peaceful compromise with Portuguese included the Sultan himself and prominent members of the ruling class. Thus the Asian kingdoms too were divided amongst those who favoured unfettered trade and those who did not.[15]

Thus in the taxonomy of states into agrarian-based, prebendally organised states, and trade oriented ones,[16] Bengal represented the typical case of the period, that was one occupying a space between the two ends of the spectrum or distribution of states. Thus historically the rulers of Bengal have been mercantilists, or had developed a comportment quite comparable to the merchants, since the Hussain Shahi rule in Bengal. The seventeenth century examples of the same sort were Mir Jumla,

Shaista Khan and Prince Muhammad Azam. The latter carried out trade under royal prerogative or *sauda-yi khass*.[17] However in almost a parallel manner there was growing assertion of state power over trade and traders, and use of coercion and influence over traders and producers.[18] Very often this took the form of overt hostilities, on pretexts different from trade, against Europeans, whose primary objective was trade. The Portuguese were at the receiving end of such hostilities during the last days of Hussain Shahi rule, and, then again during the Karrani rule in 1562, and the Mughals in 1632. The English came in for such treatment under Shaista Khan. It was these engagements which began the curious discourse regarding trade in the Asian world, and on the attitude of the rulers of Asian states towards it. Sanjay Subrahmanyam stated that, "it is almost as if these traders, usually employees of chartered trading companies, whose very basis was state sponsored monopoly, are articulating an early argument for the 'imperialism of free-trade'."[19]

This encounter became protracted as the prerogatives of *subahdars* and *nawabs* became entrenched in internal trade, and as the interest of the Companies too veered around procurement of investments from the producers and merchants directly from the hinterland. For the better part of the 18th century there is not much evidence regarding the *Nawabs* of Bengal exercising the rights of *sauda-i khass* or being involved in external trade. But there is evidence that internal, *sair* duties formed an important component of the revenue base of the *Nizamat*, and trade in products such as salt, betel-nut and tobacco - farmed out amongst royal favourites - were *Nawab's* monopoly.

The Indian Ocean Region and Bengal's Economy.

Ever since the "basic alteration in the organizational structure of Asian trade" in the fifteenth century, which was based on the segmentation of Asian trade into different maritime geographical divisions,[20] Bengal's internal economy had closely responded to impulses of overseas current. By the days of the early colonial occupation Bengal's internal economy had developed a closely integrated internal trade network. One should take note of the fact that during this period significant changes were taking place in the province of Bengal, internally. The agrarian frontier of the province moved eastwards, as new river systems gave access to new tracts of land and deposited on them the generative silt that was necessary to fertilize the soil. Areas formerly covered by dense forests were transformed into rice fields, and provided the basis for settlement of new agrarian communities.[21] The western part of the delta in which was located the major trading centre of Satgaon, slackened its pace of growth, as did the northwestern part of the province. These developments since the fifteenth century made the economy of Bengal an adjunct to its adjacent maritime zone the Bay of Bengal. However antecedents to this development, in the tenth and eleventh centuries suggest that south-east Bengal had strong linkages with neighbouring Arakan where gold and silver issues from Bengal were in circulation.[22] Moreover Bengal procured precious metals from Pegu and south-east Asia in exchange of textiles, earthenware and rice.[23] However there was a recession in this commercial contact between 11th and 13th centuries, and this situation underwent a transformation after 1400 when Malacca gained sufficient importance as stapling centre.

Thus it was with the rise of Malacca that one finds the Bay of Bengal, with the province of Bengal situated at its northern edge, became an economic unit.[24] The other alteration that took place in the Indian Ocean economy was the alteration in the status of ports like Calicut and Cambay from victualling and stopping points to terminal points.[25] By sixteenth century Bengal was supplying textiles, rice, sugar, conserves and *sinbafo* textiles within the Bay of Bengal orbit up to Pegu and Malacca, and imported from that zone Borneo camphor, pepper, Moluccan spices, sandalwood, Chinese porcelain, silk and most importantly silver.[26] Mukundaram Chakrabarti in *Chandimangala* of the sixteenth century gave a vivid description of exchange taking place in the story of the merchant or *sadagar* Dhanapati.[27] The links of the province with middle and western Indian ocean were quite old in the 16th century, as we know Arab traders were visiting Bengal since three centuries earlier.[28] The intervention of the Portuguese in the course of sixteenth century probably heightened the contacts. The items exported included mainly staples, while imported commodities were pepper, *cowry*, and silver that was much needed in Bengal. Thus Bengal's position as a supplier of staple products to parts of Bay of Bengal was confirmed by the 16th century. The fact is well attested from the list of items that the King of Bakla pledged to offer as tributes to Viceroy of Goa. This included rice, butter, country oil, white sugar, textiles and tar.[29] The export of rice from Bengal was an important aspect of Bengal's external trade in the 18th century. This item was exported to south India and Indonesia, and around 1773 Noakhali exported 115000 maunds of paddy out of its total production of about 500000 maunds, and Chittagong exported 550 tons out of 40000 tons.[30]

The development of the region or the province of Bengal as an important export zone in the Bay of Bengal and Indian Ocean economy, at large, did have a correspondence to its emerging stature as a state whose members had mercantilist pretensions (or comportment), and determined its varying relations with merchants, especially European commercial interests, beginning with the Portuguese in the 16th century, down to the English in the 18th century. From 13th century till the end of the 14th century when Bengal was under the rule of the Turkish dynasties one does come across references to maritime contact with Bengal of the merchants from west - the Arabs - and the east - the Chinese, but one is not on sure ground about the role of the state and its members in maritime trading endeavours. We have it on the good authority of M.R.Tarafdar that maritime trade in this period was sluggish till the rise of Malacca at the beginning of the fifteenth century.

The situation was certainly different in the late fifteenth and sixteenth century when one finds that the Hussain Shahi dynasty maintaining extensive trading contacts with ports down the littoral of the Bay and other regions. The ruler of Bengal as the anonymous Portuguese interpreter of the 1521 mission narrated, owned ships and sent merchandise to Malacca, and even had an admiral to conduct trading and maritime operations.[31] For such a state it was indispensable to develop an awareness regarding maritime politics. And from this point of view the accommodation of Portuguese was vital, as the presence of their fleet on the seas and ports was always an important consideration. One finds further evidence of the fact that for economic reasons particularly, external powers and the rulers of Bengal were inclined to deal with each other, though on an unequal basis. This evidence is provided again by the treaty between Paramananda, the Raja of Chandradwip or Bakla, and Dom Constantino de Braganza, the viceroy of Goa, in 1559. The viceroy agreed to provide four *cartazes* to the Raja for trade to Malacca, Goa and Ormuz against the supply of provisions and permission to the Portuguese to trade duty-free in the kingdom.[32]

Engagement with Europeans and dealings with them in the internal sphere was heightened in the 17th century due to a number of factors. One was the involvement of state officers and members of the ruling class like Abul Hassan Asaf Khan, Mirza Muhammad Ardestani, Mirza Abu Talib Shaysta Khan and Prince Muhammad Azim. Some of them used the royal prerogative to trade in certain products. This was called the *sauda-yi khass*. The second important factor was the inflow of precious metal or bullion through the channel of investments made by the Dutch VOC, and the English East India Company. The European companies requirement of converting bullion into *sicca* rupees or other currency of the region, necessitated access to mints, which were under royal control. This was very often a source of irritation for the companies. The third important factor was the ebb and flow in the procurement of exportable commodities and investment through a network of agents, and merchants which often came into conflict with royal rights exact revenue and its and the prerogatives of the state officials.

In the course of these developments during the 17th century, when the mercantile orientation of the members of the state machinery became quite pronounced, the resource base of the state had been expanding. Extension of frontiers of agriculture in the eastern side, monetisation in the countryside particularly through taxation measures, increase in output and employment in the secondary sector, and consequent growth of demand internally as well as externally, had created conditions for further surplus extraction through the revenue mechanism. Land-revenue and revenue from the collection of duties on movement and sale of goods formed the mainstay of government's finance, and the source of royalty's personal consumption. Thus one notices that in the 18th century there was a shift in the posture of the ruling group - from a mercantilist comportment to the position of a revenue farmer in land and internal trade revenue, both. One does not come across much evidence of royalty making investments in overseas trade or engaging in financial dealings. Such functions were taken up by specialised merchant houses and financiers like the Jagat Seth, Omichand and Armenian merchants like Khwaja Serhud and Khwaja Wajed who had close links with politics of the *Nawab's* court.

Since the conjunction of Bengal's economy with the world-maritime cum economic sphere through the Portuguese in the 16th century, or even earlier, the region had provided textiles, saltpeter, opium and other items of provision within the intra-Asian and trade to Europe. However empirical data on the subject is scanty and scattered. For the seventeenth century we have data more systematically arranged, and from this we can say that the internal economy of Bengal was active and able to provide for the European demand, though volume of trade with them was growing slowly. The average share of Bengal goods in English trade was 22% between 1674 and 1687[33], while that in VOC's trade with Japan - a much lower volume of trade than with Europe - was 43.8%[34]. Share in VOC's trade with Europe was very low. However the eighteenth century witnessed the heydays of Bengal's European trade. Between 1700 and 1720 the share of Bengal in VOC's Europe bound trade was 40%, while for the English the same figure for the period of 1710-1756 was 54%, and from 1725 onwards 58.5%.[35] Another side to this picture presented by the export figure was that Bengal goods accounted for a high percentage share in times of low all-India exports. This was true for VOC and East India Company both. In 1665-66, Bengal goods accounted for 49.4% of a rather small value of goods exported to Europe by VOC,[36] and similarly in 1691, 1693, 1694 and 1695 Bengal goods accounted for 45%, 31%, 74% and 95% of the share of a rather small amount of export to Europe by East India Company.[37]

We can come to a few conclusions from this picture. One that Bengal's share was rising significantly by the turn of the seventeenth century. For the VOC this buoyancy in trade continued till 1735-36, while for the East India Company it continued till 1756, and then after sharp fall in 1757, continued to rise. Second, and this is tentative and impressionistic conclusion - that Bengal was able to provide goods for export during times of political and consequent economic elsewhere in the country. This can be attributed to the relatively stable political condition in Bengal *subah*, compared to other parts of the country in late 17th century.

However one should not lose sight of the fact that, though the same economic forces that had "moulded and shaped the Company's commercial organisation" at the beginning of Company's activities were active in beginning and the later periods of its history in the 17th and 18th centuries, from 1709 onwards a new period had begun. This was on account of the fact that from 1709 onwards the English Company attained a stability and peak of organizational efficiency that needed little fundamental innovation.[38] K.N.Chaudhuri stated that:

> The essential continuity of the Company's post-1709 history is revealed in the maintenance of the same trading centres, operational plans, and procedural rules. It is doubtful whether a comparison of the Company's structure between 1710 and 1750 would show anything other than differences of finer details. The preceding period, on the other hand, was one of vigorous experiments, of continuous search for new trade routes, of new commodities, and fresh outlets for both exports and imports.[39]

However Chaudhuri's contention is that Company had been emerging strong from the mid-17th century onwards on account of a greater capital stock and financial liquidity.[40]

The sluggish nature of the trade in the early and mid 17th century could be partly due to the nature of relation between the Company and the government in Bengal. The English translations of the *nishan* of Shah Shuja, the *farman* of Shaista Khan, and, their address to Mughal authority, mentions various wrongs, abuses and oppressions upon them but never touched upon any question of principle or norm. They claimed through these translated *nishan* and *farman* that they had been granted redress, and that their claim to trade without oppression from the governors and custom-free had been admitted by authorities. But in case of any violation of orders by the local governors, who they alleged had hindered trade with the country merchants, demanded English at their chosen rates and demanded 4% duty on all goods imported and exported, their plea was nothing more than an intervention by the central authority who would give orders for resumption of "free", unhindered and normal trade.[41] The main purpose was to clear the routes of trade, by a message through the *farman* to the local governor that trade of the Company would pass through a particular route. The translated *farman* from Shaista Khan had some special features like instructions to local authorities to help the Company to recover debts from weavers or merchants, or at least not grant them protection of the government.[42] To what extent these instructions had been obeyed is not certain. However the representation before the Mughal in 1686 put the record of exactions and obstructions in quite straight forward manner. It detailed the conduct of the governor of Patna in demanding presents, and the losses of the Company. It detailed particularly the problem the Company faced with regard to the *pycars* refusal to bring cloth according to the contract price or the *bazar* price, or, supply of low quality cloth with the support of local authorities especially the courts.[43] Such instances of obstruction of trade or personal harassment was more openly represented and not clandestinely settled - at least not on record - as in the eighteenth century. The Company tried to meet its objectives perhaps by adding a twist to the language of translation which could further their claims, but could hardly display any strategic maneuver. By the mid 18th century Company was in a position to do that.

An important factor influencing the relation between the chartered Companies and the government in Bengal was the participation of Mughal state officials in trade, in their private capacity. It was an indication of the growing commercial potential of the *subah*, which could not have excluded participation of European trading companies. Nor could the inevitable tensions with them be avoided. The state officials used their official position to enhance their commercial interest. Amongst them one finds a number of small and big officers like *subahdar* Shaista Khan, his sons Buzurg Umed Khan and Abu Nissar Khan, the *dewan* of Orissa, the *faujdar* of Hooghly, and many other officers[44]. This was evidently a reflection of the fact that commercial possibilities presented by the province's resources were high. However assuming that there existed a "certain amount of slack" in the economy, as Om Prakash has postulated, the investments and exports by the companies did contribute to the enhancing production and commercial possibilities, through an increase of output and income in the economy.[45] From the estimates made by Om Prakash, of the looms required to produce textiles, and full time jobs created by the raw silk production sector we know that there was a considerable expansion of output and employment in Bengal's economy by the late 17th century, when the province emerged as a major trading partner of Europe.[46]

The major implication of the growth of Company's trade in Bengal was the displacement effect on Asian traders in Bengal. First this had political implications, important for understanding the nature of relation and tensions between the Company and political authorities in Bengal. Second, the nature of displacement also raises the question regarding the changing nature of the political ruling class of Bengal. In the first half of the 17th century the merchants operating from Bengal, particularly in the eastward ventures, were Mughal state officials.[47] Om Prakash has argued with enough evidence, that the outstanding feature of the decline of this trade in Bengal was the changing participation of these officials. Their domination in trade had continued from 1653 to the 1680s. But from the late 1690s "state officials virtually disappeared from this trade".[48] This was in spite of the fact that the volume of trade carried on by ordinary merchants in this direction did not decline. Similarly in Bengal-Maldives trade, though it grew around the turn of the century, the participation of state officials declined markedly. Om Prakash has argued that this change was not on account of either a growing dominance of chartered companies trade in the 17th century, or, the pass policy on maritime routes that the VOC operated from Batavia. He has left the question of displacement rather open-ended, linking the disappearance of Mughal state officials in trade to the developments that took place in the domain of relation between the state and the economy in general, that unfolded itself as the *jagirdari* crisis which involved a flow of incomes of the *mansabdar* officials.[49]

East India Company's Response to Changing Economic and Political Compulsions.

A feature of the consultations of the English East India Company was its pre-occupation and engagement with political authority which they perceived as peculiarly oriental, and hence despotic. Further, they found this characteristic of Asian states incompatible with what they held to be normal commercial ethic. This perception became acute in the post-Plassey days. The clamour for "freedom" reached a crescendo during the virtual revolt led by private trading lobby amongst Company servants in Vansittart's Council, during Mir Kasim's regime.[50] Though it is possible to suggest that such characterisation of governments in India was largely among English private trader circle, that was in conflict with different states in the eighteenth century, the Company's official view also veered around this idea. It was that the principle of governance in Bengal (or India) was arbitrary and it "ruined the country, depopulating many towns and villages" and hence antithetical to sound economic policies that could further trade.[51]

It can reasonably be argued that this idea was a mid 18th century construction in the Company's official viewpoint, and a reflection on the growing practice of revenue farming within the settled revenue domain of the Nizamat of Bengal. This was also a part of the growing discourse in the Company circle regarding the legitimacy and illegitimacy of institutions, legal documents and finally the locus of sovereignty in Bengal (and India). Thus the growth of the practice of revenue farming and the construction of an official viewpoint based on the experience of it played an important role in the formulation of policy regarding commercial strategies in mid 18th century involving procurement of investments through *dadni* or contract system to direct procurement through *gomastas*.

The perception of authority and the nature of construction it had lend itself to, registered a marked change in the mid 18th century. In 1753 the Board in Calcutta recorded that extortion were very unwarrantable, especially as those had been practiced without any legal authority,[52] while John Zephania Holwell talked about the Nizamat being in a virtual state of war with the Calcutta settlement of the East India Company, when it decided to impose an embargo on the importation of grain into the settlement.[53] The markedly acerbic nature of these minutes were caused by many factors. One was that the grant of the *farman* by emperor Farukhshiyar to the Surman Embassy in 1717 made the Company insist on prerogatives which they deemed they were "constitutionally" entitled to.

Second, as the Company's settlements came to be located further down than Hooghly since 1704-05, there had been the problem of hold-ups and exactions by *chowkies*, even on the Company's goods. This added to the delays in procuring goods for which investments were made. It resulted in accruing balances, particularly in a situation where made.[54] Holwell felt the necessity of representing to the *Nawab* in the strongest possible terms the nature of oppressive exactions of the several *chowkies* that rendered the merchants incapable of undertaking Company's business in future.[55] The problem was more acute in the *aurungs* up the country, while in those close to the settlement of Calcutta there seems to have been fewer hold-ups.[56]

Thirdly, the farming of revenue through collection of duties from trade in grain to Calcutta from Bakharganj (or Bakla), and other adjoining areas of the settlement was an important factor in the relation with authorities in Bengal and formed an important aspect of the construction of its power. The contra-positioning of revenue farming and "freedom" to trade was brought out in the most acute form through this tussle, because the Company's settlement in Calcutta was dependent on supply of provisions from these regions.

Regarding the first point, that is the obligation of the rulers of the country towards the Company, Company officials like Holwell insisted that *Nawab* be always addressed representing the tenor of the *farman* "by which (we) are excused from all taxes whatever"[57] If the trade continued to be harassed by exorbitant contributions then the Company would be obliged to retract.[58] The Company demanded that *muchleka* be taken from the farmers of *chowkies* to let all goods with *dastaks* pass unmolested both by land and water. Regarding small *chowkies* adjacent to the settlement of Calcutta, the Board was urged to remove those by force directly as they were construed illegal.[59]

However diplomatic parleys or show of force in some instance or other could not have been a part of long term strategy to continue uninterrupted trade. Hindrances of different sorts came up the way of Company's trade in mid 18th century, and officials of the *Nawab's* court, taking advantage of many violations of treaty by the Company itself laid many exactions on them.[60] On one occasion the Kasimbazar officials reported that a solution had been reached, but the death of the adopted son of the Chhota *Nawab* impeded all business.[61] On another occasion a demand for a new King's accession to throne was used as a pretext for demanding money,[62] while on another occasion money was demanded from traders carrying sugar to Calcutta.[63]

As a general response to the situation the Company had to enunciate a policy. This policy was that of a switch over from the *dadni* method of procurement of exports to a more direct method of procurement through *gomastas*, who were native Bengalis. It may be an exaggeration to state that the change in the method of procurement was directly a result of impediments to trade, posed by the country authorities. But undoubtedly this factor had played a crucial role. In general however the reason and the context was provided by a falling - though dominant - share of Bengal's goods in exports from Asia to Europe.[64] In 1754 the share had come down to 41% from 70% fifteen years ago. The amount contracted in one season in Calcutta, in 1753, did not exceed Rs.15 lakhs, which in bygone years had always been Rs. 25 lakhs or more.[65] However the greater problem was that 85% of this investment was advanced, "within a limited time" and even if the country was free from trouble (i.e. depredation by Marathas) the whole amount delivered and prized would not amount more than Rs.8 lakhs. One of the principal reason was exaction by *chowkies* but the Company wanted a more wholesale change.

This was evident from the opinion expressed in the Board meeting of June 1753. On 10th June 1753 Holwell gave his reasons for dismissing the *dadni* merchants from operation completely and opting for *gomastas*. On the question of risk incurred by the Company in sending money and material to the *aurungs*, he stated that he believed the *gomastas* would be as reliable as *dadni* merchants, because the latter had always carried on business at the *aurungs* through their own *gomastas*. He felt that the government could exact any sum of money at anytime from the Company, but there was no special risk of plunder on the way to the *aurungs*, and the cost of protecting the investment was never very high.[66]

Though the Board averred that the original intent and design of conducting investment by means of *dadni* merchants were founded on good reason, that is, lessening the Company's risk at the *aurung* by advancing money to such merchants as were able to give security for delivery of goods contracted for, these expectations were not fulfilled. This was particularly due to circumstances which were related to the general climate of the politics of the province and exactions by the *chowkies*. Therefore the Board was willing to take into consideration the representation of only those *dadni* merchants whose investments were not sorted and prized, though ready in the warehouses only if those goods provided at distant *aurungs* where their boats were liable to detention or exaction, could be included in the contracts of the last year i.e. for the recovery of previous year's balances.[67] But this did not apply to those who procured goods from *aurungs* adjacent to Calcutta where such impediments could have little or no influence.[68] Those goods were to be received and prized as ready money purchases.

Therefore regarding the new method of procurement of goods the Company set new guidelines. Preference was given to those *gomastas* who had for a term of years been conversant with those *aurungs* to which they were sent.[69] Holwell was certain that many of such *gomastas* could be employed. They were to be of "proper rank", so as to be "worthy" of receiving the credit and honour from the Company. They should also have a fair character, and should be from a modest background. People of such "rank" were generally found to have greater fidelity and diligence than those of a higher stamp and affluence. They were also required to reside within the settlement of Calcutta.[70]

A point of crucial importance particularly in view of exaction by the *chowkies*, was the distance between *aurungs* and the settlement of Calcutta. *Gomastas* were to be sent to different *aurungs* with orders to purchase goods, as directed by the list of investments on the best and most reasonable terms conformable to the muster.[71] But if the *aurungs* were at a distance of thirty or forty days from the settlement, in which case a large sum of investments had to wait till the purchase was over, it was proposed that a Company should accompany the *gomasta*. In *aurungs* at a distance of five or six days journey from the settlement occasional visits by Board members were proposed. The rules governing the *gomastas* employment were: (a) they should give sufficient security for performance, (b) every *gomasta* appointment be approved by the whole Board, (c) *banian* or servants of any member were not eligible to be a *gomasta*, (d) sorters be sent with *gomastas* to examine the cloth, particularly its length, (e) *gomastas* were to give information of all occurrences in their *aurung*.[72]

Asian States and Mercantilism in the Indian Ocean Economy

The Board rejected the first application for *gomasta*, that came their way, on the ground that his offer of his son as security was not sufficient, and that he did not offer his possessions in Calcutta seemed intriguing to the authorities in the Board. Many *gomastas* employed by the Company asked them to inspect the cloth that had been purchased, and were instructed to depend on the "country" *gomastas* employed under them. Yet the Company decided to trust the *gomastas* because "honourable Company's money being under their care will be great security for they can deliver it out by small sums and there be no ways of deceiving of them in drawing more out of their hands till the produce of that is brought in".[73] Besides, the Company decided to have occasional inspection and watch "for if they are not strictly watched they will in time be both purchasers and sellers to the Company, by entertaining poor *dalals* for their servants by which means they will have the best part of the *dalali* and besides from their buying directly from the weavers will have it in their power to pass the cloth at an advance price and we not able to prevent or detect it."[74]

Thus having fixed the mode of business to be carried out in the interiors of the country along these lines, the Company thus put in place a strategy to combat revenue exactions on their inland trade, and the manipulations of the *dadni* merchants, both. However more exactions took place within the proliferating internal trade revenue or *sair* revenues, and not through the regular channels of customs, the *bakshbandar* and *shahbandar* that controlled "trade by sea".[75] Therefore along with all the instructions, directions and rules mentioned above, the Board also decided to apprise the Kasimbazar officials of the "motives of our conduct and directed to use all means in their power to obviate any objection or demand. And as the adjacent Rajas and zamindars may have power either to assist or impede our business a proper conduct towards them must be observed according to their behaviour".[76]

But in those days when farming of revenue was the norm, either in response to a financial crisis, or as a means of looking for profit by the officials of the state, there could be no guarantee

541

against exaction. In 1753 such uncertainties regarding the conditions in which the Company carried out trade were expressed by Holwell in the meeting of the Board :

> The Company's business has been and always will be as liable to be obstructed by the government, when their estates are advanced to the merchants as *dadni* as if it had been sent by the *gomastas* of their own *aurungs*.

Further....

> Nor has it been at all clear to me that Company would ever have run the risk by sending their estates to the *aurungs* the plundering of which was a method never thought of by the government, nor I am persuaded never will; when it has been determined to exact a sum of money, an unjust pretext for obstructing your business has hitherto been sufficient without their taking a step at once so impolitic and needless - and any risk the Company would run of being plundered by the Rajas, *faujdars* and zamindars is still more improbable, as they are very sure they would in that case be plundered and sold by the government who would want no better pretence for fleecing them. [77]

Thus it was clear that regular levy of duties rather than direct plunder brought more revenue to the state. From such observations we can appraise how nature of political authority was perceived. Observations became even more acute and focussed in its presentation of the nature of political authority, when it reflected on the effect of revenue farming practices on trade in grain and other staples. Substantial quantities of grain were exported overseas to Madras in the early 18th century.[78] But unlike other commodities exported by the Company through sea-route, grain was liable to exaction and levy of duty by zamindari and government *chowkies* in the interiors of the country. Trade in grain was mostly in the hands of local traders who supplied the markets of Calcutta. Thus in order to keep the settlement supplied with provisions the Company could not have simply depended on the politics of the *farman*, that is questioning the legality of state action. It now had to take stock of real situation and play the politics of intrigue.

In this politics of intrigue officers of the court of the *Nawab* of Bengal like the *daroga* of the *Pachotrah* emerge as key players. This position was held by Hakim Beg in the mid 18th century.[79] It seems that the *daroga* was in charge of the operation of a network of *chowkies* within a well defined region where grain moved from areas of production to markets, in southern and central Bengal, through a grid of river-ways. Though the Company records attributed motives to the *darogas* action in an attempt to distinguish him from actual political authorities, it clearly admitted that farming out the revenue posts were a part of the general government policy, and the Nawabs were interested in receiving the proceeds.

The farmer of the *ganj* at Hooghly Jibbon Kour and Tilluck Kour laid an embargo on the grain trade in Bakharganj and prevented that from reaching Calcutta, to increase the customs of the *ganj*. They had official support of Murshidabad court which was secured through the misrepresentations made by Kanks Narain, the *dewan* of Aga Bakhar, a substantial landholder of Bakharganj. Aga Bakhar laid the embargo in Bakharganj by refusing permission to the *gomastas* of the Company from departing the markets of Bakharganj without sufficient security. This embargo was continued for three months in 1752 and finally they were allowed to carry grain to Azimgunje and Chandernagore, those being centres close to Murshidabad and Hooghly. For importation of quantity of grain to Calcutta Kanks Narain was to be indemnified.[80] The grain merchants of Calcutta thus suffered losses and withdrew from business. The Company servant at Kasimbazar William Watts negotiated the whole affair with *Nawab's* court throughout 1753 to 1756 regarding exactions by the *chowkies*.[81] By 1756 such exactions by the farmer of Hooghly had become general, and all *chowkies* located between Buddal and Jalangi, and Jalangi to Calcutta was under the control of *pachotrah daroga* who operated through a number of farmers. These exactions especially those

543

under Jibbon Kour, farmer of Hooghly and Shacogunge affected Company's trade, and their goods from different *aurungs* were detained at *ghats* close to the settlement of Calcutta. (Similar complaints of levy of *mangan* or *churagee* by the *faujdar* were received from Midnapur and Jellasore, and also from Rajmahal, where the Company's salt petre boat was detained by Nawajees Muhammad Khan)[82]. In 1754 the Board recorded in their minutes:

> that many of the *chowkies* are set up by the Prime Minister and *Pachotrah Daroga* Hukumbeg and the Chhota *Nawab*, who farm them out and who support these farmers in their extortions in order to raise theiron (sic) revenues

These instances of detention of boats carrying goods on the river routes particularly - because in Bengal internal trade was through river route mainly - and the demands issued from the *Nawab's* court as conditions for their release, as well as regular levy of duties does suggest that members of the state did not consider it necessary to maintain conditions for an easy conduct of commerce. Rather revenue gathering was more important. How far the state or the *subah* was compelled to farm out its revenue resources, - though revenue assignments like *jagir* were annulled by Murshid Quli Khan - to delegate the functions of supervision, and control in administration amongst state officials and other underlings of the state is a matter of further research. But growing income within the province in the eighteenth century might have caused a greater emphasis being laid on the policy of maintaining revenue farms rather than initiating policies that could work towards a general augmentation of wealth.

In the history of the relation between the Company and the merchants the departure from *dadni* mode of procurement was definitely an important event. But this decision was not prompted by a simple calculus of the falling, though dominant share, of Bengal's goods in Asian trade with Europe around 1750s. Perhaps a more impelling cause the necessity to extend the social basis of the whole mode of procurement, supply and delivery of goods from and within the country. This aspect of distribution of goods, in situation when the state was turning towards revenue farming on a greater scale had definite significance. Thus we find the East India Company caught in a tangle. It had to attack the monopolies of the *Nawab* in the trade of some commodities that its private merchants were interested in, and also the right to exact taxes within revenue farms like trade in grain which were protected as monopoly rights.

References:

1. K.N.Chaudhuri, *The Trading World of Asia and the English East India Company*, CUP, 1978, p. 41
2. Carl Hanson, *Economy and Society in Baroque Portugal*,
3. Chaudhuri, *op.cit.* p.11
4. Jacob Viner, *Theories of International Trade*, p. 87.
5. Chaudhuri, *op.cit.* p.41
6. ibid.p.20
7. ibid. pp.20, 44
8. Chaudhuri, *op.cit.* pp.110-11.
9. Sanjay Subrahmanyam, "Persianization and Mercantilism: Two themes in Bay of Bengal History, 1400-1700" (henceforth "Persianization and Mercantilism") *Paper presented at the ICHR seminar on Bay of Bengal, Delhi,1994*, p.5.
10. ibid. p. 5
11. ibid. p. 27
12. *HPPC*, 10th June, 1753
13. Simon Digby
14. Genevieve Bouchon and L.F.F.R. Thomaz, (ed.) *Voyage dans les Deltas du Gange et de l' Irraudy du 1521*, 1988, Paris, pp. 329-332
15. Sanjay Subrahmanyam, *Portuguese Empire in Asia: Political and Economic History*, Orient Longman, 1992, pp. 11-13
16. ibid. p. 13
17. Sanjay Subrahmanyam, "Persianization and Mercantilism", p.4, 27.
18. ibid. pp.26-27.See also, Home Miscellaneous Series, vol.629, Letter from Fort St. George 10th March, 1686-87, to His Majesty The Great Mogul.
19. ibid. p.27.
20. Om Prakash, *European Commercial Enterprise in Pre-Colonial India*, (henceforth *ECEPCI*), CUP, p.9.

21	Richard Eaton, *The Rise of Islam and the Bengal Frontier*, Oxford, 1998, 194-98.
22	M.R.Tarafdar
23	ibid.
24	ibid.
25	Om Prakash, *ECEPCI*, pp.9-12.
26	Sanjay Subrahmanyam, *Improvising Empire* (henceforth *IE*), pp.99-102.
27	Mukundaram Chakrabarti,
28	M.R.Tarafdar
29	Surendra Nath Sen *op.cit.* pp. 6-7
30	P.J. Marshall, *East Indian Fortunes: The British in Bengal in the Eighteenth Century*, p. 107
31	Bouchon and Thomaz, *op.cit.* pp. 333-34.
32	Sen, *Studies in Indian History*, AES publication, pp. 3-10.
33	Chaudhuri, *op.cit.* pp. 507-10, Appendix 5, Table C.1.
34	Om Prakash, *The Dutch East India Company and the Economy of Bengal, 1630-1720*, (*DEICEB*), p.80, Table 3.6.
35	Chaudhuri, *op.cit.* pp. 507-10, Appendix 5, Table C.1.
36	Om Prakash, *ECEPCI*, p.198, Table 5.4
37	Chaudhuri, *op.cit.* pp.508-09
38	ibid. p. 43.
39	ibid. pp. 43-44
40	ibid. p. 43.
41	Home Miscellaneous Series, vol. 629, Translate of the *nishan* of Shah Shuja.
42	Home Miscellaneous Series, vol. 629, Translate of Nawab Shaista Khan's *farman*.
43	Home Miscellaneous Series, vol. 629, Letter from Fort St. George 10th March, 1686, to His Majesty the Great Mogul.
44	Om Prakash, *DEICEB*, pp. 32-33
45	ibid. p.240
46	ibid. pp.243-247, Tables 8.1, 8.2 & 8.3
47	Om Prakash, *DEICEB*, pp. 229-30
48	ibid. p. 230
49	ibid. p. 234
50	Henry Vansittart, *Narratives of Transactions in Bengal,* (A.C.Banerjee ed.) pp. 286-327
51	Home Public Proceedings and Consultations, National Archives of India, (henceforth *HPPC*)7th June 1753
52	*HPPC*, 19th October, 1753
53	*HPPC*, 24th May, 1753

54	HPPC, 18th April, 1755
55	HPPC, 10th June 1753
56	HPPC, 7th June, 1753
57	HPPC, 19th October, 1753
58	ibid.
59	ibid.
60	HPPC, 3rd December, 1753; HPPC, 2nd February, 1756; HPPC, 15th January, 1756; 22nd January, 1756.
61	HPPC, 30th August, 1756.
62	HPPC, 18th November, 1754
63	HPPC, 10th November, 1755
64	Chaudhuri, op.cit. p. 510
65	HPPC, 7th June, 1753
66	HPPC, 10th June, 1753
67	HPPC, 7th June, 1753
68	ibid.
69	HPPC, 10th June, 1753
70	ibid.
71	HPPC, 7th June, 1753
72	ibid.
73	HPPC, 18th June, 1753
74	ibid.
75	For an explanation of this phrase, see P.J.Marshall, *East Indian Fortunes: The British in Bengal in the Eighteenth Century*, p. 111. James Grant, *Appendix to the Fifth Report from the Select Committee on the Affairs of the East India Company*, pp. 404-406, divided the *sair* of Dewani under three general heads (a) *sair Chunakhali*, levied in the environs of Murshidabad, including *pachotrah* or inland customs, arising from taxes on houses, shops, bazaars; licences for vending spirituous liquors etc.; duties on exports of raw silk and piece goods manufactured in or about the city of Murshidabad, and passing by the *pachotrah* stations on either branch of the Hooghly river forming the island of Kasimbazar; ground rents; customs or tolls of established gunjes or granaries at bridges, ferries, passes etc. (b) *sair bakshbandar*, export and import, customs, foreign merchandise (c) the mint or *darulzerb*.
76	HPPC, 7th June, 1753
77	HPPC, 10th June, 1753
78	Bengal Public Consultations, February 12th 1704,
79	James Grant wrote that Shahmat Jang, was the *daroga* superintendent of the *pachotrah* in 1757.
80	HPPC, 24th May, 1753

81 For negotiations with the *Nawab's* court and Hakim Beg by the English Company to secure a *parwana* and relieve the traders through an order to the *faujdar* of Bakharganj, refer, *HPPC*, 14th August, 1753, *HPPC*, 30th August, 1753, *HPPC*, 25th October, 1753, *HPPC*, 8th November, 1753, *HPPC*, 3rd December, 1753, *HPPC*, 11th April, 1754, *HPPC*, 17th October, 1754, *HPPC*, 28th October, 1754, *HPPC*, 11th November, 1754, *HPPC*, 18th November, 1754, *HPPC*, 28th November, 1754, *HPPC*, 30th October, 1755, 10th November, 1755, *HPPC*, 15th January, 1756, *HPPC*, 2nd February, 1756.

82 *HPPC*, 21st October, 1754, *HPPC*, 10th July, 1755.

34

MILESTONES OF THE MUGHAL PERIOD IN THE HAIDARABAD REGION[1]

Jean Deloche

We know that the demarcation of roadways existed in the northern plains of Hindusthan from the Mauryas to the Mughal Period.[2] In the South of the peninsula, the usage of lining the roads with markers also existed in the Tamil Country, and several milestones indicating specific units of road measurement have been found in the Baramahals and in the Tiruvannamalai region.[3] Regarding Andhra Pradesh, route indicators have been mentioned in the vicinity of Haidarabad and Machilipattanam by Father Coeurdoux and Colonel Upton, both 18th century travellers.[4]

Now, in December 1968 while travelling by car from Haidarabad to Vijayavada, I was surprised to find, to the east of the capital city, masonry columns, arranged by pairs, on either side of the road, or in the fields nearby, having the shape of the markers described by the two visitors. As I was in a hurry, I just noted down their location in relation to the modern milestones. For different reasons I had to wait until January 1986 for starting a systematic survey of these structures. During that period, this highway had been rebuilt, considerably broadened and, in several places, had been given a new course, describing a large curve, at some distance from the old road. The result was that some columns seen in 1968 had disappeared in 1986, especially those which were on both sides of the narrow old roadway.

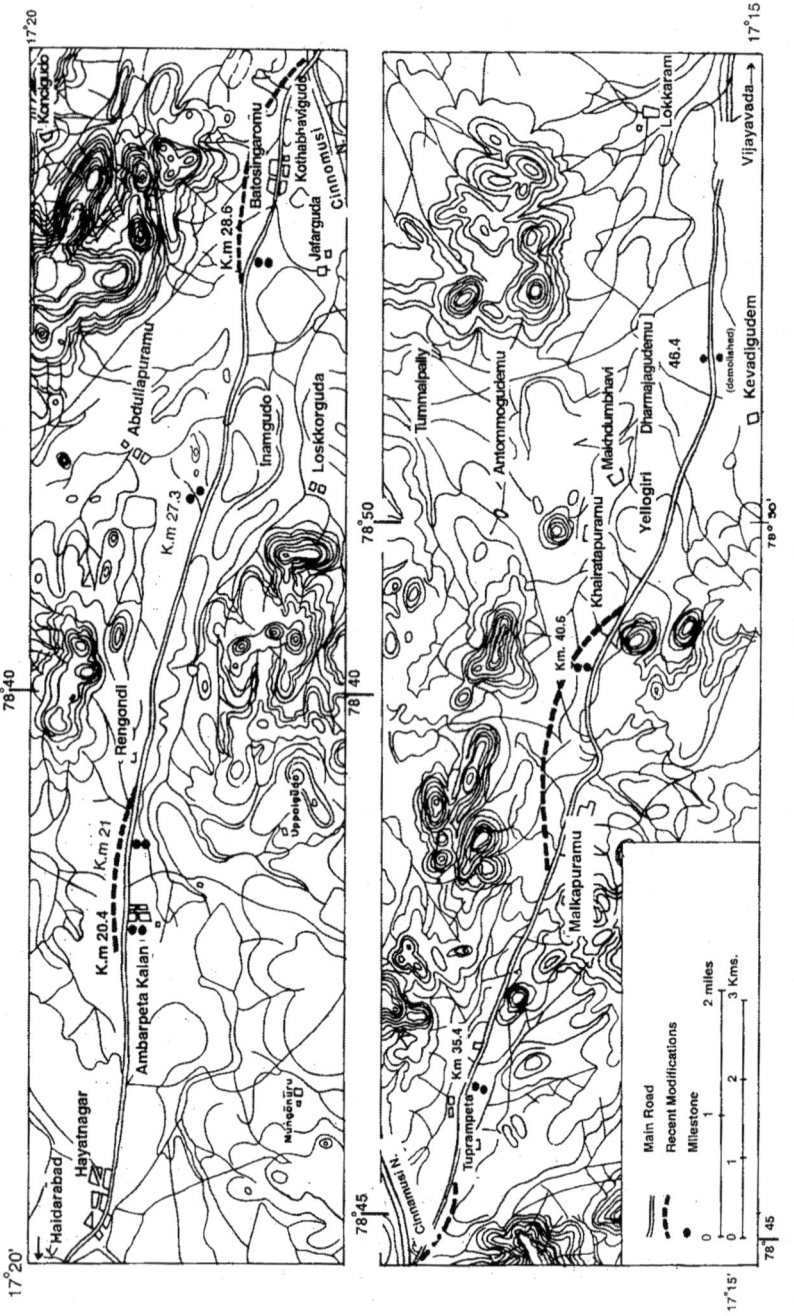

Fig. 1: Map of the region

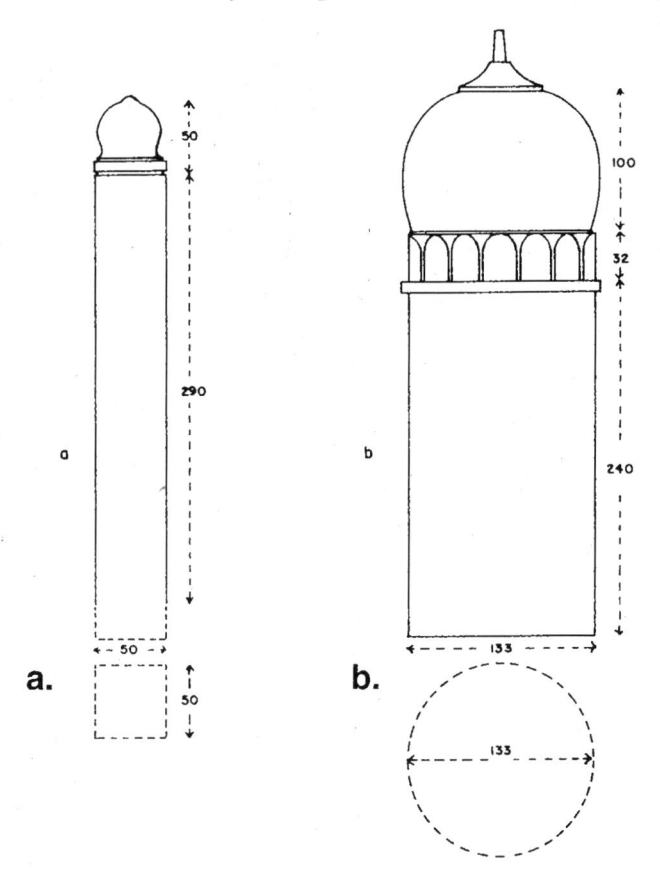

Pillars and Turrets

Let us consider the details of each structure: In order to locate them easily, their site will be mentioned in relation to kilometre-and hectometre-markers of the recent highway. We shall proceed from Haidarabad eastwards (see the map of the region, fig.1).

- Km 20 (to the east of Haidarabad), inside the village of Ambarpeta Kalan, to the right of the old roadway, are 2 square stone pillars, 3.40 m high, 0.50 m broad and 11.20 m distant from each other *(see fig.2,a & photo 1)*

551

- Km 21, to the right of the old roadway, 2 masonry turrets are seen, 3.47 m high, with a diameter of 1.33 m, separated by a span of 12 m. One is in good condition, the other is almost destroyed *(see photo 2)*

- Km 27.3, to the left of the highway, on either side of a narrow trail leading to rocky hills, 2 turrets are standing, well preserved, 3.10 m high and 14.70 m distant from each other *(see photo 3)* According to the shepherds residing in this place, there were two other turrets on either side of the highway which have been demolished.

- Km 28.6, on the right side of the old roadway, in a field, are found 2 well-built turrets, slightly higher than the former (3.70 m) and separated by the same span *(see fig. 2, b & photo 4)*. Here the new highway describes two curves crossing the old one before reaching Tuprampeta.

- Km 35.4, on the right side of the road, in a field, 2 turrets of the same type, but smaller (3,20 m) and separated by a larger span (17.50 m) *(see photo 5)* are erected.

In 1968, we had noticed, a few yards further, on the left side, a square stone pillar which does not exist any more.

- Km 40.6, after Malkapuramu, between the old and the new roadways, are found the same turrets, but higher (3.35 m) and separated by a smaller span (12.80 m only) *(see photo 6)*.

- Afterwards, there is no trace of the old road and the turrets seen in 1968 have disappeared.

Km 46.4, however, the basement of 2 turrets and some pebbles are found, the only remains of these structures.

- I was told by a villager that 2 km before that place, opposite Kevadigudem, near the mosque, 2 other turrets were destroyed when the highway was rebuilt.

Characteristics of the Structures

The stone pillars (granito-gneissic) are cut from the rocks and are bulb-shaped at the top. The turrets are cylindrical structures made of several layers of cut stones with lime, crowned with a top piece also in the form of a bulb surrounded by petals. Their height varies from 3,40 m to 4.20 m and the distance which separates them varies from 11.20 m to 17.50 m (*see fig. 2 ,a&b*).

Identification

What was the use of these structures ? In 1968, I informed my old friend, Dr P. Saran, then Professor of Medieval History at Osmania University, of our discovery. He was not convinced by my description and wrote to me that "most of those pillars seem to be the gates of the mansions or country castles of the feudal barons of Nizam's days". This is obviously a wrong identification, since several "country castles" could not have been built on the same line and at regular intervals. The opinion of the local villagers is different. They all say that these turrets mark out the old roadway of the jaghir time, that they not only show the course of the track (between two turrets), but have served as milestones. They call them *gummatalu*, plural of *gummatamu* which means dome, cupola, but which is here understood in the sense of giant (like *Gummata* or *Gomata*, the gigantic statue of the jain tirthankara, Bahubali)[5] and consider them as village guardians.

There is no doubt that these structures were route-indicators. A letter from Father Coeurdoux, dated February 1760, confirms this identification :

These pillars are located to the right and left, six toises (11.64 m) distant from each other ; at certain places they are stone masonry structures, 2 toises (3.88 m) high, with a top in the form of a globe in the style of the mosque minarets ; they are round and their diameter is about 3 feet (0.972 m). In other places they are ordinary stones, very high, of one piece roughly cut ; in other regions these pillars are hardly 3 feet high. But however they have been built, they show the number of cos (kos) from one place to the other".[6]

This description tallies with the monuments we have mentioned, except on one point : the indication of distance has disappeared with the plaster covering the stones.

Colonel Upton also noticed them in 1777, while coming from Haidarabad :

"From the Nullah to Mulkapore is an entire jungle ; and almost the whole of this day's journey at about the distance of every coss we observed two small pillars between which the road runs. These pillars are about 18 feet high and appear to have been put on purpose as a guide to travellers through the jungle. They are now falling down"". [7]

Milestones in the Deccan

Father Coeurdoux also says that these turrets existed in the vicinity of Machilipattanam and not in other places :

"It should not be thought that these pillars are to be found throughout India. I have not seen a single one on my various journeys, and Father Montjustin, who has travelled the Deccan in all directions, as you can recognise by the road map of the French army drawn up from his memoirs, assures me that these pillars are indeed rare, that he encountered them in the proximity of Masulipatam and Héderabad and almost nowhere else" [8]

We have travelled most of the roads radiating from the ancient harbour of the Golkonda kingdom. They are today broad highways paved with asphalt, running along canals and rice fields. Nowhere were milestones found and the local people, villagers and scholars, do not remember having seen these structures along the roads of the district.

The Problem of the Stones Arranged by Pairs

In South India it is the second time we notice milestones arranged by pairs. In Tamilnad we have found double stones on the road skirting the Tiruvannamalai Hill and we suppose that the few *kadam* -stones we have seen in the Baramahals region were very likely arranged in the same manner.[9] Now, in the North, from the Mauryas to the Mughals, each marker was represented by a single stone. Should we infer from this fact that, in the south of the peninsula, there was a different system for demarcating roadway ?

Conclusion

To conclude, it can be said that the picturesque *gummatalu* erected during the Mughal Period are endangered monuments. To save the last which have survived (we do not know how many turrets have been destroyed since 1986), the State Department of Archaeology should look into the matter and take the neccessary steps in order to protect them.

References:

1   This paper is based on my article entitled : Bornes milliaires de l'Andhra Pradesh, published in *Bulletin de l'Ecole française d'Extrême-Orient*, t. 75, 1986, 37-42.

2   See the detailed study of these structures we have made in our book, *Transport and Communications in India prior to Steam Locomotion*, vol.I, Delhi, 1993, 149-159.

3   See our paper, "Itinerary Measures and Milestones in thirteenth Century Tamil Country", in *Pandit N.R. Bhatt Felicitation Volume*, Delhi, 1994, 596-603.

4   Father Coeurdoux in *Lettres édifiantes et curieuses*, ed. 1810-11, Paris, t. XV, 154-155 and col.Upton in *Asiatic Annual Register, 1804, Miscellaneous Tracts*, 26

5   According to N.R. Bhatt.

6   Father Coeurdoux in *op.cit.*, 154.

7   Col. Upton in *op.cit.*, 26.

8   Father Coeurdoux in *op.cit.*, 154-155.

9   See our paper in *Pandit N.R.Bhatt Felicitation Volume*, Delhi, 1994, 603.

Jean Deloche

Photo 1. Km 20.

Photo 2. Km 21

Photo 3. Km 27.3

Milestones of the Mughal Period in the Haidarabad Region

Photo 4. Km 28.6

Photo 5. Km 35.4

Photo 6. Km 40.6

35

WEST EUROPEAN AND MUGHAL INTERACTION DURING THE REIGN OF AURANGZEB

J.B.P. More

Much has been written on Indo-European maritime interaction and history. But still much remains to be done. In this paper we intend to add a little more to our knowledge of this interaction, by dealing with some of the salient features of the confrontation and interaction between the small but upcoming west European nations and the mighty Mughal empire, when it was at its height in the second half of the 17th century, during the reign of Emperor Aurangzeb, mainly on the basis of French sources. We will limit ourselves to Mughal interaction with the Portuguese, Danes, French and the English. The Mughal empire was no doubt a territorial superpower during this period. Emperor Aurangzeb himself was incessantly engaged not only in quelling the rebels like the Marathas on the western coast, and also in pushing his territorial limits further into South India at the expense of the Deccan sultanates, but also in interacting with the west Europeans established in his territory and keeping them under check, with an eye on promoting the commercial interests of the Indian merchants and his vast empire. But before going into all these aspects in some detail, it would be worthwhile to glance through the evolution of Indo-European history from the arrival of the Portuguese in India in 1498 to the ascension of Aurangzeb on the Mughal throne in 1658.

Historical Background :

The accounts of Marco Polo about the wealth, opulence and splendour of the East had aroused the curiosity and cupidity of the relatively small and upcoming west European States, who incessantly quarrelled and fought with one another. Their subsequent expansion across the world was not the outcome of any accident. It was generally a pre-meditated and organised affair which took place originally with the blessings of the Pope who actually divided the world between the Spaniards and the Portuguese.

Very soon the other west European nations contested this unilateral decision and wanted a share not only in the spoils of the East but of the whole world. Generally speaking, west European expansion across the world was never imbued with any altruistic intentions. Instead they seem to have inaugurated their expansion on a wrong footing, which very soon resulted in the wiping out of whole populations and civilisations from the face of the globe in many parts of the world.

When they showed themselves up in India in 1498, after rounding the Cape, it was certainly not just as peaceful traders. Actually, Vasco da Gama, belonging to Portugal, a small maritime nation, with a population of just one million,[1] was at the head of a Portuguese squadron when he arrived off Calicut on the Malabar coast. He very soon realized that Indian ships were no match to the Portuguese which were superior not only in fire-power and navigation, but also in strength and solidity.[2]

This realization seems to have given way in the Indian Ocean waters to what may be known as the "Gun boat trade era", ie., trade backed by force and fire-power. Vasco da Gama and his successors like Cabral and Albuquerque seem to have been the chief architects of the "gun boat trade " in the Indian Ocean waters, for the Arabs, Chinese, Jews, Armenians and others who traded with peninsular India before the Portuguese never seem to have resorted to such strong-arm methods in a systematic manner. In fact, till the arrival of the Portuguese,

Indians used only stitched vessels for peaceful navigation and trading. They never used nails and bolts to render their ships sturdier, though they knew the use of iron and even exported it.[3] But they never also knew that it was the official policy of the Portuguese to use force, especially against the Muslim traders.[4]

The Portuguese were followed by other west European nations. Accustomed as they were to hatred, enmity and jealousy of one another back home in Europe, they could not help carrying the same all the way to the relatively peaceful Indian Ocean waters.[5] Professor K.S. Mathew, the prominent maritime historian, had described these western nations during this period as belonging to the "third world".[6]

A few years after the Portuguese set foot in south India, the dreaded Mongols, who had earlier struck terror across Asia and Europe, entered the Indian continent by capturing Kabul in 1504. Babar, of Turkish-Mongol descent brought northern India under his control by 1526 and established what came to be known as the Mughal dynasty. But Babar like his ancestor, Genghiz Khan, probably the greatest conqueror and also devastator till date, were land-based conquerors. They never seem to have possessed any idea or experience in maritime conquest and warfare.

The Zamorin (Hindu ruler) of Malabar and his Mappila (Muslim) traders and seamen, who were outside the sphere of influence of the great northern Indian Mughal empire, confronted the Portuguese during the 16th century. Though the Portuguese got the upper hand in this tussle, mainly on account of their superior fire-power,[7] yet they were unable to make inroads further north into the territories of the Mughals. In fact, the Portuguese who established a certain superiority at sea by vanquishing the Mappilas, were never in a position to confront militarily overland the mighty Mughal empire.

The Mughals in their turn, accustomed as they were with the spirit of conquest and domination, indulged in incessant quarrels and warfare in order to expand or maintain their territorial control in the various parts of the Indian continent.

This naturally brought them into confrontation with the west European powers during the 16th and 17th centuries, when the latter had somewhat established their naval supremacy in the Indian Ocean waters.

After vanquishing the Mappilas, the Portuguese had established themselves on the Malabar coast. In 1510, they founded a settlement in Goa and subsequently established settlements at Daman, Salsette, Bassein, Bombay, further up the Malabar coast and also at Santhome on the Coromandel and Hughli in Bengal. The Mughals did not really attempt to confront them, as they did not really feel threatened by them overland. Instead Portuguese Jesuit missionaries even tried to convert Emperor Akbar(1556-1605) to Chrisitianity.[8]

With the destruction of Mappila power on the Malabar coast, the Portuguese were left almost unchallenged in the high seas around India during the 16th century. At this time, Surat, further up on the western coast on the bank of the river Tapti came within the sphere of influence of the Mughals and was fast emerging as one of the greatest ports of world trade. Abbé Carré had reported that Surat had become famous from the 16th century itself. He added that by the second half of the 17th century it had become extremely powerful through its wealth and the number of its inhabitants which included foreigners like the Persians, Turks, Chinese, Armenians, French, English, etc and the Indian Hindu and Muslim merchants.[9]

At the dawn of the 17th century the Portuguese lost out to the Dutch and the English. Subsequently the Dutch established factories at Surat, Pulicat, Cochin, Nagapattinam and at Hughli, Kazimbazar and Dacca in Bengal during the 17th century. All these settlements were placed under the authority of the Dutch in Batavia. In 1609, the English had approached Emperor Jehangir, the son of Akbar to grant permission to trade at Surat. But the Portuguese Jesuit missionaries used their influence in the Mughal court and got the grant cancelled in 1611. But the very next year the English defeated the Portuguese squadron at Swally near Surat. Probably, sensing the ascendancy of the

English, Emperor Jehangir allowed the English through a royal *firman*(charter) to trade at Surat and some other places.[10] In 1639, they acquired Madras on the Coromandel coast. It was only in 1651 that the English opened their first commercial house at Hugli in Bengal, a Mughal territory which was a major outlet into the Bay of Bengal and south-east Asia. Soon they founded other settlements at Patna and at Kazimbazar in Bengal.[11]

It was only in 1661, three years after Aurangzeb had become the Mughal emperor that the Portuguese ceded Bombay to the English king. In 1668, the king handed it over to the English East India company on payment of an annual rent of 10 pounds.[12] This transfer seems to have taken place without seeking the accord of Emperor Aurangzeb. In 1687, Bombay superseded Surat and became the headquarters of the English factories in India during the residency of John Child.

Meanwhile the Danes also had founded a settlement at Tarangapadi(Tranquebar) on the Coromandel coast in 1620 and extended it to Bengal. Though the French Capuchin missionaries were at Surat from 1639, the French obtained a royal *firman* from Emperor Aurangzeb to trade at Surat only in 1668, the same year when the English East India company acquired Bombay from the Portuguese.[13] Earlier King Louis XIV of France sent his ambassadors to Emperor Aurangzeb. Wanting to impress the Mughal Emperor, he sent a fleet of 8 vessels, 1 frigate and 3 transport ships, loaded with 238 canons and 2800 men.[14]

In 1674, they founded Pondicherry on the Coromandel coast which became their headquarters in India. In 1690, they obtained another *firman* from Ibrahim Khan, the Mughal governor of Bengal for founding another trading settlement at Chandernagore in Bengal. The same governor had given the right to the English to found a trading settlement in Calcutta.

Thus when the Mughal empire was at its height during the second half of the 17th century, west Europeans had established themselves at various coastal points. They were especially present at Surat, the principal port of the Mughal empire on the western coast and at Bengal, known to be the richest of the Mughal provinces, where silk, sugar and saltpeter were produced.[15] Therefore it is necessary to assess the interaction between the Mughal empire under Aurangzeb and the west Europeans belonging to the preceding five nations. The west Europeans were not only in competition with one another, but also in competition with the Indian merchant classes, backed especially by the mighty Mughal emperor. During this period Aurangzeb was so strong that he possessed an army of 400000 men.[16]

Aurangzeb like his predecessors had retained the arrangement of having two governors at Surat, one for the port and the other for the town, who was in charge of collecting customs duties and other taxes.[17] The revenue of Surat not only supported these two governors and their subordinates, but also the admiral of the Mughal fleet which was composed of the Sidis of East African descent and based at Danda Rajapuri, to the south of Bombay.

According to a firman issued by Aurangzeb himself, the Sidis were to receive Rs.300000 a year out of the sea customs of the port, in exchange for offering protection to Indian shipping against piracy, etc., and maintaining the security of the seas.[18] The master of the customs house was a Muslim and had his commission from the Governor of Surat. The clerks were Hindu banias while the rest of the officers or rather peons of the Customs house as waiters, porters and others, were also Muslims.[19] These very facts show how much Aurangzeb and his Mughal predecessors had attached importance to sea-borne trade and its organization and how much they counted upon revenues derived from such trade.

It has to be noted at this juncture that the west European ventures in India were generally State-sponsored like the Portuguese and French East India company or had the blessings and backings of the State like the English East India company. It has also to be noted that during the second half of the 17th century, Emperor Aurangzeb was pushing the limits of his empire deep into the south. During the last quarter of the 17th century the sultanates of Deccan of which the most prominent were Golconda and Bijapur succumbed to Aurangzeb's might and Mughal power and influence reached the deep South. In fact, in 1687 the Mughals defeated Sultan Ali Abdul Shah of Golconda and annexed his kingdom. But during the same period, Aurangzeb had to contend with the rebellious Marathas under their leader Shivaji in the western flanks of his empire in which the Mughal port of Surat was located. In 1664, the Marathas had raided Surat to the detriment of Mughal political and trade interests.[20] Shivaji had died in 1684 leaving his kingdom to his son, Sambaji. Aurangzeb was able to vanquish the Marathas and kill Sambaji in 1689.

The west Europeans based in their settlements, generally allotted to them by the Indian rulers, were no doubt conscious of the territorial conflicts in the Indian continent and the troubles of Emperor Aurangzeb especially. But they were not still in a position or did not probably have the means to take part directly in these conflicts, though they were masters of the high seas to a great extent. Generally, the Mughal emperors and the other Indian rulers seems to have also been conscious of the conflicts between the west Europeans. They had now and then tried to play one west European power against the other. But their overriding concern during this period at one stage or the another seems to have been to have European settlements in their territories.[21] They wanted somehow to trade and augment their revenues in the short-term. In Bengal for instance, it appears that the Mughals had allowed west Europeans to establish settlements there with the hope of deriving various customs duties from trade and thus increase their budgetary resources.[22]

In fact, it seems that it was only during Aurangzeb's reign that Indian merchants' role in the maritime trade and navigation increased prodigiously. It appears that with the arrival of more Europeans to Surat in the 17th century, Indian merchants had taken full advantage to increase their participation in maritime trade. In March 1669, when the French squadron arrived at Surat, it appears that there were only about 14 to 17 vessels belonging to the merchants of Surat. It also appears that the Indian merchants traded ordinarily with European ships at that time. But within a short period of about 15 years, that is, during the 1680s, there were about 72 ships with three masts, apart from many other small vessels, belonging to Surat merchants.[23] Besides, it appears that this time, the Indians traded mostly with their own ships, while 20 years before they used to trade by freighting west European ships. During this period, the most prominent Hindu merchant of Surat was a certain Virji Vora, while one of the most prominent Muslim merchant was Abd al Gafur.[24] A French account relates that the richest inhabitants of Surat were the Hindu *banias*, who were masters in trade, though the Muslims appeared more magnificent.[25] The French colonizer, François Martin had noted that Surat was among the very few cities in the world where such a huge trade took place. He added that more gold and silver entered Surat than any other city in the world. Besides in Bengal during the 17th century we have Mir Jumla, an administrator cum monopolist trader with wide maritime interests, whose commercial empire stretched from Persia to Pegu.[26]

In the light of the above it would be completely incorrect to maintain that the arrival of the west Europeans had weakened Indian maritime enterprise in the 17th century at Surat and by implication also elsewhere. It should be noted in this context that the noted maritime historian Arasaratnam had earlier dismissed the theory that the Portuguese weakened Asian maritime enterprise, especially on the Coromandel coast, as just an assumption.[27] P.J. Marshall had also held that the Asian trading world before 1800 with its huge volume of shipping was too complex for even the most belligerent Europeans to impose effective control on it.[28]

Aurangzeb and his policies towards international maritime trade in general and towards the west Europeans in particular seems to have been responsible to a great degree for the phenomenal increase in Indian trading, shipping and navigational might, in spite of the dominance of west Europeans in the high seas. It is simply impossible to imagine that the spectacular increase in the trading might of the Surat merchants during

Aurangzeb's rule was not due to Mughal State patronage and policies. Presently we are in a position to tackle the interaction between the Mughal empire under Aurangzeb and the west Europeans restricted to their settlements.

Mughal-Portuguese Interaction :

As noted earlier the Portuguese were the first to reach India and establish settlements by vanquishing the Mappilas. Very soon they proved themselves to be a menace to Indian trading and shipping further up to the western coast, for it was in order to ward off Portuguese piracy that a fort was built at Surat in 1524. A Persian inscription on the door of the fort reads as follows : 'This fort was built to stop the *Firangis*'.[29] Though the Dutch put an end to Portuguese dominance in the Indian Ocean waters in the 17th century, yet the latter continued to maintain their presence in some of their settlements on the western coast like Diu, Goa and Daman. and were issuing passes to Indian ships sailing from Surat. During Emperor Aurangzeb's reign itself, the Portuguese were earning about 4000 rupees annually by issuing passes to the Indian ships. It appears that this was needed to assure the protection of Indian ships on the high seas.[30]

The Mughal emperors themselves, from the time of Akbar, seems not to have objected to the delivery of these passes and the collection of customs duties by the Portuguese,[31] for as long as they protected Indian ships, it could only serve the interests and promotion of Indian maritime trade. In any case, he would have been conscious of the Dutch and English ascendancy in the Indian Ocean waters at the expense of the Portuguese. So as long as the Portuguese served the interests of the empire, there was no reason to antagonise them unnecessarily, especially when their strength had depleted considerably. Besides the Portuguese were not in a position to challenge Mughal power over land. This stands justified by the fact that Emperor Shah Jahan had thrown out the Portuguese from their trading post at Hughly in 1631, which seems to have pushed some Portuguese to take to piracy in the Bengal waters, along with the Arakanese pirates, even during the reign of Emperor Aurangzeb.[32]

With the conquest of the Deccan Sultanates by the Mughals, Goa became vulnerable to Mughal power.[33] But Emperor Aurangzeb never had the intention of throwing the Portuguese out from Goa. Instead, they were allowed to maintain their settlements on the western coast, because they served to some extent Mughal and Indian merchant interests, especially as they offered some protection to Indian ships on the high seas. Moreover throwing the Portuguese out would push them to take to piracy and other aggressive actions which would not serve in any way Mughal and Indian merchant interests.

But anyhow the Portuguese by virtue of the control that they had over seas, were able to confiscate ships belonging to Surat merchants, whenever they wanted the redressal of some grievances. For instance in the 1670s, the Portuguese governor of Diu wanted to get back 40000 rupees that a Muslim merchant owed to the Portuguese. As the merchant had sought refuge in Mughal territory, the Portuguese thought that it was right to confiscate Indian merchant ships. Moreover they wanted all Indian ships going to the Persian Gulf to obtain passports from the Portuguese at Diu, though it had been agreed earlier that the merchants would get their passports from Daman.[34] Besides, the Portuguese were not in good terms with the Sultan of Muscat and the King of Persia. Indian merchants who had good trading relationship with both Muscat and Persia naturally feared for the safety of their ships and goods, at the hands of the Portuguese.[35]

During the second half of the 17th century, the Mughal empire had to face the rising menace of the Marathas under Shivaji. In 1664, Shivaji at the head of 4000 cavalry ransacked Surat, the richest Mughal city, with a population of 200000 inhabitants, for 6 days. Wealthy Muslim merchants like Baharji Borah, were looted, while the Mughal governor of Surat fled to the safety of the Surat fort. It had been reported that except for the Dutch and the English, all the rest including the Hindu banias were subjected to general looting.[36] Shivaji repeated the same in 1670.[37]

The Portuguese too were threatened by Shivaji. In 1683, Shivaji's son, Sambaji, was well set on the road to throwing out the Portuguese from India. But a Mughal attack seems to have diverted his attention from this enterprise.[38]

But, it also appears that the Portuguese were not very happy with the expansion of the Mughal empire into the south. Actually, this expansion was not in their interests, both political and economical. If the Mughals became stronger, the Portuguese would naturally feel the pressure. So when Shivaji passed away in 1684, the Portuguese wanted to maintain peace and good relationship, with Sambaji, the son of Shivaji, to the great displeasure of Emperor Aurangzeb. In doing so, the Portuguese seem to have embarked upon the policy of siding with one Indian power against another.

Aurangzeb instructed the governor of Surat to prevent the Indian merchants from taking passports from the Portuguese for their ships. The merchants were alarmed by this move which was obviously detrimental to their trade interests on account of the piracy in the high seas. Aurangzeb retracted when he was made to realise the dangerous implications of his move.[39] This instance brought to light the real value of the Portuguese in the Indian Ocean waters, especially off Surat during this period. They survived because of a certain naval superiority in the high seas, which they put to good use in order to have a foothold on land and extract at the same time some revenue by delivering passes to Indian ships, for their upkeep.

On the other hand, Emperor Aurangzeb, however mighty he was overland, was unable to assure the protection of Indian ships overseas. This obliged him to tolerate the Portuguese in their settlements, in spite of their anti-Mughal activities and though he was in a position to drive them away. But the point that has to be noted is that a small nation, Portugal, whose subjects were operating in far away India, in spite of their acute limitations in men, money and other resources,[40] were able to hold in check, Emperor Aurangzeb, the mightiest of the Mughal emperors. They persisted in their efforts to stop Indian ships from sailing without Portuguese passports even in the 18th century. In 1705, the Governor of Surat was obliged to invade Portuguese territories, because the Portuguese had confiscated three Indian Muslim ships on the pretext that they did not have passports. It seems that the Portuguese continued to refuse passports to Indian ships because of these incursions and it was one of the reasons which prevented Surat ships from venturing out into the high seas during this period.[41]

Mughal-Danish Interaction :

Another small nation with which the Mughals had some relationship was Denmark. They had established themselves at Tranquebar in the deep South, outside the range of Mughal power. As a result a great part of their trade was carried on from Tranquebar and the adjoining regions, though they had established settlements at Pipely and Balasore (1636) in Bengal, with the permission of the Mughal governor of Bengal. They seem to have always lacked in men and money to compete effectively with the other west European nations as well as the Indian merchants. They borrowed heavily from Indian and Armenian merchants in order to carry on with their trade. But it seems that they were never able to repay much of their debts, which caused them immense problems.[42]

Like the Portuguese, the Danes had taken to piracy, very soon after their arrival in the Indian ocean waters. Mughal ships from Bengal seems to have been targeted from the 1640s itself. The Mughal governor reacted violently by raiding and throwing the Danes out of their settlements in Bengal. The Bengalis plundered the Danes and killed a good number of them. It appears that the Dutch disapproved Danish piracy, for often the Bengalis turned against them for damages as a sort of compensation for the losses provoked by the Danes on the high seas. It was reported in Dutch quarters that the Mughals were furious not only against the Danes but also against the English and the Dutch, because of Danish piracy.[43]

Danish piracy in the Bay of Bengal continued even after Aurangzeb became the Mughal emperor. By 1674, with only an insignificant number of ships that they had in their possession, they had intercepted about 40 Indian ships from Bengal, laden with goods.[44] It appears that the Danes generally sold the goods. They also sold the Bengali crew as slaves in Aceh and Sumatra and used the captured ships for commercial operations. The English joined the Danes in the slave trade. François Martin seems to have refused to involve the French East India company in this trade and reported that in two years about 15 to 20 thousand Indian slaves were exported to Aceh alone.[45]

The Bengalis were never in a position to counter the Danish ships. This in spite of the fact that the Mughal governor of Bengal, Shaista Khan, was reported to have possessed during this period a navy comprising of about 200 galleys, accompanied by many other smaller vessels, which went about the whole of the Bay of Bengal.[46] The Mughal fleet does not seem to have engaged the Danish ships in any naval battle. Probably, the Danes avoided such a battle as they had only few ships, though they were better in navigation and were equipped with formidable canons, which outclassed the small and rudimentary canons of the Bengali ships.[47] Finally in 1674, a peace treaty seems to have been signed.[48] Subsequently the Danes were allowed to settle at Serhampore on the Hughli in 1676.

The Danes also indulged in piracy in the Arabian sea off Surat, where they intercepted in 1686, Indian merchant ships from Surat, laden with arms and ammunitions, gold, silver and other goods worth many thousands of rupees.[49] In 1687, Danish pirates had intercepted three Indian ships off Surat and took them straightaway to Tranquebar, along with the Hindu merchants and crew. Many other Indian ships seems to have been intercepted by the Danes. The Surat merchants were alarmed very much by such a situation. To top all this, the pirated goods found their way from Tranquebar to Copenhagen.[50]

In 1698, the Danes were allowed to erect a factory near the French settlement of Chandernagore. They called it Dannemarksnagore. But this attempt was short-lived for the Mughals devastated it in 1714, eight years after the death of

Aurangzeb.[51] Thereafter the Danes seem to have concentrated on their trade in Tranquebar, until all their settlements in Asia were sold to the British in 1845.

From the preceding it is quite clear that Danish relationship with the Mughal empire was never very important. They had been thrown out of Bengal twice by the Mughals. But they managed to survive in the Indian ocean waters by indulging in piracy at the expense of Indian ships, especially from Surat and Bengal. At the most, they seem to have been more of a nuisance value to the Mughal empire under Emperor Aurangzeb than anything else.

Mughal-French Interaction :

Another west European nation whose presence in India seems to have been not of much significance for the Mughal empire under Aurangzeb, was the French. They were the last to arrive in India. Emperor Aurangzeb issued a firman for them to settle at Surat in 1668 and trade.[52] They established themselves in Pondicherry in 1674. Though they seem to have been not short of men like the Danes, they were certainly short of money to carry on their trade in a profitable manner.[53] They had also borrowed much money from Indian and Armenian merchants, for the survival of their company's factories and men in India.[54] The French were continuously harassed by the Hindu *bania* money-lenders for the debts they had incurred in Surat. It appears that during the 1680s, they were even unable to get out of their factory, due to the impossibility of repaying the debts. This situation seems to have continued well into the second half of the 18th century that the French ships rarely dared to show up at Surat.[55]

In a way it appears that in order to make up for the shortage of money, the French too were obliged to take to piracy. But their piracy seems to have targeted largely at the Golcondan ships ie., the ships sailing in and out of Masulipatam.[56] It appears that during the last quarter of the 17th century, when the Dutch dominance of the Indian ocean was at its height, mostly all the goods that arrived in France from India were goods seized by pirates and probably shipped to France from Pondicherry.[57] This situation seems not to be very different from the Danes during this period.

When Emperor Aurangzeb conquered the Sultanate of Golconda, during the last quarter of the 18th century, the French who were hitherto operating against Golcondan interests, as seen precedingly, came to terms with Aurangzeb and obtained permission from him to trade from the Coromandel coast, especially from Masulipatanam.[58] Therefore, they seem to have refrained from attacking Mughal ships.

It has been reported in 1709 that the French owed to Indian merchants and bankers 1100000 pounds in Surat, 300000 pounds in Bengal and 450000 pounds in Pondicherry. In fact, Om Prakash had remarked that in 1716, the French were under debt at Surat to the tune of 3 million rupees. Three years later, Pondicherry itself, the headquarters of the French in India was so desperate financially that its governors could only carry on with the aid of loans from leading Indian merchants.[59] and also Armenian merchants. In Bengal it was no different. Even during Aurangzeb's reign, the French had borrowed huge sums from Indian merchants and bankers of Bengal.[60]

It appears that when Dupleix was nominated as Director of the French trading station in Bengal in 1721, he had repaid some of the debts of the French company, but continued to trade with the help of Indian bankers like Sukurama, especially from Bengal, as the company funds were never adequate.[61] But during this period, it appears that Indian merchants and bankers were not willing to lend money to Dupleix, probably because the former felt that the French would shortly abandon their settlements due to shortage of money, losses, etc.[62]

During the 17th century, west Europeans were generally dependent upon their Indian agents, brokers and middlemen to carry on with their maritime trade. Thus the French were totally dependent on Gujarati and other merchants and brokers at Surat. François Martin in his *Mémoirs* had remarked about the dominating presence of Hindu banias either as merchants or as intermediaries, without whom no trade was possible at Surat. No wonder the prime intermediary and agent of the French during the early years of their trade at Surat was a bania, known in French circles as Samson.[63]

These banias were also great money-lenders. They seem to have lent money to all and sundry, especially west Europeans, without restrictions. The French seems to have taken advantage of this Hindu bania liberality, for they always suffered from an acute shortage of capital. This seems to have been primarily because King Louis XIV embroiled in European wars was never in a position to allocate adequate funds for the French East India company, though he had great ambitions to outstrip smaller west European nations like Holland in the trade and arms and ammunitions fronts.[64]

Next to these ubiquitous banias, there were the affluent Muslim traders, especially of the Borah sect, who seem to have enjoyed State patronage to some extent unlike the Hindu banias. Very soon the French probably in order to be in the good books of the Mughal officials of Surat who were more favorable to Muslims and sometimes even openly hostile to Hindu traders as in 1669 when the Qazi of Surat extorted money from Hindu merchants,[65] appointed Borahs to act as their Indian intermediaries.[66] But for borrowing money on interest, the French could not depend upon Muslim merchants. Naturally they were at the mercy of the Hindu banias and other non-Muslim merchants and bankers like the Armenians, who lent usually at 10% interest.

When the money-lenders did not get back their money, they including the Armenians complained to the Mughal officials, which naturally had the potential to cause great trouble to west European trading interests.[67] On the other hand, it also appears that the French were not only in a position of not paying the debts, but they did not also want to repay their debts.[68] Some merchants even complained to King Louis XIV, in order to get their debts repaid. French missionaries in India even thought that the French were being unjust towards their Indian and other creditors.[69]

573

The base of operations for the west European pirates in the Arabian sea was Madagascar, a French colony. They particularly targeted the ships going in and out of Surat.[70] It is strange to note that Azam Tara, the second son of Emperor Aurangzeb and Governor of Ahmedabad, had sought French help to eradicate piracy, when it was well known that Madagascar was a French colony and the pirates could operate from Madagascar only with the connivance or tolerance of the French authorities there.[71] In fact the French seem to have been one of the greatest beneficiaries of this piracy when the Dutch dominance of the Indian Ocean was at its height, for as we have seen earlier, mostly all the goods that arrived in France from India were goods that were seized by the pirates from Indian ships and shipped to France. In all probability, Azam Tara and even Emperor Aurangzeb seem not to have been fully aware of this crucial factor of French presence in the Indian Ocean, especially in Madagascar, that they even tried to rope them in their efforts to eradicate piracy by offering incentives. In fact Azam Tara offered the port of Goga to the French.[72]

So one can say that west European piracy had in a way the blessings of the French authorities both in Madagascar and in India and the Mughals were either not fully aware of this connivance of the French with the west European pirates or they preferred to shut their eyes. The Mughals probably thought that as the French were highly indebted in Surat to the point of not being able to get out of it, they could put pressure on them, (which they did) to get rid off the pirates. But what they seem to have probably never known was the French dependency on the pirates to procure goods for the French and European markets, during this period.

However the debts that they had incurred in Surat and elsewhere seems to have severely spoilt their reputation as serious and viable traders, at least during the reign of Emperor Aurangzeb. In fact, they seem to have been a liability in the trading circles of Surat. If at all they were of any value to the Mughals in the 17th century and even a little later, it must only be marginal and very limited. This certainly was not the intention of Louis XIV when he decided to send his men to India.

Anglo-Mughal Interaction:

King James I of England probably realizing the importance and greatness of the Mughal empire sent Thomas Roe as ambassador to the Mughal court of Emperor Jehangir as early as 1615. Surat was the headquarters of the English in India until 1687, when Bombay superseded it. Though the English had gained in importance at the expense of the Portuguese as noted earlier, yet they were still not in a dominant position, especially overland. They faced stiff opposition not only from the other west Europeans, but also from Indian merchants, both Hindu and Muslim, who of course had increased their trading might during Aurangzeb's period as never before. The west Europeans including the English naturally felt the pressure of Indian trading might, in spite of their dominance in the high seas.

It appears that since the reign of Emperor Shah Jahan, the English like the Dutch traded freely in Bengal and enjoyed exemption from payment of transit duties. Such privileges accorded to west Europeans continued to prevail during Emperor Aurangzeb's reign. The English as well as other west Europeans made regular gifts in cash and kind to help local Mughal officials sympathetic to them and to be sure that royal exemptions were obeyed.[73]

But the Mughal imperial treasury collected high customs duties in Bengal which went upto 4%.[74] This was not the case at Surat where it was just 2.5% until at least 1679. In that year, probably in order to buttress the sagging finances of the State, Emperor Aurangzeb imposed the infamous *jiziya* on all non-Muslims including the west Europeans. As the west Europeans protested against the imposition of this tax, the customs duties at Surat was raised to 3.5% from 2.5% to compensate the loss of revenue from *jiziya*. Probably with the objective of uniformizing taxation, the customs duties in Bengal was brought down to 3.5% also.[75] But anyhow there was cause for discontent among

575

the west Europeans due to the increase in customs duties at Surat.

On the other hand the English in Bengal had obtained exemption even from the payment of customs duties. Such exemptions seem to have been obtained by fraudulent means, probably by bribing the local Mughal officials, as noted earlier. From 1656, the English factors were obliged to pay to the port authorities at Hughli an annual tribute of Rs.3000 as the price for continued exemption from customs duties.[76] The English stood to gain enormously from this arrangement at the expense of the Mughals. Naturally any attempt to alter this situation had the potential to be resisted by the English.

Besides the English, though it was illegal, were allowing other European companies and even Indian merchants to make use of their flag to trade freely with Bengal on the basis of a profitable arrangement between themselves, without paying any customs duties to the Mughals. Naturally the Mughals were extremely unhappy with this situation, where they faced a considerable loss of revenue. Finally, the Mughals decided to suppress the *firman* given to the English, on account of gross misuse.[77]

The French traveller Thevenot had asserted that the true port of Surat was Swally. It was four and a half leagues away from Surat town. But because the customs were often stolen at Swally, the Mughals had prohibited ships from going there since 1660. But the English and the Dutch were still based there and their several godowns were also in that place.[78]

The situation of Swally offered the English (and the Dutch), a fair opportunity of getting ashore what they pleased, though not in large quantities customs free. This was a great opportunity for them to escape the 3.5% customs duties at the Surat bar(sand-banks). Other nations including Indian merchants never enjoyed this advantage. In spite of the prohibition to anchor at Swally, customs duties at the Surat bar never stopped increasing. In fact, the governor of Surat was extremely proud that in 1685, the customs duties had yielded Rs.903000. This was 50 or 60 thousand more than in 1684.[79] Later it seems to have increased still more and yielded an annual revenue of 12 lakh rupees, every lakh being worth about 100000 French livres.[80] Sometimes the Mughals increased unilaterally the customs duties according to their wish.[81] It appears that many, including Indian merchants made use of this opportunity to escape customs duties at Surat.[82] Naturally the Mughal authorities were not very happy with this situation. Thus the English were at loggerheads with the Mughals both at Surat and in Bengal and in both these places, it was the English who held the advantage.

However in spite of such advantages, the English probably unable to withstand the heavy competition in the Indian Ocean waters, especially from Indian merchants, whose trading might have had multiplied many times, as noted earlier, and also certainly encouraged by a superior naval and artillery might, took increasingly to piracy, during Aurangzeb's reign, especially when it was difficult to trade profitably.

The arrival of the Portuguese in the Indian ocean region seems to have greatly contributed to piracy, both west European and Indian.[83] The Portuguese, Danes and the French had resorted to it, as we have seen. The English were not lagging behind. They seized Indian merchant ships off the Surat port and the Malabar coast.

For instance in 1684, an Indian merchant ship sailing from Congo to Sind with a cargo worth Rs. 300000 was seized by Englishmen. Two years later two ships laden with gold, silver and other articles worth 400000 ecus, belonging to Surat merchants were seized by the English and Danish pirates.[84] Indian merchants and the Mughal emperor were alarmed by these acts. Aurangzeb held the west European nations responsible for the piracy and prohibited them from trading at Surat. It appears that the Mughal governor of Surat had embarked upon a policy of harassing the English for the latter's anti-Mughal and anti-Indian activities.[85] It appears that English piracy was the immediate cause that triggered the hostilities between the Mughals and the English.

The relationship of the Mughals and the English was also worsening in Bengal, where the English enjoyed tax exemptions, as we have seen. When the Mughals sought to suppress these privileges, the English reacted violently by sending in troops and ships to protect its rights.[86] Thus an open war seems to have broken out between the English and the Mughals in 1686.

John F. Richards had advanced the theory that because the Mughal authorities at Surat were not willing to stop the trading of private English traders, the English had embarked upon a war with the Mughals. Om Prakash had toed the line of John F. Richards in this respect.[87] Though this might be one of the reasons for the war, it remains to be established more firmly. Actually the English East India company had obtained permission from King James II of England to wage war on the Mughal empire. Om Prakash has asserted that the main aims of the war was to make territorial conquests in the coastal areas of India and to fortify the new settlements.[88] But neither he nor John F.Richards tell us how and why the attempt to stop English private traders from trading at the Mughal ports had led to an all-out war.

In the light of the above, it appears more plausible that the fear of losing their privileges both at Surat and in Bengal and the belief acquired in the course of time, that they could undo the Mughals both at sea and on land, seems to have pushed Englishmen like John Child, the Governor of Bombay, to adopt an aggresive posture against the Mughal empire.

Subsequently English company vessels entered into open warfare against Indian ships, especially Muslim-owned ships. They captured and held 80 Indian vessels at Surat.[89] They deployed ten of their ships at the mouth of the Ganges to blockade Bengal.[90] Besides west European pirates, especially English plundered Indian merchant ships and goods on the high seas in order to put pressure on the Mughals not to abolish the privileges that they enjoyed until then.[91]

Trade suffered heavily due to this hostile action of the English. Emperor Aurangzeb naturally retaliated and ordered his Mughal officers to seize all English trading missions. Efforts by an Armenian merchant to mediate between the Mughals and the English failed. In June 1687, the English confiscated another Indian ship bound to Siam from Surat.[92] In September 1687, an English ship received orders, probably from John Child, to capture 3 ships belonging to a wealthy Muslim merchant of Surat. John Child seems to have been particularly infuriated against the Borah merchant, Abd al Gafur, who had complained to Emperor Aurangzeb that English pirates were responsible for the capture of Indian ships.[93] A similar situation prevailed in 1688, when the English intercepted many Muslim ships returning to Surat from Moka and Jedda. Indian merchants naturally implored Emperor Aurangzeb to intervene more effectively and put an end to these depredations. [94]

Trade suffered heavily due to these hostile actions of the English. Emperor Aurangzeb naturally retaliated and ordered the Mughal officers to seize all English trading missions.[95] Efforts by an Armenian merchant to mediate between the Mughals and the English failed.[96]

On the western coast, the Mughal fleet led by the Sidis attacked Bombay. The island of Bombay succumbed. The Mughals seem to have not pressed forward the advantage in order to occupy the citadel, because by then the English had surrendered and had agreed to pay reparations.[97] But, François Martin had noted in his *Memoirs* that the Sidis' troops had actually disembarked and ravaged the whole island of Bombay in 1689. He added that the English were not strong enough to resist the Mughal troops, commanded by the Sidis.[98]

In Bengal, the Mughals threw out the English successfully from Hughli. The latter had to flee to a safer place known later as Calcutta. Om Prakash tells that from this place, the English tried to inflict damage on the Mughals in a variety of ways, including an attempt to overrun Chittagong and offering their services to the King of Arakan in his offensive against the

Mughals. But here too the English were not successful in undoing the Mughals. In the Bay of Bengal, even ships belonging to high Mughal officers and to members of the Great Mughal's family were seized by the British between 1686 and 1688. The Mughal Governor of Surat confiscated the goods of the English and the Dutch at Surat in order to reimburse the losses incurred by the Muslim merchants because of European piracy. He even went to the extent of arresting the brokers and their family members and imposing a total blockade of the European settlements and extracting the maximum compensation for the piratical activities of the Europeans.[99]

This tug-of-war between the Mughals and the English lasted for 3 years. In 1689, the Mughals gained the upper hand and a good many of the English factors and others surrendered. The following letter written from a Mughal camp near Bijapur to Martin (probably François Martin, the founder of French Pondicherry), by a certain Suard, a Parisian jeweller, at the court of Emperor Aurangzeb in 1689 reveals the humiliation suffered by the English at the hands of the Mughals:

> "I intimate you that peace between the English and the Mughal (emperor) has just been concluded. The envoys (English) were led by Azad Khan, the prime minister (wazir of Emperor Aurangzeb). The English followed him, their hands tied to a belt as if they were imploring; they remained standing in that position for half an hour; they then knelt down, kissing the floor and asking for forgiveness with a loud voice three times; they then stood up and their hands were untied by the minister; they(English) gifted 150000 rupees."[100]

A peace treaty was then concluded. Its terms was one of the most humiliating to the English. Aurangzeb taking into consideration the repentance of the English for having insulted his subjects and their institutions, forgave the English for their mistakes and spared their lives in exchange for 150000 rupees and the withdrawal of the Mughal fleet, manned by the Sidis, from Bombay.[101]

The Parisian jeweler at the court of Aurangzeb adds that the three years war and hostilities between the English and the

Mughals, thus came to an end.[102] As the war was fought in the name and with the permission of the English king James II, it could be said that the latter had lost out to Emperor Aurangzeb in this war that had lasted three years and had ended with the capitulation of the English. Not only had the English lost prestige on account of this war, but they had lost several of their ships and had spent several millions on arms and ammunitions. The Bengal theatre of war alone had cost them 3 millions in arms and ammunitions. Besides, their trade was severely interrupted and all their trading stations were ransacked. Thus the English aims of territorial conquest and strengthening their coastal settlements were nullified by Mughal might. The English were thoroughly beaten not only overland, but also their naval supremacy was successfully challenged and routed by the Mughal fleet both at Surat and in Bengal.

I would say that this defeat of the English at the hands of the Mughals was not just a simple miscalculation, as John F.Richards had asserted, but it was actually a gross underestimation of the strength of the Mughals both at land and at sea by the English. They had to pay the price for it. Besides, this was not a brief war as John F.Richards and Om Prakash after him had wanted us to believe.[103] Instead in the light of the above, especially the eye-witness account of the Parisian jeweler, it was a long war that lasted for three years, at the end of which the Mughals emerged victorious.

In fact, Emperor Aurangzeb was in a position to drive the English away from India once for all. Instead, he forgave them, accepted their presents and allowed them to re-establish themselves in their trading posts in India. This he seems to have done not because he had a soft corner for the English, but because he seems to have been always aware of the necessity of having west Europeans in his gigantic empire not only in order to derive trade benefits and to extract the maximum revenue from them, but also to provide a huge market and outlet to Indian goods, producers and merchants and to procure gold, silver and other imported goods necessary to his empire.[104] It has to be noted here that India produced no silver and not much gold. Hence it was only natural that the need for international trade was felt by the Mughals in general and Emperor Aurangzeb in particular.

In the light of the preceding, it is simply impossible to accept the assertion of Stuart Gordon of Cambridge that the Mughals, especially Emperor Aurangzeb were in the main unconcerned with sea-borne trade.[105] But they very well knew that foreign trade had a direct bearing on the general economy and welfare of the empire, its merchants, manufacturers, artisans and workers. Besides, revenue yielded by foreign trade was no doubt considerable, especially at Surat, as we have seen.

Though Jadunath Sarkar had claimed that the condition of the economy and the people was not at all bright during Emperor Aurangzeb's reign,[106] yet in the light of the above, it appears that at least in the foreign trade front the balance-sheet was positive at least till the end of the 17th century. Indian trading and shipping seems to have increased very much during Aurangzeb's reign, in spite of the arrival of the west Europeans and their increasing presence in the Indian Ocean waters. Revenue derived through foreign trade had also increased during Aurangzeb's reign. In fact, Emperor Aurangzeb and the Mughal officials had resorted to various methods to augment their revenues even by suppressing certain privileges accorded to the English. This had led to war with the English as we have seen.

Not only the English were no match to the Mughals during this period, but it seems that Emperor Aurangzeb had tolerated the Portuguese, Danes, French and even the Dutch in his empire, mainly in order to derive trade benefits and to contribute to the protection of Indian merchant ships on the high seas. The Danes were only of nuisance value to the Mughals as we have shown, while the French were more of a liability in Indian trade circles and the Portuguese trade value was limited, in spite of their presence in the high seas. As for the English and the Dutch, they were held in check by the Mughals and the former was actually routed and humiliated. But things were in for a change especially during the first decade of the 18th century, when the Mughal empire declined and the aged Emperor Aurangzeb passed away in 1707, abandoning the Indian continent to the greed and the lust for power of the west Europeans.

References:
1. Pearson, M.N., *The Cambridge History of India-The Portuguese in India*, Cambridge, 1987, p.24
2. Moreland, W.H., "The Ships of the Arabian coast", *Journal of Royal Asiatic Society*, Part I, Jan 1939, pp.63-190
3. Ibid.
4. Pearson, M.N., *op.cit.*, p.73
5. Mss. Inde, volume 983, Më moire de la côte de Malabar, 1752, p.41, Archives Des Missions Etrangères(henceforth AME), Paris
6. Mathew, K.S., " A note on the historiography of nationalsm in India", n.d., Unpublished paper(copy in my possession)
7. See Rowlandson, M.J., *Tohfut al Mujahideen*, London, 1833; Nambiar, O.K., *The Kunjalis- Admirals of Calicut*, Bombay, 1963
8. Pearson, M.N., *op.cit.*, pp.324-325
9. See Mss. Abbë Carrë, " Le Courrier du Roy en Orient", 1666-1672, pp.186-190
10. Collins, Maurice, *British Merchant Adventurers*, London, 1942, p.46
11. Burn, Richard (ed.), *The Cambridge History of India, IV*, London, 1937, p.73; Mukherjee, R., *The Rise and Fall of the East India Company*, Berlin, 1957, p.108.
12. Leena, P.K., "English East India Company`s Settlement at Anjengo", Ph. D. Dissertation, August 1989, Calicut University, p.7ff.
13. Bruce, John, *Annals of the Honourable East India Company*, III, London, 1810, p.136; Mss.Fr.6231, Mëmoire de la compagnie des Indes Orientales, 1642 à 1720, f.4, Bibliothèque Nationale de Paris(henceforth BNP)
14. Guet, M.I., *Origines de l'Inde Française*, Paris, 1892, pp.3,6
15. Martineau, A., *Dupleix et l'Inde Française,1722-1741*, I, Paris, 1920, p.101
16. Feynes de Henri, *Brieve Descrition faites en Levant, Perse, Indes Orientales, Chines & c., XVIIe siècle*, pp.43-44, BNP
17. Thevenot, J., *The Travels of Monsieur de Thevenot into the Levant*, Part iii, London, 1687, p.19; Tavernier, *Les Six Voyages de Jean Baptiste Tavernier*, seconde partie, Paris, MDCLXXIX, p.4
18. Alam, Muzaffar and Subrahmanyam, S.,(eds.), *The Mughal States, 1526-1750*,Delhi, 1998, p.378
19. Thevenot, *op.cit.*, p.27
20. Duperron, Anquetil, *Zend Avesta*, Tome I, Part I, Paris, 1771, p.cclxvj
21. See for eg. Martineau, A.,(ed.), *Mëmoires des François Martin*, vol III, Paris, 1934, p.122

583

22. Martineau, A., *op.cit.*, 1920, p.170; More, J.B.P., "Some Maritime Aspects of the Indian Ocean Region, 1660-1760", K.S.Mathew(ed.), *Indian Ocean and Cultural Interaction, A.D.1400-1800*, Pondicherry, 1996, pp.134-135
23. Mss.Fr.6231, *op.cit.*, ff.5,13; Martineau, A.,(ed.), *op.cit.*, II, Paris, 1932, pp.268, 435
24. Mss.Fr.6231, *op.cit*, ff.13. 32; Martineau,A, (ed.),III, op.cit,, p.168
25. Dellon, *Nouvelle Relation d'un voyage fait aux Indes Orientales*, Amsterdam, 1699,p.53
26. Arasaratnam, S., 'A Note on Periathamby Marikkar', *Journal of the Academy of Tamil Culture*, vol.XI, No.I, Jan-Mar 1964, p.51; Richards, John, F., *The New Cambridge History of India, The Mughal Empire*, Cambridge, 1993, pp.156-57
27. Arasaratnam, S., *Merchants, Companies and Commerce on the Coromandel coast, 1650-1740*, Delhi, 1986, pp.103-148
28. Marshall, P.J., *Trade and Conquest, Studies on the Rise of British dominance in India*, Hampshire, 1993, p.282
29. Duperron, A., *op.cit.*, p.cclxiv
30. Martineau, A.,(ed.), *op.cit.*, II, Paris, 1932, p.358; Mss.Fr., *op.cit.*,, ff.34,37,42
31. Pearson, M.N., *op.cit.*,pp.52-53
32. Richards, John, F., *op.cit.*, p.202; Leena, P.K., *op.cit.*, p.8
33. Martineau, A., (ed), *op.cit.*, III, p.38
34. Martineau, A., (ed.), *op.cit.*, I, Paris, 1931, pp.238-239
35. *Ibid;* Martineau, A.,(ed.), *op.cit.*, II, pp.293-294
36. Richards, John,F., *op.cit.*, p.209
37. Pearson, M.N., "Shivaji and the Decline of the Mughal Empire", *Journal of Asian Studies*, No.35, 1976, pp.221-235
38. Pearson, M.N., *The New Cambridge History of India, op.cit.*, p.138
39. Martineau, A.,(ed.), *op.cit.*, II, p.358
40. Mathew, K.M., *History of the Portuguese Navigation in India*, Delhi, 1988, pp.320-22
41. Mss.Fr.6231, *op.cit.*, ff.34,37,42
42. Macau, Jacques, "L'Inde Danoise- La Première Compagnie, 1616-1670",Aix en Provence, n.d., pp.85-92; Krieger, Martin, "Danish country Trade in the Indian Ocean in the 17th and 18th centuries", K.S.Mathew, (ed.), *op.cit.*
43. Macau, *Ibid.*, pp.86,92,96; Mathew,K.S.,(ed.), *op.cit*
44. Macau, *Ibid.*, p.93
45. *Ibid.*, p.118; Martineau, A., (ed.), *op.cit.*, II, pp.493-494
46. Martineau, A.,(ed.), *op.cit.*, II, p.502; Tavernier, *op.cit.*, p.88
47. Macau, *op.cit.*, pp.92-93
48. *Ibid.*, p.93; Krieger, Martin, *op.cit.*, p.125
49. Martineau, A.(ed.), *op.cit.*, II, pp.451,476, 480; III, p.93
50. Martineau, A.(ed.), *op.cit.*, II, pp.476,480,502
51. Krieger, Martin, *op.cit*, p.125

52. Mss.Fr.6231, *op.cit.,* f.4
53. See for eg., Mss.Inde, vol.980, Letter dated 17 Feb 1720, Pondicherry, AME
54. Mss.Inde, vol.99, Letter dated 20 September 1717, AME; Ms.Inde, vol.980, Letter Dated 17 Feb 1720, AME
55. Duperron, A., *L'Inde en Rapport avec l'Europe,* Tome II, Paris, 1778, p.38; Mss.Fr., 6231, op.cit., f,13
56. Martineau, A.,(ed.), *op>cit.,* I, pp.59-63, 419,448,451-484; II, pp.40,231,490
57. Sottas, Jules, *Histoire de la Compagnie Royale des Indes Orientales, 1664-1719,* Paris, 1905, p.396
58. Richards, John, F., *op.cit.,* p.241
59. Om Prakash, *The New Cambridge History of India – European Commercial Enterprise in Pre-colonial India,* Cambridge, 1998, p.253; Mss.Inde, vol. 991, Letter dated 20 September 1717, Pondicherry, p.581, AME; Mss. Fr. 6231, *op.cit., f.42*
60. Mss.Fr. 6231, *op.cit.,* f.40; Martineau, A.,(ed.), *op.cit.,* II, p.332
61. Martineau, A., *op.cit.,* 1920, pp.36, 71-72
62. *Ibid.,* p.346; Duperron, A., *op.cit.*
63. Martineau, A.(ed.), *op.cit,* I, pp.224-225
64. Martineau, A., *op.cit.,* 1920, pp.21,36
65. Chaudhury, Sushil, "The Surat crisis of 1669; A case Study of Mercantile Protest in Mediaeval India", *Calcutta Historical Journal, No.5,* 1983, p.140; Martineau, A. (ed.), *op.cit.,* II, p.407
66. Martineau, A., (ed.), *op.cit.,* II, pp.363-64; Alam, M., Subramaniam, S., *op.cit.,* p.370
67. Mss.Inde, vol.960, Letter dated 17 Feb 1720, p.163, AME; Mss.Inde,vol.991, Letter Dated 20 September 1717, p.586, AME
68. Mss. Inde, vol.960, Letter dated 20 sept 1717, p.5,AME
69. Mss.Inde, vol 996, Letter dated 20 September 1717, p.5 and letter dated 7 Feb 1720, p.483, AME
70. Mss. Fr.6231, *op.cit.,* f.33; Richards, John, F., *op.cit.,* p.145
71. Mss.Fr.6231, *Ibid.,* f.35
72. *Ibid.,* ff.33-34
73. Richards, John, F., *op.cit.,* pp.203-204
74. *Ibid.*
75. Om Prakash, *op.cit.,* p.132
76. *Ibid.,* p.134
77. Maritneau, A., (ed.), *op.cit.,* II, p.464; Marshall, P.J., *East India Fortunes; The British in Bnegal in the 18th century,* Oxford, 1976, pp.6-7
78. Thevenot, J., *op.cit.,* p.27
79. Martineau, A., (ed.), *op.cit.,* II, p.410
80. Thevenot, J., *op.cit.*
81. *Ibid.;* Martineau, A., (ed.), *op.cit.,* II, pp.163,410
82. Martineau, A.(ed.), *op.cit.,* II, p.354

83. See for eg., More J.B.P., *op.cit.*, pp.130-44
84. Martineau, A.,(ed.), *op.cit.*, II, pp.354, 451-52, 486
85. Mss.Fr.6231, *op.cit.*, f.16
86. Martineau, A., (ed.), *op.cit.*, II, p.464; Marshall, P.J., *op.cit.*, pp.6-7
87. Richards, John, F., *op.cit.*, p.225; Om Prakash, *p.cit.*, p.150
88. Om Prakash, *op.cit.*, p.150
89. Richards, John, F., *op.cit.*, p.225
90. Mss.Fr. 6231, *op.cit*, f.16
91. Martineau, A.,(ed.), *op.cit.*, II, pp.476,480
92. *Ibid.*, p.486
93. *Ibid.*, p.496
94. *Ibid.*, pp.517-18
95. Richards, John, F., *op.cit.*, p.240; Om Prakash, *op.cit.*, III,p42
96. Martineau, A., (ed.), *op.cit.*, II, p.468
97. Richards, John, F., *op.cit.*, p.240; Om Prakash, *op.cit.*, p.151
98. Martineau, A., (ed.), *op.cit.*, p.240
99. Om Prakash, *op.cit.*, p.151; Richards, John, F., *op.cit.*, p.240; Kulke, H, Rothermund, D., *A History of India*, London, 1992, p.219; Mss.Fr.6231, *op.cit.*, ff.29,31; Martineau, A., (ed.), *op.cit.*, III., pp.168,212,252
100. Mss, Fr.6231, *op.cit.*, f.16; Kulke,H., Rothermund, D., *op.cit.*, p.219; Rothermund, D., *An Economic History of India*, London, 1973, p.13
101. Mss.Fr. 6231, *op.cit.*, f.16
102. *Ibid.*
103. Richards, John, F., *op.cit.*, p.225; Om Prakash, *op.cit.*, p.150
104. See for eg., Kulke, H. Rothermund, D, , *op.cit.*, p.211; Martineau, A., (ed.), *op.cit.*, p.122; Mss. Fr., 6231, *op.cit.*,f.17
105. Gordon Stuart, *The New Cambridge History of India. The Marathas, 1600-1818*, Cambridge, 1993,p.65
106. Sarkar, Jadunath, *History of Aurangzeb*, 5 volumes, Calcutta, 1973 (reprint).

36

THE FRENCH AT SURAT, 1693-1701

Aniruddha Ray

Since the arrival of the French at Surat in 1666, their political activities had been narrated by S.P. Sen till 1693[1]. Earlier J.B. Malleson had given us a brief summary of their activities in India[2]. He was however too brief on the activities of the French for their first one hundred years in India. There is therefore a need to look at the activities of the French at Surat particularly in the background of the gradual declining situation of the Company. The well-known French scholar, Paul Kaeppelin[3], in his monumental study on the French in India, published in the early part of the twentieth century, had presented such activities of the French in India.

In this brief paper, we would see the functioning of the French factory at Surat from 1693 till 1701. Here, we would see not only the problems of the French at Surat, particularly during the European war that lasted till 1697, but we would see also the problems faced by the merchants of Surat as well as the pressure brought on the French by the Mughal authorities. In his classic study, Ashin Dasgupta[4] had narrated the gradual decline of Surat from 1700. In the French view, not seen so far by the Indian historians, the root of the decline could be traced earlier than 1700. Thus one would get not only a picture of hitherto unknown activities of the French at Surat, but also some of the characteristics of typical European view that blamed the Mughal authorities for all the ills. This narrative is based mostly on the unpublished French correspondences from Surat.

In September 1693, in the wake of the European war, Pondicherry fell to the Dutch, who had kept it under their occupation till the Treaty of Ryswick of 1697. Although Surat, a Mughal port, was spared the Dutch attack, the fall of Pondicherry saw the French concentrating at Chandernagore in Bengal. The condition of the Company had begun to worsen as they could not sent any ship due to the fear of the Dutch attack. The French commercial activities begun only after 1698, but by that time, the Company was running a huge debt both in India and in France. Despite this, as we would see, there was a brief revival of French commerce at Surat that was rudely suspended by the outbreak of another European war.

II

François Martin had been appointed the Director of the Coromandel Coast and Bengal and had left Surat in May 1686. His letter of 26 April 1686[5] showed that the situation of the French had much improved at Surat. The debt contracted earlier had been paid and commerce was well established. The assessment of Martin was not acceptable fully. A letter of the French from Surat in the middle of June 1686[6] showed this. The principal problem was that the Governor of city was continually demanding money from the European Companies. On behalf of the French, Roques and Deslandes had represented to the Governor of the injustice in the custom house. The Governor had seized a ship and the house of a dead Armenian merchant, Khoja Minas[7]. A merchant of Patan was charged twice in the custom house against which the merchants of the city had assembled and decided to write to the Mughal Emperor[8].

By that time, the French Company in France had prohibited the importation of painted cloth from India that had come as a rude shock to the French factors at Surat. They could cancel some orders but had to take delivery of some goods. Around then, the pirates had been operating in front of Surat and had been seizing ships coming from West Asia[10]. The Mughal campaigns in Bijapur and Golconda had created difficulties for

Surat as well. Despite a Mughal victory, the French thought that the Mughal state was in the last stage of dissolution[11].

By 1690, the French were in difficulties at Surat. The European war had practically stopped the French commerce, which forced them to take loans[12]. They could get some fund by selling their ship *St. Louis*. A severe pest had started at Surat carrying away nearly 400 persons per day[13]. No ship had come from France for long time, although Pilavoine, the Director, had assured Paris that they would be able to sell European goods at Surat. Even then, by January 1692, he wanted money to pay the debts, to load the ships and to be able to live[14]. Surat had put it clearly and rather bluntly to Paris : "We have neither money nor ship....."[15].

The only relieving feature for the French at Surat was the arrival of the Dandennes squadron from France[16]. By the end of October 1692, it had seized an English ship with goods and money and had brought it to Surat. The Governor and the merchants of the city wanted to take revenge on the English for their piracy in front of Surat. Pilavoine therefore wanted the squadron to attack Bombay, but Dandennes refused. Pilavoine still hoped that this would be possible and as late as the end of January 1693, he cherished the idea. Although the Governor of Surat was friendly to Pilavoine, he wanted to seize the drapes found in the captured English ship. Pilavoine therefore decided to send the drapes to the Coromandel Coast. Finally he brought fifty bales of drapes to Surat and distributed them among the merchants[17].

Despite such spectacular victory of the French over their rival and the usual show of force, the situation of the French had not improved much in early 1693. There was neither fund nor ship for the French and they felt that there was no point in preparing the cargo. The sale of goods had produced only 3,17,000 livres while the debt of the factory had gone up to 12,00,000 livres[18]. The situation was complicated by another factor. The Armenian merchants claimed that they had goods in the captured English ship and they prayed to Governor of Surat to return these goods to them. Pilavoine threatened that in that case, the French would seize all the ships of the Indian merchants standing at the roadstead. This declaration led the Governor to reject the claim of the Armenian merchants[19].

Since the sale of goods had brought some fund to the French, the creditors had begun to press for payment. But Pilavoine managed to get some cargo of white cloth, Ahmedabad silk, pepper, cotton yarn, indigo, porcelain and other sundry goods, including 27 bales of painted cloth that they had at the warehouse[20]. The Company had sent 3,00,000 livres for the cargo in a Portuguese ship destined for Goa. By the end of January 1693, this ship had not arrived while the squadron, without doing much commerce, was getting ready to leave. Pilavoine warned that without fund, it would be difficult to sustain the factory[21].

Financially, the French were not so desperate as Pilavoine made it out. The letter of Roques in early January 1693 showed that they had sold the English ship of a private merchant for 2,500 livres[22]. Since the English were considered to be the principal pirates, the Governor and the Emperor were favorable to the French. The crew of the captured English ship were taken as pirates and on the basis of the recommendation of the chief Qazi of Surat, the Mughal Emperor had rejected the Dutch demand of punishment to the French for their attacks on the Dutch ships. This was a favorable opportunity for the French squadron to attack Bombay, but Dandennes once again refused to attack [23], thus failing to exploit a golden opportunity.

Naturally Pilavoine was depressed. In a letter written in the third week of January 1693, he wrote: "We, in this factory, had been left in such a state that our creditors persecute us to reimburse them, in such a way that we had to use all sorts of tricks not only to keep them quiet, but also to stop them from arresting us....when we go out of Surat to collect our goods...."[24]. Pilavoine even suggested to seize the badly equipped Dutch fleet, which generally came in April to Surat. Quite understandably, he was asking for leave to go back to France, but the Governor of Surat, on the demand of the creditors, had stopped him from leaving Surat [25].

Given such a precarious resource position and the insecurity of life at Surat, some of the French were leading "scandalous" lives, compared to their pompous style of living nearly twenty years back[26]. Texivand, a merchant of the Company, was forced to marry the wife of one Ode Dummer, who suddenly died on "an unknown cause", but suspected of being poisoned. Pilavoine managed to keep them separate for three weeks and wanted to do an autopsy, but he was obstructed. He finally forced the examination on 27 March 1692, but it revealed nothing as to the cause of his death. The widow, with two infants, was found to be pregnant again and Pilavoine suspected that the "black mestizo" was responsible. The poor man was then sacked from the job without evidence. Pilavoine, who already had a strong opinion on inter-racial marriages in India, wrote that the Company should not permit marriage among the employees. He now wanted an ordinance from the Company forbidding such marriages[28].

The Dandennes squadron did not have an impact. The French of course wrote that its success had reverberated all over India[29]. That it was not so could be seen from the order of the Mughal Emperor prohibiting the commerce of the Europeans in India due to continuous complaints of European piracy. According to the French, the Governor of Surat was highly embarrassed as the Indian merchants were involved in the European commerce. The Governor was also afraid that without commerce, the Europeans would take revenge on the Indian shipping. He was worried with the arrival of Dandennes' squadron. But since the squadron had given protection to about fifteen ships at Surat roadstead, the Governor suspended the execution of the order till it was confirmed by the Emperor. He was good enough to leak this information to Pilavoine so that he could lade ships before the confirmation would arrive. On the recommendation of the Qazi, the Emperor modified the order, excluding the French from the purview of this order [29].

While the French squadron was at the roadstead, the Shahbandar of Surat had suggested to Pilavoine to seize two English ships then in anchor. Pilavoine refused as the Shahbandar wanted half of the cargo of the English ship, while the Governor was not willing to give this cargo to the Shahbandar. Pilavoine suggested to Paris that it was the policy of the Company to live in peace, which had prevented him from seizing the English ships[30].

By the middle of February 1693, the French could lade goods worth Rs. 9,00,000. The squadron would go to Mangalore to take some more goods. Only one of its ships would go to Goa first and would join the rest at Mangalore[31]. Given the situation of the French, this collection of cargo was exceptionally good, but it showed that Surat, as a commercial centre of the Mughal Empire, had still its old vitality. Obviously, the arrival of the squadron gave Surat much needed boost, both morally and physically. It had also created an ephemeral illusion of triumph to the French at Surat. The fall of Pondicherry to the Dutch in September 1693 shattered that illusion and perhaps created problems for the French, which they could not envisage then. It was their second loss since the fall of San Thomé nearly twenty years earlier to the combined forces of Golconda and the Dutch.

After the departure of the squadron, the credit of the French at Surat had gone down as quickly as it had soared. The Dutch ships had blocked the Sually roadstead, stopping the entry and exit of the French ships, thus denying any effective support reaching the French at Surat. One of the reasons of the Dutch blockade was that they had come to know of the arrival of a huge fund of the French by a Portuguese ship at Goa. The Dutch thought that this fund would be transferred to the French at Surat by the Portuguese *armada* and the four Dutch ships were stationed to stop this. To overcome this problem, the French decided to send people by land to Daman. Regnard of the French Company was asked to lead the party [32].

By the third week of December 1693, Regnard had reached Daman, where the Portuguese ship had arrived with

50, 500 pieces of Eight. He had taken six soldiers and peons under Godehu. The French at Surat now hoped for the return of peace in Europe to start their commerce in India [33].

At the time when the squadron had arrived at Surat, the Dutch were controlling the sea. There was much disunity among the Dutch then. The arrival of the squadron had brought the unity among the Dutch. The Dutch even contemplated of seizing the Portuguese ships so as to gain the complete command of the sea. However, the possibility of the arrival of the Portuguese *armada* near Surat turned out to be a mere rumour[34].

III

The sudden departure of the French squadron had left the mastery of the sea to the Dutch. The French factors at Surat had therefore no alternative but to wait. Only the ship *Jeux*, leaving France in April 1694, had managed to reach Goa, after eluding the pirates[35]. The arrival of another French squadron, led by Serquigny, at Goa on June 22, 1695[36], gave some hope to the distressed French factors at Surat. Some of the officers of the squadron reached Surat by land and found that the Mughal Emperor had declared war against the English. The squadron then approached the roadstead of Surat on 14 January 1696. Two English ships fled at their approach and one Dutch ship had entered the River of Surat[37]. But then the French were in trouble at Surat.

At Surat, the position of the Europeans had deteriorated. The Indian merchants had strong sentiments against all Europeans due to piracy. The Dewan had prohibited the supply of food to the European ships at Surat. The Dutch had eight ships and they used to bring provisions from Batavia. But they could not lade 2000 bales lying in the quay of the river and in their factory of the city. The Indian merchants had welcomed the arrival of the French squadron at Surat, since they thought that it would protect their ships. Once again they urged the French to seize Bombay, which had only thirty Europeans then. Since the Mughals had declared war against the English, this was a golden opportunity to the French to strike a blow to their English protagonist. Once again, the squadron refused to act[38].

Instead the French secretly proposed to the Mughal Governor that their squadron would escort the ships of the Surat merchants to the Red Sea on condition that the French would be given complete liberty to have their commerce. With Pondicherry under the Dutch occupation and the river mouth of Bengal blocked by the Dutch ships, this was a move to revive their dormant commerce. The French therefore proposed that the liberty of commerce would be given on payment of a sum of money, but far more important, that the Mughals would help in giving a safe passage to two French ships lying in front of Chandernagore for last two years. The Governor wanted some time to consider the proposals[39].

This was the version accepted by Kaeppelin on the basis of the report of Serquigny. The contemporary French letters from Surat had given a different version. The letters stated that the proposal first came from the Governor of the city. The comment of Kaeppelin on the political aims of the Europeans in India would be difficult to accept at this stage[40].

Since there was the prohibition on the commerce of the Europeans, the squadron found it difficult to collect the cargo, without which it would be costly to go back. In the meeting of the French war Council at Surat, it was decided to send the squadron to Bengal to escort the two blocked French ships to France with cargo. At the same time, Pilavoine was asked to continue the negotiation with the Governor of Surat on the question of escorting the Surat ships to the Red Sea in exchange of territorial and commercial advantages. The negotiation had already started and lasted six weeks[41].

Meanwhile on 7 February 1696, the three French ships of the squadron along with some Portuguese ships had a fight with eight Dutch ships. It appears that the fight was indecisive and the French ships returned to Surat unscathed[42]. This may suggest that the Dutch had forced the French to leave the command of the sea to the Dutch and to retreat. On the 26th of

February, Serquigny, after his return, found that the Mughal Emperor had not approved the proposal till then and the prohibition had remained in force. They also managed to supply food to the ships by bribing the Governor [43].

Once again the squadron had failed to wrest the command of the sea from the Dutch and they failed to get the necessary cargo from Surat. They did not try to extricate the French ships in Bengal, which they could have done by April as there were not many Dutch or English ships in Bengal then. It was only in July that eight Dutch ships had arrived at Balasore. The decision of the war Council, held on 28 April 1696, for the return was a faulty one from the interest of the French in India and had been described by Father Tchard among others. In his letter to France in the middle of August 1697, Pilavoine suggested that the officers of the squadron did not dare to go to Bengal as there was the information of the presence of eight Dutch ships, which in reality were not there. Perhaps the real reason was, as written by François Martin in his letter of 1699, that the officers had bought goods on their personal account for sale in France. They were therefore in a hurry to go back and not risk a fight[44]. The failure of the squadron had a major effect on the French establishment in India during the period.

In September 1695, the Mughal ship, *Ganj-i Sawar*, was returning to Surat from Mocha with five million rupees. It was plundered in the high-seas. Even some Muslim women were violated. The mob fury was against the English and they had besieged the English factory with the intention of setting it on fire. The astute Governor managed to quieten them by imprisoning the English factors including their President. The Mughal Emperor then had imposed total prohibition on European commerce[44]. Pilavoine, who was returning from Goa, was not allowed to enter the city. It was on the express wish of the principal merchants of the city that Pilavoine was allowed to enter Surat in January 1696[46].

The Dutch had also suffered as they could not lade their eight ships lying on the roadstead. They had goods worth two million rupees to go through the customs. They finally managed to get the permission by paying a huge amount to the Governor and the officials[47]

In November 1696, the Governor asked all the European Companies to give two ships as escort to the Surat ships bound for Haj. He had asked the French to get the squadron in exchange of the permission for another French establishment and exemption from taxes. Since the squadron was at Goa then, the French wanted time to consult the captain. The Governor asked for a small French boat to send to Bengal, obviously for his own private trading. The French wanted more details on the parties who would be sending goods [48].

The French were then in a delicate situation as six Frenchmen, all pirates, had just been arrested[49]. The French however delayed the reply to the proposal of the Governor on the ground that their squadron was still at Goa. Actually they were waiting for the fund brought by the squadron to pay for the cargo. To the French, it appeared that in case of their refusal, the prohibition would be extended to Bengal. This would mean that the squadron would return to France without cargo. On the other hand, if they would accept the proposal, they could ask Mughal help in liberating the two ships blocked on the Ganges[50].

As related earlier, in the meeting of the Council of 20 January 1696, Pilavoine was asked to negotiate with the Governor. On the 21st, Pilavoine and J.B. Martin had gone to the Governor, who met them the next day. The Governor proposed that two French ships would escort the Surat ships to Mocha and Jedda. Pilavoine agreed and gave a written assurance. However the entire French squadron should go. The Governor forwarded to the Emperor the French view that two of their ships would be sufficient. The reply would take five to six weeks and the Governor asked the French to wait. Besides, he was expecting the arrival of ten English ships from China soon[51].

As explained earlier, the squadron had come to Surat but had gone out again. They had returned to Surat on March 26, 1696 to find twenty-two Surat ships waiting on the roadstead.

Most of them were destined for the Red Sea. While waiting, the French, as seen, could lade goods[53].

There was however another problem for the French escort. It was reported that a Dutch squadron had arrived at Cochin and were looking for the French ships. In that case, the French did not want to hazard an action and there would be no problem for the Surat ships either since the Dutch fleet was there. In the meeting of the Council at Surat on the 19th of April, the French decided to send the squadron back. It left on the 26th of April through the artillery fire from the Dutch ships. Pilavoine wanted to go back but he missed the embarkation as the squadron had to leave hurriedly due to the Dutch fire [54].

The Council had further resolved that one French ship would go to Goa and leave for France from there. Pilavoine wanted to take this ship from Goa but he could not make the overland journey through Bijapur. The French ship *Pontchartrain* had come to Goa to buy pepper. Since the Dutch ships were waiting, the French decided to sell the ship to the Portuguese, who would give passage to the French officers and crew to France. Meanwhile the Mughal Emperor had ordered that two European ships would escort the Surat ships, which would mean the beginning of commerce. But the Surat merchants were still afraid of the English pirates[55].

The English at Surat pompously accepted the proposal in return of which the Governor had released the English factors. But there was strong resentment against the English among the merchants of the city. The French expected that the English would be further exposed when the Mocha and Jedda ships of Surat would return in September[56].

The Governor had asked the French to lend two ships. The French reply was that they had promised for the last monsoon when they had the squadron at Surat. Since the squadron had left without cargo and without getting any reply, the French at the moment had no ship to lend. The Governor who was heavily bribed by the English, according to the French, began to press. But the principal merchants were against the English. They were led by Abdul Gaffur, the wealthy merchant of Surat, who had lost nine to ten ships in the last few years, including their last ship with two lakh rupees. In the background of this strong resentment against the English, the Governor could not take steps against the French, excepting asking Pilavoine not to leave the city. Besides, Pilavoine had contracted debts at Surat, which he was not in a position to pay. Meanwhile, the merchants, led by Abdul Gaffur, had begun to agitate against the Governor for liberating the English [57].

Before the order of the Governor could come, Pilavoine had left Surat for Goa to embark from there. Commerce had started at Surat for the Europeans, but the Governor was insisting that it was subject to the lending of escort ships. The French did not have any ship at Surat and represented to the Governor the impossibility of accepting this condition. The Dutch had agreed to lend ships but they were looking for an excuse to break it. They refused to give passport to the ship of Abdul Gaffur, who duly complained to the Governor. He sent a captain immediately to the Dutch factory to warn them that in case of the refusal to give passport, he would send guards to besiege the factory. Such a threat had never been given to the Europeans at Surat before and the Dutch were stunned. They immediately issued the passport. The French now demanded that they should be permitted to lade goods to their small boat, since such permission had been given to the English and the Dutch. Following the Dutch, the French refused to give passport to five Surat merchants. The Governor threatened the French, who then submitted. Meanwhile two Turkish ships were plundered of three lakh rupees in cash. Information also came that five English private ships were waiting to seize some ships of the Muslim officials belonging to Gogo and Cambay. Once again, this created an uproar at Surat and the English Governor of Bombay had to send escort ships to Surat [58].

In this charged atmosphere at Surat, the French and other European merchants were not permitted to go to Sually even for a change of air, quite a change from the earlier years. At that time a terrible plague was raging at Surat with the continuous immigration of people from the rural areas due to persistent Maratha plunder. With the drought around Ahmedabad, about 25,000 people, carrying 300,000 cattle were leaving for better areas like Surat. The wells had dried up and water had become very scarce. There was a complete desertion of the countryside that had stopped cultivation. The price of millet, the staple food of the poor people, had increased by 400%.

The English had captured some French pirates and brought them to Surat, blaming the French publicly for piracy. The Governor had called Pilavoine to explain but he managed to calm the Governor. The English did not trust the Governor as they thought that he was friendly to Pilavoine and had kept the French as prisoners in the English factory. The French factors managed to contact these prisoners by letters by bribing one of the peons of the English factory. It was learnt that these prisoners were chained and were kept at a room, which had big grilled window. The French factors managed to introduce grill-cutters and it was arranged that they would escape at night and would be taken to a safe house. On the night of 29 November, the French prisoners managed to escape and they were taken to the French factory [60].

On the morning of November 30, the English found out about the escape. They then rushed to the French factory and maltreated the servants. They had then complained to the Governor, who sent soldiers to look for the escaped prisoners in the city. Meanwhile the English promised a reward of Rs. 1000 to anyone who would find them, which was quite considerable in a city where people generally gained 4 to 5 Ps. per month. The English then decided to send the French prisoners to Bombay after their capture [61].

Actually the English in the beginning had arrived at the right place. The prisoners were given some disguise and were kept in the French factory where the English had failed to recognize them. At that time the soldiers had visited everywhere in the European *mahalla* but could not find them. Irritated, the English suggested to the Governor that these men, had taken refuge in the house of the Jesuits. The Governor sent a captain and some soldiers to the Jesuit house, which was close to the French factory. The Jesuits objected to the visit of the soldiers inside the house. The French factors had also come out and objected on the ground that they considered this religious house as part of the French factory. While the English factors accompanying the soldiers were planning to use force next day, the French factors suddenly relented and had allowed only the captain to visit the house. At the same time, the French were preparing to resist the English plan of attack next day. Evidently the sentiment of the Mughal soldiers were against the English as an Arab officer of the Mughals had offered the French to come to their help with 300 soldiers in case of the English attack. The visit of the captain produced nothing and the English abandoned their plan of attack. The Governor of the city was aware that those French were in the French factory, but he did not push the search there. The French were waiting for a suitable opportunity to send those French to the Portuguese [62].

Although the Governor had been accused by the French as siding with the English, he did not actually favor the English. One of the reasons could be that the English had taken justice in their hands. They had not produced the French pirates in the court of the Governor nor they had taken the permission of the Governor to keep those French imprisoned under chains in the English factory. The rescue of these pirates by the French factors showed that they had links with those pirates, a view propagated by the merchants of Surat, particularly by Abdul Gaffur[63]. Also, the French claim of extra-territoriality extended to the religious house was quite new. The entire version was written to show to Paris the popularity of the French in the city and the hatred of the people towards the English.

That year was particularly bad for Surat. The French complained that there was acute scarcity of money in the city as they had to wait ten days to get a loan of Rs. 1000 from the richest shroff of the city. The Red Sea and the Persian Gulf fleet of the Surat merchants had not gone out due to the fear of the pirates, thus failing to bring bullions. The Arabs of Muscat were fighting with the Persian King, which had prevented normal business. To the French, the rich commerce of the city had declined considerably [64].

Such a situation had affected the French at Surat. After getting money brought by the squadron, Surat factors had sent Rs. 10,000 to Bengal by letter of change. They could have sent more but the cost of the letter of change had gone up considerably. Even they tried to get from Ahmedabad, but there was no proper shroff who had money to send to Bengal. Also, the broker of the French did not want to get involved, since there was no security in the route. Recently, a caravan of silk coming from Bengal had been plundered on the way. The French then had gone to their old friends Bohra brothers, who had arranged their agent at Agra to send this amount. In the process, the French had lost 6 to 7%. The insecurity of the route, as recounted by the French, was not always there. Bengal had sent coral against which Surat had sent Rs. 20,000 by country boat that had reached Bengal safely [65].

With the money from the squadron and the coral from Bengal, the French at Surat had a breathing space. They had also some coral at their warehouse for sale for Rs. 6000. With all these, they had nearly Rs. 60,000. The problem was to change money at Surat, whose charge had gone up to 11%. The transfer of money was hazardous since Rajaram had forty armed barges hovering between Goa and Surat looking for Mughal ships. The Malabar and the Sangam Pirates often seized vessels, which did not have much of defense [66].

The difficulties of the French at Surat continued to aggravate as they failed to sell the European goods, which always had a ready sale at Surat. They had sent Flacourt to Goa, but he could not sell most of the goods. One of the reasons however was that the woollen products got damaged by humidity. Surat still had 35 bales of coarse drapes and 15 bales of fine drapes. They had sent fine drapes to Bengal but they could not sell these [67].

Meanwhile the Governor of Surat was insisting that the French should send escort ships to Mocha. The French replied that they were waiting for their ships to come to Goa. The ship *Potchartrain*, a king's ship and commanded by the officers of the King, was at Goa. But he had refused to follow the advice of Pilavoine, who had gone to persuade him. Surat wanted to send a barge with goods to Goa to lade goods in that ship, even after paying 10% custom duties at Goa[68]. The Governor had not given the permission to transfer these goods. The French then had approached the Portuguese to send a frigate to Surat to take these goods. But the Portuguese were then busy fighting at Mozambique and did not accept the request. The French at Surat had no alternative but to appeal to France to send six ships in December[69].

Without commerce, the situation of the French had worsened at Surat, where their debt continued to mount. However the creditors had understood the situation and were waiting for the French ships to come. They had left the French in peace for the moment[70]. By the end of April 1697, the English and the Dutch got the permission of the Governor to lade their ships in lieu of their escort to Mocha[71] The French at Surat had ordered Flacourt to send the goods, including coral and drapes from Goa to Bengal. Since no French ship had come to Goa, Flacourt could not send the goods. An exasperated Surat asked Flacourt to send the goods by a Portuguese ship[72]. Surat was unwilling to send money to Bengal for changing. Cosmo Gomez, a Portuguese merchant, could easily change the money in Bengal up to Rs. 25,000. But the problem was that Surat might not get this money back due to possible piratical attacks. Recently the pirates had plundered a richly laden English ship coming from China, among others. Even the ship of the Mughal Emperor going to Mocha was plundered. These had created again a panic in the city and had further heightened tension between the Indians and the Europeans, that had further tightened financial dealings[73]. Under the circumstances, the French at Surat thought of a ruse to elude the Dutch blockade of the French ships at Surat. They had sent a ship to Bengal under the name of the Danish Governor. The plan was actually adopted in the Council meeting at Surat in May 1696, but they were not implemented earlier. The ship

The French at Surat

carried the goods of the English as well as those of the other banians of Surat. The Dutch blocked it but thought it to be a Malabar ship and sent it to Goa. The situation at Surat had improved somewhat with the arrival of goods and bullion of the English and the Dutch ships. The situation further improved on 15 September 1697, when fifteen ships of Surat including the one of the Mughal Emperor, had arrived at Surat, duly escorted by an English and a Dutch ship. The event, almost unheard of at Surat in recent years, was celebrated throughout the city. They had brought nearly 13 million of French livres that eased the financial situation at Surat[74].

The French at Surat found themselves in the worse situation. The creditors had begun to press for payment, but they were persuaded to wait for the arrival of the French ship. The French had to sell their ship *Jeux* for Rs. 14,300. It was however a mere pittance. They could not sell the drapes despite the improved financial situation of the port-city. Only their old friend, Samuchan Bohra, had bought some drapes[75]. Meanwhile a new Governor of Surat had come and had begun to take money by force. He asked the French to pay Rs. 80,000 for non-payment of taxes of earlier years. This was during the period of Anglo-Mughal war when the valuation had not been done properly. The French tried to persuade him to change his order or at least delay it since their commerce had been stopped for several years. The only saving grace, although it did not affect the French much, was that rains had been falling regularly at Ahmedabad side and work on textile had started again. Actually the price of textile was falling, but the French had no money to take advantage [76].

The situation of the French debt had been gradually going beyond the control of the French. They owed to Samuchan Bohra, brother of Samuchan Bohra, a staggering sum of Rs. 1,66,907 only till 31 October 1697. He had visited the French factory several times pressing for the payment. But the French could persuade him to wait a bit further till the arrival of their ships. He suggested to the French that they should take loan from somebody else and pay him as he needed money badly.

After sometime, he began to come daily and began to press for payment of even a part[77]. Flacourt had suggested that they should start commerce in pepper in country boats in the area around Goa. But the French feared that the English and the Dutch would seize these boats as they had factories in all places. Flacourt had started this commerce with few bales in the land of a Prince near Goa. The Prince had agreed that Flacourt should pay the custom duty of one and half percent.[78].

From the position of a global trader, the French had been reduced to a country merchant at Surat hiding from the creditors. Although they were going in procession with a large retinue of servants holding umbrella over the head of the Director in the city, they had no money to pay the creditors or to pay for the cargo. The miserable condition of the French at Surat, underlying the colourful paraphernalia, had been noted by J.B. Martin in letter after letter. Unfortunately for the French, the circumstances had gone against them in the European war at a time when they had began to prosper. The peace in Europe in 1697 gave Pondicherry back to the French, but by then, the Company was totally exhausted, running a huge debt in India and in France. The death of J.B. Martin, then acting as chief in the absence of Pilavoine, in June 1697 did not improve their condition. His second, Regnard, was a mediocre man and the French faced tremendous difficulties at Surat in the years to come.

IV

Although the Treaty of Ryswick was signed in Europe on 21 September 1697, the information took a long time to come to India. The Mughal Emperor, as seen earlier, had permitted the European Companies to start commerce.

With the peace in Europe, situation seemed to improve for the French at Surat. Three ships, *Pontchartrain, Princesse de Savoie* and *Marchand des Indes* had arrived at Surat. Regnard wanted to utilize *Pontchartrain* for coastal trading. Surat had some goods at the warehouse and they had begun to lade the *Princesse*. It could not be done properly as the Governor began to demand the arrear payment while loading was going on. Once again, Regnard persuaded the Governor to allow the departure of ships. Only the *Marchand* could leave in May 1699 with cargo and with the complaint of Regnard against the Governor [79].

The piracy however had continued. The pirates had plundered the ship of a Surat merchant coming back from Java and this led the Mughal Emperor to issue order to Amanat Khan, the Mughal Governor of Surat. The order was that the European ships escorting the Surat ships, in case of plunder, should compensate the loss, failing which they would not be permitted to do commerce. From 12 January 1699, Amanat Khan besieged the European factories, preventing any exit or entry, including food stuff, till they would sign the acceptance of the order. This included the French also. A French Jesuit was arrested on the charge of bringing food to the factory and was whipped by the order of the Governor. On 16 January 1699, Regnard had gone to meet the Governor as he was loading his ships. After a heated exchange, Regnard announced that the French would leave Surat within five days. But Amanat Khan paid no heed and forced Regnard to sign for him as well as for his sucessors a letter of change that would be used as a caution money along with a note. In the note, Regnard had to write that the French would prevent piracy between Surat and the Persian Gulf. In case of plunder, the French would pay the damage. The Dutch had to sign the same kind of note for the ships going from Jedda and Mocha. The English had to sign for the ships going to Coromandel, Malabar, Bengal, Acheh and China. Regnard sent the information to Pondicherry by the Brigantin *St. Louis* leaving Surat on May 13 [80].

Under the circumstances, Regnard and other merchants decided to send a representation to the Mughal Emperor, then in the Deccan, to highlight their grievances against the Mughal officials at Surat. Perhaps without the concurrence of Pondicherry, they called Alexander de l'Estoile from Bandar Abbassy. Estoile arrived at Surat on 25 April 1699 and was asked to go to the Mughal Emperor as envoy of France. The principal complaint would be against the Mughal Governor, who, the French felt, was out to ruin the European commerce at Surat.

Estoile was an adept in diplomacy as he had already been in the court of Persia as well as to that of the Nawab of Bengal. Before leaving for the Deccan, he sent a letter to the French Company in France explaining his mission [81]

Estoile had left Surat on 9 June 1699 and had gone to Burhanpur where the Mughal Emperor was camping. He had to wait three months to find some one to present him to the Emperor as per the etiquette of the Mughal court. Obviously none of the Mughal nobles wanted to go against Amanat Khan. Finally on 19 September, he found one who presented him to the Emperor, who interviewed him for more than an hour on France and on Louis XIV. The Emperor then gave the order to his Wazir Asad Khan to write to Amanat Khan to leave the French in peace [82]. On October 5, 1699, the order was conveyed to Amanat Khan by Asad Khan by one *Hasb-ul Hukum*, on which the Emperor had scribbled a few lines on the top in his own hand to convey the sense of urgency and authenticity. It clearly ordered Amanat Khan to restore to the French the earlier liberty of free entry and exit to and from the city. The order arrived at Surat on 13 November 1699 while Estoile could reach Surat only on 23 December 1699 [83]

That the fortune of the French had begun to smile could be seen when the two French ships, *Florissant* and *Aurore* had arrived at Surat with cargo and bullion worth 1,290,000 livres. Regnard claimed that there was a loss of nearly 80,000 livres in exchange, probably an exaggeration. However he could not get the goods passed through the custom house since Dianat Khan, the successor of Amanat Khan, could take charge only on 17 December 1699. The goods were finally cleared in March 1700 and the merchants of Surat found that most of the wines, mirror, crystal etc., had been damaged. The loss was estimated at 300,000 livres. But what irked the French most was the refusal of the new Governor to allow the French to go to Ahmedabad to give advance to the weavers. With the goods found at Surat, the French decided to lade only *Aurore* and keep the other ships at Surat. They collected cargo for *Aurore* worth Rs. 3,27,700, a rather small amount, compared to the huge fund brought from

The French at Surat

France. Although the Surat letters did not mention it, the reason of the weak cargo was perhaps due to the opposition of some creditors who were very influential merchants of Surat [84].

The restriction on the movement of the French at Surat was still there. This could be seen when Augiers, with a small squadron of two ships, had arrived at Surat from Pondicherry on 4 December 1699. He found that Regnard could not go out of the factory and the French employees of Sually could reach Surat after great difficulties. Obviously they were helped by the presence of two French warships and three other French ships then at the roadstead. Regnard, now encouraged by their presence, protested to Dianat Khan, who requested him not to go out of Surat. Regnard hinted to the Governor that Augiers might seize some Surat ships if such restrictions were to continue. The Governor climbed down and returned the letter of change to Regnard [85], which would have become invalid in any case after sometime.

Fearing that the Governor would retaliate after the departure of Augiers, Regnard met the governor on 21 December and managed to calm him. In the meeting, Regnard had also used the threat that France might send warships to Surat if freedom was not given to them. For evidence, he handed over the letter of Minister *Pontchartrain* written two years earlier. The Governor promised to treat the French well[86].

On 26 January 1700, Dianat Khan replied to the letter of the Minister *Pontchartrain*. He stated that the French were at complete liberty at Surat and whatever oppression had been done, it was during the time of his predecessor. He confessed that the French were having problem at the custom house since the son of the previous Governor was the custom officer. He was trying to improve the situation. The fact was that despite the presence of two French warships, the situation of the French had not improved much at Surat [87]

On the 27th January 1700, Augiers left Surat for Goa on the way to France with *Aurore* and *Castina* well laden. Regnard was still closeted in the factory while Tisserand and Grangement had supervised the lading at Sually. In the letter of the Council to France written on 30 January 1700, they complained bitterly on the absence of liberty of entry and exit, that was affecting commercial transactions [88]. There was therefore a difference of perception between the Mughals and the French on the question of liberty or freedom of movement. To the Mughals, it seems, given the sentiment of the city merchants against the Europeans, the liberty for some French to work at Sually was a big concession. The French believed that an united resistance of the Europeans at Surat would have brought more freedom; but there was no unity among the Europeans given their acute rivalry for goods. The inherent contradiction within the system of competition had been an essential element of weakness of the Europeans in India during the late seventeenth century, which had been cleverly exploited by the Mughal authorities.

V

With the arrival of fund, the French had begun to pick up coastal trading that was essential for the collection of cargo for Europe. An Armenian had freighted the ship *Pontchartrain* for Rs. 28,000 and sent it to Bengal. In May 1700, *Florissant* left for Persia. Bengal had sent a small ship *Fathemurad* to Surat in January 1700. It was sent to the Malabar coast to establish a post and to collect pepper. After its return, it was sent to China in May 1700 to study the commercial situation there. Fuet was made in charge and cargo worth Rs. 50,000 was given to him. In this the share of the Company was Rs. 15,000. This was the first French attempt from India to exploit the China trade[89].

Martin's long report from Pondicherry, which had become the headquarter of the French establishments in the East, written in the middle of February 1700, reiterated the problem of French commerce in India. With the limited fund sent by France, it was difficult to maintain the factories and expand the commerce. Martin explained that a limited commerce would not be able to maintain the factories. He emphasized that Surat factory had certain advantages over others, since European goods could be sold from Surat, where "everything is sold". It was the meeting place of all nations from October to the end of May. To Martin, Surat was still the wealthiest city, with many wealthy merchants, whose commerce with the Persian Gulf, the Red Sea, Malabar coast, Acheh and other places were going on in full steam. The custom duties at Surat had given the amount of twenty million livres annually. It was easy to get loans with interest ranging from 10% a year. People often offered at less interest as the Dutch got once the loan between 4 to 5% a year. The English piracy had brought the violence of the Governor towards the Europeans. In the last few years, twelve Surat ships were plundered, including the one of the Mughal Emperor. Martin was not happy with Regnard and suggested to place a good man at Surat, who would be able to deal with the merchants as well as with the Mughal officials. But he insisted that the Company should pay the debts first[90].

On 14 November 1700, Pilavoine, who could not enter Surat, wrote to the son of Amanat Khan. The *Dewan-i Suba*, who was favourably inclined towards the French, made arrangements for his entry to Surat. At Sually, Pilavoine was told of the tyranny of the Governor, which showed that the Mughal officials did not pay much heed to the order of the Mughal Emperor[91].

In the third week of September 1700, the French sent some demands to the Governor, Dianat Khan. Perhaps this had unnerved the Mughal officials, who came to Sually to escort Pilavoine and his family to Surat, an unheard gesture by the Mughal officials towards the Europeans. The French returned the gesture by visiting the Governor with a horse and other presents. Pilavoine took charge of the factory from 20 November 1700[92].

If one looks at the earlier French letter from Surat, one would notice a significant change of the situation at Surat at the end of 1700. The letter of 30 January 1700, from Surat, spoke of the depressing condition of the Europeans since there was no liberty of commerce at Surat. The letter also mentioned the arrival of the order of the Mughal Emperor [93]. By the third week of

March 1700, there was a significant change in the commercial atmosphere of Surat as reported by the French in their letter of 20 March 1700 [94]. They reported that the commerce of Surat had been made "open to all the world" and mentioned that the chief of the English Company had entered in last February "with much magnificence". But it was a temporary reprieve. By November 1700, the English pirates had seized a ship of a Surat merchant and restrictions had been imposed on the exit of the English from the city [95].

Fortune however continued to smile on the French. The two French ships, *St. Louis*, commanded by Mayer and *Etoiles d'Orient* had arrived at Surat. Mayer immediately accused Pilavoine for wasting time and money in displaying magnificence. Pilavoine had entered Surat with pomp, riding a horse and surrounded by the Mughal officials and the principal merchants of the city. Obviously it was the principal merchants who had forced the officials to come to a compromise with the European Companies, showing a different perception from those of the officials [96].

The two ships were sent to Calicut to buy pepper after which they had come back to Surat via Goa along with *Agreeable* and *Mutiny* on 22 December 1700. The Governor immediately proposed to the French to send these four ships out to fight the pirates. Pilavoine was against it since there were no pirates in front of Surat in the first place. Secondly, Pilavoine felt that it would create a precedence, although the liberty of commerce had been accorded by the Emperor on this condition. Yet with the arrival of four ships at Surat, the situation was favourable for the French as the Mughal Governor was on the defensive. With no intention to escort the Surat ships, Pilavoine decided to recover the note of caution from the Governor. He asked the commander Chateaumorant to get it. Meanwhile another ship *Florissant* freighted by the Surat merchants had come back to Surat with profit [97].

Actually the problems of the French at Surat were linked to the wider problems of Surat - the piracy, the disgust of the population towards the Europeans, the restrictions imposed by the Mughal Governor etc. Often, the French linked such problems with the coming civil war on the approaching death of the aged Mughal Emperor. The suspicion of the Surat merchants towards the Europeans was too deep to be removed and would come out in trivial incidents. In September 1700, two Dutch ships freighted by the Surat merchants, coming from Mocha with bullion, were scuttled near Daman. It was widely believed at Surat that the Dutch had done it deliberately to get the huge amount of bullion. The Dutch had to pay 75% of the loss, but it created a tension between the Europeans and the local merchants at Surat [98].

Chateaumorant was at Sually, where the son of Dianat Khan, met him and had brought him to Surat [99]. Dianat Khan also met him at Surat [100]. While the negotiation started, the French had a Council meeting at the factory on 11 January 1701. It was decided to ask for the return of note. In the meeting with the Governor, a draft agreement was drawn up, in which Chateaumorant inserted a threat. If the note was not delivered in time, the King of France would be free to send ships or to take other measures to get it by force. The negotiation almost broke up as Dianat Khan refused to accept it. With four ships to lade, Pilavoine agreed to the reconciliation and the uncertainty was removed. Dianat Khan agreed to request the Mughal Emperor for the return of the note, which he put in writing [101]. Obviously Dianat Khan wanted to delay it, since the French ships would have to leave in a few days time. Pilavoine was aware of the tactic of Dianat Khan and expressed to Paris that the note could not be recovered without force. However, even after the departure of ships, the old liberty continued for the French. Perhaps this was partly due to the costly presents given by Pilavoine to Dianat Khan and his son [102].

All these troubles led Pilavoine to propose to Paris to have a territorial establishment in the Western coast. He thought Diu would be most convenient due to its links with the Red Sea, the Persian Gulf and the Mughal Empire. This was not new. The commandant Mayer was already suggesting an establishment on the Island of Karanja near Bombay. Mayer thought that the Portuguese would willingly give it up. Pilavoine wanted to get away from the Mughal control and felt that the Hindus would willingly change their masters from the declining Portuguese and that they were merely waiting for a capable master to maintain them in their possessions as well as in their religion[103]- an idea that the later colonial writers took up earnestly. Once again the outbreak of another European war prevented any discussion on the French plan of expansion in the Western Coast of India.

In all the senses, it was a happy return of Pilavoine at Surat. The French had got back some semblance of their earlier liberty at Surat sanctified by an order of the Mughal Emperor. The French commerce at Surat was at the threshold of opening into a new and prosperous future. It is no wonder that Pilavoine was thinking of a new territorial enclave beyond the reach of the Mughal officials. But the flicker of a prosperous commerce was extinguished soon by another European war that saw the Company completely exhausted in France. A few merchants of St. Malo took over the Indian commerce from the French Company on payment of 10% on the return. They did not send any ship to Surat resulting in the total stoppage of French trade at Surat till another Company was formed in France in 1719. Pilavoine ultimately died broken-hearted at Surat leaving a huge debt. Surat gradually went into the backwater of French commerce with the emergence of Pondicherry and Chandernagore in Bengal.

In this brief narrative, one would notice the sudden changes of fortune of the French, linked to the politics in Europe. It had been shown that the fortune of Surat was linked to the political vicissitudes of Western Asia that had affected the markets there and the prosperity of Surat[104]. In case of the French, it was more of the political fluctuations in Europe that had influenced the position of the French at Surat. From the narrative however the increasingly dominant role of the Surat merchants could be traced. Sometimes, the political authority at Surat had to accept the decisions of Surat merchants that showed that the world of commerce and the political world were coming closer in the wake of the declining fortunes of Surat. It would also show that the problems of Surat had begun to affect its commerce from the last decade of the seventeenth century in which piracy had played a significant role. As seen from the French eyes, the decline of Surat had started well before 1700.

References:

1. S.P. Sen, *The French in India*, Calcutta, 1984
2. C.B. Malleson, *History of the French in India*, Delhi, 1984, reprint of 1909 ed.
3. Paul Kaeppelin, *La Compagnie des Indes Orientales et François Martin*, Paris, 1908 (Kaeppelin hereinafter).
4. Ashin Dasgupta, *Indian Merchants and the Decline of Surat, c. 1700 - 1750*, Weisbaden, 1979.
5. François Martin, *Memories*, ed. by A. Martineau, Paris, 1931-34, 3 Vols., II, 431.
6. *Archives Nationales et Coloniales* (France), (AN hereinafter), *Colonie* C(2) 63, Surat to Paris, 26 April 1686, ff 65-65v.
7. Ibid., f 75
8. *Ibid*, Surat to Paris, 17 June 1686, ff 75-75v.
9. *Ibid*, ff 75 -7 5v.
10. Kaeppelin, 248
11. Martin, *op.cit.*, II, 451. He thought that these pirates were Danes. The estimated loss of two ships was according to Martin, 400,000 ecu (1 ecu = 2 sicca Rs. See, V. Ball in his editon of J.B. Tvarnier,*Travels in India*, ed., New Delhi, 1977, 327-29).
12. AN, Colonie C(2) 63, Surat to Paris, 17 January 1688, ff 112-122v: "........the country is nearly destroyed; the war has contributed to this misfortune....." (my translation).
13. Martin, op.cit., III, 43-48
14. *Ibid*, 76-77
15. AN, Colonie C(2) 64, Pilavoine from Surat to Paris, 29 January 1692, f 31 v.
16. *Ibid*, letter of Roques, 30 January 1692, f 38v.
17. Kaeppelin, 300-301
18. AN, Colonie C (2) 64, Pilavoine from Surat to Paris, 24 January 1693, ff 58-59v.
19. *Ibid*; also, letter of Roques from Surat, 6 January 1693, f 50.
20. *Ibid*, letter of Pilavoine, 24 January 1693, ff 58, 63-63v, 72-72v.
21. *Ibid*, Pilavoine from Surat, 20, January 1693, f 52v; letter of Pilavoine, 24 January 1693, f 62.
22. *Ibid*, letter of 24 January 1693, f 63.
23. *Ibid*, Roques from Surat, 6 January 1693, ff 50-50v.
24. *Ibid*, f 51
25. *Ibid*, letter of Pilavoine from Surat, 20 January 1693, f 52v.
26. *Ibid*, f 54v.

27. For details, see the article of Aniruddha Ray entitled "The Growth of the city of Surat, 1610-1671" in *The Journal of the Asiatic Society of Bangladesh* (Humanities), Dhaka, Vols. XXIV-VI, 1979-81, 95-107.
28. AN, Colonie C(2) 64, Pilavoine from Surat, 20 January 1693, ff 55v-56.
29. *Ibid*, f 52
30. *Ibid*, letter of 24 January 1693, ff 73v-74.
31. *Ibid*, ff 74v-75
32. *Ibid*, Pilavoine from Surat, 15 February 1693, f 80.
33. *Ibid*, letter from Surat, 24 December 1693, f 85v.
34. *Ibid*, letter from Surat, 26 December 1693, ff 86-86v.
35. *Ibid*, letter from Surat, 24 December 1693, f 85v.
36. *Kaeppelin*, 326-327. The squadron had six ships and 1266 men with 256 canons.
37. AN, Colone C (2) 64, Relation by the commandant M. de Serquigny, 1695-97, ff 136v post.
38. *Ibid*, f 138
39. *Ibid*, ff 137-137v : "The entire city showed so much joy since we can guarantee the protection to their ships from the Red Sea, disturbed since a few years."
40. *Ibid*, ff 137-137v.
41. *Ibid*, Martin & Deslandes from Hughli to Surat, 10 July 1696, ff 143v-144; Kaeppelin, 328
42. *Kaeppelin*, 328
43. AN, Colonie C(2) 64, Relation, ff 137v-138; *Kaeppelin*, 329
44. *Koeppelin*, 329-30
45. Full discussion in *Ibid*, 331 & note 1.
46. Jadunath Sarkar, *History of Aurangzeb*, Calcutta, 5 Vols., V, 5th ed., 365.
47. AN, Colonie C(2) 64, letter of Pilavoine from Surat, 19 January 1696, ff 19-149v.
48. *Ibid*, f 19v.
49. *Ibid*, 150-150v.
50. *Ibid*, f 150; Serquigny wrote that eight French pirates were seized (Ibid, ff 136v-137).
51. *Ibdi*, letter of Pilavoine, 19 January 1696, f 150.
52. *Ibid*, letter of Pilavoine, 24 January 1696, f 152.
53. *Ibid*, f 153v.
54. *Ibid*, f 154v.
55. *Ibid*, letter of Surat, 25 July 1696, ff 185v-186.
56. *Ibid*.
57. *Ibid*, ff 186v-187.
58. *Ibid*, letter of Surat, 30 November 1696, ff 188-188v.
59. *Ibid*, f 190.
60. *Ibid*, f 190v.
61. *Ibid*.
62. *Ibid*, ff 190v-191
63. *Ibid*, f 192

64. *Ibid*, ff 192-192v.
65. *Ibid*, ff 194v-195.
66. *Ibid*, f 195
67. *Ibid*, f 196v.
68. *Ibid*, f 199.
69. *Ibid*, f 202.
70. *Ibid*, 202v.
71. *Ibid*, letter from Surat, 28 April 1697, f 222.
72. *Ibid*, ff 222v-223.
73. *Ibid*, ff 225v-226.
74. *Ibid*, letter from Surat, 15 February 1697, f 231.
75. *Ibid*, ff 231-234.
76. *Ibid*, f 236.
77. *Ibid*, f 238.
78. *Ibid*, f 239.
79. *Ibid*, Colonie C(2) 65, letter from Surat, 30 January 1700, f 197v.
80. Kaeppelin, 450-451.
81. AN, Colonie C(2) 65, letter of Estoile to Paris, 25 April 1699, f 17.
82. *Ibid*, for the request to the Mughal Emperor in Persian, ff 18-19; letter of Deslandes from Hughli, 8 February 1700, ff 121-123.
83. *Ibid*, also, *Kaeppelin*, 451.
84. *Kaeppelin*, 452-453.
85. *Ibid*, 453-454.
86. *Ibid*, 453.
87. *Ibid*, 453-454
88. AN, Colonie C(2) 65, letter from Surat, 30 January 1699, ff 199-199v.
89. *Kaeppelin*, 455.
90. AN, Colonie C(2) 65, letter of Martin from Pondicherry, 15 February 1700 ff 49v051.
91. *Ibid*, Pilavoine from Surat 27 November 1700, f 223
92. *Ibid*, f 224.
93. *Ibid*, letter from Surat, 30 January 1700, ff 199-201.
94. *Ibid*, letter from Surat, 20 March 1700, f 210v.
95. *Ibid*, letter from Surat, 22 November 1700, f 227v.
96. *Kaeppelin*, 476
97. AN, Colonie C (2) 66, letter from Surat, 15 January 1701, f 119v.
98. *Ibid*, letter from Surat, 2 January 1701, f 111v.
99. *Ibid*.
100. *Ibid*, letter from Surat, 31 January 1701, f 127v.
101. *Ibid*, letter from Surat, 15 January 1701, f 115.
102. *Ibid*, letter from Surat, 31 January 1701, f 127.
103. *Ibid*, Pilavoine from Surat, 1 February 1701, ff 131-131v.
104. See the well known view of Ashin Dasgupta *op.cit*.

37

FRENCH NOTICES ON THE DRUGS AND MEDICAL PRACTICES OF MEDIEVAL INDIA

P. Hymavathi

India became a centre of attraction to the travellers from the very ancient days. Many travellers from far and near came as the merchants, embassadors, pioneers, writers, physicians and philosophers and spent long time in this country travelling throughout its length and breadth and left valuable and very interesting accounts behind them. During the medieval period, especially in the 16th and the 17th centuries, many European travellers from Portugal, Italy, Holland, France and England visited the country. Among them, interestingly we can find some physicians and surgeons, who were appointed to serve the trading company of the respective country. In the initial days, these Europeans were alien to this land and they had to face many health problems from its climate. Such developments started on their journey over the seas. Therefore each ship used to carry at least a physician and a surgeon to look after the staff on the board of the ship. These medical scholars observed the local systems and practices and recorded them as they had understood. Some botanists like Clusius from France, Garcia da Orta from Portugal and Linschoten, the Dutch traveller and a friend of Palludanus, a doctor-cum-botanist, collected valuable information regarding the Indian *materia* medica and collected plant species to rear them in their respective countries, left valuable accounts which were published with rapid speed with translations into various European languages. Their accounts contain references to the social customs and traditions with regard to health care, the tropical diseases, their cures, trade in medicinal goods, etc. In this essay, an attempt is made to trace out the contribution of French travellers and physicians to the heuristic lot which helps in reconstructing the medical history of India during the sixteenth and the seventeenth centuries.

Clusius

Before going to discuss about the contribution of the French scholars to the spread of Indian medical or pharmacological knowledge in the west, it is very important to glance at the attempts of the Portuguese, to whom the French had indebted much in this respect. The first French writer on Indian plants and drugs was Clusius, who translated the work of Garcia da Orta, the Portuguese physician, entitled *"Coloquies dos simples e drogas he cousas medicinais da India compostos pello Doutor Garcia da Orta"* in the form of a dialogue. Garcia da Orta reached Goa in September 1534 and stayed at Diu for some time as a physician and later he visited the places like Kathiawar, Ahmad Nagar, Cochin and Ceylon. He does not seem to have visited the places on the east coast. At Goa, he had a house and a garden with a variety of medicinal plants. He was in medical practice for a long time on the west coast and after gaining about 25 years of experience as a physician in India, he was induced by his friends who were scholars in Botany (Dr. Rauno and Markham) and medicine (Dimas Bosque) to compose a work on Indian drugs and drug-substances for the benefit of future generations. Garcia da Orta fulfilled their desire by adding a lot of knowledge on simples (the meaning according to the context and content of the text is individual drug-substances) and drugs after "indifatigable enquiries from native physicians and in his examinations of Yogis from the kingdom of Delhi, and of traders and others from all parts - Deccanis, Guzeratis, Cingalese, Moors, Persians, Arabs and Malays." His book printed in A.D. 1563 was the first medical work printed in India. Later it was translated into many European languages.[1]

The French scholar to trnaslate this work was Clusius. Clusius translated Garcia da Orta's work into Latin adding annotations and new illustrations and is free with many additions and looks like a different one from the original. It gained far-reaching influence and much appreciation in the learned circles of Europe, when it was published in 1567. It was further reprinted with rapid speed in the successive years, i.e., 1574, 1579, 1593 and 1605 testifying its significance and wide popularity. With regard to the biographical details of Clusius, we can get some information from Arbar, who later edited his work. According to the information given by him, Clusius or commonly known as Charles de I ecluse was born in 1526 at Arras in France. He studied at various Universities and specialised in Botany in Montpeller University under the guidance of Guillaume Rondelet, Platter, Bauhim, etc. Especially, Clusius was much indebted to Rondelet, who inculcated a greater love for botany in Clusius which continued throughout his life like a "ruling passion".[2]

As the family of Clusius belonged to the reformed faith, it was exposed to religious persecution and one of his relatives was burnt alive at the stake. Their family property was confiscated. In addition to this, ill-health also haunted him. Inspite of all these troubles, he did not cease the study of plant life. Though he was a licensed physician, he was much interested in Botany rather than in medicine.

Clusius also translated the work of Acosta Christovole, a Spanish work on Drugs of India. Acosta's work was written on the lines of Garcia da Orta. He had personal touch with Garcia da Orta when he was at Goa. Though Clusius became immortal by his translations, he had his credit of composing some original works and investigating contributions in the history of plant-life. He published a work entitled *"Rariorum aliquot stirpium per Hispanias Observatarum Historia"* which is considered his *magnum opus*.

The translations of Garcia da Orta and Acosta into Latin by Clusius helped for the rapid spread of medicinal and botanical knowledge of India in the western countries as Latin was the classical language known to the elite sections in all the western countries. Sooner translations appeared in many European languages such as French and Italian which made available the knowledge of Indian drugs in the language of the common people in Europe. Such developments influenced the herbalists and botanists of the renaissance Europe.

François Bernier:

Among the travelogues left by the Europeans recording their experiences in Mughal India, the account of François Bernier is the most useful work as it projects a multi-faceted view of the life in Mughal Empire. As he was a Doctor of medicine, it is more useful to the researcher or Indian medical history.

After completing his education (born in 1620) in his homeland, he travelled across Europe. He went to Montpellier to obtain a medical degree and received it in August 1652. He came to India in 1659 and spent many years at the Mughal capital and later moved to Lahore and Kashmir with Mughal army. Later, he travelled eastward and stayed in Kasim Bazar about the year 1666. From there, he moved towards the south. He stayed for some time in Machilipatnam and Golconda and recorded his experiences in the South. In 1667, he reached Surat and left for his homeland via Persia and Morseilles. He reached Paris in 1669 and got his work published in 1670. He died at the age of 68 in 1688.[3]

Bernier was well received in India probably due to the good repute of the Dutch and French physicians and who already had good practice in India and who started spreading the new ideas of renaissanc Europe. The first noble to receive Bernier with much admiration was Prince Dara Sukhov. The French physician treated the wound of the wife of Dara Sukhov. The Mughal Prince was much impressed over this and asked him to join as a physician in his military camp. But as the Prince himself was in troubles at that time, moving from place to place in search of protection, it became difficult for him to retain the French physician.[4] Later Bernier was received by Aurangzeb and became a court-physician. Bernier treated the women in the harem and

619

the Padshah himself. The descriptions given by Bernier in his account regarding the manners, customs and the way that he was treated indicate the position of physician in the society.

The manner in which he was taken into the harem was described by him thus:[5] "I have sometimes gone into it when the King was absent from Delhi, and once pretty far, I thought, for the purpose of giving my professional advice in the case of a great lady, so extremely ill that she could not be moved to the outward gate, according to the customs observed upon similar occasions; but a Kachemire Shawl covered my head, hanging like a large scarf down to my feet and an eunuch led me by hand, as if I had been a blind man."

In his opinion, most of the diseases in India are due to the extremities in the climatic conditions, especially, the extreme heat of the country causes fatigue and common illness. He describes the Indian summer, its extremity, and the steps that he took thus:[6] "My Indian servants, not withstanding their black, dry and hard skin, are incapable of further exertion. The whole of my face, my feet and my hands are flayed. My body too is entirely covered with small blisters, which prick like needles. Yesterday, one of our poor troopers, who was without a tent, was found dead at the foot of a tree where he had crept for shelter. I feel as if I should myself expire before night. All my hopes are in four or five limes still remaining for lemonade, and in a little dry curd which I am about to drink diluted with water and with sugar. Heaven bless you! The ink dries at the end of my pen and itself drops from my hand."

Once he suffered from dysentery when he was at Lahore. As a physician, experiencing the tropical disease, explains this distemper thus:[7] "When at Lahor I was seized with a flux, accompanied by acute pains in my limbs, in consequence of having passed whole nights on a terrace in the open air, as is commonly done in Delhi without danger. My health was suffering; but since we have been on the March, the violent perspirations, which continued for eight or nine days, have dissipated my bad humours, and my parched and withered body has become a mere sieve, the quart of water, which I swallow at a drought passing at the same movement through every one of my pores, even to my fingers' ends. I am sure that today, I have drunk more than ten pints. Amid all our sufferings, it is a great consolation to be able to drink as much water as we like with impunity provided it be of a good quality."

Bernier narrates the diseases caused by impure water. The impure and contaminated water of Delhi causes "worms to be bred in the legs which produce violent inflamation, attended with much danger. If the patient leaves Delhi, the worm is generally soon expelled although there have been instances where it has continued in the system for a year or more. They are commonly of the size and length of the treble string of a violin, and might be easily mistken for a sinew. In extracting them great caution should be used lest they break. The best way is to draw them out little by little, from day to day, gently winding them round a small twig of the size of a pin."[8]

With regard to his observations on principles of Indian medicine and some of the therapeutic methods, his glance was superficial and could not go through the medical works as they were in Sanskrit verse form and regional commentaries. He observed the practices at a time and place where Indian system was not much patronised. That's why, sometimes his observation on the principles of medicine are very brief. He writes, "On Physic, they have a great number of small books, which rather collections of recipes, than regular treatises. The most ancient and the most esteemed is written in verse."[9]

Bernier's remarks on the medical practices of Hindus and Muslims, similarities of both the systems and the comparative observation of the Indian and the western systems are very valuable. He says, "I shall observe, by the way, that their practice differs essentially from ours, and that it is grounded on the following acknowledged principles; a patient with a fever requires no great nourishment; the sovereign remedy for sickness is abstinence; nothing is worse for a sick body than meat broth, for it soon corrupts in the stomach of one afflicted with fever; a patient should be bred only on extra-ordinary occasions, and where the necessity is most obvious as when there is reason to apprehend a brain fever, or when an inflamation of the chest, lever or kidneys, has taken place. Whether these modes of treatment be judicious, I leave to our learned physicians to decide; I shall only remark that they are successful in Hindustan, and that the Mughal and Mohometan physicians, who follow the rules of Avicenna and Averroes, adopt them no less than do those of the Gentiles, especially in regard to abstinence from meat broth. The Mughals it is true, are rather more given to the practice of bleeding than the gentiles for where they apprehended the inflammations just mentioned, they generally bleed once or twice, not in the trifling manner of the modern practitioners of Goa and Paris, but copiously, like the ancients, taking eighteen or twenty ounces of blood, sometimes even to fainting; thus frequently subduing the disease at the commencement, according to the advice of Galen, and I have witnessed in several cases."[10]

Bernier could not properly grasp the developments in Ayurvedic medicine that took place during the medieval period. At many places he looked down on the knowledge of the physicians in India, probably guided by the general ill-treatment meted out by the pandits during the fanatic rule of Aurangzeb. He narrates the way that he came in touch with the indigenous medical knowledge thus:[11] "Do not be surprised if, notwithstanding my ignorance of Sanskrit (the language of the learned, and possibly that of ancient Brahmens, as we may learn further on), I yet say something of books written in that tongue. My Agan, Danechmendi - Khan, partly from my solicitation and partly to gratify his own curiousity, took into his service one of the most celebrated Pandits in all the Indies, who had formerly belonged to the household of Dara, the eldest son of the king Chah-Jehan; and not only was this man my constant companion during a period of three years, but he also introduced me to the society of other learned Pendets, whom he attracted to the house." This statement makes it clear that he was in touch with a Brahmin with "whom he attracted to the house." However it is a fact that he could not go through the medical works such as

Bhavaprakasa, Lolambarajiyam, Vaidyacintamani, Sarabharajiyam, Arkaprakasa, Yogaratnakara, etc, which were composed during the later medieval period. If he had gone through these works which contained the latest findings of the period, he could not have made such a weak and superficial comments on the therapeutic methods like an ordinary itinerant. Perhaps it might be the language that stood as a barrier preventing him to have an access to the valuable works which contained valuable prescriptions for many diseases including the venereal diseases which appeared due to the contact with the Portuguese and the other Europeans. He writes, "the venereal disease, common as it is in Hindustan, is not of so virulent a character, or attended with such injurious consequences as in other parts of the world."[12] As a matter of fact, in the works of Bhavamisra and Sarabharaja, we find the mention of *Phirangiroga* (syphilis) with many varieties found out within a short period and wonderful cures to these diseases.

The Ayurvedic scholars give more importance to *swathavritta* than to *aturavritta* and prescribed ideal daily and seasonal regimen to keep oneself healthy. Bernier appreciated this characteristic feature in the social life of the people and states,[13] "I have no doubt that happy ignorance which prevails of many distempers is fairly ascribable to the general habits of sobriety among the people, and to the profuse perspiration to which they are perpetually subject. The gout, the stone, complaints in the kidneys, catarrhs and quartan agues are nearly unknown; and persons who arrive in the country afflicted with any of these disorders, as was the case with me, soon experience a complete cure."

Though Ayurvedic medicine achieved successes with incessant investigations and innovations, it lost its significance in the opinion of Bernier at its weakness in analysing anatomical detail and blood circulation system in a scientific way. He brought to India the findings of William Harvey who scientifically explained the blood circulation system and the ideas of other western philosophers like Gassendi and Descartes. He discussed their scientific philosophy with the Brahmin scholars in a debate where according to Bernier, the Brahmin scholars failed to satisfy Bernier with their explanations in the philosophical ideas of medicine.[14] Surprisingly we can observe a development during the seventeenth century that the Indian physicians, both Unani and Ayurvedic, suffered from a complex that their systems were being looked down by the Mughal government and also by the foreign physicians who came out with new ideas and started criticising certain therapeutic methods and anatomical knowledge of the natives. That is why, when Bernier tried to explain the new doctrine of Harvey and their anatomical principles, they were not properly received by the native doctors or rather the western physicians like Bernier could not convincingly or amicably convey their advanced knowledge on the mutual respect basis.

Charles Dellon :

Born in 1649 in France, Charles Dellon, a French surgeon left for India in 1668. He served as a surgeon on the French ships and French factories of the Company for sometime. In 1673 he resigned his job in the Company and started medical practice at Daman, which was under the Portuguese rule. He was arrested in 1674 and was in prison for two years and then left for his native country.

Dellon wrote two books on his experiences in India, which were published in 1685 and 1686 respectively. The first work entitled *"Relation d'un Voyage fait an Indes Orientales"* is an account of his travels in India, which was translated into English under the title *"Voyage to the East Indies"*. The second book entitled *"Relation de l'Inquisition de Goa"* and this also was translated into English once in 1688 and again in 1812.

"Voyages to East Indies" contains the description of the diseases that occur in the eastern countries and as commonly happen in the voyages into these parts of the countries with their remedies. The contents of this medical treatise are: "of vomiting, of Scurvey, of the Colicks, of Medagascar, of the Venereal Distemper in the Daubhin, of the Distemper of the Indies and the first of their fevers, of the Distemper called by the Indian,

Mordechi, of the Bloody Flux, of the Distempers called by the Portuguese *Effalsados*, of Small-pox, of the Biting of Adder, of the Distemper called by the Portuguese, *Bicho*." Among these, Chapter V of the Distempers of the Indies, and first of their fevers"[15] is useful to know the health conditions in the society, the common fevers which occur with the change of seasons, the physicians at their work, the therapeutic methods, food habits, diagnostic methods followed by the native physicians, the quacks and their failures, etc.

On the common diseases, he says, "Malignant fevers are not frequent in the Indies, but the simple continual fevers are much in vogue. Among the intermitting fevers, the Tertians and double Tertians are not most common and their cure is very difficult in those parts, for they prove often mortal." He points out the weak point in Indian medicine thus: "The Pagan physicians whom they call Pandites, are a sort of people without learning or any knowledge of insight into anatomy." His observations over the professional skills of the indigenous physicians indicate the deteriorating condition of professional ethics and the prevalence of quacks in the regions where he moved about.

Though chemico-mineral and herbo-mineral drugs gained much popularity in South India during the medieval period, it is quite surprising when Dellon says, "Chymical preparations are unknown to the Pandites, they are surprised when they see us foreigners to produce such evacuations as we do, by the help of such small quantity of physick."[17] Perhaps, the physicians of the western coast might not have prepared the chemico-mineral drugs or might be that Dellon could not observe their usage within the short span of his stay there.

As regards the examination of urine to diagnose the factor causing distemper, Dellon made a criticism saying that the native physicians stress only on the examination of urine, but ignore the other signs such as delirium appearing on the patient and opines that blood-letting is inevitable in such cases.[18] He has his own discretions in making observations and expresses," I lived

625

at Daman for several months, where inspite of all the Pandites there, who were envious at me, I was employed as physician in all the best families." It was the inherent complex of superiority and the endeavour to establish it in the alien land that prompted him to express some biased or hasty views regarding the medical practices in India. It must also be an attempt to support his self-respect against the envious looks of the indigenous physicians that generally the western physicians and surgeons looked down on the knowledge of the traditional doctors in India. It is also to be remembered that they could not differentiate between a quack and a good physician.

It is also important to note here two facts - 1. the native physicians preferred to diagnose the case basing on the examination of urine. 2. but the people preferred the old system of blood-letting for any distemper such as high fever in which the characteristics of delirium can be observed. In the native medical works written in South India during the medieval period, we find more advanced methods in *astasthana pariksa* and especially in the examination of urine. The native physicians in the light of these developments did not prefer to let blood in many cases. But the people from the very ancient days were used to blood-letting in such cases and they expected a cure with it. According to the indigenous system of medicine, any disease or distemper cannot be cured without the implicit faith of the patient on the physician. That is why, when they observed any suspicion on the part of the patient or his family, they used to leave the case. Such observations of the Europeans like Dellon indicate the signs of the penetration of European medicine in deep roots in India.

Inspite of some reservations, Dellon, like the other European physicians and travellers could not remain silent on some of the most meritorious features in the medical profession. He appreciates the dietetic habits and the regimen prescribed by the Indian physicians to their patients. He describes the prescription of "Cange" (*ganji* in Telugu and Kannada which means the vital liquid essence of rice) to patients and the method of its preparation, its usefulness, etc. On blood-letting, he says,

"Letting of blood is much used among the Indians, and that with good success; the Pandites being by long experience, convinced by the usefulness of this remedy, will some times let blood twenty times one after another, without the least reluctancy to be observed in the patient, who never grumble here at what their physicians do, but are exactly observant to their orders, much beyond what practised in most parts of Europe where the patients, their friends and the nurses propose their own remedies, before the physicians' prescriptions."[19]

"They let blood commonly with extraordinary good success. ......The Indians prescribe cupping and leeches in those distempers where they don't think it proper to let blood."

At the beginning of the Chapter V of his work, *"Voyages to East Indies"*, Dellon says, "Nevertheless it is observable that by their long experience, they have made such observations concerning certain distempers peculiar to those countries, that they practise with better success than the most learned foreign physicians, who upon certain occasions must follow the footsteps, if they expect to succeed in their cures in this climate."[20]

Tavernier

Jean Baptiste Tavernier, born in A.D. 1605 in France, made six voyages to India during 1639-'43, 1645-'48, 1651-'54, 1659-'61 and 1665-'67. He recorded his experiences and observations during his travel in various parts of India in his Travel account. His first publication appeared under the title *"Nouvelle Relation du serrail du Grand Signior"*. His great book the "Six Voyages" appeared in French in 1676. The first authentic and scientific translation of that work into English was rendered by Dr. Valentine Ball, F.R.S., a famous geologist and the same was published by Messrs. Macmillan Co., London in 1889. Dr. Ball was interested in Tavernier's account because they dealt with the economic mineral resources, mainly diamonds of India. Besides Dr. Ball had long experience of travelling in India, in connection with his official duties and he could thus supply useful notes, appendices, etc. to Tavernier's work. William Crooke edited Dr. Ball's translation entitled *"Travels in India by Jean*

Baptiste Tavernier, Baron of Aubonne", and the second edition of that work was published, in two volumes, by Messrs. Oxford University Press, London, in 1925.[21]

Tavernier had travelled extensively in all the islands of the east and the Indian sub-continent and recorded an eye-witness account of the conditions prevailed in those days. From his travel account we will get a picture of the social customs, religious beliefs, medical practices, *materia medica*, trade links of the region with other islands, etc. Though Tavernier, being a trader, gave much place in his book to the description of various industries, including agro-industries, methods of testing precious stones, the practises of adulteration in every industrial product, etc., we find valuable information regarding the condition of medical profession and the allied matters. We have the detailed description of some of the medicinal stones obtained from the animals such as goats, cows, snakes, monkeys, etc. in this region, their demand in the commercial transactions, etc. He had referred to the method of collecting drug-substances, trade in drugs, the health precautions taken at the industrial areas etc. His medical observations such as letting blood, venesection, etc also are quite relevant to be discussed here.

Tavernier gives a graphic description of venesection done in the royal palace of the Qutb Shahis of Golconda in his travelogue. He narrates, "On reaching Golconda, we stayed at the house of a Dutch man named Petre de Lan whom Chatter, whom the Batavian ambassador had kept at Golconda. He was the Royal Surgeon. With great importunity the King had taken him from the ambassador because the king was suffering from chronic headache and the royal physicians had diagnosed and suggested that it was necessary to have venesection to be performed at four places under the tongue. But no efficient surgeon was present to perform it, because the people of this country were utterly ignorant of surgery."[22]

Regarding the appointment of the Dutch surgeon and the fees fixed, Tavernier writes, "De Lan's pay was fixed at 800 pagodas. ......after waiting for a few days, the king called the surgeon and told him that the physicians were of the opinion that four venesections should be performed under the tongue and not more than 20 *tolas* (8ounces) of blood should be let out. The surgeon expressed his willingness to undertake the operation and he was ordered to appear the next day."

On the precautionery hygienic steps taken before performing the surgery (Chirurgy in his words), he mentions that three eunuchs took him to a room and four old women took him to bath and took of his cloths and gave him a bath and especially washed his hands fully. Then his body was made fragrant with scents and thereafter instead of his European dress, he was made to wear the courtier's dress. The vessels made of gold which were meant to cup the blood let, were weighed in front of the court-physicians, so that the quantity of blood as fixed might be weighed and calculated after venesection. After the venesection, it was found out that the blood which was let was exactly the same as fixed previously. The King was much pleased and gave the surgeon 300 pagodas as a reward. Tavernier also mentions that "The young Queen and the Queen mother also resolved to be let blood too" and the surgeon performed it.

Tavernier mentions that there were no physicians in the villages and the common people cured their petty diseases in their homes only by taking the drugs given by elderly women.[23] Though this statement is not fully correct, we cannot set aside the fact that the women were experts in curing the petty physical troubles like cold, cough, vomiting sensation, head-ache, stomach-ache, pains in the body, children's ailments, ill-health of the pregnant women, the newly delivered women, etc. Tavernier, in another place, refers to the priest physicians[24] and also the physicians in towns and cities.[25] He describes the procedure of collecting herbs by the common people thus: "As for the common people, after the rains are fallen and that it is time to gather herbs, you shall see every morning the good women of the town going into the fields, to gather such simples which they know to be proper for such diseases as reign in the family. Thus it seems that the common people, especially, the women used to collect the necessary herbs which were available in their surroundings and in a particular season when they were available in a ready to use condition. They might have preserved them for the other seasons.

Tavernier refers to the availability of some of the medicinal stones in this region and describes the procedure of their collection thus: "Bezoar comes from a province of the kingdom of Golconda towards the northeast. It is found among the orduse in the paunch of a wild goat that brouzes upon a certain tree, the name whereof I have forgot. This shrub bears little buds, round about which and the tops of the boughs, he bezoar engenders in the man of the goat. It is shaped according to the form of the buds of tops of the branches which the goats eat; which is the reason there are so many shapes of bezoar stones. The natives, by feeling the belly of the goat, know how many stones she has within and sell the goat according to the quantity." He referred also to the adulteration committed by the traders trading in bezoar. He narrates that in the east-coast, bezoars bred in cows were extensively available which the Portuguese mostly favoured and kept always with them as "their guard for fear of being poisoned."[26] He described another stone known as "the Porcupine stone, which that creature is said to carry in its head and is more precious than bezoar against poison"[27]

About the serpent stone, he says "There is the serpent-stone not to be forgotten, about the bigness of a double and some are almost oval, thick in the middle and thin about the sides. The Indians report that it is bred in the head of certain serpents. But I rather take it to be stone of the idolators, priests and that the stone is rather a composition of certain drugs. Whatever it be, it is of excellent virtue to derive any person out of those that are bit by venomous creatures."[28]

About its application and functioning, he narrates, "If the person bit be not much wounded, the place must be incised, and the stone be applied, will not fall off till it has drawn all the poison to it. To cleanse it, you must steep it in woman's milk, or for want of that, in cow's milk, after the stone has lain 10 or 12 hours, the milk will turn to the colour of an apostemated matter."[29]

Travernier also gives a list of drugs and their prices under the heading "Concerning the drugs obtainable at Surat, and those imported from foreign countries, with the price of each, per mound." Among them can be seen both the drug-substances and the commercial goods like gum-lac, salt-petre, coffee, tobacco, sugar, dyes, etc. Regarding the old sugar, he narrates the belief of the natives thus: "I was told a fact by many old people of the country which should be recorded: It is that sugar kept for thirty years becomes a poison, and that there is nothing more dangerous or rapid in producing this effect."[30] Thus the account of Tavernier is very useful to know the beliefs and practices of the common people regarding the art of healing.

Basing on his observation, of course of Dellon also, regarding the position of surgery in India, we cannot come to the conclusion that Indian doctors were not capable of taking up the surgical operations. Many doctors in the seventeenth century also were experts in surgery attending the war-camps. Some doctors like Panakala Raya, the author of *Netra Darpanam* were experts in eye operations also. There are still now some people, who cure the piles by surgical methods with traditional technique which they have inherited from their ancestors. Then the doubt arises why the king of Golconda called for the Dutch surgeon while there were court physicians who could do such things. Perhaps, the fame of the Dutch doctors which attracted the attention of the Portuguese might have also created a good impression in the mind of the Golconda ruler, who generally much appreciated foreign things. Not only this, the Dutch physicians were more famous, it seems, specially for their talent in blood-letting. Sometimes they do it even if there was not much necessity. The quantity of blood they used to extract also seems to be very high that the Portuguese feared so much and complained the same thing to their governor of the region. About it, Fryer writes, "the physicians here are great Bleeders, in so much that they exceed often Galen's advice, an deliquium, in Fevers; hardly leaving enough to feed the Currents for

Circulations; of which cruelty some complain invidiously after Recovery." It is because of this reason that the Golconda Sultan got the diagnosis done by his court-physicians. Then only he called for the surgeon and told him that he should let blood from four places and not more than eight ounces of blood, should be let out.

Manucci, the Venetian physician, who came to India during the same period (of Travernier), described the method of plastic surgery as practised by the doctors in the Deccan. In 1670, when a war broke out between the Mughals and the Bijapur, the Bijapur soldiers cut off the noses of Mughals who had committed depredations on the war-field. Describing the treatment of the native surgeons, Manucci says: "The surgeons belonging to the country cut the skin of the forehead above the eyebrows, made it fall down over the wounds on the nose. Then, giving a twist so that the live-flesh might meet the other live surface, by healing applications, they fashioned for them other imperfect noses. There is left above, between the eyebrows, a small hole, caused by the twist to the skin to bring the two live surface together. In a short time, the wounds heal up some obstacle being placed beneath to allow of respiration. I saw many persons with such noses and they were not so disfigured as they would have been without any nose at all."[31]

Anyway, the above observations of the French medical scholars and travellers make it clear that the physicians of India were not great bleeders like the European doctors. They tried their best to heal the physical and mental ailments with the herbs only. They considered most of the diseases as a result of the imbalance of the *tridhatus* (humours) and gave herbal treatment to reinstate the equilibrium. Especially after the development of the examination of pulse and the *astasthana pariksa*, (especially advanced methods in urine testing), it became easier for the physicians to identify the cause for ill-health. They identified many new diseases and discovered many prescriptions. After these developments, it seems that they considered it not necessary to let blood in most of the cases even though they were cured previously by the method of extracting blood from the vitiated part. The development of yoga as a therapeutic method also made surgery not necessary in many of the cases. *Rasa* system of medicine also achieved wonderful cures. That is why, except in war camps, major operations did not seem to be felt necessary in general cases. Both the indigenous literary sources and the texts on ophthalmology testify to the prevalence of the most common operation on eye i.e., cataract. A persian record belonging to the Bijapur dynasty gives an allusion to the existence of rhinoplasty performed by a barber.[32]

Thus the accounts of the French physicians practised in India and the observations of the other travellers help us in tracing the art of healthy living and healing techniques of the people of later medieval India. Sometimes, they were led by hearsay and sometimes they could not understand the deep-rooted underlying aim of traditional practices. That's why, we can observe some biased views which can be proved wrong when studies in corroboration with other sources. Sometimes we find their observations very apt especially with regard to their comments on the quacks whom they considered in general as the doctors of the land. Therefore, they are to be studied in comparison with the notices of the other contemporary European travelogues and also the general literary and medical works of the land. But there is no doubt that the French travelogues form an important part in the heuristics of Indian medical history.

References:

1. Subba Reddy, D.V., "XVI Century European Writers on Indian Drugs", *Bulletin of Indian Institute of History of Medicine*, Vol. IV (2), 1974, pp.102-109.
2. *Ibid.*, pp. 111-112.
3. Bernier, François, *Travels in Moghul Empire*, New Delhi, 1989, pp. xix - xxi.
4. *Ibid.*
5. Bernier, *op.cit.*, p.267
6. *Ibid.*, p.253.
7. *Ibid.*, p.388.
8. *Ibid.*, p.355.
9. *Ibid.*, p.338.
10. *Ibid.*
11. *Ibid.*, p.323.

633

12. *Ibid.*, p.254.
13. *Ibid.*, p.253-54.
14. *Ibid.*, p.347.
15. Subba Reddy, D.V., "Charles Dellon, a French Surgeon of XVII Century: His Popularity and his Misfortunes in India", *Bulletin of IIHM*, Vol.II, 1964, pp. 191-'92.
16. *Ibid.*, p. 193.
17. *Ibid.*, p.195.
18. *Ibid.*, pp.195-'96.
19. *Ibid.*, pp. 194-'95.
20. *Ibid.*, p. 193.
21. Tavernier, Jean Baptiste, *Travels in India*, Atlantic Publishers & Distributors, New Delhi, 1989, pp.xii-xxv.
22. *Ibid.*, pp.232-'34
23. *Ibid.*, p. 231.
24. *Ibid.*, p.250.
25. *Ibid.*, p.231.
26. *Ibid.*, p. 368-'69.
27. *Ibid.*, p. 370.
28. *Ibid.*, p.371
29. *Ibid.*
30. Tavernier, *Travels in India*, Vol. II, pp.16-21.
31. Niccolao Manucci, *Storia Da Mogor*, London, 1907, Vol. II, p.301.
32. *Bulletin of IIHM*, Vol. XVI, 1986, p.6.

COLBERTISM AND THE FRENCH EAST INDIA COMPANY'S TRADE WITH INDIA DURING THE SEVENTEENTH AND EIGHTEENTH CENTURIES

B. *Krishnamurthy*

The age of sails and discoveries, followed by the commercial revolution, that extended roughly between 1500 and 1750, is termed as 'mercantile or mercantilist era', since 'mercantilism' was the guiding principle of economic policy during this period, known politically for 'royal absolutism'. Mercantilism was the term applied to this type of economic thinking by its subsequent critics like Adam Smith and not the one adopted by its advocates and practitioners, who were never a self-conscious school of economists. Indeed, they were practical politicians, statesmen and merchants of the genre of Jean Baptiste Colbert, Dupleix, Thomas Mun and a score of others, who wrote on and acted in defense of their favoured economic policies and programmes. The French variety of mercantilism came to be known as 'Colbertism', as Colbert, the French Finance Minister under Louis IV, turned out to be its great exponent and "embodied French State power in the economic field".[1]

An attempt is being made in the following pages, to study and analyse the main features of 'mercantilism', with special reference to 'Colbertism' and how far these economic policies influenced the thinking and invigorated the economic activities of the French East India Company in France as well as in India and to what result.

Mercantilism, as the name implies, attached greater significance to trade than to industry and agriculture. Later, when they understood and appreciated the inevitability of manufactured goods to satisfy the demand of the native market and to export to foreign countries, which would attract the inflow of precious metals, the practitioners of mercantilism started encouraging industry, but, still their despise for agriculture continued throughout. Antonio Sera (1580-1650) in his treatise *'On the causes which can make gold and silver plentiful in Kingdoms where There Are No Mines'* mentions that manufacture was superior to agriculture, since industrial goods could more readily be sold abroad thus bringing in money.[2]

In the same way, the mercantilists preferred foreign trade to domestic trade. D' Avenant, writing in 1697, argued that in domestic trade the nation in general did not grow richer, only a change in the relative amounts of wealth of individuals took place; but foreign trade made a net addition to a country's wealth. The mercantilists always projected merchant's profit in the overseas trade as beneficial to the nation as a whole.

Mercantilism had an essentially static view of the world and its resources. To the mercantilist, the world contained a fixed quantity of trade and material prosperity. As such, if a particular country wished to prosper, it could only be achieved at the expense of other nations. This has givenforth to the idea of economic nationalism and subsequent *guerre de commerce* (trade war). The fact that trade could be mutually beneficial was quite incomprehensible to the mercantilists.[3]

The mercantilists suffered from an insatiable thirst for precious metals or 'Midas Mania', as Oncken puts it. " 'Gold' is a wonderful thing! Whoever possesses it is master of everything he desires. With gold, one can even get souls into paradise" asserts Columbus in his letter written in 1503 from Jamaica. The precious metals were considered as of paramount importance and the most convenient and tangible form of wealth. There was a growing tendency to accumulate and maintain a 'national bullion hoard'.

This 'mania' quite naturally resulted in aiming at the augmentation of the inflow of bullion - the nerves and support of the kingdoms and the monarchs - and restriction of its outflow. Clement Armstrong of England writing in the early sixteenth century maintains that it is 'better to have plenty of gold and silver in the realm than plenty of merchants and merchandises'. Monchretien, a Frenchman echoes the same view a century later: 'We live not so much from trade in raw materials as from gold and silver'.[4]

The fear, which Prof. Heckscher refers as 'fear of goods' or 'fear of buying', that the balance of trade, if not favourable to the country concerned would result in the outflow of bullion, always charecterised mercantilist thought. Martin Luther lamented that "the Germans were making all the world rich and beggaring themselves by sending their gold and silver to foreign countries; Frankfurt, with its fairs, was the hole through which Germany was losing her treasure".[5] Johann Joachim Becher of Germany too maintains 'that it is always better to sell goods to others than to buy goods from others, for the former brings a certain advantages and the latter inevitable damage'.

Thomas Mun also reiterates the same view by saying that "the ordinary means therefore to increase our wealth and the treasure is by foreign trade, wherein we must ever observe this rule: to sell more to strangers yearly than we consume of theirs in value". Thus, the mercantilists believed that the favourable balance of trade by the export of more goods to other countries than import from outside would ensure continuous inflow of precious metals and therein laid the power and prosperity of the particular nation state.

E. Misselden went a step ahead and he was anxious to restrict commerce 'within Christendom' in order to preserve treasure.[6] His idea was to control the movement of gold within the boundaries of Christendom if not within the national boundaries.

However, Mun tried to distinguish between the general balance i.e. the balance of a nation's total exports compared with its imports and the particular balances in the different branches of its trade with separate countries. He advocated that if the general balance was favourable, there was no need for anxiety should one or other of the particular balances be adverse. He defended the Indian trade in which the export of bullion is inevitable, on the ground that an unfavourable particular balance might be an essential factor in procuring a favourable general balance.[7] In spite of Mun's efforts, bullionism continued to shook the conscience of entire Europe in connection with its East Indian trade relations during the decades to come.

Mercantilism is generally identified with state-making and Heckscher calls it 'a phase in the history of economic policy' designed to secure political unification and national power.[8] The essence of mercantilism is, "the total transformation of society and its organisation, as well as of the state and its institutions, in the replacing of a local and territorial economic policy by that of the national state."[9] It was a system of economic nationalism conditioned and governed by national economic policies and programmes. It called for the sacrifice of individual, group, local and regional interests at the altar of national interest and power.

The Crown saw in this economic nationalism means to strengthen royal absolutism against both rivals abroad and the remnants of medieval particularism at home.[10] The monarchs calculated and worked on the long held and little questioned assumptions of economic life, "... that there was a more or less fixed volume of commerce, money and economic activity generally, that the circumstances of both supply and demand were normally fairly inelastic, and that Governments should govern in economic matters as in political."[11] As such, they considered that the "economic matters are too serious to be left to take their natural course" and they aimed to secure for their country "the largest possible slice of the cake."[12] To achieve this, the Crown imposed a policy in the interest of the State which coincided with the interests of dynastic power and the regard for fiscal returns.[13] This resulted in state intervention in all walks of economic life of a nation, especially industry and long-distance trade.

II

Colbert, who served Louis XIV of France as his Superintendent of Finance for twenty two long years from 1661 to 1683, sincerely believed in the mercantilist doctrines. He strictly held the view that "the might and greatness of a state are measured entirely by the quantity of silver it possesses."[14] He was of the opinion that commerce was 'the source of (public) finance' and competition for foreign trade 'the money war' and as such, "the commerce causes a continuous struggle among the participants-the Dutch, the English and the French-on who would secure a major share of it, in peace as well as in war times."

In his ambition to place his country in the premier position in all the fields of economic activity, Colbert introduced a threefold programme of embracing the monopoly of overseas trade for the French marine, the improvement of domestic industry and the erection of a protective tariff against the manufactures of foreign countries.[15] He considered manufactured goods as the mines of the kingdom and so, based his industrial policy on monopoly and privilege. He revived the guild system with full vigour. French industry thrived on his system of bounties.

To deprive the English and the Dutch of their profits on their trade of Indian goods with France and to secure a share in the lucrative sea-borne trade, Colbert established numerous chartered companies. '*La Compagnie Française des Indes Orientales*' (the French East India Company) was founded in 1664 by his initiative and encouragement. On his persuasion, Louis XIV conferred on it an exclusive privilege of navigation and trade from the Cape of Good Hope onwards in the Eastern waters for fifty consecutive years.[16] The king invested his own resources in the Company and coerced the noble, ecclesiastical and bourgeois state functionaries to take part in it.[17] The state not only provided the incentive for colonial trade but it also put up the bulk of the risk capital and paid most of the operating expenses.[18]

To keep the regionalistic tendencies, which proved to be the bane of French national economic enterprises, under control, Colbert organised the French East India Company as a federal set up with local chambers, on the line of the Dutch model.[19] This step was taken to satisfy the claim of regional commercial centres like Rouen, Nantes, Lyon, La Havre and St. Malo and to project the Company as a national enterprise. Thus, an earnest effort was made by Colbert to involve all sections of society and all regions of France in this venture.

III

As the initiator of the Company, the French Crown especially Colbert, formulated and played an active role in the French diplomacy of trade. To be precise, the French strategy of trade was, what Colbert conceived about trade and what he had done to achieve it. As this was the case, the first two decades of the existence of the French East India Company could be rightly called the 'era of Colbert.'

In India, Baron, François Martin, Dumas and Dupleix had acted on the line, which Colbert had chalked out for them. Colbert, the 'Financial Wizard' of the seventeenth century France, was in no way less sagacious in the art of diplomacy. He started screwing up the French diplomatic machinery in the service of the company. Through the French ambassador stationed at London, he secured an order from the English ruler to their countrymen in India, which goaded them to assist the French in India.[20] The French ambassador at La Haye (Holland), was expected to furnish the details about the commercial activities of the Dutch and also to recruit experienced Dutchmen for the service of the French company.[21] Moreover, Colbert planned to form an alliance between the French and the Portuguese in the East, against their common enemy, the Dutch and to share their resting and refuelling facilities.[22]

The King of France by his declaration of August 1664 empowered the French Company to send ambassadors in his name to the Eastern Sovereigns and also to declare war and conclude peace with them.[23] The Company had sent M. M. Beber, Mariage and Dupont and the king ordered S[r]. de la lain and S[r]. de la Boullaye le Gouz to accompany them and the remain as his ambassadors in the courts of the Shah of Persia and the Emperor of Delhi, respectively.[24] Louis XIV wrote letters of recommendation addressed to Aurangzeb seeking his protection and privileges to the French company.[25] Fr. Ambrosse de Peruilly, a Capuchin Superior at Surat, stood surety for the French good conduct and cleared the doubts created by the Dutch in the native minds about the French as peaceful traders and Jacquies de la Palisse, a French doctor in the service of Aurangzeb at Agra helped the ambassadors in their dealings at the Mughal Court.[26] Aurangzeb, by his *firman* dated August, 11, 1666, offered the French the same rights and privileges enjoyed by the Dutch and English at Surat and permitted them to trade with his empire.[27]

On the recommendation of La Boullaye le Gouz and François Caron, in whose hands the fortunes of the French Company was left initially,Louis XIV and Colbert had sent out a powerful fleet under the command of M. de la Haye to the East Indies in 1671, to gain for the French their rightful share in the coveted East India Trade.[28] However, the mission turned into a fiasco.

The French attempts to establish and to trade in India were stoutly opposed by other Europeans, especially by the Dutch. The wars in Europe between France and Holland had their repercussions here in India and the Dutch succeeded in ousting the French out of Pondicherry, their commercial headquarters in India, by 1693. The French Crown intervened on behalf of the Company and secured the restoration of Pondicherry to the French Company by the treaty of Ryswick (1699), in spite of the fact that the Dutch in India have evicted the French only after purchasing Pondicherry from the Marathas.[29]

Moreover, viewing the individual achievements in the field of trade and commerce as well as colonization in no way inferior to the victories in wars, the French Crown created a sort of commercial nobility by conferring titles like *Marquis* on people like François Martin, Dumas and Dupleix, who served the French Company with zeal. Even the natives like Guruvapillai, Ananda Ranga Pillai and Kanagaraya Mudaliar secured the cross of St. Michael and gold medals bearing the figure of the king of France on one side and the Company's Coat of Arms on the other, for their meritorious services for the cause of the Company. All these facts go to prove beyond doubt the involvement and the interest taken by the French Crown in the affairs of the Company.

IV

Due to the efforts of Caron, Baron and especially François Martin, the 'Founder of Pondicherry', the French secured trading stations and commercial privileges in both the Western and Eastern Coasts of India and started their commercial activities. Though they came to India to procure spices, especially pepper, soon they understood that their company could not have profitable trade on spices alone and they had to take back varieties of cotton and silk textiles, referred to as piece goods in the French Company records, also from India.

The Indian piece-goods, due to their good quality, attractiveness, durability and above all to their incredible cheapness, commanded a favourable market in France.[30] The French protectionists and manufacturers of linen, wool, hemp and silk fabrics, every now and then raised hue and cry about the transport of several million *livres* out of the kingdom for the procurement of these textiles, which adversely affected the French manufacturers and ruined the workers, who had to desert and leave the kingdom in search of livelihood.[31] The Crown, by the edict of October 26, 1686, prohibited the entry of silk fabrics embroidered in gold and silver as well as white cotton cloth from India and China and their sale and purchase were declared illegal after December 1687.[32] The edict imposed on the offender, a fine of 3000 *livres* as well as the confiscation and burning of the stock.

The royal decree of January 27, 1687, gave a concession to the Company to bring into France the Indian textiles worth 150,000 *livres*. Against this favour, it was expected to export to India 500,000 *livres* worth of the French products.[33] The Company had to declare its stocks of painted, printed and white cotton cloth to the Lieutenant General of Police, who got them marked by the seals carrying an impression of the arms of the Company in top and bottom of the cloth.[34] This step was taken to prevent the entry of these varieties back into France from Holland, clandestinely. The royal decree of April 6, 1688, empowered the authorities to inspect the shops in Paris and elsewhere and to burn all the unmarked cloth.[35]

The decree of January 22, 1695, relaxed the prohibition and the Company was allowed to bring in some painted cloth to the tune of 150,000 *livres* per year for three consecutive years. The directors had to declare to the Fermier General on the arrival of the ships about the quantity of cloth brought in and to store them separately; mark them appropriately and to send them abroad for disposal, within six months of their arrival.[36] In 1702, the king again set up a dead line on the use of Indian cotton and silk fabrics till December 31, 1704.[37] Lieutenant General of Police of Paris, Intendants and other officials were ordered to take severe action against those who wore them after the deadline.

In 1709, the Company was prevented from bringing in the textiles from India even for re-exportation.[38] The users of prohibited cloth were fined up to 1000 *livres*. But the decrees of December 10, 1709 and April 28, 1711, by way of concession and compensation, permitted the sale of muslin and white cotton cloth during the ongoing war.[39]

At the same time, the king through series of decrees interdicted the local artisans like printers and painters of cloth, tailors, couturiers and tapestry-makers from working on the cloth brought from India.[40] A fine upto 3000 *livres* was imposed on them, besides confiscation of the stock of the Indian textiles. The royal decree of July 29, 1710, forbade the production of cloth in France imitating the print and texture of the Indian textiles.[41]

The royal decree of September 27, 1719, (article XIII) announced cash award to the informant, inspectors and clerks of the customs department, who worked for the success of the prohibition programme. *Ten sols* were given on the confiscation of *an ell* of white and painted cotton cloth; twenty *sols* on *muslin*, satin, *gazes* and *taffetas* and three *livres* on *Damas* or the silk stuffs embroidered with gold and silver thread.[42] Article XII of the same *arrêt* prohibited the export and use of cotton cloth from India even in the French colonies on pain of fine and other such punishments. In 1720, the Crown imposed an exorbitant amount of 20,000 *livres* as fine. Later, on pain of death, it tried to curb the use of prohibited cloth among the French.[43]

But the royal decree of May 9, 1724, reversed the crown's stand on the total prohibition of Indian textiles, as they had become somewhat a necessity and none of the French products could supplant the cotton hand kerchief brought from India. So the Company was allowed to bring in and to retail, the cotton and silk handkerchief after due marking according to the *decree* of April 28, 1711.[44] It seems that white (guinea cloth and *percales*), stripped and checked cotton cloth and muslin were also allowed to be exported and disposed of in France after due marking.[45]

The protectionist policy followed by the French Crown and implemented ruthlessly by the officials had seriously affected the commercial prospects of the French Company in India.[46] The Company officials found it highly impossible to run their business here with prohibition on Indian textiles back home.

V

Again, the realities of the Indian economic scene have thrown up a stiff challenge to the French Company and its commercial activities. The market for the European goods in India was small and thus could be very easily saturated. All the European companies as well as the interlopers brought the same kind of commodities to India. This resulted in their phenomenal price fluctuation, under-pricing and on several occasions the French Company found it highly impossible to dispose off its European Commodities in the Indian market. To avoid this, the only solution was to bring precious metals, for which India has always shown an insatiable thirst.[47] Thus, the French had to import into India the precious metals, mainly silver, in coins as well as in ingots. In 1665, they had sent about 174,695 *livres* of silver to the East and in 1667, 385,768 *livres* of silver was imported.[48]

To encourage the French East India Company to export more manufactured goods of France to the East, the King offered it an incentive of fifty *livres tournois* (81 fr. 50) on every ton of merchandise that was exported out of France and seventy five *livres tournois* (122 fr. 25) on every ton imported into France.[49] Later, in 1687, it was forced to import the local manufactures to the tune of 500,000 *livres* annually, for the concession given to the Company to bring into France the Indian textiles worth 115,000 *livres*.[50] All these incentives failed to achieve the desired goal and the French Company had to import silver into India.

The resultant outflow of precious metals was squarely unacceptable to the French mercantilists in the government as well as in the Company. In their effort to avoid the export of silver, the French authorities in India chalked out an innovative plan. Martin aimed at increasing the territorial possessions of the Company with his intention to finance its trade through the revenue collected from its landed possessions. By intervening in the local politics in support of one party against the other the French could secure considerable territories in India. The French Company also indulged in tax-farming to augment its revenue. Again, by giving loans to the native potentates against landed possessions as mortgage, the French Company could acquire some more territories.

In spite of these efforts, the French found it impossible to prevent the import of silver to India and this trend continued to be an unavoidable feature of the French trade with India.

For a period of about twenty years from October 1, 1724 to June 30, 1743, the French imported merchandise including the victuals for the crew to the value of 28,364,969 *livres* while silver worth 150,741,022 *livres* was imported during the same period.[51] Thus, the proportion of bullion and merchandise was approximately 5:1. Moreover, according to their agreement with the Nawab of Carnatic they had to give 50,000 *pagodas* worth of silver of each ship arrived at Pondicherry directly from France, in return of the permission accorded to mint Arcot silver rupees at Pondicherry.[52]

VI

Joseph François Dupleix, in whose able and efficient hand the fortunes of the French Company was left in early 1740s, turned out to be a staunch believer of 'Colbertism' and what it stood for. His thinking process was highly influenced and conditioned by mercantilist ideals. In spite of his personal experience in India for about three decades, Dupleix writes in his memoir dated October 16, 1753, that the French Company must avoid the exportation of gold and silver. While acceding to the reality that it was very hard in China and in India without exporting specie, Dupliex even preferred that the export could be done with some European power that was trading with India. "In a choice between the evils, it would be preferable to buy from our neighbours, because through other channels a certain proportion of it will come back into France, whereas the exportation of specie to China and India means its total loss for all Europe".[53] Here, Dupleix simply echoes the feelings of Misselden referred to earlier and his intention was to restrict the flow of gold within the continental, if not within the national, boundaries.

As the second-best solution, Dupleix tried to restrict and minimise the out flow of precious metals from Europe as much as possible. It seems that he was successful in this count to a considerable extent. For a period of four years from 1750 to 1754, about 35,049,000 *livres* worth of silver and merchandise for 13,605,000 *livres* were imported into India. Thus, to the great relief of the French Government and the Company, a comparatively low proportion of less than 3:1 was achieved by the activities of Dupleix in India.[54]

Again, Dupleix sincerely believed that the Indian trade was restricted and could not be greatly increased by one company without seriously affecting the interest of all other contenders and competitors. Likewise, he presumed that the European consumption of the oriental merchandise was also fixed and invariable and so increase of investments in India by one company would only serve to ruin the rival companies.[55] In short, Dupleix thought that no one could have trade with India without war and war without trade.[56]

Dupleix firmly held the view that East India companies could not subsist solely on the profits derived from its commerce but, a "fixed and assured revenue is essential" for its continued operation.[57] "If Europe cannot insure this, we must get it somewhere else and nowhere better than in India", he believed. He has chosen the path of war with the natives as well as with his European competitors on the basis of the assumption that the Dutch too acquired their revenue through war. Dupleix clearly mentions in his memoir that he planned "to secure a revenue of ten millions for the French in India and the turn of events made him to think of securing at least five millions." As there was a competition among the Europeans, not only in seeking trading rights and privileges from the Indian rulers, but also in enhancing their territorial possessions in the Indian soil, which would ensure larger income, they looked upon each other with the jealousy of the fox in the fable, as Dupleix puts it.[58]

Dupleix, in his eagerness to practice 'Colbertism' had involved the French Company in the local politics and he took sides with certain native powers against others. Initially, he was successful in achieving his goals. Later, the English too jumped into the fray and played his game more successfully than he himself and with stunning effect. Moreover, Dupleix's activities had drawn the French Company into *guerre de course* or commerce-destroying war against the English, to the detriment of its economic interests. In short, Dupleix caused a whirlwind, which he was not in a position to contain, at a later stage.

It is generally believed that Dupleix's struggle with the English for supremacy in India during the mid-eighteenth century has practically brought the commercial activities of the French here in India, to a grinding halt. This view calls for some explanation. For a period of twelve years from 1742-1754, during which Dupleix was at the helm of affairs in Pondicherry, the French money and merchandise were imported to India through 225 of the vessels of the Company, of which 148 reached the shores of France in return.[59]

Moreover, for four years from 1750-54, thirty five vessels of the Company had brought to India bullion and merchandise worth 35,049,000 *livres* and 13,606,000 *livres*, respectively. These figures clearly prove that Dupleix's wars have affected the French trade only marginally, and not brought it to a standstill, as some detractors of Dupleix tend to make us believe.

On the other hand, on some counts, Dupleix acted against the ideals of Colbertism. While Colbert was against the private enterprise of individuals or associations in the East India trade and reserved it for the French East India Company alone, Dupleix himself has involved and indulged neck-deep in private trading ventures. While Colbert displayed utter disregard and contempt for accumulation of wealth by individuals, Dupleix accumulated huge wealth at the cost of the Company and his country. In defense of Dupleix, it may be said that he intended to concentrate more on the development of the country trading ventures of the Company as the only solution for its difficulties in raising funds for the purchase of Indian goods. But, private trading interests were always uppermost with Dupleix.[60]

By way of conclusion, it may be said that 'mercantilism' or 'Colbertism' was the outcome of the political and economic conditions of the age during which it sprang up and the vested interests-merchants at the first instance and absolute monarchs later-utilised it as an instrument for achieving their own goals-profit, in the case of former and power, in that of latter. In their over-enthusiasm, the kings of France and their faithful guardian angels like Colbert, instead of leaving the Company master of its own destiny under broad state control, groomed it under strict dependence on the State. Under Colbertism, the French Company evolved into an organisation that was more royal than mercantile in its approach and attitude towards the Indian trade.

In India, Dupleix's advocacy of 'Colbertism' had earned for the French more enemies than friends, among the native potentates as well as among their European counterparts. In their dream of carving out a colonial empire in India, the French were out-manoeuvered by the English. The failure of Dupleix, if we may say so, lies in the fact that he tried to act upon 'Colbertism' without having *le roi soleil* (the Sun King) Louis XIV and Colbert back at home, to back his projects in India.

References:

1. Eli F. Heckscher, *Mercantilism*, trans. Mendel Shapiro, London, 1935, vol.1, p.346.
2. As quoted by Harasankar Bhattacharyya, *Aspects of Indian Economic History (1750-1950)*, Calcutta, 1980, (Second Edition), p.40.
3. Samuel Pepys (*Diary*, February 2, 1664) refers about a certain Captain Cocke's words that 'the trade of the world is too little for us (the English and the Dutch) two, therefore one must down'.
4. Bhattacharyya, *op.cit.*, p.40.
5. Eric Roll, *A History of Economic Thought*, London, 1953, p.65.
6. *Ibid.*
7. Arthur Birnie, *An Economic History of the British Isles*, London, 1948, (Sixth Edition), p.176.
8. Heckscher, *op.cit.*, vol.1, p.19.
9. Gustav Schmoller, *The Mercantile System*, New York, 1914, p.51.
10. Roll, *op.cit.*, p.62.
11. D.C. Coleman, "Economic problems and Policies" in F.L. Carsten (ed.), *The New Cambridge Modern History – The Ascendancy of France (1648-88)*, vol.V, Cambridge, 1964, p.44.
12. William Doyle, *The Old European Order 1660-1800*, Oxford, 1978, p.64.
13. Kristof Glamann, "European Trade 1500-1750" in Carlo M. Cipolla (ed.), *The Fontana Economic History of Europe - The Sixteenth and Seventeenth Centuries*, vol.II, Glasgow, 1974, p.521.
14. C.W. Cole, *Colbert and A Century of French Mercantilism*, New York, 1939, vol.I, p.337.
15. Frank Arnold Haight, *A History of French Commercial Policies*, New York, 1941, p.5.
16. Bibliothèque Nationales, Departément des Manuscrits Française (hence- forth B.N.Mss.Fr.) 8972, *Declaration du Roy du Aoust, 1664 et Registrées en Parlement le Premier Septembre, 1664*, Article XXVII.

17. *Declaration du Roy...* 1664, Articles I, VI and VII. The French nobles hitherto stood aloof from trade and commerce, as they thought that it was degrading to indulge in them. They also feared that they would lose the favours and concessions due to their noble birth, if they did so. The French King Louis XIV tried to efface the relic of the public opinion universally prevalent that maritime commerce was incompatible with nobility and assured time and again that participation in trade would not degrade or denude them of their nobility and its due favours and privileges.

18. Pierré H. Boulle, "French Mercantilism, commercial companies and Colonial profitability" in L. Blusse and F. Gaastra (eds.), *Companies and Trade*, Leiden, 1981, p.107.

19. Henri Weber, *La Compagnie Française des Indes 1664-1875*, Paris, 1904, p.190.

20. E.B. Sainsbury (ed.), *A Calendar of the Court Minutes etc. of the East India Company 1671-73* (Oxford, 1907-27). Pp.257-259; Paul Kaeppelin, *La Compagnie des Indes Orientales et François Martin*, 1664-1719, Paris, 1908, p.527.

21. Weber, *op.cit.*, p.151. François Caron, who was earlier in the Dutch company's service, but left it in disgust and disappointment, was wooed into service of the French Company by M. de Thou, the French ambassador for Holland. Colbert believed that Caron, with his considerable experience in the Eastern trade would be of great help for the nascent French company affairs in India.

22. Weber, *op.cit.*, pp.152-3, Abbé Carré, *Travels of Abbe Carre in India and the Near East 1672 to 1674* (Lady Fawcett tr.), (London, 1947-1672, vol.II, pp.390-1, 447. It seems that the French had secured the right to approach Lisbon to rest and refuel on their way, from and to, India. The following developments in India prove that Colbert's efforts to seek the Portuguese co-operation against the Dutch had failed miserably. The Portuguese in India were not prepared to pardon the French, for their breach of the so-called Portuguese monopoly of trade and considered them their deadly enemies. They even expected that their ruler should declare war against France and punish the French for their impunity.

23. Declaration du Roy... Article XXXVI.

24. Castonnet des Fosses, *L'Inde Française avant Dupleix* (Paris, 1887), p.80, n.1.

25. *Ibid.*, p.80.

26. Thevenot, *Indian Travels of Thevenot and Careri*, (S.N. Sen ed.), New Delhi, 1949, pp.29-31; Castonnet des Fosses, *op.cit.*, p.75.

27. Edmond Guadart, *Les Privileges du Commerce Français dans L'Inde*, (Pondicherry, 1935), p.2.

28. Bibliothèque Nationale Fond Nouvelles Acquisitions Français (henceforth B.N.N.A.) 9352, f.76. (Carré's letter dated January 22, 1674.).

29. B.N.N.A. 9353, fls.185v, 227v., B.N.N.A.9352. fls.196-197. It was really a diplomatic feat for the French Crown and his ambassadors to gain the restoration of Pondicherry from the Dutch as the treaty of capitulation of Pondicherry of 1693 (Article 8) was specifically against restoration after the end of the war and even the peace treaty that would be signed in due course called for it, since the Dutch got it purchased from Rajaram, the Maratha King and had not snatched it simply from the French as a prize of war.

30. B.N.N.A. 9353, f.134v.

31. B.N.N.A. 21778, f.6; B.N.N.A. 9353, f.133v.

32. B.N. Mss. Fr.16737, f.125v.

33. B.N. Mss. Fr.16737, f.126; B.N. Mss. Fr.6231, f.27v.

34. Weber, *op.cit.*, p.236.

35. B.N. Mss. Fr.16737, f.126v.
36. B.N. Mss. Fr.16737, f.129; J. Barbier, "*La Compagnie Française des Indes*" in *Revue Historique de l'Inde Française*, vol.3, (Paris-Pondicherry, 1919) p.72.
37. B.N.N.A. 21778, f.42.
38. *Ibid.*, fls.48-9. (Royal decree of August 27, 1709).
39. *Ibid.*, f.57.
40. B.N. Mss. Fr.16737, f.125v; B.N.N.A.21778, fls.42, 44, 48-9.
41. B.N.N.A. 21778, f.53.
42. *Ibid.*, f.85.
43. *Ibid.*, fls.93-4.
44. *Ibid.*, f.119.
45. Barbier, *op.cit.*, p.72.
46. *Proces – Verbaux des deliberations du Conseil Superieur de Pondichéry* (hereafter C.S.P.V.) tome II, p.101.
47. François Bernier, *Travels in the Mogul Empire, 1656-68*, trans. Irving Borck and ed. V.A. Smith, London, 1914-16, p.202.
48. B.N.N.A. 9353, f.30; Kaeppelin, op.cit., p.55.
49. *Declaration du Roy 1664*, Article: XLVI.
50. B.N.Mss. Fr. 16737, f.21v; 6231, f.27v.
51. B.N.N.A. 9354, f.423.
52. C.S.P.V., tome III, p.53; Alfred Martineau, *Lettres et conventions des Gouverneurs de Pondichéry avec les divers Princes Hindous 1666-1793*, Pondichéry, 1914, pp.41-44.
53. B.N.N.A. 9355, f.366v. (Dupleix's *Memoire* dated October 16, 1753, in which he tried to take his higher-ups, both in the Government and in the Company, into confidence about his ambitious plans in India. Unfortunately for France, and especially for Dupleix, this memoir reached their hands too late, to fetch any meaningful support for him in realising his projects.
54. *Archives Coloniales*, C^2 40, f.28, as cited by Wilbert H. Dalgleish, *The Company of the Indies in the days of Dupleix 1722-54*, Philadelphia, 1933, p.80. It may be recalled that during 1724-1743, the proportion of bullion and merchandise imported into India was approximately 5:1.
55. B.N.N.A. 9355, f.359.
56. La Boullaye la Gouz, who was deputed by Louis XIV to the Court of Aurangzeb to take care of the French interest there, advocated in his memoir of April 1, 1666: "...*de n'epargner ni poudre ni boulets, pour abattre l'orgueil des Hollandais... fomenter la guerre entre Anglais et Hollandais et secourir toujours le plus faible...*". (to spare neither powder nor bullets to humble the pride of the Dutch... to foment war between the English and the Dutch and always help the most week...). It was Dupleix, who took la Gouz more seriously than any of his predecessors and followed him systematically and sincerely.
57. B.N.N.A. 9355, f.343.
58. B.N.N.A. 9355, fls.358-359.
59. Kaeppelin, *op.cit.*, pp.653-661.
60. C.S.P.V., Tomes I, II and III, passim.

39

FRENCH CONNECTIONS WITH MAHE IN THE EIGHTEENTH CENTURY

Joy Varkey

Mahe was the centre of French colonial administration and mercantile activities on the Malabar coast during the eighteenth century. Like other European powers, the French realised that the exercise of political influence was essential to the establishment of commercial monopoly. Nevertheless, Versailles had no intention of carving out a vast territorial empire in India. The metropolitan plan was to build up trading counters at strategic coastal locations. The officials of these trading centres were instructed to maintain diplomatic relations with local rulers in such a way that would support and promote France's commercial interests in the region. The establishment of the French factory at Mahe was in line with this metropolitan policy. The following discussion in this paper will make some brief notes on the role and significance of Mahe in the commercial, political, military and communication programmes of the French in India in the eighteenth century.[1]

Mahe is situated at the mouth of the river Mayyazhi, which provided safe harbour for vessels upto eighty tons[2]. This river has a total courses of about thirty-four miles from its origin in the forests of the Wayanad ghats to its merger with the Arabian sea. It was navigable in all seasons for country boats (*Thonis*) for a distance of about twelve miles from Mahe to Parakkadavu[3]. It was the principal route of transportation to and from different pepper producing areas in the Kingdom of Kadathanad.

This river navigation also facilitated the import of goods from Kurungot, Kottayam and Iruvinad kingdoms. Cardamom, sandal, wood, turmeric, ginger and other commodities collected from farther hinterlands and the Wayanad ghats were brought along land routes as far as Parakkadavu in order to transport them to Mahe by country boats. It was the Mayyazhi river navigation that enabled the French to obtain the major share of spices produced in the Kingdom of Kadathanad. The convenient location of Mahe, which provided easier accessibility to the hinterland, had attracted the French as early as the beginning of the eighteenth century. They established commercial relations with the Kurungot Nair in 1702.

The establishment of a trading counter at Mahe was part of the grand scheme of overseas commerce and colonisation launched by the newly organised *Companies des Indes*. In 1721 the company obtained permission from the Vazhunnavar, rule of Kadathanad, to erect a loge at Mahe. The company also received monopoly right to the pepper trade in this country on condition that it would pay a tax of thirteen *fanoms* of Calicut per *candi* pepper and twenty-six same *fanoms* per candi cardamom to the Vazhunnavar[4]. In addition the French and the Vazhunnavar agreed to support each other in case of offensive and defensive actions against their enemies. These commercial and political agreements were reaffirmed by a treaty settlement between the Vazhunnavar and the chief of Mahe, André Molladin in 1722 [5]. Eventually, the French established their trading posts in Peringattoor, Poythara, Chembra, Mylath and Ramanthali.

The erection of French trading counter at Mahe led to the beginning of a series of Anglo-French military conflicts. The English at Tellicherry, about four miles north of this pepper emporium, began to worry about the future of their commercial enterprises in North Malabar. Officials at Tellicherry were determined to remove this French obstacle out of their way. In 1725 they persuaded the Vazhunnavar to expel the French from Mahe. By this time he had become discontented with the French for their failure in purchasing the pepper produced in his country and, hence, for not fulfilling the conditions of the monopoly contract. The Vazhunnavar, therefore, welcomed the English as the potential party to conduct the trade. Following their advice and contravening the terms of agreements with Molladin, the Vazhunnavar ejected the French from Mahe in 1725. Yet, to the surprise of the English, Mahe was recaptured by the French in the same year. This successful event, challenging the diplomatic dexterity of the English, strengthened France's political foundation on the Malabar coast. Consequently, the Vazhunnavar was forced to sue for peace with the French and finally a formal treaty was established on 8th November 1726[6]. This treaty reaffirmed the previous agreements between the French and the Vazhunnavar. Moreover, the French received permission to fortify their settlement of Mahe and unchangeable monopoloy right to the pepper trade. The French, however, felt doubtful about the loyalty of the local ruler.

In 1728 the authorities of Mahe and Tellicherry decided to conclude a peace treaty for the safe operation of their commercial ventures in North Malabar [7]. The treaty proposed that both the French and the English should not interfere in the local politics to the detriment of each other. The most important proposal was that the purchasing price of pepper should be fixed by their bilateral negotiations and consent; unilateral decision on this matter should not be made. Nonetheless, in practice, this principle had been discarded because of competition from Calicut. The English often offered a higher price than the fixed price of seventy rupees. In 1737 when the French protested against this purchase, a new price was fixed at eighty-four rupees for one *candi* pepper based on their mutual agreement. However, in 1738 Stephen Law, Chief of Tellicherry factory, wrote to the commander of Mahe, Bunel, that "although we have hitherto mutually kept our purchases of pepper at eighty-four rupees per *candi*, it is evident now that it is impracticable to obtain it for less than eighty-six"[8]. In the same year the Calicut market offered eighty-nine or ninety rupees per *candi* pepper [9].

In the competitive pepper market of North Malabar the French had always been in a disadvantageous position due to the lack of sufficient funds. Absence of proper warehouses facilities and irregular arrival of ships also affected their commercial activities. Yet they were able to maintain a flourishing trade with Mahe. Alfred Martineau stated that the annual export of pepper created a profit rate of 300 per cent; whereas the average profit from total annual French export from India constituted only 200 per cent [10]. However, this business trend did not exist throughout the eighteenth century. The British occupation of Mahe between 1761 and 1765 and later from 1779 to 1785 had adverse impact on the trade. In 1785 Commander of Mahe Louis Martin argued that *"le comptoir de Mahé n'avait jamais e'té d'un grand revenu pour la nation"*[11]. Other contemporary officers had also expressed the same viewpoint.[12]. In short, there was opposition to the establishment of a factory and fort at Mahe as early as 1727-28.[13]. But it should be noted that this critical report on Mahe did not say that the French could not make any profit from the pepper trade. Rather, it was based on the fact that this trade could not generate sufficient income in order to meet France's total expenditure in Mahe. Although not getting the anticipated benefit was a disappointment, the metropolitan government wanted to train Mahe because it was the only source from where they could directly purchase the best quality pepper, an item highly demanded in Europe[14]. In the 1783-84 period the Minister of Marine and Colonies at Versailles was even thinking of transferring the capital of French India from Pondicherry to Mahe. This idea was abandoned later, but it exemplified French considerations on this pepper emporium[15].

Mahe was also a centre of slave trade in North Malabar. The French in Mahe, both the officials and merchants, purchased local slaves-men, women and children - for domestic works and for export to other French settlements. Francis Day wrote: "one of the horrors of Malabar ... was the kidnapping of children by gangs of Moplahs, who sold them to the super cargoes of European vessels, more especially to the French at Mahe and the Dutch at Cochin"[16]. A register of slaves maintained by the Government of Pondicherry for the period from 1781 to 1791 stated that about 166 children between seven and fifteen years of age were sold at a price ranging from three to twenty rupees.[17] Besides local slaves, the French in Mahe were interested in purchasing black slaves from Africa. T.R. de Souza explained that the Mhamaya merchants of Goa were the chief suppliers of slaves from Mocambique to Mahe[18]. French officials in Mahe, De Canaple, Louis Marin, de Court and Boyer purchased black slaves. De Canaple, who was more intrested in commerce than in administration, demanded honest and healthy cafres belonged to an age group of 15-20 years from Goa. De Court requested the Mhamayas to pick up about thirty slaves from Mahe and transport them to Isle de France[19]. These references indicate the role of Mahe in French slave trade, a topic which requires further research for more information.

Mahe had a crucial role in the maintenance of French diplomatic relations with native kingdom. It was successful in establishing French dominance of political affairs in North Malabar until 1761. In 1751 the Rajah of Kolathunad wrote to Governnor of Pondicherry Fancois Dupleix: "we need your protection, the greatness of the French is famous throughout the country, we therefore seek shelter under it"[20]. The Vazhunnavar of Kadathanad, Kurungot Nair, and other local rulers as well as the most powerful Maharajah of Travancore Marthanda Varma had cordial relations with Mahe. Marthanda varma wrote to Dupleix: "if we had ships, we would have helped you with all our heart and sent a large army. Even now we are ready to send what men we can" to assist the French[21]. These diplomatic relations were dependent upon France's commercial and political interests on the one hand and local political complexity and instability on the other hand. Political dynamics of North Malabar was profoundly influenced by the interaction between these two factors. In addition to official diplomacy, the French offered special gifts to local rulers on the occassions of festivals such as Onam, Vishu and others[22]. Exchange of presents and protocols further strengthened the political foundation of the French in Mahe.

Dupleix had realized the uselessness and impracticability of traditional trading system in conditions of competition in the

Indian Ocean region. He rejected the French East India Company's and the home government's commercial policy of coastal-posts predicated on hinterland trade by means of bullion imported from France. Dupleix found that the only profitable way of conducting Eastern trade was through creating local capital as introduced by the Portuguese and adopted by the Dutch and the English. He proposed a policy of an imperialistic mercantilism which was based on his belief that "no commercial company whatsoever can subsist solely on the profits derived from its commerce, but a fixed and assured revenue is essential, especially when such a company maintains a large number of trading centres[23]. Furthermore, Dupleix explained: "it is often said that every commercial Company should concern itself solely with the purchase and sale of merchandise and never make war... If the Dutch had shared that limited and narrow viewpoint, their Company would long ago have ceased to exist.... It was war which won them their revenues... We also can acquire ours only by war. It can make ours more powerful than any European Company"[24]. In line with this policy the Government of Mahe tried to exert its hegemonic influence over local kingdoms and use such diplomatic relations to fight against the English at Tellicherry. Although Mahe was successful to some extent in such endeavours, with the recall of Dupleix in 1754 the programme of French imperialistic mercantilism disappeared from India.

Subsequently, the policy of Mahe with regard to the kingdoms of Mysore and Marathas was to maintain peace and friendship. In the absence of an imperial policy the French thought that friendly relations with these major Indian powers would help them to assert their domination over local rulers of Malabar and, hence, to threaten the English at Tellicherry. Mahe had always preserved friendship with Haider Ali and Tipu Sultan. In 1766 Haider Ali made a friendly visit to Mahe and in 1766 he granted the villages of Palloor, Pandakkal and Naluthura to the French. For the Government of Mysore, Mahe was the only nearest port under French control for importing supplies from abroad. His son and successor Tipu Sultan wrote to the French officials in 1797 : "you cannot be ignorant of the friendship which my father ... and myself have ever entertained for the French". During the last Mysore war "the English, the ambitious English, not having sufficient confidence in their own strength and courage to attack me singly, formed an alliance with the Maharattas[and] the Nizam, and attacked me every quarter...If you will assist me, in short time, not an Englishman shall remain in India"[25]. It is needless to discuss further the diplomatic contacts and co-operation between the French and rulers of Mysore. However, it is noteworthy that during the time of Tipu Sultan the French in Mahe were not very much satisfied with their relations with Mysore. Commander Canaple explained that, unlike Haider Ali, Tipu Sultan was "not trustworthy; his attitude was contradictory". His invasions into Malabar disturbed Mahe's commercial activities and encourged the Moplahs to menace the French.[26] Yet Mahe retained friendship with Mysore in tune with the general policy of peace and trade.

Illustrating the French policy with regard to the Marathas, King of France Louis XVI wrote to King Ramaraja in 1776 that "I have no intention to acquire territories in Hindustan... All that I desire is the establishment of reciprocal trade between your subjects and mine"[27]. Mahe had tremendous responsibility in dealing with the Marathas and implementing this policy. In 1771 when the Marathas were planning for an expedition to the Coromandel coast via Malabar, Commander of Mahe, Picot de la Motte requested Governor of Pondicherry, Law de Lauriston, to give advice on necessary policy and approach that he had to follow towards the Marathas. The French were afraid of the Maratha power. The Council of Pondicherry informed Picot de la Motte that neutrality was the best policy for the French in case of a Maratha military campaign. The council further explained to him: "this power, Sir, the most formidable and most solidly established in the whole of India, requires most tactful handling." It added that, despite the policy of neutrality, the Marathas would be able to force Picot de la Motte to adopt a course of action at their choice. Therefore, if the Marathas asked for any assistance, he was instructed to obey them without any reluctance[28]. This policy directive from Pondicherry was a crystal-clear illustration of France's political weakness in India. Fortunately, the proposed Maratha exepedition did not take place. In any way, the fear and concern developed in Mahe and the burden of responsibility on the shoulder of its commander indicate the diplomatic significance of this coastal town to the survival of French India.

Mahe was a principal source of sepoys for French military service in India. It seems that most of them were Moplahs of North Malabar. They were first employed at Mahe in the war against the Vazhunnavar in 1739-40. In 1742 Governor of Pondicherry, Dumas, ordered three companies of sepoys to come to the Corromandel coast to assist the French soldiers in defending Karaikkal against the Tanjoreans[29]. From this time onwards the Mahe sepoys had a notable part in the defensive as well as offensive programmes of the French empire. They attacked the English at different places on the Coromandel. In March 1747 six hundred Mahe sepoys participated in an expedition against Fort St.David at Cuddalore. Earlier about one thousand sepoys had assisted the French in the capture of Madras from the English. After occupying the city of Madras, it was reported that "all was plundered by those Mahe sepoys" Commander of the sepoy troops Abdul Rahman and his brother Shaikh Hassan "seized palankins, elephants, horses etc...Abdul Rahman got all the plunder of the thousand sepoys under him and became rich"[30]. In 1750 the farmers of Olukkari complained that the sepoys had cut their crops to feed their horses[31].

The main reason for plunder by the sepoys was their poverty. Although they had been serving the French, they were not paid enough salary for their survival, nor paid them regularly either. In 1750 Shaikh Hassan complained to Governor Dupleix: "I can not describe the abuse given me by my sepoys for their being six or seven months in arrears... The sepoys declare, they do not demand their pay but desire only to give back their muskets and be dismissed"[32]. This elucidates the hardships and poverty suffered by ordinary Mahe sepoys in the French military service. It appears that both the French and the English had similar policies with regard to the payment of salary to the sepoys. The difference between the French and the English was that the latter appointed British drill-sergeants and adjutant in their sepoy cops but the former left the leadership and discipline completely in Indian hands except when the sepoys were co-operating with French troops[33].

Mahe had a remarkable position in the communication network between France and its colonies in India. Vessels coming from France to Pondicherry often anchored at this port of call before proceeding to their destinations. At this time letters and other correspondences to Pondicherry were transferred to Mahe for quicker despatch. Ships coming from Isles de la France et Bourboun and the Persian Gulf region also followed this practice. There was an overland route from Mahe to Pondicherry via Palaghat, Coimbatore, Selam, Namagiripetta, Attur, Ulundur and Perumakkal[34]. The Brahmins were regularly employed to carry French correspondences to and from Pondicherry. They normally took twelve days for one way journey, whereas one way sailing took longer time, about three weeks at least. Information about political, military and diplomatic developments in Malabar were also brought to Pondicherry by the Brahmin messengers. The French believed that the Brahmins were more trustworthy in managing confidential matters. There were, however, occassions when others were appointed as messengers.

It also appears that some time Pondicherry was dependant upon Mahe for obtaining information about important events in Europe and India. As it was situated on the Malabar coast the colonial office of Mahe had got the first opportunity to know about such events in one way or another. In 1748 it was Commander Louet of Mahe who received the first news about the Treaty of Aix-la-Chappelle through English officials at Tellicherry[35]. In 1776 when Pallebot de St. Lubin conducted negotiations with the Marathas and concluded a treaty of alliance and trade with them the Commander of Mahe followed these developments and informed the Pondicherry government about them form time to time[36]. Thus Mahe acted as a linchpin of communication system in French India.

In brief, the history of Mahe in the eighteenth century shows the interplay of French colonial policy with local conditions. The geographic location of Mahe, resources of the hinterland and local political factors together with France's financial constraints determined the nature of French commercial ventures in Malabar. Mahe's role as a seaboard emporium of pepper trade, as a source of sepoys to the French military, as a motor of diplomatic interactions with local rulers and as an intermediary point in the exchange of communication had great importance to the sustenance of the French empire in India.

References

1. It should be noted that Mahe is one of the overlooked topics in the history of French colonialism in India. The pioneering study of Mahe was done by Alfred Martineau in his *Les Origins de Mahe de Malabar*, Paris, 1916. Following this the historiographical contribution to the study of eighteenth century Mahe has been limited to the publication of a few articles. M.P. Sreedharan, "Mahe: The Formative Years, 1721-1765" in *Revue historique de Pondicherry* (hereafter R.H.P.), vol XVI, 1989-90, pp.23-25; He published another essay : "Formative Years of French Colonial Settlement in Kerala" in his own edited book *Papers on French Colonial Rule in India*, Calicut, 1997, pp. 15-25. Another work on Mahe has been done by K.K.N. Kurup, " The Origin of the French Settlement at Mahe". In R.H.P. op.cit., pp. 19-22. It is also worthwhile to go through T.R. de Souza,. " Goa-Mahe Trade Links (Late 18th Early 19th Centuries): A New Source-Material" in K.S. Mathew, ed., *Studies in Maritime History*, Pondicherry, 1990, pp. 165-174.
2. "Memoire sur Mahe" par Simon Lagrenée de Mezieres, 4 July, 1784, in Edmond Gaudart, ed., *Catalogue des Manuscrits des Anciennes Archives de l'Inde Française: Mahe et loges de Calicut et de Surate*, Paris, 1934, vol. 5, pp. 47-48. The same memoir is published in R.H.P. vol 17, 1991, pp. 27-30.
3. William Logan, *Malabar Manual*, New Delhi, 1989, vol. 2., p. cccxix
4. Martineau, *Origins de Mahe*, p. 29
5. For the text of treaty see ibid., appendix no. 5, pp 283-285.
6. *Ibid.*, appendix no. II pp. 296-300.
7. *Ibid.*, pp. 300-304; William Logan, *A Collection of Treaties, Engagements and other Papers of Importance*, New Delhi, 1989, pp. 15-16.
8. Cited in Ashin Das Gupta, *Malabar in Asian Trade, 1740-1800*, Cambridge, 1967, p. 25.
9. *Ibid.*, p. 25.
10. Martineau, *Origins de Mahe*, p. 200.
11. "Mémoire..... sur la colonie de mahe et des revenus" par marin, 17 August., 1785, in Gaudart, Catalogue des Manuscrits, vol. p.50.
12. "Mémoire sur Mahe" par Simon Lagrenee, op. cit.

13. AC. C2. vol. 74, pp. 254-255, Extrait d'un mémoire de M. Desboisclairs sur l' e 'tat des e' stablishments de la Compagnie dans L'Inde en 1727, n.d, August, 1728;- pp. 260-276, Me'moire de M. Lenoir, 6 October, 1727.
14. Duarte Barbosa gives a description of the quality of pepper and its areas of production in North Malabar in his *The Book of Duarte Barbosa*, trans. and ed. by Mansel L. Danes, London, 1967, vol.2, pp. 80-83.
15. It seems that Simon Lagrenée's memoir (op.cit) had an important role in changing the metropolitan idea.
16. Francis Day, The Land of Perumals, Madras, 1863, p. 183
17. National Archives of India, Pondicherry, No. 16, vente d' enfants et d' esclaves, 25 November 1781 - 22 December, 1791. This register did not identify the number of children from Mahe.
18. T.R de Souza, "Goa-Mahe Trade Links (Late 18th -Early 19th Centuries): The New Source Material" in K.S. Mathew, ed., *Studies in Maritime History*, Pondicherry, 1990, pp. 165-174
19. *Ibid.*, 170-171
20. The Private Diary of Ananda Ranga Pillai (hereafter D.A.R.P.) .ed. by J.F. Price and P.K. Rangachari, New Delhi, 1985, vol. 8, p.44.
21. Ibid., vol. 6, p.23
22. Gaudart, *Catalogue des Manuscrits*, vol. 5, pp. 290-293; Lettre et Conventions des Gouverneurs de Pondicherry avec different Princes Hidous, 1666-1793, Pondicherry, 1911- 14, p. 391; see also National Archives of India, Pondicherry, Record No. 471.
23. Dupleix's Memoir, 16 October, 1753 in V.M. Thompson, Dupleix and His Letters 1742-1754, New york , 1933, p.801
24. Ibid., pp. 818-19 see also Dupleix's Letter to Savalette, 15 February, 1753, ibid, p. 793.
25. Kabir Kausar, Secret Correspondence of Tipu Sultan, New Delhi, 1980. pp. 163-164.
26. Gaudart, Catalogue des Manuscrits, vol, 5, pp..91-92
27. V.G. Hatalkar, trains., ed., French Records Relating to the History of the Marathas, Bombay, 1983, vol.2.p.34.
28. *Ibid.*, vol. 3 pp. 97-99, Picot to Law de Lauriston, 31 December, 1771; the Supreme Council of Pondicherry to Picot, 21 January, 1772.
29. D.A.R.P., vol. 1, p. 168.
30. *Ibid.*, p. 169.
31. *Ibid.*, p. 50
32. *Ibid.*, p. 265
33. *Ibid.*, p. 168
34. D.A.R.P. is the basic source for tracing the overland route from Mahe to Pondicherry.
35. *Ibid.*, vol 6 pp. 82-83.
36. Hatalkar, French Records, vol. 2 p 116, passim.

APPENDIX : K.S. MATHEW - A BIBLIOGRAPHY

Books

1. *Prasadvaram* (Malayalam), Alwaye, 1966.
2. *Iswaranum Darsanikarum* (Malayalam) Co-authored, Alwaye, 1966.
3. *Society in Medieval Malabar,* Jaffee Jo Books, Kottayam, 1979.
4. *Chronica do Reyno de Gusarate* (Chronicle of Gujarat, a Portuguese Manuscript of the Early Sixteenth entury edited jointly with Prof. S.C. Misra), Baroda, 1981.
5. *Portuguese Trade with India in the Sixteenth Century,* Manohar Books, New Delhi, 1983.
6. *Portuguese and the History of the Sultanate of Gujarat,* Mittal Publications, New Delhi, 1985.
7. *Studies in Maritime History,* Pondicherry, 1990
8. *Emergence of Cochin in the Pre-Industrial Era* (A Study of Portuguese Cochin), Pondicherry, 1990.
9. *Mariners, Merchants and Oceans: Studies in Maritime History,* Manohar Book Service, New Delhi, 1995.
10. *Indian Ocean and Cultural Interaction A.D. 1400-1800,* Pondicherry, 1996.
11. *Ship-building and Navigation in the Indian Ocean Region A.D 1400-1800,* Munshiram Manoharlal, New Delhi, 1997.
12. *Indo-Portuguese Trade and the Fuggers of German,* Manohar Book Service, New Delhi, 1997.
13. *Canada: Its Region and People,* Michael D. Behiels and K.S. Mathew eds., Munshiram Manoharlal Publishers Pvt. Ltd., New Delhi, 1998.
14. *Indo-French Relations,* edited jointly with S. Jeyaseela Stephen, ICHR Monograph Series 2, Pragati Publications, Delhi, 1999.
15. *French in India and Indian Nationalism (1700-1963 A.D.),* 2 vols, New Delhi, 1999
16. *Medieval and Modern Deccan: Felicitation Volume in Honour of Professor A.R. Kulkarni,* jointly edited with Professor Aniurdha Ray and M.A. Nayeem, New Delhi, 2000.
17. *The Portuguese and the Socio-Cultural Changes in India, 1500-1800,* jointly edited with Dr. Teotonio R. de Souza and Dr. Pius Malekandathil, Pondicherry, 2001.

Research Articles

1. "Financiers of the Portuguese Trade with India in the Sixteenth Century", *Journal of the Maharaja Sayaji Rao University of Baroda*, Humanities Number vols. XXVII-XXVIII, 1978-79., No. 1, pp.87-99.

2. "Portuguese Trade with India and the Theory of Royal Monopoly in the Sixteenth Century". *Proceedings of the Indian History Congress* (40th Session, Waltair), pp.389-398.

3. "Commodity composition of Indo-Portuguese Trade in the Early Sixteenth Century", *Proceedings of the Indian History Congress* (41st Session, Bombay), 1980, pp. 297-305.

4. "Indo-Portuguese Trade and the Italian Financiers in the Sixteenth Century", *Proceedings of the Indian History Congress* (42nd Session. Bodhgaya), 1981, pp. 570-575.

5. "Khwaja Saffar, the Merchant - Governor of Surat and the Indo-Portuguese Trade in the Early Sixteenth Century", *Proceedings of the Indian History Congress* (43rd Session, Kurushetra), 1982, pp. 232-242.

6. "The King of Tanur on the Malabar Coast and the Indo-Portuguese Trade in the Early Sixteenth Century", *Journal of Kerala Studies*, Vol. X, Parts 1-4 Trivandrum, 1983, pp. 147-165.

7. "Portuguese Trade on the Malabar Coast" in S.N. Sen (ed.), *Western colonial Policy*, Calcutta, 1984, pp.302-317.

8. "Indian Merchants and the Portuguese Trade on the Malabar Coast during the Sixteenth Century", in T.R. De Souza (ed.), *Indo-Portuguese History: Old Issues and New Questions*, New Delhi, 1984, pp.1-12.

9. "The Portuguese in the Indian Ocean during the Sixteenth and Early Seventeenth Centuries", *Tamil Civilization*, Vol. 11, No.3, 1984, pp.74-86.

10. "Indo-Portuguese Coinage in the Sixteenth and Early Seventeenth Centuries", *Journal of the Numismatic Society of India*, Varanasi, Vol. XLVI, Parts 1&2, 1984, pp. 120-129.

11. "Indo-Portuguese Trade and the Gujarat Nobility in the Sixteenth Century: A Case Study of Malik Gopi", *Proceedings of the Indian History Congress*, (45th Session), Annamalai, 1984, pp. 357-66.

12. "Portuguese Relationship with Shivaji" *Lokarajya* Bombay, April 1985, pp. 167-172.

13. "The South Indian Apostolate of St. Thomas and the Portuguese in the Sixteenth Century", *Christian Orient*, Kottayam, Vol. VI, No. 1, March 1985, pp. 5-12.

14. "The First Mercantile Battle in the Indian Ocean 1508-09: Afro-Asian Front against the Portuguese", II *Seminario Internacional* de Historia Indo-Portuguesa, Lisbon, 1985, pp.177-186.

15. "India Contract of Indo-Portuguese Trade in the Last Quarter of the Sixteenth Century", in V.K. Chavda, ed., *Studies in Trade and Urbanisation in Western India*, Baroda, 1985, pp.163-171.

16. "Nationalism and Secularism" in *Nationalism in Crisis,* Bangalore, 1985, pp. 9-28.

17. "Agricultural Production in the Deccan during the Seventeenth Century and Overseas Markets", *Tamil Civilisation,* Vol. III, No. 4, 1985, pp. 76-83.

18. "Trade and Economy of Coastal Gujarat in the Sixteenth Century", *Journal of the Oriental Institute,* Baroda, Vol. 34, Nos. 3-4, 1985, pp. 76-83.

19. "Maritime Trade of the Portuguese with North Western Coast of India in the Seventeenth Century", *Tamil Civilisation,* Vol. III, No.1, pp. 10-22.

20. "Trade in the Indian Ocean and the Portuguese System of Cartazes" in Malyn Newitt (ed.), *The First Portuguese Colonial Empire,* University of Exeter Publication, Exeter. 1986, pp.69-83.

21. "Business in Portuguese India: The Sixteenth and Seventeenth Centuries" in Dwijendra Tripathi (ed.), *State and Business in India,* Delhi, 1987, pp.22-58.

22. "Economy of Bassein in the Sixteenth Century", *Indica,* Bombay, Vol. 24, No.2, 1987, pp.131-140.

23. "Indian Shipping and the Maritime Power of the Portuguese in the Seventeenth and eighteenth Centuries", *Purabhilekh Puratatva",* Goa, vol. IV, No.2, 1986, pp.1-12.

24. "Masulipatnam and Maritime Trade of India during the Seventeenth Century", *Proceedings of the Andhra Pradesh History congress",* (11th Session), Nagaram, 1987, pp. 76-89.

25. "Church Economics in the Sixteenth Century", in P.P. Shirodkar (ed.), Goa: *Cultural Trends,* Panaji, 1988, pp. 123-130.

26. "Khwaja Saffar, the Merchant Governor of Surat and the Indo-Portuguese Trade in the Early Sixteenth Century" in *Vice-Almirante A Teixeira Da Mota in Memoriam,* Vol. 1, Lisboa, released in 1988, pp. 319-328.

27 "Goa: Past and Present", in *Purabhilekh Puratatva,* Vol.V, No.1 released in October 1988, pp.1-14.

28 "Nobility in Gujarat Sultanate and the Portuguese during the Sixteenth Century", *Proceedings of the Indian History congress"* (48th Session), Goa, released in November 1988, pp.275-283.

29. "Money Economy in the Portuguese India" *Journal of Gujarat Itihas Parishat* released in January 1989, pp.23-33.

30 "Nobility in Gujrat Sultanate and the Portuguese during the Sixteenth Century" in Dr. G. Victor Rajamanickam and Dr. Y. Subbarayalu (eds.), *History of Traditional Navigation,* Tamil University, Thanjavur, released in 1989, pp.129-140.

31. "Masulipatnam on the Coromandel Coast and the Maritime Trade of India during the Seventeenth Century A.D." in *Tamil Civilisation,* Vol.5, No.4, released in 1989, Thanjavur, pp. 45-60.

32. "Cochin and the Portuguese Trade with India during the Sixteenth Century", *Indica,* Vol. 26, Nos.1 & 2, Bombay, 1989, pp. 77-91.

33. "Cochin and the Maritime Trade of India during the Sixteenth Century", in *Purabhilekh Puratatva*, Vol. 6, No.4, 1989, pp.1-10.

34. "Socio-Economic History of Medieval South India and Portuguese Historians" *Purabhilekh Puratatva*, Vol.7, No.1, January-June 1989, pp. 1-17.

35. "Maritime Trade of Masulipatnam on the Coromandel Coast of India during the Second Half of the Eighteenth Century" in Lewis R. Fischer and Helge W. Nordvik (eds.) Shipping and Trade, 1750-1950: *Essays in International Maritime Economic History*, Pontefract, 1990, pp.1-14.

36. "Trade and Commerce in Sixteenth Century Goa" in T.R. De Souza (ed.), *Goa Through the Ages*, Vol. II, 1990, Goa, pp. 137-145.

37. "The Portuguese and the Malabar Society during the Sixteenth Century: A Study of Mutual Interaction" in *STUDIA*, No. 49, Lisboa, pp. 36-69.

38. "Khwaja Shams-ud-din Giloni: A Sixteenth Century Entrepreneur in Portuguese India", in *Emporia, Commodities and Entrepreneurs in Asian Maritime Trade, C.1400-1750*, Roderich Ptak and Dietmar Rothermund eds., Beitrage zur Suedasienforschung Suedasien-Institut, Universitaet Heidelberg, Franz Steiner Verlag, Stuttgart, 1991, pp. 363-371.

39. "Maritime Trade of India and the Germans in the Sixteenth Century", in the *Souvenir of the Second International Symposium on Maritime Studies*, Department of History, Pondicherry Univeristy, Pondicherry 1991, pp. 37-47.

40. "Cuddalore in the Eighteenth Century", in Indu Banga and J.S. Grewal (eds.), *Ports and their Hinterlands in India, 1700-1950*, New Delhi, 1992, pp. 77-87

41. "Freedom Movement and National Integration", in S.Manickam (ed.) *Reflections on Trends and Themes in History*, Madurai, 1992, pp. 76-89.

42. "German Merchant Financiers in Goa during Sixteenth and Seventeenth Centuries", in P.P. Shirodhkar (ed.), *Goa's External Relations*, G. 1992, pp. 32-56

43. "Urban Development of Portuguese Cochin in the Sixteenth and Seventeenth Centuries", *Proceedings Volume of the Eleventh Annual Session of the South Indian History Congress*, Calicutt, 1991 (Released in January 1993), pp. 79-84.

44. "Medieval Deccan and the Maritime Trade of India", *Proceedings of the Andhra Pradesh History Congress*, Vol. XVI, Karimnagar, 1992 (released in 1993), pp. 39-53.

45. "Freibriefe fuer den Handel an Indiens Kueste", in Wolfgang Knabe, *Auf den Spuren der ersten deutschen Kaufleute in Indien*, Anhausen (West Germany), 1993, pp. 30 ff.

46. "Die Konkurrenten der dedutschen Haendler" in Wolfgang Knabe, *Auf den Spuren der ersten deutschen Kaufleute in Indien*, Anhausen (West Germany), 1993, pp. 107 ff.

47. "Trade and Navigation in the Indian Ocean under Portuguese and Akbar", *Purabhilekh Puratatva*, Vol. IX, No.1, pp. 3-22.

48. "Maritime History of Andaman and Nicobar Islands" in V.Suryanaran & V. Sudarsen eds., *Andaman and Nicobar Islands: Challenges of Development*, Delhi, Konark Publishers, 1994, pp. 51-58.

49. "Reflections on the Portuguese *Lusiadas* as Source for Indian History" in *Journal of Indian History*, Vol. LXV, Parts 1-3, Trivandrum, released in February 1995, pp. 27-34.

50. "Age of Discoveries and the Emergence of French Canada" in *Indo-Canadian Relations: Future Perspectives*, Berhampur University Publication, released in March 1995, pp. 11-24.

51. "Indian Shipping and the Maritime Power of the Portuguese in the Seventeenth and Eighteenth Centuries" *Proceedings of the Indian Historical Records Commission*, New Delhi, 1995, pp.25-34.

52. Differential Reactions to the Portuguese Monopoly of Trade in the Indian Ocean Region during the Sixteenth Century" in *Felicitation Volume of Prof. Agam Prasad Mathur*, Vol. III, *Recent Trends in Humanities and Social Sciences*, Hazuri Bhawan, Peepal Mandi, Agra, 1995, pp. 65-87.

53. "The Portuguese Trade and State in the Sixteenth Century India" in R.L.Hangloo, ed., *Situating Medieval Indian State*, New Delhi, Commonwealth Publishers, 1995, pp.33-45.

54. "Maritime Trade of Gujarat and the Portuguese in the Seventeenth Century", *Mare Liberum*, Number 9, Lisbon, 1995 (released in 1996 June),pp.187-195.

55. "The Private Diary of Ananda Rangapillai and the Study of Maritime History of India in the 18th Century", *Revue Historique de Pondicherry*, October 1996, pp.256-265.

56. "Akbar and the Portuguese Maritime Dominance" in Irfan Habib, *Akbar and His India*, OUP, Delhi, 1997, pp.256-265.

57. "Indian Naval Encounters with the Portuguese, Strength and Weakness" in K.K.N. Kurup, *India's Naval Traditions: The Role of Kunhali Marakkars*, New Delhi, 1997.pp.6-25.

58. "Portuguese Sources and Medieval Indian History", *Proceedings of Indian History Congress*, Presidential Address (Medievel Section), Madras section, 1997.

59. "Indian Independence and Integration of the Portuguese Pockets in India", *Souvenir of the 58th Session of Indian History Congress*, Bangalore, 1997, pp.114-124.

60. "The Portuguese and the Study of Medicinal Plants in India in the Sixteenth Century", *Indian Journal of History of Science*, No.32 (4), New Delhi, 1997, pp.369-376.

61. "Indo-Portuguese Trade under Dom Philip I of Portugal and the Fuggers of Germany", *A Carreira da India e as Rotas dos Esreitas*, Angra do Heroisma, 1998, pp. 563-580.

62. 'Indian Ocean and Cultural Interaction", *Indica*, Mumbai, 1998, pp.97-133.

63. "Life on Board a Portuguese Ship during the Sixteenth Century" *Samvada*, New Delhi, 1998, pp.23-35.

64. "Indian Entrepreneurs and Maritime Trade in the Bay of Bengal during the Eighteenth Century with special reference to Ananda Ranga Pillai", in Om Prakash and Denys Lombard, *Commerce and Culture in the Bay of Bengal 1500-1800*, New Delhi, 1999, pp. 221-232.

65. "Trade and Commerce in Andhra Desa and Masulipatnam during the Second Half of the Eighteenth Century", *Trade and Commerce in Andhra Desa 17th & 18th Centuries* A.D., ed. by R. Soma Reddy, Mr. Radhakrishna Sarma and Dr. A. Satyanarayana, Hyderabad, 1998, pp. 1-21.

66. "Akbar and the Europeans - A Study of Changing Perspectives", *Akbar and His Age*, ICHR Monograph Series-5, Iqtidar Alam Khan, ed., Northern Book Centre, New Delhi, 1999, pp.114-131.

67. "Ship Building on the Malabar Coast and the Portuguese during the 16th & 17th Centuries", *Perspectives on Kerala Traders*, ed. T. Jamal Mohammed, Sree Sankaracharya University of Sanskrit, Kalady, Kerala, 1999, pp.6-33.

68. "Portuguese Trade in Indian Ocean Regions under Philip II of Spain and the German Merchant Financiers" in Artemio D. Palongpalong & Sylvano D. Mahiwo (eds.), *Society and Culture: The Asian Heritage Festschrift for Juan R. Francisco*, Metro Manila, 1999, pp. 128-145.

69. "Syrian Catholics in India" in S. Settar and P.K.V. Kaimal, *We Lived Together*, ICHR Monograph Series 3, Delhi, 1999, pp. 156-172.

70. "Vasco da Gama and the German Merchants" in *Proceedings of the International Seminar* held in Paris in May 1999.

71. "The Germans and Portuguese India" in João Pedro Garcia, ed., *Vasco da Gama e a India*, Fundação Calouste Gulbenkian, Lisboa, 1999, pp. 281-293.

List of Contributors

1. Late Prof. Dr. A.R. Kulkarni
   Former UGC Chairman and
   Professor Emeritus of History
   University of Pune, Maharashtra

2. Prof. Dr. Eberhard Schmitt
   Founder of Forschungsstiftung für
   Europäische Überseegeschichte
   and Professor Emeritus of
   History
   Bamberg University
   Hans-Wölfel-Str.6
   D-96049 Bamberg
   Germany

3. Prof. Dr. M.N. Pearson
   Professor Emeritus of History
   The University of New South Wales
   Sydney 2052, Australia

4. Prof. Dr. Luis Filipe F.R. Thomaz
   Professor Emeritus of History,
   Universidade Nova de Lisboa
   Av. Amadeu Duarte, 249-1
   2775 Parede, Portugal

5. Stephan B.G.C. Michaelsen
   Sölder Waldstraße-29
   D-44289 Dortmund, Germany

6. Prof. Dr. Joseph Velinkar
   Former Professor of History
   St. Xavier's College
   5, Mahapalika Road
   Bombay 400001, India

7. Prof. Dr. K.K.N. Kurup
   Former Vice Chancellor
   Calicut University
   Calicut University P.O.
   Malappuram Dt. Kerala, India

8. Prof. Dr. Jan Kieniewicz
   Former Professor of History
   Centre for Studies on the
   Classical Tradition,
   Warsaw University
   Warsaw, Poland

9. Late Prof. Dr. Kenneth McPherson
   Former Professor of History
   Indian Ocean Centre
   Curtin University of Technology
   Perth, Western Australia

10. Prof. Dr. John G. Everaert
    Former Professor of Colonial and
    Maritime History
    University of Ghent
    2 Blandijnberg, B-9000 Ghent
    Belgium

11. Prof. Dr. Carlos Alonso Vañes
    Professor, Estudio Teologico
    Augustiniano
    Paseo de Filipinos, No. 7
    47007 Valladolid, Spain

12. Late Prof. Dr. George Winius
    Professor Emeritus of History
    University of Florida
    North Carolina, USA

13. Late Prof. Dr. A.J.R. Russell-Wood
    Professor Emeritus of History
    The Johns Hopkins University
    3400 North Charles Street
    Baltimore, Maryland 21218
    USA

14. Prof. Dr. S. Jeyaseela Stephen
    Former Professor of History
    Viswa Bharati University
    Santiniketan, Bengal

List of Contributors

15. Late Prof. Dr. Glenn J. Ames
    Former Professor of History
    University of Toledo,
    Ohio 43606-3390, USA

16. Prof. Dr. Pius Malekandathil
    Former Professor of History, CHS,
    JNU, New Delhi

17. Prof. Dr. João Teles e Cunha
    Professor of History
    Institute of Asian Studies,
    Universidade Católica
    Portuguesa,
    Lisbon, Portugal

18. Prof. Dr. Nagendra Rao
    Professor in History
    Goa University
    Goa 403206, India

19. Prof. Dr. K.M. Mathew
    Former Dean of Social Sciences
    Goa University, Goa 403206

20. Prof. Dr. Hannes Stubbe
    Professor, University of Cologne
    Herbert Lewinstr. 2
    D-50931 Köln, Germany

21. Prof. Dr. Maria de Jesus dos
    Martires Lopes
    R. Americo Durão, 4-2ª dto
    1800 Lisboa, Portugal

22. Dr. Fatima Gracias
    C-86 Altinho
    Panjim, Goa 403001
    India

23. Late Prof. Dr. B. Arunachalam
    Professor of Geography
    University of Bombay, Maharashtra,
    India

24. Late Dr. Haraprasad Ray
    Former Associate Professor of
    Chinese Studies
    JNU, New Delhi, India

25. Dr. T. Jamal Mohammed
    Former Syndicate Member
    Sree Sankaracharya University of
    Sanskrit, Kalady
    Kerala.India

26. Prof. Dr. Juan R. Francisco
    Former Professor of Indology
    Asian Centre
    University of the Philippines-Diliman
    1101 Quezon City, Philippines

27. Prof. Dr. Francis Arakal
    Professor of Sanskrit
    Sree Sankaracharya University of
    Sanskrit, Kalady
    Kerala, India

28. Late Prof. Dr. Teotonio R. de Souza
    Former Professor of History
    Universidade Lusofona de
    Humanidades e Tecnologias
    Lisboa. Portugal

29. Prof. Dr.M.O.Koshy
    Former Pro-Vice Chancellor
    Kannur University, Kannur, Kerala,
    India

30. Late Prof. Dr. Dietmar Rothermund
    Professor of History
    South Asian Institute of Heidelberg
    University
    D-69120 Heidelberg
    Germany

31. Prof. Dr. B. Sobhanan
    Professor of History
    University of Kerala
    Trivandrum, Kerala, India

List of Contributors

32. Prof. Dr. Ujjayan Bhattacharya
    Professor of History
    Vidyasagar University
    Midnapur 721102, Bengal

33. Late Prof. Dr. Jean Deloche
    École Française d'Extrême Orient
    Centre de Pondicherry
    16&19, Dumas Street
    Pondicherry 605001, India

34. Prof. Dr. J.B.P. More
    30 rue Francoeur
    Viry Chatillon-91170, France

35. Late Prof. Dr. Aniruddha Ray
    Professor of Islamic History and Culture
    University of Calcutta, Bengal, India

36. Prof. Dr. Hymavathi
    Professor of History
    Kakatiya University
    Warangal, 506009
    India

37. Prof. Dr. B. Krishnamurthy
    Professor, School of International Studies
    Pondicherry Central University
    Pondicherry 605014
    India

38. Dr. Joy Varkey
    Dept. of History
    N.A.M.College, Kallikandy P.O
    Kannur. Kerala. India